Lecture Notes in Computer Science 3711

Commenced Publication in 1973
Founding and Former Series Editors:
Gerhard Goos, Juris Hartmanis, and Jan van Leeuwen

Fumio Kishino   Yoshifumi Kitamura
Hirokazu Kato   Noriko Nagata (Eds.)

Entertainment Computing – ICEC 2005

4th International Conference
Sanda, Japan, September 19-21, 2005
Proceedings

 Springer

Volume Editors

Fumio Kishino
Yoshifumi Kitamura
Osaka University, Graduate School of Information Science and Technology
2-1, Yamadaoka, Suita-shi, Osaka 565-0871, Japan
E-mail: {kishino, kitamura}@ist.osaka-u.ac.jp

Hirokazu Kato
Osaka University, Graduate School of Engineering Science
1-3, Machikaneyama, Toyonaka, Osaka 560-8531, Japan
E-mail: kato@sys.es.osaka-u.ac.jp

Noriko Nagata
Kwansei Gakuin University, School of Science and Technology
2-1 Gakuen, Sanda, Hyogo 669-1337, Japan
E-mail: nagata@ksc.kwansei.ac.jp

Library of Congress Control Number: 2005932210

CR Subject Classification (1998): H.5, H.4, H.3, I.2, I.3, I.7, J.5

ISSN   0302-9743
ISBN-10   3-540-29034-6 Springer Berlin Heidelberg New York
ISBN-13   978-3-540-29034-6 Springer Berlin Heidelberg New York

Springer is a part of Springer Science+Business Media

springeronline.com

© 2005 IFIP International Federation for Information Processing, Hofstrasse 3, 2361 Laxenburg, Austria
Printed in Germany

Typesetting: Camera-ready by author, data conversion by Scientific Publishing Services, Chennai, India
Printed on acid-free paper   SPIN: 11558651   06/3142   5 4 3 2 1 0

Foreword

First of all, we appreciate the hard work of all the authors who contributed to ICEC 2005 by submitting their papers. ICEC 2005 attracted 95 technical paper submissions, 8 poster submissions and 7 demo submissions, in total 110. This number is nearly equal to ICEC 2004.

Based on a thorough review and selection process carried out by 76 international experts from academia and industry as members of the senior and international program committees, a high-quality program was compiled. The program committee consisted of experts from all over the world: 1 from Austria, 3 from Bulgaria, 2 from Canada, 4 from China, 1 from Finland, 4 from France, 10 from Germany, 1 from Greece, 1 from Ireland, 1 from Israel, 1 from Italy, 26 from Japan, 1 from Korea, 4 from The Netherlands, 1 from New Zealand, 1 from Norway, 1 from Singapore, 1 from Thailand, 4 from the UK, and 8 from the USA. In this number, reviewers are included.

The final decision was made at the senior program committee meeting based on three reviewers' feedback, available online via the conference management tool. Through earnest and fair discussion at the meeting, 25 technical papers were accepted as long papers and 32 technical papers were accepted as short papers from 95 submitted technical papers. Moreover, 3 poster papers and 5 demo papers were accepted.

Although accepted, 3 long papers and 7 short papers were unfortunately withdrawn during the registration process. Finally 47 technical papers, 3 poster papers, 5 demo papers and 1 keynote paper were compiled and are presented in this book. A total of 56 contributions are included from Australia, Austria, Canada, China, Denmark, Finland, France, Germany, Japan, Korea, The Netherlands, Singapore, the UK, and the USA. All these papers could be allocated to one of the following topics: (1) interactive digital storytelling; (2) graphics; (3) advanced interaction design; (4) social impact and evaluation; (5) seamful / seamless interface; (6) body and face; (7) robot; (8) music and sound; (9) mixed reality and mobile; (10) education; (11) virtual reality and simulation; and (12) theory. Papers per topic are ordered as follows: a keynote paper, technical papers, demo papers, and poster papers.

September 2005

Fumio Kishino
Yoshifumi Kitamura
Hirokazu Kato
Noriko Nagata

Preface

Entertainment has come to occupy a very important part of our life by refreshing us and activating our creativity. Recently, with the advances made in computers and networks, new types of entertainment have been emerging such as video games, edutainment, robots, and networked games. Unfortunately, until recently, entertainment has not been among the major research areas within the field of information processing. Since there are huge industries and markets devoted to entertainment, this unbalance seems very strange. The new forms of entertainment have the potential to change our lives, so it is necessary for people who work in this area to discuss various aspects of entertainment and to promote entertainment-related research.

With this basic motivation, the General Assembly of the International Federation of Information Processing (IFIP) approved in August 2002 the establishment of the Specialist Group on Entertainment Computing (SG16). The responsibility of SG16 is to monitor and promote research and development activities related to entertainment computing throughout the world. One of the major activities of SG16 is to organize and support the International Conference on Entertainment Computing (ICEC). The ICEC is expected to bring together researchers, developers, and practitioners working in the area of entertainment computing. The conference covers a wide range of entertainment computing issues, such as theoretical studies, hardware/software development, integrated systems, human interfaces, and applications.

Let's take a brief look at the history of ICEC. The annual conference started in 2002 as the International Workshop on Entertainment (IWEC 2002), which was held May 14–17, 2002 in Makuhari, Japan. The workshop attracted more than 100 participants, and 60 papers were published in the proceedings by Kluwer. Based on the success of IWEC 2002, SG16 upgraded the workshop to a conference and organized ICEC 2003. ICEC 2003 was held May 8–10, 2003 at the Entertainment Technology Center of Carnegie Mellon University, Pittsburgh, USA. ICEC 2003 was also successful, with more than 100 attendees and 20 highly select papers. All of the papers of ICEC 2003 were accepted by ACM for inclusion in their ACM online digital library. In the next year, ICEC crossed the Atlantic Ocean to move to Europe, and ICEC 2004 was held September 1–3, 2004 at the Technical University of Eindhoven in The Netherlands. The conference attracted more than 150 attendees, and 27 full papers were published by Springer in the Lecture Notes in Computer Science (LNCS) series. In 2005, ICEC came back to Japan, and ICEC 2005 was held at Kwansei Gakuin University, Sanda, Japan. We selected more than 50 papers, and these papers are published in this LNCS volume.

For the success of ICEC 2005, we express our special thanks to the following people who worked so hard to organize the conference: Michihiko Minoh and Akihiro Yagi as co-chairs, Fumio Kishino, Yoshifumi Kitamura and Hirokazu Kato as program committee chair and co-chairs, Haruhiro Katayose as local organization committee chair, and other local organization committee members. We are also grateful for the contribution of all the paper reviewers as well as the sponsors and cooperating societies.

September 2005   Ryohei Nakatsu

Organization

Chair

Ryohei Nakatsu   Kwansei Gakuin University, Japan

Co-chairs

Michihiko Minoh   Kyoto University, Japan
Akihiro Yagi   Kwansei Gakuin University, Japan

International Organizing Committee

Marc Cavazza   University of Teesside, UK
Adrian David Cheok   National University of Singapore, Singapore
Takchiko Kamae   NICT, Japan
Donald Marinelli   Carnegie Mellon University, USA
Matthias Rauterberg   Technical University of Eindhoven, The Netherlands

Program Committee

Chair:
Fumio Kishino   Osaka University, Japan

Technical Paper Chair:
Yoshifumi Kitamura   Osaka University, Japan

Poster and Demo Chair:
Hirokazu Kato   Osaka University, Japan

Senior Program Committee Members:
Galia Angelova   Bulgarian Academy of Sciences, Bulgaria
Bruno Arnaldi   IRISA-INRIA, France
Brad J. Bushman   University of Michigan, USA
Natanicha Chorpothong   Assumption University, Thailand
Paolo Ciancarini   University of Bologna, Italy
Sidney Fels   The University of British Columbia, Canada
Jaap van den Herik   University of Maastricht, The Netherlands
Ville-Veikko Mattila   Nokia Research Center, Finland
Junichi Hoshino   University of Tsukuba, Japan

Qunsheng Peng	Zhejiang University, China
Theresa-Marie Rhyne	North Carolina State University, USA
Yasu Santo	Hong Kong Polytechnic University, China
Nikitas Sgouros	University of Piraeus, Greece
Arik (Ariel) Shamir	The Interdisciplinary Center Herzliya, Israel
Ehud Sharlin	University of Calgary, Canada
Scott Stevens	Carnegie Mellon University, USA
Norbert Streitz	Fraunhofer IPSI, Germany
Demetri Terzopoulos	New York University, USA
Tsutomu Terada	Osaka University, Japan
Frans Vogelaar	Academy of Media Arts Cologne, Germany
Lars Wolf	IBR, Germany
Peter Wright	University of York, UK
Volker Wulf	Fraunhofer Institute, Germany
Tatsushi Yamasaki	Kwansei Gakuin University, Japan

Reviewers:

Marc Bechler	IBR, Germany
Svetla Boytcheva	Sofia University "St. Kliment Ohridski", Bulgaria
Jens Brandt	IBR, Germany
Emanuil Djerassi	Bulgarian Academy of Sciences, Bulgaria
Xiaoyuan Gu	IBR, Germany
Zefir Kurtisi	IBR, Germany
Carsten Rocker	Fraunhofer IPSI, Germany
Denis Zorin	New York University, USA

Local Organizing Committee:

Chair:
Haruhiro Katayose   Kwansei Gakuin University, Japan

Secretary (Student Volunteers Director):
Tatsushi Yamasaki   Kwansei Gakuin University, Japan

Secretary:
Mitsuyo Hashida   Kwansei Gakuin University, Japan

Treasurer:
Takeshi Kawabata   Kwansei Gakuin University, Japan

Publication:
Noriko Nagata   Kwansei Gakuin University, Japan

Web Design and Publicity:
Yasuhiko Kitamura   Kwansei Gakuin University, Japan
Helmut Prendinger   National Institute of Informatics, Japan

Liaison:

Michio Chujo   Kwansei Gakuin University, Japan
Masataka Hashimoto   Future Laboratory, Japan

Special Advisors:

Kozaburo Hachimura   Ritsumeikan University, Japan
Tadahiro Kitahashi   Kwansei Gakuin University, Japan
Katsuhide Tsushima   Osaka Electro-Communication University, Japan

Sponsors

International Federation for Information Processing (IFIP)
Information Processing Society of Japan (IPSJ)
Kwansei Gakuin University
Embassy of France in Japan
Commemorative Organization for the Japan World Exposition '70
Tsutomu Nakauchi Foundation
Support Center for Advanced Telecommunications Technology Center
Hyogo Prefecture

Cooperating Societies

Acoustical Society of Japan
Human Interface Society
IEEE Kansai Section
IEICE Human Communication Group
Japan Ergonomics Society
TC of Virtual Reality, China Society of Image and Graphics
The Institute of Image Electronics Engineers of Japan
The Institute of Image Information and Television Engineers
The Japanese Society for Artificial Intelligence
The Robotics Society of Japan
The Virtual Reality Society of Japan

IFIP SG16

SG16 (Specialist Group on Entertainment Computing) was established at the General Assembly of IFIP (International Federation on Information Processing) in 2001. The outline of SG16 is described below.

Aims:

To encourage computer applications for entertainment and to enhance computer utilization in the home, the technical committee will pursue the following aims:
- to enhance algorithmic research on board and card games
- to promote a new type of entertainment using information technologies
- to encourage hardware technology research and development to facilitate implementing entertainment systems, and
- to encourage haptic and non-traditional human interface technologies for entertainment.

Scopes:

1. Algorithms and strategies for board and card games
   - algorithms for board and card games
   - strategy controls for board and card games
   - level setups for games and card games
2. Novel entertainment using ICT
   - network-based entertainment
   - mobile entertainment
   - location-based entertainment
   - mixed reality entertainment
3. Audio
   - music informatics for entertainment
   - 3D audio for entertainment
   - sound effects for entertainment
4. Entertainment human interface technologies
   - haptic and non-traditional human interface technologies
   - mixed reality human interface technologies for entertainment
5. Entertainment robots
   - ICT-based toys
   - pet robots
   - emotion models and rendering technologies for robots
6. Entertainment systems
   - design of entertainment systems
   - entertainment design toolkits
   - authoring systems

7. Theoretical aspects of entertainment
   - sociology, psychology and physiology for entertainment
   - legal aspects of entertainment
8. Video game and animation technologies
   - video game hardware and software technologies
   - video game design toolkits
   - motion capture and motion design
   - interactive story telling
   - digital actors and emotion models
9. Interactive TV and movies
   - multiple view synthesis
   - free viewpoint TV
   - authoring technologies
10. Edutainment
    - entertainment technologies for children's education
    - open environment entertainment robots for education

SG16 Members (2005)

Chair:
Ryohei Nakatsu   Kwansei Gakuin University, Japan

Vice-Chair:
Matthias Rauterberg   Technical University of Eindhoven, The Netherlands

Secretary:
Claudio Pinhanez   IBM, USA

National Representatives:

Galia Angelova	Bulgarian Academy of Sciences, Bulgaria
Sidney Fels	The University of British Columbia, Canada
Zhigeng Pan	Zhejiang University, China
Ville-Veikko Mattila	Nokia Research Center, Finland
Bruno Arnaldi	IRISA-INRIA, France
Richard Reilly	University College Dublin, Ireland
Paolo Ciancarini	University of Bologna, Italy
Takehiko Kamae	National Institute of Informatics, Japan
Hyun S. Yang	KAIST, Korea
Matthias Rauterberg	Technical University of Eindhoven, The Netherlands
Geir Egil Myhr	University of Troms, Norway
Adrian David Cheok	National University of Singapore, Singapore
Pedro Gonzalez Calero	Complutense University of Madrid, Spain
Natanicha Chorpothong	Assumption University, Thailand
Marc Cavazza	University of Teesside, UK
Donald Marinelli	Carnegie Mellon University, USA

WG Chair persons:

WG16.1	Marc Cavazza University of Teesside, UK
WG16.2	Hitoshi Matsubara Future University-Hakodate, Japan
WG16.3	Matthias Rauterberg Technical University of Eindhoven, The Netherlands
WG16.4	Jaap van den Herik University of Maastricht, The Netherlands
WG16.5	Andy Sloane University of Wolverhampton, UK

Working Groups (WG) Under SG16

WG16.1 Digital Storytelling

Storytelling is one of the core technologies of entertainment. Especially with the advancement of information and communication technologies (ICT), a new type of entertainment called video games has been developed, where interactive story development is the key that makes those games really entertaining. At the same time, however, there has not been much research on the difference between interactive storytelling and conventional storytelling. Also as the development of interactive storytelling needs a lot of time and human power, it is crucial to develop technologies for automatic or semiautomatic story development. The objective of this working group is to study and discuss these issues.

WG16.2 Entertainment Robot

Robots are becoming one of the most appealing forms of entertainment. New entertainment robots and/or pet robots are becoming popular. Also, from a theoretical point of view, compared with computer graphics-based characters/animations, robots constitute an interesting research object as they have a physical entity. Taking these into consideration, it was decided at the SG16 annual meeting that a new working group on entertainment robots is to be established.

WG16.3 Theoretical Basis of Entertainment

Although the entertainment industry is huge, providing goods such as video games, toys, movies, etc., little academic interest has been paid to such questions as what is the core of entertainment, what are the technologies that would create new forms of entertainment, and how can the core technologies of entertainment be applied to other areas such as education, learning, and so on. The main objective of this WG is to study these issues.

WG16.4 Games and Entertainment Computing

The scope of this workgroup includes, but is not limited to, the following applications, technologies, and activities.

Applications:
- Analytical games (e.g., chess, go, poker)
- Commercial games (e.g., action games, roleplaying games, strategy games)
- Mobile games (e.g., mobile phones, PDA's)
- Interactive multimedia (e.g., virtual reality, simulations)

Technologies:
- Search techniques
- Machine learning
- Reasoning
- Agent technology
- Human-computer interaction

WG16.5 Social and Ethical Issues in Entertainment Computing

The social and ethical implications of entertainment computing include:
- actual and potential human usefulness or harm of entertainment computing
- social impact of these technologies
- developments of the underlying infrastructure
- rationale in innovation and design processes
- dynamics of technology development
- ethical development
- cultural diversity and other cultural issues
- education of the public about the social and ethical implications of entertainment computing, and of computer professionals about the effects of their work.

WG 16.5 explicitly cares about the position of, and the potentials for, vulnerable groups such as children, the less-educated, disabled, elderly and unemployed people, cultural minorities, unaware users and others.

Anyone who is qualified and interested in active participation in one of the working groups is kindly invited to contact one of the WG chairs.

Table of Contents

Social Impact and Evaluation

Seamful/Seamless Interface

Body and Face

Robot

Music and Sound

Mixed Reality and Mobile

Education

Virtual Reality and Simulation

Theory

Posters and Demonstration

A New Framework for Entertainment Computing: From Passive to Active Experience

Ryohei Nakatsu[1], Matthias Rauterberg[2], and Peter Vorderer[3]

[1] School of Science and Technology, Kwansei Gakuin University,
Kobe-Sanda Campus 2-1, Gakuen, Sanda Hyogo, Japan
nakatsu@ksc.kwansei.ac.jp
http://ist.ksc.kwansei.ac.jp/~nakatsu/
[2] Department of Industrial Design, Technical University Eindhoven,
Den Dolech 2, 5612AZ Eindhoven, The Netherlands
g.w.m.rauterberg@tue.nl
http://www.idemployee.id.tue.nl/g.w.m.rauterberg/
[3] Annenberg School for Communication, University of Southern California,
3502 Watt Way, Los Angeles, CA 90089-0281, USA
vorderer@usc.edu
http://ascweb.usc.edu/
http://www.ijk.hmt-hannover.de/

Abstract. In this paper a new framework for entertainment computing is introduced and discussed. Based on already existing models and concepts the different links and relationships between enjoyment, flow, presence, and different forms of experiences are shown and their contributions to the new framework reviewed. To address the more fundamental and theoretical issues regarding entertainment, we have to utilize existing theories in information processing, enjoyment and flow theory. Some already possible and probably important conclusions for the design of new entertainment system are drawn.

Keywords: Adaptivity, active experience, complexity, enjoyment, entertainment, flow, incongruity, information, integrated presence, learning, play.

1 Introduction

The application and research domain of entertainment technology can be separated in different fields: (1) game, (2) sport, (3) novel and movie, and (4) art (see Altman and Nakatsu, 1997). With upcoming developments of advanced technology (Nakatsu, 1998), new media applications can be realized (e.g. Nakatsu, Tosa and Ochi, 1998; Cavazza, 2003). The *characteristics of new media* are:

▲ New types of experiences (e.g. Ono, Imai and Nakatsu, 2000)
▲ [Inter-]active experiences, compared to passive experiences
▲ Integration of spatial, social, mental and physical presence

Although a variety of theories has been advanced in communication and media psychology that describe and explain specific experiential states commonly understood as 'entertainment' or 'enjoyment', it seems to be very challenging to achieve a

F. Kishino et al. (Eds.): ICEC 2005, LNCS 3711, pp. 1–12, 2005.
© IFIP International Federation for Information Processing 2005

coherent, integrative view on entertainment. The main reasons for these difficulties are the huge variety of experiences called 'entertainment' (e.g., curiosity, exhilaration, tenderness, pride, melancholy, sexual arousal, perception of being in control or holding power) and the procedural dynamics of entertainment, that is, the strong variability of cognitive and affective dimensions of entertainment over time within the course of media use (Vorderer, Klimmt and Ritterfeld, 2004).

Looking back, various types of considerations on *play* are already published: Groos (1901/1899), Huizinga (1980/1939), Caillois (1961/1958), Piaget (1969/1947), Csikszentmihalyi (1975), Kauke (1992), Scheuerl (1997), and Raessens and Goldstein (2005). While Groos (1901) argued that children's play is a preparation for life, this was later often credited with the idea that children need to run off their surplus energy. The *classification of play* by Caillois (1961) is given as follows: (1) **Competition** (Greek: Agon): Boxing, Soccer, Chess, etc.; (2) **Chance** (Latin: Alea): Dice, Roulette, etc.; (3) **Mimicry** (Greek: Mimicry): Actor, Theatrical play, etc.; and (4) **Ecstasy** (Greek: Ilinx): Swing, Thrill ride, etc. What is missing in Caillois' classification? Ecstatic immersion (Ilinx) is an essential factor in **all** plays, and Csikszentmihalyi (1975, 1990) has noticed this. Caillios confuses physical presence and mental presence. Does it really make sense to classify soccer and chess into the same group? According to the flow concept by Csikszentmihalyi (1990), flow is an essential factor of play in the following sense: (1) flow is same as immersion based on engagement (Douglas and Hargadon, 2000), and (2) the strict border between work and play is eliminated (Rauterberg and Paul, 1990; Rauterberg, 2004a).

1.1 Curiosity, Arousal and Pleasingness

Curiosity is defined as a need, 'thirst' or desire for *knowledge*. The concept of curiosity is central to motivation in relation to mental presence. The term can be used as both a description of a specific behavior as well as a hypothetical construct to explain the same behavior to achieve mental presence. Berlyne (1960) believes that curiosity is a motivational prerequisite for exploratory behavior. Exploratory behavior refers to all activities concerned with gathering information about the environment and/or changing the environment. This leads to the conflict and question of whether exploratory behavior should be defined (1) in terms of the movements that a human performs while exploring, or (2) in terms of the goal or purpose of the observable behavior. A clear distinction between these two seems to be not always possible (Fjeld, Lauche, Bichsel, Voorhorst, Krueger and Rauterberg, 2002).

According to Berlyne (1960) arousal is a function of collative stimulus properties such as complexity, novelty, incongruity (incompatible, discrepant), and surprisingness (unexpected). Environments with medium level of uncertainty (and a positive hedonic tone) produce the most positive aesthetic judgments. Sufficient empirical support exists for Berlyne's curvilinear, inverted U-shape relationship that has been obtained at least for the complexity dimension that determines the arousal level (see Figure 1; based on former work of Wundt, 1874). Similar relationships have been obtained for other dimensions: more novel, more surprising, and less incongruous environments are preferred. Although Berlyne's research was pioneering, he did not sufficiently investigate the relationship to *individual* skills and preferences. This was addressed by Csikszentmihalyi's research (1975, 1990) about 'flow'.

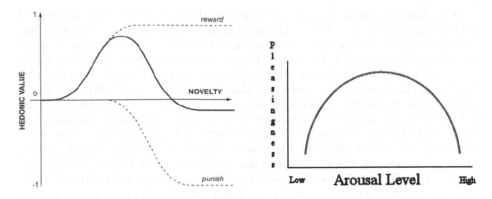

Fig. 1. The Wundt Curve (1874, left) shows the hedonic function used to calculate interest; the hedonic function is shown as a solid line, the reward and punishment sigmoidal curves summed to form the hedonic function are shown dashed. Relationship between cortical *arousal level* and *pleasingness* (right, adapted from Berlyne, 1960, p. 201).

1.2   Conceptual Models of Flow

All flow component segmentation models are based upon Csikszentmihalyi's defini-tion of flow in terms of skills and challenges (Csikszentmihalyi, 1990, p. 74). How-ever, the segmentation models attempt to account for all possible combinations (com-ponents) of high/low skills and challenges. Underlying all of the flow component segmentation models is the central role of skill and challenge as predictors of flow. Novak and Hoffman (1997) compare two flow component segmentation models. The original three component model from Csikszentmihalyi (1990; shown in Figure 2 left) identifies flow as congruent skills and challenges, both high and low; *anxiety* is iden-tified as the combination of high challenges and low skills, and *boredom* as high skills and low challenges.

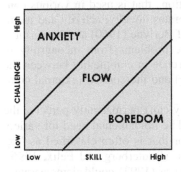
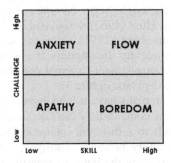

Fig. 2. Three component flow model (left; adapted from Csikszentmihalyi, 1990, p. 74); four component flow model (right; adapted from Novak and Hoffman, 1997)

In the four component model from Novak and Hoffman (1997; shown in Figure 2 right) identifies flow only in the combination of high skills and high challenges. They separate *apathy* from flow in the combination of low skills and low challenges. Sufficient empirical support has been found for the reformulated four component model shown in Figure 2 (right). An extension of this four component model is an extended eight component model (Massimini and Massimo, 1988; Ellis, Voelkl and Morris, 1994), which also allows for intermediate (moderate) levels of skills and challenges, and identifies four additional components: arousal, control, relaxation, and worry. As the arousal-relaxation distinction is collinear with challenge, and the control-worry distinction is collinear with skill, the eight component model does not provide any additional information that allows one to predict flow only based upon skill and challenge, over and above the four component model from Novak and Hoffman (1997). All these different multi-component models rely on a non-learning human with an almost fixed level of skills. But humans can and do learn and therefore change their skills and capabilities based on their actions taken.

We are compelled to learn and to make experiences our whole life. Human information processing can not be independent of this life-long learning process. In this sense, humans are open systems. In his law of requisite variety Ashby (1958) pointed out, that for a given state of the environment, an open system has to be able to respond adaptively, otherwise the adaptability and the ability of the system to survive is reduced. A learning system, without input or with constant input, either decays or (in the best case) remains fixed. Learning and the need for variety implies, that with constant input variety from context the requisite variety of the system tends to be not satisfied over time. This is a strong argument against 'one best way' solutions in system design to achieve a sufficient level of enjoyment (Csikszentmihalyi and Hunter, 2003).

1.3 Information Processing Framework

Based on the work of Streufert and Streufert (1978), Rauterberg (1995) extended their concepts into a general information processing framework by including learning of adaptive systems. Information and information processing are one of the most important aspects of dynamic systems. The term 'information', that is used in various contexts, might better be replaced with one that incorporates novelty, activity and learning. Hunt (1963) designated the 'arousal potential' of Berlyne (1960) as 'incongruity'. Rauterberg (1995) shifts the semantic and theoretic problems from incongruity to complexity. Incongruity is now defined as the difference in complexity between the learning system (internal complexity of the memory) and the context (external complexity) (see Figure 3).

Humans have a fundamental need for variety: they can't permanently perceive the same context, they can't do always the same things. The fundamental need for variety leads to a different interpretation of human behavior that is often classified as 'exploratory behavior' (Berlyne, 1960) or even 'errors' (Rauterberg and Felix, 1996). Variety is the basis to measure complexity. Rauterberg (1993) could demonstrate a promising approach of measuring behavioral and cognitive complexity in a fully automated way (see also recently Fromm, 2004). We can distinguish two different situations: (1) positive incongruity, and (2) negative incongruity (see Figure 3). If the context complexity of the environment is fixed then the learning process will automatically decrease the amount of incongruity, and at the end will turn positive incongruity into negative incongruity. If the actual amount of positive incongruity is below an individual specific threshold then this individual system can either start to actively increase the context complexity or looking for another context with sufficient complexity.

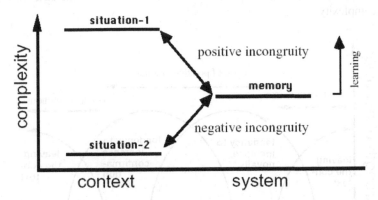

Fig. 3. The difference between the complexity of the system's mental model and the complexity of the situational context is called *incongruity* (adapted from Rauterberg 1995, p. 59)

Ulich (1987) differentiates between 'boredom' and 'monotony'. *Boredom* emerges from the feeling of not having enough possibilities to be active (fixed context complexity; see Figure 3). *Monotony* emerges from the feeling of doing always the same things ('fixed' system complexity; see Figure 3). If the context does not provide sufficient action affordances and opportunities (e.g. context complexity), we are condemned to boredom; if we are not allowed for sufficient variety and learning, we are condemned to monotony, and this monotony effect seems to be independent from the complexity of the system's knowledge structure (memory). Monotony can exists on any level of memory complexity and is mainly caused by insufficient learning and/or action opportunities.

Traditional concepts of information processing are models of homeostasis on a basic level *without* learning (e.g., Shannon, 1949). Human activity and the irreversible learning process are the main driving forces that cause permanently in-homeostasis in the relationship between a learning system and its context. A suitable model for information processing for learning systems must be conceptualized on a higher level: a homeostatic model of 'in-homeostasis'. The concept to information processing from Rauterberg (1995) includes action and learning and shows an inverted U-shaped function between positive incongruity and strength of particular behavior to keep the positive incongruity level optimized (see Figure 4).

First we have to accept that actual amount of incongruity is individual, context and situation specific; further is this situation specific incongruity permanently drifting based to learning. To keep the incongruity in an optimal range, the learning system has to be provided with a context in which the complexity should permanently increasing as well to provide a sufficient amount of positive incongruity (Csikszentmihalyi and Hunter, 2003). This contextual adaptation rate should be similar or close to the individual learning rate[1]. If any of these conditions are not given, then each individual will enter the range of negative emotions and will start actions to re-establish a situation within the range of positive emotions (see Figure 4). If the incongruity increases (e.g., too fast increase of context complexity), the human starts actions to increase confirmation and therefore to decrease external complexity. If the incongruity decreases, the human would react with exploratory or other actions to increase novelty and external complexity.

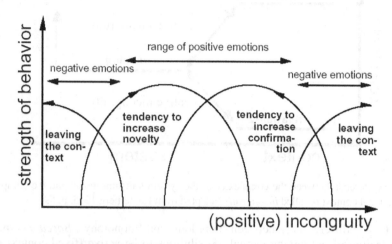

Fig. 4. The coherence between positive incongruity, emotions and strength of observable behavior (taken from Rauterberg 1995, p. 66)

Future research will show how this model will be able to provide important design recommendations for entertainment systems with dynamic and adaptive behavior, beyond game levels with different complexity (see also Fabricatore, Nussbaum and Rosas, 2002). The work of Spronk (2005) looks very promising.

1.4 Conceptual Model of Flow

A conceptual model of flow in relation to skill, challenge and presence is described in detail by Hoffman and Novak (1996) and Novak, Hoffman and Yung (2000). Key features of this model are that flow is determined by skills, challenges and presence. Challenges and presence are prerequisites for flow and exploratory behavior. The latest revised version of Hoffman and Novak's structural model is shown in Figure 5. Novak, Hoffman and Yung (2000) indicate the construct of exploratory behavior parallel to flow. Control in Figure 5 refers to Ajzen's (1988) construct of perceived behavioral control, and is indicated as an antecedent, rather than a consequence, of flow. Challenge determines flow directly, and via attention and presence indirectly (see Figure 5). This model of Novak, Hoffman and Yung (2000) is one of the first concepts in which (1) individual skill level (including learning), (2) external challenges, and (3) presence is related to exploratory behavior and flow.

---

[1] This is the central concept and challenge of any kind of didactic (Heiman, 1962).

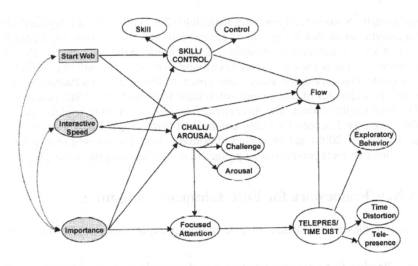

Fig. 5. Structural model of presence and flow in relation to other dimensions (adapted from Hoffman, Novak and Yung, 2000, p. 34)

In the model of Novak, Hoffman and Yung (2000, p. 34; see Figure 5) the direct paths to flow from skill, challenge, and presence are positive and statistically significant. However, there was no support for the hypothesis that greater focused attention corresponds directly to greater flow, although focused attention was found to correspond to greater presence and time distortion. Interactive speed exerts a direct positive influence on flow, but greater speed did not correspond to greater focused attention or presence and time distortion. Greater importance was positively associated with greater focused attention, and the longer the usage was, the greater the users' skill and control in the virtual environment.

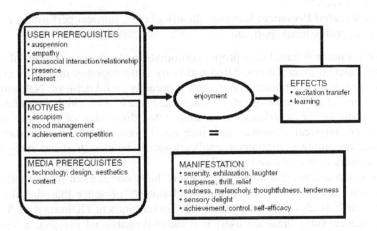

Fig. 6. Enjoyment as the central concept for entertainment experience (adapted from Vorderer, Klimmt and Ritterfeld, 2004, p. 393)

Additionally Vorderer, Klimmt and Ritterfeld (2004) propose an integrated view of media entertainment that is capable of covering more of the dimensional complexity and dynamics of entertainment experiences than existing theories can do. Based on a description of what is meant by complexity and dynamics, the authors outline a conceptual model that is centered around enjoyment as the core of entertainment, and that addresses prerequisites of enjoyment which have to be met by the individual user and by the given media product. The theoretical foundation is used to explain why people display strong preferences for being entertained (motivational perspective; see Vorderer and Bryant, 2005) and what kind of consequences entertaining media consumption may have (effects perspective, e.g., facilitation of learning processes; Figure 6).

2 A New Framework for Entertainment Computing

Human activities in the context of entertainment experiences can be related to two major classes:

▲ **Passive Experiences:** Reading novels, watching movies; people watch experiences of others, etc.; sometimes called 'lean back' entertainment.
▲ **Active Experiences:** Doing sports, creating art; people are active participants in the dynamic situation (e.g. Nakatsu, Tosa and Ochi, 1998) ; sometimes called 'lean forward' entertainment.

Passive and active experiences are the two poles of the 'activity' dimension. Active experience is mainly correlated with 'physical' presence, and passive experience mainly with 'mental' presence. Nakatsu (2004) combines 'physical' and 'mental' presence into 'integrated' presence.

▲ **Physical Presence:** hear sound, look at image, utter speech, move body, exercise, etc.
▲ **Mental Presence:** use language, read a book, listen to music, watch picture or movie, etc.
▲ **Integrated Presence:** Karaoke, theatrical play, musical performance, sculpture, professional sport, etc.

Integrated presence is based on a proper combination of a certain amount of physical activity and mental imaginations. Mind and body come together in a more enjoyable form of experiences and presence than each separately could achieve. Nakatsu (2004) proposed a *new classification of entertainment applications* in which the dimension of 'passive versus active experience' is related to the dimension of presence which is separated into 'physical', 'mental' and 'integrated' forms. In this new framework all existing and upcoming entertainment applications can be classified and categorized in a comprehensive new way (see Figure 7).

Virtual environments and new entertainment have added even more challenges to entertainment theory. Clearly, the amount and state of presence that virtual environments can elicit is closely connected to new entertainment (Klimmt and Vorderer, 2003). However, since presence itself is a multi-dimensional concept, a very large number of connections between (dimensions and precursors of) presence and (dimensions / manifestations of) entertainment is conceivable. For example, interactivity, which is a key element of virtual environments and an important determinant of integrated presence, holds fundamental implications for the quality and intensity of new entertainment, primarily for individuals who can cope with the additional learning challenges of interactive media (Vorderer, Knobloch and Schramm, 2001).

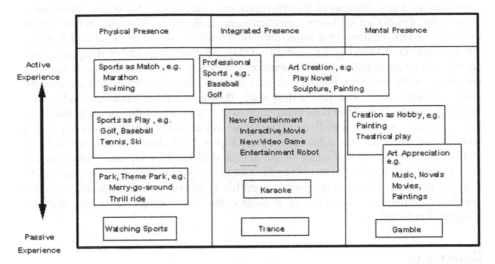

Fig. 7. Classification framework for entertainment applications (adapted from Nakatsu, 2004)

Klimmt (2003) and Klimmt and Hartmann (2005) has linked interactivity to such diverse dimensions of enjoyment as *effectance, suspense, curiosity, pride*, and simulated experience of *attractive action roles*. Vorderer, Hartmann and Klimmt (2003) have discussed the implications of interactivity for *competitive* forms of entertainment. On the other side based on an intensive literature search (Rauterberg, 2004b), Rauterberg could find that *collaborative* forms of entertainment have significant positive effects on human growth and development. Other key characteristics such as sensuous richness (Turner, Turner and Caroll, 2005), audio-visual realism (Shirabe and Baba, 1997), digital narratives (Cavazza, 2003), aesthetics (Overbeeke and Wensveen, 2004; Wensveen and Overbeeke, 2004), and intercultural differences (Rauterberg, 2004a) have not yet been systematically connected to entertainment theory.

Another important link between presence and new entertainment refers to the assumption that enjoyment only occurs in situations when users perceive themselves as being in *control* (Früh and Stiehler, 2003). However, very immersive new entertainment applications could induce very captive and overwhelming feelings of presence, which in turn might lead to a reduction of perceived control and thus diminish enjoyment. From this perspective, entertainment experiences can only unfold if users achieve a balance between inner distance to and 'being captivated' by a virtual environment, which preserves a required minimum of perceived control over the situation (Kiili, 2005). The relationship between 'overwhelming' presence, perceived control and entertainment is thus another key objective of future theoretical and empirical investigations.

3 Conclusions

In this paper we have several theoretical concepts presented and discussed which can contribute to a new framework for entertainment computing. One major optimization criteria for the design of future entertainment applications (e.g. interactive movie, new type of video games, entertainment robots, etc) is *enjoyment* (Tosa and Nakatsu, 1998; Vorderer, Klimmt and Ritterfeld, 2004). To reach enjoyment integrated presence has to be combined with active experience. Active experience is mainly based on sufficient motor behavior involved in user actions: the cognitively and emotionally enhanced body! If the user is in a flow state, then active experience can lead to integrated presence. One of the remaining questions is how to get the user into the flow? Let us assume, we have a sufficient interactive environment which involves physical and mental presence (to achieve integrated presence), how should we link the challenges from this action space to the actual skill level of the user? One possible and promising answer is a sufficient adaptive system behavior to the user's learning progress. Enabling the user to keep his or her optimal incongruity (= proper match of challenges to skills), is probably the best design to reach enjoyable integrated presence.

References

Ajzen, I. (1988). *Attitudes, Personality, and Behavior*. Chicago: Dorsey Press.
Altman, E. & Nakatsu, R. (1997). Interactive Movies: Techniques, Technology and Content. *Course Notes, No. 16*, ACM SIGGRAPH'97.
Ashby, R.W. (1958). Requisite variety and its implications for the control of complex systems. *Cybernetica*, Vol. 1, No. 2, pp. 83-99.
Berlyne, D.E. (1960). *Conflict, Arousal, and Curiosity*. New York: McGraw Hill.
Caillois, R. (1961). *Man, Play and Games* [Translated from 1958]. New York: Free Press.
Cavazza, M. (2003).Virtual Unreality: Storytelling in Virtual Environments. In: *Proceedings of the ACM Symposium on Virtual Reality Software and Technology VRST'03* (pp. 4-5), New York: ACM.
Csikszentmihalyi, M. & Hunter, J. (2003). Happiness in everyday life: the uses of experience samples. *Journal of Happiness Studies*, Vol 4, pp. 185-199.
Csikszentmihalyi, M. (1975). *Beyond boredom and anxiety: experiencing flow in work and play*. San Francisco: Jossey-Bass Publishers.
Csikszentmihalyi, M. (1990). *Flow: the psychology of optimal experience*, New York: Harper Perennial.
Douglas, Y. & Hargadon, A. (2000). The pleasure principle: immersion, engagement, flow. In: *Proceedings of ACM Conference on Hypertext'00* (pp. 153-160), New York: ACM.
Ellis, G.D., Voelkl, J.E. & Morris, C. (1994). Measurement and analysis issues with explanation of variance in daily experience using the flow model. *Journal of Leisure Research*, Vol. 26, No. 4, pp. 337-356.
Fabricatore, C., Nussbaum, M. & Rosas, R. (2002). Playability in action videogames: a qualitative design model. *Human-Computer Interaction*, Vol. 17, pp. 311-368.
Fjeld M., Lauche, K., Bichsel, M., Voorhorst, F., Krueger, H. & Rauterberg, M. (2002). Physical and virtual tools: activity theory applied to the design of groupware. *Computer Supported Cooperative Work*, Vol. 11, Nos. 1-2, pp. 153-180.
Fromm, J. (2004). *The emergence of complexity*. Kassel: Kassel University Press.

Früh, W. & Stiehler, H.-J. (2003; Eds.). Theorie der Unterhaltung-ein interdisziplinärer Diskurs [Translated: Entertainment theory–an interdisciplinary discourse]. Köln: van Halem Verlag.

Groos, K. (1901). *The play of man* [Translated from 1899]. New York: D. Appleton.

Heimann, P. (1962). Didaktik als Theorie und Lehre. *Die deutsche Schule*, Vol. 54, No. 9, pp. 407-27.

Hoffman, D.L. & Novak, T.P. (1996). Marketing in hypermedia computer-mediated environments: conceptual foundations. *Journal of Marketing*, Vol. 60, pp. 50-68.

Huizinga, J. (1980) (translated from 1939). *Homo Ludens: a study of the play element in culture.* London: Routledge and Kegan Paul.

Hunt, J.M.V. (1963). Motivation inherent in information processing and action. In: O.J. Harvey (Ed.) *Motivation and social interaction: the cognitive determinants* (pp. 35-94). New York: Ronald Press.

Kauke, M. (1992). Spielintelligenz: spielend lernen-spielend lehren? [Translation: Play intelligence: playful learning-playful teaching]. Heidelberg: Spektrum Press.

Kiili, K. (2005). Digital game-based learning: towards an experimental gaming model. *Internet and Higher Educations*, Vol. 8, pp. 13-24.

Klimmt, C. & Hartmann, T. (2005, in press). Effectance, self-efficacy, and the motivation to play computer games. In P. Vorderer & J. Bryant (Eds.), *Playing video games: Motives, responses, and consequences.* Mahwah: Lawrence Erlbaum Associates.

Klimmt, C. & Vorderer, P. (2003). Media Psychology 'is not yet there': introducing theories on media entertainment to the Presence debate. *Presence: Teleoperators and Virtual Environments*, 12 (4), 346-359.

Klimmt, C. (2003). Dimensions and determinants of the enjoyment of playing digital games: A three-level model. In M. Copier & J. Raessens (Eds.), *Level Up: Digital Games Research Conference* (pp. 246-257), Utrecht: Utrecht University.

Massimini, F. & Massimo, C. (1988). The systematic assessment of flow in daily experience. In M. Csikszentmihalyi and I. Csikszentmihalyi (Eds.), *Optimal Experience: Psychological Studies of Flow in Consciousness*, (pp. 288-306), New York: Cambridge University Press.

Nakatsu, R., Tosa, N. & Ochi, T. (1998). Interactive movie system with multi-person participation and anytime interaction capabilities. In: *Proceedings of the 6th ACM International conference on Multimedia: Technologies for interactive movies* (pp. 2-10), New York: ACM.

Nakatsu, R. (1998). Nonverbal information recognition and its application to communication. In: *Proceedings of the 6th ACM International Conference on Multimedia: Face/gesture recognition and their applications* (pp. 2-9), New York: ACM.

Nakatsu, R. (2004). Entertainment computing. Retrieved March 2005 from: http://www.idemployee.id.tue.nl/g.w.m.rauterberg/presentations/Nakatsu(2004)/Nakatsu%5 B2004%5D_files/frame.htm

Novak, T.L., Hoffman, D.P. & Yung, Y.F. (2000). Measuring the customer experience in online environments: a structural modeling approach. *Marketing Science*, Vol. 19, No. 1, pp. 22-42.

Novak, T.P. & Hoffman, D.L. (1997). Measuring the flow experience among web users. Retrieved from http://elab.vanderbilt.edu/research/papers/pdf/manuscripts/Flow-MeasuringFlowExpJul1997-pdf.pdf

Ono, T., Imai, M. & Nakatsu, R. (2000). Reading a robot's mind: a model of utterance understanding based on the theory of mind mechanism. *Advanced Robotics*, Vol. 14, No. 4, pp. 311-326.

Overbeeke, C.J. & Wensveen, S.A.G. (2004). Beauty in use. *Human-Computer Interaction*, Vol. 19, No. 4, pp. 367-369.

Piaget, J. (1962). *Play, dreams and imitation in childhood* [Translated from 1947]. New York: Norton.

Raessens, J. & Goldstein, J. (2005, Eds.). *Handbook of Computer Game Studies.* Cambridge: MIT Press.

Rauterberg, M. & Felix, D. (1996). Human errors: disadvantages and advantages. In: *Proceedings of 4th Pan Pacific Conference on Occupational Ergonomics PPCOE'96* (pp. 25-28). Hsinchu: Ergonomics Society Taiwan.

Rauterberg, M. & Paul, H.-J. (1990). Computerspiele - Computerarbeit: Spielerische Momente in der Arbeit. In: F. Nake (Ed.), *Ergebnisse der 9. Arbeitstagung "Mensch-Maschine-Kommunikation"* (Informatics Report No. 8/90, pp. 13-49). Bremen: University Bremen.

Rauterberg, M. (1993) AMME: an automatic mental model evaluation to analyze user behaviour traced in a finite, discrete state space. *Ergonomics*, Vol. 36, No. 11, pp. 1369-1380.

Rauterberg, M. (1995). About a framework for information and information processing of learning systems. In: E. Falkenberg, W. Hesse & A. Olive (Eds.), *Information System Concepts--Towards a consolidation of views* (pp. 54-69). London: Chapman & Hall.

Rauterberg, M. (2004a). Enjoyment and Entertainment in East and West. In: M. Rauterberg (ed.), *Entertainment Computing ICEC'04* (pp. 176-181). *Lecture Notes in Computer Science*, Vol. 3166, Springer Press.

Rauterberg, M. (2004b). Positive effects of entertainment technology on human behaviour. In: R. Jacquart (ed.), *Building the Information Society* (pp. 51-58). IFIP, Kluwer Press.

Scheuerl, H. (1997, 12th edition, Ed.): Theorien des Spiels [Translation: Theories of Play]. Weinheim: Beltz.

Shannon, C.E. (1949). The mathematical theory of communication. In: C.E. Shannon & W. Weaver (Eds.) *The mathematical theory of communication* (pp. 29-125). University of Illinois Press.

Shirabe, M. & Baba, Y. (1997). Do three-dimensional real-time interfaces really play important roles?. In: M.J. Smith, G. Salvendy & R. Koubek (Eds.) *Design of computing systems: social and ergonomic considerations* (pp. 849-852), Amsterdam: Elsevier.

Spronk, P. (2005). *Adaptive Game AI.* PhD Thesis, University of Maastricht, Netherlands

Streufert, S. & Streufert, S.C. (1978). *Behavior in the complex environment.* Washington: Winston & Sons.

Tosa, N. & Nakatsu, R. (1998). Interactie poem system. In: *Proceedings of 6th ACM International Conference on Multimedia* (pp. 115-118), New York: ACM.

Turner, P., Turner, S. & Carroll, F. (2005) The Tourist Gaze: Towards Contextualised Virtual Environments. In: P. Turner & E. Davenport (Eds.) *Spaces, Spatiality and Technology.* (The Kluwer International Series on Computer Supported Cooperative Work, Vol. 5), Springer.

Ulich, E. (1987). Umgang mit Monotonie und Komplexität [Translation: Dealing with monotony and complexity]. *Technische Rundschau*, Vol. 5, pp. 8-13.

Vorderer, P. & Bryant, J. (2005, in press, Eds.). *Playing video games: Motives, responses, consequences.* Mahwah, NJ: Lawrence Erlbaum Associates.

Vorderer, P., Hartmann, T. & Klimmt, C. (2003). Explaining the enjoyment of playing video games: the role of competition. In: *Proceedings of the 2nd IFIP International Conference on Entertainment Computing ICEC'03* (online). New York: ACM.

Vorderer, P., Klimmt, C. & Ritterfeld, U. (2004). Enjoyment: At the heart of media entertainment. *Communication Theory*, Vol. 14, No. 4, pp. 388-408.

Vorderer, P., Knobloch, S. & Schramm, H. (2001). Does entertainment suffer from interactivity? The impact of watching an interactive TV movie on viewers' experience of entertainment. *Media Psychology*, Vol. 3, No. 4, pp. 343-363.

Wensveen, S.A.G. & Overbeeke, C.J. (2004). The role of balance and symmetry in the expression of valence, arousal and urgency in interaction design. *Bulletin of Psychology and the Arts*, Vol. 4, No. 2, pp. 77-80.

Wundt, W. (1874). *Grundzüge der physiologischen Psychologie* [Translation: Principles of physiological psychology]. Leipzig: Engelmann.

Cultural Computing with Context-Aware Application: ZENetic Computer

Naoko Tosa[1], Seigow Matsuoka[2], Brad Ellis[1], Hirotada Ueda[3],
and Ryohei Nakatsu[4]

[1] Kyoto Univeristy, Academic Center for Computing and Media Studies,
Yoshida-Nihon-Matsu, Sakyo, 606-8501 Kyoto, Japan
tosa@mm.media.kyoto-u.ac.jp,
bellis@deepthought.org
[2] Editorial Engineering Laboratory, 7-6-64 Akasaka Minato-ku,
107-0052, Tokyo, Japan
[3] National Institute of Information and Communications Technology,
Keihanna Human Info-Communication Research Center,
3-5 Hikari-dai, Seika-cho, Soraku-gun,
619-0289, Kyoto, Japan
hiro-u@nict.go.jp
[4] Kwansai Gakuin University, School of Science and Technology,
2-1 Gakuen, 669-1337 Sanda, Japan
nakatsu@ksc.kwansei.ac.jp

Abstract. We offer Cultural Computing as a method for cultural translation that uses scientific methods to represent the essential aspects of culture. Including images that heretofore have not been the focus of computing, such as images of Eastern thought and Buddhism, and the Sansui paintings, poetry and kimono that evoke these images, we projected the style of communication developed by Zen schools over hundreds of years into a world for the user to explore – an exotic Eastern Sansui world. Through encounters with Zen Koans and haiku poetry, the user is constantly and sharply forced to confirm the whereabouts of his or her self-consciousness. However, there is no "right answer" to be found anywhere.

1 Introduction: Cultural Computing

Since involving various kinds of media technology in our everyday lives, we have built a sphere of communication that reaches to all parts of the globe. However, on the other hand, we are starting to feel the danger that, as the communication network expands, the level of personal communication has become shallow.

In this situation, a new communication medium that will convey personal depth of feeling across long distances has become urgently necessary. Within this context, we decided with this project to pursue the possibility of a communication medium that incorporates a new kind of interactivity, with editorial engineering [1] and art and technology [2] as a foundation, and including research on the operation in which interactions of multiple cultures come to fruition, and research on the "intelligence" that appears in between the user and the system.

F. Kishino et al. (Eds.): ICEC 2005, LNCS 3711, pp. 13–23, 2005.

Human communication is originally something cultivated in an environment comprising localities, national customs and language. Therefore, the fruits of these cultures have strong roots in their unique histories.

However, the media that developed in order to convey these peculiarities across cultures were communication media such as writing, music and film. Now, as the computer society covers the earth, the task that computers must take on is the clear and accurate intercommunication between local and global cultures. Toward that end, it is first necessary for those involved with computer technology to bring to life local characteristics.

Thus, the authors focused on the cultural roots of their native country, Japan. This includes Buddhist culture, the *kanji* culture, *haiku* and other Japanese poetry and song, and traditional Japanese dress (*kimono*). They decided especially to dig into the unique communication space and imagery methods developed in Zen Buddhism and landscape ink painting (*sansui* painting).

Within the traditional relationship between culture and computers, emphasis has been placed on the preservation of decaying traditional cultures for the sake of future generations, restoration of artifacts, and computer graphics simulations recreating lost relics. However, the authors struck on the possibility of computing the previously unquantifiable essence of culture inherent within people, such as personal subjectivity, feeling, emotion and cultural personality. [3]

With this research project, the authors offer the concept and direction of "cultural computing" as above, and describe, in simple terms and through the realization of an actual interactive system, a computing method reflecting the differences of emotion, consciousness and memory that will be indispensable for the future communication abilities of computers.

As Cultural Computing is a very broad field, in order to produce a specific example, one must pick out a single local culture and use that as a base for building a real system. In this case, we chose Zen, a special area of Buddhism, and developed and evaluated ZENetic Computer as a system in which people can experience Zen culture firsthand.

2 ZENetic Computer Artistic Concept

We developed ZENetic Computer as a specific example of Cultural Computing. We focused on the roots of Japanese culture, including Buddhist culture, kanji culture, waka and haiku poetry. [8] We decided to especially focus on the unique communication space Zen and sansui ink painting create.

Below is explained the scenario a user experiences within ZENetic Computer. First, the user builds a three-dimensional sansui ink painting on the display using an intuitive and user-friendly interface, constructing her own virtual space.

These images express the natural world that characterizes the East and Japan and their philosophical concepts, providing the user with a dramatic experience very different from the images seen in modern-day life. [9] In this way, in the introduction, the system brings about a kind of awakening within the user, and encourages their unconscious imagination.

Next, as the system classifies the user's state of consciousness based on the composition of their sansui landscape design, it generates a story appropriate for the user, drawing her through the display into this alternate world.

Within the story are included mechanisms to shake the user's consciousness developed from haiku poetry and Zen riddles (koan). The story built from these elements is not a complete linear story like those found in movies or novels, but rather a nonlinear collection of short story-fragments. A user who experiences these inconclusive story-fragments feels a kind of uncertainty, and holds an expectation and desire to build a complete story by connecting these fragments. Because of this desire, the user, in being asked questions without a "correct" answer, may hesitate somewhat but cannot help but try to answer these questions.

Through several such triggers lurking within the center of culture, the user connects these stories and builds her own unique narrative. Next, as the user uses a virtual brush, a rake for the rock garden, and images within the screen in response to questions posed by the system via images and voice, she begins to realize that the system is demanding that she meet it face-to-face. This means the door to her "unified consciousness" has begun to open further. As our desire to connect the story fragments mixes with the system's user interface, the distance between our every-day self and our true hidden self begins to shrink.

Ma interaction plays an important role in the process of fusing together these two selves. Ma is a very Japanese concept; it is one that places a high value on ephemeral events – the here-and-now – within every experience.

The user, having thus traveled through several stages and several scenes, now coming to the end of the trip, interacts with a bull, which is used in Zen as a metaphor for expressing one's true self. Through this dialogue, the user can experience the process in which the everyday self and the subconscious self fuse together to bring about a unified self-consciousness.

Fig. 1. ZENetic Computer at SIGGRAPH 2004 Emerging Technologies

As the surrounding environment plays a very important role in this experience, we have made an effort to conjure an Eastern atmosphere for the ZENetic Computer installation. (Fig. 1)

3 Story Generated from Symbols

3.1 Creation of a Typical *Sansui* Painting

We divided sansui painting into twelve hieroglyphic characters (rock, mountain, moon, traveler, bridge, bird, tree, flower, wise man, cloud and water) and made them into icons. The user drags any 2D icon and constructs his or her own 3D *sansui* painting. Fig. 2 is an example user-constructed *sansui* painting.

Fig. 2. Making a 3D Sansui Ink Painting

3.2 *Sanen* Design

As one can see in the Sesshu painting in Fig. 3, there is a unique method of perspective for *sansui* paintings called *sanen*. Within the painting are three perspectives: koen, lying far away with a view from below; heien, with a straight-on view; and shinen, close-up and viewed from above. Depending on the position of the user's icons, graphics corresponding to the sanen area are displayed, increasing the realism of the user-created sansui painting.

Fig. 3. Composition of *sanen* perspective in Sesshu's work

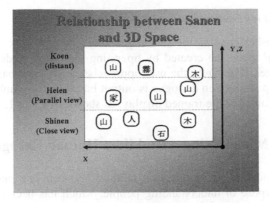

Fig. 4. Composition and distance within 3D space

Fig. 5. Interaction with the rock garden interface

Table 1. Relationships between *Sansui* symbols and Haiku

Haiku Output	Icon Priority		
The day passes slowly; A pheasant comes down onto the bridge.	Bird	Bridge	House
The rush thatched roof looks cool, even from the bridge one can make out the aroma of tea.	Bridge	Mountain	Cloud
Advancing through pebbles, there flows a rivulet running from a spring.	Water	Cloud	Rock
An old quiet pond/A frog jumps into the pond/Splash! Silence again	Moon	House	Water
The autumn moon; I wandered round the pond all night long.	Moon	Traveler	House

3.3 Interactive Story Generation

When the user finishes creating the *sansui* painting, she can walk through the three-dimensional *sansui* space she created by operating the "rock garden interface" containing a touch panel. (Fig. 5) As the user approaches any *sansui* painting icon within the space, a *haiku* poem or Zen dialogue is output based on the combination of *sansui* painting icons contained in the framed display, as shown in Table 1.

4 Interaction Model Using a Buddhist Human Recognition Model

We include the Buddhist communication method between Zen master and pupil, a fashion for the purpose of understanding people, which has been followed for over 2,000 years. This kind of interaction based on the deep understanding of people is a field not yet researched within Western science.

4.1 *Sansui* World Expression Based on World Model *"Godai"* (sky, water, fire, wind, earth)

In Buddhism, the directions and the five elements (godai) constructing the world are closely related. Upon walking through the sansui painting world, changes in weather based on godai appear depending on the direction of movement. For example, weather changes such that if one goes north, it snows; south, a thunderstorm appears; east, it gets foggy; and west, it rains.

4.2 Classification of User Personality Based on Personality Recognition Model *"Goun: shiki, jyu, sou, gyou, shiki"*

Goun are the elements that make up the core of the Buddist thought in which five basic physical and mental elements make up the world; in this interactive system, we apply these elements in the classification of personality. The five personality categories are as follows:

色 (Shiki)   How nature and materials actually exist
受 (Jyu)   Intuitive impression
想 (Sou)   Perceived image
行 (Gyou)   Process of mind that activates behavior
識 (Shiki)   Deep mental process reaching beyond the above processes

We prepare a two-dimensional *goun* space made up of 10 areas with these values along the vertical axis and their strength (positive or negative) along the horizontal axis. When the user generates a *sansui* landscape according to her preferences, the system classifies the user's individuality through the combination of *goun* categories assigned to the icons that make up the landscape. (Table 2) Through this process, the user's individuality is expressed as a *goun* value, and the initial value is determined as described above.

Table 2. Relationships between symbols, *Sanen* perspective and *Goun*

Icon	Koen	Heien	Shinen
Rock	Jyu	Sou	Siki
Mountain	Jyu	Gyou	Siki
Moon	Siki	Jyu	Shiki

4.3 Zen Dialogue Interactions

When the user approaches certain objects within the *sansui* painting, a Zen event occurs. Every event is constructed such that one can have an interactive pseudo-real experience with a Zen *koan*. The User, Target and Zen Master agents exist within each interaction, and the content of the interaction changes based on their interrelationships.

For example, the *koan* "Dharma Anjin" (Fig. 6) is a dialogue where once, in response to a pupil's complaint that his inner spirit is in turmoil even after training, Dharma replied "Alright, then show me your troubled spirit." We have translated this into an interaction in which one draws one's inner spirit. The *koan* "The Lotus

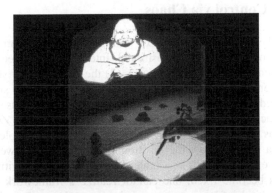

Fig. 6. Zen dialogue "Dharma Anjin," where the user draws herself using the touch screen

Fig. 7. Zen dialogue "The Lotus Smiles," where the user's *goun* state increases with successful matching of Noh Theater masks

Fig. 8. Zen dialogue "The sound of one hand clapping"

Smiles" (*nengemisho*), shown in Fig. 7, holds the meaning of telepathy. In order to express this, we made an interaction like a matching game, hiding Noh Theater masks beneath lotus leaves, such that the leaves change to flower petals when the user finds matching masks. Fig. 8 is the *koan* "the Sound of One Hand Clapping," wherein the system judges the calmness of the user's spirit by measuring the regularity of the user's hand-clapping.

5   Interaction Control via Chaos

One can think of the interaction for the Zen dialogues as being controlled by a combination of both cooperative and oppositional interactions between three different states: (1) the current state of the user (User), (2) the goal the user should reach (Target), and (3) the Zen master that guides the user (Zen Master). To simulate this process, a model is used such that the reaction of the system during user interactions depends on the interaction of the three elements of User, Target and Zen Master, which are all expressed as points within *goun* space. As a method to implement this model, one can think of a way to show the positional relationships between the three elements and the system's reactions as a table. However, because with this method the system's reactions become fixed, one cannot realize a framework allowing the enjoyment of various kinds of interactions spanning several uses. In order to allow many users to experience various interactions each time they interact with the system, it is helpful to introduce an appropriate element of "fluctuation."

   The system uses a method for the dual synchronization of chaos to realize this fluctuation. [10] The method for dual synchronization of chaos is a model handling the synchronization of two or more chaos states. In this case, the system adopts a model containing three chaos states, corresponding respectively to the User, Target and Zen Master. Each chaos state corresponds to a point in *goun* space. Under the method for dual synchronization of chaos, if one applies an initial value and an appropriate input value, the three chaos states relate to one another, moving through *goun* space, and generate an output corresponding to their interactions. For the chaos input, the system uses data from the user's interactions. With the basis of Zen, activity, as the axis, the *goun* value rises (in the plus direction) the more active a user's interaction, and falls (in the minus direction) the less active he is. The data output from the chaos model is used after transformation into the system's reaction data for the user. For example, in the *koan* "Dharma Anjin," the position of the Target chaos changes depending on the curvature and density of the drawing the user sketches. The higher the density and curvature are, the better *goun* state achieved. In other words, the Zen "*enso*" (circle) is the best. Also, in "The Lotus Smiles," the *goun* state rises with a higher accuracy in matching images of Noh theater masks.

6 The Flow of the Story Experience Within Sansui Space

The story process a user walks through is as follows: (Fig. 9)

1. Generate a *sansui* painting
2. *Haiku* are generated related to the icons on the *sansui* painting
3. When the user approaches objects in the *sansui* painting, associated Zen dialogues appear
4. Depending on the interaction results from the four Zen dialogues, a form matching the user's personality is determined from the following four forms of Japanese culture:

   kisoi: comparative design   *mitate*: choice and metaphor

   awase: design in pairs   *soroe*: design based on sets

   The interaction for kimono pattern choice is executed according to the above forms.
5. In conclusion, the "Ten Ox Story" corresponding to the user's interactions is displayed.

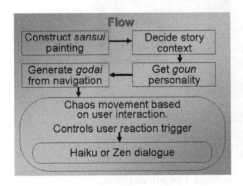

Fig. 9. Interaction process and context generation

7 Application in Context-Aware Environment

We installed this system in the Ubiquitous Home at the National Institute of Information and Communications Technology, making use of RFID (Radio Frequency IDentification) and floor pressure sensors, as well as computer-controlled displays, to transform ZENetic Computer into a context-aware interactive experience. We took advantage of the context-aware environment to recognize the presence of people in the room, their entrance and exit, and their movement around the room.

Using these embedded sensors as an interface enriches the interactive experience by allowing the user to communicate with the system indirectly. For example, when someone walks into the living room, the display turns on and a voice welcomes the user. The user's identity is detected by reading the RFID tag she's wearing, so she may choose to work on a previous painting or start a new one by clicking on a wireless tablet-computer interface.

After the user begins painting with the tablet computer, a voice encourages her to stay if she tries to leave before finishing the painting. However, once the painting is finished, ZENetic Computer allows free interaction with the system. The system watches movement on certain areas of the living room floor, using people's movement as a trigger to play haiku poems or natural sounds related to the elements of *sansui*. Walking front of the display triggers the painting's perspective to shift in the direction of movement, transforming the three dimensional *sansui* ink painting into a dynamic work of art.

By taking advantage of RFID and pressure sensors, displays and speakers embedded in this kind of "house of the future", the ZENetic Computer experience opens up from a single touch-screen interface and display to a physical space encompassing an entire room.

Fig. 10. ZENetic Computer at the NICT Ubiquitous Home

8   Evaluation and Future Outlook

At the 32nd UNESCO General Conference, the meaning of culture was defined once again. Culture encompasses all of customs, images, expressions, knowledge, skills, as well as related tools, goods, artificial objects and cultural spaces. Not only physical cultural relics, but also information exchange systems, communal, spiritual, and philosophical systems are included in the definition of culture.

In 2004, ZENetic Computer received second place in the UNESCO-sponsored Digital Storytelling Competition of Intangible Heritage. In the future, as the processing power of computers, high quality displays and input devices approach the limits of human perception, it is expected that high technology will enter the spiritual domain. In the West, Japanese Zen is an old and mysterious philosophy. Indeed, although books try their hand at explanation, it is difficult to truly understand Zen by reading alone. ZENetic Computer tries to convey the spirit of a culture through experiences such as participating in Zen dialogues, listening to *haiku* and exploring *kimono* patterns.

In the future, there will likely be a strong desire for the thought and design of cultural computing for universal communication, boldly making this kind of cross-cultural connection. ZENetic Computer was planned with this intent in mind, and for its realization the authors made use of advanced game design, graphics, and interactive displays. We are certain that the methods used in ZENetic Computer will flourish in the broad field of education and will make possible experience-based cross-cultural understanding.

References

1. Balazs, Bela: Theory of Film. Japanese Trans.: Gakugei Shorin (1992) 200
2. Isbister, K., Nakanishi, H., Ishida, T., Nass, C.: Helper Agent: Designing Assistant for Human-Human Interaction in a Virtual Meeting Space. In: CHI Letters, Vol. 2 Issue 1. ACM Press, New York (2000) 57-64
3. Matsuoka, Seigow: *Chi no Henshukogaku*. Asahi Shimbunsha (2001) (Japanese)
4. Tosa, N: Chapter 19, AFFECTIVE MINDS. In: ELSEVIER (2000) 183-201
5. Murray, Janet H.: Digital Storytelling. Arima, Tetsuo (trans.). Kokubunsha (2000)
6. http://www.astem.or.jp/digital/
7. Levoy, Marc, et al. The Digital Michelangelo Project: 3D Scanning of Large Statues. In Proceedings of SIGGRAPH 2000, pp. 131-144, August 2000.
8. Matsuoka, Seigow: *Kachofugetsu no Kagaku*. Chuko Bunko (2004)
9. Matsuoka, Seigow: *Sansui Shisou*. Gogatsu Shobo (2003)
10. Liu, Y. and Davis, P.: Dual synchronization of chaos. In: Physical Review E, 61 (2000) R2176-R2179
11. Tosa, N., Matsuoka, S., and Miyazaki, K.: Interactive storytelling system using behavior-based non-verbal information: ZENetic computer. In: Rowe, L., Vin, H., Plagemann, T., Shenoy, P., and Smith, J. (eds.): Proceedings of the Eleventh ACM International Conference on Multimedia, November 2-8, 2003, Berkeley, CA, USA. ACM (2003) 466-467.
12. http://portal.unesco.org/culture/en/ev.php-URL_ID=1698&URL_DO=DO_TOPIC&URL_SECTION=201.html

Automatic Conversion from E-Content into Animated Storytelling

Kaoru Sumi[1] and Katsumi Tanaka[1,2]

[1] National Institute of Information and Communications Technology,
Interactive Communication Media and Contents Group,
3-5 Hikaridai, Seika-cho, Soraku-gun, Kyoto 619-0289, Japan
Kaoru@nict.go.jp
http://www2.nict.go.jp/jt/a133/indexe.html
[2] Kyoto University, Graduate School of Informatics,
Yoshida Honmachi, Sakyo, Kyoto 606-8501, Japan
ktanaka@i.kyoto-u.ac.jp

Abstract. This paper describes a medium, called *Interactive e-Hon*, for helping children to understand contents from the Web. It works by transforming electronic contents into an easily understandable "storybook world." In this world, easy-to-understand contents are generated by creating 3D animations that include contents and metaphors, and by using a child-parent model with dialogue expression and a question-answering style comprehensible to children.

1 Introduction

We are awash in information flowing from the World Wide Web, newspapers, and other types of documents, yet the information is often hard to understand; laypeople, the elderly, and children find much of what is available incomprehensible. Thus far, most children have missed opportunities to use such information, because it has been prepared by adults for adults. The volume of information specifically intended for children is extremely limited, and it is still primarily adults who experience the globalizing effects of the Web and other networks. The barriers for children include difficult expressions, prerequisite background knowledge, and so on. Our goal is to remove these barriers and build bridges to facilitate children's understanding and curiosity. In this research, we are presently considering the applicability of systems for facilitating understanding in children.

This paper describes a medium, called *Interactive e-Hon*, for helping children to understand difficult contents. It works by transforming electronic contents into an easily understandable "storybook world." *Interactive e-Hon* uses animations to help children understand contents. Visual data attract a child's interest, and the use of concrete examples like metaphors facilitates understanding, because each person learns according to his or her own unique mental model [1][2], formed according to one's background. For example, if a user poses a question about something, a system that answers with a concrete example in accordance with the user's specialization would be

F. Kishino et al. (Eds.): ICEC 2005, LNCS 3711, pp. 24–35, 2005.

very helpful. For users who are children, an appropriate domain might be a storybook world. Our long-term goal is to help broaden children's intellectual curiosity [3] by broadening their world.

Attempts to transform natural language (NL) into animation began in the 1970s with SHRDLU [4], which represents a building-block world and shows animations of adding or removing blocks. In the 1980s and 1990s, HOMER [5], Put-that-there [6], AnimNL [7], and other applications, in which users operate human agents or other animated entities derived from natural language understanding, appeared. Recently, there has been research on the natural behaviour of life-like agents in interactions between users and agents. This area includes research on the gestures of an agent [8], interactive drama [9], and the emotions of an agent [10]. The main theme in this line of inquiry is the question of how to make these agents close to humans in terms of dialogicality, believability, and reliability. Our research aims to make contents easier for users to understand, not for agent humanity. WordsEye[18] is text to scene generating system including special data. Our system generates animation but not scene.

Little or no attention has been paid to media translation from contents with the goal of improving users' understanding.

2 Interactive e-Hon

Figure 1 shows the system framework for Interactive e-Hon. Interactive e-Hon transforms the NL of electronic contents into a storybook world that can answer questions and explain of the answers in a dialogue-based style, with animations and metaphors for concepts. Thus, in this storybook world, easy-to-understand contents are created by paraphrasing the original contents with a colloquial style, by creating animations that include contents and metaphors, and by using a child-parent model with dialogue expression and a question-answering style comprehensible to children.

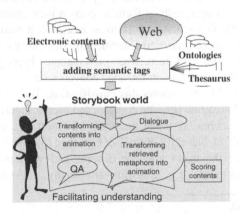

Fig. 1. Interactive e-Hon: This system transforms the natural language of electronic contents into a storybook world by using animation and dialogue expression

Interactive e-Hon is a kind of word translation medium that provides expression through the use of 3D animation and dialogue explanation in order to help children to understand Web contents or other electronic resources, e.g., news, novels, essays, and so on.

For a given content, an animation plays in synchronization with a dialogue explanation, which is spoken by a voice synthesizer.

This processing is based on text information containing semantic tags that follow the Global Document Annotation (GDA)[1] tagging standard, along with other, additional semantic tags. Tags with several semantic meanings for every morpheme, such as "length," "weight," "organization," and so forth, are used. To provide normal answers, the system searches for tags according to the meaning of a question. To provide both generalized and concretized answers, after searching the tags and obtaining one normal answer, the system then generalizes or concretizes the answer by using ontologies. Recently, the Semantic Web [11] and its associated activities have adopted tagged documentation. Tagging is also expected be applied in the next generation of Web documentation.

In the following sub-sections, we describe the key aspects of Interactive e-Hon: the information presentation model, the transformation of electronic contents into dialogue expressions, the transformation of electronic contents into animations, and the expression of conceptual metaphors by animations.

2.1 Content Presentation Model

Our system presents agents that mediate a user's understanding through intelligent information presentation. In the proposed model, a parent agent (mother or father) and a child agent have a conversation while watching a "movie" about the contents, and the user (or users in the case of a child and parent together) watches the agents. In this model, the child agent represents the child user, and the parent agent represents his or her parent (mother or father). For this purpose, the agents take the form of moving shadows of the parent and child. There are agents for both the user or users (avatars) and others (guides and actors), and the avatars are agentive, dialogical, and familiar [12]. Thus, we designed the system for child users to feel affinities with ages, helping them to deepen their understanding of contents. According to the classification scheme of Thomas Rist [13], a conversational setting for users and agents involves more cooperative interaction. This classification includes various style of conversation, e.g., non-interactive presentation, hyper-presentation/dialogue, presentation teams, and multi-party, multi-threaded conversation.

The horizontal axis of Figure 2 shows this classification. The vertical axis of Figure 2 shows the grain size of Interaction between contents and agents. Figure 2 shows the position of the agent related researches, in which there are Microsoft Agent at Microsoft Office, Talking Head[15], BEAT[8], Steve[10], Kairai[9], Ego chat[16], and Agent Salon[17].

With its agents for the users and for others, and with its process of media transformation from contents (e.g., question-answering, dialogue, and animation),

---

[1] http://i-content.org/GDA
Internet authors can annotate their electronic documents with a common, standard tag set, allowing machines to automatically recognize the semantic and pragmatic structures of the documents.

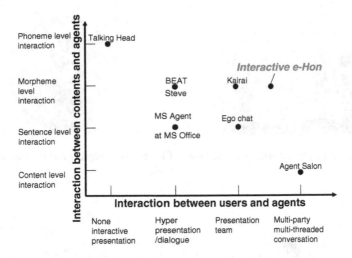

Fig. 2. Interaction among users, agents and contents

Interactive e-Hon corresponds to between a multi-party, multi-threaded conversation and a presentation team. Interactive e-Hon has Morpheme level Interaction, because it has a close relationship with the contents being explained.

2.2 Transformation from Contents into Dialogue Expressions

To transform contents into dialogues and animations, the system first generates a list of subjects, objects, predicates, and modifiers from the text information of a content. It also attempts to shorten and divide long and complicated sentences.

Then, by collecting these words and connecting them in a friendly, colloquial style, conversational sentences are generated. In addition, the system reduces the level of repetition for the conversational partner by changing phrases according to a thesaurus. It prepares explanations through abstraction and concretization based on ontologies, meaning that it adds explanations of background knowledge. For example, in the case of abstraction, "Antananarivo in Madagascar" can be changed into "the city of Antananarivo in the nation of Madagascar," which uses the ontologies, "Antananarivo is a city," and "Madagascar is a nation." Similarly, in the case of concretization, "woodwind" can be changed into "woodwind; for example, a clarinet, saxophone, or flute." These transformations make it easier for children to understand concepts.

In the case of abstraction, the semantic tag "person" adds the expression, "person whose name is"; "location" adds "the area of" or "the nation of"; and "organization" adds "the organization of". In the case of concretization, if a target concept includes lower-level concepts, the system employs explanations of these concepts.

2.3 Transformation of Contents into Animations

Interactive e-Hon transforms contents into animations by using the word list described in the previous subsection. In an animation, a subject is treated as a character, and a

Fig. 3. The public official sternly warned the presidents

Fig. 6. The company did the traffic accident hiding

Fig. 4. The company announced the fact of untruth

Fig. 7. The Teddy bear crossed America

Fig. 5. It attracts the buyer's attention

Fig. 8. The boy always have a disadvant age

predicate is treated as the action. An object is also treated as a character, and an associated predicate is treated as a passive action. One animation and one dialogue are generated for each list, and these are then played at the same time.

Many characters and actions have been recorded in our database. A character or action involves a one-to-many relationship. Various character names are linked to each character. Various action names are linked to each action, because often several different names indicate the same action. Actions can be shared among characters in order to prepare a commoditized framework of characters.

Representation of animation is from real motions, gestures, emphasized behaviors and cartoon like deformation. Figure 3 is from a human behavior which is close to real motions. Figure 4 is an emphasized behavior representing announcing untruth fact. The lighting fairy lamp of Figure 5 is cartoon like deformation. Figure 6 represent the traffic accident hiding by cartoon like deformation of that the man close the rolling door and hide the background of the traffic accident. Figure 7 is also cartoon like deformation by using the map. Figure 8 is representing expression of feeling from the text of *disadvantage*.

If there is a word correspondence between the name of a character and a subject or object in the list, the character is selected. If the subject or object is a company or government and other public offices, a man in suit is selected. If there is no word correspondence, in the case of the semantic tag "person," the system selects a general person character according to an ontology of characters.

The background file is selected by the order of priority of the semantic tag "location", "pur"(purpose), "sbj"(subject).

2.4 Searching and Transformation of Metaphors into Animations

If a user does not know the meaning of a term like "president," it would be helpful to present a dialogue explaining that "a president is similar to a king in the sense of being the person who governs a nation," together with an animation of a king in a small window, as illustrated in Figure 9. People achieve understanding of unfamiliar concepts by transforming the concepts according to their own mental models [1][2]. The above example follows this process.

The dialogue explanation depends on the results of searching world-view databases. These databases describe the real world, storybooks (with which children are readily familiar), insects, flowers, stars, and so on. The world used depends on a user's curiosity, as determined from the user's input in the main menu. For example, "a company president controls a company" appears in the common world-view database, while "a king reigns over a country" appears in the world-view database for storybooks, which is the target database for the present research. The explanation of "a company president" is searched for in the storybook world-view database by utilizing synonyms from a thesaurus. Then, the system searches for "king" and obtains the explanation, "A company president, who governs a company, is similar to a king, who governs a nation." If the user asks the meaning of "company president," the system shows an animation of a king in a small window while a parent agent, voiced by the voice synthesizer, explains the meaning by expressing the results of the search process.

In terms of search priorities, the system uses the following order: (1) complete correspondence of an object and a predicate; (2) correspondence of an object and a predicate, including synonyms; (3) correspondence of a predicate; and (4) correspondence of a predicate, including synonyms.

Commonsense computing [14] is an area of related research on describing world-views by using NL processing. In that research, world-views are transformed into networks with well-defined data, like semantic networks. A special feature of our research is that we directly apply NL with semantic tags by using ontologies and a thesaurus.

For example, there is one of explanations of *a house servant*, in which "a house servant is similar to a pupil of a wizard in the sense of obeying someone" together with an animation of that in a small window. There is one of explanations of *a bear*, in which "a bear is similar to a wolf in the sense of attacking someone" together with an animation of that in a small window.

Fig. 9. A sample view from Interactive e-Hon

In this case, e-Hon is explaining the concept of a "president" by showing an animation of a king. The mother and child agents talk about the contents. The original text information can be seen in the text area above the animation. The user can ask questions to the text area directly.

The original text:

"President Roosevelt went bear hunting and he met the dying bear in autumn of 1902. However, the President refused to shoot to death and helped the bear. With the caricature of Clifford Berryman, the occurrence was carried by Washington Post as a heartwarming story."

The following is a dialogue explanation for this example:

Parent Agent: President Roosevelt carried out to bear hunting. Then, it met with dying small bear.

Child Agent: The President is having met the small bear which is likely to die.

A real child: What is a president, mummy? (Then, his mother operate e-Hon system by clicking the menu)

(Here, an animation using the retrieved metaphor is played.)

Parent agent: A president is similar to a king as a person who governs a country.(With king's animation in a small window)

A real parent: A president is a great man, you know?

Parent Agent: Do you know what did it carry out after this?

Child Agent: No. what did it carry out after this?

Parent Agent: the President refused to shoot to death. And, the President helped the small bear.

Child Agent: The President assisted the small bear.

Parent Agent: The occurrence was carried by Washington Post as a heartwarming story, with the caricature of Clifford Berryman.

Child Agent: The episode was carried by News paper as a good story.

3 Application to Web Contents

Web contents can easily be created by anybody and made available to the public. These contents differ from publications, which are written by professional writers and edited by professional editors, in that they are not always correct or easy to understand. Because these contents may include errors and unknown words (like neologisms, slang words, and locutions), they tend to be ill-defined. In this section, we thus discuss practical problems and solutions in transforming Web contents into a storybook world.

For example, we might try to transform the actual content, "the origin of the *teddy bear*'s name," from a Web source into an animation and a dialogue (Figure 9) Web contents can easily be created by anybody and made available to the public. These contents differ from publications, which are written by professional writers and edited by professional editors, in that they are not always correct or easy to understand. Because these contents may include errors and unknown words (like neologisms, slang words, and locutions), they tend to be ill-defined. In this section, we thus discuss practical problems and solutions in transforming Web contents into a storybook world.

For example, we might try to transform the actual content, "the origin of the *teddy bear*'s name," from a Web source into an animation and a dialogue (Figure 9).

3.1 Transformation of Web Contents into Dialogues

As described above, the system first generates a list of subjects, objects, predicates, and modifiers from a content's text information; it then divides the sentences in the text. For example, it might generate the following lists from the long sentences shown below:

(Original Sentence 1)
"It is said that a confectioner, who read the newspaper, made a stuffed bear, found the nickname "Teddy," and named it a "Teddy bear.""

(List 1) MS: modifier of subject; S: subject; MO: modifier of object; O: object; MP: modifier of predicate; P: predicate.

- S: confectioner, MS: who read the newspaper, P: make, O: stuffed bear;
- S: confectioner, P: find, O: nickname "Teddy," MO: his;
- S: confectioner, P: name, MP: "Teddy bear";
- S: it, P: said.

(Original Sentence 2)
"But, the president refused to shoot the little bear and helped it."
(List 2)

- S: president, P: shoot, O: little bear;
- S: president, P: refuse, O: to shoot the little bear;
- S: president, P: help, O: little bear.

The system then generates dialogue lines one by one, putting them in the order (in Japanese) of a modifier of the subject, the subject, a modifier of an object, the object, a modifier of the predicate, and the predicate, according to the line units in the list. To provide the characteristics of storytelling, the system uses past tense and speaks differently depending on whether the parent agent is a mother or a father.

Sometimes the original content uses reverse conjunction, as with "but" or "however" in the following example: "but.... what do you think happens after that?"; "I can't guess. Tell me the story." In such cases, the parent and child agents speak by using questions and answers to spice up the dialogue. Also, at the ending of every scene, the system repeats the same meaning with different words by using synonyms.

3.2 Transformation of Web Contents into Animations

In generating an animation, the system combines separate animations of a subject as a character, an object as a passive character, and a predicate as an action, according to the line units in the list.

For example, in the case of Original Sentence 2 above, first,

- president (character) shoot (action)
- little bear (character; passive) is shot (action; passive)

are selected. After that,

- president (character) refuse (action)

is selected. Finally,

- president (character) help (action)
- little bear (character; passive) is helped (action; passive)

are selected.

This articulation of animation is used only for verbs with clear actions. For example, the be-verb and certain common expressions, such as "come from" and "said to be" in English, cannot be expressed. Because there are so many expressions like these, the system does not register verbs for such expressions as potential candidates for animations.

3.3 Handling Errors and Unknown Words

One problem that Interactive e-Hon must handle is dealing with errors and unknown words from Web contents, such as neologisms, slang words, locutions, and new manners of speaking. The text area in the system shows original sentences. Erroneous words and unknown words are thus shown there, but they are exempt from concept explanation by metaphor expression.

In generating dialogue expressions using such words, the resulting dialogues and animations may be strange because of misunderstood modification. In the case of a subject or predicate error, an animation cannot be generated. In the Interactive e-Hon system, if an animation is not generated, the previous animation continues to loop, so errors may prevent the animation from changing to match the expressions in a dialogue. If both the animation and the dialogue work strangely, the text area helps the user to guess the original meaning and the reason for the problem. In addition, new or unknown words can be registered in the NL dictionary, the animation library, and the ontologies.

In fact, our example of "the origin of the teddy bear's name" from the Web may exhibit some errors in Japanese, such as the equivalent of "Teodore Roosevelt" or

"Othedore Roosevelt". In such cases, since the original text is shown in the text area, and most of the variant words corresponding to "Roosevelt" are related to "the president," this was not a big problem.

4 Experiment Using Subjects

We conducted an experiment using real subjects to examine whether Interactive e-Hon's expression of dialogue and animation was helpful for users. We again used the example of "the origin of the *teddy bear*'s name.". Three types of content were presented to users and evaluated by them: the original content read by a voice synthesizer (content 1), a dialogue generated by Interactive e-Hon and read by a voice synthesizer (content 2), and a dialogue with animation generated by Interactive e-Hon and read by a voice synthesizer (content 3). The subjects were Miss T and Miss S, both in their 20s; child K, five years old; and child Y, three years old. Both women understood content 2 as a dialogue but found content 1 easier to understand because of its compaction. They also thought content 3 was easier to understand than content 2 because of its animation. T, however, liked content 1 the best, while S favored content 3. As T commented, "Content 1 is the easiest to understand, though content 3 is the most impressive." In contrast, S commented, "Content 3 is impressive even if I don't hear it in earnest. Content 1 is familiar to me like TV or radio." She also noted, "The animations are impressive. I think the dialogues are friendly and may be easy for children to understand."

K, who is five years old, said that he did not understand content 1. He first felt that he understood content 2 a little bit, but he did not express his own words about it. He found content 3, however, entirely different from the others, because he felt that he understood it, and he understood the difficult word *kobamu* in Japanese, which means "refuse" in English. Child Y, who is three years old, showed no recognition of contents 1 and 2, but he seemed to understand content 3 very well, as he was able to give his thoughts on the content by asking (about President Roosevelt), "Is he kind?".

In this experiment, we observed that there was a difference between the results for adults and children, despite the limited number and age range of the subjects. At first, we thought that all users would find it easiest to understand content 3 and would like it and be attracted by it. In fact, the results were different.

We assume that contents that are within a user's background knowledge are easier to understand by regular reading, as in the case of the adults in this experiment. In contrast, for contents outside a user's background knowledge, animation is expected to be very helpful for understanding, as in the case of the children. Further experiments may show that for a given user, difficult contents outside the user's background knowledge can be unde rstood through animation, regardless of the user's age.

5 Discussion

Interactive e-Hon's method of expression through dialogue and animation is based on NL processing of Web contents. For dialogue expression, the system generates a plausible, colloquial style that is easy to understand, by shortening a long sentence and extracting a subject, objects, a predicate, and modifiers from it. For animation expression, the system generates a helpful animation by connecting individual animations selected for the subject, objects, and predicate. The result is expression through dialogue with animation that can support a child user's understanding, as demonstrated by the above experiment using real subjects.

In the process of registering character data and corresponding words, or an action and its corresponding words, which are one-to-many correspondences, certain groups of words that are like new synonyms are generated via the 3D contents. These groups of synonyms are different from NL synonyms, and new relationships between words can be observed. This can be considered for a potential application as a more practical thesaurus based on 3D contents, as opposed to an NL thesaurus.

Reference terms (e.g., "it," "that," "this," etc.) and verbal omission of a subject, which are open problems in NL processing (NLP), still remain as problems in our system. As a tentative solution, we manually embedded word references in the GDA tags. A fully automatic process knowing which words to reference will depend upon further progress in NLP.

As for the process of transforming dialogues, Interactive e-Hon generates all explanations of locations, people, and other concepts by using ontologies, but granular unification of the ontologies and user adaptations should be considered from the perspective of determining the best solution for a given user's understanding.

6 Conclusion

We have introduced Interactive-e-Hon, a system for facilitating children's understanding of electronic contents by transforming them into a "storybook world." We have conducted media transformation of actual Web contents, and demonstrated the effectiveness of this approach via an experiment using real subjects. We have thus shown that Interactive e-Hon can generate satisfactory explanations of concepts through both animations and dialogues that can be readily understood by children.

Interactive e-Hon could be widely applied as an assistant to support the understanding of difficult contents or concepts by various kinds of people with different background knowledge, such as the elderly, people from different regions or cultures, or laypeople in a difficult field.

As future work, we will consider expanding the databases of animations and words, and applying Interactive e-Hon to several other kinds of contents.

References

1. Philip N. Johnson-Laird: Mental Models, Cambridge: Cambridge University Press. Cambridge, Mass.: Harvard University Press (1983).
2. D. A. Norman, *The Psychology of Everyday Things*, Basic Books (1988).
3. Hatano and Inagaki: Intellectual Curiosity, Cyuko Shinsho (in Japanese) (1973).
4. Terry Winograd, Understanding Natural Language, Academic Press (1972).
5. Vere, S. and Bickmore, T: A basic agent. Computational Intelligence, 6:41-60 (1990).

6. Richard A. Bolt: "Put-that-there": Voice and gesture at the graphics interface, International Conference on Computer Graphics and Interactive Techniques archive, Proceedings of the 7th annual conference on Computer graphics and interactive techniques, ACM Press (1980).
7. N. Badler, C. Phillips, and B. Webber, Simulating Humans: Computer Graphics, Animation and Control. Oxford University Press (1993).
8. Justine Cassel, Hannes Hogni Vilhjalmsson and Timothy Bickmore: BEAT: the Behavior Expression Animation Toolkit, Life-Like Characters, Helmet Prendinger and Mitsuru Ishizuka Eds., pp. 163-187, Springer (2004).
9. Hozumi Tanaka et al: Animated Agents Capable of Understanding Natural Language and Performing Actions, Life-Like Characters, Helmet Prendinger and Mitsuru Ishizuka Eds., pp. 163-187, Springer, (2004).
10. Stacy Marsella, Jonathan Gratch and Jeff Rickel: Expressive Behaviors for Virtual World, Life-Like Characters, Helmet Prendinger and Mitsuru Ishizuka Eds., pp. 163-187, Springer (2004).
11. D. Fensel, J. Hendler, H. Liebermann, and W. Wahlster (Eds.) *Spinning the Semantic Web*, MIT Press (2002).
12. Toyoaki Nishida, Tetsuo Kinoshita, Yasuhiko Kitamura and Kenji Mase: *Agent Technology,* Omu Sya (in Japanese) (2002).
13. Thomas Rist, Elizabeth Andre, Stephan Baldes, Patrick Gebhard, Martin Klesen, Michael Kipp, Peter Rist and Markus Schmitt: A Review of the Development of Embodied Presentation Agent and Their Application Fields, Life-Like Characters, Helmet Prendinger and Mitsuru Ishizuka Eds., pp. 377-404, Springer (2004).
14. Hugo Liu and Push Singh: Commonsense reasoning in and over natural language. Proceedings of the 8th International Conference on Knowledge-Based Intelligent Information & Engineering Systems (KES-2004) (2004).

Key Action Technique for Digital Storytelling

Hiroshi Mori and Jun'ichi Hoshino

University of Tsukuba,
Graduate School of Systems and Information Engineering
{hmori, jhoshino}@esys.tsukuba.ac.jp

Abstract. Building story-based interactive systems are important for entertainment and education. In the storytelling system, a user can change the discourse of the story by talking with the character. The problem is that the scene goals in the realistic situations are complex and often multiple goals make effects to decide the current action. When a user asks something to the character, the character needs to arbitrate multiple goals based on the priorities, the current action plan, and the contents of the conversation. In this paper, we propose the method for controlling multiple temporal goals of the story character. The character controls its reaction to the user interactions by using temporal key action (TKA). TKA is a temporal sub-goal setting with time constraint and a priority value. When the TKA is newly added, the action sequences are interpolated using an action network. We created a story-based animation example in which the user can be a detective in the virtual London city.

1 Introduction

Controlling interactions of multiple characters are important for story-based interactive animation and computer games. Fig. 1 shows the example of typical story-based interactive animation. In the story environment, characters typically have multiple goals defined by the story settings. When a user interacts with the character, character's new goals are generated and spontaneous action sequences begin. For example, when the user asks the character to do something, the character needs to decide if the character can accept the request by considering its current goals and time constraints described in the story in advance. The character might reject the user's request due to the time limitations, or its mental status such as emotion and interpersonal relationships. When the character accepts user's request, the planned action sequences should be recalculated based on the user's requested temporal goals.

To construct such a complex story environment, interactive characters should have the following functions:

Generating time and location constraint action plan: When user and the character decides to meet at the specific location, the characters needs to plan action sequences by referencing time stamps. For example, when the user asks a character to "meet with person A at B street on C o'clock", the character should proper action sequences to satisfy that time and location conditions. By sharing the time and location specifications between multiple characters, synchronized action can be generated.

F. Kishino et al. (Eds.): ICEC 2005, LNCS 3711, pp. 36–47, 2005.

Arbitrating multiple temporal goals: A character has multiple temporal goals in story environment with different priorities. For example, when a user request an information about the accidents to a resident in a town, the resident might be busy due to his works. The user needs to change the priority by talking with the character.

In this paper, we propose the story-based interaction synthesis technique based on conversational control of temporal key actions. We control character's actions by using a key action technique. The key action specifies the important action and timing that characterize the discourse of the story. Key actions are interpolated using an action network.

The character controls its reaction to the user interactions by using temporal key action (TKA). TKA is a temporal sub-goal specification with time constraint and a priority value. When the TKA is newly added, the action sequences are interpolated using an action network. By integrating TKA and template-based language synthesis technique, the character can explain the current and future action plan. The user can dynamically change the priority of TKA through the conversation with the character. We created a story-based animation example in which the user can be a detective in the virtual London city.

Fig. 1. Snapshots from multiple character animation using key interaction control method. A user can change the discourse of the story by making a conversation with characters.

2   Previous Works

Behavior control of virtual humans has been one of the important topics in computer graphics. [Noser et al. 1995, 1996] presented a navigation model for animation characters using synthetic visions, whilst [Bandi and Thalmann 1998] discretized a synthetic environment into a 3D uniform grid to search paths for autonomous characters. IMPROV uses script language to control the actor's interactive motion[Perlin and Goldberg 1996]. [Faloutsos et al 2001] proposed a composer able controller for physically-based character animation. Goal directed action control using behavior network was proposed by [Maes 1989]. The proper behavior modules are selected by propagating activation from the goal behavior. [Swartout2001, Martinet2003] proposed story-based virtual reality systems using interactive characters.

[Funge 1999] proposed the cognitive modeling technique for virtual characters. Characters can control its actions by using goal specifications and planning technique. [Mori 2004] has proposed the early concept of key action control method. The previous method provides static goal setting, and temporal goal arbitrations are not considered. In this paper, we focus on the problem of time constrained multiple goal arbitrations in the complex story situations.

Human motion synthesis techniques have also been extensively investigated. [Rose et al. 1998] introduced the framework of "verbs and adverbs" to interpolate example motions with a combination of radial basis functions. [Kovar et al. 2002] introduced a motion graph to represent transitions between poses of the captured motion data. A node of this graph represents a pose, and two nodes are connected by a directed edge if they can be followed from one to the other. [Lee et al. 2002] represented motion data with a graph structure, and provided a user interface for interactive applications. [Pullen and Bregler 2002] developed a method for enhancing roughly-keyframed animation with captured motion data. [Li et al. 2002] developed a two-level statistical model by combining low-level linear dynamic systems with a high-level Markov process. Generating gestures from natural languages was developed by [Cassell 1994, 2000].

In the narrative theory field, [Propp1958] proposed that classic folktales can be constructed by series of typical character actions. Propp named the character's typical action prototype functions. A function is an abstracted character action such as "The hero leaves home" and "The villain harms a member of the community". [Sgouros 1999] proposed a dynamic generation technique of interactive plots. The framework supports an Aristotelian plot conception, in which conflict between antagonistic forces develops out of an initial situation. Our multiple key action technique is useful for filling the gap between animation and the logic-based plot control technique because continuous animations can be produced from abstract story descriptions with motion-level consistency.

3   Key Action Technique

3.1   Overview of the Key Action Method

Story can be considered as a collection of character's composite actions with a proper order and timing. Character's composite acting is modeled by a sequence of small actions. When the user interacts with the character, the character's actions locally changes, but we would like to maintain global consistency of actions.

To generate improvisational action with global consistency, we introduce *key actions* that corresponds to the important action in the story. Fig. 3 shows the Story's

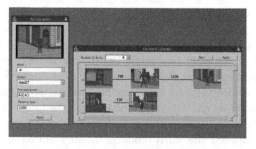

Fig. 2. Storyboard interface for key action setting

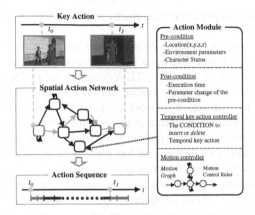

Fig. 3. Interpolating key action using spatial action network

structure is described using series of key actions like Propp's functions [Propp1958]. Actor's action has degree of freedom between key actions. For example, if there is a key action describing "actorA find object B in room C", there are a lot of variations how actorA finds object B. Another actor or user may happen to talk to the actorA while it is searching in the room.

Key action interpolation is a function that generates action sequences between key actions. There are many possible interpolated actions. Proper action sequences are selected by referencing current situations and internal actor's status such as emotion parameters.

3.2 Story Descriptions Using Key Action Network

Fig. 2 is the example of storyboard interface to visually describe key actions[MORI04]. A key action *k* is defined by

k: Actor[Actor ID] Do [Action ID] at [Previous Key Action ID, Relative time]

Actor ID is actor identifier, *Action ID* is action module identifier to output actor motion(Details are described in 4.1.), *Previous Key Action ID* is identifier of the key action that become standard in providing execution time of this key action *k*. *Relative Time* is the specification of relative interval of time from *Previous key Action* to this key action *k*.

There are two categories of key actions. *Static key actions* define the story actions described by creators in advance. *Temporal key actions* are determined by the actor's internal module. Key actions are more like human actor's script in movie scenes because characters need to add various actions between key actions.

4 Key Action Interpolation Using Spatial Action Network

4.1 Action Modules and Action Network

Key actions are interpolated with sequence of actions using action network. Action modules are abstract functions representing what and where the actions take place.

Action modules consist of *pre-condition, post-condition, temporal key action controller, and motion controller.*

Temporal action controller(TKAC) controls the reaction of the character by temporarily control sub-goal settings. TKA has priority value in addition to the KA definition in Sec. 3.2. The priority value of the TKA is calculated in TKAC.

Action modules are connected by spatial action networks that represent possible connections of actions. An action network consists of a directed graph connecting action modules. Arcs represent direction of the module connections.

An action network is automatically generated from a collection of action modules. Continuity of the action is evaluated and the possible action modules are linked together. First the possible action modules are selected by the scene descriptions. For example, there is a suitable class of actions in breakfast scenes. Then, we evaluate the two types of continuity: 1) spatial continuity, and 2) pose continuity. Spatial continuity means that not all actions are executable in all the positions. Spatial continuity is evaluated by referencing a precondition of the action modules. Pose continuity means that the end of one action module and beginning of the other action module is connectable.

Action modules are abstracted by a controller, and we separate the actual implementation of the motion synthesis technique. In the experiments in this paper, we use a simple motion transition graph to connect roughly the continuous motion segments.

Action network is represented as $N^{\alpha}{}_M =(G=(M, A), length_M)$ where node $m \in M$ is action module, graph G consists of directed arc $a \in A$, and $length_M(a)$ corresponds to execution time T_{tail} . Execution time of an action sequence can be represented by the total length of a partcial graph.

$$length_p(P) = \Sigma length_M(a) \tag{1}$$

4.2 Multiple Path Finding over Action Networks

Actors can improvise behaviors to satisfy key actions by searching optimal path in the action network. Fig. 4 shows the concept of key action interpolation. To interpolate key action, possible action sequences are evaluated based on time constraints. Key action interpolation can be done by extending Dijkstra method [Dijkstra1958].

In original Dijkstra method, only minimum cost path is selected. Therefore we apply Dijkstra method twice in forward and backward. We reverse directed graph when we apply Dijkstra method in backward. By adding cost of each nodes obtained by backward and forward search, we can obtain the minimum path of three nodes {begin node, relay node, end node}.

Let us m_i is an action module specified by a key action k_i . When we thinks an action sequences to satisfy two key actions k_i and k_{i+1} , the time constraint condition can be represented by

$$length_k(k_i, k_{i+1})= length_p(P_i) +\Delta T \quad (-T_e <T<T_e) \tag{2}$$

where ΔT is an margin time, and T_e is maximum time tolerance. Action sequences are calculated using the above time constraint conditions.

Using the time constraint conditions, the proper action sequence $P_i = (m_i, m_k, m_{k+1}, ..., m_{i+1})$ is generated using the following steps:

Apply Dijkstra method from k_i to k_{i+1}, and then from k_{i+1} to k_i. In the Dijkstra method, the minimum distances from the beginning node are stored in each node in the action network. Let $C^j_{forward}$, C^j_{back} be the minimum distance at node j.

Let action sequence P_i be the minimum path that satisfy the begin and end key actions, and relay key actions. The total length is $length_M(P_j) = C^j_{forward}+C^j_{back}$

$$length_k(k_i, k_{i+1}) \leq length_p(P_j) + \Delta T \quad (\Delta T>0) \tag{3}$$

Consider the action modules that are executable repeatedly. The original Dijkstra method does not count such nodes. When N repeating nodes are included in candidate path P_j,

$$length_p(P_j^?) = length_p(P_j) + \sum_{n=0}^{N-1} \sum_{k=0}^{K_{r+n}} k \cdot length_M(m_{r+n}) \tag{4}$$

where K is

$$K_{r+n} = length_k(k_i, k_{i+1}) - length_p(P_i) / length_M(m_{r+n}) \tag{5}$$

The minimum distance is selected as

$$|length_k(k_i, k_{i+1}) - length_p(P_i) - \Delta T| \rightarrow min \tag{6}$$

4.3 Sharing Key Actions for Cooperative Actions

We need to synchronize the multiple characters' actions in most of the story. For example, when Actor_A meets Actor_B at location C on time D, two actors need to move to the location C and improvise actions until time D. The characters might spend time by shopping, having a coffee, or talking with friends. In this case, we use key action association. When two characters (actorA and actorB) meet and talk, the actorA and actorB have key actions of the same location and the same time.

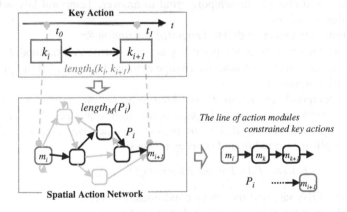

Fig. 4. Key action interpolation using the action network

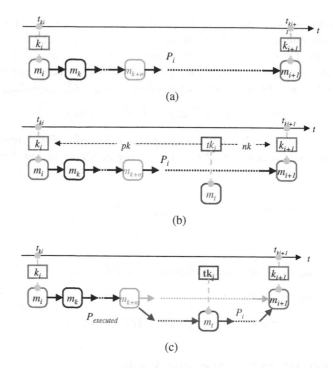

(a)

(b)

(c)

Fig. 5. Example of temporal key actions. Action modules can create temporal key actions to dynamically change the course of the actions, whilst maintaining the global story structure.

4.4 Controlling Temporal Key Actions

Key actions are used to control the character's action by the consequence of the user's interactions. The character is capable of controlling the temporal key actions. For example, when the user asks the character to do something, and the character has enough time, it will changes its temporal goal to answer. Temporal key action rules can be described as follows:

If (condition) then **insert** *or* **delete** *Temporal key action #n*

Fig. 5 shows the example of temporal key action control. Action modules can create temporal key actions to dynamically change course of actions, yet the global story structure is still maintained.

When new temporal key action tk_j is added to an action sequences $P_i = (m_i, m_k, m_{k+1}, ..., m_{i+1})$ between key actions $k_i \square k_{i+1}$, new action sequences $P_i = (m_i, m_k, m_{k+1}, ..., m_{k+m}, ..., m_{i+1})$ is generated. Let the action sequence between m_i and m_{k+m} be $P_{executed}$, the application condition of tk_j is as follows:

$$Length_p(P_t) \le length_p(P) - length_p(P_{executed}) \qquad (7)$$

When a new TKA satisfied the above conditions, the TKA is inserted in the action sequence, and the new action sequence is dynamically generated.

5 Conversational Control of Multiple Temporal Key Actions

Characters typically have multiple scene goals described in the story. These pre-defined multiple goals contain daily sequences and story events. When a user talks with the character, the character needs to arbitrate the priority of multiple goals based on the current action plans and the contents of the conversation. The character controls its reaction to the user interactions by using temporal key action (TKA). TKA is a temporal sub-goal setting with time constraint and a priority value. By integrating TKA and template-based language synthesis technique, the character can explain the current and future action plan.

5.1 Arbitrating Multiple TKA Using Priority Values

When there are many possible TKAs at the current situation, the character can not adopt all TKAs within limited time. Therefore the character needs to select proper TKA to generate a proper action sequence.

TKA has a priority value as described in Sec. 4.1. We examine the possibility of adding a new TKA by dynamically calculate a temporal action sequences. If the temporal action sequences are executable, the character add a new TKA in the current action sequences. Let us the current action sequences be calculated from two KA and one TKA : $\{KA_a, TKA_a, KA_b\}$. When new TKA_b is generated, the character temporarily generate an action sequences $\{KA_a, TKA_a, TKA_b, KA_b\}$. If the new action sequence is executable, the current action sequence is replaced to the new one.

Arbitrating process of multiple TKAs can be done by the following steps:

1) Sorting TKAs by using priority values within the planning scope $T_{planing}$. Select candidates by thresholding sorted TKA with threshold value C.
2) Calculate a temporal action sequence by applying the TKA with the highest priority.
3) Check the time constraint of the new temporal action sequence. If the action sequence is executable, remove the TKA from the candidate list. Then, go to 2) and apply new TKA with the second priority value.
4) Apply 3), 4) to the all candidates TKAs in the list.

In step 2), the generation of a temporal action sequence can be done as follows. Let m_{execut} be the action module that are currently executing. Let the sorted and thresholded temporal key actions are $tka=(tk^{(1)}, tk^{(2)}, ..., tk^{(n)})$. First, we calculate the action sequence from m_{execut} to a closest story key action KA with $tk^{(1)}$. If it is possible to calculate a temporal action sequence considering time constraint, $tk^{(1)}$ is adopted. When the priority values of TKAs are changed by the situation change or user's utterance, the sorted order of TKAs are changed. Then the new action sequences are re-computed.

5.2 Conversational Control of TKA

The user can dynamically change the priorities of TKAs by the conversation with the character. We created a story-based animation example in which a user can be a detective in the virtual London city. 5.2.1 describes an interactive action planning technique using an utterance from the user. 5.2.2 describes a template-based conversation synthesis technique using an action plan.

5.2.1 Changing the Priority of TKA by User's Utterance

User's utterance gives an influence to the priority of TKA. When a user talks to a character, TKA controllers analyze the utterance by using a standard lexical analyzer. Priority control rules in TKA controller decide the influence value on effect value. When the priority value changes, the action sequence is updated using the arbitration method in Sec. 4.3.

5.2.2 Generating Character's Conversational Response

Characters respond to user's requests by generating conversation. When a character received a user's utterance, the character matches the input text and condition of the conversation templates. Conversation template consists of user's utterance, a history of executed action sequence, story key action, TKA, and non-executed TKA. For example, in the detective RPG game, when the user asks "Could you let me know about A?", and the character's priority is low, the character may select an answer "Could you come back later because I'm busy doing X".

6 Examples

We applied the proposed method to a multi-user RPG game. In this game, the user plays the role of Sherlock Holmes in a virtual London city. User can control the locomotion of the character using a keyboard or a game controller pad. The system displays the candidate utterances to the user. In this example, 6 characters are controlled.

6.1 Key Action-Based Behavior Generation

We show the example of key action control of a café stuff and a male character. Table 1 and 2 show story key actions in the café scene. We would like to have a scene that the café staff and the make character bumps each other before the café. The characters should improvise actions between the specified actions based on their roles.

To create such a scene, we specify the key actions of going out an office ($k_0^{(Male)}$), stagger before the cafe ($k_1^{(Male)}$), standing at the crossings ($k_2^{(Male)}$) for a male actor. For staff's key actions, standing before a counter ($k_0^{(staff)}$), picks up a garbage ($k_1^{(staff)}$). By specifying "stagger before the cafe ($k_1^{(Male)}$)" and "picks up a garbage ($k_1^{(staff)}$)" at the same time stamps, we can generate the action sequences that satisfy the time constraint.

We show snapshots of the produced animation in Fig. 6. The animation sequence with action networks is in the video. Red nodes in the action network are key actions, green nodes are TKA, and orange lines show the action sequences that satisfy key action settings.

6.2 Changing Character's Priority via Conversation

The user controls Holmes, and asks information about the incident from the café staff. First, the café staff answers "I'm busy" because of TKAs created by the customer characters inside the cafe. However, after Holmes explains about the importance of the hearing, the priority of café staff's TKA changes. The action sequences are re-computed, and action modules to answers the questions are selected. The result of the generated animation sequences are in the video.

Table 1. Key action example of a make actor

Key action	Script
$k_0^{(Male)}$	**Actor**(*Male*) **Do**(*open_door:18*) **at**(*none, 0*)
$k_1^{(Male)}$	**Actor**(*Male*) **Do**(*collide:32*) **at**($k_0^{(Male)}$, *780*)
$k_2^{(Male)}$	**Actor**(*Male*) **Do**(*stand:3*) **at**($k_1^{(Male)}$, *1500*)

Table 2. Key action example of a café stuff

Key action	Script
$k_0^{(Staff)}$	**Actor**(*Staff*) **Do**(*counter:1*) **at**(*none, 0*)
$k_1^{(Staff)}$	**Actor**(*Staff*) **Do**(*pick_up:31*) **at**($k_0^{(Staff)}$, *750*)

Fig. 6. Correspondence of key actions and snapshots of the generated animation sequence

7 Conclusion

In this paper, we propose the story-based interaction synthesis technique based on conversational control of temporal key actions. Behaviors of the characters are controlled by changing the priorities of the characters. Discourse of the story is changed by accumulating such changes.

The limitations of the current technique may be the conversation synthesis tech-nique is still limited. Integration with the more sophisticated conversation modules will be useful. In future, we extend our approach to the more complex story situations and interactions with many characters.

References

ICKMORE, T., CAMPBELL, L., VILHJ´ALMSSON, H., AND YAN H.,. Conversation as a system framework: Designing embodied conversational agents. 2000. In J. Cassell, J. Sullivan, S. Prevost, and E. Churchill, editors, Embodied Conversational Agents. MIT Press, Cambridge, MA

COHEN, M. F. 1992. Interactive spacetime control for animation. ComputerGraphics(Proc.SIGGRAPH'92)26, 293–302.

DIJKSTRA, E. W. 1959. A note on two problems in connection with graphs. Numerische-Mathematik1, 269–271.

FALOUTSOS, P., PANNE, M. TERZOPOULOS, D..2001. Composable Controllers for Physics-based Character Animation. Proceedings of ACM SIGGRAPH 2001, pp 251–260

FUNGE, J, TU, X. , TERZOPOULOS, D. , "Cognitive Modeling: : Knowledge, reasoning and planning for intelligent characters," Proc. ACM SIGGRAPH 99 Conference, Los Angeles, CA, August, 1999, in Computer Graphics Proceedings, Annual Conference Series, 1999, 29-38.

KOVAR, L., GLEICHER, M., AND PIGHIN, F. 2002. Motion graphs. ACMTransactionson-Graphics(Proc.SIGGRAPH2002)21,3, 473–482.

LEE, J. AND SHIN, S. Y. 1999. A hierarchical approach to interactive motion editing for human-like figures. *Computer Graphics (Proc.SIGGRAPH'99)33*, 395–408.

LI, Y., WANG, T., AND SHUM, H.-Y. 2002. Motion texture: A two-level statistical model for character motion synthesis. *ACM Transactions on Graphics(Proc.SIGGRAPH2002)21,3*, 465–472.

MAES, P.1989. How to do the right things. Connection Science Journal, Special Issue on Hybrid Systems

MATEAS, M.. STERN, A. 2000. Towards Integrat-ing Plot and Character for Interactive Drama, Socially Intelligent Agents: The Human in the Loop, AAAI symposium.

MARTIN K, MICHAEL K, PATRICK G, THOMAS R. 2003. Staging Exhibi-tions: Methods and tools for modelling narrative structure to produce interactive performances with virtual actors, In: Special Issue of Virtual Reality on Story-telling in Virtual Environments, Springer-Verlag .

MORI, H, HOSHINO, 2005, Key Action Control of Virtual Actors, Proceedings of IEEE VR 2005, (accepted as a poster)

NOSER, H., PANDZIC, I. S., CAPIN,T.K., THALMANN, N. M., AND THALMANN, D. 1996. Playing games through the virtual life network. In Proc.Alife'96.

NOSER, H., RENAULT, O., THALMANN, D., AND THALMANN, N. M. 1995. Navigation for digital actors based on synthetic vision, memory, and learning. ComputersandGraphics19,1, 7–19.

PERLIN,K. GOLDBERG,J A. 1996. Improv:a system for scripting interactive actors in virtual worlds, SIGGRAPH'96, pp. 205 – 216

PROPP, V. 1958 . Morphology of the Folktale", University of Texas Press

PULLEN, K. AND BREGLER, C. 2002. Motion capture assisted animation: Texturing and synthesis. *ACM Transactions on Graphics (Proc.SIGGRAPH2002)21,3*, 501–508.

RICKEL, J., JOHNSON, W., 1999. Animated agents for procedural training in virtual reality: Perception, cognition, and motor control. Applied Artificial Intelligence, 13:343–382

RICKEL, J., JOHNSON,J L.. 1999. Virtual humans for team training in virtual reality. In Proceedings of the Ninth International Conference on Artificial Intelligence in Education, pages 578–585. IOS Press

ROSE, C., COHEN, M. F., AND BODENHEIMER, B. 1998. Verbs and adverbs: Multidimensional motion interpolation. *IEEE Computer Graphics and Applications 18,5,* 32–40.

TOWNS, S. VOERMAN, J. ,CALLAWAY,C. LESTER, J. 1997. Coherent gestures, locomotion, and speech in life-like pedagogical agents, Proceedings of the 3rd international conference on Intelligent user interfaces. pp. 13-20

SGOUROS, N. M. 1999. Dynamic Generation, Management and Resolution of Interac-tive Plots, Artificial Intelligence, vol. 107, no. 1, pp.29-62.

SWARTOUT, W., HILL, R., GRATCH, J., JOHNSON, W.L., KYRIAKAKIS, C., LABORE, K., LIND-HEIM, R., MARSELLA, S., MIRAGLIA, D., MOORE, B., MORIE, J., RICKEL, J., THIEBAUX, M., TUCH, L., WHITNEY, R., and DOUGLAS, J. 2001. Toward the Holodeck: Integrating Graph-ics, Sound, Character and Story. ,Proceedings of the Fifth Interna-tional Conference on Autonomous Agents 2001, ACM Press, pp.409-416.

A New Constrained Texture Mapping Method

Yan-Wen Guo[1,2,*], Jin Wang[1], Xiu-Fen Cui[1], and Qun-Sheng Peng[1,2]

[1] State Key Lab of CAD&CG, Zhejiang University, Hangzhou 310027, China
[2] Department of Mathematics, Zhejiang University, Hangzhou 310027, China
{ywguo, jwang, xfcui, peng}@cad.zju.edu.cn

Abstract. The validity of texture mapping is an important issue for point or mesh based surfaces. This paper provides a new constrained texture mapping method which is capable of ensuring the validity of texture mapping. The method employs the "divided-and-ruled" strategy to construct a direct correspondence between the respective patches of the texture image and 3D mesh model with feature matching. The mesh model is segmented based on the "approximate shortest path". Further, a "virtual image" relaxation scheme is performed to refine the rendering effect. We show how mesh morphing can be conducted efficiently with our constrained texture mapping method. Experiment results demonstrate the satisfactory effects for both texture mapping and mesh morphing.

Keywords: Texture mapping; Approximate shortest path; Morphing.

1 Introduction

Texture mapping plays an important role in computer graphics and virtual reality. Without this technique, it would be a time-consuming task to render the details of complex models and the nature scene with realistic appearance. To accomplish texture mapping from a texture image onto a 3D face mesh model, the fundamental issue is to construct a one-to-one correspondence between the model and texture plane. Conventionally, this is achieved by parametrization of the mesh surface. Furthermore, some applications demand rigid correspondence between the features of model and those of the texture image during the parametrization process, for example, when mapping an image of a face to a 3D face model, the details of the eyes, nose, etc must be mapped precisely to the correspondent parts on the face model. This problem is commonly referred to as constrained texture mapping. The constrained texture mapping of a 3D mesh is a tedious work since no intrinsic parametrization of the 3D mesh satisfying these constraints is available. Although several constrained texture mapping approaches were proposed in recent years, most of them make no guarantee of the validity of the parametrization.

1.1 Related Work

Continuous efforts were made concerning constrained texture mapping in the past several years [3] [4] [6] [14] [15]. Most of the proposed methods mainly deal

---

** Corresponding author.

F. Kishino et al. (Eds.): ICEC 2005, LNCS 3711, pp. 48–58, 2005.

with the mesh model with disc topology, since a complicated mesh model can always be decomposed into several "meaningful" disc topological patches and all current texture mapping methods can be applied to a patch with disc topology.

Levy proposed a method capable of dealing with iso-parametric curves [3]. Subsequently Levy solved the problem of feature mapping by respecting an arbitrary set of constrained features [4] and enabled the method to satisfy the constraints. Levy's method works well for a small number of constraints but can lead to invalid parametrization when dealing with a large set of constraints. The main drawback of the above approaches is that both of them cannot always ensure the validity of the texture mapping. Validity is an essential and important issue for constrained texture mapping which can be regarded as a problem of special parametrization of the mesh surface.

In a recent work, Kraevoy *et al* brought forward a method [6] called Matchmaker. This method adopts the "divided-and-ruled" method to parameterize the 3D meshes onto the planar region. Although this method can ensure the validity of texture mapping, it needs to parameterize the mesh model onto the planar region as a pre-processing, which is in fact a difficult work. On the other hand, it incurs incorporating with steiner vertices and the number of steiner vertices may vary from several tens to thousands according to the complexity of the mesh model. The process is therefore tedious. Furthermore, if the 3D mesh model is of low density or the mesh quality is poor, the decomposed triangular patches are usually jagged, and the matching between the irregular patches and the triangles on the texture plane must undergo a refinement operation as a post-process.

1.2   Our Work

This paper provides a new constrained texture mapping method ensuring the validity of parametrization. The method employs also the "divided-and-ruled" strategy; however it does not need to parameterize the 3D mesh model as a preprocess, rather it applies directly a decomposition scheme to the 3D mesh model and parameterize each divided 3D patch. The texture image is segmented based on the same feature set. Texture mapping is then preformed between each pair of corresponding mesh region and texture triangle.

Besides the validity of the texture mapping, our method has two advantages over the previous methods. Firstly, our method does not inquire a global parametrization of the entire mesh as a preprocess, instead, it performs a local parametrization over each segmented region on the mesh, thus both the complexity and computation of the parametrization are greatly reduced; Secondly, our method supports direct mapping between each pair of corresponding parts on both the 3D mesh and the texture image, user can intuitively adjust the locations of the feature points to get the desired mapping result.

The rest of this paper is organized as follows: In Section 2, we describe our constrained texture mapping method in detail. Section 3 shows some experimental results. In Section 4 we show how the proposed method can be extended to solve mesh morphing. The last section summarizes our method and discusses the future work.

2   A Divided-and-Ruled Algorithm

The main steps of our algorithm can be summarized as follows (see Fig. 1):

Step 1 Interaction: Specify the same set of feature points on both the mesh model and the texture image. This is the only interaction involved in our method.

Step 2 Decomposition and Matching: Triangulate the texture plane based on the feature points by Delaunay triangulation, decompose the mesh model accordingly using "approximate shortest path" on meshes.

Step 3 Embedding: Embed each patch on the mesh to the corresponding triangle on the texture plane to generate the texture coordinates.

Step 4 Refinement: Refine the texture mapping effect using a virtual image relaxation approach for vertices along the boundaries.

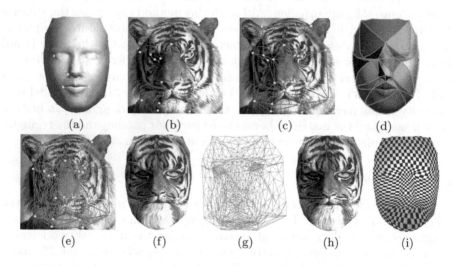

Fig. 1. The stages of the method. (a) feature vertices on the mesh model; (b) feature points on the texture image; (c) triangulation of the feature points; (d) decomposed different patches; (e) the embedding result; (f) the direct mapping result without a further refinement; (g) texture mesh after refinement; (h) the final rendering effect; (i) the effect of mapping grids with the same texture coordinates as (g).

2.1   Notations

For description convenience, we introduce some notations:

- $V = \{v_i | i = 1, ..., n\}$: the specified feature vertices set on the mesh model.
- $P = \{p_i | i = 1, ..., n\}$: the corresponding feature points set on the texture image, v_i corresponds to p_i.
- T_P: the triangle set obtained by triangulating the texture plane with feature points set P.
- E_P: the edge set of T_P.

2.2 Interaction

For a disc topological model, our method first specifies some feature vertices on its surface, including some selected vertices along the boundary of 3D mesh denoted by $V_b = \{v_{bi} | i = 1, ..., m\}$. It is obvious that V_b is a subset of V. Accordingly, some feature points are specified on the texture image, some of which are denoted by $P_b = \{p_{bi} | i = 1, ..., m\}$, p_{bi} corresponds to v_{bi} in V_b.

2.3 Decomposition and Matching

The purpose of this step is to construct the correspondences between the patches of mesh model and those of the texture image. So the mesh model and texture image must firstly be segmented.

The texture image is triangulated based on the feature points of P with boundary constraints, which means that two ordinal points p_{bi}, $p_{b(i+1)}$ of P_b compose a boundary edge of the triangulation so as to preserve the same connectivity as the vertices in V_b. Suppose that $E_b = \{e_{bi} = (p_{bi}, p_{b(i+1)}) | i = 1, ..., m\}$ stands for the edge set consisting of the vertices in P_b, E_b is defined as boundary constraint for the Delaunay triangulation of the feature points on the image (see Fig. 2). It is sure that E_b is included in E_P.

After triangulating the texture plane with the feature points, the mesh model is decomposed accordingly by a kind of precise shortest path called "approximate shortest path" on meshes.

Unlike the Dijsktra shortest path which connects two specified vertices consisting of the edges on mesh, *approximate shortest path* [7] [8] is a more precise shortest path passing through the surface of the mesh. We employ an algorithm similar to the one proposed by Zhang *et al* to compute the *approximate shortest path* [8]. Their method represents the triangle mesh by a weighted graph, each node of the graph denotes a vertex of the mesh and each edge represents an edge of the triangular mesh. Traditional Dijsktra algorithm is then applied to calculate the shortest path between two feature points on the graph, by iteratively subdividing the related triangle edges and constructing new weighted graph, the

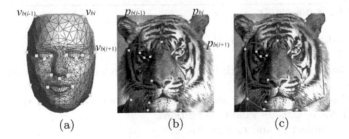

(a)   (b)   (c)

Fig. 2. Boundary constraint for triangulation. Since v_{bi} has direct topology relation with $v_{b(i-1)}$ and $v_{b(i+1)}$ in some sense (a), there should be two edges linking p_{bi} with $p_{b(i-1)}$ and $p_{b(i+1)}$ respectively (b). The edge set in order linking $p_{b(i-1)}$ with p_{bi} is the boundary constraint for Delauny triangulation (c).

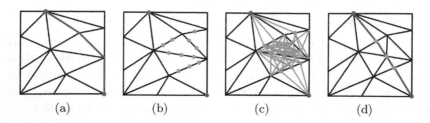

(a)   (b)   (c)   (d)

Fig. 3. The process for computing *approximate shortest path*. (a) Dijsktra shortest path on original mesh connecting two points (red dots); (b) subdivision on the related edge; (c) the constructed new graph for subdivision; (d) the final shortest path by applying Dijsktra algorithm to the new graph and the remeshed meshes.

shortest path between points on the graph finally approaches the shortest path on the mesh surface. Rather than subdividing the related edges iteratively, we adopt a more straightforward method and subdivide the related edge on the graph only once according to the length of the edge. Given a constant length, each edge is inserted with several intermediate points and the number of inserted points amounts to the ratio of the edge length to the given length. Thus a long edge is divided into more fragments compared with a short edge. This method of computing the shortest path is highly efficient and quite suitable for our demand. Note that remeshing is needed on the correlative region of the shortest path. Fig. 3 gives an example of computing the shortest path.

For each edge $e_i = (p_j, p_k)$ in E_p, if e_i is in E_b, then v_j, v_k are connected by the boundary, otherwise, we connect v_j, v_k by the *approximate shortest path*. The pathes connecting adjacent feature vertices are generated one by one so as to maintain the same topology as the triangulation result of the texture image. When generating one new shortest path, a number of validity conditions must be taken into account as suggested by Kraevoy *et al* in [9], such as, the new path must not intersect with existing paths except at the ends of the path;

Table 1. Algorithm: Matching process

---

while E_p is not empty
begin
    Pop edge $e=(p_j, p_k)$ from E_p;
    if $e \in E_b$
        Connect v_j and v_k with boundary vertices lying between them;
    else
        Compute *approximate shortest path* S_{Path} between v_j and v_k;
        if S_{Path} satisfies validity conditions
            Connect v_j and v_k with S_{Path};
        else
            Utilize the method propose by Kraevoy *et al* [9] to generate the path
            between v_j and v_k;
  end

---

the new path must not block necessary future paths, etc. In case that one of these conditions is violated, additional Steiner vertices must be introduced for generating new path between two feature vertices.

Nevertheless, the invalidity situations seldom occur in our experiments. This is because our approach adopts the *approximate shortest path* which is a kind of relatively precise shortest path independent of the density of meshes. Note that, the Dijsktra shortest pathes advocated by Kraevoy's paper may incur unforeseen situation since the Dijsktra shortest path may be highly irregular if the concerned mesh is of poor quality and low sampling density.

The above algorithm can be described by the codes presented in **Table 1**.

2.4   Embedding and Refinement

The correspondence between the texture plane and mesh model is constructed by decomposing them into consistent triangular patches, and then the texture coordinates of each point on the 3D mesh can be determined by embedding its triangular patch of the mesh onto the corresponding triangle on the texture plane. We use the convex combination parametrization method [1] [2] with mean value coordinates [5] to compute the embedding.

Up to now, we are ready to map the texture image onto the mesh model precisely. As shown in Fig. 1, (f) is an initial mapping result. Although this effect is remarkably well in some sense, the distortion of the initial embedding is relatively high especially near the boundary of each patch due to boundary constraints of the local parametrization. To handle this problem, we can optimize the texture meshes (the embedding mesh in the Fig. 1 (e)) to generate more ideal rendering effect.

We conduct the mesh optimization by applying the similar method proposed in [16] to every unstrained point on the texture mesh. Each planar texture coordinates are recomputed by averaging its neighboring coordinates with some weighted value, such as the mean value [5], while the new coordinates should guarantee the triangles incident on this vertex without foldovers.

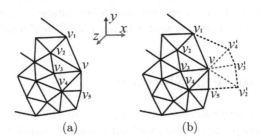

(a)   (b)

Fig. 4. The "virtual image" scheme. (a) $v_1, ..., v_5$: the neighbors of a boundary vertex v. (b) v_2', v_3' and v_4': the virtual reflection. With this scheme, we in fact obtain an weighted form of v about v_2, v_3 and v_4 that will facilitate the refinement operation.

Nevertheless the mean value coordinates of the boundary vertex is difficult to compute, since its neighboring vertices cannot form a circuit. We propose here a "virtual image" scheme to deal with this situation.

Suppose that a boundary vertex v has a number of incident vertices $v_1, ..., v_n$, where v_1 and v_n are also boundary vertices. For the interior vertices $v_2,...,v_{n-1}$, we calculate their "virtual images" $v_2', ..., v_{n-1}'$ which are the symmetrical vertices of $v_2', ..., v_{n-1}'$ about v. Connecting them with v_1, v and v_n as show in Fig. 4 (b) will create a circuit around v and we can thus compute the mean value coordinates of v with its neighbors and their "virtual images". Note that since $v_2', ..., v_{n-1}'$ are the linear combination of v with $v_2,...,v_{n-1}$ respectively, we can obtain a weighted value form of v based on $v_1, ..., v_n$, which facilitates the optimization operation. (Fig. 4).

3   Experimental Results

We adopted several examples to test the validity of our texture mapping algorithm on an Intel Pentium IV 2.0GHz PC with 512MB main memory under the Windows XP operating system (In Figs. 5, 6, 7 the yellow dots are the specified feature points). Table 2 gives the performance results, among which the 2th, 3rd and 4th columns present the time for computing the *approximate shortest path*, embedding and refinement. It can be seen that the total time varies from several seconds to less than 20 seconds, among which the computation of shortest path and embedding consume much more time.

Fig. 5 demonstrates the process of seamlessly mapping two images of a girl from different viewpoints onto the Igea model which is composed of 4442 triangles and 2223 vertices. Different from traditional methods, we do not need to segment the Igea model into two parts and parameterize each path as pre-processing. The sole interaction is to specify 58 feature points on the texture image Fig. 5 (b) and 45 feature vertices on Igea Fig. 5 (a), among which 13 are located on the imaginary bisection line of the mesh model. Fig. 5 (f) shows the rendering results of the model after applying our constrained texture mapping approach.

Fig. 6 shows the results of mapping the texture of a rabbit and its mirror image onto a 3D rabbit model (850 triangles and 462 vertices), while Fig. 7 concerns the mapping of a tiger texture and a boy image onto a cow head model (1891 triangles and 968 vertices) and a human head model (2923 triangles and 1532 vertices) respectively.

4   Extension to Mesh Morphing

Mesh morphing is an interesting research topic for mesh based models. To achieve a natural smooth morphing between the source model and the target model, it is essential to set up a correspondence between the feature points on both models. This is accomplished in current approaches [10] [11] [13] by conducting a global parametrization of the two mesh surfaces. The parametrization of the source model is then embedded into the parametric domain of the target mesh and

Table 2. Performance results

Model	Shortest path (s)	Embedding (s)	Refinement (s)	Total time (s)
Rachel	1.71125	0.755625	0.023625	2.490500
Igea	7.011625	9.179875	0.773250	16.96475
Rabbit	1.232200	0.562523	0.013320	1.808043
Cow	2.959125	2.508000	0.029250	5.496375
Face	2.947500	3.621000	0.036750	6.605250

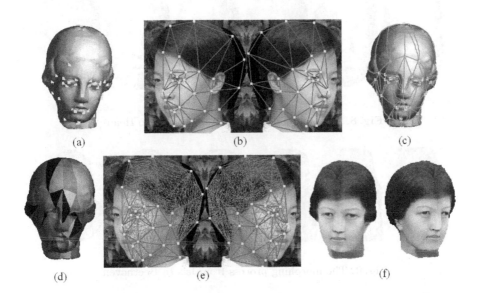

(a)   (b)   (c)

(d)   (e)   (f)

Fig. 5. The rendering effect of mapping two charts of mirrored image onto the Igea model

(a)   (b)   (c)   (d)   (e)

Fig. 6. The rendering effect of mapping two charts of mirrored rabbit onto the Rabbit model

warped to yield a new version which is consistent with that of the target model with feature alignment. No wonder that the above process is complicated and time-consuming.

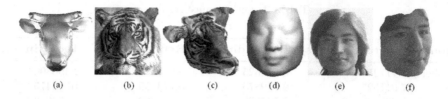

(a)   (b)   (c)   (d)   (e)   (f)

Fig. 7. Other texture mapping results for mesh model with disc topology

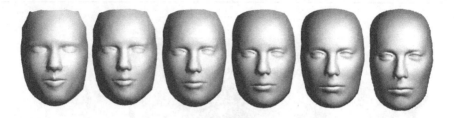

Fig. 8. The morphing process from Rachel to Head

Fig. 9. The morphing process from Isis to Beethoven

Since the fundamental issue of mesh morphing is also feature alignment, we can easily extend our method for constrained texture mapping to mesh morphing. Instead of parameterizing both the source mesh and the target mesh simultaneously, our method need only parameterize the target mesh. This 2D global parametrization result is regarded as a texture image and triangulated based on specified feature points. The souce mesh is then decomposed into segments accordingly. After a process similar to constrained texture mapping applying to both the source mesh and target texture, each segmented patch of the source mesh is embedded into the corresponding triangle in the parametric domain of the target mesh. Finally, resampling and remeshing operation is performed to generate the same topology between the source mesh and target mesh. Note that our morphing method also employs the "divided-and-rules" ideology, the correspondence is constructed precisely and efficiently.

Fig. 8 and Fig. 9 show two morphing results generated by our method. Note that the feature on the intermediate model is well preserved since the feature region on the source model is precisely matched with that on the target model by our method.

5 Conclusions and Future Work

In this paper a new constrained texture mapping method is presented. The method maps precisely the texture image onto the mesh model, discarding the parametrization of the model as a pre-processing adopted by most of the previous methods, at the same time guarantees the validity of constrained texture mapping which is often a problem of constrained parametrization. Instead of Dijsktra shortest path, *Approximate shortest path* is employed to generate the path between feature vertices, which can indeed alleviate the distortions incurred by mapping and runs in interactive time. Since only the feature points on the texture image and the mesh model are needed to be specified, the interaction involved in this method is also simple, especially for the close model. Experiment results show the satisfactory effect of this method.

The provided algorithm can be easily extended to process other feature matching problem, such as mesh morphing, we treat it as an application of our proposed approach. Part of the processing in our algorithm, such as computing the shortest path, can be ported to the Graphics Processing Unit (GPU) that may realize real-time texture mapping. The problem of how to determine a limited set of feature points with the best morphing effect remains as a future work to be concerned. Some other applications such as expression colon for meshes and image driven meshes etc., are also the works in the future.

Acknowledgement

Some of the models for experiments are fetched from [12].

This paper is supported by National 973 program (No. 2002CB312101) and NSFC grant (No. 60033010)&(No.60403038).

References

1. Floater, M.S.: Parametrization and Smooth Approximation of Surface Triangulations. Computer Aided Geometric Design. Vol. 14(3), (1997) 231-250
2. Eck, M., DeRose, T., Duchamp, T., Hoppe, H.: Mutiresolution Analysis of Arbitrary Meshes. In: Proceedings of ACM SIGGRAPH 1995. Los Angeles, CA, (1995) 173-183
3. Levy, B., Mallet, J.L.: Non-Distortion Texture Mapping for Sheared Triangulated Meshes. In: Proceedings of ACM SIGGRAPH 1998. Orlando FL, (1998) 343-352
4. Levy, B.: Constrained Texture Mapping for Polygonal Meshes. In: Proceedings of ACM SIGGRAPH 2001. Los Angeles CA, (2001) 417-424
5. Floater, M.S.: Mean Value Coordinates. Computer Aided Geometric Design. Vol. 20(1), (2003) 19-27
6. Kraevoy, V., Sheffer, A., Gotsman, C.: Matchmaker: Constructing Constrained Texture Maps. In: Proceedings of ACM SIGGRAPH 2003, ACM Transactions on Graphics. Vol. 22(3), (2003) 326-333
7. Kanai, T., Suzuki, H.: Approximate Shortest Path on a Polyhedral Surface and its Applications. Computer-Aided Design. Vol. 33, (2001) 801-811

8. Zhang, L.Y., Wu, X.: Approximate Shortest Path on Triangular Mesh Surface. Journal of CAD&CG. Vol. 15(5), (2003) 592-597
9. Kraevoy, V., Sheffer, A.: Cross-Parameterization and Compatible Remeshing of 3D Models. In: Proceedings of ACM SIGGRAPH 2004, ACM Transactions on Graphics. Vol. 23(3), (2004) 861-869
10. Alexa, M.: Merging Polyhedral Shapes with Scattered Features. The Visual Computer. Vol. 16(1), (2000) 26-37
11. Praun, E., Hoppe, H.: Spherical Parameterization and Remeshing. In Proceedings of ACM SIGGRAPH 2003, ACM Transactions on Graphics. San Diego. Vol. 22(3), (2003) 340-349
12. CYBERWARE INC., http://www.cyberware.com
13. Shapiro, A., Tal, A.: Polyhedron Realization for Shape Transformation. The Visual Computer. Vol. 14(8), (1998) 429-444
14. Matsushita, K., Kaneko T.: Efficient and Handy Texture Mapping on 3D Surfaces. In Proceedings of EUROGRAPHICS 1999, Computer Graphics Forum. Vol. 18(3). (1999) 349-358
15. Ecksteinl, L., Surazhsky, V., Gotsman, C.: Texture Mapping with Hard Constraints. Computer Graphics Forum. Vol. 20(3), (2001) 95-104
16. Sander, P., Gortler, S., Snyder, J., Hoppe, H.: Signal Specialized Parametrization. In Proceedings of Eurographics Workshop on Rendering 2002. (2002)

Protect Interactive 3D Models via Vertex Shader Programming

Zhigeng Pan[1,2], Shusen Sun[1], Jian Yang[3], and Xiaochao Wei[1]

[1] College of Computer Science, Zhejiang University,
310027 Hangzhou, China
{zgpan, sss, weixch}@cad.zju.edu.cn
http://www.cad.zju.edu.cn/vrmm/index.htm
[2] Institute of VR and Multimedia, Hangzhou Dianzi University,
310012 Hangzhou, China
[3] Centrality Communications Corp. 201206 Shanghai, China
jyang@centralitycomm.com.cn

Abstract. In 3D games, virtual museum and other interactive environments, 3D modes are commonly used interactively. Many of these models are valuable and require protection from misuse such as unlawful exhibition, vicious distribution etc. A practical solution is to avoid the interactive user to reconstruct precise 3D models from data stream between applications and 3D APIs (such as Direct3D, OpenGL, etc) under condition of not affecting interaction. The scheme proposed in this paper protects 3D modes via vertex shader programming. The data of 3D models are encrypted in 3D application first and then decrypted in vertex shader.

1 Introduction

Today, with fast development of computer in software and hardware, the graphics capabilities of computers have achieved great advance. Personal computers have been becoming competent for running 3D games, interactive cruise of 3D scene (VRML), online exhibition of virtual cultural relics [7], entertainment and so on. Under these interactive environments, 3D models are commonly used.

Most of these 3D models need to be protected for various reasons. In 3D games, it will take many artists and lots of financial resources to create 3D models using 3D modelling software such as MAYA, 3DS Max, etc [6]. If the competitive companies acquire these models, the loss is hard to imagine. In addition, some models in virtual museum are created from cultural heritage under contract. For instance, the Stanford Digital Michelangelo Project [7] created many 3D models of large statures of Michelangelo. The contact with the Italian authorities permits these models are distributed to established scholars for noncommercial use. Again, the 3D models recovered and created from the Terra Cotta Warriors and Horses, which represent China's cultural institutions, can be exhibited [21]. But it is a critical problem to avoid malicious audience's creating accurate physical objects from these 3D models. More examples can be

F. Kishino et al. (Eds.): ICEC 2005, LNCS 3711, pp. 59–66, 2005.

found here [1,3]. In a word, most of 3D models should be protected for different reasons.

This paper is organized as follows. In next section, the related works are disccused first. Then, Section 3 talks about the factors affecting the security of 3D models. In Section 4, the detail of protecting 3D models via vertex shader programming is presented, followed by Section 5, the system implementation. Conclusions and future work are given in Section 6.

2   Related Works

To protect the 3D models, some solutions are adopted such as image based remote rendering not using 3D APIs [5], 3D model watermarking technology [8,14,15,16,19], matching technology for copyright protection [4].

Ohbuchi introduces 3D watermarking in 1997 [13]. Watermarking techniques for 3D models are faced with many difficulties and challenges [9]. First of all, it is unacceptable for 3D models to import slight distortion under some conditions such as cultural archaeological artifacts. Secondly, the nature of 3D data (no implicit order, not regular sampling, etc) makes it hard to extend 2D analysis methods and watermarking algorithms to 3D. In addition, most of the current 3D models watermarking algorithms are not blind, i.e. it requires the original 3D models to detect watermarks. Under some conditions, it is impossible or impractical to get original 3D models. It is a content-based retrieval (CBR) problem to get original model according to watermarked one. And CBR itself is a challengeable work. Another challenge for 3D watermarking is there are too many attacks for 3D watermarking. So far there is no blind, robust and readable 3D watermarking algorithm.

Ko presented an object-matching methods for the point vs. NURBS surface and the NURBS surface vs. NURBS surface cases [4]. Matching techniques needs to deal with CBR problem as 3D watermarking does. Moreover, many 3D models are not represented by NURBS surface. At SIGGRAPH'2004, Koller etc presented a remote rendering system to protect interactive 3D graphics from reconstruction[5]. To avoid the live-end user to reconstruct 3D models from received information, the snapshots of the rendering results are shown according to users' requirement in client machine using a remote rendering system, which does use 3D APIs like OpenGL or Direct3D. The limitation of this solution is that the reaction time of the system is affected by the bandwidth of network. It is not suit for real time application (3D games).

3   Possible Hijacking Methods

From 3D model file to images displayed on the screen, there occur many chances that the data of 3D models can be hijacked. Koller described the possible attacks in traditional graphics pipeline in [5]. Here we study the total process from 3D model data to display device including programmable vertex shader and fragment shader as shown in Fig. 1, which has some differences with traditional graphics pipeline. The possible hijacking points including:

Hijack Original 3D Model Data Stream Fig. 1(I). 3D data stream used by 3D applications comes from local storage or Internet. Now most of the 3D games locate the 3D models in local computer. Most of the live-ends get the model data though Internet in culture heritage exhibition system. If the local files and network packets are encrypted, it is very difficult to recover 3D models using reverse-engineering from encrypted local file or network packets.

Hijack 3D API Commands Fig. 1(II). Most of 3D games,CAD development suites and other 3D applications use 3D APIs, either Direct3D or OpenGl, to render 3D models. For diverse purposes such as tracing, debugging or implementing distributed graphics architecture, many users, malicious or not, replace the original dynamic library with instrumented versions. For example, Jian Yang's AnyGL system [18], Mohr's stylized rendering system [10,11]. Nunn's Direct3D benchmark [12], Yan's interactive controlling of Direct3D based games [17], and so on. For 3D Direct3D or OpenGL, there are standard formats for their APIs. Once the original dynamic library is replaced, the 3D models can be reconstructed accurately. Shaping from Rendering Results Fig.1(XII) Framebuffer holds the rendering result which is not transmitted to the display devices. The image displayed on the screen is the last rendering result. Since the first shaping-from-shading technique was developed in early 1970s by Horn, many different algorithms have been emerging. The details are described in [20]. For any interactive 3D system, the goal is to show some pictures on the screen. So the 3D model can be reconstructed if there are enough rendering results. The problem is that the reconstructed model is accurate or not.

4 Our Solution

It is impossible to implement absolute security unless the interactive system does not show any results on the screen. In [5], Koller proposed a scheme to

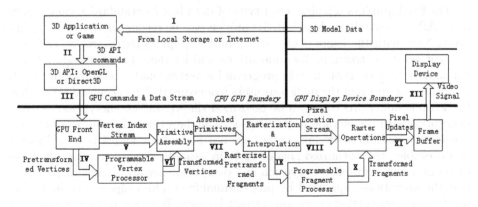

Fig. 1. Programmable Graphics Pipeline

protect interactive 3D graphics which uses remote rendering system to prevent attackers from reconstructing accurate 3D models from rendering results. What displayed on live-on terminal is the snapshots of the rendering results in remote server machina rather than the results rendered with Direct3D or OpenGl. The method cannot be used to protect 3D data of games running in local computer. Here, what we concerned is how to protect 3D API interfaces from being hijacked to reconstruct 3D models. Considering most 3D application need hardware acceleration, the approaches such as software-only rendering, image-based rendering or remote rendering are not appropriate. On the other hand, graphics hardware developed very fast in last few years. Now many graphics cards have programming ability. The architecture of programmable graphics pipeline is shown in Fig. 1. The programming ability of the graphics card can be used to protect 3D models. Our solution encrypts the data of 3D models in 3D application and decrypts the encrypted data in vertex shader.

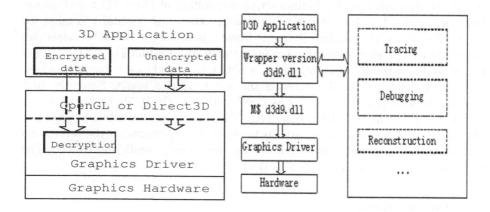

Fig. 2. En-/De-cryption Architecture **Fig. 3.** Advanced D3D Wrapper Architecture

For fixed graphics pipeline, each type of data has its standard format. Only if 3D API commands are hijacked, 3D models can be reconstructed without any error. Now, with the support of programmable graphics hardware, we can first encrypt 3D data stream in 3D applications and let them pass through 3D API commands, then decrypt them in programable vertex shader, as shown in Fig. 2. In addition, to prevent the malicious users from constructing accurate 3D models from frame buffer, 3D data can be deformed slightly before encryption or after decryption with the method in [5]. Thus stream data through interfaces between application and 3D rendering engines are not plain data, and it is very difficult to disasmbley the optimized shader code in assemble language after all. Base on modern cryptography, encryption and decryption are not a difficult problem. But the operations supported by programmable graphics pipeline is limited so far. So many encryption operations cannot be used. With the quick development of GPU, this problem will be solved soon.

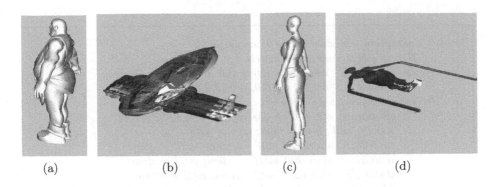

(a)   (b)   (c)   (d)

Fig. 4. The models reconstructed from non-encrypted/encrypted data stream. (a) and (c) are models reconstructed from unencrypted data stream passing through Direct3D APIs; (b) and (d) are models reconstructed from encrypted data stream corresponding to (a) and (c) passing through Direct3D APIs.

5   System Implementation

In order to test our ideas, we implement our method. An advanced Direct3D wrapper is developed to reconstruct models through hijacking 3D APIs. Fig.3 illustrates the architecture of the wrapper. The models shown in Fig. 5 (a) and (c) are reconstructed models with the advanced Direct3D wrapper from 3Dmark03. It is obvious that the reconstruction is accurate if the data passing through Direct3D APIs are not encrypted.

Considering the limitation of the operations supported by graphics processor [2], the geometry information of one vertex is processed as a group. In fact, the texture coordinates can also be processed in same way.

The encryption/decryption procedures include nonlinear and linear operations. Encryption matrix Men and decryption matrix Mde are used to implement linear operation. This way makes full use of the advantages of GPU in matrix processing. The nonlinear operation is used to avoid linear equation based attacks.

The encryption procedure is part of 3D applications. To finish encryption, the 3D data stream are multiplied by encryption matrix and then processed with nonlinear operation. Fig. 5 gives the pseudo code of the encryption procedure in C++ language.

The decryption procedure is implemented as part of vertex shader. On the whole, decryption is the inverse process of encryption. The pseudo code of the decryption procedure is given in Fig. 6 in CG language.

6   Conclusion

The copyright protection of 3D models attract people's great attention in recent years. Many techniques are tried to cope with this problem. There is no perfect

```
//Encryption procedure in C++ language
// Men is 4 by 4 encryption matrix
vector <double, 4> dVector = { 0.0, 0.0, 0.0, 1.0 };
vector <double, 4> dTem = { 0.0, 0.0, 0.0,1.0 };
for(int i=0;i<vertexcount; i++){
        absmean=( abs(vi[0])+ abs(vi[1])+ abs(vi[2]) )/3.0;
        xtem = vi[0]; ytem= vi[1]; ztem= vi[2];
        abs(vi[0])< absmean? vi[0] =- ytem: vi[0] = ytem;
        abs(vi[1])< absmean? vi[1] =- ztem: vi[1] = ztem;
        abs(vi[2])< absmean? vi[2] =xtem: vi[2] = -xtem;
        dTem[0] = vi[0]; dTem[1] = vi[1]; dTem[2] = vi[2];
        D3DXMatrixMultiply(&dVector,&dTem ,&Men);
        vi[0] =dTem[0]; vi[1] =dTem[1]; vi[2] =dTem[2];
};
......
```

Fig. 5. The pseudo code of encryption procedure

```
//Decryption procedure in CG language
struct OUTPUT{
     float4 position : POSITION;
     float4 color : COLOR;
};

OUTPUT vshader(float4 position : POSITION,...){
        OUTPUT Output;
        float x,y,z,x1,y1,z1;
        //Mde is 4 by 4 decryption matrix Mde = Men⁻¹
        float4 PosTem;
        ......
        PosTem = mul (position, Mde);
        x1= PosTem.x;
        y1=PosTem.y;
        z1= PosTem.z;
        absmean =( abs(x1) + abs(y1) + abs(z1))/3.0;
        abs(y1)> absmean? Output.x= z1 : Output.x =-z1;
        abs(z1)> absmean? Output.y= -x1 : Output.y=x1;
        abs(x1)>absmean? Output.z= -y1 : Output.z=y1;
        ... ...
        return Output;
}
```

Fig. 6. The pseudo code of decryption procedure

technical solution to this problem so far. In this paper, a new solution based on GPU's programmability is proposed. The latest achievement in computer graphics is employed in the scheme. The prototype system shows that the method is promising.

However, the operations provided by GPU has many limitations now. For example, neither bitwise operators nor pointer operations are supported currently by vertex shader. Many advanced encryption algorithm cannot be applied. In addition, only one vertex's data can be accessed, so it's impossible now to encrypt the topology of the model. With the improvement of programming capabilities of GPU, it will be more convenient to implement more complex encryption algorithms. It will be ideal if 3D APIs supply secure mechanism.

Acknowledgment

The research work is supported by National Science Foundation of China (No. 60473111) and the Excellent Young Teacher Program of MOE, PRC.

References

1. Corcoran, J. Demaine, M. Picard, L. G. Dicaire, and J. Taylor. Inuit3d: An interactive virtual 3d web exhibition. Museums and the Web 2002, Apr. 18-20 2002.
2. R. Fernando and M. J. Kilgard. *The Cg Tutorial: The Definitive Guide to Programmable Real-Time Graphics.* Addison-Wesley Longman Publishing Co., Inc., Boston, MA, USA, 2003.
3. Janson and etc. Web3d security discussion. http://www.sandyressler.com/about /library/weekly/aa013101a.htm.
4. K. H. Ko. *Algorithms for Three-Dimensional Free-Form Object Matching.* Phd. thesis, Massachusetts Institute of Technology, March 2003.
5. D. Koller, M. Turitzin, M. Levoy, and etc. Protected interactive 3d graphics via remote rendering. *ACM Trans. Graph.*, 23(3):695–703, 2004.
6. D. F. Kosak. Sid meier's pirates: Behind the scenes. http://archive.gamespy.com/ articles/march04/pirates/index.shtml, March 8 2005.
7. M. Levoy, K. Pulli, B. Curless, and etc. The digital michelangelo project: 3D scanning of large statues. In K. Akeley, editor, *Siggraph 2000, Computer Graphics Proceedings*, pages 131–144. ACM Press, 2000.
8. L. Li, D. Z. Z. G. Pan, and J. Y. Shi. Watermarking 3d mesh by spherical parameterization. *Computers & Graphics*, 28(6):981–989, 2004.
9. C. M., M. Barni, and F. Bartolini. Towards 3d watermarking technology. In *Proceed-ings of the IEEE Region 8 EUROCON 2003 Conference*, pages 393 –396, 2003.
10. A. Mohr and M. Gleicher. Non-invasive, interactive, stylized rendering. In *SI3D '01: Proceedings of the 2001 symposium on Interactive 3D graphics*, pages 175–178, New York, NY, USA, 2001. ACM Press.
11. A. Mohr and M. Gleicher. Hijackgl: reconstructing from streams for stylized rendering. In *NPAR '02: Proceedings of the 2nd international symposium on Non-photorealistic animation and rendering*, pages 13–18, New York, NY, USA, 2002. ACM Press.

12. R. A. Nunn. Unamed direct3d benchmarking tools. http://www.users.on.net/triforce/d3dbench.zip.
13. R. Ohbuchi, H. Masuda, and M. Aono. Watermarking three-dimensional polygonal models. In *Proceedings of the ACM International Conference on Multimedia '97*, pages 261–272, Seattle,USA, November, 1997. ACM Press.
14. R. Ohbuchi, A. Mukaiyama, and S. Takahashi. A frequency-domain approach to watermarking 3d shapes. *Computer Graphics Forum*, 21(3):373–382, 2002.
15. E. Praun, H. Hoppe, and A. Finkelstein. Robust mesh watermarking. In A. Rockwood, editor, *Siggraph 1999, Computer Graphics Proceedings*, pages 49–56, Los Angeles, 1999. Addison Wesley Longman.
16. S. S.Sun, Z. G.Pan, L. Li, and J. Y. Shi. Robust 3d model watermarking against geometric transformation. In *Proceeding of CAD/Graphics'2003*, pages 87–92, Macao, Oct.29-31, 2003.
17. W. Yan. Direct3D pipeline wrapper platform. Bachelor thesis, Zhejiang University, 2004.
18. J. Yang. *AnyGL: A Larger Scale Hybrid Distributed Graphics System*. Phd. thesis, Zhejiang University, 2001.
19. K. K. Yin, Z. Pan, and J. Y. Shi. Texture watermarking in vrml scenes. *Journal of Engineering Graphics*, (3):126–132, 2003. (in Chinese).
20. R. Zhang, P. S. Tsai, J. E. Cryer, and M. Shah. Shape from shading: A survey. *IEEE Transac-tions on Pattern Analysis and Machine Intelligence*, 21(8):690–706, 1999.
21. J. Y. Zheng. Virtual recovery and exhibition of heritage. *IEEE MultiMedia*, 7(2):31–34, 2000.

An Optimized Soft 3D Mobile Graphics Library Based on JIT Backend Compiler

Bailin Yang[1,2], Lu Ye[1,3], Zhigeng Pan[1], and Guilin Xu[1]

[1] State Key Lab of CAD&CG, Zhejiang University,
310027 Hangzhou, China
{ybl, LuYe, zgpan, xuguilin}@cad.zju.edu.cn
http://www.cad.zju.edu.cn/vrmm/index.htm
[2] Zhejiang Gongshang University, Hangzhou, 310035, P.R. China
[3] Department of Computer and Electronic Engineering,
Zhejiang University of Science and Technology, Hangzhou 310012, P.R. China

Abstract. Mobile device is one of the most widespread devices with rendering capabilities now. With the improved performance of the mobile device, displaying 3D scene becomes reality. This paper implements an optimized soft 3D mobile graphics library based on JIT backend compiler, which is suitable for the features of the mobile device. To deeply exploring the advantages of JIT technology, this paper improves the traditional rasterization model based on JIT technology and proposes a hybrid rasterization model which integrates the advantages of both the per-scanline and per-pixel rasterization models. As we know, the backend compiler is the critical factor in running 3D application programme. In this paper, we implement a backend compiler for certain CPUs and propose some optimization techniques accordingly. The experimental results indicate that our 3D graphics library has achieved fine performance.

1 Introduction

Mobile graphics is the 3D and 2D graphics which are used in the embedded devices such as the PDA, mobile phone etc. For the 3D graphics, there are the following standards: OpenGL ES constituted by Khronos, JSR 184 by Nokia and Direct3Dm by Microsoft. OpenGL ES, current specification version is 1.13, is a well-defined subset of desktop OpenGL and supported by many mobile manufacturers, companies and research institutes. The specification is targeted primarily at embedded devices that have the drawbacks including lacking of float point, small amounts of memory, little bandwidth, and limited power consumption. Therefore, it deletes many unusually used functions and modifies some APIs according to the embedded devices' features [1].

There are two kinds of implementation based on the OpenGL ES specification: hardware implementation and soft implementation. Now, many manufactures such as ATI, NVIDIA and PowerVR have developed different embedded video cards. In contrast to soft implementation, hardware can greatly improve the performance of 3D rendering, but it also has some disadvantages such as the

F. Kishino et al. (Eds.): ICEC 2005, LNCS 3711, pp. 67–75, 2005.
© IFIP International Federation for Information Processing 2005

high cost and long research period. For the soft implementation, the greatest advantage is its cheap price and satisfactory effect if we achieve excellent design and implementation. There also have some excellent implementations in the market including Hybrid's OpenGL? ES API Framework[2] and HI's Micro3D[3]. In our research group, we also have implemented our soft implementation M3D. Now, Hybrid has good corporations with Nokia, Philips and other mobile devices manufacturers, which indicates that soft implementation has a bright future.

In our research group, we have implemented a soft mobile graphics library, M3D, conformed to the OpenGL ES Specification 1.0 and worked out many 3D games based on M3D. The most critical disadvantage of soft implementation is the low performance, which leads to the slow running speed and screen flicker. To solve these problems, many techniques, algorithms and architecture have been put forward. At present, there exist mainly two ways to improve the performance: pipeline architecture and system level optimization.

(1) 3D pipeline optimization. There are many different algorithms and pipeline architecture suitable for the mobile graphics such as Tile-based rendering [4], Early Culling and Deferred Shading[5,6], Vertex caching technology and its optimization[7], inexpensive multisampling scheme and texture compressing[8], etc.

(2) System level optimization. This method is very important for soft implementation. In practice, we often adopt the following techniques. a) High programming language optimization for certain embedded device CPU. b) Using the assembly language to rewrite source code instead of the high-level language which consumes more CPU resources. c) Adopting JIT backend compiler to improve the performance [2,9,10].

JIT compiler, which is often used in Java language, dynamically translates the high-level language code into the machine code during runtime. JIT compiler produces different machine codes for different types of CPU chips dynamically to meet the portability requirement. In 3D graphics pipeline, the JIT technology is often used due to the following characteristic. From the most abstract point of view, a renderer is a state machine. In the whole rendering, testing the states can actually take longer than the real rendering. But these states don't change all that often in fact. Thousands of pixels are all rendered using the same state. Using the JIT compiler, we can successfully eliminate the redundant state checking, and only execute the functions that perform the render operation corresponding to current state.

This paper focuses on adopting JIT technology, rasterization model and backend compiler to improve the M3D performance. It is organized as follows. First, some traditional rasterization models are introduced. Second, a hybrid rasterization model which is suitable for the JIT technology is presented. Then the JIT backend compiler we implemented is introduced and some techniques and methods are proposed to improve its performance. After that, the experimental result is illustrated and discussed. Finally, a conclusion and future work are offered.

2 Improved Rasterization Model Based on JIT

2.1 Traditional Rasterization Model

The rendering process consists of two stages: geometry processing, and rasterization. In the geometry processing stage, triangle vertices are transformed from object space into screen space. In the rasterization stage, a triangle is converted into pixels, which are depth buffered into the frame memory. Because rasterization stage consumes more CPU resources [11], how to improve its performance is the most important problem for 3D soft implementation. In Section 1, some common techniques are introduced to solve this problem. Then, we will further analyze it from both the rasterization pipeline and JIT compiler in the following sections.

Basically there are two models for the rasterization, which are per-scanline and per-pixel. In the per-scanline case, there is an early test for whether each operation (texturing, shading, etc.) will contribute to the pixels in question and later these textured pixels are combined with the resultant pixels of other operations, such as shading, fog, etc. In the early test, Z-test is to be done at the very end after all other operations have already been executed. This means that although a complete scanline might not be visible we still have to texture, shade, fog every pixel. The disadvantage of this solution is that it is quite slow. It is easy to see that this buffer filling and combining takes a lot of memory bandwidth, which is a serious bottleneck on mobile platforms [12]. Per-pixel based rasterization is a popular model in the hardware 3D rasterization pipeline.

In this model, we would have to do some different tests for each pixel such as z-test, texturing-test, shading-test, fogging-test, blending-test, etc. Generally, this model is slower than the per-scanline model for soft implementation. However, we can adopt some ways to improve it for example bringing forward the Z-test operation. To this model, the most amazing benefit is that the advantages of JIT technology can be fully explored for soft implementation. JIT backend compiler can execute all the pixel related operations, which are the most time-consuming operations during the whole rasterzation stage.

2.2 Hybrid Rasterization Model Based on JIT Backend Compiler

As introduced in Section 1,, JIT backend compiler has been used in the 3D graphics pipeline because of its particularity. The per-pixel model employs the JIT backend compiler to dynamically compile and translate the intermediate code into machine code. First, it rewrites the fragment functions with intermediate language, which are the most time-consuming function. Second, the different fragment functions are compiled when they are needed. Finally, the machine code corresponding to the fragment function will be executed by the application.

This technique improves the program running speed and achieves better result. Unfortunately, this method has the following shortcomings. 1) The machine code for different fragments functions seems too lengthy. Function cache is used to store the machine code. Comparing with PC device's cache, the capacity of mobile devices' cache is limited even less of 1M. 2) Lots of repeated codes exist in the fragment function, which is not beneficial to the cache performance. 3) The function schedule algorithm is not the best. 4) The frequently-used state functions have not been made the best use.

To solve the above problems, we propose a hybrid model that is based on both the per-scanline and per-pixel model. This method employs the JIT technology just like the per-pixel model, which dynamically compiles the fragment function. Furthermore, we adopt the fixed function, which is often used by 3D soft implementation, to advance the performance [13].

During the running of general 3D scene, for instance, running the real-time 3D game, some pipeline state combinations are often invoked. These state combinations have a fixed set of state setting, such as only the shading, shading and texturing combined. There exists a certain frequently-used function corresponding to each state combination in the programme,. To make for improving the programme performance greatly, we put these frequently-used functions into the function cache and store them permanently.

Before the geometry stage, the pre-compiler stage is introduced into our hybrid model, in which the JIT backend compiler is used to compile the frequently-used functions. These functions are directly written into the function cache like the per-scanline model rather than per-pixel model. By this way, we can make best use of these frequently-used functions, which are executed fast because they are stored in the function cache all the time. What's more, this method saves the code space efficiently, since the frequently-used functions' source code is smaller than the fragment functions'.

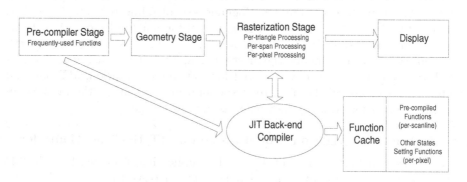

Fig. 1. Framework of hybrid rasterization model

The hybrid rasterization model consists of three stages including pre-compiler stage, geometry processing stage and rasterization stage. The framework of our model is illustrated in Fig. 1. A typical 3D application will go through the process as follows.

– **Step I:** Pre-compiler stage. When the 3D application begins to run, we utilize the JIT back-end compiler to translate the intermediate code of frequently-used functions into machine code and store it in the cache.

- **Step II:** Geometry stage. This stage is independent of the JIT backend compiler. We just operate it as usual.
- **Step III:** Rasterization Stage. In this stage, we first perform the prepare operation, that is to obtain certain function's address from the cache if current state setting is the same as this function's state setting. Otherwise we will compile the function corresponding to current state. We can use the function cache schedule algorithm to decide how to do it. Second, we perform the following steps: per-triangle processing, per-span processing, and per-pixel processing.
- **Step IV:** Display the result.

Function Cache Schedule Algorithm can be described as follows.

1) When the combined state setting appears, it should be compared with the state settings for the frequently-used functions. If the result is equal, then the function in the cache will be executed later. Otherwise the current state setting will be compared with the other state settings of the functions again. If there exists the same state setting, we will also execute this function corresponding to the current state setting later.

2) If we can't find any same state as the current's after two comparisons, the JIT back-end compiler will compile this function and store the machine code in the function cache.

3) As we know, the function cache's capacity is limited. There are so many different combined state settings for the whole 3D pipeline that we can not store all the machine code of the function into the function cache. Therefore, we should design a high performance schedule algorithm to replace and adjust the functions in the cache. In our implementation, we use an advanced LRU (Least-Recently Used) algorithm to replace the function which has not been used or frequently used recently when the cache is full. The difference between our algorithm and the common LRU algorithm is that we classify all functions in the cache with different priorities. The pre-compiled frequently-used functions are assigned the top priority and the others are assigned different priority according to their executive numbers. When the RUN algorithm is performed, we will replace certain function with current compiled function according to the priority. In this way, the pre-compiled frequently-used functions usually will not be replaced.

3   JIT Backend Compiler

3.1   Efficiency Analysis

JIT backend compiler is one of the dynamically compile technology which compile the source code into the machine code. We define the total execution time for certain function in the function cache, which consists of two main parts.

$$T(total) = Tc + n * Te \tag{1}$$

Tc is the time for compiling this function. Te is the time for executing the function's binary code in the cache. In order to get the minimum T(total), we must decrease both the Tc and Te . However, there seems to be a relationship between Tc and Te. Generally, when compiler time is short, the execute time will be long and vice versa [14]. To optimize the programme fully, we should find a balance between both sides. Considering the features of 3D application's execution and our hybrid model, decreasing the Te is the key factor for optimizing our application, because of the following reasons: 1 As indicated in Section 2, the functions in the cache will be called many times and then the number of n will be up to 100 or more, especially for the pre-compiled function. When n is large enough, the total time T(total) will be equal to n* Te.2 The Tc for pre-compiled function does not occupy the application execution time. This case is just like the static compile function, whose compile time is ignored by the user.

3.2   Framework of Our JIT Backend Compiler

Fig. 2 is the framework of our JIT backend compiler (BJIT). As a backend compiler, there is no need for the BJIT compiler to do the lexical parsing, grammar parsing and semantic parsing, just only to convert the intermediate code into target machine code. In BJIT compiler, we redefine intermediate code which is similar to assembly language and related to the target machine's CPU instruction set. For the purpose of implementing our BJIT on both the ARM processor and Bird Company's special processor, we should define two sets of intermediate code. To produce the target machine code, we first rewrite the origin function with the intermediate language.

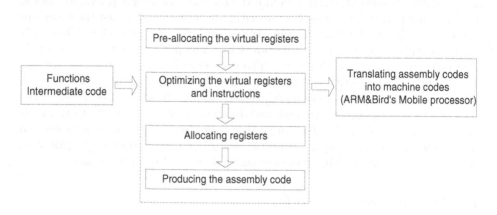

Fig. 2. Framework of JIT backend Compiler

Secondly, these functions will be compiled into the corresponding assembly language for different processor by our BJIT. This process consists of the following steps. 1) Pre-allocate the virtual register. 2) Optimize the virtual register and pseudo instruction. 3) Registers allocate using the Graph Coloring algorithm. 4) Producing the assembly code suitable for the target machine processor. This stage is the key factor for improving the performance of BJIT. We will perform

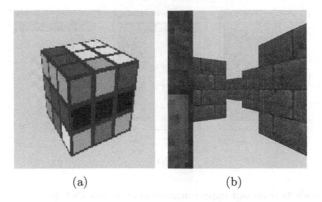

(a)   (b)

Fig. 3. Screen shots from our 3D mobile game Maze and Magic

most of our optimizations in this stage. After getting true assembly codes, we translate them into machine codes suitable for ARM or Bird Company's processor and store the generated codes in the function cache.

3.3   Optimization of BJIT Compiler

Because there are frequent memory write and read operations in our programme, we could do the optimizations from several aspects including Register Allocate algorithm, Copy propagation and spill elimination. We will adopt the linear-scan algorithm [13] instead of the Graph Coloring algorithm, which is not so well for the register allocating in our programme. Copy propagation and spill elimination are classical optimizations in compiler technology, which are used to delete the redundant copy and store operations. The optimizations play an important role for our programme, because a large numbers of copy and store operations exist. Up to now, we have finished this BJIT compiler successfully. The optimizations for the BJIT are the future work.

4   Experiments and Results

Our work in this paper is based on the M3D, which is conformed to the OpenGL ES 1.0 speciation and runs on Bird E868 and HP iPaq Pocket PC. M3D is implemented with standard C language rather than C++ language for portability because some mobile's compilers do not support C++ language. The motivation for us to explore the M3D is to provide the 3D library for developing 3D mobile game. To evaluate our hybrid rasterization model's performance, we use two games, which are the maze and the magic cube, and different number of points, lines and triangles as our benchmarks. The hardware for our experiment is on HP iPaq equipped with ARM processor, which can reach 400MHz frequency at most.

Table 1 shows the performance comparison for the above benchmark. The second column is the performance data for our hybrid rasterization model of

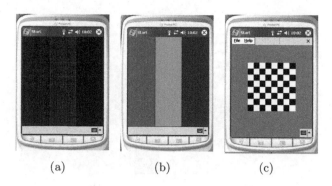

(a)   (b)   (c)

Fig. 4. Screen shots from our experiments. (a) contains 1960 points. (b) contains 960 lines. (c) contains 2 triangles with texture.

Table 1. The Performance Comparison of our hybrid model library and M3D library

	Hybrid Rasterization model	M3D library without JIT
2 Triangles	22.546667	61.375000
960 Lines	45.000000	156.060608
1920 Points	160.409088	189.615387

M3D library with our BJIT, while the third column is for M3D library without JIT. The performance data in the table is the running time for each frame in ms (micro second).

Comparing the two columns, we see that the performance has been improved greatly by means of our hybrid rasterization model based on JIT backend compiler. For rendering two triangles with texture, the efficiency increases almost 2.72 times. For lines, it achieves a more significant improvement to 3.47 times. However, there is no remarkable effect for points. As a result of our experiments, triangle rendering, which is the primary operation in 3D application, achieves promising efficiency with our hybrid model based on BJIT. Due to this improvement, the maze game, developed on our M3D library, runs more smoothly than before.

5   Conclusion and Future Work

We have implemented an optimized soft 3D mobile graphics library based on JIT backend compiler. In this novel 3D library, a hybrid rasterization model, which fully makes use of the JIT backend compiler and integrates the advantages of both the per-scanline and per-pixel rasterization models, is proposed for improving its performance. Furthermore, we have implemented our own BJIT backend compiler, which is targeted at the ARM and Bird Company's mobile processor.

However, there is still much work to do in the future for improving M3D's performance. The better management of function cache is important especially the function schedule algorithm during the execution of global programme. Furthermore, the optimization for our BJIT backend compiler is the urgent task for us in the next phase.

Acknowledgment

This project is co-supported by 973 project (grant no: 2002CB312100), Excellent Youth Teacher Program of MOE in China, and the Bird Company. We would like to thank Mr. Shijie Wang and Mrs. Yuanjun Liu from Bird Company for their kind help in this project. They have given us some good suggestions and methods on improving the 3D library. Also, I would like to thank Mrs. Haihong Wu for her kind help in writing this paper.

References

1. van Leeuwen, J. (ed.): Computer Science Today. Recent Trends and Developments. Lecture Notes in Computer Science, Vol. 1000. Springer-Verlag, Berlin Heidelberg New York (1995)
2. OpenGL ES Overview. http://www.khronos.org/embeddedapi/.
3. OpenGL ES API Framework, http://www.hybrid.fi/main/esframework/index.php.
4. Mascot Capsule Engine Micro3D Edition,http://www.hicorp.co.jp/.
5. D. Crisu, S. D. Cotofana, S. Vassiliadis, P. Liuha, Efficient Hardware for Tile-Based Rasterization, Proceedings of 15th Annual Workshop on Circuits, Systems, and Signal Processing (ProRISC 2004), pp. 352-357, Veldhoven, The Netherlands, November 2004.
6. S. Kumar, D. Manocha, B. Garrett, and M. Lin. Hierarchical back-face culling. In 7th Eurogmphics Workshop on Rendering, pages 231-240, Porto, Portugal, 1996.
7. S. Kumar, D. Manocha, William F. Garrett, Ming C. Lin: Back-Face Computation of Polygon Clusters. Symposium on Computational Geometry 1997: 487-488.
8. Alexander Bogomjakov, Craig Gotsman: Universal Rendering Sequences for Transparent Vertex Caching of Progressive Meshes. Computer Graph Forum 21 (2): 137-148 (2002)
9. T. Akenine-Moller and J. Strom, "Graphics for the Masses: A Hardware Rasterization Architecture for Mobile Phones", ACM Trans. on Graph.,vol 22, nr 3,2003, pp. 801-808.
10. swShader, http://sw-shader.sourceforge.net/technology.html.
11. A 3-D Rendering Library for Mobile Devices, http://ogl-es.sourceforge.net/architecture.htm.
12. D. Crisu, S.D. Cotofana, S. Vassiliadis, and P. Liuha,"GRAAL- A Development Framework for Embedded Graphics Accelerators", Proc. Design, Automation and Test in Europe (DATE 04), Paris, France, February 2004.
13. Klimt software architecture overview, http://studierstube.org/klimt/documentation.php .
14. I.H. Kazi, H. H. Chen, B. Stanly, D.J. Lilja,"Technique for Obtaining High Performance in Java Programs,"ACM Computing Surveys,2000, Vol.32, No. 3, September,pp.213-240.
15. M. Polwrro, V. Sarkar, Line scan register allocation, ACM transactions on Programming Languages and System, vol.21, no.5, Sep.1999, pp.895-913.

Frame Rate Control in Distributed Game Engine

Xizhi Li[1] and Qinming He[2]

[1] CKC honors School, College of Computer Science,
Zhejiang University, Hangzhou, China 310027
lixizhi@zju.edu.cn,
http://www.lixizhi.net
[2] College of Computer Science,
Zhejiang University, Hangzhou, China 310027
hqm@cs.zju.edu.cn

Abstract. Time management (or frame rate control) is the backbone system that feedbacks on a number of game engine modules to provide physically correct, interactive, stable and consistent graphics output. This paper discusses time related issues in game engines and proposes a unified time management (or more specifically frame rate control) architecture, which can be easily applied to existing game engines. The frame rate system has been used in our own distributed game engine and may also find applications in other multimedia simulation systems.

1 Introduction

Several new challenges arise in the visualization and simulation of distributed virtual environment of unsteady complexity, such as in a computer game engine. Time management (including time synchronization and frame rate control) is the backbone system that feedbacks on a number of game engine modules to provide physically correct, interactive, stable and consistent graphics output.

Timing or frame rate in game engines is both unpredictable and intertwined. For example: some scene entities are animated independently, whereas others may form master-slave animation relations; simulation and graphics routines are running at unstable (frame) rate; some of the game scene entities are updated at variable-length intervals from multiple network servers; and some need to swap between several LOD (level-of-detail) configurations to average the amount of computations in a single time step. In spite of all these things, a game engine must be able to produce a stable rendering frame rate, which best conveys the game state changes to the user. For example, a physically correct animation under low frame rate is sometimes less satisfactory than time-scaled animation, which will be discussed in the paper. A solution to the problem is to use statistical or predictive measures to calculate the length of the next time step for different time-driven processes and game objects. In other words, time management architecture (such as the one proposed in this paper) should be carefully integrated to a computer game engine.

It is also important to realize that timing in computer games is different from that of the reality and other simulation systems. A computer game prefers (1) interactivity or real-time game object manipulation (2) consistency (e.g. consistent game states for

F. Kishino et al. (Eds.): ICEC 2005, LNCS 3711, pp. 76–87, 2005.

different clients) (3) stable frame rate (this is different from interactive or average frame rate). For technical reasons, it is unrealistic to synchronize all clocks in the networked gaming environment to one universal time. Even if we are dealing with one game world on a standalone computer, it is still not possible to achieve both smoothness and consistency for all time related events in the game. Fortunately, by rearranging frame time, we can still satisfy the above game play preferences, while making good compromises with the less important ones, such as physical correctness.

Section 2 discusses time related issues in game engine as well as related works. Section 3 formulates the time management problem and proposes the frame rate control architecture. Section 4 evaluates the system by examples in our own game engine. Section 5 concludes the paper.

2 Timing in Game Engine and Related Works

Game related technologies have recently drawn increasing academic attention to it, not only because it is highly demanding by quick industrial forces, but also because it offers mature platforms for a wide range of researches in computer science.

Time management has been studied in a number of places of a computer game engine, such as (1) variable frame length media encoding and transmission (2) time synchronization for distributed simulation (3) game state transmission in game servers (4) LOD based interactive frame rate control for complex 3D environments. However, there have been relatively few literatures on a general architecture for time synchronization and frame rate control, which is immediately applicable to an actual computer game engine. To our knowledge, there have been no open-source game engines which directly support time management so far. In a typical game engine, modules that need time management support include: rendering engine, animation controller, I/O, camera controller, physics engine, network engine (handling time delay and misordering from multiple servers), AI (path-finding, etc), script system, in-game video capturing system and various dynamic scene optimization processes such as ROAM based terrain generation, shadow generation and other LOD based scene entities. In addition, in order to achieve physically correct and smooth game play, frame rate of these modules must be synchronized, and in some cases, rearranged according to some predefined constraints.

In the game development forums, many questions have been asked concerning jerky frame rates, jumpy characters and inaccurate physics. In fact, these phenomenons are caused by a number of coordinating modules in the game engine and cannot be easily solved by a simple modification.

This section reviews the current implementations of a number of time-related modules in game engines. We have discussed them in a way that practitioners can figure out how to address them with the proposed frame rate control architecture, which is presented in Section 3.

2.1 Decoupling Graphics and Computation

Several visualization environments have been developed which synchronize their computation and display cycles. These virtual reality systems separate the graphics and computation processes, usually by distributing their functions among several platforms or system threads (multi-threading). Bryson's paper [6] addresses time management issues in these environments.

When the computation and graphics are decoupled in an unsteady visualization environment, new complications arise. These involve making sure that simultaneous phenomena in the simulation are displayed as simultaneous phenomena in the graphics, and ensuring that the time flow of computation process is correctly reflected in the time flow of the displayed visualizations (although this may not need to be strictly followed in some game context). All of this should happen without introducing delays into the system, e.g. without causing the graphic process to wait for the computation to complete. The situation is further complicated if the system allows the user to slow, stop or reverse the apparent flow of time (without slowing or stopping the graphics process), while still allowing direct manipulation exploration within an individual time step.

However, decoupling graphics and computation is a way to explore parallelism in computing resources (e.g. CPU, GPU), but it is not a final solution to time management problems in game engines. In fact, in some cases, it could make the situation worse; not only because it has to deal with complex issues such as thread-safety (data synchronization), but also because we may lose precise control over the execution processes. E.g. we have to rely completely on the operating system to allocate time stamps to processes. Time stamp management scheme supported by current operating system is limited to only a few models (such as associating some priority values to running processes). In game engines, however, we need to create more complex time dependencies between processes. Moreover, data may originate from and feed to processes running on different places via unpredictable media (i.e. the Internet). Hence, our proposed architecture does not rely on software or hardware parallelism to solve the frame rate problem.

2.2 I/O

The timing module for IO mainly deals with when and how often the engine should process user commands from input devices. These may include text input, button clicking, camera control and scene object manipulation, etc. Text input should be real-time; button clicking should subject to rendering rate. The tricky part is usually camera control and object manipulation. Unsmooth camera movement in 3D games will greatly undermine the gaming experience, especially when camera is snapped to the height and norm of the terrain below it. Direct manipulation techniques [6] allow players to move a scene object to a desired location and view that visualization after a short delay. While the delay between a user control motion and the display of a resulting visualization is best kept less than 0.2 seconds, experience has shown that delays in the display of the visualization of up to 0.5 seconds for the visualization are tolerable in a direct manipulation context. Our experiment shows that camera module reaction rate is best set to constant (i.e. independent of other frame rates).

2.3 Frame Rate and LOD

The largest number of related work [4] [5] [7] lies in Frame rate and LOD. However, the proposed framework does not directly deal with how the LOD optimization module should react to feedbacks from the current frame rate; instead it aims to provide a preferred activation rate to modules not limited to LOD optimization.

Frame Rate and Scene Complexity. In many situations, a frame rate, lower than 30 fps, is also acceptable by users as long as it is constant. However, a sudden drop in frame rate is rather annoying since it distracts the user from the task being performed. To achieve constant frame rate, scene complexity must be adjusted appropriately for each frame. In indoor games (where the level geometry may be contained in BSP nodes), the camera is usually inside a closed room. Hence, the average scene complexity can be controlled fairly easily by level designers. The uncontrolled part is mobile characters, which are usually rendered in relatively high poly models in modern games. Yet, scene complexity can still be controlled by limiting the number of high-poly characters in their movable region, so that the worst case polygon counts of any screen shot can stay below a predefined value. In multiplayer Internet games, however, most character activities are performed in outdoor scenery which is often broader (having much longer line-of-sight) than indoor games. Moreover, most game characters are human avatars. It is likely that player may, now and then, pass through places where the computer cannot afford to sustain a constant real-time frame rate (e.g. 30 FPS). The proposed frame rate controller architecture can ease such situations, by producing smooth animations even under low rendering frame rate.

2.4 Network Servers

Another well study area concerning time management is distributed game servers. In peer-to-peer architecture or distributed client/server architecture, each node may be a message sender or broadcaster and each may receive messages from other nodes simultaneously. In Cronin's paper [2], a number of time synchronization mechanisms for distributed game server are presented, with its own trailing state synchronization method. Diot [1] presented a simple and useful time synchronization mechanism for distributed game servers.

In order for each node to have a consistent or fairly consistent view of the game state, there needs to be some mechanism to guarantee some global ordering of events [8]. This can either be done by preventing misorderings outright (by waiting for all possible commands to arrive), or by having mechanisms in place to detect and correct misorderings. Even if visualization commands from the network can be ordered, game state updates on the receiving client still needs to be refined in terms of frame rate for smooth visualization. Another complication is that if a client is receiving commands from multiple servers, the time at which one command is executed in relation to others may lead to further ordering constraints.

The ordering problem for a single logical game server can usually be handled by designing new network protocols which inherently detects and corrects misorderings. However, flexible time control cannot be achieved solely through network protocols. For example, in case several logical clocks are used to totally order events from multiple game servers, the game engine must be able to synchronize these clocks and use them to compose a synthetic game scene. Moreover, clocks in game engines are not directly synchronized. For example, some clocks may tick faster, and some may rewind. Hence, time management in game development can be very chaotic if without proper management architecture.

2.5 Physics Engine

The last category of related works that will be discussed is timing in physics engine, which is also the trickiest part of all. The article [3] provides a comprehensive overview about the time related problems with the use of a physics engine in game development.

The current time in the physics engine is usually called simulation time. Each frame, we advance simulation time in one or several steps until it reaches the current rendering frame time (However, we will explain in Section 4 that this is not always necessary for character animation under low frame rate). Choosing when in the game loop to advance simulation and by how much can greatly affect rendering parallelism. However, simulation time is not completely dependent on rendering frame time. In case the simulation is not processing fast enough to catch up with the rendering time, we may need to freeze the rendering time and bring the simulation time up to the current frame time, and then unfreeze. Hence it is a bi-directional time dependency between these two time-driven systems.

Integrating Key Framed Motion. In game development, most game characters, complicated machines and some moving platforms may be hand-animated by talented artists. Unfortunately, hand animation is not obligated to obey the laws of physics and they have their own predefined reference of time.

To synchronize the clocks in the physics engine, the rendering engine and the hundreds of hand-animated mesh objects, we need time management framework and some nonnegotiable rules. For example, we consider key framed motion to be nonnegotiable. A key framed sliding wall can push a character, but a character cannot push a key framed wall. Key framed objects participate only partially in the simulation; they are not moved by gravity, and other objects hitting them do not impart forces. They are moved only by key frame data. For this reason, the physics engine usually provides a callback function mechanism for key framed objects to update their physical properties at each simulation step. Call back function is a C++ solution to this paired action (i.e. the caller function has the same frame rate as the call back function). Yet, calculating physical parameters could be computationally expensive. E.g. in a skeletal animation system, if we want to get the position of one of its bones at a certain simulation time, we need to recalculate all the transforms from this bone to its root bone. With time management, we can use two synchronized frame rate controllers to reduce the amount of computations. One controller is assigned a low frame rate for updating the physical parameters of an animated object; the other is assigned the same (high) frame rate as the simulation time to interpolate the object's physical parameters and feed to the physics engine.

2.6 Conclusion to Related Works

Section 2 discussed a number of places in the game engine where time management is critical, as well as related works on them. Time management should be carefully dealt with in a computer game engine. In fact, we believe it will soon become common in the backbone system of distributed computer game engines.

3 Frame Rate Control Architecture

In this section, we propose the Frame Rate Control (FRC) architecture and show how it can be integrated in an actual computer game engine.

3.1 Definition of Frame Rate and Problem Formulation

In the narrow sense, frame rate in computer graphics means the number of images rendered per second. However, the definition of frame rate used in this paper has a broader meaning. We define frame rate to be the activation rate of any game process. More formally, we define f(t) → {0,1}, where t is the time variable and f(t) is the frame time function. We associate a process in the game engine to a certain f(t) by the following rule: f(t) is 1, if and only if its associated process is being executed. The frame rate at time t is defined to be the number of times that the sign of f(t) changes from 0 to 1, during the interval (t-1,t].

Let $\{t^{s_k} \mid k \in N, \lim_{\delta x \to 0}(\dfrac{f(t^k)-f(t^k-\delta x)}{\delta x}) = +\infty\}$ be a set of points on t,

where the value of f(t) changes from 0 to 1. Let

$\{t^{e_k} \mid k \in N, \lim_{\delta x \to 0}(\dfrac{f(t^k+\delta x)-f(t^k)}{\delta x}) = -\infty\}$ be a set of points on t, where the

value of f(t) changes from 1 to 0. Also we enforce that $\forall k(s_k < e_k < s_{k+1})$.

$\{t^{e_k}, t^{s_k}\}$ is equivalent to f(t) for describing frame time function.

With the above formulation, we can analyze and express the frame rate of a single function as well as the relations between multiple frame rate functions easily. Fig. 1 shows the curves of three related frame rate functions: i, j and k.

The curve of f(t) may be unpredictable in the following ways.

- In some cases, the length of time when f(t) remains 1 is unpredictable (i.e. $|t^{e_k} - t^{s_k}|$ is unknown), but we are able to control when and how often the f(t) changes from 0 to 1 (i.e. t^{s_k} can be controlled). The rendering frame rate is often of this type.
- In other cases, we do not know when the value of f(t) will change from 0 to 1 (i.e. t^{s_k} is unknown), but we have some knowledge about when f(t) will become 0 again (i.e. we know something about $|t^{e_k} - t^{s_k}|$). The network update rate is often of this type.
- In the best cases, we know something about $|t^{e_k} - t^{s_k}|$ and we can control t^{s_k}. The physics simulation rate is often of this type.
- In the worst cases, only statistical knowledge or a recent history is known about f(t). The video compression rate for real-time game movie recording and I/O event rate are often of this type (fortunately, they are also easy to deal with, since these frame rates are independent and do not need much synchronization with other modules.).

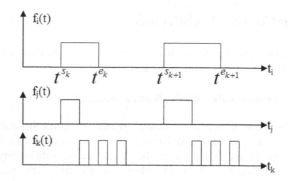

Fig. 1. Sample curves of frame rate functions

Let $\{f_n(t_n)\}$ be a set of frame time functions, which represent the frame time for different modules and objects in the game engine and game scene. The characteristics of $f(t)$ and the relationships between two curves $f_i(t)$ and $f_j(t)$ can be expressed in terms of constraints. Some simple and common constraints are given below, with their typical use cases. (More advanced constraints may be created.)

1. $|t_i - t_j| < \text{MaxDiffTime}, (\text{MaxDiffTime} \geq 0)$. Two clocks i, j should not differentiate too much or must be strictly synchronized. The rendering frame rate and physics simulation rate may subject to this constraint.

2. $(t_i - t_j) < \text{MaxFollowTime}, (\text{MaxFollowTime} > 0)$. Clock(j) should follow another clock(i). The rendering and IO (user control such as camera movement) frame rate may subject to it.

3. $\forall_{k,l}((t_i^{s_k}, t_i^{s_{k+1}}) \bigcap (t_j^{s_l}, t_j^{s_{l+1}}) = \varnothing)$. Two processes i, j cannot be executed asynchronously. Most local clocks are subject to this constraint. If we use single-threaded programming, this will be automatically guaranteed.

4. $\max\{(t^{s_k} - t^{s_{k-1}})\} < \text{MaxLagTime}$. The worst cast frame rate should be higher than 1/MaxLagTime. Physics simulation rate is subject to it for precise collision detection.

5. $\forall k (|t^{s_{k+1}} + t^{s_{k-1}} - 2t^{s_k}| < \text{MaxFirstOrderSpeed})$. There should be no abrupt changes in time steps between two consecutive frames. The rendering frame rate must subject to it or some other interpolation functions for smooth animation display.

6. $\forall k ((t^{s_k} - t^{s_{k-1}}) = \text{ConstIdealStep})$. Surprisingly, this constraint has been used most widely. Games running on specific hardware platform or with relatively steady scene complexity can use this constraint. Typical value for ConstIdealStep is 1/30fps, which assumes that the user's computer must finish computing within this interval. In in-game video recording mode, almost all game clocks are set to this constraint.

7. $\forall k((t^{s_k} - t^{s_{k-1}}) <= ConstIdealStep)$. Some games prefer setting their rendering frame rate to this constraint, so that faster computers may render at a higher rate. Typical value for ConstIdealStep is 1/30fps; while at real time $(t^{s_k} - t^{s_{k-1}})$ may be the monitor's refresh rate.

3.2   Integrating Frame Rate Control to the Game Engine

There can be many ways to integrate frame rate control mechanism in a game engine and it is up to the engine designer's preferences. We will propose here the current integration implementation in our own game engine called ParaEngine [9]. ParaEngine is an experimental game engine framework aiming to bring interactive networked virtual environment to the Internet through game technologies.

Table 1. The Game Loop of ParaEngine [9], which drives the flow of the engine, providing a heartbeat for synchronizing object motion and rendering of frames

```
Main game loop callback function {
    Time management: update and pre calculate all timers used in this frame.
    Process queued I/O commands (IO_ TIMER) {
        Mouse key commands: ray-picking, 2D UI input
        Key stroke commands
        Animate Camera (IO_ TIMER): Camera shares the same timer as IO
    }
    Environment simulation (SIM_TIMER) {
        Fetch last simulation result of dynamic objects
        Validate simulation result and update scene object parameters, accordingly.
        Update simulation data set for the next time step:
            Load necessary physics data to the physics engine; unload unused ones.
            Calculate kinematic scene objects parameters, such as player controlled
                character (this usually results from user input or AI strategies.).
            Update necessary simulation data affected by kinematic scene objects.
        Start simulating for the next time step (this runs in a separate thread than the
        game loop).
        Run AI module (SIM_TIMER) {
            Run game scripts (SIM_TIMER): Currently networking is handled trans-
            parently through the scripting engine.
        }
    }
    Render the current frame (RENDER_TIMER) {
        Advance local animation (RENDER_TIMER)
        Render scene (RENDER_TIMER)
        Render 2D UI: windows, buttons …
    }
    In-game video capturing (RENDER_TIMER)
}
```

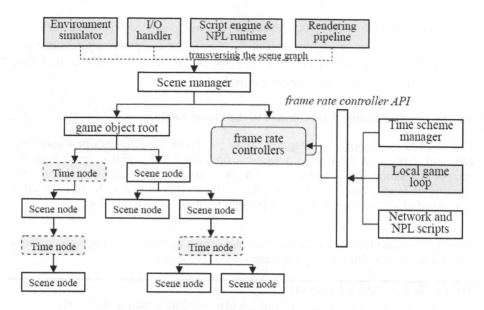

Fig. 2. Integrating time control to the game engine

In ParaEngine, we designed an interface class called FRC Controller and a set of its implementation classes, each of which is capable to manage a clock supporting some constraints listed in Section 3.1. Instances of FRC Controller are created and managed in a global place (such as in a singleton class for time management). A set of global functions (see Time Scheme Manager in Fig. 2) are used to set the current frame rate management scheme in the game engine. Each function will configure the frame rate controller instances to some specific mode. For example, one such function may set all the FRC controllers for video capturing at a certain FPS; another function may set the FRC controllers so that game is paused but 2D GUI is active; yet a third function may set controllers so that the game is running normally with an ideal 30 FPS frame rate.

Like in most computer game engines, a scene manager is used for efficient game object management. For each time-driven process (see Table 1) and object in the scene, the game engine must know which FRC controllers it is associated with. One way to do it is to keep a handle or reference to the FRC controllers in every scene object. However, it is inefficient in terms of management and memory usage. Moreover, most present day games are composed by commercial engines whose base programming interface is fixed or unadvised for modification. A more efficient way to do this is to take advantage of the tree hierarchy in the scene manager and its transversal routines during rendering and simulation. This is done by creating a new type of dummy scene node called time node (see Fig. 2), which contains the reference or handle to one or several FRC controller instances. Then they are inserted to the scene graph like any other scene nodes. Finally, the following rules are used to retrieve the appropriate FRC controllers for a given scene object:

- The FRC controllers in a time node will be applied to all its child scene nodes recursively.
- If there is any conflict among FRC controllers for the current scene node, settings in the nearest time node in the scene graph are adopted.

Since frame rate controllers are managed as top-layer (global) objects in the engine (see Fig. 2). Any changes made to the FRC controllers will be immediately reflected in the next scene traversal cycle. Table 1 shows the game loop. Three global frame rate controllers are used: IO_TIMER, SIM_TIMER and RENDER_TIMER. These are the initial FRC controllers passed to processes in the game loop. As a process goes through the scene graph, the initial settings will be combined with or overridden by FRC controller settings contained in the time nodes.

4 Evaluation

This section contains some use cases of the proposed framework in our own game engine. The combination of FRC controller settings can create many interesting time synchronization schemes, yet we are able to demonstrate just a few of them here. Readers are welcome to download our game demo from links in the thesis [9].

4.1 Frame Rate Control in Video Capturing

The video system in ParaEngine can create an AVI video while the user is playing the game. When high-resolution video capture mode (with codec) is on, the rendering frame rate may drop to well below 5 FPS. It's a huge impact, but fortunately it does not get run at production time. The number of frames it will produce depends on the video FPS settings, not the game FPS when the game is being recorded.

Now a problem arises: how do we get a 25 FPS output video clip, while playing the game at 5FPS? In such cases, the time management scheme should be changed for the following modules: I/O, physics simulation, AI scripting and graphics rendering. Even though the game is running at very low frame rate, it should still be interactive to the user, generate script events, perform accurate collision detection, run environment simulation and play coordinated animations, etc, as if the game world is running precisely at 25 FPS. ParaEngine solves this problem by swapping between two sets of FRC controller schemes for clocks used by its engine modules. In normal game play mode, N-scheme is used; whereas during video capturing, C-scheme is used. See

Table 2. Frame rate control schemes

	N-scheme	C-scheme
ConstIdealFPS	30 or 60	20 or 25
Rendering	FRC_CONSTANT	FRC_CONSTANT
I/O	FRC_CONSTANT	FRC_CONSTANT
Sim & scripting	FRC_FIRSTORDER	FRC_CONSTANT

Table 2. In C-scheme, the simulation and the scripting system use the same constant-step frame rate controller as the rendering and I/O modules. The resulting output of C-scheme is that everything in the game world is slowed but still interactive.

4.2 Coordinating Character Animations

In computer game engine, a character's animation is usually determined by the combination of its global animation and local animation. Global animation determines the position and orientation of the character in the scene, which is usually obtained from the simulation engine. The local animation usually comes from pre-recorded animation clips. In order for the combined motion of the character to be physically correct, the simulation time is usually strictly matched with the local animation time using constraint (1) in Section 3.1. However, this is not the best choice for biped animation with worst case rendering frame rate between 10FPS and 30 FPS. Our experiment shows that setting simulation time to constraint (5) and the local animation time to constraint (6) will produce more satisfactory result. This configuration does not generate strictly correct motion, but it does produce smooth and convincing animation. The explanation is given below. Suppose a biped character is walking from point A to B at a given speed. Assume that the local "walk" animation of the biped takes 10 frames at its original speed (i.e. it loops every 10 frames). Suppose that the simulation engine needs to advance 20 frames in order to move the biped from A to B at the biped's original speed. Now consider two situations. In situation (i), 20 frames can be rendered between A and B. In situation (ii), only 10 frames can be rendered. With constraint (1), the biped will move fairly smoothly under situation (i), but appears very jerky under situation (ii). This is because if the simulation and the local animation frame rates are strictly synchronized, the local animation might display frame 0, 2, 4, 6, 8, 1, 3, 5, 7, 9 at its best; in the actual case, it could be 0, 1,2, 8,9, 1,2,3,7,9, both of which are missing half the frames and appears intolerable jumpy. However, with constraint (5) and (6) applied, the local animation frame displayed in situation (i) will be 0,1,2,3,4,5,6,7,8,9, 0,1,2,3,4,5,6,7,8,9, and under situation (ii), 0,1,2,3,4,5,6,7,8,9, both of which play the intact local animation and look very smooth. The difference is that the biped will stride a bigger step in situation (ii). But experiment shows that users tend to misperceive it as correct but slowed animation. The same scheme can be used for coordinating biped animations in distributed game world. For example, if there is any lag in a biped's position update from the network, the stride of the biped will be automatically increased, instead of playing a physically correct but jumpy animation.

5 Conclusion

Time management is very important in the visualization and simulation of distributed virtual environment, such as networked computer game worlds. The paper reviews a number of time-related issues in computer game engines and proposes a unified frame rate control architecture which can be easily applied to a computer game engine. The frame rate system has been successfully used in our own distributed game engine and may also find applications in other multimedia simulation systems.

References

1. C. Diot and L. Gautier.: A Distributed Architecture for MultiPlayer Interactive Applications on the Internet. In IEEE Network magazine, 13(4), August 1999
2. E. Cronin, B. Filstrup, and A. R. Kurc.: A distributed multiplayer game server system. UM EECS589 Course Project Report, http://www.eecs.umich.edu/~bfilstru/quakefinal.pdf, May 2001
3. Outsourcing Reality: Integrating a Commercial Physics Engine. Game Developer Magazine, Aug. 2002
4. Thomas A. Funkhouser, Carlo H. Séquin.: Adaptive Display Algorithm for Interactive Frame Rates During Visualization of Complex Virtual Environments. Computer Graphics (SIGGRAPH '93 Proceedings), vol 27, 247--254, Aug. 1993
5. Xia, Julie, and A. Varshney.: Dynamic View-Dependent Simplification for Polygonal Models. Proceedings of IEEE Visualization 96, 1996
6. S. Bryson and SandyJohan.: Time management, simultaneity and time critical computation in interactive unsteady visualization environments. Published in proceedings IEEE Visualization '96, 1996
7. Markus Grabner.: Smooth High-quality Interactive Visualization. Proceeding of SCCG 2001, pages 139-148, April 2001
8. Lamport, L.: Time, Clocks, and the Ordering of Events in a Distributed System. Communications of the ACM 21(7), 558-565. 1978
9. Xizhi Li.: Distributed Computer Game Engine – research and implementation. B.C. thesis, Zhejiang Univ. http://www.lixizhi.net/paraworld/DisGameEngineThesis.pdf, June 2005

A Universal Interface for Video Game Machines Using Biological Signals

Keisuke Shima, Nan Bu, Masaru Okamoto, and Toshio Tsuji

Graduate School of Engineering, Hiroshima University, Japan
{keisuke, bu, okamoto, tsuji}@bsys.hiroshima-u.ac.jp
http://www.bsys.hiroshima-u.ac.jp

Abstract. This paper proposes a universal entertainment interface for operation of amusement machines, such as video game machines and radio control toys. In the proposed interface system, biological signals are used as input, where users can choose some specific biological signal and configuration of signal measurement in accordance with their preference, physical condition (disabled or not), and degree of the disability. From the input signals, users' intention of operation can be estimated with a probabilistic neural network (PNN), and then, control commands can be determined accordingly. With the proposed interface, people, even those with severe physical disabilities, are able to operate amusement machines. To verify validity of the proposed method, experiments were conducted with a video game machine.

1 Introduction

Recently, a variety of amusement machines, such as video game machines, radio control toys, and entertainment robots, have been rapidly developed, and has found wide application in people's daily lives. It has been confirmed that amusement machines can be used as a method of rehabilitation therapy for people with physical disabilities [1]-[3]. However, operation of amusement machines might be difficult for the disabled, since movements of the users' body are necessary to operate input devices, such as switches and buttons. To deal with this problem, universal entertainment interfaces are required, with which even people with severe physical disabilities can enjoy amusement machines.

In the field of entertainment interfaces, a lot of research has been carried out to enable people with physical disability to operate amusement machines [4], [5]. Most of this research attempts to design dedicated input devices according to the users' physical condition and their capability for controlling the movements of the head, feet, hands, and other parts of the body. An interface for Play Station 2 (PS2) was proposed by replacing PS2's controller with large buttons or the use of shifting body weight for operation [4]. Also, according to the IN-TERCOMUNICANDO project, games can be controlled using various switches (hand operated, foot operated, and so on), which can be chosen depending on the users' capability of body movement [5]. However, these interfaces require

F. Kishino et al. (Eds.): ICEC 2005, LNCS 3711, pp. 88–98, 2005.
© IFIP International Federation for Information Processing 2005

some (specific) body movements, which are difficult for people with severe physical disabilities, such as patients who have cervical spine injuries and those with
amyotrophic lateral sclerosis.

On the other hand, in the literature of human machine interfaces, systems
using biological signals have been intensly studied [6], [7]. Krepki et al. proposed
a brain computer interface as a pointing device of computers, and this system
can control simple computer games based on the users' intention estimated from
electroencephalogram (EEG) signals [6]. Also, Betke et al. proposed a vision-
based human-computer interface. This system tracks users' movements with a
video camera and *translates* them into the movements of a mouse pointer on
screen, and it has been successfully applied to several computer games [7]. However, these interfaces have not been applied to other amusement machines, e.g.,
video games. Also, it has been widely accepted that users have to take a long-
term training process to gain dexterous skill for operation, because estimation
of the users' intention from EEG features is extremely difficult.

In this paper, a novel entertainment interface is proposed, and operation of
video game machines is presented to illustrate validity of the proposed method.
With this system, users can choose some specific biological signals and measurement configuration with respect to their preference and degree of physical
disabilities. The users' intention of operation is estimated from the biological
signals using a probability neural network (PNN), and the differences in biological signals among individuals can be covered by using adaptive learning. Then,
operation commands are set according to the users' physical conditions and the
selected video game. Also, many kinds of video game machines can be incorporated, since the control and communication functions are implemented on a
reconfigurable hardware, field programmable gate array (FPGA).

This paper is organized as follows: In Section 2, the proposed entertainment
interface system and a prototype are described. Section 3 presents experimental
results of healthy subjects and a patient with a cervical spine injury. Finally,
Section 4 concludes this paper.

2   A Universal Entertainment Interface

The proposed universal entertainment interface system is shown in Fig. 1. This
system consists of four parts: (1) signal measurement, (2) operation estimation,
(3) command encoding, and (4) signal conversion. In this section, a prototype
of the proposed system is introduced.

2.1   Signal Measurement

A variety of biological signals such as electromyogram (EMG) signals and EEG
signals can be used to extract the intention of operation and to detect motions of the human body. These signals reflect the physiological information on
movement and the internal state of users. Also, movements of the body can be
detected from acceleration (ACC) signals. In the proposed method, users can
choose some specific biological signals and measurement configuration according

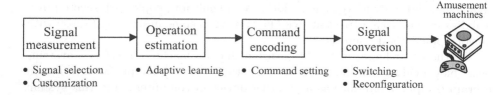

Fig. 1. The proposed entertainment interface system

to their preferences and degree of the disability. Because of this flexible choice of input signals, it is expected that the number of potential users of amusement machines would greatly increase.

2.2   Operation Estimation

In this part, probabilistic neural networks (PNNs) are used for discrimination of operation from biological features. In the context of pattern discrimination, a large amount of research has been carried out using PNNs [9]-[13]. It is widely accepted that, due to the prominent nonlinear approximation capability, PNNs can estimate the posterior probability distribution of input patterns with arbitrary accuracy by training the network architecture and the weights appropriately. So far, PNNs have been used as an important tool for pattern discrimination, and have been proven to be efficient especially for complicated problems such as discrimination of biological signals [12], [13].

Features extracted from biological signals are inputted into PNNs. Let us take EMG signals for example. L pairs of Ag/AgCl electrodes with conductive paste are attached to muscles. The L channels of EMG signals inputted are rectified and filtered by a second-order Butterworth filter. The filtered EMG signals are defined as $EMG_l(t)$ $(l = 1, \cdots, L)$. Then, these EMG signals are normalized to make the sum of L channels equal 1:

$$x_l(t) = \frac{EMG_l(t) - EMG_l^{st}}{\displaystyle\sum_{l'=1}^{L}(EMG_{l'}(t) - EMG_{l'}^{st})} \tag{1}$$

where $EMG_l^{st}(t)$ is the mean value of $EMG_l(t)$ which is measured while relaxing the muscles. Feature vector $\boldsymbol{x}(t) = [x_1(t),\ x_2(t),\ \cdots,\ x_L(t)]^{\mathrm{T}}$ is used for pattern discrimination.

In the prototype system, a log-linearized Gaussian mixture network (LL-GNM) [12] is used. LLGMN is based on a Gaussian mixture model (GMM) and a log-linear model of probability distribution function (pdf). By applying the log-linear model to a product of the mixture coefficients and the mixture components of GMM, a semiparametric model of pdf is incorporated into a three-layer feedforward NN, as shown in Fig. 2. For details of LLGMN, please refer to [12]. LLGMN estimates probability distribution from the input vector $\boldsymbol{x}(t)$, and outputs posterior probability of operation k $(k = 1, \ldots, K)$.

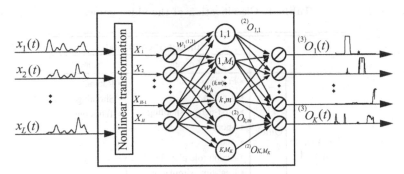

Fig. 2. EMG pattern discrimination using LLGMN

To determine when the operation occurs, force information $F_{EMG}(t)$ is calculated from EMG signals,

$$F_{EMG}(t) = \frac{1}{L} \sum_{l=1}^{L} \frac{EMG_l(t) - EMG_l^{st}(t)}{EMG_l^{avg}(t) - EMG_l^{st}(t)} \tag{2}$$

where $EMG_l^{avg}(t)$ is the mean value of $EMG_l(t)$ measured under an average contraction level that is determined by the user. Since we plan to integrate the signal processing part into a hardware platform, the power level $PL(t)$ is set as $[0, 1]$ to simplify the data representation:

$$PL(t) = \begin{cases} F_{EMG}(t) & (F_{EMG}(t) \leq 1) \\ 1 & (F_{EMG}(t) > 1) \end{cases} \tag{3}$$

Then, $PL(t)$ is compared with a threshold M_d. When $PL(t)$ is more than M_d, intention of operation would be discriminated. In addition, entropy of the output of LLGMN is used to avoid misdiscrimination [14]. The entropy is defined as

$$E(t) = - \sum_{k=1}^{K} {}^{(3)}O_k(t) \log {}^{(3)} O_k(t) \tag{4}$$

where $O_k(t)$ indicates the posterior probability of operation k. If $E(t)$ is less than a threshold E_d, an operation, which has the largest posterior probability, is determined. In contrary, when $E(t)$ is more than E_d, discrimination should be suspended, since large entropy suggests that the network's output is ambiguous.

2.3 Command Encoding

In the step of command encoding, commands of amusement machines are encoded based on the estimated operations. The prototype system uses video games as controlled objects. Because video games differ in the numbers of commands and the response speed required for operation, different protocols are needed for different kinds of games. In the proposed method, a direct mapping or a

Table 1. Classification of the video games

		Number of commands	
		Large	Small
Response speed	Quick	• Fighting • Rhythm • First-person shooting • Sports • Action • Action role playing • Real-time simulation	• Racing • Shooting • Tetris type
	Slow	• Role playing • Simulation role playing • Simulation	• Puzzle • Table • Board • Adventure

shift-group method is used. The direct mapping assigns each operation to a different command. For the shift-group protocol, commands are divided into several groups. In each group, operations are directly mapped into commands. By shifting these groups, objective commands can be achieved, with a smaller number of operations.

In this paper, games are classified according to response speed of operation and the numbers of commands (see Table 1). In Table 1, games with a large number of commands and quick response speed are classified as Type 1. Similarly, definitions of the other types are given as: Type 2 (small-quick), Type 3 (large-slow), and Type 4 (small-slow). For games of Type 3, to perform all the commands with a limited a number of operations, the shift-group protocol can be applied. In the case of Type 4 games, direct mapping can be used. However, patients with severe physical disabilities may conduct very small number of operations, say just one or two. For such users, the shift-group protocol is applicable.

In addition, the command encoding part uses an operation threshold α to avoid errors of operation. Given the number of consecutive estimations of the same operation (R_{count}), the operation is discriminated when R_{count} exceeds α.

2.4   Signal Conversion

In the signal conversion, the control signals are determined based on commands, and then transmitted to the target game machine following communication protocols. However, since communication protocols vary largely among amusement machines, the signal conversion part needs to be reconstructed whenever the game machine is changed. In the proposed interface system, a reconfigurable hardware is used as an implementation platform for signal conversion. In the prototype system, a field programmable gate array (FPGA) chip is used. FPGA

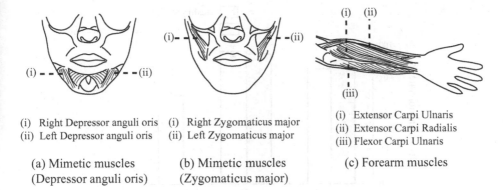

(i) Right Depressor anguli oris   (i) Right Zygomaticus major
(ii) Left Depressor anguli oris   (ii) Left Zygomaticus major

(i) Extensor Carpi Ulnaris
(ii) Extensor Carpi Radialis
(iii) Flexor Carpi Ulnaris

(a) Mimetic muscles   (b) Mimetic muscles   (c) Forearm muscles
(Depressor anguli oris)   (Zygomaticus major)

Fig. 3. Locations of electrodes

is chosen since it allows easy reprogrammability, fast development times, and reduced efforts with respect to large-scale integration (LSI) design. When the game machine is changed, FPGA can be reconfigured at will. Consequently, a variety of amusement machines can be operated with a single hardware device.

3 Experiments

To examine validity of the proposed method, EMG discrimination experiments and video game operation experiments using PS2 were performed with five subjects (A, B, C, and D: healthy people, E: a patient with a cervical spine injury).

3.1 Experimental Condition

In the experiments, electrodes were attached to the following three different locations: (a) depressor anguli oris muscles ($L = 2$; on the right and left sides), and (b) zygomaticus major muscles ($L = 2$; on the right and left sides), (c) forearm muscles ($L = 4$; right hand: extensor carpi ulnaris, extensor carpi radialis, and flexor carpi ulnaris; left hand: extensor carpi ulnaris), as shown in Fig. 3. For subject E, operation with forearm muscles was not conducted, because his arms are paralyzed. The EMG signals after rectification and smoothing were digitized using the 8bit AD converter with a sampling frequency of 50 Hz. The feature pattern, $x(t)$, was used to train LLGMN. In the learning process of LLGMN, 20 EMG patterns were extracted from EMG signals for each operation, and the teacher signals consisted of $K \times 20$ patterns, where K is the number of operations. In addition, the operation threshold α was set as 30, the threshold M_d as 0.6, and the threshold E_d as 0.2.

Also, we implemented the signal conversion part on a development board (Xtreme DSP Development Kit-2, Nallatech), which hosts a Xilinx Virtex family FG676 FPGA chip (XCV3000-4FG676). The signal conversion circuit was

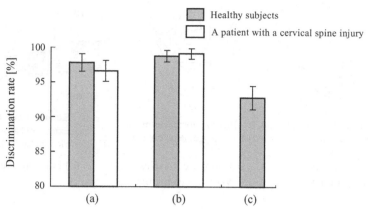

EMG measurement locations :

(a) : Depressor anguli oris; (b) : Zygomaticus major; (c) : Forearm muscles

Fig. 4. EMG pattern discrimination rates

described in Verilog-HDL. The game machine was PS2 (Sony Computer Entertainment Inc.), and the "Othello" game (SUCCESS Corp.) was used for experiments, which can be classified into Type 4 (see Table 1). In this setup, five commands are necessary for operation: up, down, left, right, and stone arrangement.

3.2 EMG Discrimination Experiments

The EMG patterns measured during users' operation were discriminated using LLGMN. In the experiments using depressor anguli oris muscles and zygomaticus major muscles, three motions ($K = 3$; contracting muscles on the right side, the left side, and both sides) were discriminated. For forearm muscles, the classes were five motions ($K = 5$; right hand: flexion, extension, grasping, and opening; left hand: grasping). The EMG pattern discrimination rates for three measurement locations are shown in Fig. 4. It can be seen that all of the discrimination rates are in a relatively high level. Using LLGMN, high discrimination accuracy can be achieved, and it is applicable for practical game operation, even if the experimental conditions such as the number of operation and measurement positions were changed.

3.3 Operation Experiments

In the experiments, subjects were asked to follow a predefined route and place the stone at a *goal* (see Fig. 5). EMG signals were measured from depressor anguli oris muscles (see Fig. 3(a)), and three operations can be discriminated ($K = 3$): contracting muscles on the right side, the left side, and both sides. In this experiment, the shift-group protocol was used for game control, because the number of operations was less than that of commands. Command groups are shown in Fig. 6. In this figure, operation 1 means contracting muscles on

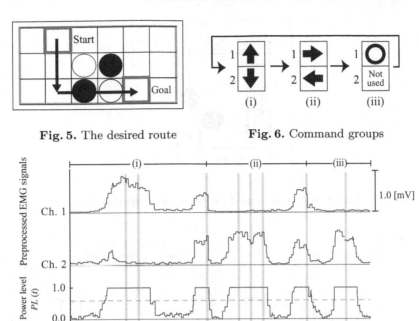

Fig. 5. The desired route   **Fig. 6.** Command groups

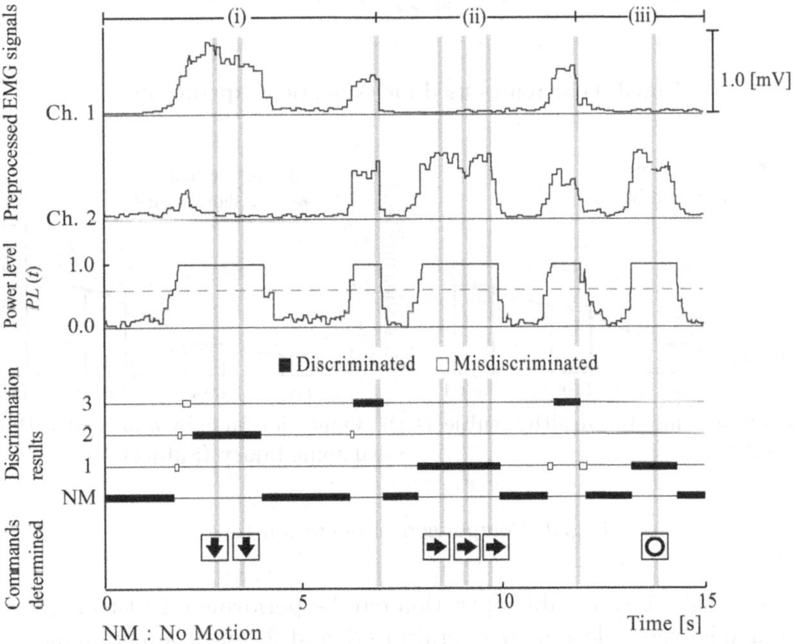

Fig. 7. An example of operations using EMG measured from depressor anguli oris muscles (Subject E)

the right side, operation 2 means contracting muscles on the left side. Also, by contracting muscles on both sides users can shift groups of commands. With this method, five commands can be selected using only three operations.

An example of operations by subject E is shown in Fig. 7. In this figure, two channels of the preprocessed EMG signals, the power level $PL(t)$, the discrimination results, and control commands are plotted. The gray areas indicate the operations the subject made in the Othello game. The discrimination results were set as no motion (NM) when the power level $PL(t)$ was less than M_d.

The EMG signals corresponding to the users' operation were discriminated by LLGMN. In this method, misdiscrimination can be reduced using the power level $PL(t)$ and the entropy $E(t)$. However, during the transient phases of users' operations, some misdiscrimination can still be found. Commands corresponding to the users' operations are decided when the same discrimination continues α

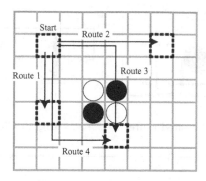

Fig. 8. Four routes used for evaluation experiments

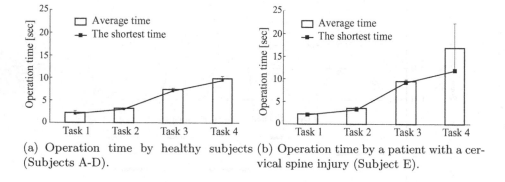

(a) Operation time by healthy subjects (Subjects A-D).

(b) Operation time by a patient with a cervical spine injury (Subject E).

Fig. 9. Comparison of operation time

times. Using this rule, a stable operation can be performed. In this experiment, the commands were selected by operations 1 and 2, and the command groups were shifted by operation 3. It should also be mentioned that since the shift-group method was utilized, some additional commands can be added. From the experimental results, it can be confirmed that the proposed system can work according to subject's intention even when the number of operations were very small.

Then, evaluation experiments were conducted with four predefined routes (see Fig. 8). Subjects were asked to perform these four tasks, and the operation times were recorded. In tasks 1 to 4, a cursor is moved from the start to three different *goals*, and in task 4, users are asked to arrange stones on target positions. For each task five trials were performed.

Comparison of operation time in video game operation experiments using depressor anguli oris muscles is shown in Fig. 9. The command groups were set as Fig. 6. In Fig. 9, the bar graph indicates the average operation time, and the sequential line graph indicates the shortest time for each task. It can be seen that, for both healthy subjects and subject E, average time and the shortest time increase when the complexity of the task increases. For subject E, the operation time of task 4 has a large standard deviation. The cursor path in

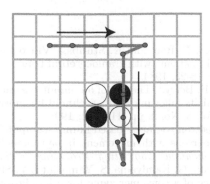

Fig. 10. The most time-consuming trial by Subject E (Task 4)

the most time-consuming trial is plotted in Fig. 10. The cursor control took a long time, because he could not stop at the desired position in this trial. This problem could be related to how to set the parameters such as M_d, E_d, and α.

In the experiments, it was confirmed that all subjects could conduct tasks successfully. Further insights are necessary focusing on parameter setting according to the user's profile.

4   Conclusion

In this paper, we have proposed a novel entertainment interface using biological signals, and a prototype system has been constructed. In this interface system, a variety of biological signals can be used as input, and users can choose input signals with respect to their conditions, so that a lot more people are able to enjoy video games. Also, the users' intention of operation is estimated from the input signals using a PNN. Due to the adaptive learning capability of neural networks, a high level of discrimination accuracy is achieved. Moreover, video game machines can be easily changed, so that various amusement machines can be incorporated into the proposed system.

To verify validity of the proposed interface, EMG discrimination experiments and video game operation experiments have been carried out with five subjects. In the experiments, discrimination rates of all subjects were about over 90%. With this interface system, subjects can operate games at will.

The game "Othello" used in the experiments is classified into Type 4, and the operations are comparatively easy. In cases of Type 1 games, the proposed method may have some limitations, because Type 1 games are very fast paced and require a variety of complex commands. Thus, it will be necessary to first confirm the feasibility of the proposed method with those games. Also, in future research, we would like to improve the decision algorithm of the operation parameters, and apply the proposed method to other input signals and other amusement machines.

98   K. Shima et al.

References

1. J. Malec, R. Jones, N. Rao, and K. Stubbs, "Video game practice effects on sustained attention in patients with craniocerebral trauma," *Cognitive Rehabilitation*, Vol. 2, No. 4, pp. 18-23, 1984.
2. R.J. Taylor, and E. Berry, "The use of a computer game to rehabilitate sensorimotor functional deficits following a subarachnoid haemorrhage," *Neuropsychological Rehabilitation*, Vol. 8, No. 2, pp. 113-122, 1998.
3. K. Coleman, "Electromyography based human-computer-interface to induce movement in elderly persons with movement impairments," *Workshop on Universal Accessibility of Ubiquitous Computing: Providing for the Elderly*, pp. 75-79, 2001.
4. M. Suzuki, Y. Niida, G. Kamiyama, S. Yamashita, Y. Shiota, T. Tamagaki, and E. Ito, "The interface of a consumer game for a handicapped parson," *Transactions of the Japanese Society for Medical and Biological Engineering*, Vol. 42, p. 140, 2004. (In Japanese)
5. J.B. Lopes, "Designing User Interfaces for Severely Handicapped Persons," *IEEE Transactions on Automatic Control*, Vol. 23, No. 4, pp. 538-544, 2001.
6. R. Krepki, B. Blankertz, G. Gurio, and K.R. Muller, "The Berlin Brain-Computer Interface (BBCI)," *IEEE Transactions on Automatic Control*, Vol. 23, No. 4, pp. 538-544, 2003.
7. M. Betke, J. Gips, and P. Fleming, "The Camera Mouse: Visual Tracking of Body Features to Provide Computer Access for People With Severe Disabilities," *IEEE Transactions on Neural System and Rehabilitation Engineering*, Vol. 10, No. 1, pp. 1-10, 2002.
8. D. Specht, "Probabilistic Neural Networks," *Neural Networks*, Vol. 3, No. 1, pp. 109-118, 1990.
9. A. Hiraiwa, K. Shimohara, and Y. Tokunaga, "EMG pattern analysis and classification by neural network," *Proceedings of IEEE International Conference on Systems, Man and Cybernetics*, pp. 1113-1115, 1989.
10. A. Hiraiwa, U. Uchida, and K. Shimohara, "EMG/EEG pattern recognition by neural networks," *Proceedings of the Eleventh European Meeting on Cybernetics and Systems Research*, pp. 1383-1390, 1992.
11. M.F. Kelly, P.A. Parker, and R.N. Scott, "The Application of Neural Networks to Myoelectric Signal Analysis A Preliminary Study," *IEEE Transactions on Biomedical Engineering*, Vol. 37, No. 3, pp. 221-230, 1990.
12. T. Tsuji, O. Fukuda, H. Ichinobe, and M. Kaneko, "A Log-Linearized Gaussian Mixture Network and Its Application to EEG Pattern Classification," *IEEE Transactions on Systems, Man, and Cybernetics-Part C: Applications and Reviews*, Vol. 29, No. 1, pp. 60-72, 1999.
13. T. Tsuji, N. Bu, M. Kaneko, and O. Fukuda, "A Recurrent Log-linearized Gaussian Mixture Network," *IEEE Transactions on Neural Networks*, Vol. 14, No. 2, pp. 304-316, 2003.
14. T. Tsuji, H. Ichinobe, K. Ito, and M. Nagamachi, "Discrimination of Forearm Motions from EMG Signals by Error Back Propagation Typed Neural Network Using Entropy," *Transactions of the Society of Instrument and Control Engineers*, Vol. 29CNo. 10Cpp. 1213-1220, 1993. (In Japanese)
15. S. Shitamori, T. Tsuji, O. Fukuda, Y. Uchida, and N. Mitoda, "Development of Barrier Free Interface: BIO-REMOTE," *SICE System Integration Division Annual Conference*, pp. 415-416, 2002. (In Japanese)

Development of a System to Measure Visual Functions of the Brain for Assessment of Entertainment*

Akihiro Yagi[1], Kiyoshi Fujimoto[1], Tsutomu Takahashi[1], Atsushi Noritake[1], Masumi Iwai[2], and Noriyuki Suzuki[2]

[1] Department of Psychology, Kwansei Gakuin University,
Uegahara, Nishinomiya, Hyogo, 662-8501, Japan
http://www.dips-kwansei.gr.jp/Yagi's%20HP/top.htm
[2] Melon Technos Co., Ltd., Riverside Building.6F 8-24,
Naka-cho, 1-chome, Atsugi-shi, Kanagawa 243-0018, Japan
http://www.melontechnos.co.jp/

Abstract. The unique event related brain potential (ERP) called the eye fixation related potential (EFRP) is obtained with averaging EEGs at terminations of saccadic eye movements. Firstly, authors reviewed some studies on EFRP in games and in ergonomics and, secondly introduced a new system for assessment of visual entertainments by using EFRP. The distinctive feature of the system is that we can measure the ERP under the conditions where a subject moves eyes. This system can analyze EEG data from many sites on the head and can display in real time the topographical maps related to the brain activities. EFRP is classified into several components at latent periods. We developed a new system to display topographical maps at three latent regions in order to analyze in more detail psychological and neural activities in the brain. This system will be useful for assessment of the visual entertainment.

Keywords: ERP, eye movement, attention, game, movie.

1 Introduction

Entertainment computing brings great benefits to the people. Recently, however, ill effects on the brain by playing a game are reported sensationally by journalisms in Japan. Of course, playing a simple game for a long time is not good for healthy development of the child's brain and mind. On the other hand, some of the games and new medias have possibilities to activate and recover an aged brain function in an old person. And new types of digital contents are developed to activate cognitive activities for an adult person [1].

Positive psychology is becoming a big topic in the field of clinical psychology [2]. The positive psychology deals with the well-being in the human life. Many researchers who study positive psychology are interesting in the creation of the good relation between people. They study positive emotion and motivation related to cognitive factors. Not only a good human relation, but also a new relation between the human and

---

* This research was supported by a Grant-in-Aid for Scientific Research in Academic Frontier Promotion Project provided by MEXT and a Grant-in-Aid for Scientific Research, (14310046) by MEXT. Correspond to Prof. A. Yagi, (yagi@kwansei.ac.jp).

F. Kishino et al. (Eds.): ICEC 2005, LNCS 3711, pp. 99–105, 2005.

such artifacts as games, robots and digital contents bring great benefits for high quality of life. Therefore, scientific assessment of the entertainment is required in many fields; e.g. psychology, medicine, education, information science and engineering.

When a person watches a display, movies or something, psychological and physiological changes occur in the brain and the body. Psychological phenomena; e.g. perception, cognition, emotion and motivation are studied as indices by using performance, verbal responses and physiological responses.

The author found the specific brain potential associated with eye movements [3]. The potential varies with visual functions [4]. We developed a system to measure cognitive phenomena with the brain potential. The system is applicable to assess the visual function. In this paper, firstly we reviewed some studies of the brain potentials and, secondly introduced a new system to measure the brain potential for assessment of the visual entertainment.

2   ERP and EFRP

Brain potentials (e.g. EEG; the spontaneous brain wave and ERP; the event related brain potential) can be measured from electrodes placed on the scalp. ERP is a sequence of electrical changes elicited by sensory or perceptual stimuli, and cognitive events. ERP is a very small change in electrical activity of the brain. The direct observation of ERP is very difficult, because ERP is intermingled with EEG. In order to obtain an ERP, successive stimuli or events have to be presented to a subject. The EEG is triggered by the onset of a stimulus or event and EEG epochs associated with the onsets are averaged. Because the spontaneous EEG is assumed to be a random process, the averaged value of EEG gradually approaches to zero. On the other hand, ERP linked to the events becomes increasingly clear as the number of trials averaged increases. Therefore, in order to obtain ERP, signals associated with repeatable stimuli, responses or events are required to trigger EEGs for averaging. A researcher must prepare intermittent visual stimuli with a fixation point on the display to obtain the visual ERP. The researcher asks to a subject to watch the fixation point and not to move eyes. Therefore, it is very hard to apply the visual ERP to situations where eyes move.

When a subject looks at something, the eye movement record shows step-like pattern consists of saccadic eye movements (saccade) and eye fixation pauses. Since saccadic suppression occurs during the saccade, information concerning the nature of the visual object is sent from the retina to the brain during the fixation pause. When EEGs are averaged time-locked to fixation pause onset; i.e. offset of saccades, a unique ERP is obtained. The author found the potential and named it the eye fixation related potential (EFRP). EFRP is a kind of ERPs measurable in situations requiring eye movements. EFRP like the ERP consists of some components that are classified with the latent time (latency) and the distribution on the scalp of the brain (Fig.1). The most prominent component with latency of about 80-100 ms is called the lambda response. Some components of EFRP change as a function of stimulus properties as well as subjective factors [5]. The late component with long latency (300 ms) appears at around the central region on the scalp, when the subject detects a given target at visual search tasks. The component is identical the so-called P3 (P300) component.

3   Application of EFRP to Entertainment

The technology of EFRP is applied to assessment of attention in ergonomics. For instance, assessment of lighting environments [6], a visual display [7], a computer graphic (CG) task [8] and so on [9, 10, 11]. Further, the technology is also applied to assessment of the visual fatigue [12] or attention in computer games [13]. In ERP studies, many intermittent stimuli are repeatedly presented at the same point. The ERP gradually decreases by habituation, if a response to the stimulus is not assigned in the experiment. However, EFRP showed very small decrement during the CG task and a playing game. We observed increment of the EFRP in amplitude during a computer graphic task [8]. The subjects who were novices of a CG task reported that they were interested in the task and enjoyed the painting task. They felt that the task was a kind of games rather than the work.

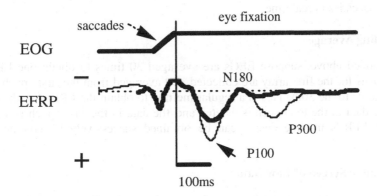

Fig. 1. Model of EFRP. EFRP consists of several components, (upward negativity) EOG shows Eye movement.

In the studies on games, a real time analyzer is required to develop to assess temporal variation of the EFRP. And topography of EFRP also is useful to observe the regional activities of the brain associated with cognitive phenomena. We developed a system to make a real time topographical map of EFRP [14]. In the system, amplitudes of only one component (P80) of the EFRP from 32 sites on the scalp can be displayed in real time. Recently, we developed a new system to display in real time the topographical maps of three components; for instance P80, N150 and P200 (these parameters are optionally changeable).

4   Outline of the System

4.1   Detection of Onset of an Eye Fixation Pause (Offset of a Saccade)

EOG data for the eye movements are digitized with a given sampling time by an A-D converter. The waveform of EOG consists of saccades (big deflections), slow drift and small noises. There are small noises by EMG (muscle potential) even during eye fixation pauses. At the first stage, a saccade is discriminated from the noise. And at the second stage, the point where a big deflection changes into flat is defined as onset of the eye fixation pause. The vector value is computed form the horizontal EOG and the vertical EOG to detect the absolute value of the saccade.

4.2 Averaging EEGs

In the detection of the regular ERP, EEG epochs time-locked to the stimulus onset are averaged several ten times to increase the ratio of the signal to noise. In EFRP detection, EEG epochs time locked to onset of the eye fixation pause are averaged several ten times. One EFRP can be obtained by this procedure similar to the regular ERP. When an eye blink (spike) occurs, the trigger signal is canceled from the subsequent analysis.

Further, when EMG or an irregular eye movement occurs, the EEG sample is canceled. Therefore, EEGs without artifact and noise are averaged automatically at offset of saccades in real time.

4.3 Sliding Average

As mentioned above, suppose EEGs are averaged 30 times to obtain one ERP. 30 EEG epochs for the first array are collected and averaged from the first epoch for the first stimulus to the 30th. This is a regular method to obtain the ERP. For the second array, the data in the top epoch is deleted and the data in the 31st epoch is added. A series of EFRPs in time course can be obtained successively by continuing the procedure.

4.4 Monitor Screen of Low Data

Fig.2 shows windows of real time monitors of low data. The upper left shows the current waveform of EFRP at the occipital region. The upper right shows the current saccade offset. The trigger point indicates by a vertical line. EEG and EOG data are shown in the lowest window. We can check the trigger point and the effect of noise and artifact.

4.5 Display of the EPRPs

When a series of topographies of EFRPs can be displayed continuously, we can observe the dynamic changes of EFRPs like an animation. Fig. 3 shows the topographical maps in three time zones of EFRPs. Each topographical map indicates the distribution of potentials on the brain. The upper side of each topography is the frontal region and the bottom side is the occipital region.

Three bigger maps at the left side show the current topographical maps at three time regions; an early component, a middle component and a late component. Since each topographical map is displayed at the same position, the maps show dynamic changes of EFRP on the scalp. We can observe in real-time the dynamic movement of the EFRP. The dynamic movement was like an animation movie.

Smaller maps at the right side presented one by one at each time region. Therefore, the final map is the same as the right big one. We can observe the trend of the maps at three time regions. The map with the number of 1 indicates the earliest map in each component.

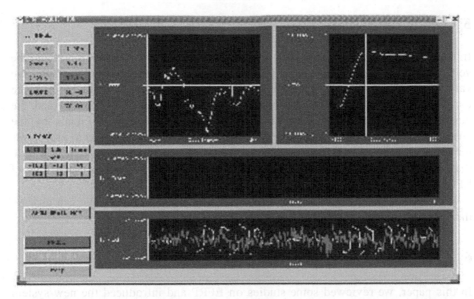

Fig. 2. Monitor screen. A waveform in the upper left shows typical EFRP. The upper right shows a current saccade. A vertical line indicates the point of saccade offset: i.e., onset of an eye fixation. The lowest window shows EEG and EOG.

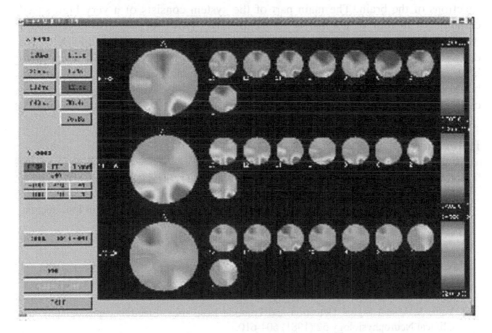

Fig. 3. Shows topographies of EFRP in three latent periods. The left three are current topographies. Red means high positive potential and blue means negative potential.

5 Test of the System

In the test of the system, EEGs were measured from 14 sites. The horizontal and the vertical EOG were measured and amplified. EEGs were averaged 30 times to observe variation in the amplitude of EFRP in neatly real time. The amplitudes of three components; i.e. the positive component (70 ms), the negative (120ms) and the positive (180ms) after an eye fixation were measured and made maps by the analyzing system. In this test, the subject, who was a student, was asked to move eyes between two targets on the strips every 1sec. The distance between two targets was 20 deg. The task was very simple. Topographical maps show dynamic variations of EFRP in time course.

Fig. 3 shows an example of the topographical changes of EFRP. We can observe the temporal changes of EFRP.

6 Conclusion

In this paper, we reviewed some studies on EFRP and introduced the new system that was developed very recently. In the most of the past studies on the brain function, mass data in a session for a long time have been analyzed while subjects are playing games. However, the new system is useful to analyze in real time the functions of the brain. The main part of the system consists of a very high speed computer with four CPUs that is very expensive. However, we also developed a more economical system that works with a personal computer of Window-XP. We can analyze EFRP and can obtain a topography of EFRP in offline [15]. The system is already on sale. It will be useful for a convenient analysis of EFRP. The authors believe those two systems will be useful for assessment of such visual entertainment as game, movies and so on.

References

[1] Kawashima, R. (Supervising Editor): "Nou o Kitaieru Otonano DS Training" (Training of the Adult Brain with Nintendo DS), Nintendo Soft (2004) (in Japanese).
[2] Seligman, M.E.P., & Csikszentmihalyi, M., 2000, Positive Psychology: An Introduction, American Psychologist 55 (2000) 5-14.
[3] Yagi, A. Averaged Cortical Potentials (lambda responses) Time-locked to Offset of Saccades. Physiological Psychology 9 (1981) 318-320.
[4] Yagi, A. Eye Fixation-related Potential as an Index of Visual Function, In: Kikuchi, T., Sakuma, H., Satio, I., & Tsuboi, K. (eds.): Biobehavioral Self-Regulation; Eastern and Western Perspectives, Springer-Verlag, Tokyo (1995) 177-181.
[5] Yagi, A. Visual Signal Detection and Lambda Responses. Electroencephalography and Clinical Neurophysiology 52 (1981) 604-610.
[6] Yagi, A., Imanishi, S., Akashi, Y., & Knaya, S. Brain Potentials Associated with Eye Fixations during Visual Tasks under Different Lighting Systems, Ergonomics, 41 (1998) 670-677.

[7] Yagi, A., & Ogata, M. Measurement of Workload Using Brain Potentials during VDT Tasks, In: Anzai, Y., Ogawa, K., & Mori, H. (eds.): Symbiosis of Human and Artifact: Human and Social Aspects of Human-Computer Interaction, Elsevier Science B. V.. Amsterdam (1995) 823-826.

[8] Yagi, A., Sakamaki,E. & Takeda, Y. Psychophysiological Measrement of Attention in a Computer Graphic Task. Proceedings of WWDU '97 (1997) 203-204.

[9] Yagi, A. Application of Eye Fixation Related Potentials in Ergonomics. In: C. Ogura, Y. Koga & M. Shimokochi (eds.): Recent Advances in Event-Related Brain Potential Research, Elsevier. Tokyo (1996) 586-592.

[10] Moriyama, Y., Matsuo, N., Tomita, Y., Honda S. Simultaneous Identification of Eye Fixation Related Potential and Reaction Related Potential from Single Trial Signals. Medical & Biological Engineering & Computing 35 (1997) 671-677.

[11] Matsuo, N., Ohkita, Y., Tomita, Y., Honda, S., Matsunaga, K. Estimation of an Unexpected-Overlooking Error by Means of the Single Eye Fixation Related Potential Analysis with Wavelet Transform Filter. International Journal of Psychophysiology, 40 (2001) 195-200.

[12] Hirata, K. & Yagi, A. The Variability of Eye Fixation Related Potentials with Task. Demand and Time Course, Psychophysiology in Ergonomics, 1 (1996) 36-37.

[13] Yagi, A., Tanaka, H., Kanamori, N., & Kazai, K., Event Related Potential during a Driving Simulation Task, Proceedings of the XV the Triennial Congress of the International Ergonomics Association（IEA2003）(2003) 588-589

[14] Yagi, A. Moving Topography for ERPs Associated with Terminations of Saccades, NeuroImage, Special Issue, lii, 20052 (2002).

[15] Yagi, A., Kazai, K., Fujimoto, K, et al., A New System to Analyze the Temporal Changes of the Event Related Potential Associated with Offset of Saccades. In: Tsuji, S., Tobimatsu, S. & Barber, C. (eds.): Brain Science Series, Unveiling the Mystery of the Brain, Elsevier, Amsterdam (2005) 437-430.

SportsVBR: A Content-Based TV Sports Video Browsing and Retrieval System

Liu Huayong[1] and Zhang Hui[2]

[1] Department of Computer Science, Central China Normal University,
Wuhan 430079, Hubei, PR China
hyliuwuhee@hotmail.com
[2] Finance Department of Business School, Wuhan University,
Wuhan 430072, Hubei, PR China
zhanghui994@sohu.com

Abstract. An advanced content-based sports video browsing and retrieval system, SportsVBR, is proposed in this work. Its main features include event-based sports video browsing and keyword-based sports video retrieval. The paper first defines the basic structure of our SportsVBR system, and then introduces a novel approach that integrates multimodal analysis, such as visual streams analysis, speech recognition, speech signal processing and text extraction to realize event-based video clips selection. The experimental results for sports video of world cup football games indicate that multimodal analysis is effective for video browsing and retrieval by quickly browsing event-based video clips and inputting keywords according to a predefined sports vocabulary database. The system is proved to be helpful and effective for the overall understanding of the sports video content.

1 Introduction

With the deep development and abroad application of multimedia technology, video digital has become a very important information expressing form in the information system. With the remarkable increase of video data, it is becoming important to index and store them considering their retrieval and recycling. In order to enable detail retrieval, understanding the semantic contents of the video is inevitable. And automatic indexing and retrieval of video information based on content is a very challenging research area with many research efforts addressing various relevant issues [1, 2, 3, 4, 5]. The most difficult problem is: what does content mean? Or, more specifically, how should one characterize visual or auditory content present in a video, and how to extract them for building useful, high-level annotations to facilitate content-based indexing and retrieval of video segments from huge digital video libraries? It is generally accepted that content is too subjective to be characterized completely because it is often concerned about objects, background, domain, context, etc. This is one of the main reasons why the problem of content-based access is still largely unsolved. Ref. [6] has presented a video browsing method, which is conducted through a VCR-like

F. Kishino et al. (Eds.): ICEC 2005, LNCS 3711, pp. 106–113, 2005.

interface. It is tedious and time-consuming, and is not concerned about high-level semantic content understanding. Ref. [7] has presented a video's structured browsing and querying system called videowser, but it also has not realized effective content-based retrieval and just considers the image analysis, so it is not a really content-based video browsing and retrieval system.

Sports video of TV programs is an important resource for the sports fans or the special sports analysis experts. But what the consumer wants to see are the interesting segments of the sports video, and so how to extract the interesting segments, that is to say, how to index and retrieve the content of events is the problem that we want to solve in this paper. There are lots of related works that are concerned with the retrieval of sports video such as Y. Gong et al. [8] that presents a method to automatic parse the soccer programs using domain knowledge, Yoshinori Ohno et al. [9] that describes a system to track soccer players and a ball by using color information from video images, etc. But most of the recent reported work related to sports video focus on one of video features and do not truly constitute a content-based multimedia research method.

Though much research work has been made towards developing automatic video searching system in recent years, however, because of the numerous video program variations, it is still a very difficult work to design a general-purpose system for all types of video programs. In this paper, we focus on TV sports video as a particularly important category of video programs and design a content-based sports video browsing and retrieval system, SportsVBR, which is convenient for users to fast browsing and retrieving sports video. Combining audio-visual features and caption text information, the system can automatically selects the interesting events. Then using automatically extracted text caption and results of speech recognition as index files, SportsVBR supports keyword-based sports event retrieval. The system also supports event-based sports video clips browsing and generates key-frame-based video abstract for each clip.

The rest of the paper is organized as follows. In Sec. 2, we present an overview of our system. We first present an algorithm in Sec. 3 to select video clips that may contain events. Then we describe how to get keywords such as "goal" or "penalty kick" by speech recognition and detect interesting segments by computing the short time average energy and other parameters of audio. At last, a method of extracting textual transcript within video images is introduced to detect events and use these textual words to generate the indexing keywords. Based on sections above, we present the approach of content-based browsing and retrieval of sports video in Sec. 4, and in Sec. 5, the interface of SportsVBR and its functions are given, and conclude the paper in Sec. 6.

2   Overview of the System

Fig. 1 shows the block diagram of our system. The modules shown within the dotted lines form the core part of our system and also are the main subject of this paper. Our system analyzes the sports video by dividing it into video and audio streams respectively. In video streams, it processes the visual features and extracts the textual transcripts to detect the shots that probably contain the events. Visual features are not sufficient for detecting events, so the textual transcripts detection can improve the accuracy and it also use to generate the textual indices for users to query the video events clips. In audio streams, we realize the speech recognition of special words such as "goal" or "penalty kick" and use these words to generate the textual indices, too. In audio signal processing module, we compute several parameters of audio signal to find the interesting parts of sports video more accurately. After we find the video events clips, we organize them in our system for content-based browsing and retrieval.

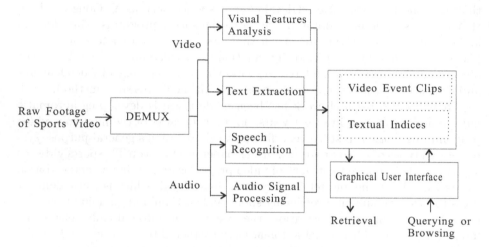

Fig. 1. The block diagram of our system

3   TV Sports Video Multimodal Analysis

Sports video indexing based on events is a kind of indexing by semantical contents, and we think that an event is defined over a time interval, not just a time point. Further, a current event is closely related to preceding events or subsequent ones. In football games, there are lots of events can be considered from different points of view. In our research work, we are particularly concerned with the events that maybe change the score and are interesting for fans and coaches or kinematics researchers: i) penalty kicks (PK), ii) free kicks next to goal box (FK), and iii) corner kicks (CK). These are typical events shown in TV news and magazine programs summarizing a match: they thrill the speakers and the audience, as they embody attack actions in proximity of the goal box area that might eventually lead to the scoring of a goal. Hence, penalty kicks and corners are also often used to calculate statistics supporting the evaluation of the degree of aggressiveness of the two teams.

3.1 Visual Streams Analysis

For video analysis, visual streams processing are aimed at shot-by-shot indexing, so we try to discover a shot that is similar to the target event by matching of feature vectors. First, the sports video stream is segmented into shots. The fundamental element in video processing is usually a shot, which is defined as image sequence what the pickup camera records during one continuous movement. The shots are given by detecting shot change operations such as cuts or dissolves. Second, a shot to be matched is selected from all the segmented shots. For the shot, we extract $N1$ image frames from its head and $N2$ frames from its tail. Because for the events described above, the ball is set to a steady state for kick in the starts of these events, and the ends are the goal box scene or a field scene taken behind a goal post. So the scenes are transitions from a camera-steady frame containing a steady ball to a scene containing goal box or scene taken behind a goal post. Each frame is divided into 4×4 rectangular blocks. Color distribution in each block is given as feature parameters. A feature vector f_n of an image frame n is formed as

$$f_n = (R_{1 \times 1}^n, G_{1 \times 1}^n, B_{1 \times 1}^n, R_{1 \times 2}^n, G_{1 \times 2}^n, B_{1 \times 2}^n, ..., R_{4 \times 4}^n, G_{4 \times 4}^n, B_{4 \times 4}^n) . \qquad (1)$$

where $R_{k \times l}^n, G_{k \times l}^n, B_{k \times l}^n$ are average RGB values in the kth$\times l$th block. We build a feature vector F of a shot by concatenating each vector of $N(= N1 + N2)$ image frames. In symbols

$$F = (f_1, f_2, ..., f_N) . \qquad (2)$$

Finally, we measure the distance between the vector of the shot and that of the example image sequence, which may be viewed as a temporal image model of the target event. Let G denote the latter vector. Of course, the dimension of both vectors is identical. In the matching, the distance is given by

$$d(F, G) = \|F - G\|^2 . \qquad (3)$$

If d is smaller than some threshold, the shot is indexed by the target event: PK, FK, or CK. The example sequence is provided for each target event. It is a crucial problem how we should obtain it. The ideal way may be learning from example stream. At the current stage, we employ a simple way, selecting a sequence randomly from the concerned stream.

3.2 Audio Streams Analysis

The fundamental purpose of this method is to detect segments from TV sports programs where interesting events described above occur. Because only use the visual streams analysis, it is not so sufficient to detect these interesting events exactly. Adding audio streams analysis can improve the accuracy rate of event detect greatly. This typically means increased crowd activity manifested as increased energy level in audio. However, energy level alone is not sufficient in detecting meaningful segments; further processing for recognition of keywords such as "goal" or "penalty kick" is necessary in order to detect the interesting events.

Our algorithm can run with sequences sampled at rates much lower than the typical rates. For that, we sub-sample the 44.1kHz data and work with 441Hz sequences. This further improves the computational efficiency and makes it possible to implement this method on platforms with less computation power. We process the audio streams in units of segments that are one second long. We use a form of audio energy that we call $InterestingLevel$, $X(A)$ which is computed as average absolute amplitude for each segment: if A is a segment of the audio level, the interesting level, $X(A)=\text{Ave}(\text{Abs}(A))$ where Abs is the absolute value function. Then, a sliding window of five units (equivalent to five seconds) is used to compute the average levels, as in most situations true events last for at least five seconds. Then segments with averages above a certain threshold are combined to form a sequence. The threshold we used is half of the max value over the entire program (approximately three hours). The measure of importance used in ranking for each segment is the summation of all average energy values through the range. This ensures that energy as well as the duration is taken into account in picking that segment. The parameters used in the algorithm such as the five second interval or the level of threshold is experimental and further optimization may be possible.

Recognition of keywords such as "goal" or "penalty kick" is helpful to detect these interesting events. In our framework we integrate the speech recognition engine that is compiled with the API functions, which are provided by the speech recognition development kit Microsoft Speech SDK 5.0 of Microsoft corps. This engine recognizes the commentator's voices in each shot to get the frame containing the interesting events.

3.3 Text Extraction

For retrieval of sports video, we should extract the meaningful texts appeared in the frames within interesting events and other situations. Because these specific texts including explain an athlete or reflect the score change, etc, and they appear in a fixed subregion of an image frame, contain textual information that expresses the on-going scenes. An example is displayed in Fig. 2. The text segmentation and extraction algorithm is described in detail in another paper of mine [10].

Fig. 2. An example of the meaningful texts

Using test data set, world cup football games selected from our video database randomly, which lasts three hours or so in total, we obtain an accuracy rate of 91.3% and a recall rate of 97.5% for sports video event clip selection.

4   Content-Based Browsing and Retrieval of Sports Video

According to analysis of sports video above, we present content-based sports video browsing and retrieval. For this paper, we combine the method of content-based browsing event-based video clips and the method of querying by inputting keywords.

Browsing video is an important retrieval method to obtain video content. Through the event detection of sports video, we can get the three interesting events: PK, FK and CK. Then the clips containing the three events are stored into the system database for users' browsing. Key frame can let users know general meanings of a video clip quickly, and now there are lots of algorithms that introduce how to extract key frame. Considering the specification of TV sports programs, we select three kinds of frames as key frames in our framework. The first is the frame that is closest to the middle point in temporal space in $N1$ frames of every event shot. The second is the corresponding frame in $N2$ frames. And the third is the frame that is closest to the middle point in temporal space in every event shot. So the key frames and the video clips of interesting events forms a kind of video abstract for users' retrieval.

Querying by users' inputting keywords is another efficient method for video retrieval. Keywords obtained from the speech recognition module and text extraction form full-text search indices, and some keywords are predefined in a small sports video vocabulary database that are built according to our observation results for a month of CCTV sports programs and the database can be expanded in future work. When users input keywords whatever they thought about such as "goal" or "corner kick" to query sports video, and then the system can provide the exact video abstracts.

5   The Interface of SportsVBR and Its Functions

Fig. 3 shows the interface of our system. It consists of four sections, the display window, the video control window, the sports event clips display window and the key word inputting query window. User is able to input sports video files, and set the start and end of the video files. Clicking the play button in the video control window, the sports video event clip selection of the video files is automatically finished. The results of extracted key frames of the selected event clips are shown in the sports event clips display window. The display window is used to play a video file in realizing event clip selection. And also is used to play a event clip selected from the selected results or to show a key frame selected from the extracted key frames. User is able to input keywords to search event clips, for example, the word "goal", and then the retrieval result is shown in the display window. Click the key frame and the corresponding event clip can be played in the display window.

Fig. 3. The interface of our system

6 Conclusions

Content-based video browsing and retrieval for video flows is a hot spot in the recent researches of video database. This paper develops a system, called SportsVBR, to realize fast and efficient sports video browsing and querying based on event-based video clips selection. The system is designed for parsing TV sports video, but its integration strategy of audio-visual cues, the analysis of text event detection, as well as the methods of content-based video browsing and retrieval can also be applied to the scene segmentation and video retrieval of other video types in future work.

References

1. S.W.Smoliar and H.J.Zhang: Content-Based Video Indexing and Retrieval. Multimedia (1994) **1**(2): 356–365
2. Michael G. Christel: Visual Digests for News Video Libraries. In Proc. of the ACM Multimedia'99 Conference (1999) 303–311
3. Alexander G.Hauptmann, Michael J. Witbrock: Story Segmentation and Detection of Commercials In Broadcast News Video. In ADL-98 Advances in Digital Libraries Conference (1998) 168–179
4. Cuneyet Taskiran, Jau-Yuen Chen, Charles A.Bouman et al: Compressed Video Database Structured for Active Browsing and Search. In Proc. of IEEE Int'l Conf. on Image Processing (ICIP'98) (1998) 133–137
5. H.J.Zhang, Y.H.Gong, S.W.Smoliar et al: Automatic Parsing of News Video. In Proc. of IEEE Int'l Conf. on Multimedia Computing and Systems (1994) 45–54
6. Y.H.Chang, D.Coggins, D.Pitt et al: An Open-Systems Approach to Video on Demand. IEEE Communications Magazine (1994) 68–80
7. Wu Lingqi, Li Guohui: Video's Structured Browsing and Querying System: Videowser. Mini-Micro System (2001) 112–115
8. Y.Gong, L.T.Sin, C.H.Chuan et al: Automatic Parsing of TV Soccer Programs. ICMCS'95 (1995) 167–174

9. Yoshinori Ohno, Jun Miura and Yoshiaki Shirai: Tracking Players and a Ball in Soccer Games. In Proc. of the 1999 IEEE Int'l Conf. on Multisensor Fusion and Integration for Intelligent Systems (1999) 147–152
10. Liu Huayong, Zhou Dongru. Content-based News Video Story Segmentation and Video Retrieval. In Proc. of SPIE Second International Conference on Image and Graphics (2002) 1038–1044

Online Community Building Techniques
Used by Video Game Developers

Christopher Ruggles, Greg Wadley, and Martin R. Gibbs

Department of Information Systems,
The University of Melbourne,
Parkville 3010, Australia
cj.ruggles@gmail.com,
{greg.wadley, martin.gibbs}@unimelb.edu.au

Abstract. Online fan communities are an important element in the market success of a videogame, and game developers have begun to recognize the importance of fostering online communities associated with their games. In this paper we report on a study that investigated the techniques used by game developers to maintain and promote online communities within and around their games. We found that game developers consider online communities to be important to the success of both single-player and online multiplayer games, and that they actively support and nourish these communities. Online community building techniques identified in the study are categorized and discussed. The results represent a snapshot of current developer thinking and practice with regards to game-based online communities. The study augments existing research concerning the relationship between design features, online community and customer loyalty in new media, Internet and game-related industries.

1 Introduction

Video gaming is increasingly a social pastime and social interaction has become an important motive for many players. These players are drawn to games that enable cooperative and competitive interaction with other people. Multiplayer games such as LAN games, online shooters and MMORPGs are salient examples of social gaming and comprise a rapidly growing segment of the game market [7].

Many games acquire a large following of fans who want to come together to discuss the game, share information and resources, and where possible play together. Fan communities form around both single- and multi-player games. Vendors recognize that having a community of fans based around a game has a significant impact on a game's commercial success [7]. Communities can promote a game by encouraging and supporting new users, developing strategies, plots and content and by simply talking about the game. Discussion in gamer communities takes place in online forums and chat rooms, both vendor- and player-operated, and of course offline; for example at school and at LAN game cafes.

Though recent reports make it clear that online fan communities are an important element in the market success of a game [7], it is less clear how vendors can go about promoting a community of fans supportive of their games. In this project we sought to discover and document the techniques used by game developers to promote such

F. Kishino et al. (Eds.): ICEC 2005, LNCS 3711, pp. 114–125, 2005.

communities. We interviewed individual game designers and developers at five successful game companies. All interviewees believed that online community was important to a game's success, and that they were able to influence the formation of communities around their games. Through analysis of interview transcripts we identified a number of techniques that developers use or intend to use to promote online communities around games. We categorized them as 'in-game' or 'out-of-game' according to whether they can be implemented within the game software or not. Our results, presented here, represent a snapshot of current developer thinking, and current and planned practice, with regards to online community. It augments previous research concerning the relationship between design features, online community and customer loyalty, with relevance especially to new media, Internet and game-related industries.

2 Online Communities and Videogames

A 'community' can be thought of as a group of people who share informal relationships that are intimate, enduring, intense, and emotional [6, 16, 19]. Communities form around a shared interest, need or expertise [16, 19].

Widespread Internet access has enabled the formation of online communities whose members communicate using facilities such as e-mail, newsgroups, message boards, and chat. An online community is often ad-hoc; its membership fluctuating as people come and go [6]. Members generally have loose ties with many people rather than strong ties with a few and can participate more comfortably without the commitment, pressure, and emotional investment associated with face-to-face contact [18]. However, relationships can be formed online, even deep supportive relationships characterized by frequent, long term, intimate contact [18]. The Internet has supported the formation of many types of communities, including those based on business, research, and leisure [9].

Videogame vendors have taken advantage of the Internet to connect players, both in- and out-of-game, for the purpose of discussion and sharing resources related to games, and sometimes to allow geographically dispersed players to play together [8, 12]. The way in which the Internet is utilised varies between single-player games (no involvement of the Internet to play the game), multi-player games (using a server to host non-persistent sessions), and massively multiplayer games (players connect via the Internet to a persistent virtual world) [8]. Although single-player games do not require players to be connected to the Internet to play the game, players can still benefit from membership in online communities through which hints and tips are shared, strategies discussed, and stories, experiences and content exchanged. Online communities have flourished around Internet-enabled multiplayer games, especially massively multiplayer persistent-world games. A primary motive for playing these games is to be part of an online community.

Online communities provide a number of benefits to their members, including an opportunity to meet like-minded people and discuss common interests. They are abundant in resources such as personal experience, knowledge and opinions, and give members the opportunity to share and gain status in their community [5]. But online communities based around use of a commercial product can also be valuable to the companies that make and sell the product. They can provide new ways to market a product and reinforce customers' relationships with the product.

Online communities typically form spontaneously, but community-building techniques can encourage their formation and growth, and these communities are often more successful if nurtured [2]. To foster online community both the usability and the sociability of the medium supporting it must be considered [16]. Usability concerns ease of use, learning and navigation, efficiency and consistency of the technology. Sociability concerns the policies and mechanics that guide social interaction. Policies define the community's purpose, membership and style of governance [16].

Online communities have often formed around videogames. While many researchers have examined the dynamics of online game communities [4, 11, 12, 13, 14], we seek to understand what game developers can do to promote communities, through features designed into game software, or community management strategies.

3 Method

We used a practitioner-oriented approach comprising face-to-face interviews with game producers, developers and designers at five different Australian companies. The companies were all successful vendors of online videogames, varying in size from 6 to 60 staff, producing single-player, multi-player and massively-multiplayer games in a variety of genres for PC, console, handheld and mobile platforms (see table 1).

Table 1. Case study organizations

Company	Company Profile
A	40 staff; developing arcade, sim and FPS games, on PC, Xbox, and mobile platforms
B	6 staff; developing arcade, racing, platform, RPG; on PC and mobile
C	60 staff; developing RTS, simulation, RPG; on PC
D	25 staff; developing racing, arcade, children's, FPS, strategy; on PC
E	40 staff; developing racing, arcade, sports; console, handheld, mobile; on PC

The interviews lasted one to two hours, and were mostly conducted at the companies' premises. Participants were asked questions including:

• Are online communities important for the success of a game?
• Do game development techniques influence the formation of online community?
• What techniques have you used to promote online community?
• What techniques are used in industry to promote online community?

Open-ended discussion was also encouraged, to allow unanticipated issues to be discovered. Interviews were transcribed and analyzed using open, axial, and closed coding, to identify the techniques used and the issues raised by the participants. Interview excerpts relevant to each technique were identified. The list of techniques thus categorized and annotated is presented below.

4 Results

All of the participants in our study believed that online community contributes to the success of games, and that the techniques they use in the design and development of a game can influence the formation of online community associated with the game.

We identified a number of techniques that game developers use to promote community in and around their games. The techniques can be categorized according to a number of factors. The participants distinguished between those techniques that are implemented within the game software and those implemented externally to the game, and we have followed that categorization in presenting the techniques below. Whereas in-game techniques are likely to be considered during game design and implemented by the game designers and programmers, out-of-game techniques may be implemented after the release of the game, and involve staff other than the developers, such as web administration staff and community managers, which may be employed by a separate company. Some of the techniques identified are in widespread use already, while others are planned for future projects.

4.1 In-game Techniques

Support formation of player organizations. Players often form groups within a particular game. In some games these groups can register as organizations or guilds while in others they remain informal. Membership within an organization is often based on a common interest, goal, play style, or friendship outside the game [10]. However, not all members necessarily know each other outside the game. In some games membership in a player organization is necessary to achieve high levels of play. Guilds and clans allow players to be a member of a visibly defined group, to socialize and relate with other players and to co-operate to achieve in-game success. They introduce social dynamics such as intra- and inter-group politics, hierarchies, rivalry, competition, loyalty, trust, and pride [10].

Guilds provide a structure for coordinating players. They primarily cater to dedicated players, and often require commitment and responsibility from members, especially leaders, to maintain group coherence (Company B, D). They can form naturally if a game provides features that assist players in running the guild. Some basic features that provide this assistance are summarized in Table 2.

Players can be provided with a simple guild-like structure, without the responsibility of having to run it, by providing a system of 'factions', whereby players join the game as members of a race or group of NPCs. "If you are a goblin, your friends are the goblins - [it's] cutting away some of the complexity while at the same time trying to give you the same sort of mechanism" (Company B).

Interdependence can also be encouraged using a class/skill system that requires players to seek others with skills they do not possess, in order to complete game goals. For example, a warrior may require a healer character to survive a battle, or an engineer to manufacture weapons. Player interdependence can be made "a barrier to entry where you have to interact with a player to get anything done" (Company A).

Reciprocal help between guild members is a powerful community builder, but opens the possibility for exploitation by some players (Company A). It is important to enforce rules in the game world concerning player interactions, such as when players borrow items. "The Internet is anonymous, [and] bonds of trust are going to get strained quite quickly. Hard-coded rules are a way of guaranteeing that when a player invests something they get a return" (Company A).

Table 2. Summary of Basic Game Features to Assist Players with Guild Management

Feature	Purpose
Guild Tag	Display group affiliations to other guild members and other players.
In-game comm. Channel	Allow members to communicate in game with the entire guild. Used for chat, announcements, and co-ordination.
Communicate with players offline	Allow members to communicate with others who are offline, either through a message that they will receive when they next log on, or through another medium such as e-mail or SMS.
Management functions	Allow certain members to invite or promote other members, form or disband the guild.
Hierarchical structure	Allow players to appoint, nominate, or elect positions of leadership who have greater power over guild management functions.
Guild split and merger	Allow guilds to split or merge as circumstances change or conflicts occur (Company A). These mechanisms should allow players to preserve time, effort and resources invested in the group when a split or merge occurs
Item borrowing	Allow members to preferentially share their resources with other members. Mechanics to enforce return of items that have been loaned should help promote sharing (Company A).
Guild progression / statistics	Allow members of the guild to keep track of the progression and vital statistics of the guild and members of the guild.

Encourage competition between players. Competition encourages players to interact socially, develop rivalries and friendships, and "gets people talking about the game and communicating with other people who are playing" (Company D).

Single-player games can facilitate competition by allowing players to upload their scores to a website (Company D, E). In multiplayer games, player vs. player (PvP) competition is often a key aspect of game play and the most common source of competition between players. Although some players prefer not to participate in PvP, others relish it (Company B). To cater to PvP players without making the game unpleasant for players who do not wish to compete, it is important that PvP action happens "in a particular defined context, so that it is always opt-in, and you know the moment you walk across that boundary that you're fair game" (Company A). Safe areas, where players are unable to engage in PvP, can also be created (Company B).

'Griefing' is the exploitation of game mechanics or imbalances to harass other players. Rules may be necessary to ensure players behave fairly and do not ruin the game experience for other players. Experienced players can be deterred from killing new players by removing any rewards that they would receive (Company B). Depending on the kind of game, developers may choose to minimize the rules governing PvP because it "adds to the element of fear" in the game; newer players are not protected but have to fight (Company B).

Design effective player matching systems. Simple player matching systems can include ways for players to register their interests or goals (Company D), or indicate that they wish to collaborate, attempt a particular mission, or join a guild. This enables players to search for and contact people who meet their preferred criteria. Player profiles can be built for more fine-detailed matching based on behavior in the game (Company D). An alternative to implementing these in game software is to employ a 3rd party multiplayer client such as GameSpy, which provides player matching and game management services (Company D).

Consider both casual and hardcore play styles. Casual and hardcore players have differing needs and goals and enjoy different aspects of a game. "The mechanics you use to foster community for the different types of groups are quite different" (Company A). "One of the challenges at the moment is coming out with massively multiplayer persistent game worlds that appeal to the more casual player" (Company C). Developers should "find ways for the more casual players and the more dedicated players to have a common purpose in the clan" (Company A). One way is to create inter-dependence between players of different styles. However hardcore and casual players may need distinct goals and rewards.

Consider different types of player-to-player communication. Members of a community need to be able to communicate in-game. Many games provide a typed-text channel that allows within-group chat, and private messaging between individuals. Channels are often based on a game context, limiting group chat for example to players within a particular area of the game world, or to players in a guild. IRC-style functionality can be provided to allow players to create their own channels, invite and kick specific players, password protect their channel, and moderate it. Although it may be desirable to be able to chat with others anywhere in the world, developers may choose not to allow this, as "it breaks some of the realism of the game" (Company B).

Increasing uptake of broadband Internet has made voice-over-IP feasible in games. Voice allows players to communicate more easily and quickly and "amplifies emotion" in games (Company A). However it may also reduce immersion. "The emotional experiences and kind of experience you have while playing a game using voice to communicate with your teammates is very different from text" (Company A). Voice chat may also breach the comfort zone of players, "there is a layer that you lose", "people are left a bit more open", and is generally a "more aggressive and less welcoming environment" than text (Company D). The effectiveness and appropriateness of voice communication depends on the type of game in question [3].

Asynchronous communication methods allow players to leave messages for others who are not in-game at time of communication (Company A). In-game classifieds allow players to place notices, news, advertisements, and messages for other players (Company A). Providing a variety of communication methods allows "players to communicate at a tempo that suits them better" (Company A).

Report on and applaud player actions. Publicizing player achievements encourages participation in the game and the community. Earning respect within the community increases a player's sense of belonging, gives them an identity, and increases the community's trust in them (cf. [15]). Well-known players can become role models, mentors, and champions for the community.

Systems can automatically generate news based on game events (Company A). Alternatively players can be encouraged to report on each other's actions. This news when collected can be the history, story, and lore of the game. In this way a player's newsworthy actions have a lasting effect on the game (Company A).

Allow players to modify the world in-game. Modifications to the game world cause a player's presence to be felt by others, and encourage players to continue playing the game to avoid losing the effort they have invested. Quests can be implemented that on completion produce a change in the game story. Developers can run events and implement storylines that allow players to have an impact on the future of the game world (Company B). Players can be involved by allowing them to suggest and vote on game rules, allowing them to affect not only how the game world looks, but how it works. This alleviates developers' work and increases player involvement.

Allow a player's character to participate in the game while offline. Persistent-world gamers can suffer a "tyranny of absence" (Company A). When they are not logged in, they do not have a presence in the game: their characters cannot trade, interact, or communicate, and are not affected by in-game events. In many current games the player's character simply disappears from the world, only to reappear in exactly the same condition and location when the player next logs in.

Some techniques allow a player's character to participate in the game when the player is not logged in. For example, an NPC can buy and sells items on the player's behalf, or their character may continue to work on menial tasks such as resource gathering, allowing the player to complete more interesting tasks later (Company A).

Pervasive computing techniques can allow players to interact with the game at more times and locations (Company D). "Mobile phones and web interfaces [provide] casual, low-cost, instantaneous access to a game to provide players with ways of interacting with a game when they're not online" (Company A).

Design the world with social spaces in mind. The layout of a game world affects how people interact within it [11]. "There is great value in creating social spaces that are meaningfully laid out to help players [socialize]" (Company A). The sociability of a space depends less on aesthetic design than on "where players go on a recurring basis with the intention of hanging around for a period of time" (Company A), for example places that players must visit frequently to acquire goods or missions. Casual conversations happen where people trade items and seek services (Company B).

Factions can be provided with their own 'home' or 'town' area where they will encounter fellow faction members (Company A, B). Designers should consider travel routes and where players will encounter each other (Company B). However, casual contact is an inefficient way of finding other players and cannot be solely relied on to initiate community (Company A), so player matching and communication systems should be used as well.

Instancing involves creating a private area of the world for a group of players to enter and complete a task. While it allows content to scale to the volume of players, it restricts player interaction. Therefore it can be "acid for that shared world experience" (Company A). Travel, trading, interaction with players and NPCs, and game progression should be retained in the shared world, and instancing used for specific tasks or missions (Company A). Instanced space should also be "notionally real": if a group enters a certain instanced area of the world, they are the only group in that area at that time (Company A). "We are trying to avoid the sense that 10 teams walk through a magic door simultaneously into their own copy of the world" (Company A).

Encourage players to participate in community events. Players can participate in the online community through staged community events such as in-game meetings with developers, quests, battles, tournaments, or social events (Company A). Developers may also periodically run a mission or quest involved with the storyline, with associated rewards, to give players new goals and introduce competition as players collaborate or compete to complete the task (Company B).

Implement trade systems and encourage a virtual economy. "Virtual economies" have appeared in some persistent-world games, trading goods, services, and currencies that are meaningful within the game [1], and this can contribute to online community, as players seek trading partners. Symbolic value such as graphical design and sentimental value has less impact on the value of an item than its utility; however uniqueness and rarity can play a large role (Company C). In-game trading systems can be implemented to facilitate a virtual economy, although at the present time, out-of-game auction websites such as eBay have also provided an effective trading system (Company A). Secure trading systems can be implemented to prevent players 'scamming' each other (Company B). Players can be provided with unattended trading so that they can place items up for sale while offline.

4.2   Out-of-Game Techniques

Provide an official website and forum. The game vendor or developer's official website and discussion forum are the primary point of contact with players (Company B), and are a basic requirement of every game (Company D). Forums provide a place for players to discuss the game and other topics, debate the current state and future of the game with developers, help each other with technical problems, share game play hints and tips, and collaborate on content creation and other projects (Company C).

Support and encourage fan websites. Like the official website, player-created sites allow players to discuss the game, relate experiences, share information, and share content or utilities. However players perceive an opportunity to more truly express themselves, especially to criticize the game, vendor or developer without fear of censorship.

Fan websites are more likely to continue to be updated even after the developer has moved on to other projects (Company D). Forums run by the developer can become a magnet for complaints as the players have direct access to the developers (Company A), and developers cannot respond to these discussions without being "seen to beat up on some poor fan" (Company C). There is also an expectation that the developer will respond to complaints, and suggestions within a short period of time, which is often not viable due to the volume of messages (Company C). Forums run by fans still allow developers to gain feedback and information (Company D), and allows them to be selective about when they want to interact with the community (Company C).

Developers may choose to empower popular fan sites to host the majority of community discussion on their own forums. Developers can give fan websites interesting content (Company A) and make themselves available for interviews (Company D). Developers can browse fan websites to identify common suggestions to enhance the game (Company D), notify them of important changes, or reply to discussions.

Ensure effective interaction between developer and players. Developers can go beyond simply providing a website, by employing community managers who encourage community associated with a game and maintain contact between developer and community. One interviewee held the position of online community manager, and another participant employed people in that role. "The biggest thing as a developer in these online communities is the element of trust" (Company C). In order to build trust, players must feel that their issues are being heard and not being ignored, and that the commitments made to them by the developer are being fulfilled. Developers must ensure that they are communicating changes being made in the game and what the plans are for the future to the community (Company C).

Players can be encouraged to form groups within the community based on character choices or collaboration in content creation (Company C). The developer can then communicate with a representative of the group. However, this can create a hierarchy within the community as leaders gain influence with the developers and have the power to choose which issues are raised (Company C). Players who hold an opinion different to the majority of players or do not fall into a definable group may feel their issues are not being addressed.

Attain an early critical mass of players. Multiplayer games have little value to a player if few other people play. "An online game will suck if there are no other online players there" (Company B). It is important to create community early, before the release of a title, and reach a critical mass of players shortly after release (Company A, B).

Building a community early depends on both game development techniques and traditional marketing techniques. "Forums and a decent website that can communicate the basis of the game are crucial" (Company A). Providing fan sites and community with content, and allowing them contact with the developer, fuels interest in a title before release. Building interest through viral marketing can be effective on the Internet (Company A, B). "The single greatest resource you have for a good massively multiplayer game is word of mouth" (Company A). Running an open beta is a technique that can help seed an early community and gain valuable feedback from the players to enhance the game before release (Company B).

Developers and publishers whose previous titles have already built an online community have a valuable resource that can be used to promote a new game. Advertising to existing players "goes straight to the people most likely to be interested in the game" (Company B). Games based around hobbies or movie licenses can take advantage by marketing to existing online or offline communities (Company B, C). Running an open beta can seed an early community and give valuable feedback (Company B).

Encourage key players to become champions for the community. High-ranking players can be harnessed as advocates who help promote the game and nurture the community. Champions become leaders in the community, organizing other players, championing their issues, and providing feedback. "They know the game better than you do" (Company A). It is important to choose the right players to be community champions: "The people who are the noisiest people, the people who volunteer to be game moderators, they aren't the people you want. The people who volunteer are usually volunteering for the wrong reasons. The reluctant people, who you see and are doing all the right things naturally ... those are the ideal community people, because they are fair and honest about how they go about things" (Company A).

Involve players in design and development decisions. Player feedback allows developers to improve a game before and after its release (Company B). Knowing that comments are received by developers encourages players to participate in the game's online community.

Developers may choose to focus on developing the game engine and managing the community, leaving creation of game content to players, through a combination of user feedback, content creation, and modification of the world in-game (Company C).

Encourage and support the creation of player-generated content. Player-created content expands the size and re-playability of a game and allows players to express themselves creatively, and to collaborate and share with others. To encourage players to create and share content, developers can: (Company C, E)

- provide tools that allow users with limited technical knowledge to easily create game content;
- allow content-creators access to the development team, to resolve technical problems via email, the official forums, or chat session;
- manage content creators by organizing groups to work on common projects;
- make it easy for players to package, transmit, and install content;
- be aware that intellectual property disputes can arise with content creators, resulting in ill-will, and therefore ensure that terms are communicated clearly;
- encourage high-quality content by rewarding its creators with extra benefits, such as access to the development team or inclusion in a commercial release.

5   Discussion and Conclusion

Community is clearly important within MMOGs, yet contributes to the success of single player and multi-player server-based games as well. The opportunity to play with and against people rather than artificial intelligence is a major motivation for all forms of online multiplayer gaming [17]. Online player communities also allow developers to maintain contact with existing players and to promote their games to new players through word of mouth and similar activities.

All of the game developers we interviewed believed that having a successful online community contributes to the success of a video game. They also believed that game developers can influence the formation of online communities; that is, the appearance and maintenance of communities is not entirely spontaneous, or dependant on factors beyond the developer's control. They described a number of techniques which can be used to actively promote and sustain game communities. We have discussed these techniques and, in doing so, provided a snapshot of current thought and practice concerning online game communities. Following the participants, we differentiated between in-game and out-of-game techniques.

Our preference for face-to-face interviews restricted our population to Australian game developers. However the participants in this study represented a broad range of companies of different size, age, development platform, and type of games developed. They all compete in the global video game market and all have international game player communities associated with their products. Thus our findings should be generalizable to the global video game industry.

The study presented in this paper was an initial foray into the issues surrounding the promotion of online communities associated with videogames. Given the novelty of this area our research was necessarily exploratory, and we have limited our investigation to capturing and understanding the current practices of game developers. Now that a range of techniques used by developers has been identified and described, a study of how these techniques are operationalized, and an assessment of their effectiveness, is possible.

A fruitful avenue for future work would be to explore the connection between game genre and online community. Many different types of games exist, focused for example on violent battle, problem-solving, role-playing, story-telling, strategy, or socializing. Likewise many types of communities exist: they can be aggressive, welcoming, guarded, collaborative or competitive. Certain types of communities may be suited to certain types of games and not to others. The challenge for game developers is to use techniques that foster the kinds of communities that complement their games. Research examining the connection between game genre and community style can usefully inform these choices as well as improve our understanding of how and why online communities take particular forms and not others.

While there is a growing research interest in online communities in general, there remains broad scope to understand online communities associated with video games, and how these communities can shape and influence the game development process. The research offered in this paper provides a starting point for further analysis of the role of player communities in the video game industry.

References

1. Castronova, E. (2003). On Virtual Economies. Game Studies 3 (2)
2. Cothrel, J. and Williams, R.L. (1999). On-line communities: helping them form and grow. Journal of Knowledge Management 3 (1)
3. Gibbs, M., Hew, K., Wadley, G. (2004). Social Translucence of the Xbox Live Voice Channel. In Proceedings of The International Conference on Entertainment Computing 2004. Springer-Verlag: Berlin.
4. Herz, J.C. (2002). Multi-Player Worlds Online. In King, L. (ed): Game on: the history and culture of videogames. Laurence King: London

5. Holland, J. and Baker, S.M. (2001). Customer Participation in Creating Site Brand Loyalty. Journal of Interactive Marketing 15(4)
6. Jankowski, N.W. (2002). Creating Community with Media: History, Theories and Scientific Investigations. Handbook of New Media. Sage Publications
7. Jarett, A. and Estanislao, J. (2002). IGDA Online Games White Paper 2002. International Game Developers Association.
8. Jarett A., Estanislao, C., Dunin, E., MacLean, J., Robbins, B., Rohrl, D., Welch, J., Valadares, J. (2003). IGDA Online Games White Paper 2nd Edition. International Game Developers Association.
9. Leiner, B., Cerf, V., Clark, D., Kahn, R., Kleinrock, L., Lynch, D., Postel, J., Roberts, L., Wolff, S. (2003). A Brief History of the Internet. Internet Society Website http://www.isoc.org
10. Lin, H., Sun, C., Tinn, H. (2003). Exploring clan culture: social enclaves and cooperation in online gaming. In Copier, M. and Raessens, J. (eds.): Level Up: Digital Games Research Conference, Universiteit Utrecht
11. Manninen, T. (2003). Interaction Forms and Communicative Actions in Multiplayer Games. GameStudies.org 3(1)
12. Morris, S. (2004). Co-Creative Media: Online Multiplayer Computer Game Culture. In SCAN:: Journal of Media Arts and Culture, http://scan.net.au
13. Morningstar, C. and Farmer, F.R. (1990). The Lessons of Lucasfilm's Habitat. In Benedikt, M. (ed): Cyberspace : first steps. MIT Press: Cambridge
14. Mulligan, J. and Patrovsky, B. (2003). Managing An Online Game Post-Launch. GamaSutra: The Art and Science of Making Games. http://www.gamasutra.com
15. Preece, J (2000). Online communities: designing usability, supporting sociability. John Wiley: New York
16. Preece, J. and Maloney-Krichmar, D.(2003). Online Communities: Focusing on Sociability and Usability. In Jacko, J.A. and Sears, A. (ed): The Human-Computer Interaction Handbook: Fundamentals, Evolving Technologies and Emerging Applications. Lawrence Erlbaum Associates: Mahwah, New Jersey
17. Wadley, G., Gibbs, M., Hew, K., Graham, C. (2003) Computer Supported Cooperative Play, "Third Places" and Online Videogames. In S. Viller and P. Wyeth (eds), Proceedings of the Thirteenth Australian Conference on Computer Human Interaction. University of Queensland: Brisbane
18. Wellman, B. (1998). Networks in the Global Village: Life in Contemporary Communities. Westview Press, Boulder
19. Wenger, E.C. and Snyder, W.M. (2000). Communities of Practice: The Organisational Frontier. Harvard Business Review 78 (1)

Aggregation of Action Symbol Sub-sequences for Discovery of Online-Game Player Characteristics Using KeyGraph

Ruck Thawonmas* and Katsuyoshi Hata

Intelligent Computer Entertainment Laboratory,
Department of Human and Computer Intelligence,
Ritsumeikan University, Kusatsu, Shiga 525-8577, Japan
ruck@ci.ritsumei.ac.jp

Abstract. Keygraph is a visualization tool for discovery of relations among text-based data. This paper discusses a new application of Key-Graph for discovery of player characteristics in Massively Multiplayer Online Games (MMOGs). To achieve high visualization ability for this application, we propose a preprocessing method that aggregates action symbol sub-sequences of players into more informative forms. To verify whether this aim is achieved, we conduct an experiment where human subjects are asked to classify types of players in a simulated MMOG with KeyGraphs using and not using the proposed preprocessing method. Experimental results confirm the effectiveness of the proposed method.

1 Introduction

The market size of Massively Multiplayer Online Games (MMOGs) continues to experience surging growth. According to the Themis Group [1], estimated worldwide revenues of MMOGs will rise from 1.30 Billion USD in 2004 to 4.10 Billion USD in 2008, and to 9 Billion USD in 2014. At the same time, competitions among MMOGs are also becoming very high. Besides acquisition of new players, retention of current players is also very important. For player retention, tools are needed that discover player characteristics, so that tailored contents or supports can be provided to players. One of such tools is KeyGraph [2] that was originally proposed for extracting keyword terms in a document. Its underlying concept is based on a building construction metaphor. KeyGraph has been later applied to visualizing the relations among Web pages, among products in markets, and among earthquake faults, etc. [3].

In this paper, we apply KeyGraph to discovery of MMOG player characteristics. However, typical MMOG player data consist mainly of sequences of

---

* The author has been supported in part by Ritsumeikan University's **Kyoto Art and Entertainment Innovation Research**, a project of the 21st Century Center of Excellence Program funded by Ministry of Education, Culture, Sports, Science and Technology, Japan; and by Grant-in-Aid for Scientific Research (C), Number 16500091, the Japan Society for Promotion of Science.

F. Kishino et al. (Eds.): ICEC 2005, LNCS 3711, pp. 126–135, 2005.

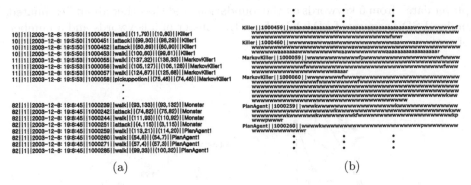

(a)   (b)

Fig. 1. (a) MMOG player data from an MMOG simulator Zereal and (b) action symbol sequences of players

action symbols (Fig. 1) that are not fit for KeyGraph. This is because an action symbol in such sequences does not represent important concepts, but a group of them might do, in analogy to characters and terms in a document, respectively. We therefore propose a preprocessing method for iteratively aggregating sub-sequences of consecutive action symbols into more informative forms. Experimental results from simulated MMOG player data show that KeyGraph using preprocessed MMOG player data has a higher visualization ability to distinguish player types than KeyGraph using the original player data.

2 KeyGraph

Here rather than giving a detailed explanation of it, we briefly describe an outline of KeyGraph. KeyGraph consists of three major components derived based on building construction metaphor. Each component is described as follows:

Foundations − sub-graphs of highly associated and frequent terms that represent basic concepts in the data,

Roofs − terms that are highly associated with foundations,

Columns − associations between foundations and roofs that are used for extracting keywords, i.e., main concepts in the data.

In KeyGraph, associations between terms are the co-occurrence among them in same sentences, and keywords are the terms in either foundations or roofs that are connected to strong columns. In addition, foundations are depicted by solid lines and their touching black nodes, columns by dotted lines, roofs excluding those in the foundations by red nodes, and keywords by double circles.

Fig. 2 shows an example of KeyGraph[1] when it is applied to the text data taken from Section 1 of this paper. From the result, one can see that there are two main concepts in Section 1, i.e., the concept about "KeyGraph for MMOG

---

[1] In this paper, we use a commercial KeyGraph tool developed by Kozo Keikaku Engineering Inc.

player data" from 5 keywords on the foundation, and the other about "estimated billion USD revenues of MMOGs" from the cluster of 3 keywords and a number of roofs.

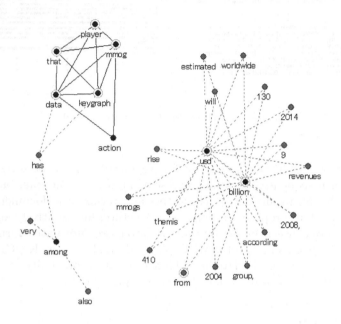

Fig. 2. KeyGraph applied to Section 1 of this paper

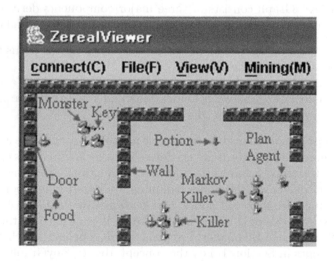

Fig. 3. Screenshot of a game world in Zereal

3   MMOG Simulator and Player Modeling

To obtain MMOG player data, we use Zereal [4], a Python-based multiple agent simulation system. Figure 3 shows the screen shot of a game world in Zereal. Zereal was designed for testing player modeling, artificial intelligence, and data analysis techniques for MMOGs. We focus on three types of player agents, as done in [5], i.e., Killer, InexperiencedMarkovKiller, and Experienced-MarkovKiller, each having 9 actions listed in Table 1. Three player types have different characteristics and different intelligence levels, as summarized in the following descriptions; the last two use a probability matrix following a Markov model for deciding the next action:

- **Killer (K)** roams among game worlds and pursues the closest player or monster and kill them; it has no sociability and thus does not chat with others.
- **InexperiencedMarkovKiller (IMK)** randomly equally attempts all possible actions in a given situation; it models a novice player.
- **ExperiencedMarkovKiller (EMK)** prefers particular actions over others in a given situation and tends to attack monsters nearby; this player type models a veteran player.

In this study, we ran 16 Zereal game worlds, 300 simulation-time cycles each. In each game world, there were 50 player agents for each type, 50 monster agents, and 50 items for each game object (food, potion, and key).

Figure 4 shows KeyGraphs for the three player types when action symbol sequences of players from Zereal are not preprocessed with our method, discussed in the next section. Though their foundations are slightly different, these KeyGraphs have the same keywords, except the KeyGraph for **K** that has no keywords associated with "talk". As a result, it is hard to distinguish one player type from others with these KeyGraphs.

Table 1. Summary of player agent actions in Zereal

Action	Symbol	Description	Precondition
walk	w	walks from one place to another	not blocked by other objects
attack	a	attacks other players or monsters	targets available nearby
talk	t	talks to other players	other players available nearby
pick up food	f	picks up food items	food items available nearby
pick up potion	p	picks up potion items	potion items available nearby
pick up key	k	picks up key items	key items available nearby
leave the world	l	leaves the current world through a door	has a key of the door
enter the world	e	enters the current world through a door	has a key of the door
removed	r	removed from the game	hit points reaches 0

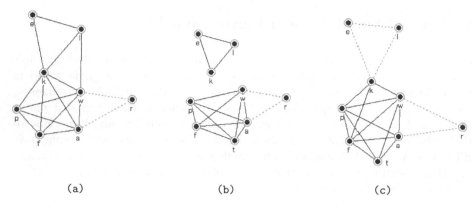

(a)   (b)   (c)

Fig. 4. KeyGraphs for the three player types, from left to right, (a) Killer, (b) Inexperienced MarkovKiller, and (c) ExperiencedMarkovKiller, when player data are not preprocessed with the proposed method

4   Action Symbol Sub-sequence Aggregation

As shown in Fig. 1, the action symbol sequence of a player contains many repetitive portions. One action symbol does not represent that much information on agent characteristics. On the contrary, we conjecture that a sub-sequence of consecutive action symbols, for example, "..wwaa..aaww.." as frequently seen in **K** indicates that the objective of this type of player is to look for targets to attack. Based on this conjecture, we propose an algorithm that aggregates a frequent sub-sequence of consecutive symbols into a more informative symbol called a chained symbol. The proposed algorithm interactively performs aggregation of frequent sub-sequences until they are no longer found.

The proposed algorithm below mainly consists of two parts, i.e., frequent sub-sequence detection (Step 1-2) and frequent sub-sequence aggregation (Step 3-4). The rest of the algorithm (Step 5-6) is for formatting final results.

Step 1. Obtain n-grams[2] from each sequence, and calculate the occurrence frequency in all sequences of each n-gram.
Step 2. Flag all n-grams whose occurrence frequency is T times above the average.
Step 3. For each sequence, find from left to right any sub-sequence that matches with one of the flagged n-grams, and aggregate that sub-sequence into a new symbol called a chained symbol.
Step 4. Count a chained symbol as one symbol in n-grams and repeat Step 1 to Step 3 until there are no n-grams to flag.
Step 5. For each chained symbol in a sequence, replace a portion having consecutive identical action symbols by the capital letter of that action symbol.

---

[2] An n-gram is an n-long sub-sequence of consecutive symbols. It is called a bi-gram if $n = 2$.

Step 6. For each sequence, put spaces between chained symbols and remaining action symbols.

The example below shows the result from the above algorithm with $n = 2$ and $T = 2$, for the action symbol sequences:

```
sequence #1 -- wwwwwwwwwwwawwpwwa
sequence #2 -- wawwwwwwwwfwpwwa
sequence #3 -- wwaawwawwwwwwaww
```

At Step 1, the following bi-grams and their occurrence frequencies are obtained.

```
ww:27, wa:7, aw:5, wp:2, pw:2, wf:1, fw:1, aa:1
```

At Step 2, since the average occurrence frequency is 5.75, only the bi-gram ww, the occurrence frequency of which is above 2 times of the average, is flagged.

At Step 3, the resulting sequences are as follows:

```
sequence #1 -- [ww][ww][ww][ww][ww]a[ww]p[ww]a
sequence #2 -- wa[ww][ww][ww][ww]fwp[ww]a
sequence #3 -- [ww]aa[ww]a[ww][ww][ww]a[ww]
```

where and henceforth a chained symbol is surrounded by brackets for the sake of illustration.

Step 1 at the next iteration gives the following bi-grams and their occurrence frequencies.

```
[ww][ww]:9, [ww]a:6, a[ww]:5, p[ww]:2, [ww]p:1,
wa:1, [ww]f:1, fw:1, wp:1, aa:1
```

At Step 2, since the average occurrence frequency is 2.8, the two bi-grams [ww][ww] and [ww]a, the occurrence frequency of which is above 2 times of the average, are flagged.

At Step 3, the resulting sequences are as follows:

```
sequence #1 -- [wwww][wwww][wwa][ww]p[wwa]
sequence #2 -- wa[wwww][wwww]fwp[wwa]
sequence #3 -- [wwa]a[wwa][wwww][wwa][ww]
```

Since there are no bi-grams for being flagged at the next iteration, the algorithm goes to Step 5.

At Step 5, the resulting sequences are as follows.

```
sequence #1 -- [W][W][Wa][W]p[Wa]
sequence #2 -- wa[W][W]fwp[Wa]
sequence #3 -- [Wa]a[Wa][W][Wa][W]
```

At Step 6, the following sequences are obtained.

```
sequence #1 -- [W] [W] [Wa] [W] p [Wa]
sequence #2 -- w a [W] [W] f w p [Wa]
sequence #3 -- [Wa] a [Wa] [W] [Wa] [W]
```

5   Experimental Results

We set n and T to 2 and 10, respectively, for the proposed algorithm.

5.1   KeyGraphs for Player Data Preprocessed with the Proposed Method

Figures 5(a), 5(b), and 5(c) show KeyGraphs for **K**, **IMK**, and **EMK**, respectively, when action symbol sequences of players are preprocessed with the proposed method. Each KeyGraph represents well the characteristics of the corresponding player type. They are summarized as follows:

Fig. 5(a): It is the only KeyGraph that has keywords associated with "attack" on the foundation. In addition, it has no nodes associated with "talk". Apart from the foundation, there is a cluster of keywords associated with "leave the world", "enter the world", and "pick up key".

Fig. 5(b): Its foundation is formed by keywords associated with "walk" and "talk". Apart from the foundation, there is a cluster of keywords associated with "attack" and "walk" in the right top corner. Other keywords outside of the foundation do not form clusters among themselves, showing randomness in selection of actions.

Fig. 5(c): Compared with the above two KeyGraphs, there are more clusters of keywords here. This implies that they are patterns in selection of actions. Such clusters are a cluster associated with "pick up potion" and "walk" in the left bottom corner, a cluster associated with "pick up food" and "walk" in the left middle part, and a cluster associated with "attack" and "walk" in the right middle part.

5.2   Player-Type Classification by Human Subjects

Since KeyGraph is a visualization tool, we conducted an experiment to see whether human subjects can classify resulting KeyGraphs correctly according to player types when the proposed preprocessing method was and was not used. First, we had 10 subject read Section 2 and Section 3, with the last paragraph (on Fig. 4) being excluded, of this paper. This was done in order to provide them the necessary information on KeyGraph and player types. Then, each subject was shown in a random order the group of KeyGraphs in Fig. 4 and the group of KeyGraphs in Fig. 5. For each group, each KeyGraph was also shown in a random order to the subject. Finally, they were asked to label the player type of each KeyGraph in a given group.

Tables 2 and 3 show the classification results not using and using the proposed method, respectively. The classification rate of the latter is higher than that of the former for **IMK** and **EMK**. For **K**, they have the same classification rate, as expected since most subjects should easily detect non-presence of nodes associated with "talk".

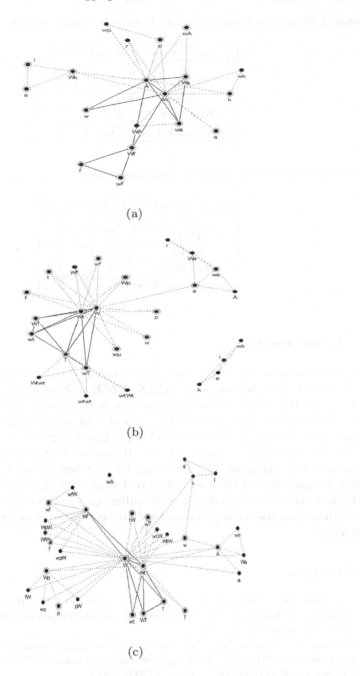

Fig. 5. KeyGraphs for the three player types, from top to bottom, (a) Killer, (b) InexperiencedMarkovKiller, and (c) ExperiencedMarkovKiller, when player data are preprocessed with the proposed method

Table 2. Player-type classification results by human subjects for KeyGraphs in Fig. 4

Answers\Types	K	IMK	EMK
K	9	0	0
IMK	0	3	3
EMK	0	3	3
Not Sure	1	4	4
Classification Rate	0.9	0.3	0.3

Table 3. Player-type classification results by human subjects for KeyGraphs in Fig. 5

Answers\Types	K	IMK	EMK
K	9	1	0
IMK	0	7	3
EMK	1	2	7
Not Sure	0	0	0
Classification Rate	0.9	0.7	0.7

6   Conclusions

We have shown in this paper that KeyGraph is a powerful tool for discovery of the player characteristics of **K**, **IMK**, **EMK** in Zereal, provided that player data are preprocessed with the proposed method. Example applications for real MMOGs include discovery of the characteristics of players who belong to a same social group (guild), who have a same level, who get bored soon after starting the game, etc.; once such characteristics are discovered, better communication tools or proper levels of game difficulties can be provided to corresponding players. After incorporation of DNA analyzing techniques, we plan to test our approach with real data from an edutainment online game called The ICE [6], under development at the authors' laboratory, to be released soon to students of our university.

References

1. Alexander, K., Bartle, R., Castronova, E., Costikyan, G., Hayter, J., Kurz, T., Manachi, D., Smith, J.: The Themis Report on Online Gaming 2004. www.themis-group.com/reports.phtml (2004)
2. Ohsawa, Y., Benson, N.E., Yachida, M.: KeyGraph: automatic indexing by co-occurrence graph based on building construction metaphor. Proc. Advanced Digital Library Conference (IEEE ADL'98) (1998) 12-18
3. Ohsawa, Y., McBurney, P. (eds.): Chance Discovery - Foundation and Its Applications. Springer Verlag (2003)
4. Tveit, A., Rein, O., Jorgen, V.I., Matskin, M.: Scalable Agent-Based Simulation of Players in Massively Multiplayer Online Games. Proc. the 8th Scandinavian Conference on Artificial Intelligence (SCAI2003), Bergen, Norway, (2003)

5. Matsumoto, Y., Thawonmas, R.: MMOG Player Classification Using Hidden Markov Models. In: Rauterberg, M. (ed.): Lecture Notes in Computer Science, vol. 3166, 429-434 (Third International Conference on Entertainment Computing (ICEC 2004), Eindhoven, The Netherlands, Sep. 2004)
6. Thawonmas, R., Yagome, T.: Application of the Artificial Society Approach to Multiplayer Online Games: A Case Study on Effects of a Robot Rental Mechanism. Proc. of the 3rd International Conference on Application and Development of Computer Games (ADCOG 2004), HKSAR, 12-17 (2004)

Agreeing to Disagree – Pre-game Interaction and the Issue of Community

Jonas Heide Smith

Dept. of Digital Aesthetics and Communication, IT University of Copenhagen,
Rued Langgaards Vej 7, 2300 Copenhagen S, Denmark
smith@itu.dk

Abstract. Playing online multiplayer games entails matching oneself with other players. To do so, players must typically employ various types of communication tools that are part of the game or of game-external matching services. But despite the centrality of these tools they receive little attention in discussions of game design and game HCI. This paper seeks to rectify this situation by presenting an in-depth analysis of two pre-game interaction systems which represent influential approaches. Whereas one of these games allows for high player control and thus inspires negotiation, the other allows player communication mainly to help players pass time between matches. The two approaches are discussed in the light of HCI researcher Jenny Preece's concept of "sociability" and zoologist Amotz Zahavi's demonstration of criteria for "honest signalling". The paper concludes with a discussion of the trade-off facing game designers between efficiency and community-supporting social interaction.

1 Introduction

Finding allies and opponents for multiplayer online games is central to enjoying the game experience. The players found must be of appropriate skill level [6] and depending on the game, the player may also be concerned with the moral fibre of opponents; i.e. he or she may wish to avoid "cheaters", "grief players" and other types of saboteurs [14, 16].

This underlines the importance of pre-game player matching systems and makes it unfortunate that these systems have received little attention in the literature on game design and game HCI. By analyzing two highly different approaches to player matching this paper seeks to illustrate the consequences of design choices determining the ways in which players can interact prior to the actual game.

The first game analyzed is the real-time strategy game *Age of Empires II – The Age of Kings* (Ensemble Studios, 1999; see Fig. 1). Here, one player sets up a game, inviting others to join and determining settings which may be changed until the actual game starts. This makes room for negotiation and also paves the way for potential cheating which may in turn increase suspicion among the other players. On the other hand, this approach also invites considerable communication affording some sense of community among the players.

The other game analyzed is the small-scale racing game *Turbo Sliders* (Jollygood Games, 2004; see Fig. 2). As is increasingly common with online action games little

F. Kishino et al. (Eds.): ICEC 2005, LNCS 3711, pp. 136–147, 2005.

decision space is left to the players themselves as settings are determined on the game server level. This approach has multiple advantages in terms of establishing "swift trust" [8] between players but also creates a mostly functionalistic social space where inter-player communication is highly limited.

Fig. 1. *Age of Empires II* is a traditional war-oriented real-time-strategy game in which players vie for control over the game map

Fig. 2. *Turbo Sliders* is a top-down racing game where 2-16 players compete to finish a given number of laps first

These two games are chosen for analysis since their approaches arguably constitute two very different sets of opinions regarding the importance of community and the issue of trust in online gaming. While not representative of the entire population of online games they are positioned at each end of a spectrum.

In order to inform this game design sub-discipline and to illuminate links between game studies and other fully established fields, the analyses are discussed in the light of HCI researcher Jenny Preece's work on "sociability" [10] and zoologist Amotz Zahavi's theory of honest signalling [18, 19].

The analyses follow a brief discussion of related work and a general introduction to the functions of pre-game interaction. After the analyses, the paper briefly discusses opportunities for further research.

2 Related Work

Computer-supported communities not directly game-oriented have been examined under the lens of collective action theory, a school of thought interested in the obstacles faced by groups whose individual members are torn between personal and collective goals [9]. Most directly, Kollock and Smith have studied USENET interaction from this perspective [5] and later commented upon other types of computer-mediated communication (CMC) [17] arguing that the principles emerging from the works of political scientists could be used to shape online social interaction. In a similar vein, Judith S. Donath, borrowing theoretical framework from Amots Zahavi whom I'll return to later, has described how CMC design features relate to trust as they make deception and subterfuge more or less likely [2]. However, these analytical tools have not (or have only indirectly) been brought to bear on games.

As regards games more directly, the observation that games often display novel approaches to interface design has sparked some interest within HCI circles over the years [3, 7, 11][1]. Such analyses, however, tend to focus on efficiency in terms of task-completion rather than how design influences social dynamics or the broader relationship between players. These latter questions have only been dealt with sporadically [4, 15].

In essence, game studies have yet to seriously consider games in the light of social dimensions not directly related to the actual in-game player status (fully competitive, semi-cooperative etc.) particularly for game types other than massively multiplayer games. Such attention would enable designers to make more informed choices about the tools made available to players for communication and for finding others to play with.

3 Pre-game Interaction

It is common to conceptualize games as competitive structures[2]. While not technically wrong, such a definition downplays the fact that multiplayer games rely on a form of social contract between players who must not only agree to disagree but also agree on *how* this disagreement should be played out. This is perhaps most obvious in analogue games. *Monopoly* players must not only agree to actually play the game (at the same time, in the same room etc.) but must also agree on an interpretation of the written game rules, negotiate house rules and manage to deal with rules that are implicit [13]. They are assisted in this process by the multi-modal nature of face-to-face communication.

Largely the same goes for offline multiplayer games (LAN or console-based) although here the core rules are processed by a computer rather than by the players. In online gaming, however, players must largely make due with the tools supplied by the designers[3]. These tools may vary greatly and their exact functions depend on the concrete game. Nevertheless, they share a number of common functions briefly described below. The relative importance of each function depends on the actual game setup – in general their importance correlate with the time requirement of the game (the player may care less if a single game requires a minimal time investment), the importance attached to winning or losing (matching skill levels attains high importance in games which save scores, for instance), and the perceived possibilities for in-game cheating etc.

[1] For a brief review, see Jørgensen, A.H., Marrying HCI/Usability and computer games: a preliminary look. in *Proceedings of the third Nordic conference on Human-computer interaction*, (Tampere, 2004), ACM Press.
[2] See for instance the definitions analysed by Salen and Zimmerman in their *Rules of Play* (p71-83).
[3] Some players make use of third-party CMC tools while playing but these will not concern us here.

3.1 Matching

Players must find allies and/or opponents, and generally look for others who match their own skill level. Some systems provide players with data on the prowess of others to let them choose for themselves, while other games offer more automated matching (see Fig. 3 and Fig. 4).

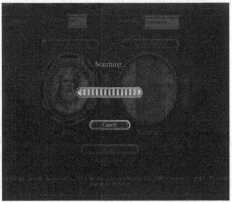

Fig. 3. A *Chess* player at Zone.com matches him- or herself with other players manually based on their scores

Fig. 4. *Age of Mythology* (Ensemble Studios, 2002) players may choose to have the game automatically set them up against suitable opponents

In order to increase the universe of suitable opponents many systems calculate points as a function of the difference between the skill levels of the players. Thus, a highly experienced player may receive but a small number of points for defeating a newcomer while the newcomer may be extravagantly rewarded should he or she defeat the far more experienced opponent.

3.2 Negotiation of Settings

Players look for games with settings matching their preferences. Different games offer different ranges of settings from particular victory conditions to team options, map types, game length etc. Settings are typically adjustable by the player hosting the game or by server administrators. In the former case players may demand that certain options be changed (map size, for instance) and depending on the host player's eagerness to get started he or she may or may not comply with such requests/demands. When playing on game servers outside individual player control changing settings may require contacting the server admin (if he or she is not active in the actual game) or rallying support from the community to vote for a permanent change of settings. The latter is a common procedure in first-person-shooter communities concentrated around particular servers.

3.3 Negotiation of "House Rules"

As noted above, computers do not eliminate the need to settle for certain "soft" rules. Generally, the more complex the game, the more soft rules are needed. In the first-person-shooter *Battlefield 1942* (Digital Illusions CE AB, 2002) players usually consider certain tactics (such as attacking the enemy home base in certain ways) very bad style or even grounds for banishment [16]. Similarly, abuse of in-game communication channels is almost always frowned upon even if such behaviour is arguably made possible by the game code (and thus could be construed as a game tactic).

3.4 Evaluating Opponent Attitude

If stakes are high, either in terms of rating system or in terms of time invested in a single game, players may be interested in other players' sense of responsibility. In rated games having one's allies suddenly drop from the server may mean a loss of points and in more casual but still lengthy games having someone (either ally or opponent) drop may spoil the fun rendering the game outcome moot. Thus, pre-game interaction may allow players to gauge whether others are worth spending time with or whether it would be more prudent to seek out alternative players.

3.5 Other Functions

Finally, pre-game interaction may serve much more indirect, even unplanned, functions. Firstly, chat may itself entertain as players strike up conversations, tell jokes or discuss the game. But it may also give the player a sense of social presence not achievable through systems which do not enable players to communicate. Thus, while negotiating settings etc. may be time-consuming and technically inefficient it may also be a catalyst for the formation of community and a sense of sociability within the game space. We shall return to this design trade-off after the game analyses below.

4 Two Approaches: Game Analyses

As mentioned *Age of Empires II* and *Turbo Sliders* represent remarkably different approaches to pre-game interaction. Below the two systems will be analysed primarily in terms of their structure and flow, after which the observations will be discussed in a theoretical framework.

4.1 Letting Players Speak: *Age of Empires II*

The real-time-strategy game *Age of Empires II - The Age of Kings* (*AOK* henceforth) is supported by the web-based Zone.com, a Microsoft-owned gaming portal. Here players create accounts through which their team affiliation and results are stored and to a large degree shared with other players (see Fig. 5 and Fig. 6).

Fig. 5. "Info" page of a Zone.com player profile

Fig. 6. "Ratings" page of a Zone.com player profile

Thus, by accessing another player's profile with a thorough understanding of the rating system one may get a reasonably accurate idea of that player's skill level.

Upon logging in, players are presented with an overview of current game "rooms" some of which have different victory conditions (see Fig. 7). Upon entering a room, the player gains access to the room chat channel and may join one of the existing "games" or choose to host a new one of his or her own (see Fig. 8).

Age of Empires II	
Room	**Population**
Dark Ages	2 players
Hunt The Royal	0 players
Deathmatch Room 1	129 players
Deathmatch Room 2	1 players
Deathmatch Room 3	0 players
Deathmatch Room 4	0 players
Deathmatch Room 5	0 players
Deathmatch Room 6	0 players
Custom Scenario Room 1	1 players
Custom Scenario Room 2	117 players
Non-Patch Room 1	34 players
The Plains (Rookie)	106 players
Battlefield (Expert)	2 players

Fig. 7. The player chooses between available rooms

Fig. 8. The player is then presented with a list of actual games and a general chat channel

Fig. 9. Upon choosing a game the player is presented with information on game settings, other players and with a game chat channel

The general chat channel is typically used for aggressively advertising individual games rather than for dialogue.

Meanwhile, once inside a "game" (see Fig. 9), discussion generally becomes more focused revolving around game settings or suggestions for "soft" rules not imposable through the settings [15]. For instance, a player may suggest that certain in-game strategies such as very early attacks should not be used.

Interestingly, at this point the game host may still choose to leave certain settings unsettled. This may be done in order to more easily attract players to the game but it may also have the consequence that those players who do enter will turn out to have incompatible game preferences. When enough players have entered the game the host chooses to launch the game. This leads to yet another setup screen, the final one before the actual game (see Fig. 10).

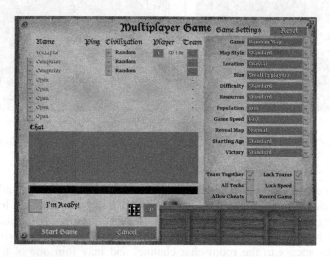

Fig. 10. The final setup screen. Settings not previously settled upon must now be set.

Again, players are given a chat channel and thus the chance to discuss the final game settings. Typically, once things have progressed this far discussions will not centre on basic issues like victory conditions but revolve around map type or size and team setup. Once players have progressed to this point they will often have spent considerable time searching for a suitable game and most are reluctant to leave even if game settings do not turn out to match their preferences entirely.

Over all, it is clear that actually starting up an *AOK* game requires considerable patience and effort[4]. From a functionalistic point of view the process is less than efficient. Thus, we might assume that online *AOK* play is less than attractive. It may surprise us, in this light, to observe how online play remains popular even today, more than four years after the game's release (although most now play with the game expansion *Conquerors* from 2000). The number of players online rarely drops below 1000 and one of the game's most popular web forums (at http://aok.heavengames.com/) still sees considerable activity and has received a total of well over 400.000 posts. Although surely this must partly be attributed to the qualities of the game it also suggests that while technically quite inefficient, the pre-game interaction system has other qualities. We'll return to this point after examining the very different approach used by Turbo Sliders.

---

[4] Add to the processes described above the considerable technical difficulties encountered in many sessions, revolving around router port settings, firewalls and incompatible versions of the game.

4.2 Hard-Coded Interaction: *Turbo Sliders*

The low-budget, and quite technologically modest, top-down racing game *Turbo Sliders* is usually played on one of around 15 publicly available game servers[5]. The servers are not under player control and hence settings are not up to debate. From a central list the player is informed of server settings, player population etc. and chooses which one to access (see Fig. 11). Since the game depends on fast reflexes and motor skill, server latency will clearly be of importance (second column on Fig. 11). Next, players will generally look for populated servers and avoid those with no other players (fourth column). Column seven and eight shows whether cars can collide on the track ("Gho"=no means that cars are not ghosted; that they *can* collide) and whether "Pro rules" are activated on the server.

The Pro rules are a somewhat controversial feature introduced to combat certain playing styles thought to be detrimental to the enjoyment of other players. Before this feature was introduced, some players would find it entertaining to drive in the non-intended direction to ram into other players who would then be seriously disadvantaged. However, the new feature could not simply disable such behaviour as one must sometimes backtrack to get free of obstacles etc. Thus, instead the new rules punish players who collide with another player who is too far ahead (on the assumption that this difference is a sign of someone not really trying to compete). This approach, however, has some unfortunate consequences as being far behind another car can also be a sign of inexperience, in which case the superior player may use the Pro rules as a weapon.

Fig. 11. The server list (selective enlargement)   **Fig. 12.** Chat room where players wait between races

The implementation of the Pro rules is an example of an approach which seeks to avoid anti-social play through code.

As players join a server they can usually enter the ongoing cup even if arriving between races. As players on a server wait for the next race to begin (a process fully

---

[5] Players may also run their own servers but this is rarely done. At least such servers are rarely accessible through the central server list.

controlled by the server) they are offered a chat channel. This channel is quite often used for brief spouts of small-talk and frequently carries offensive comments directed at named players.

Generally, actually getting to play *Turbo Sliders* online is a simple and fast process. Compared to the choices and multiple screens facing *AOK* player the *Turbo Sliders* system is far more efficient. However, the gaming experience is also quite different in another sense as one's interaction with the other players is extremely limited. Now, obviously this is partly a function of the gameplay. In general action gameplay does not allow for much in-game communication as this would not be compatible with trying to win the game. But it is also obvious that recent action games tend to prioritize ease of access and to downplay pre-game interaction if that is even made possible by the game designers. Popular games like *Counter-Strike* (Valve, 2000) and *Battlefield 1942* for instance, use a setup quite similar to that of *Turbo Sliders*.

The limited pre-game interaction caters to a certain, rather functionalistic style of play. If getting to the actual game is considered the prime task facing players then this highly automated approach will surely do best from a usability perspective. However, making players interact may carry with it different advantages.

5 Pre-game Interaction, Community and Trust

In the following, I will argue that while the *Turbo Sliders* approach solves many of the problems inherent in the *AoK* approach, it does so at the expense of the social atmosphere of the gamespace. While the *Turbo Sliders* system is high on trust, it is low on sociability, which suggests that lessons learned from game-spaces that are more open may not be unproblematic and that the issue should be given more careful consideration.

One reason why game designers may be tempted to eliminate pre-game communication is the problem of distrust between players.

The *AoK* approach clearly leaves room for strategic communication and downright subterfuge. This structural property is likely to affect a player's perception of statements (or actions) made by others. In terms of signalling, statements from *AoK* players are generally not trustworthy as players have few options to actually back up their claims. For instance, claiming to be a responsible player (e.g. one who does not suddenly leave his keyboard), claiming that one's custom made map is fair etc. may be met with scepticism as the system does not grant the player ways to support his or her claims [15].

More formally, zoologist Amots Zahavi has distinguished between *conventional signals* and *assessment signals* [19]. The former are mere statements (e.g. "I am honest"), while the latter are statements, in a broad sense, which prove themselves (e.g. spending large amounts of money as a signal of wealth). Sending trustworthy signals generally involves some cost or handicap (in terms of energy expended, time used, money spent etc.) since an uncostly signal is one that anyone can send. A common way to send such trustworthy signals is by actually limiting one's options, for instance by having a mutually trusted third party (such as a bank) actually carry out an exchange. Another is to place oneself in a situation where breaking a promise would bring down a punishment on one's head (as when two parties sign a legally binding contract). Within the structure of the *AoK* pre-game system it is quite difficult to incur such a cost even if one is quite willing. To a large degree statements within this system cannot be backed up by clear evidence.

The opposite is true in the *Turbo Sliders* system. Here, the very process of logging on to a server can be described as an assessment signal about one's intended behaviour. Logging on to a server where all settings are essentially hard-wired means limiting one's options almost entirely and there will be little reason for players to be wary of each other as one person's actions do not seriously affect the other people's game outcomes[6].

But while trust is important in online play, we may also consider the issue in terms of community. Now, initially one might be tempted to think that players go online to *play* and not to *talk* but in fact a large majority of online gamers find communication/chat with other players to be an appealing part of online gaming [14]. And given the fact that at least some players presumably go online to play (while they could also have chosen single-player entertainment in the comfort of their homes) *because* of the social nature of the former experience, the characteristics of the social experience arguably become important. Put differently, the notion of "sociability" becomes relevant. Sociability, according to Jenny Preece [12], is the way in which a multi-user software product supports favourable social interaction – particularly such interaction as inspires the formation of community. As Preece has noted, designing for sociability is often quite different from designing for usability:

> "... many communities have joining requirements. Though still open to everyone, having to register, provide a login name and password, and then wait several hours or days for acceptance does deter less-serious and unscrupulous people from casually dropping into the community." [12]

While this process is clearly quite difficult and inefficient in terms of task-completion it may have community-beneficent side-effects. While one may design a highly efficient pre-game process it should be emphasised that stripping away requirements or possibilities for inter-player communication is not only a solution to a problem but also a trade-off between improvement on the functional level and possible negative effects on the social level.

In this light, it becomes interesting that *AoK* developers Ensemble Studios chose an approach quite similar to that of *Turbo Sliders* for their subsequent title *Age of Mythology* (see Fig. 4). This indicates an attempt to avoid the social problems accompanying the earlier system, but it is thought-provoking that this was achieved by eliminating the possibility, and certainly the need, for communication altogether.

For future designers of pre-game interaction systems it may be worthwhile attending to the possibility of combining the virtues of these two approaches; to support both trust and sociability. As I have argued elsewhere [15] there is nothing *inherently* impossible in raising the level of trust in a gamespace reliant on player communication.

---

[6] This is a slightly idealized description as the earlier description of the Pro rules indicates.

6 Discussion and Suggestions for Further Research

In 1996 Judith Donath argued that

> "...the future success of virtual communities depends on how well the tools for social interaction are designed. If they are poorly designed, the on-line world may feel like a vast concrete corporate plaza, with a few sterile benches... If the tools are well designed, the on-line world will not only be inhabited, but will be able to support a wide range of interactions and relationships, from close collaboration to casual people watching." [1]

Since then great strides have been taken in the design of social software and in research within Computer-Supported Cooperative Work. But with the possible exception of MMORPGs it is not obvious that this development has fully benefited the design of multi-player games.

Clearly, the two games discussed above differ on a host of variables other than those of the matching systems. Hence, it is not reasonable to compare the popularity of the two games to determine which approach appeals more to players in general. Nevertheless, although the initial observations made above are theoretically founded, it is important that the actual behavioural effects of various approaches to pre-game interaction be studied empirically in future work. Due to the vast number of variables which potentially influences player behaviour (genre preferences, expectations of the concrete title, online gaming experience, input devices, time since game launch etc.) such studies would most likely have to combine quantitative and qualitative methodological approaches. By doing so, such research would shed light on a much under-appreciated aspect of online game design and would help pave the way for the sharing of experience between the areas of game design and the design of social software more broadly.

Furthermore, the value placed on social interaction in gamespaces should be further investigated. It is important to examine how players value different types of interaction outside the core game and equally interesting to discover how much players agree on the relative importance of communication and core-game activities. It might well be the case that player preferences differ greatly on this issue which would make the design challenge one of catering to very different interaction styles.

7 Conclusions

This paper has argued that player interaction outside the core game is too important to be ignored by those involved in designing games. Pre-game interaction has a number of crucial functions, but while many of these can be automated in a way that makes the interaction flow much more streamlined such streamlining does not come without sacrifice in the form of diminished communication and sense of community.

This has been illustrated by an analysis of two radically different approaches to pre-game interaction. Whereas one invited problems related to trust the other is merely a pseudo-solution to this problem as it represents the stripping away of almost all non-game interaction between players, interaction which we know to be appealing to many players.

The design of many modern games seems to suggest that game designers concern themselves mainly about classical usability in a very limited sense. Since players also come online to interact with others, and indeed to have a social experience, such a narrow focus may have unfortunate consequences.

References

1. Donath, J. Inhabiting the Virtual City – The design of social environments for electronic communities, Massachusetts Institute of Technology, 1996.
2. Donath, J.S. Identity and deception in the virtual community. in Kollock, P.S., Marc ed. Communities in Cyberspace, Routledge, New York, 1999.
3. Dyck, J., Pinelle, D., Brown, B. and Gutwin, C., Learning from Games: HCI Design Innovations in Entertainment Software. in 2003 Conference on Graphics Interface (GI'03), (Halifax, 2003).
4. Koivisto, E.M.I., Supporting Communities in Massively Multiplayer Online Role-Playing Games by Game Design. in Level Up - Digital Games Research Conference, (Utrecht, 2003), Utrecht University.
5. Kollock, P. and Smith, M. Managing the Virtual Commons – Cooperation and Conflict in Computer Communities. in Herring, S.C. ed. Computer-Mediated Communication: Linguistic, Social, and Crosscultural Perspectives, John Benjamin, Amsterdam, 1996.
6. Koster, R. A Theory of Fun. Paraglyph Press, Scottsdale, 2005.
7. Malone, T.W., Heuristics for designing enjoyable user interfaces: Lessons from computer games. in Proceedings of the 1982 conference on Human factors in computing systems, (Gaithersburg, Maryland, 1982), ACM Press.
8. Meyerson, D., Weick, K.E. and Kramer, R.M. Swift Trust in Temporary Groups. in Kramer, R.M. and Tyler, T.R. eds. Trust in Organizations - Frontiers of Theory and Research, SAGE Publications, London, 1996.
9. Olson, M. The Logic of Collective Action - Public Goods and the Theory of Groups. Harvard University Press, London, 1971.
10. Ostrom, E. Governing the Commons – The Evolution of Institutions for Collective Action. Cambridge University Press, New York, 1990.
11. Pausch, R., Xerox, R.G., Skelly, T. and Thiel, D., What HCI Designers Can Learn From Video Game Designers (in Conference Companion). in CHI '94, (Boston, 1994).
12. Preece, J. Online Communities - Designing Usability, Supporting Sociability. John Wiley & Sons, Ltd., New York, 2000.
13. Salen, K. and Zimmerman, E. Rules of Play - Game Design Fundamentals. MIT Press, London, 2004.
14. Smith, J.H. Avatars you can trust - A survey on the issue of trust and communication in MMORPGs, www.game-research.com, 2003.
15. Smith, J.H. The games economists play - implications of economic game theory for the study of computer games. In review.
16. Smith, J.H., Playing Dirty - Understanding Conflicts in Multiplayer Games. in 5th annual conference of The Association of Internet Researchers, (The University of Sussex, 2004).
17. Smith, M.A. and Kollock, P. Communities in Cyberspace. in Smith, M.A. and Kollock, P. eds. Communities in Cyberspace, Routledge, London, 1999.
18. Zahavi, A. The cost of Honesty (Further Remarks on the Handicap Principle). Journal of Theoretical Biology, 67. 603-605.
19. Zahavi, A. and Zahavi, A. The Handicap Principle: A Missing Piece of Darwin's Puzzle. Oxford University Press, 1999.

Keyword Discovery by Measuring Influence Rates on Bulletin Board Services

Kohei Tsuda and Ruck Thawonmas*

Intelligent Computer Entertainment Laboratory,
Department of Human and Computer Intelligence, Ritsumeikan University,
Kusatsu, Shiga 525-8577, Japan
ruck@ci.ritsumei.ac.jp

Abstract. In this paper, we focus on relations between comments on Tree-style Bulletin Board Services (BBSs), and propose a method for discovering keywords by measuring influence rates thereon. Our method is based on an extended model of Influence Diffusion Model (IDM) proposed by N. Matsumura et al. in 2002, where they discussed the influence diffusion of a term in a comment to all succeeding comments that include that term and reply to that comment. Here we additionally consider the influence diffusion of a term over comments that include that term and all reply to a same comment, as well as the influence diffusion of a term over nearby comments that include that term, regardless of their reply relation. Evaluation results using Tree-style BBS data related to Massively Multiplayer Online Games (MMOGs) show that the proposed method has higher precision and recall rates than IDM and a classical method based on term frequencies. As a result, keywords discovered by the proposed method can be effectively used by MMOG publishers for incorporating users' needs into game contents.

Keywords: Keyword Discovery, Tree-style BBSs, Comments, MMOGs.

1 Introduction

Online contents such as Bulletin Board Services (BBSs) have recently gained a lot of attention as new tools for market analysis [1]. In Massively Multiplayer Online Games (MMOGs), their contents must be accordingly updated after the first release in order to retain users [2]. It is therefore important to grasp user demands, and for this task BBSs outside of the game are a good candidate. With the increasing number of documents in such BBSs, automatically discovering keywords is a very challenging and important issue.

We focus on relations between comments on Tree-style BBSs, where the reply relation of comments (who replies to whom) is clear. For keyword discovery

---

* The author has been supported in part by Ritsumeikan University's **Kyoto Art and Entertainment Innovation Research**, a project of the 21st Century Center of Excellence Program funded by Ministry of Education, Culture, Sports, Science and Technology, Japan; and by Grant-in-Aid for Scientific Research (C), Number 16500091, the Japan Society for Promotion of Science.

F. Kishino et al. (Eds.): ICEC 2005, LNCS 3711, pp. 148–154, 2005.

on such BBSs, we extend Influence Diffusion Model (IDM) [3], [4] and propose our method based on it. The main concept behind our method is that an influential term in a comment should be also used in succeeding comments. In our method, three types of influence diffusion of a term over comments that include that term are considered, namely, the influence diffusion from a comment to all succeeding comments that reply to that comment (originally discussed in IDM), the influence diffusion over comments that all reply to a same comment, and the influence diffusion over nearby comments, regardless of their reply relation. In our case study using Tree-style BBS data related to MMOGs, the proposed method, IDM, and a classical method based on term frequencies are compared. Thereby the superiority of the proposed method over the others is confirmed in terms of both the precision rate and the recall rate.

2   Measuring of Influence Rates

In this section, we describe the definition of comment relations and our algorithm for measuring influence rates. On BBSs, communication is done by exchanging comments, via posting a new comment and its reply comments. The influence of a term is diffused from a comment in which the term resides to succeeding comments that include also that term.

2.1   Comment Relations

We consider that there are three types of comment relations, via which the influence of a term is diffused over comments that include also that term, as follows:

Comment Chain. (Fig. 1(a)) that shows the influence diffusion of a term from a comment, say comment **X**, to all succeeding comments that reply to comment **X**;

Parallel Chain. (Fig. 1(b)) that shows the influence diffusion of a term from a comment that replies to a preceding comment, say comment **Y**, to all succeeding comments that also reply to comment **Y**; where terms residing in Comment Chain are excluded from consideration;

Cross Chain. (Fig. 1(c)) that shows the influence diffusion of a term from a comment, say comment **Z**, to up to its α succeeding comments; where terms residing in either Comment Chain or Parallel Chain are excluded from consideration;

where in Fig. 1 comment numbers indicate the order where the comments are posted.

2.2   The Proposed Algorithm

Treating each term equally, we define the influence rate of term t on comment k as follows:

$$i_{t,k} = \frac{1}{|w_{c,k}| + |w_{p,k}| + |w_{x,k}|}, \tag{1}$$

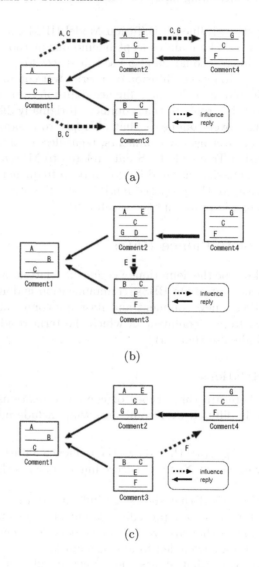

Fig. 1. Examples of (a) Comment Chain, (b) Parallel Chain, and (c) Cross Chain

where $w_{c,k}$, $w_{p,k}$, and $w_{x,k}$ are the set of terms whose influence on comment k is via Comment Chain, Parallel Chain, and Cross Chain, respectively.

In practice, the above three chain types should have different effects in calculation of influences. Our heuristic is as follows:

Effect of Comment Chain $\geq$ Effect of Parallel Chain $\geq$ Effect of Cross Chain

We further analyzed a targeted BBS in our case study discussed in Section 3 and found that in a given comment, the number of terms whose influence is via a particular chain type basically fits the relation in the above heuristic. We therefore define the influence rate of term t on comment k via Comment Chain, Parallel Chain, and Cross Chain, respectively, as follows:

$$i_{c,t,k} = i_{t,k} \cdot \frac{|w_{c,k}|}{|w_{c,k}| + |w_{p,k}| + |w_{x,k}|} \tag{2}$$

$$i_{p,t,k} = i_{t,k} \cdot \frac{|w_{p,k}|}{|w_{c,k}| + |w_{p,k}| + |w_{x,k}|} \tag{3}$$

$$i_{x,t,k} = i_{t,k} \cdot \frac{|w_{x,k}|}{|w_{c,k}| + |w_{p,k}| + |w_{x,k}|} \tag{4}$$

Due to the definition of each chain type, the influence of a term on a given comment is via either of the three chain types. As a result, the total influence rate of term k diffused from comment 1 to comment n can be given below as:

$$I_{t,n} = \sum_{k=1}^{n} j_{t,k}, \tag{5}$$

where $j_{t,k}$ is defined as

$$j_{t,k} = \begin{cases} i_{c,t,k} & \text{if via Comment Chain} \\ i_{p,t,k} & \text{if via Parallel Chain} \\ i_{x,t,k} & \text{if via Cross Chain} \end{cases} \tag{6}$$

Now we are ready to give the algorithm for measuring influence rates. Our algorithm is as follows:

1. Decide the first comment and the last comment for measuring influence rates in a given BBS, and then move to the first comment
2. Move to the next succeeding comment
3. Select all terms in the current comment whose influence is via Comment Chain
4. Select all remaining terms in the current comment whose influence is via Parallel Chain
5. Select all remaining terms the current comment whose influence is via Cross Chain
6. Calculate the influence rate of each selected term using (5)
7. Repeat 2 to 6 if the current comment is not the last one.

3   Case Study

We analyzed 1697 comments in Japanese that were posted on Yahoo!BBS [5] (Fig. 2) during June 22, 2002 and August 15, 2004. The main topic of this BBS is on MMOG systems, especially on new ideas and dissatisfactions of users. From

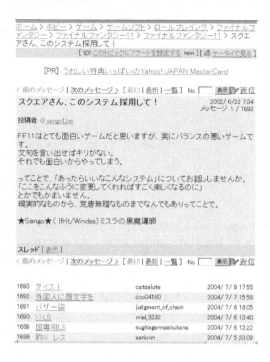

Fig. 2. Yahoo!BBS used in our case study

these comments, 4906 terms (only nouns) were extracted. We compare the result of the proposed method with that of IDM and that of a classical method using Term Frequencies (TF)[1].

3.1   Influential Terms

The top 10 influential terms from each method, with $\alpha = 2$ for our method, are listed in Table 1.

3.2   Precision and Recall Rates

We asked 10 human subjects, 5 veteran players playing MMOGs more than 100 hours monthly and 5 novice players playing less, to thoroughly read all comments. We then separated the subjects into two groups, i.e., a group of the veteran players and a group of the novice players. For each group, its members were asked to individually select 100 important terms, and the terms selected in common by all members were considered influential terms of that group. By this, 6 influential terms were decided by the former group, and 5 influential terms by the latter group. Because there was one influential term decided in common

---

[1] In TF, terms are simply ranked according to their occurrence frequency in all comments.

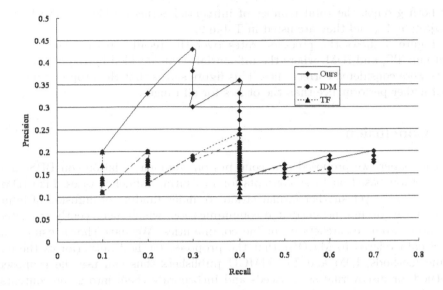

Fig. 3. Precision/Recall curve of each method

Table 1. Influential terms from each method

Ranking	Ours	IDM	TF
1	System	Human	System
2	Human	Level	Human
3	Level	Magic	Level
4	Game	Warrior	Game
5	Balance	Experience	Magic
6	Item	Equipment	Charm
7	Equipment	Red (magic)	Warrior
8	Experience	Attack	Experience
9	Self	White (magic)	Equipment
10	Magic	Charm	Black (magic)

Table 2. Influential terms decided by human subjects

	Term		
Veteran	Item Cure	Equipment	
	Individual Quest	Solo	
Novice	Balance Charm		
	Combination	Casino	

by both groups, the total number of influential terms decided by the human subjects is 10, and they are listed in Table 2.

Figure 3 shows the precision rates over the recall rates of the proposed method, TF, and IDM, where the influential terms decided by the human subjects were considered correct ones. This figure shows that the proposed method is of higher performance than the others for all ranges.

4   Conclusion

In this paper, we proposed new concepts on comment relations on BBSs and the method based on these concepts for measuring influence rates. Like IDM, our method is yet another formalization to understanding of diffusion of influential terms on internet-mediated communication, which has recently attracted attention from researchers on online communities. We have shown using real BBS data related to MMOGs that the proposed method outperforms the existing methods, IDM and TF. MMOG publishers thus can use the proposed method for discovering users' needs and incorporate them into game contents. In our future work, we plan to modify and apply our method to other types of entertainment-oriented text-based communities, such as blogs, chat rooms, and social networking services.

References

1. Hanson, W.: Principles of Internet Marketing. South-Western Pub. (1999)
2. Alexander, T. (ed): Massively Multiplayer Game Development. Charles River Media, Inc., Massachusetts (2003)
3. Matsumura, N., Ohsawa, Y., Ishizuka, M.: Influence Diffusion Model in Text-Based Communication. Proc. Int'l World Wide Web Conf. (WWW02), Hawaii (2002)
4. Matsumura, N., Ohsawa, Y., Ishizuka, M.: Influence Diffusion Model in Text-Based Communication. Journal of the Japanese Society for Artificial Intelligence, Vol. 13, No. 3, 259–267 (2002) (in Japanese)
5. Yahoo!BBS. http://messages.yahoo.co.jp/bbs

Seamful Design for Location-Based Mobile Games

Gregor Broll[1] and Steve Benford[2]

[1] Institute for Informatics, Embedded Interaction Research Group,
Amalienstr. 17, 80333 München, Germany
gregor@hcilab.org
[2] Mixed Reality Laboratory, The University of Nottingham,
Nottingham, NG8 1BB, UK
sdb@cs.nott.ac.uk

Abstract. Seamful design is a new approach to reveal and exploit inevitable technical limitations in Ubiquitous Computing technology rather than hiding them. In this paper we want to introduce its general ideas and apply them to the design of location-aware games for mobile phones. We introduce our own seamful trading-game called "Tycoon" to explore seams on this platform and show how to incorporate them into the design of mobile games. We want to evaluate how applications for the mobile phone platform which use cell-positioning can exploit seams for better interaction, gameplay and usability.

1 Introduction

Devices and applications for mobile communication and computing usually suffer more from their technical limitations than other systems of Ubiquitous Computing. Patchy network coverage, fluctuating signal strength, deviations in positioning and the generally limited resources provided by mobile devices are an everyday reality for their users. Usually they experience these limitations indirectly as sketchy and slow mobile internet access, variations in the quality of speech transmission, loss of connections or ambiguities in positioning. As mobile applications and services will offer more sophisticated and demanding services e. g. for multimedia and entertainment, those seams in both technology and interaction-design are even more likely to come to the users' attention.

Despite the efforts of seamless design to smooth over these bumps and cracks in ubicomp systems and their infrastructures using costly investments in better and more reliable technology, we think that mobile applications could greatly benefit from exploiting those seams rather than abandoning them. Contrary to seamless design, seamful design tries to reveal inevitable seams in ubicomp systems and use them to increase the awareness for system infrastructures, their heterogeneous components and otherwise neglected yet useful information within the system.

We want to explore the possible benefits of seamful design and show how to apply it to mobile applications in general and mobile games in particular as they provide a very flexible and playful environment for an easy evaluation of seamfulness. We in-

F. Kishino et al. (Eds.): ICEC 2005, LNCS 3711, pp. 155–166, 2005.
© IFIP International Federation for Information Processing 2005

troduce our own design for a seamful location-based game for mobile phones called "Tycoon" and want to explore how to exploit the seams on this platform – especially in cell-based positioning, network coverage and data inconsistencies – as resources for better usability, interaction and gameplay.

2 Designing Ubiquitous Computing Systems

2.1 From Seamlessness to Beautiful Seams

Both seamfulness and seamlessness can guide the design of ubicomp systems and are more or less derived from Mark Weiser's vision of Ubiquitous Computing. As part of this vision Weiser called for invisibility as a general design goal of Ubiquitous Computing and especially for invisible tools that don't intrude on the user's consciousness but let him focus on the task and not the tool itself (see [1]). According to [2] this postulation seems to have "been translated into requirements for seamless integration of computer system components, as well as the interactions supported by those components". Since then seamless design became the ruling paradigm for realizing Ubiquitous Computing systems.

The infrastructures of ubicomp systems and applications usually contain many different heterogeneous components and devices. Seamless design advocates knitting these components tightly together and assembling them into one single entity in order to hide the complexity of the infrastructure caused by the heterogeneity of its components. The invisibility of the individual parts enables seamless interaction and allows users to unconsciously interact with them through the whole entity which itself becomes "literally visible, effectively invisible" [1].

An everyday example of interacting with a (seemingly) seamless system is the handover between adjoining GSM-cells while using a mobile phone. Though being an essential feature of mobile communication technology, handover between cells is kept hidden in the infrastructure of service provider networks. Because of this, handover is automatically and seamlessly handled while people simply use their mobile phones unaware of handover, changing cells or even the concept of cells.

Despite its benefits of comfort and simplicity, the paradigm of seamlessness is questioned. [3] points out that Mark Weiser actually opposed it as a misleading concept. Instead of making everything the same, reducing different components in a seamless system to the level of a "lowest common denominator" [4] and sacrificing their uniqueness for the goal of overall compatibility, he calls for "seamful systems" which [2] paraphrases as: "making everything the same is easy; letting everything be itself, with other things, is hard". Weiser also advocates seamful systems with "beautiful seams" [4] meaning that seamfully integrated parts of a system could still provide seamless interaction with the whole system while openly retaining their individual features.

2.2 Seams and Seamfulness

An approach to seamfulness and seamful design becomes even more intelligible as infrastructures of ubicomp systems still have limitations and boundaries despite their efforts for seamless integration and interaction.

Just as seamless design refers to both the technical joints between infrastructure-components and the overall experience of smooth, seamless interaction, the concept of seams in ubicomp systems comprises the technical cracks and bumps in the joints between those components as well as the user's experience of them in the system. Seams can be seen as deviations in actual use from a notional ideal of technological continuity or uniformity including discontinuities in technologies themselves and discontinuity between what actually happens and what the system observes.

Seams in ubicomp systems are mostly caused by technical limitations and differences between heterogeneous components in the underlying infrastructures. Among them are finite resolution and sampling rates of sensors, fluctuating signal strength, limited connectivity, defective transformations or delays in communication. These technical constraints in the infrastructure come to the user's attention when they interact with a supposedly seamless system. Seams then reveal themselves as uncertainties, ambiguities or inconsistencies.

Probably the most common seams can be found in systems for navigation and mobile communication where they include inaccurate positioning, sketchy internet-access or patchy network coverage. For example infrastructures for outdoor- and indoor-positioning with GPS- or ultrasonic-trackers are notorious for their literally built-in deviations. These are due to technical constraints like finite coarseness of sensing-technology as well as non-technical restraints like "urban-canyons" or reflecting surfaces which make accurate sensing difficult. People using positioning systems experience those seams as uncertainties about their current position.

2.3 Seamful Design and Designing for Appropriation

Often enough seams can't be completely hidden and undermine the ideal of a totally seamless system. Instead of trying to iron these bumps out of an ubicomp application, seamful design tries to incorporate its heterogeneous components while recognizing and maintaining their characteristics and uniqueness without giving up the overall goal of seamless interaction. In order to accomplish the goal of "seamless interaction but seamful technology" [5] outlines the process of seamful design by identifying its 3 key-problems as "understanding which seams are important", "presenting seams to users" and "designing interactions with seams".

The first step to turn seams into a helpful feature is to identify those seams that can enhance a system's functionality, understand them and find out how they can become a resource for user-interaction. Seamful design reveals and recognises the infrastruc-ture's influence on user-interaction and increases the awareness for features that cause seams in applications. If designers know how certain seams affect interactions, they can decide how to incorporate them into an application, how to channel their effects into useful features and include them in the process of interaction design itself. That way seamful design allows users to use seams, accommodate to them and even ex-ploit them for their own advantage.

The less the presentation of seams is restricted in the way people can interact with them, the more can users harness those seams and adapt to them. Giving them the opportunity and freedom to play with seams, explore how to use and exploit them in new ways adds a flexibility to seamful interaction that increases the depth of an application. This new quality may ultimately lead to the more general concept of designing for appropriation. Users are given a presentation of seams that increases their awareness for them but are not restricted to interact with them in a compulsory way. Design for appropriation allows users to interact with seams individually, take advantage of the gaps and limitations in ubicomp infrastructures and develop new patterns of behaviour that have not been considered during the initial design of the system.

The use of mobile phones offers intuitive examples of appropriation: Among their most common seams are patchy network coverage and local variations in signal strength which are commonly accepted as reasons for not answering or dismissing a call. Users can exploit their knowledge about those seams and adapt their behaviour by pretending to be outside of network coverage (e. g. in tunnels) or to have a bad reception which - unfortunately - forces them to dismiss a call.

2.4   Bill – A Seamful Mobile Game

Being one of the first seamfully designed mobile games, "Bill" was developed at the University of Glasgow by Matthew Chalmers et al. [6], exploring seams in 802.11 wireless networking. Bill is a seamful mobile multiplayer game in which two teams of players compete against each other by collecting virtual coins in a designated gaming-area. This area features wireless access points connected to the game server which distributes information about the game. Each player is equipped with a PDA supporting GPS-positioning and 802.11 wireless internet-access. The GUI of Bill displays information about the locations of coins, players and network covered areas on a pan- and zoomable map of the gaming-area (see Fig. 1).

During the game, players roam the gaming-area, discover access-points and collaboratively build up a shared map of network covered areas. Local coverage and quality of wireless network access are displayed as transparent squares on the GUI's map with different colours indicating different levels of signal strength. Players use GPS-positioning to collect coins but have to get inside the coverage of a wireless access point in order to upload them to the game server and earn credits for their team. A simultaneous, collaborative upload with several other team-mates earns players a cumulative amount of credits for the same amount of coins. An additional pick pocket-feature lets players steal coins from each other if thief and victim are close enough (according to GPS) and within access point coverage.

The main seams in Bill are the patchy coverage of the wireless access points and the dynamic boundaries of the network covered areas. Presenting information about them to players as a part of the game's interface turns the negative seams into a helpful visual feature of the game's interface. Players can use it and develop an understanding of network coverage and signal strength in order to succeed in the game. They can even use this information to adapt their behaviour by staying out of network covered areas in order to avoid pickpockets, by knowing where to gather with team mates for a collective upload or by specializing as pickpockets themselves.

Other seams in Bill include inaccurate GPS-positioning that allows players to collect coins which are actually out of their reach and data inconsistencies that let different players find the same coin independently from each other as they see different subsets of the available coins at different times unless they are regularly updated.

 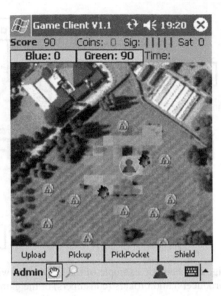

Fig. 1. Bill's GUI includes general information about the game (e.g. scores), icons for invoking interactions (e. g. "Upload", "Pickup") and a map of the gaming-area with the positions of coins as well as colored squares visualizing wireless network coverage and signal strength (screenshots taken from [6], [7])

3 Seamful Design for Mobile Phone Games

3.1 Introducing Tycoon

The "Bill"-game showed how to turn the seams in a mobile application supporting GPS and 802.11 into helpful features of a game, how seamful design can drive its gameplay and how players can exploit seams in order to win. We want to extend the ideas of seamful design to games for mobile phones, explore which seams occur on this platform and how to apply seamful design in order to exploit them for better gameplay, interaction and appropriation.

For this purpose we developed our own seamful game for mobile phones called "Tycoon". Tycoon is a location-based multiplayer trading game with a simple producer-consumer-cycle that uses the different GSM-cells of a service provider network within a designated gaming-area, e. g. the centre of a city. Each of these cells in the physical area is virtually mapped to either a producer or a consumer in the game (see Fig. 2). Tycoon uses the metaphor of a wild west scenario to communicate its central mechanisms of collecting resources from producers which are called "mines" and using them to buy objects from consumers which are called "brokers" and have the names of cities or counties in California (see Fig. 2). These cells are called "brokers" because they sell objects in their areas in exchange for collected resources.

While playing the game, players are travelling between the cells in the gaming-area, collect local resources in mines, use them to buy global objects from brokers and get credits for claiming them. Each mine produces an unlimited amount of one of the

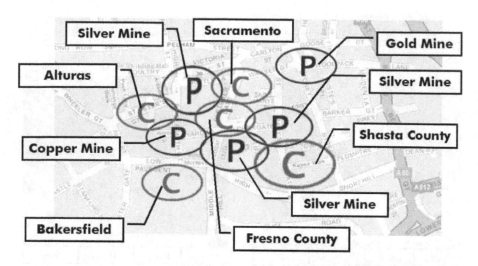

Fig. 2. Schematic example of the GSM-cells within a gaming-area and their mapping to mines (producers) and brokers (consumers) of the game

three *local resources* in the game – gold, silver or copper. They are called local resources because players can collect them independently of each other and don't compete for them. Each broker has a list of *global objects* e. g. different buildings or estates in towns and counties that players can buy with their local resources. There is only a limited number of unique global objects in the game (e. g. there is only one saloon in Sacramento) and players compete against each other for claiming them, since every global object can only be claimed once by one player. Each global object has a combined price of two local resources and a value in credits. Players have to enter a broker's cell and pay an object's price in order to claim it and earn its value in credits. The objective of the game is to gather as many credits as possible; it ends when all objects are sold and the player with the most credits wins.

The responsibility for the maintenance of the game-state and its overall correctness is split between the global game-server and the local clients on players' mobile phones. These clients tell players where they are, help them navigate through the gaming-area and supervise the collecting of local resources. The clients connect with the game-server via GPRS in order to buy global objects from single brokers and ask for updates on the *global game-state*, which comprises the general availability of all global objects of all brokers in the game. The game-server processes and answers client-requests, manages the global game-state and runs the game by controlling its logic. It doesn't know anything about individual resource-collecting of different clients and clients only have a limited knowledge about the global game-state unless they ask the game-server. In short, the cell-phone clients each manage individual local game-states and the game-server manages the shared global game-state.

3.2 How to Play Tycoon

Unlike Bill Tycoon doesn't provide a general map of the gaming-area including the locations of the different mines and brokers. Mobile phone displays are often too small to be useful for map-navigation and a map of the Tycoon gaming-area would be significantly bigger than the map in Bill. We want the players to start Tycoon by having to explore the gaming-area and discover mines, brokers and their locations by themselves. That way the players can gather their own knowledge about the gaming-area, where to find resources and where to claim objects.

Two features of Tycoon help players to navigate in the gaming-area: Whenever a player changes from one cell into another, an alert is triggered and he gets a notification about him entering a new cell. Afterwards the main screen displays the name of the new cell (Fig. 3).

Fig. 3. The main screen of Tycoon's GUI which is updated whenever a player crosses boundaries between adjoining cells. It is the central screen of Tycoon and shows the amount of collected resources and earned credits as well as the current location.

A log containing annotations about mines, brokers and their different locations is intended as an aid to memory in order to remember where their cells can be found. When a new log-entry is created, Tycoon automatically logs the current cell and the player can add a short description about the location (e. g. [gold mine] near book shop). During the game each player will eventually build up his own log of locations.

Collecting local resources is only possible in suitable mines and the return depends on the time a player spends in the cell which is virtually mapped to a mine. A player can start and stop a counter on his mobile client and will be collecting the current resource until he decides to stop or until he leaves the cell. Collecting local resources is completely managed by the mobile client without the game-server's knowledge.

Each player starts Tycoon with a list containing the names of all brokers in the gaming-area but without showing which objects each of them is offering. A broker's initial list of objects will be revealed to the player once he discovered the appropriate cell and enters it for the first time.

In order to earn credits a player has to enter the cell of a broker, choose one or several entries from his list of available objects and claim them from the game-server. If his choice is still available according to the global game-state the player gets the object's credits added to his account. If objects have already been claimed by other players and are no longer available the player keeps his resources for future claims. In either case the player gets an update on the availability of all objects for the current broker.

Players can ask the game-server for a separate update on the global game-state anytime and anywhere in order to soften the possible inconsistencies between the game-server and the mobile clients concerning the availability of global objects. An update has to be paid with a certain charge in local resources since it gives players a considerable advantage in the game. A player will receive the update only for the lists of global objects of brokers whose cells he has already discovered. This way no player can skip the discovery of all the brokers by simply getting an update.

While a player can ask the game-server for updates anytime and anywhere, collecting resources and claiming objects are location-dependent functionalities of Tycoon and are only available when a player is within an appropriate cell.

3.3 Understanding Seams in Mobile Phone Applications

The design of Tycoon tries to cope with three seams which we consider to be characteristic for the mobile phone platform especially when compared to a seamless approach: dynamic cell-coverage, expensive internet-access and data-inconsistencies.

Usually mobile phone users are unaware of their current cell when using their phones, since the handover between different cells is handled seamlessly. Contrary to the symbolic presentation in Fig. 2 the coverage of GSM-cells is not static and has no neatly defined borders. Fig. 4 shows coverage and propagation of GSM-cells in an area of London based on samples of cell-ids and their GPS-positions. Their coverage is depending on many factors, cells' boundaries and propagation are rather dynamic and fluctuating and as Fig. 4 shows, cell-coverage has irregular shapes and adjoining cells often overlap and don't share exact borders.

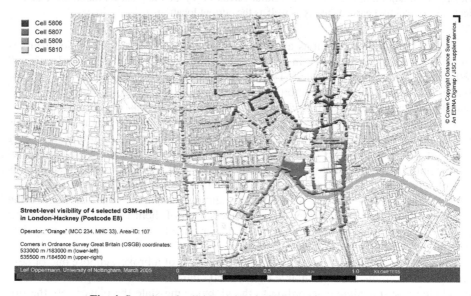

Fig. 4. Samples of cell-ids and their GPS-positions in London

The invisible handover between cells is handled seamlessly so that users don't get any information about their current cell and don't have to worry about their position, dynamic cell coverage and propagation or flipping cells. While seamless design usually hides this information, we would like to present it to players and make them aware of this information so that they can take advantage of it during the game and use it as a valuable resource. In a location-based mobile game players are dependent on knowing where they are and dynamic boundaries and propagation of cells may raise interesting design-issues concerning the influence of positions and relations between GSM-cells on the behaviour of the users during the game.

Tycoon is a multiplayer game for cell phones and the driving part of its gameplay is the competition between several players with mobile clients. In order to compete with each other including asking for claims, having the availability of objects confirmed, scores compared or the end of a game announced, players have to be able to turn to a central entity which controls a shared global game-state. Mobile internet-access is most convenient and almost indispensable for accessing a shared game-server on the internet and synchronising its data with the mobile clients.

A seamless approach to this synchronisation would try to guarantee as little inconsistencies between the global and all local game-states as possible. That would mean that whenever a client changes the global game-state e. g. by claiming an object, the server would have to route this change to all other clients or they would periodically have to ask the game-server for an update on the latest changes.

Either way a lot of traffic would be generated and mobile internet-access via GPRS is still quite expensive. Despite the above definition of seams, these expenses are neither rooted in technical limitations nor show themselves as uncertainties or ambiguities and may therefore be considered as an artificial seam. But it still constrains the uniformity and continuity of a mobile application and we think that's why costly internet-connections can be treated as a considerable seam. We would like to turn this seam into a rewarding feature of the game by encouraging players to use less online-connections to the game-server without examining the technical limitations of GPRS-connections like delays or its general availability.

The question of whether to use more or less GPRS-connections to synchronise game-states goes hand in hand with the probability of data-inconsistencies. Those would be an immediate consequence of insufficient synchronisation between a server and its clients. Inconsistencies could occur when individual clients synchronise data with the central server that maintains the global game-state which is shared between all clients. When one of these individual clients updates globally shared data, local copies of that data on other clients become inconsistent with the shared data.

As mentioned, a seamless approach to Tycoon would try to prevent data-inconsistencies through frequent updates. But when tackling the seam of costly GPRS-connections by making less of them, we also have to cope with the seam of increasing data-inconsistencies between mobile clients and the global game-server. While a seamless approach would try to guarantee a persistent globally correct game-state we want to enrich Tycoon's gameplay by turning inconsistencies into a gambling-element that rewards players for taking the risk of them during the game.

3.4 Combining Tycoon's Gameplay and Seamful Design for Appropriation

Tycoon uses the unique cell-id of GSM-cells in its gaming-area to support navigation and to determine its location-dependent behaviour during the game. The alert-mechanism is a monitor for the current location and its changes, it improves the visualisation of cells' boundaries and decreases the players' uncertainties about their whereabouts by presenting otherwise neglected seamful information about cell coverage and propagation. It is an effective and flexible means of navigation in the gaming-area especially since the propagation of its virtual areas dynamically changes with the coverage of the physical cells they are mapped to. A static map of the gaming-area would need an expensive mechanism to continuously sample cell coverage and display their propagation in real time.

The alert-mechanism makes players not only aware of dynamic changes in the cell-propagation but is also part of Tycoon's interaction with the seam of dynamic cell-coverage. Tycoon's behaviour is partly location-dependent. It changes with the current location and adapts to it, e. g. collecting local resources automatically stops when a players leaves a mine and enters another cell. The functionalities of collecting resources and claiming objects are exclusively available in mines or broker-cells. The log that helps players remember where to find different mines and brokers only logs information in cells within the gaming-area.

Like in the Bill-game players can use their spatial knowledge about the gaming-area to adopt their own strategies of how to move between cells and how to find the most efficient tactics of which resources are needed to buy which available objects and where to find them in nearby mines. They can also exploit ambiguities caused by dynamic cell propagation and boundaries more effectively when they find an area where adjoining cells overlap and flip after some time without moving. This is also an interesting issue for designing the gaming-area of Tycoon and assigning mines and brokers to different cells.

In order to cope with the seams of expensive internet-connections and data-inconsistencies, Tycoon encourages players to spend more time offline and synchronize their local game-state (individual clients' knowledge about available global objects) less often with the game-server's global game-state (the overall availability of global objects). Its trading-mechanism features a simple economic model that offers players an incentive to engage in extended offline-play and spend more time on collecting a greater number of (more valuable) resources.

As mentioned before, global objects each have a price in local resources and earn a player a certain amount of credits when claiming them. Both values are related to each other as the credit-values of objects rise with their prices in local resources. The local resources have different values themselves which is indirectly expressed by the time it takes to collect one unit of each (2,4,8 seconds to collect 1 copper-, silver-, gold-nugget). That way the credit-value of a global object is also related to the time it takes to collect the resources that are necessary to buy the object. But the values of resources, the values of objects and their prices don't rise proportionally. The economic model is tuned in a way so that the more time a player spends offline to collect more and more valuable resources in order to afford more and more valuable objects the more credits per second could he possibly earn than by collecting less resources for smaller, less valuable objects during the same time. Additionally a player gets a discount for successfully claiming several objects from a broker with the same request to the game-server. Of course in order to afford buying several objects, players have to spend even more time offline to collect more and more valuable resources.

The goal of this economic model is to give players an incentive to spend more time offline between connections to the game-server and collect local resources which is more profitable than spending less time offline collecting less and less valuable resources for claiming less valuable objects.

Extended offline-play increases the danger of inconsistencies between the global game-state and a player's local list of available global objects. Other players can claim objects on that list which are then no longer globally available but are still shown as available on a player's local list. Since players can't rely on getting constant updates of the global game-state which would require regular expensive connections to the game-server, they have to consider the growing probability of inconsistencies between local and global game-state when deciding how much time they spend offline for collecting local resources.

This is where the gambling-approach of Tycoon comes into play: It recognizes these inconsistencies in the gameplay and rewards players not only for spending more time offline but also for taking the risk of inconsistencies. Players are free to collect as many local resources as they want but can only turn them into credits when they successfully buy and claim global objects with them. The more time they spend offline, the more profit is possible but the greater becomes the probability of inconsistencies. Players have to adopt their own individual strategies and consider their chances of earning more credits during the same time against the risk of data inconsistencies.

4 Conclusion

Seamful design is a rather new approach to ubicomp applications other than seamless design. We showed how to use and exploit seams on the mobile phone platform by incorporating them into our own seamful game. Instead of hiding these seams we revealed them and integrated them into the game's interaction design for a better gameplay. Based on our experience with designing and implementing a seamful trading-game we think that seamful design is a rewarding approach for realizing applications of Ubiquitous Computing and a considerable alternative to seamless design whose efforts often result in expensive improvements of infrastructure-technology but not always in better applications.

Acknowledgements

This project was supported by EQUATOR, an Interdisciplinary Research Collaboration (IRC), funded by the UK Engineering and Physical Sciences Research Council.

We would like to thank Leif Oppermann (MRL, University of Nottingham) for providing us with a map of cell coverage and propagation based on GSM-samples and their GPS-positions taken during a workshop in London. We would further like to thank Albrecht Schmidt (Institute for Informatics, Embedded Interaction Research Group, Munich) and Holger Schnädelbach (MRL, University of Nottingham) for their support and making this project possible.

References

1. Weiser, M.: *The world is not a desktop*. ACM Interactions 1(1) (1994) 7-8.
2. Chalmers, M., MacColl, I.: *Seamful and Seamless Design in Ubiquitous Computing*. Technical Report Equator-03-005, Equator [Technical Reports] (2003)
3. Chalmers, M., MacColl, I., Bell, M.: *Seamful Design: Showing the Seams in Wearable Computing*. Eurowearable 2003, University of Birmingham, UK. International Conference Proceedings (2003)
4. Weiser, M.: *Creating the invisible interface (invited talk)*. ACM Conf on User Interface Software and Technology (UIST94) (1994), 1
5. Oulasvirta, A.: *Notes on Seams, Seamfulness and Seamlessness*. http://www.hiit.fi/u/oulasvir/Haninge (2004)
6. Chalmers, M., Bell, M., Hall, M., Sherwood, S., Tennent, P.: *Seamful Games*. http://www.ubicomp.org/ubicomp2004/adjunct/demos/chalmers.pdf (2004)
7. Chalmers, M., Bell, M., Brown, B., Hall, M., Sherwood, S., Tennent, P.: *Seamful Game*. http://www.seamful.com (2004)

A Display Table for Strategic Collaboration Preserving Private and Public Information

Yoshifumi Kitamura[1], Wataru Osawa[1,*], Tokuo Yamaguchi[1],
Haruo Takemura[2], and Fumio Kishino[1]

[1] Osaka University, Graduate School of Information Science and Technology,
2-1 Yamadaoka, Suita, Osaka, Japan
http://www-human.ist.osaka-u.ac.jp
[2] Osaka University, Cybermedia Center 1-32 Machikaneyama,
Toyonaka, Osaka, Japan

Abstract. We propose a new display table that allows multiple users to interact with both private and public information on a shared display in a face-to-face co-located setting. With this table users can create, manage and share information intuitively, strategically and cooperatively by naturally moving around the display. Users can interactively control private and public information space seamlessly according to their spatial location and motion. It enables users to dynamically choose negotiation partners, create cooperative relationships and strategically control the information they share and conceal. We see the proposed system as especially suited for strategic cooperative tasks in which participants collaborate while attempting to increase individual benefits, such as various trading floor-like and auction scenarios.

1 Introduction

Personal equipments such as PDAs and cellular phones are widely spread in our daily lives. Although this trend provides us efficiency in our business situation, a harmful influence is also recently pointed out; there is increasing number of people in younger generation who lacks social sense. One of the solutions for this problem is to facilitate face-to-face co-located environment for collaboration or negotiation with others which requires multimodal interactions with a variety information channels.

When working in groups, we often conduct face-to-face meetings to accelerate the exchange of ideas or opinions, or to complete a cooperative task. Collaboration, a natural and efficient approach to problem solving, has been one of the most challenging topics in HCI studies. Many studies and systems have been presented to facilitate face-to-face collaboration during group meetings or discussions [e.g. 1-6]. Collaborative table displays are designed to enhance functions of ordinary meeting tables to support small-group collaborative activities and have lately considerable attention [7].

---

* Currently, with Kansai Electric Power Co. Inc.

F. Kishino et al. (Eds.): ICEC 2005, LNCS 3711, pp. 167–179, 2005.
© IFIP International Federation for Information Processing 2005

One of the most important research topics of collaborative table displays is to develop techniques to support transitions between personal and group work. For example, many systems typically use multiple displays to share information among participants in a meeting, and use one or several large wall displays to show public information. However, a special framework is often required to allow multiple users to deal with private information in addition to the public one [8-11]. Many of the current solutions to sharing public and private information between multiple users still suffer from ambiguities.

In this paper, we propose a collaborative, public and private, interactive display. It seamlessly presents the private and the public information and allows users to change the public information space and the private information space dynamically according to their spatial location and motion. With this system users can dynamically select collaborative partners and strategically control the information they share or hide during negotiation or cooperation. Our preliminary observations suggest great promise to the proposed system in tasks that require collaboration side-by-side with maintaining personal gain. We believe the proposed system can be useful in several trading floor, market-like, and auction scenarios where people need to meet and collaborate in order to exchange goods or information in an ad-hoc manner.

2 Private and Public Information

When we collaborate or negotiate with others while sharing information, we often have to be careful about which parts of the information can and cannot be shared [12]. These pieces of information can be classified into different categories [13]. The roughest classification is to divide it into private (that is not sharable) and public (that is sharable) information, a classification that can sometimes be static and sometimes dynamic. This section overviews display systems that support classification of information into public and private categories.

2.1 Related Work

Let us assume that a piece of information has an attribute that can be either private or public. When two or more people are handling information items, some of these can be private and others public. One of the most common configurations is to present private information and public information on separate displays. For example, several systems use one or several large wall displays to show public information with small displays, PDAs, or notebook PCs to show private information [8-10]. In these cases, if people want to share personal information with others electronically, they have to explicitly place these pieces of information on a display surface that can be seen by others. When one has multiple information items that can be shared with other people, putting these pieces on the shared display surface becomes cumbersome and difficult to manage. Moreover, if the physical locations of public display and the private information are separated, people tend to concentrate mostly on their personal displays rather than attending to a number of other, less handy surrounding displays. In order to avoid this forced and potentially damaging display separation we need a more intuitive way that will seamlessly handle two different types of information displayed in the same spatial locality.

One possible solution for sharing information in multiple user environments is to directly make individual private display available to another particular user with whom we wish to share information. An example is to connect personal displays together on an ad-hoc basis [11]. Although this method is simple and intuitive, all information shown on the display is shared, and it is difficult to share and hide only a part of the information on the display. One may consider temporally hiding information that is not to be shared; however, a system or mechanism that handles both private and public information equally and displays both of them simultaneously is required for the owner of that information.

Another solution is to use a technique for stereoscopic display, which provides two different peoples with a pair of images that are ordinarily provided to the left and right eye as stereoscopic images. For example, liquid crystal device shuttered glasses (LCD glasses) are used to separate private and public information displayed on a single display [14]. However, the number of users is limited to two because of the reason originating in its principle. In addition, the private information would be exposed to a non-participant who just happens to pass by the collaborative site without glasses, a fact that substantially limits the type of private data that can be displayed on the screen.

Another possible solution for such a system is to employ an automatic software filter that copies shared pieces of information on a public display [15, 16]. In these cases, information sharing forces a user of the system to be constantly alert to whether the information displayed on the user's personal display is also being displayed on the public display. The user should also remain watchful over other users accessing copies of the private information or trying to modify or copy it. This can be an important issue as such undesirable conducts may not be explicitly highlighted on the legitimate user's personal display. In such situations, users should maintain careful observation of the information being displayed on the public display area and carefully monitor other users' interest in their private information. We assume that these special attention requirements will make copying of pieces of information onto a public display much less desirable.

2.2 Collocation Using Private and Public Information

Based on the considerations outlined in the previous subsection, in this subsection we discuss a display system that allows multiple users to deal with both private information and public information seamlessly in a face-to-face environment.

If shared pieces of information were still to be displayed in proximity to the user's personal display, the user would feel that these pieces of information are owned by her and are under her control. The others, who are interested in the user's public information, would physically look into the user's own personal display. This explicit motion of other users would increase the user's awareness of the environment and the collaboration state, that is, "if she stands next to me, she can see my private information". Moreover, a user is able to know whether someone is interested in the information he or she has. These considerations lead us thinking of using a part of the user's personal display as a shared display that is visible to the other participants.

Even in this configuration, when individual shared displays are located apart from each other, a user has to visit the participants' personal displays one-by-one to seek any public information being displayed. A user has to continually visit other user displays to look for updated information when public information changes dynamically. If multiple personal displays could be integrated into a single display, the display would turn into a single working surface on which users could focus their attention at one place and time. The single display surface becomes the only reference space where users act upon or view information.

The advantage of using a single shared display for displaying both private and public information is that a relatively small number of people can work more intimately, with more productive and effective interaction. In particular, by using a tabletop-type display configuration, the display surface can also be used as a table to hold documents, stationery or coffee cups. However, how could we display private information on a tabletop-type of display without it being seen by other people? The following section describes the implementation of our display system.

3 Method

3.1 Principle

The display system consists of a normal display and a display mask, which has a hole in its center (Fig. 1(a)). The display mask is placed over the display surface at a suitable distance. Each user observes the display system through the hole. By controlling the position of the information display area for each user according to his/her viewpoint (measured by a suitable tracker), each user can always see his/her own individual area of the display. Figure 1(b) shows an example in which three users simultaneously observe information on different display areas. The information display area P in Fig. 1(b), which is derived from user P's viewpoint, is an area for showing the information for user P alone. The other users (Q and R), standing at their positions in this figure, are unable to see the P's individual information display area because the display mask adequately occludes this area. Therefore, this area can be used to show the private information of P.

On the other hand, the Q and R's information display areas overlap; therefore this overlapping area can be used to show the public information shared by Q and R. The

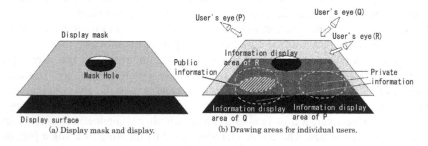

(a) Display mask and display.   (b) Drawing areas for individual users.

Fig. 1. Configuration of the display system

areas other than the overlapping area are areas where only one of them can observe information; as a result, these areas can be used to show the private information of Q or of R.

If a user moves his/her head, the information display area corresponding to the user also moves according to the motion of the viewpoint. This feature enables users to dynamically determine—by simply moving around the display—which display areas are used for private information and which display areas are used for public information that might be shared with a particular user.

The configuration of the display and the mask is along the same lines as the IllusionHole, a stereoscopic display system for multiple users [17], although stereoscopic images are not shown in this configuration. In IllusionHole the overlapping of image drawing areas among adjacent users was a weakness, which the design tried to avoid. In our current display system this weakness is turned into a key design feature.

3.2 Position and Size of Information Display Area

The position of the information display area for each user is derived from two parameters: the user's viewpoint in the display coordinate system $(x_{eye}, y_{eye}, z_{eye})$, and the distance between the display surface and the mask D. By using the display coordinate system where the center of the display surface is the origin of the coordinate, the center of the image drawing area is given by $(-x_{eye}D/(z_{eye}-D), -y_{eye}D/(z_{eye}-D), 0)$. The radius of the information display area r is determined by three parameters: the height of the user's viewpoint z_{eye}, the distance between the display surface and the mask D, and the hole radius of the mask R, as $r = R z_{eye}/(z_{eye}-D)$. These values dynamically determine the information display area for each user, which expands/shrinks as the user approaches/retreats to/from the mask hole.

If a larger hole is used, a user is expected to observe a larger area on the display. The area increases with the distance between the display surface and the mask D and the radius of the mask hole R. On the other hand, the number of users decreases according to the radius of the mask hole R or as the distance between the display surface and the mask D increases.

4 Displaying Information

In this section we detail the method of showing and handling information on our proposed display system. As representations of the virtual information items we use graphical icons and similar virtual objects to assist in the explanation.

4.1 Priority Levels of Users

The display system provides several methods for presenting the information in overlapping areas, according to the priority levels of corresponding users. When two users with equal priority levels have an overlapping area, the objects owned by these two users are shown as equals in the public information display (Fig. 2(a)). In this case, user P can see object Q2 owned by user Q in the public information display area, and user Q can see object P2 owned by user P in the same area.

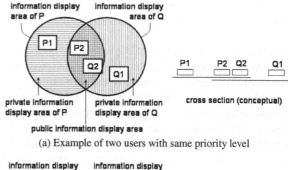

On the other hand, when two users who have different priority levels share an overlapping area, the objects will not be shown in the public information display area (Fig. 2(b)). In this example, user Q has a higher priority level than user P. Therefore, user Q can see object P2 owned by user P in the public information display area, but user P cannot see object Q2 owned by user Q.

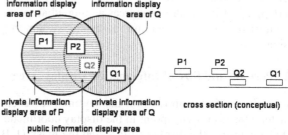

(a) Example of two users with same priority level

(b) Example of two users with different priority levels

Fig. 2. Examples of objects in the public information display area according to the users' priority levels

Here, the priority of users can be determined statically in advance or dynamically according to the users' conditions during the task. Examples of such conditions can be users' motion speed, direction, finger pointing or other behavioral patterns.

4.2 Permission Levels of Objects

Users possess and handle their own objects in their private information display area, in an association that can be considered as "ownership," allowing them to freely manipulate the objects. Here, "manipulate" means to execute, delete, copy, or edit the file identified by the object. For each object, the levels of permission can be classified as follows:

Level-1: no user other than the object's owner can either see or manipulate this object.
Level-2: the other users (non-owners) can see, but cannot manipulate this object.
Level-3: all users can both see and manipulate this object.

Here, the level-3 objects can be placed either in the private information display area or the public information display area, and every user can see and manipulate level-3 objects. The level-2 objects can also be placed either in the private information display area or public information display area. They can be seen but not manipulated by the users other than the owner if this object is placed in the public information display area. Finally, no other user besides the owner can see the level-1 objects, even if the objects are placed in the public information display area.

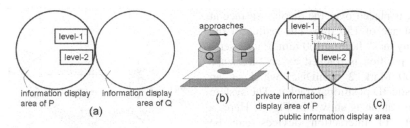

Fig. 3. A visibility change

However, these level designations are not static and can be dynamically modified in correspondence to changes in the collaboration environment. Therefore, the visibilities of the level-1 objects have to be controlled in order for them not to be seen by any other user besides the owner (we describe these control mechanisms in the following section which describes our prototype). For example, if an adjacent user approaches the user closely enough, the public information display area expands as the approached user's private information display area shrinks. In this case, the visibility of objects displayed in the user's private display area has to be changed.

Let us examine the scenario presented in Fig. 3, describing interaction between users P and Q. In Fig. 3(a) two objects one classified into level-1 and the other into level-2, are shown in the information display area of user P. If user Q approaches closely enough toward user P as shown in Fig. 3(b), the public information display area expands as user P's private information display area shrinks. In this case, the level-2 objects can remain in their original positions; however, the visibilities of the level-1 objects must change. For this purpose, a possible method would be to use the priority levels of users shown in Fig. 2(b). Another possible solution would be to change the display positions of the level-1 objects and move them outside the boundary of the expanding public information display area, as shown in Fig. 3(c). After user Q moves a sufficient distance from user P, the objects can be replaced to their previous visibility positions. This method is useful especially in an application where users' priority levels are not introduced.

5 Prototype

In order to examine our design approach we developed a fully operational prototype display system. The prototype display system enables participation and interaction of multiple users, who can all participate in collaborative tasks by manipulating displayed objects cooperatively or strategically.

5.1 Hardware

The proposed method is implemented by using a 68-inch conventional display system, i.e., BARON (Barco), to show the effectiveness of the method. The display system used in the trial system has a 1,360-mm-wide and 1,020-mm-deep display surface, and the height of the display surface from the floor is 1,000 mm. The display mask is placed over the display surface at a distance of 150 mm. The radius of the display mask hole is 200 mm. Each user's head position is tracked by an Intersense IS-600 Mark 2 SoniDisc, which is an acoustic 3D positional tracker. The system configuration is shown in Fig. 4. Here, a variety of interaction devices can be considered for manipulating objects. In this prototype, a game controller (SONY Dualshock2) is used for each user to manipulate objects.

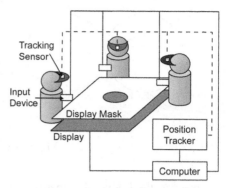

Fig. 4. System configuration

5.2 Object Manipulation Interface

Following our proposed design principles, we implemented an object manipulation interface on the prototype system.

5.2.1 Object Sharing

Users can change the priority levels of their own objects at any time. In the prototype system, clicking an object with the controller changes its priority level. Users also can change whether the object should be in the private information display area or in the public information display area to be shared with other users. If a user moves (drags and drops) an object from the private information display area into the public information display area, this object can be instantly shared with other users. In this case, if the user moves a level-1 object from the private information area to the public information display area, it is assumed that the permission level of this object changes to level-2. The permission levels of objects are shown by color changes of their borders.

5.2.2 Copying and Moving Objects

Users can change the position of an object by simple drag-and-drop actions. If a user moves a level-3 object shown in the public information display area to her own private information display area, she will become the owner of the object. Users can exchange objects between their own private information display

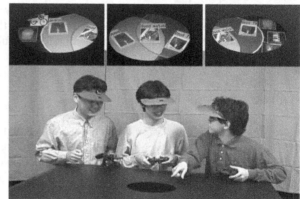

Fig. 5. An example of application

areas through the public information area. A user can also provide a copy of an object by dragging it from her private information display area to the public information area, and then changing its priority level by clicking it.

5.3 Application Example

Figure 5 shows an example of applying the proposed system to a goods-barter task. Three users (named Red, Green, and Blue, from left to right) are exchanging miscellaneous goods (such as used watches, televisions, jeans, and so on) by using their private and public display areas effectively. In this example, each user has his own miscellaneous goods to be exchanged in his private display area, and move the appropriate ones to the area shared with a particular person who is interested in the exchange. The level of each displayed object is level-1 at the beginning, and it is automatically changed to level-2 when the object is moved to the public information display area. Each user can see the other participants' faces, and the negotiations progress through eye contact and hand/body gestures, which provides subtle communication cues. A user determines the best partner with whom to exchange information by changing his standing position and face-to-face communication using oral conversation. Figure 5 shows a the green user standing at the center, considering with which partner to exchange by comparing offered goods displayed on the overlapping areas with left user (Red) and right user (Blue). The top three images in Fig. 5 are user's views for Red, Green, and Blue (right, middle and left, respectively).

5.4 Analyzing User's Movements

We analyzed how the private information display area and public information display area are used by preliminary testing multiple users in a strategic cooperative task that requires handling of both private and public spaces. Three volunteers participated in a task which required assembly of a puzzle with nine pieces made from a picture divided into 3x3 areas. Three such puzzles, each having different pictures, are used in the task, so in total there are 27 pieces in the workspace, and each user owns nine of them at the beginning of the experiment. Users are asked to complete any one of the puzzles as soon as possible before the other users do, in their own private information areas, by exchanging the pieces among users through negotiation. The level of each piece is level-1 at the beginning. When an owner of a piece moves it to a shared information display area to show it to another user, he or she changes the permission to level-2 using the controller button. After the negotiation of exchange is concluded, he or she again changes the permission to level-3.

Behaviors and utterances of users during the experimental session were video recorded, and the head position of each user measured by a tracker was also recorded. Figure 6 shows a typical part of a transition (4 minutes of a 7 minute-22 second-session) of each user's position represented by the directional angles. The vertical axis of Fig. 6 represents the time transition (seconds). The time and positions where users exchanged the pieces of the puzzles are marked with circles. In this figure, ellipses mark the time and positions where users exchanged the pieces of the puzzles. Figure 7 shows snapshots taken during an experimental session: Figure 7(a) shows the display system shared by three users (named R, G, while B), and Fig. 7(b) shows the corresponding image display areas on the proposed system.

Preliminary observations revealed that some typical behaviors of users could be found throughout the session. For example, we found that, for the purpose of negotiation or exchange of pieces, a user actively approaches with his body to another particular user in order to share the information display area. The wedges marked a1 to a10 in Fig. 7 show the time and positions where these types of behaviors occurred.

Each user puts together pieces in order to complete the puzzle within his private information display area. If the adjacent user approaches too close to him, it becomes difficult for him to place the puzzle pieces to complete the task. When a user's private information display area became too small due to the adjacent user's approaching too near, we found that he naturally tries to expand his private information display area by moving away from the adjacent, approaching user. The arrows in Fig. 6 labeled by leave1, leave2, and leave3 designate periods when the user moved away from an approaching adjacent user, under these conditions.

User's intentional actions aiming at disturbing other user private information display area and public information display area could be found in other situations. For example, at the

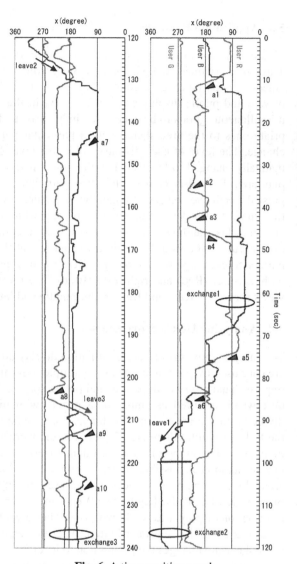

Fig. 6. A time-position graph

116th second labeled by exchange2 in Fig. 6, when two of the users (G and B) were preparing to exchange their pieces by using their public information area, the third user (R) came to disturb this exchange by approaching them and thus making their public information area shrink. Although no explanation was given to the users in advance as to how their movements around the display provide breakthroughs in their mutual situations, we found that users strategically altered both the public information display area and the private information display area by using their own body motions in order to fulfill their purposes.

(a) Display system shared by three users.   (b) Information display areas of three users

Fig. 7. Snapshots taken during experimental work

Because each user could see the other participants' faces, the negotiations among users (regardless of whether they are friendly or strategic) were naturally and intuitively advanced through eye contact, which provided an intuitive and natural communication channel. It was also helpful for users to understand the state of the task by simply monitoring the location of the other users along the round display. This seems to be an advantage of a single display that can provide public screen space as well as private screen space.

6 Discussions

The proposed system provides a face-to-face environment by using a single display in which a user can smoothly negotiate with particular partners through showing his/her public pieces of information on the area adjacent to his/her private information display area. The public information display area naturally expands when two adjacent users approach each other closely enough. Furthermore, the system design promotes intuitive collaboration through the dynamic size of overlapping areas caused by the change of distance between users. This feature cannot be obtained by other systems such as those that use multiple displays. We believe that physical distances between adjacent users, and in accordance the distribution of public and private information on the display, might change according to the intimacy level, or other psychological parameters which influence interpersonal distances [18]. Since both public and private information are presented on the same display, users do not need to divide attention between several spatially separated displays and can easily grasp the status of their private and public information. Users can communicate by using eye contact and/or face-to-face conversations; consequently, they can negotiate with each other naturally and intuitively. This is an important advantage of the proposed method using a single, round display.

Exploiting these features, our method can be applied to various collaborative tasks that incorporate strategic aspects. One example is to use it in a meeting on reshuffling of personnel in a company or an organization. At a meeting where managers or directors of some sections gather, the sharable information is general personnel matters such as careers or work experiences of the persons who are shuffled. On the other hand, some background information that does not necessarily have to be shared with all participants might be held as private by a manager. She can decide at some point that it is profitable to show the secret information to a particular participant, according to the situation. By using our proposed system, the participants can proceed through their negotiations by exchanging or sharing information with particular partners. One application example of this type is where sport team managers conduct a meeting on trading baseball players. Another possible example of this type is when negotiating the barter of goods among several participants, similar to the example shown in Fig. 5.

One of the drawbacks of our display system is the resolution of the information display areas; that is, only a part of the display surface is used for each user. A higher resolution image display will help alleviate this drawback, and it should even be possible to enlarge each user's display area by using different design parameters, e.g., employing a larger mask hole if the number of users can be limited to two. In the application example of Fig. 5, implementation was made more sophisticated, mainly to display pictures or portraits and accompanying text data of sufficiently large size by switching one after another by using the buttons of controllers.

7 Conclusion

In this paper, we proposed a round display system that enables multiple users to share private and public information following an intuitive collaboration mechanism. Through prototype implementation and preliminary evaluation, we found that the proposed system displays private and the public information seamlessly and that users can interactively control public and private information spaces by naturally changing their relative spatial location. Users can dynamically choose their collaboration partners, perform tasks which involve cooperation and negotiation, and intuitively control the information they kept private or shared publicly with their collaboration partners.

In the proposed system each user can see the other participants' faces. This support for natural eye contact provides subtle cues for communication between users. The users can proceed through their collaborative work naturally via conversation and hand and body gestures. Corresponding to the dynamically changing user locations the single display can provide public screen space as well as private screen space. The proposed method supports natural interpersonal interaction with a technique of seamless transitions between personal and group work. In addition, it provides users with a face-to-face collaborative work environment in which physical objects can also be used in the same environment.

We believe that the collaborative interaction paradigm the proposed system suggests can be easily extended to support a wide range of activities. We see the main usefulness of this interaction paradigm in human activities that combine the need to collaborate and share information on one hand, with a necessity to strategically and dynamically conceal some knowledge on the other hand. Potential applications can range from stock market and trading floor-related tasks, barter of goods, auctions, cooperative human resources meetings and many others.

Acknowledgement

This research was supported in part by "The 21st Century Center of Excellence Program" of the Ministry of Education, Culture, Sports, Science and Technology, Japan, and "Strategic Information and Communications R&D Promotion Programme (SCOPE)" of the Ministry of Internal Affairs and Communications, Japan.

References

[1] Pederson, E. R., McCall, K., Moran, T. P., and Halas, F. G., Tivoli: An electronic whiteboard for informal workgroup meetings. In *Proc. of INTERCHI*, pp. 391-398 (1993).

[2] Dietz, P. and Leigh, D., DiamondTouch: a multi-user touch technology, In *Proc. of UIST*, pp. 219-226, ACM (2001).

[3] Rekimoto, J. Pick and drop: a direct manipulation technique for multiple computer environments. In *Proc. of UIST*, pp. 31-39, ACM (1997).

[4] Streitz, N. A., Geisler, J., Holmer, T., Konomi, S., Muller-Tomfelde, C., Reischl, W., Rexroth, P., Seitz, P., and Steinmetz, R., i-LAND: an interactive landscape for creativity and innovation, In *Proc. of CHI*, pp. 120-127, ACM, 1999.

[5] Greenberg, S. and Rounding, M., The notification collage: posting information to public and personal displays, In *Proc. of CHI*, pp. 515-521, ACM (2001).

[6] Shen, C., Lesh, N. B., Vernier, F., Forlines, C., Frost, J., Sharing and building digital group histories, In *Proc. of CSCW*, pp. 324-333, ACM (2002).

[7] Scott, S.D., Grant, K.D., and Mandryk, R.L. System guidelines for co-located, collaborative work on a tabletop display. In *Proc. of ECSCW*, pp. 159-178 (2003).

[8] Rekimoto, J. A multiple device approach for supporting whiteboard-based interactions, In *Proc. of CHI*, pp. 18-23, ACM (1998).

[9] Brad A. Myers, Herb Stiel, Robert Gargiulo, Collaboration using multiple PDAs connected to a PC. In *Proc. of CSCW*, pp. 285-294, ACM (1997).

[10] Izadi, S., Brignull, H., Rodden, T., Rogers, Y., and Underwood, M. Dynamo: A public interactive surface supporting the cooperative sharing and exchange of media, In *Proc. of UIST*, pp. 159-168, ACM (2003).

[11] Tandler, P., Prante, T., Muller-Tomfelde, C., Streitz, N., and Steinmetz, R. ConnecTables: dynamic coupling of displays for the flexible creation of shared workspaces, In *Proc. of UIST*, pp. 11-20, ACM (2001).

[12] Elwart-Keys, M., Halonen, D., Horton, M., Kass, R., and Scott, P. User interface requirements for face to face groupware. In *Proc. of CHI*, pp. 295-301. ACM (1990).

[13] Tang, J.C. Findings from observational studies of collaborative work. *International Journal of Man-Machine Studies*, 34, pp. 143-160 (1991).

[14] Garth, B., Shoemaker, D., and Inkpen, K., Single display privacyware: augmenting public displays with private information, In *Proc. of CHI*, pp. 522-529, ACM (2001).

[15] Rekimoto, J. and Saitoh, M. Augmented surfaces: a spatially continuous work space for hybrid computing environments. In *Proc. of CHI*, pp. 378-385, ACM (1999).

[16] Fox, A., Johanson, B., Hanrahan, P., and Winograd, T. Integrating information appliances into an interactive workspace. *CG & A*, Vol. 20, No. 4, pp. 54-65, IEEE (2000)

[17] Kitamura, Y., Konishi, T., Yamamoto, S., and Kishino, F. Interactive stereoscopic display for three or more users, In *Proc. of SIGGRAPH*, pp.231-239, ACM (2001).

[18] Hall, E. T. The hidden dimension. Doubleday & Company, New York (1966)

Gamble — A Multiuser Game with an Embodied Conversational Agent

Matthias Rehm and Michael Wissner

Multimedia Concepts and Applications,
University of Augsburg, Germany
rehm@informatik.uni-augsburg.de, michael.wissner@web.de

Abstract. In this article, we present Gamble[1], a small game of dice that is played by two users and an embodied conversational agent (ECA). By its abilities to communicate and collaborate, an ECA is well suited for engaging users in entertaining social interactions. Gamble is used as a test bed for such multiuser interactions. The description of the system's components and a thorough analysis of the agent's behavior control mechanisms is followed by insights gained from a first user study.

1 Introduction

Entertainment computing has so far successfully focused on the technical problems of enhancing the user's experience (e.g., [23], [7], [20]). An equally important factor are the social interaction qualities of a game which play an especially crucial role in multiplayer games. Talking about multiplayer games often means talking about the interaction of multiple users mediated by a computer. In this article, we present a game instead that is played by multiple users together with an embodied conversational agent (ECA) that serves as one of the interaction partners.

Why do ECAs make sense for an application like a game? Apart from their conversational skills, the nonverbal behavior and the appearance of embodied interface agents become more and more realistic. Thus, ECAs serve as an ideal tool for engaging users in social interactions like tutoring, gaming, etc. According to Sidner [21], engagement "is the process by which two (or more) participants establish, maintain and end their perceived connection during interactions they jointly undertake." Engagement behaviors comprise spoken linguistic behavior, i.e. the ability to communicate by speech, collaborative behavior, i.e. the ability to do something together with others, and gestural behavior, i.e. the ability for multimodal interactions including body movements and eye gaze. All of these behaviors are also essential ingredients of ECAs. But most ECA systems constrain themselves to interactions with single users or with single users and other agents (e.g., [6], [11], [13]) because dealing with multiple users is much more

---

[1] This work is supported by the EU Network of Excellence HUMAINE (http://emotion-research.net).

F. Kishino et al. (Eds.): ICEC 2005, LNCS 3711, pp. 180–191, 2005.

difficult than dealing with a single user. Although the setting in a specific application might constrain the relevant interaction, such a multiuser interaction is much less predictable. The users might show any behavior, e.g., by collaborating against the agent, by discussing off topic matters, etc. In the dyadic situation the only interaction partner is the agent triggering the user to regard her "traffic rules" of social interaction. This might be not the case if there is a real human as an interaction partner available apart from the agent. There are few systems that risk dealing with multiple users and thus, the literature on the behavior of multiple users is sparse. An exception is the work of Vertegaal and colleagues, who studied gaze behavior in multiuser settings ([22]).

Collaborating or competing with others in a game has one important prerequisite: sharing the interaction space with others be they humans or game characters. One way to realize this is to use augmented reality techniques to integrate the virtual world into the real world. Impressive examples of mixed reality games are Invisible Train [23], Human PacMan [7], and MR Mystery game [20]. The Invisible Train installation aims at simplifying the technical prerequisites necessary for an augmented reality experience by employing standard hand-held devices as a window to the virtual world. The players control virtual trains on real wooden tracks. In the Human PacMan system, users play the roles of Pacman and the ghosts in a real world setting competing and collaborating to win the game. The Mixed Reality Mystery game at last takes place in an art gallery, where the user has to deal with a robbery. Real paintings of Hopper are augmented by virtual information, allowing e.g., to explore the back alley of the bar Nighthawks. All of these have one feature in common. There is no ECA involved in the interaction. If we change our focus towards ECA systems, sharing the interaction space is often accomplished by using large screens (e.g., Cassell's REA system [6]) and/or impressive sound systems (e.g., the MRE system [11]), by using a CAVE (e.g., the Multimodal Assembly eXpert (MAX) [13]), or by using head-mounted displays to join the other characters in the virtual world (e.g.,

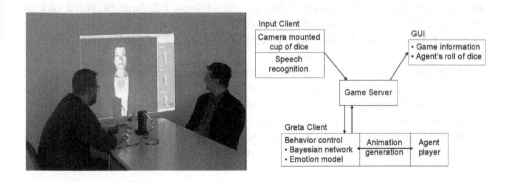

Fig. 1. The setting (left) and the system architecture (right). The agent is projected to the wall at the end of the table, thus sitting together with the other players around the table. Between the human players, the CamCup and the microphone are visible.

Rickel's Steve agent [19]). Due to the complexity of coordinating an autonomous agent with a freely moving user, the use of augmented reality techniques in ECA systems has just started (see [1] for an overview). A different approach uses the application's setting to augment the presence of the ECA and create a shared interaction space, e.g., in the MACK system [15]. The metaphor for the MACK system is an information booth in the entrance area of a building. The agent is situated on a screen that shows the real world area behind the agent making use of a video camera. Thus, the agent's screen is its booth in which it works its shifts. In Gamble, we follow a similar approach to augment the ECA's presence. Gamble is a small game of dice played at a table. This setting naturally constrains the possible interaction space. No sophisticated movements through space are supposed to take place, the agent is sitting together with the other players at the table by projecting it to a screen at the end of the table (see Fig. 1 (left)). In the remainder of this article, we will first describe the rules of the game (Sec. 2), followed by a description of the system itself (Sec. 3) and the insights gained by a first evaluation study (Sec. 4).

2   Gamble: The Game

In Gamble, two users play a simple game of dice (also known as Mexicali) with an embodied conversational agent. To win the game it is indispensable to lie to the other players and to catch them lying to you. The traditional (not computer-based) version of the game is played with two dice and a cup.

Let's assume it is the turn of player 1. He casts the dice and then inspects the dice without permitting the other players to have a look. The cast is interpreted in the following way: the higher digit always represents the first part of the cast. Thus, a 5 and a 2 correspond to a 52. Two equal digits (11, ..., 66) have a higher value than the other casts, the highest cast is a 21. Player 1 has to announce his cast with the constraint that he has to say a higher number than the previous player. For instance, if the dice show a 52, but the previous player already announced a 61, player 1 has to say at least 62. Now player 2 has to decide whether to believe the other player's claim or not. In this case, he has to cast next. Otherwise, the dice are shown and if player 1 has lied he has lost this round and has to start a new one.

Although the rules of the game are very simple, complex behaviors emerge from these simple rules. Blaming another player for an attempted deceit or getting away with such an attempt e.g., creates highly emotional situations that trigger rich social interactions allowing us to use Gamble as a test bed for investigating social behavior of an agent towards users and vice versa. Section 4 reveals insights gained from a first user study.

3   Gamble: The System

The architecture of our system can be seen in Figure 1 (right): The game server is the central element. It manages turn order, collects announcements and casts

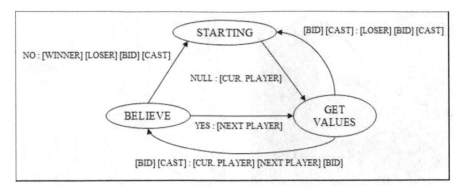

Fig. 2. The game protocol. Depending on the players input, transitions between states are initiated and corresponding output is sent by the game server to the different clients.

from both the human players and the agent, calculates the results and sends all relevant game information to the agent and the GUI. The input client gathers the user input through the CamCup (actual cast) and the speech recognition (announcements) and sends them to the game server. The Greta client contains the agent's behaviour control and animation generation. It sends the agent's announcement and cast to the game server and selects and generates the multimodal output to be displayed by the agent player.

3.1 Game Server

The communication between the game server and the other components is realized via sockets, with the game server acting as a socket server while its clients (input client, Greta client, GUI) are socket clients. It is written in Java and the server's protocol is implemented through a finite state transducer (see Fig. 2).

- STARTING: At the beginning of each round the server is in the state STARTING. The server awaits no input from the clients but broadcasts whose player's turn it is now. At the beginning of a new game, this player is randomly selected, after that it is always the player who lost the last round.
- GETVALUES: In state GETVALUES the server awaits a CAST and a BID from the current player and a simple acknowledgement from everyone else. If the bid is incorrect (i.e. it was lower than the previous player's bid) the current player loses instantly, the server broadcasts the round's result (LOSER) and switches back to state STARTING for a new round. However, if the bid is correct, the server asks the next player to rate the current player's bid and switches to state BELIEVE.
- BELIEVE: If the next player answers YES, she becomes the current player and the server broadcasts that it's her turn. The state switches to GET-VALUES. With an answer of NO on the other hand, the server compares the current player's cast and bid, determines the WINNER and switches to state STARTING in order to start a new round.

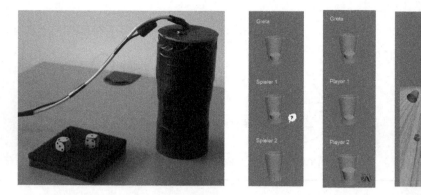

Fig. 3. The CamCup (left) and different GUI states (right). The cup is augmented by a webcam which registers the casts. Basically, three GUI states can be distinguished: (i) Rating announcements (left), (ii) casting dice by user (middle), (iii) casting dice by agent (right).

3.2 Input Client

As mentioned above the input client gathers all the human players input and sends it to the game server. There are two kinds of input: announcements and casts. Announcements (bids and believe-statements) are received through speech recognition while the dice casts are registered with the CamCup.

Speech recognition. A microphone is set between the players and records their announcements. These announcements are then processed by the speaker independent ESMERALDA speech recognition system ([10]) which was trained to recognize all possible numbers and a few variations of 'yes' and 'no' like 'I believe you' or 'Never'. The result of the speech recognition process is then forwarded to the input client.

The CamCup. The dice cup used by Gamble (see Fig. 3 (left)) contains an USB-camera in order to recognize the dice cast. Once the dice recognition is started, the camera takes one picture every 200 milliseconds and compares every pair of successive pictures. If these two pictures do not differ, the dice recognition assumes that 'the dice are cast' and begins to analyze the last picture with a blob coloring procedure. Once this procedure is complete the recognised cast is returned to the input client as a two-digit number.

3.3 GUI

Gamble's GUI is designed in Macromedia Flash and displays all relevant game information to the users (see Fig. 3 (right)). Each player's score is displayed by a jigger which is more or less filled with a yellowish liquid. There are six different 'fill-states' from empty (the player has not lost until now) to full (the player has lost five times and the game is over if he loses once more) . Besides, the current player is indicated by a small symbol next to her jigger: a pair of dice if it's her

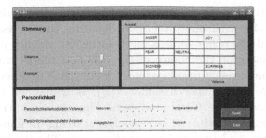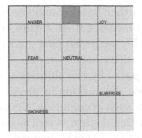

Fig. 4. Setting the agent's initial emotion (left, above) and its personality (left, below) and visualising the agent's emotional state (right)

turn to cast or a thought bubble with a question mark if it's her turn to rate another player's announcement. To indicate that the agent is currently casting the dice, a short video is shown.

3.4 Greta Client

The ECA supplied in Gamble is the Greta agent by Catherine Pelachaud[2] and colleagues ([8]). Controlling the generation of animations (facial and gestural behavior) as well as speech is conversation triggered, i.e., by augmenting utterances of the agent with special tags supplied by APML (Affective Presentation Markup Language, [5]). Based on the utterance and the given tags, corresponding facial expressions, gestures, and speech are generated and afterwards played back with the agent player. To allow for a seamless interaction in Gamble, some modifications were necessary.

Behavior control. Before generating the animations, the appropriate, i.e., context and situation specific, verbal and non-verbal behaviors have to be decided on. A Bayesian network is deployed for this reasoning process. Depending on the evidence available, the network calculates probabilities for possible actions. A turn in the game can roughly be divided into two phases: rating and announcing. First, the announcement of the previous player has to be rated. This decision is based upon (i) Greta's current emotional state, (ii) the probability of the announced result, e.g., the highest cast 21 has a probability of 0.056, (iii) the number of times that the previous player was caught lying. If the agent believes the previous player or has falsely accused him of lying, it has to cast the dice next and announce a result. The announcement is based upon (i) Greta's cast, (ii) the probability of the necessary announcement, (iii) the number of times Greta was caught lying, (iv) the agent's emotional state.

The agent's emotional state is influenced by its game success and by its personality traits. Catching another player lying, getting away with a lie, or being falsely accused of a lie and thus winning the round constitute a positive emotional influence. Falsely accusing another player or being caught lying on

---

[2] We are grateful to Catherine Pelachaud and her colleagues for their excellent support and encouragement.

the other hand constitute a negative emotional influence. The emotional model is dimensional in nature (e.g., [14]) with one dimension denoting the arousal of the accompanying emotion and the other dimension denoting its valence on a positive/negative axis. The reason for the choice of this emotion model was triggered by the abilities of automatic recognition systems for emotions to detect those dimensions in physiological ([4]) or speech signals ([2]). It is planned to test such recognition algorithms with the Gamble system. The agent's initial emotional state as well as its personality traits can be set before starting the game (see Fig. 4 (left)). Instead of using a sophisticated personality model like the big five (e.g., [12]), we take the dimensional model into account directly. The user can determine modulator values for valence and arousal. These modulators allow the agent different appraisals of a given situation. A high modulator value for valence is interpreted as a highly emotion driven decision process changing fast between positive and negative evaluation of a situation whereas a low modulator value results in a more rational decision. The arousal modulator on the other hand determines how capricious the agent reacts. A high value of the arousal modulator results in a fast increase of the arousal level in a given situation whereas a low value slows the increase down making the agent more phlegmatic. The agent's emotional state can be monitored (see Fig. 4 (right)) but is visible to the user only by the agent's behavior.

The information about the actual cast and the announcement are sent to the game server. Output of the behavior module for the animation generation is the result that will be announced by Greta, the emotional state of the agent in terms of valence and arousal, and the current ability to mask a necessary lie. Because it would be frustrating to play against an agent that is able to show a perfect poker face, we modelled some facial clues of deceit that shall allow the user to catch the agent lying (see Sec. 4.1). The ability to mask a necessary lie depends in our model on the arousal and valence value of the emotional state, on the probability for the announced result of the previous player, and on the probability of Greta's own announcement.

Animation generation. Among other things, APML allows for enriching the utterance of an agent with information on the emotional state of the agent (e.g., surprised, sad), meta information about the dialogue context (e.g., greeting, information), and gestural information (e.g., iconic for small). For the use in Gamble the gestural repertoire was extended by German emblems described in detail in the Berlin lexicon of german everyday gestures ([3]). The semantic content of emblems is well defined because they generally are used instead of words, conveying a specific meaning like the OK sign in the American culture formed by thumb and index finger. Moreover, many emblems are especially suited for a game context, because there exist specific emblems, e.g., for surprise or disbelief which occur naturally in such a context. 30 emblems have been created for Gamble.

Whereas APML allows for defining unlimited emotional facial expressions, the current lip model which relies on recorded data restricts the facial expressions to some basic emotions (anger, disgust, fear, joy, sadness, surprise, neutral). Thus, the information about the emotional state of the agent has to be mapped to these basic emotions before generating the agent's utterance. According to the current emotional state of the agent and the kind of statement (belief/disbelief, announcement, comment), an utterance and an animation is chosen from a database, which is then send to the agent player. To generate realistic utterances for the agent, video recordings of human players were analysed to gain a corpus of game relevant utterances. Next step is the use of a dynamic template based speech generation approach that takes into account the emotional state of the agent and generates appropriate utterances and animations on the fly.

Agent player. In our modified version we established a client/server connection between the animation generation and the agent player via sockets. The latter is the client and waits for play-back instructions from the generation module. Having received such an instruction the player loads the corresponding animation and audio files. After finishing the play-back it switches into an idle mode and awaits the next instruction. In order to make these idle phases look more natural we implemented some idle movements (shifting, nodding, gazing around) for the agent. When entering the idle state, the player randomly chooses and plays an idle movement, depending on the agent's current emotional state. For each emotional state, at least three different variants of the idle movement exist. Moreover, the strength of the movements can be modified, e.g., if arousal is very high, the movement can be rendered more agitated and space consuming. If the player receives a play-back instruction from the generation module while playing an idle movement, the movement is blended into the new animation within 20 frames to grant a smooth transition between the two animations.

4   Gamble: The Test Bed

Gamble is a test bed for affective multiparty interactions which allows us to investigate social behavior of an agent towards users and vice versa. The CASA paradigm (Computers Are Social Actors, e.g., [16]) claims that agents are regarded and treated as social actors. Whereas in 1:1 interactions it was shown that people tend to consider their "traffic-rules" of social interaction, we know little about scenarios in which more than one user is interacting with the same agent at the same time. Gamble serves as a test bed for aspects of social interactions and the remainder of this article we present some results from a first evaluation study on deceiving agents, multiuser and affective interactions.

24 students from computer science and from communication science participated in this first user study. They were divided in 12 groups, each pair played two sessions of 12 minutes ensuring that each participant played before and after the agent. Thus, each participant had to lie to the agent some time in the game and each had to rate the agent's announcements. To ensure the participants interest in the game, winning the game would earn them 5 Euros. The general game information like actual cast, announced result, and success was logged

during the game. The sessions were recorded on video and the videos have been annotated considering for each player – human and agent – the utterances, the gaze behavior, the role in the game at that moment in time, and if the player was laughing. This last bit of information is used to train and test a system for automatic recognition of emotion from speech.

4.1 Deceiving Agents

To win the game it is indispensable to sometimes deceive the other players and to detect such attempts by the other players. Playing with an agent that is able to conceal its attempts completely, might be not a very satisfactory experience. Ekman [9] describes facial clues to deceit, that can only be controlled by the most experienced liars. Some of these clues were modelled for the Greta agent allowing it to control the level of concealment during the game. Thus, Gamble allows us to investigate in a principled way (i) if users react at all to such facial clues of deceit when an ECA shows these clues, and (ii) if this is the case, how they react to and interpret these clues, e.g., as a malfunction of the system, as an affront, or as a useful feature that makes the interaction more engaging. Although a pilot study revealed that users react to such clues shown by an agent, in the context of the game they seem to be far more engaged in the interaction to pay any attention to these clues. A thorough discussion of the results obtained by the first user study on this account can be found in [17]. Of course, also the human players try to deceive the agent and consquently we will have to deal with the question how to handle false expressions by the user, i.e. how to react to them. Such a reaction is necessary if the agent has caught the previous player lying. At the moment this situation is handled by predefined gloating behaviors. E.g., the agent displays an emblematic gestures that is recognized as gloating in Germany (holding the hand as an extension of the nose) and says "You have lost".

4.2 Multiuser Interaction

Furthermore, Gamble allows us to study emotional interaction within a multi-party scenario with several human users – an aspect which has been largely neglected so far. Our first study revealed the high engagement of the users in the interaction with the agent and with one another. And although the game is round-based and thus allows for a thorough control of turns, all kinds of social behavior could be seen, from testing the agent's domain competence over commenting on the agent's and/or the other player's moves up to a collaboration of players against the agent. What is evident in the video recordings of the first user study is the acceptance of the agent as a competent interaction participant.

Gaze behavior is generally interpreted as an indicator of the user's engagement in an interaction. Annotating the users gaze behavior in the video recordings revealed a high interest in the agent (see [18] for a thorough discussion). Overall, users looked 1.5 times longer towards the agent than to their human interaction partner. Moreover, users accepted the agent as a social interaction partner although there is also a another real partner present. Users showed the same gaze patterns as in natural interactions ([22]). As a speaker, they first looked away and then towards the agents which was also described for human face to face interactions. As a listener, they looked towards the agent during its announcements which again is a natural behavior. At the moment, the agent shows no active gaze behavior but only randomly gazes towards the users. Thus, the results from the first user study will be used to develop a gaze model for such a multiuser setting.

4.3 Affective Interaction

Additionally, using Gamble, we can create highly emotional situations, for example when the agent blames the user for deceit or when the user detects such an attempt and the agent has to react to it. Until now, there is some anecdotal evidence from the video recordings for this effect. Reacting to an attempted lie, e.g., with the utterance "Du hast einen totalen Knall"[3] accompanied by a gesture where the agent is waving a splayed hand to and fro in front of its face, often elicits an appropriate reaction by the users, e.g., comments like "Ich wollt's mal versuchen"[4] or "Hätt ja klappen können"[5]. In another example, the agent starts swearing after the user has repeatedly caught it lying. This results always in a big laugh from the users because it is an appropriate social behavior in the context that was not expected from a technical artefact like an ECA and renders the agent even more interesting. Consequently, Gamble enables us to investigate how emotional signals employed by the agent are perceived by the human user. In particular, we want to study how emotions need to be conveyed in order to increase the user's trust in an agent. Measuring the user's affective states by means of physiological sensors and automatic speech recognition system, we will investigate how different expressive behaviors of the agent exert an influence on these states.

5   Summary

In this article we presented an ECA system that engages two users in an entertaining interaction. Because of their ability to interact in a socially appropriate manner, ECAs are well suited as a competent and natural interaction partner. The agent in Gamble provides a number of engagement behaviors that are necessary for drawing the users into the interaction. Its conversational behavior, i.e., ist ability to communicate by speech and gestures, was tailored to the domain by analyzing video recordings of human players to create game relevant utterances as well as by augmenting the agent's gestural repertoire to allow for appropriate accompanying gestures (German emblems). The agent's collaborative behavior,

---

[3] You are stupid.

[4] I just wanted to try.

[5] Could have worked.

i.e., its ability to join the human players in the game of dice, renders it a competent game partner. Enhancing the behavior control by an emotional model and some simple personality features, the agent's behavior is no longer predictable by the basic facts of the game like the probability of a cast, but becomes much more interesting by enhancing the decision process with uncertainty factors. The setting of the game (round based, played at a table) allows us to integrate the agent in a natural way. Projecting it to a screen at the end of the table creates the impression of sitting at the table together with the other players. What is lacking in terms of engagement behaviors at the moment is an active gaze behavior of the agent. The observations of the first user study show some similarities with natural multiuser communication and also some peculiarities like increased attention towards the agent. These observations will inform our gaze model for the agent allowing for an even more engaging interaction.

References

1. Elisabeth André, Klaus Dorfmüller-Ulhaas, and Thomas Rist. Embodied Conversational Characters: Wandering between the Digital and the Physical World. *it-Information Technology*, 2004.
2. A. Batliner, V. Zeißler, C. Frank, J. Adelhardt, R. P. Shi, and E. Nöth. We are not amused - but how do you know? User states in a multi-modal dialogue system. In *Proc. EUROSPEECH 2003*, pages 733–736, Geneva, 2003.
3. BLAG. Berliner lexikon der alltagsgesten. *http://www.ims.uni-stuttgart.de/ projekte/nite/BLAG/*, last visited: 22.05.2005.
4. Wauter Bosma and Elisabeth André. Exploiting Emotions to Disambiguate Dialogue Acts. In *Proceedings of the 9th International Conference on Intelligent User Interfaces*, pages 85–92. ACM Press, 2004.
5. Berardina De Carolis, Valeria Carofiglio, Massimo Bilvi, and Catherine Pelachaud. APML, a Mark-up Language for Believable Behavior Generation. In Z. Ruttkay and C. Pelachaud, editors, *Workshop AAMAS02: Embodied conversational agents — let's specify and evaluate them!*, 2002.
6. Justine Cassell, Timothy Bickmore, Lee Campbell, Hannes Vilhjalmsson, and Hao Yan. Designing embodied conversational agents. In Justine Cassell, Joseph Sullivan, Scott Prevost, and Elisabeth Churchill, editors, *Embodied conversational agents*, pages 29–63. MIT Press, Cambridge, MA, 2000.
7. Adrian David Cheok, Siew Wan Fong, Kok Hwee Goh, Xubo Yang, Wei Liu, Farzam Farzbiz, and Yu Li. Human Pacman: A Mobile Entertainment System with Ubiquitous Computing and Tangible Interaction over a Wide Outdoor Area. In L. Chittaro, editor, *Mobile HCI 2003*, pages 209–224. Springer, Berlin, Heidelberg, 2003.
8. Fiorella de Rosis, Catherine Pelachaud, Isabella Poggi, Valeria Carofiglio, and Berardina De Carolis. From Greta's mind to her face: modelling the dynamics of affective states in a conversational embodied agent. *International Journal of Human-Computer Studies*, 59:81–118, 2003.
9. Paul Ekman. *Telling Lies — Clues to Deceit in the Marketplace, Politics, and Marriage*. Norton and Co. Ltd., New York, 3rd edition, 1992.
10. G. A. Fink. Developing HMM-based recognizers with ESMERALDA. In V. Matoušek, P. Mautner, J. Ocelíková, and P. Sojka, editors, *Lecture notes in artificial intelligence*, pages 229–234. Springer, Berlin, Heidelberg, 1999.

11. Randall W. Hill, Jonathan Gratch, Stacy Marsella, Jeff Rickel, William Swartout, and David Traum. Virtual humans in the mission rehearsal exercise system. *KI – Künstliche Intelligenz*, (4):5–10, 2003.
12. O. P. John. The "Big Five" factor taxonomy: Dimensions of personality in the natural language and in questionnaires. In L. A. Pervin, editor, *Handbook of personality: Theory and research*, pages 66–100. Guilford, New York, 1990.
13. Stefan Kopp, Bernhard Jung, Nadine Lessmann, and Ipke Wachsmuth. Max — A Multimodal Assistant in Virtual Reality Construction. *KI – Künstliche Intelligenz*, (4):11–17, 2003.
14. Peter J. Lang. The Emotion Probe: Studies of Motivation and Attention. *American Psychologist*, 50(5):372–385, 2002.
15. Yukiko I. Nakano, Gabe Reinstein, Tom Stocky, and Justine Cassell. Towards a Model of Face-to-face Grounding. In *Proceedings of the Association for Computational Linguistics*, Sapporo, Japan, July 1–12 2003.
16. Byron Reeves and Clifford Nass. *The Media Equation — How People Treat Computers, Television, and New Media Like Real People and Places*. Cambridge University Press, Cambridge, 1996.
17. Matthias Rehm and Elisabeth André. Catch me if you can — Exploring lying agents in social settings. In *Proceedings of AAMAS'05*, 2005.
18. Matthias Rehm and Elisabeth André. Where do they look? Gaze Behaviors of Multiple Users Interacting with an Embodied Conversational Agent. In *Proceedings of Intelligent Virtual Agents (IVA)*, 2005.
19. J. Rickel and W. J. Johnson. Task-oriented collaboration with embodied agents in virtual worlds. In J. Cassell, J. Sullivan, S. Prevost, and E. Churchill, editors, *Embodied conversational agents*, pages 95–122. MIT Press, Cambridge, MA, 2000.
20. Jorge Santiago, Luis Romero, and Nuno Correia. A mixed reality mystery game. In *Proceedings of the second international conference on Entertainment computing*, pages 1–8, Pittsburgh, Pennsylvania, 2003.
21. Candace L. Sidner, Cory D. Kidd, Christopher Lee, and Neal Lesh. Where to look: a study of human-robot engagement. In *Proc. of the 9th Int. Conf. on Intelligent User Interface*, pages 78–84, 2004.
22. Roel Vertegaal, Robert Slagter, Gerrit van der Veer, and Anton Nijholt. Eye Gaze Patterns in Conversations: There is More to Conversational Agents Than Meets the Eyes. In *Proceedings of SIGCHI 2001*, Seattle, WA, 2001.
23. Daniel Wagner, Thomas Pintaric, Florian Ledermann, and Dieter Schmalstieg. Towards Massively Multi-User Augmented Reality on Handheld Devices. In *3rd International Conference on Pervasive Computing (Pervasive 2005)*, Munich, 2005.

Touchable Interactive Walls:
Opportunities and Challenges

Kelly L. Dempski and Brandon L. Harvey

Accenture Technology Labs, 161 N. Clark St.,
Chicago, IL 60601, USA
{Kelly.L.Dempski, Brandon.L.Harvey}@accenture.com
http://www.accenture.com/Techlabs

Abstract. Very large, high resolution, interactive screens—also known as interactive walls—can be used to deliver entertainment and advertising content that is qualitatively different from what is available in television, kiosk, or desktop formats. At a sufficient resolution and size, the touchable wall can offer the engaging interactivity of full-fledged entertainment software, but on a scale that enables new kinds of public experiences. This paper describes some of the opportunities enabled by what we believe to be a new computing medium in its own right. We also describe some of the new design challenges inherent in this medium, together with suggestions based on our own approach to those challenges.

1 Introduction

Since the advent of movies, audiences have experienced entertainment presented on large screens, with actors and events often appearing larger than life. IMAX movies take the experience one step further; the content is specifically designed to encompass the viewer's whole visual field, enveloping them in a nearly immersive experience. Despite this feeling of immersion, of course, the viewer does not participate; the audience is passive.

On the other hand, video games and computer applications are highly interactive, but are usually relegated to the smaller physical formats of monitors or televisions. A few privileged users do have access to larger-format interactive screens such as SmartBoards, but these are rarely used as a medium for public entertainment. Where large interactive screens are deployed in public, they tend to feature the same sorts of content that would be found on a desktop computer, simply magnified onto a larger area. In one type of installation, the touch interface may be simplified to its barest essentials—pressing buttons—putting a limit richness of possible interactions; in the other direction, the user can control a pointer, making for a much more flexible interface. But typically, few accomodations are made for the difference in circumstances between desktop computing and interactive touch screens. The same interface elements developed for a screen one foot wide—the menus and lists, the positioning of elements on screen and their relative proportions—are imported wholesale into a context where there is a much larger canvas, a different sort of pointer (the hand), and a different set of use cases.

F. Kishino et al. (Eds.): ICEC 2005, LNCS 3711, pp. 192–202, 2005.

We believe that large interactive displays will be effective only if the content is specifically designed to take advantage of the particular parameters of this medium. The overall scope of our research covers a range of applications, from large command and control screens, to group decision applications, to entertainment and advertising applications. The purpose of this paper is to discuss the latter, and show the opportunities and challenges involved with creating content that is large in size, highly detailed, directly interactive for multiple users, and usable by the general public.

1.1 Defining the Interactive Wall

Our definition of an interactive wall includes both physical size and resolution. Just as a true IMAX experience requires both a large screen and a higher resolution film stock, high quality large format digital experiences demand both a large size and very high resolution—a lot of pixels in a small physical area. To create a large, high-resolution screen, people typically tile together a number of high-resolution display elements. Whether this is accomplished using front or rear projection, or by stacking up special monitors with very thin bezels, two problems immediately arise. The first is the number of video inputs—what will drive all of the video ports? The second is the sheer number of pixels involved—what will compute all the screen contents? There are few if any graphics cards that can generate a canvas many thousands of pixels across, with real-time performance.

There are several approaches to these challenges, ranging from specialized signal fusion hardware [1] to low level software schemes for distributed rendering [2]. Because of limitations of these approaches, we used neither and created a higher level distributed rendering scheme (described in [4]) that allows us to distribute a very large high resolution application across a network of heterogeneous devices. Although we can scale much higher, our current screen is comprised of 8 1024x768 tiles running on 4 PCs connected with our software. This effectively creates a virtual PC capable of running at 4096x1536 resolution on a 10ftx4ft screen with very high 2D and 3D graphics performance and a low cost. This resolution will be mentioned later when we compare desktop applications to potential wall applications, although our system supports different configurations and different display resolutions.

Our approach is focused on supporting interactive content. To accomplish this, we built a very high resolution touch system, based on cameras, that senses the entire screen with a high sampling rate (greater than 120 Hz) and a precision finer than a fingertip. This setup allows us to control the virtual application with the same responsiveness one would expect from a mouse. More recently, we have developed the system's ability to detect and resolve multiple simultaneous touch inputs. We find this very exciting because it allows us to begin creating interfaces that can be used either separately or cooperatively. This aspect can be very important in public spaces where multiple people may want to interact with content simultaneously.

To date, related projects have focused on the technological infrastructure—without adapting content to fit the new form factor—or they have addressed size and resolution issues independent of interactions [3][5]. We have found that the combination of all of the features of an interactive wall, working in concert, demands new approaches to content creation and application design.

The combination of the aforementioned features comprises what we believe to be a new medium with new capabilities. In the remainder of the paper, we'll discuss the application opportunities created by the wall medium; then we will describe the related challenges and some approaches to meeting these challenges.

2 Opportunities for Interactive Walls

In this section, we will discuss how large format interactive walls are qualitatively different from standard kiosks (which facilitate user interaction) and large passive displays (which emphasize a visual experience). We will discuss each of these elements separately to better explain the value of each. However, it is important to recognize that the best applications will be the ones that blend all the elements to create rich interactive experiences.

2.1 Touch: Direct Experiences

When you interact with a computing system you become engaged in an entirely different way than when you passively absorb information from a screen or a sign. This is one of the primary reasons why computer entertainment exists, and it is also a principle that has been put to work many times in, for example, educational software.

An interactive wall that can be touched by anyone, using no special tools or skills, gives users the chance to shape an experience as they might with a computer, but on a scale similar to that of physical experiences. Interactive walls can reward sustained attention, like computers do, but they can also support a more casual interaction pattern than desktop computers do, because they forgo the small, delicate controls and the inert sitting posture. On an interactive wall, even very broad physical input—such as waving a hand over something—can create large, dramatic results, results that are instantly shareable with others because of the public nature of the display.

An interactive wall, if it allows multiple simultaneous touch inputs, may focus on bringing people together into entertaining activites in which they compete or cooperate (a life-size game of Pong); or it might allow users to interact separately (a music store could have a wall that functions as a row of "listening stations"). Interacting with users who are distant, perhaps standing at other walls, could enlarge the social dimension of the wall.

Advertisers may use interactive walls as a way to get people more involved with a campaign or a product. The content might involve: product information; games or prizes; demonstrations of a product (users could interact with virtual doubles of real products such as music players or cars); offering special functionality or "Easter eggs" to existing customers (of, say, a particular wireless device); and so forth.

2.2 Large Size: Life Size Experiences

A screen so big that it takes up a user's entire field of view provides one of the most immersive experiences we can create, short of virtual reality goggles. IMAX screens produce this effect for users who are many yards away, by deploying a truly enormous screen. In the case of an interactive wall, which is merely large, the enveloping nature of the experience is a byproduct of how close the primary users are.

Some applications benefit from a large size presentation simply because it makes more sense to present certain objects at a lifelike size. For example, human beings have seldom been represented before in an interactive medium at a true scale. With a wall, the user can be face to face with someone who appears to be standing right in front of them. (In fact, with the right setup, it is possible to stage correct eye contact between two remote users.) Because of factors like these, applications such as teleconferencing, distance learning, or remote business presentations may be more successful at wall-size than they have been in other form factors.

Conveying aesthetic details or portraying relationships in space have presented challenges in the consumer-oriented visualization area. But since even large objects such as cars can appear at near life size on a sizable interactive wall, there may be new viability for some forms of "virtual product showroom." For example, a home furnishings retailer might find a competitive advantage in offering customers an interactive experience of how their home would look, decorated and furnished differently, in a life-size virtual mockup.

The number of and kind of users anticipated to approach the wall will guide the design of the wall's size and shape. If we expect dense crowds around the wall, blocking lines of sight, we may want to make the display some feet taller than user's reach. This leaves space to display content, once the crowd has packed around the display. Conversely, a wall intended for children may be built much shorter, and set closer to the ground.

2.3 High Res: Life-Like Experiences

Data density is important not just in scientific applications, with their complex information sets, but for entertainment and advertising as well: text elements, detailed photographs, generated graphics, images of fabrics and textures, and human faces all benefit from detailed presentation. A wall might feature incredibly detailed scenes, thousands of pixels across, whether recorded, artificially generated, or streamed live from another location. Depending on the quality of the content, things onscreen may appear with near-ocular visual fidelity, as a result of a resolution that is multiples higher than what is available through DVD or HDTV.

Designers may take high resolution into account to create "stations" for individual users, within the larger canvas of the wall. When multiple users are standing shoulder to shoulder, interacting simultaneously, high pixel densities let us fit rich visual information into a manageably small space in front of each user.

At the same time, the effects of user interactions should be designed to be large enough so that secondary users, standing behind the direct users, can share the experience—suggesting actions, gleaning information, or simply being entertained or informed.

It is important to note that unlike in the case of most other screens, the person touching an interactive wall may be unable see the entire surface, except at a very steep viewing angle, and not all at the same time. Those standing farther back, of course, have a different experience: they see the whole wall at once, and for them, the users and their actions on the wall actually function as a part of the display—part of the experience. This is a feature that can inform design choices; an application (such as a puzzle) might involve a number of localized tasks for primary users to carry out, while users standing farther back have a special role because they can see the "big picture".

2.4 Multi-user: Shared Experiences

The user's interactions, and the kinds of applications a wall can offer, take on a different light when we consider that, unlike most other public computer systems, which at least try to create a certain privacy, wall interactions are completely, unapologetically public. Given the size, brightness, and the geometry of the wall, and given the fact that the users interact with relatively large motions of their hands and arms (rather than small motions of the fingers and wrists), both the input and the output of the wall are manifestly obvious to everyone around. Wall applications will automatically be spectacles.

Laptop computers, ATMs, and airport kiosks are used in public places, but in a semi-private fashion (at least hopefully), because of the personal information they convey. Wall applications, by contrast, will typically avoid any deployment of personal data. In fact, this will be one the main attractions of the medium: as with pick-up basketball games, strolling on a boardwalk, and karaoke, watching and being watched are both acceptable forms of participation in the public experience. Walls will be appropriate wherever crowds are appropriate, or wherever one wishes to try to draw a crowd.

We can define three criteria for a successful wall application: (a) it must attract—and then entertain, sell to, or educate—interacting users (b) it must keep those users happy about performing their interactions in front of an actual or potential public (c) it must also perform an entertainment, selling, or education function for onlookers.

By the lights of these criteria, interactive walls applications share more qualities with blackboards than they do with personal computers. A blackboard in a hallway is a place to write, but also to be seen writing—people occasionally write there for their own understanding, but usually on behalf of (actual or potential) others as well. It is the sense of being seen that consciously or unconsciously governs what is written. A similar sensibility can be expected to influence users' behavior as they interact with various wall applications.

The arcade game provides a successful example of public computing, and one that satisfies the same three criteria: the user is entertained by the interaction; she is conscious of, and comfortable with, her role in creating a potential or actual public spectacle; and others are free to look on. These three factors considered together define the value of the device.

2.5 Connectedness: Dynamic Experiences

Some of the examples above describe instances where the wall supercedes a non-interactive medium, and the dynamic nature of the display is used to create engaging interactions and spectacles. However, the content is also dynamic in another sense of the word; the contents of a networked display can be changed or updated more easily than standard signage. This is very important to advertisers who might want to change messages depending on audience, time of day, or business conditions.

The same might be accomplished with passive digital signage (such as plasma screens). However, it's important to note that unlike passive digital signage, touch screens also create information that can be sent back to content creators. The measurement of touch feedback patterns can give content creators immediate access to the reactions of their customers, which in turn can be used to enhance the content. For instance, one can imagine a marketing firm creating three different wall applications to advertise a new movie. These three applications can be distributed to three different test markets. After some time period, the marketing firm can use touch information to gauge the effectiveness of each application and distribute only the best application to all markets.

3 Challenges and Approaches

Having laid out some of the potential of the interactive wall as a medium, we will present some of the challenges which arise in developing content that uses the medium effectively. As we do, we will present various approaches to working through these challenges.

3.1 Touch Interaction and Multiple Users

The fact that a wall-size display can be interactive raises a number of questions for designers: how will people know how to interact with it? What will their initial expectations be, and will these be met? What sorts of places are suitable for an interactive wall?

Touch interaction going beyond simple button-pressing is somewhat novel, but it can also be quite intuitive for most users (once they recognize that the wall is actually touchable). In our system, we chose to recognize only the simplest touch inputs: touching, releasing, and dragging objects on screen with a finger or a cluster of fingers. We also support "waving away" certain items as our only supported "gesture", but the gesture is optional. Requiring users—particularly casual users in a mall, airport, street environment, or museum—to learn a vocabulary of special gestures in order to interact sets the barrier to entry needlessly high. Specialized gesture vocabularies might be suitable to a command and control environment (though we question this as well); in an entertainment context, they are probably out of the question.

The potential for simultaneous user interactions presents a new dimension for user experience—and a new design challenge. The same questions as above must be asked again in a different light: will people realize that the wall can handle multiple touches? Operating on the assumption that they are dealing with a computer—and computers have a single input point—users might assume the contrary. (A user study on questions like these would be very illuminating.) What kinds of applications will engage multiple people, and not just a single user?

There are very few standing guidelines for multi-user interactive experience, except, again, in the area of arcade games. From arcades, we do know that engaging applications, especially those that support and reward constant communication between players, can succeed. It is also important to keep learning time to a minimum, both so that newcomers feel entitled to try the game, and so that the onlookers—who themselves are crucial to attracting interest, and attracting new players—stay engaged, instead of dissipating in boredom as a new player tries to gain enough mastery to actually play the game. When no one is playing, arcade games typically feature an "attraction loop", which demonstrates various important facts: that the game is available to be played; what kinds of experiences are available in the game; and even how to play. We may want to offer a similar functionality for wall applications.

From the software design perspective, we have added a layer of complexity by accommodating multiple users, each of whom might be performing multiple touches, all within the scope of one application. Most UI tools and packages are tuned for a situation in which one event arrives at a time, in a coherent sequence that representing the behavior of a single user. We are unaware of any standard applications in which two or three mice simultaneously operate in a single application space, but that is precisely the situation that the multi-user interactive wall creates for the designer. Compounding this is the fact that unlike mouse pointers, which have an identity and a given position at all times, touches are ephemeral, disappearing and reappearing; it now becomes a task in itself to stitch together various touch signals into a coherent picture of user behavior.

These considerations rule out certain styles of interface behavior, such as, for example, anything that is modal—i.e. any interface element which assumes it can get, or has got, exclusive control over the environment. Menus, for example, are modal in most interfaces: a click opens the menu; another click, on a menu item, selects that item. What about clicks elsewhere on screen? They close the menu—in fact, that is the principal means of dismissing a menu we don't wish to use. In a multi-touch environment, this logic (now a part of every GUI user's muscle memory) is probably unsuitable, because events that are distant from me on screen should not be able to affect the state of "my" interface widgets.

In fact, most of the classic interface widgets that are the standard components of a modern desktop GUI are built on a similar logic. If we wish to use them, they need to be rewritten so that they do not assume a single-user environment. But even if this is done, some of these widgets are unsuitable for the wall interface in the first place. Some of the reasons for this will become clear in our discussion of the challenges of the wall's large size.

The assumption of modality, however, is not restricted to GUI widgets. It is a core principle of desktop software design, and we must think carefully about how to avoid accidentally re-invoking this principle in a context where it is inappropriate.

In Figure 1 (adapted from content at [6]), we show three possible software environments. The left panel of Figure 1 depicts a number of buttons arranged along the top of a screen. One of the buttons has been selected, causing a product detail window to appear below. The scheme is typical of what we might find in a Macromedia Flash application on a website. Note that the menu system takes up the whole width of the application environment. This reveals one kind of modality assumption: it assumes exclusive rights to the entire upper edge of the (single-use) viewing port. The product detail window takes up the rest of the space, again modally, covering up whatever might have previously occupied that real estate. This kind of logic works well in a single-user environment with a small screen, because it uses the limited screen real estate effectively.

Fig. 1. Layouts in different form factors

In the center panel of Figure 1, the same kind of scheme has been naively applied to an interactive wall. The buttons are still ranged along the top of the screen—but this means that now, each user is closer to some of them, and farther from others. This probably doesn't make sense if both users might like to work independently. And of course, the fact that the product detail window occupies most of the wall surface is an even greater impediment to multiple use.

In the right panel of Figure 1, the menu system has been removed—or rather, the menuing function has been spread across the canvas, in the form of a product matrix. The users can now browse independently, even though there is a single product matrix which they must share. They simply browse different parts of the matrix, without preempting one another visually. In this particular application, each user does not have total access to all the products from where he is standing; each product only exists at one spot on the matrix. But that may be a reasonable design choice in this case; perhaps as a user physically moves rightwards, along the wall, they move towards higher-priced cars. The structure of the wall space reflects the continuum of products. Now, moving one's body is a meaningful action within that space, rather than an arbitrary artifact of a UI widget. Software design in these kinds of scenarios might actually incorporate a notion of crowd flow.

3.2 Designing at Scale

Building compelling applications for a canvas the size of a wall presents a challenge which may surprise many designers. Over the past few decades, just as most interface logic has been optimized for a single pointer, as mentioned above, most GUI design has assumed a relatively small, well-bounded interaction surface. When the surface is small, we can assume that the whole space randomly accessible to the user's eye, at almost no time cost. This lets us put a clock in the corner, for example, for handy reference. What's less handy, however, is when the clock is eight feet away, and I have to move my whole body in order to read it. As the cost of viewing access goes up, a static viewing target like the clock loses some utility.

Similarly, in a compact desktop environment, designers take advantage of the small screen size and the user's muscle memory when they create static click targets, such as menu bars, that the user can visit with their mouse pointer again and again, from anywhere onscreen, at a low navigation cost. They place these targets at the edge of the screen when they can, to help the mouse pointer hit the target without overshooting. But in the new medium of an interactive wall, most of these optimizations must be undone, since the "cost structure" they are based upon has to be refigured.

For one thing, the edge of the screen is not privileged as a click target any more—the opposite is true, since the center of the screen is usually much more accessible from the average hand position. The existence of multiple users might mean that we need multiple copies of a common click target. Or, alternatively, we might do away with static click targets entirely, replacing them with controls that follow the user somehow, either by appearing in appropriate contexts, or by hovering near the area of the user's interactions.

3.3 Fleshing Out the Field of View

Almost by definition, a media wall that is touch-interactive must have a high resolution—that is, a high pixel density—because it will be experienced from arm's length, and we want to ensure significant quality and detail at that close range. Surprisingly, however, this is not always the case. We believe that designers should present the user with a rich visual experience *as they use the wall*, not afterwards, when they step back. Of course, many command center installations, projected presentations, and other large displays are only intended to be viewed from across a room, and consequently feature a fairly low pixel density. But at arm's length, those same densities translate into a sharp limit on the quality of the user's visual experience.

In our experience, single-projector interactive systems (such as Smartboard and similar solutions) suffer from a field-of-view problem—they expect users to touch the screen, but they do not offer a useful amount of visual information at that range. (See the left-hand side of Figure 2.)

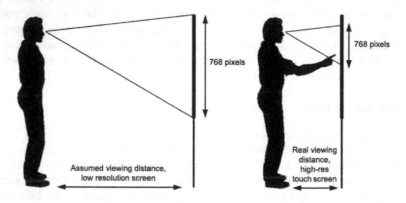

Fig. 2. Necessary visible pixels as a function of distance

We want to include enough visual information, and enough functionality, in a human see-and-touch range (perhaps three or four feet across), that a person can do something interesting, without having to walk around too much, or step back from the wall; all this requires high pixel density. Thus, the way we author any one area of a wall application, and the interactive elements we embed in the design, will often be constrained by the human viewing angle (as well as others physical factors, such as height and armspan). Density is also the feature that allows multiple users, interacting simultaneously, to have access to a reasonable amount of content even as they stand stand somewhat close together. As a rule of thumb, we feel that there should be a laptop screen's worth of pixels (1024 by 768 or so) in the user's vertical field of view as they stand at interaction distance, as shown in the right hand side of Figure 1.

But at the same time, we must expect users at all distances, at all times; the same content which might seem suitable for presentation at a distance must also stand up to the scrutiny of users who are much closer in. Imagine a wall application for a car show. The designer might put a large interactive video in the center of the wall, and smaller stations for interactive product information on either side. The interactive video is operated by a single user, but it is wide enough (perhaps six feet wide) that it can be seen by passersby.

If we were to repurpose standard DVD-quality video for this application, and simply made it "big", it would probably not be effective. Passersby would be satisfied, because of the small portion of their field of view occupied by the (relatively) small amount of visual content. But for the primary user—the one who is running the show and creating the spectacle—there isn't much visual pleasure in the experience. The effect is similar to standing too close to a TV. And for anyone interested enough to approach the wall, visual quality falls off quickly. And, in the case where the wall is not in use, running an attraction loop, the lack of visual quality may discourage interaction in the first place. If it looks like a big-screen TV, people will probably assume that it is one.

Broadly speaking, there are many situations in which the proportions of ordinary digital graphics should be reconsidered for wall-based designs Figure 1 showed a web application with a matrix of cars [6]. The web application is optimized for an 800x600 window. To fit in the available space, each car is represented by the low fidelity graphic shown on the left side of Figure 3. On a 2048x1536 wall display, the same matrix can be represented with a much larger number of pixels. If one keeps the relative sizes of all of the elements the same, each car can be—should be—represented a higher-fidelity version such as the one on the right hand side of Figure 3.

Web Content   Wall Content

Fig. 3. Different amounts of detail at different pixel densities

The possibility for much higher fidelity—which is also a demand for that fidelity— can create interesting challenges for content acquisition and creation, as all creative assets have to be created at different scales and resolutions than do web or print graphics. However, as Figure 3 shows, better art assets create better product depictions and rich user experiences.

4   Conclusion and Examples

In the previous sections, we have described some of the advantages of large format displays as they pertain to entertainment and advertising, we have discussed some of the challenges, and we've used abstract examples to describe some of our current thinking about how to approach these challenges. We are still very early in the process of understanding the medium and refining our design choices, and we hope that these ideas will help others think about how to best design content for large screens.

As with early word processing and web design, the first examples of content designed for a new medium are not necessarily the best indicators of the eventual potential of that medium. Having said that, Figure 4 shows one example of what we have designed for our 4096x1536 touchable display. The depicted application is aimed at multiple users in a public environment, provides a rich visual experience at various distances, and is driven by intuitive touch interaction.

We are using this application, and others like it, to explore the medium and define approaches that work best for the form factor. These applications also serve as a basis for user studies into the usability of large, public, multi-user displays. We hope to present the results of those investigations in the future.

Fig. 4. One example of an interactive advertising and entertainment application

References

1. Jupiter Systems. http://www.jupiter.com
2. G. Humphreys, M. Houston, Y.-R. Ng, R. Frank, S. Ahern, P. Kirchner, and J. T. Klosowski, "Chromium: A Stream Processing Framework for Interactive Graphics on Clusters," presented at SIGGRAPH, San Antonio, Texas, 2002.
3. Li, K., Chen, H. et al. Building and Using A Scalable Display Wall System. IEEE Computer Graphics and Applications, Volume 20 , Issue 4 (July 2000) Pages: 29 - 37
4. Dempski, K., Harvey, B.: Supporting Collaborative Touch Interaction with High Resolution Wall Displays. 2nd Workshop on Multi-User and Ubiquitous User Interfaces (MU3I) January 9, 2005 at IUI 2005
5. NCSA Tiled Display Wall. http://brighton.ncsa.uiuc.edu/~prajlich/wall/
6. Mercedes-Benz. http://www.mbusa.com/brand/selector/controller.jsp?filter=msrp

Generic-Model Based Human-Body Modeling

Xiaomao Wu[+], Lizhuang Ma[+], Ke-Sen Huang[*], Yan Gao[+], and Zhihua Chen[+]

[+] Department of Computer Science & Engineering, Shanghai Jiao Tong University,
HuaShan Rd. No. 1954, Shanghai, P.R.C (200030)
{xmwu, ma-lz, gaoyan, zhchen}@cs.sjtu.edu.cn

[*] Department of Computer Science, National Tsing Hua University,
Kuang Fu Rd. No. 101, Sec. 2, HsingChu, Taiwan 300 R.O.C (30013)
hks@glserver.cs.nthu.edu.tw

Abstract. This paper presents a generic-model based human-body modeling method which take the anatomical structure of the human body into account. The generic model contains anatomical structure of bones and muscles of the human body. For a given target skin mesh, the generic model can be scaled according to the skin, and then morphed to be fitted to the shape of the target skin mesh. After an anchoring process, the layered model can be animated via key-framing or motion capture data. The advantage of this approach is its convenience and efficiency comparing to existing anatomically-based modeling methods. Experimental results demonstrate the success of the proposed human-bodymodeling method.

Keywords: Anatomically-based modeling, human body modeling, generic model.

1 Introduction

Modeling and deformations of human bodies remain one of the main challenges in the field of computer graphics. The human body is biologically complex, which consists of more than 200 bones and 400 muscles [1]. Additionally, we are subconsciously sensitive to the details of human bodies because we are extremely familiar to our bodies.

Fortunately, users concern only about the skin deformations of the human body in most graphics applications. Human skin can be modeled as parametric surfaces by using existing commercial software, or be acquired via 3D laser scanners. Given a skin mesh in a static pose, animators could either employ the widely used method – skinning, or more complex anatomically-based method, to animate the skin.

Skinning is the most common method for generating of skin deformations in games and interactive systems, it has many names including SSD, enveloping, smooth skinning, transform blending, matrix blending and linear blend skinning. While this method is very fast and widely supported by commercial applications, it cannot represent complex deformations and suffers from "collapsing joint" and "candy-wrapper" defects [2,3]. At the same time, adjusting weights of the skeleton to the skin vertices is a tedious and time-consuming task.

Alternatively, anatomically based approach can also be used to animate the skin. We can insert bones, muscles, and sometimes fat tissues below the given skin mesh, and utilize physically based method to simulate skin deformations [4,5,6,7]. This anatomically-based method mimics the layered deformation way of real humans, thus can produce

F. Kishino et al. (Eds.): ICEC 2005, LNCS 3711, pp. 203–214, 2005.

detailed and realistic skin deformations. Anatomically based method is not so popular as skinning, because it requires the user designing the bones, muscles, and sometimes fat tissues individually, and fine-tuning the muscle shapes carefully, in order to fit those underlying structures to the skin mesh.

Example-based method is another competitive way for generate skin deformations. If we have obtained a series of scanned body poses via scanning, we can use the algorithm described in [8] to interpolate those poses, to produce very realistic skin deformations. While this approach can produce detailed and realistic skin deformation effects, it faces the retargeting problem: we can only capture the skin deformations of a specific human body at a time, and cannot easily retarget the captured deformations to the skin of a different human body. Furthermore, this approach is not suitable for the situation that a body shape is only in the animator's mind and doesn't exist at all, because we have no way to scan an imaginary body.

Inspired by related work on facial animation [4,5,6] and horse modeling [7,9], we present an improved anatomically-based modeling method. We uses a generic model to simplify the construction process of human anatomical structures. Our method inherits of the advantages of anatomically-based modeling approach and is easier to implement.

Our method involves the following five steps: (1) Design the generic model; (2) Obtain the target skin mesh. The target skin mesh could either be modeled with commercial modeling software, or directly obtained by scanning a real person using 3D scanners; (3) Design the skeletons of the generic model and that of the target skin by using the interactive tool we have developed for skeleton design; (4) Fit the generic model to the skin mesh; (5) Anchor skin vertices to underlying components, then animate the skin mesh.

The next section introduces related work on human body modeling. Section 3 introduces how to prepare the generic model and the target skin mesh. Section 4 introduces the method we use to fit the generic model to the target mesh. In section 5, we introduce how the final model can be animated. Experimental results are shown in section 6. We conclude in section 7 with the future work.

2   Related Work

There are many ways to classify related research work that are most related to ours. We describe them in three classes: generating skin upon underlying components; deforming pre-existing skin; and deforming skin by examples.

The first class attempts to extract the skin from underlying components such as bones and muscles, it generally use implicit surfaces to represent the skin. Implicit surfaces are frequently utilized to model organic forms. Many researchers have used implicit surfaces to represent the skin. Blinn [10] used implicit surfaces generated by point skeletons with an exponentially decreasing field function to model his "blobby man". Bloomenthal [11] modeled a hand containing veins with convolution surfaces. He used polygons and lines as primitives. Yoshomito [12] used ellipsoidal metaballs to model the skin of a ballerina which produced realistic-looking shape. More recently, Scheepers *et al.* [13] and Wilhelms *et al.* [14] also used implicit functions to extract the skin from underlying structures.

Deforming pre-existing skin is the second class of human body modeling. If we have modeled a skin with modeling system, e.g. Maya, or have acquired a skin mesh from a real person using 3D laser scanners, we may face the problem of how to deform that skin. Many researches have been done to solve this problem. Komatsu [15] applied a continuous deformation function with respect to the joint angles to deform the control points of a skin mesh represented by Bezier patches and Gregory patches. Magnenat-Thalmann et al.[16,17] introduced the concept of *joint-dependent local deformation* or JLD, to deform existing skin algorithmically. Thalmann and Shen [18] formulated skin as cylindrical contours, they obtained smooth deformations of human trunk and limbs by setting the orientation and position of each contour. Schneider and Wilhelms [9] described a hybrid modeling method based on anatomy. They specified hierarchical skeleton, individual bones, muscles and generalized tissues below an existing skin, and used a physically based method to deform the skin. Simmons et al. [7] proposed generic-model based method to deform the pre-existing skin of a horse . They first deformed the skeleton and bones, and then fine-tuned the muscle shape, in order to fit them to the skin. Skinning [19,2,20,3] is the most popular method to deform existing skin mesh, it defines the deformed vertex of the skin mesh as a weighted summation of the transformations of subspace.

The development of range scanning technologies has make it possible to scan a whole body in several minutes with satisfactory accuracy. Given a variety of scanned poses of a human body, Allen [8] successfully blended those poses, which produced smooth and highly-realistic skin deformations. Sand et al. [21] described a method for acquiring deformable human geometry from silhouettes. Body shape can be reconstructed and new body shape can be synthesized using a normalized radial basis function (NRBF).

Our method falls into the second class. We focus on how to deform a hand-made or range-scanned skin mesh efficiently and realistically, by using a generic model which contains bones and muscles of a human body. A detailed discussion on the unique of our method can be found in section 7.

3 Preparation of the Generic Model and Target Skin Mesh

The generic model plays an important role in our scheme. It consists of basic bones and muscles of the human body. The generic model will be used to semi-automatically reshaped according to a given skin mesh. The basic rules for establishing such a generic model are: Firstly, it should be general enough to represent the basic structure of bones and muscles of a human body; Secondly, anatomical accuracy of the generic model is not crucial, because our interest finally lies in the skin. More accurate anatomical structure will lead to slower speed in the final animation process; Thirdly, the generic model should stand at a muscle-relaxed pose, in which all muscles are placed on the bones in a state of relaxation. It is very helpful for simplifing the muscle animation process.

3.1 Generic-Model Design

Many ways can be used for designing the generic model (Fig. 1). It can be modeled with commercial modeling systems like Maya, SoftImage or 3DMax by artists. Basic

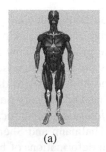 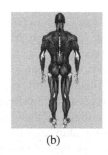 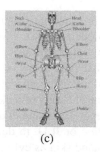

(a)   (b)   (c)

Fig. 1. The left two figures illustrate the generic model that we designed. (a) Frontal view. (b) Rear view. The right figure shows the designed skeleton of the generic model. The skeleton is designed interactively by using the graphics tool we developed. Muscles are not shown for clarity.

knowledge of human anatomy [1] is required to model the generic model properly. Alternatively, we can also make use of existing volume database of human bodies [22], and use reconstruction algorithms to construct the generic model from scanned volume data [23].

We have modeled the generic model with 3DMax referring to anatomy books [1]. Each bone or muscle are individually modeled. The final generic model consists of 176 individual bones and 186 individual muscles. Bones and muscles are modeled as triangular meshes. Currently, we only model skeletal muscles. Cardiac muscles and smooth muscles are not modeled because we do not take facial and organic animation into account.

3.2   Skeleton Design

Skeleton can be used to name the bones of a human body that are attached to each other by joints, or the stick figure representing the positions and orientations of the joints that build up the articulated figure [24]. We follow the second meaning in this paper. A skeleton should be embedded into the generic model(Fig. 1), and will be used later to transform the generic model in order to fit the generic model to the skin.

The task of skeleton design is to specify the skeleton parameters $SC_i = \{P_i, O_i\}$, $i = 0, 1, ..., n-1$, where $P_i \in R^3$ is the joint position, $O_i \in S^3$ is the joint orientation, and n is the joint number. We have developed a tool which can be used to interactively specify the skeleton parameters.

3.3   Muscle Parameter Design

Muscles of the generic model are modeled as irregular triangular meshes, several parameters should be assigned to each muscle, because those parameters are important in the muscle morphing and animating stages. Before we introduce the muscle parameters, we first introduce four terms referring to the characteristics of muscle deformations (Fig. 2(a)): *origin, insertion, belly* and *action line* [1].

A skeletal muscle may attach a bone to another bone (often across a joint) or a bone to another structure, such as skin. When the muscle contracts, one of the structures usually remains stationary, while the other moves. The *origin* of the muscle is the muscle

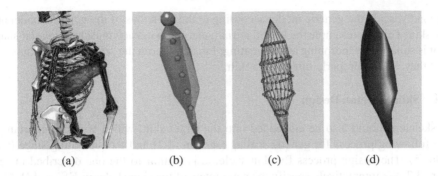

(a)   (b)   (c)   (d)

Fig. 2. (a) Muscle parameter design. The muscle is shown in red. The small green and blue sphere represent the *origin* and the *insertion* respectively. The five small yellow spheres represent the points on the *action line*. The bones shown in blue and green are the *origin bone* and the *insertion bone* respectively. (b)-(d): The muscle resampling process. (b) The original shape of bicep muscle with seven points on the *action line*. (c) Intersections between rays emitted from the middle five point on the *action line* and the original muscle mesh. (d) The reconstructed muscle shape with Phong Shading.

end that attaches to the stationary structure, usually bone. The *insertion* of the muscle is the muscle end that attaches to the moving structure.The *belly* of the muscle is that part of the muscle between the origin and insertion. The *action line* of the muscle is a spline starting from *origin* to *insertion*, it will be used to simulate muscle deformation.

The parameters of a muscle can be expressed as $M_i = \{O, I, Q_j, B_o, B_i, P_o, P_i\}$, where M_i is the parameters related to the ith muscle, O is the *origin*, I is the *insertion*, Q_js ($j \in [1, 5]$) are the five points on the *action line*, B_o is the *origin bone* which is the bone that the *origin* attached to, B_i is the *insertion bone* which is the bone that the *insertion* attached to, P_o and P_i are the *origin* and *insertion* of the muscle respectively. Those parameters are interactively designed by using the designing tool we have developed. Designing the parameter M_i for each muscle is a time-consuming task. But fortunately, it need be done only once.

3.4   Target Skin Mesh

The target skin mesh is the target mesh that we want to animate. It could be modeled with current modeling systems, or be obtained from digital skin model library produced by scanning real human bodies using 3D body scanners like CyberWare WB4 [25]. The previous method is more flexible, but is time-consuming, which requires the modeler has experience on modeling and art design; the latter method can produce more realistic human skin, but is not so flexible as the previous one. Our generic-based modeling technique is suitable for both methods. In our work, we have modeled the target skin with the latter method as an example. The target skin mesh is downloaded from Cyberware [26].

4   From Generic Model to Specific Target Skin

In this section, we introduce the method that we use to fit the generic model to an existing skin mesh. Our method consists of 4 steps: Firstly, design the skin skeleton;

Secondly, scale the generic model according to the skeletons of the generic model and the skin; Thirdly, resample the irregular triangular mesh of each muscle to regular shape that is suitable for morphing and animating; Finally, morph the scaled muscle shapes so that they will be properly fitted to the skin.

4.1   Skin Skeleton Design

A skeleton should also be embedded into the target skin, which is very important to the following process for generic scaling (section 4.2) and the animating stage (section 5). The design process for skin skeleton is similar to the one described in section 3.2. We interactively specify the parameters of the skin skeleton $SS_i = \{P_i, O_i\}$, $i = 0, 1, \cdots, n - 1$, where $P_i \in R^3$ is the joint position, $O_i \in S^3$ is the joint orientation, and n is the joint number. During the skeleton designing process, the skin is rendered translucently to assist the user specifying the location and orientation of each joint clearly. Fig. 3(b) show the designed skeleton of the skin mesh.

4.2   Generic Model Scaling

In order to fit the generic model to the skin, we first scale the bones and muscles of the generic model. The scaling algorithm consists of the following five steps:

1. Group bones of the generic model.
2. Transform bones to local joint coordinates.
3. Scale the bones of each segment.
4. Change the skeleton of the generic model.
5. Scale muscles.

We start the scaling process by grouping bones of the generic model. The bones that lie between two joints are assigned to the parent joint , e.g., bones between *hips* and *chest* are assigned to *hip* joint, and bones between *chest* and *neck* are assigned to *chest* joint.

In step 2, the grouped bones are transformed to the local coordinate system of their associated joints. If the accumulated matrix of the coordinate system of a local joint is

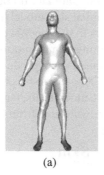
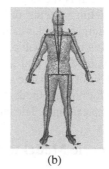

(a)   (b)

Fig. 3. (a) The target skin mesh. (b) The skin skeleton has been designed.

M_i, then the transformed bone vertices are $M_i^{-1} \cdot v_j, j = 1, 2, \cdots, n$, where v_js are the bone vertex.

In step 3, the transformed bones of each segment are scaled according to the segment lengths of the generic-model skeleton and the skin skeleton. Segment length is defined as the Euclidean distance between the two joints that a segment attached to. Each bone is scaled by $S_{ij} = LS_i/LC_i$ along the segment direction pointing from the parent joint to the children joint, where S_{ij} is the scale factor of the jth bone in ith segment, LS_i and LC_i are the lengths of the ith segment of the generic-model skeleton and of the skin skeleton, respectively. The scale factor along the other two orthogonal axises of the local coordinate system are also scaled by S_{ij}, but they can be interactively modified by the user. Fig. 5(b) and Fig. 5(c) show the bones of the generic model before and after the transformation and scaling process.

In step 4, the generic-model skeleton should be changed to have the same parameters as the skin skeleton, i.e., $SC_i = SS_i$, $i = 0, 2, \cdots, n - 1$, where SC_i and SS_i represent the skeleton parameters of the generic model and of the skin individually.

Finally, all muscles should be scaled after the scaling process of bones. Muscle shapes will be resampled and morphed. The according transformation matrix can be represented by equation 1.

$$M_i = M_R \cdot M_T \cdot M_0^{-1} \cdot M_s \cdot M_0 \cdot v \tag{1}$$

where:

M_i is the according transform matrix of the ith muscle.

M_0 is the transform matrix that transforms the origin of the muscle to the global origin ,and the $origin - insertion$ vector to the Z axis of the global coordinate system.

M_S is the scale matrix, the scale factor of Z axis is $S_z=LM_S/LM_0$, with $S_x = S_y = 0.4 * S_z$. Here, LM_S is the Euclidean length between the associated $origin\ bone\ point$ and $insertion\ bone\ point$ of the ith muscle in the scaled generic model, LM_0 is the Euclidean length between the associated $origin\ bone\ point$ and $insertion\ bone\ point$ of the ith muscle in the original generic model. The scale factor in X and Y direction is set be small enough to make sure hat the muscle would lie between the skin. We set the scale factor to 0.4 in our experiment, which produced satisfactory results.

M_0^{-1} is the inverse matrix of M_0, which translates the muscle back to its original position from the global origin.

M_T is a transform matrix that translates the muscle from its unscaled $origin\ bone\ point$ to the scale $origin\ bone\ point$.

M_R is the transform matrix that rotates the muscle along axis OA with angle θ, where $OA = OI \times O_s I_s$, and $\theta = acos(\frac{OI \cdot O_s I_s}{|OI| \cdot |O_s I_s|})$.

4.3   Muscle Resampling

Because muscles of the generic model are modeled as irregular triangular meshes, they should be resampled and changed to another form that is suitable for morphing and animation. In this section, we introduce our muscle resampling method that can sample each irregular triangular muscle shape to a regular one. It consists of five ellipses and two extreme points, say, the $origin$ and the $insertion$(Fig. 2(b)). The resampling algorithm consists of five steps:

1. Fit Bezier curve to the points on the *action line*.
2. Shoot rays from each point on the *action line*.
3. Calculate intersections between each ray and the muscle meshes.
4. Fit ellipse to the intersections.
5. Reconstruct and render the resampled muscle meshes.

First, we fit a Bezier curve to the seven *action line* points by solving a set of linear equationsusingth the Gauss-Jordan elimination method [28].

Then, we shoot rays from each point on the *action line* in their normal planes. Twenty rays are shot from each point, the angle between adjacent rays are $\alpha = 2\pi/n$, $n = 20$. More rays can produce more accurate shape but will also slow down the sampling speed.

In the following step, the intersections between the rays from each *action line* point and the skin mesh are calculated using Möller's method[29], which is one of the fastest ray-triangle intersection algorithms. A ray $R(t)$ with origin O and normalized direction D is defined as $R(t) = O + tD$, and a triangle is defined by three vertices V_0, V_1 and V_2. A point $T(u, v)$ on a triangle is given by $T(u, v) = (1 - u - v)V_0 + uV_1 + vV_2$. Computing the intersection between the ray, $R(t)$, and the triangle, $T(u, v)$, is equivalent to $R(t) = T(u, v)$, which yields:

$$O + tD = (1 - u - v)V_0 + uV_1 + vV_2 \qquad (2)$$

The final solutions can be obtained through the following equation using a trick and Cramer's rule:

$$\begin{bmatrix} t \\ u \\ v \end{bmatrix} = \frac{1}{P \cdot E_1} \begin{bmatrix} Q \cdot E_2 \\ P \cdot T \\ Q \cdot D \end{bmatrix} \qquad (3)$$

where $E_1 = V_1 - V_0$, $E_2 = V_2 - V_0$ and $T = O - V_0$, $P = (D \times E_2)$ and $Q = T \times E_1$).

In step 4, we fit ellipse to the sampled intersections calculated in the previous step using the method proposed in [30] which is ellipse-specific, extremely robust, and efficient.

In the final step, we reconstruct the resampled muscle shape and render it with Phong shading. Fig. 2(b)-(d) illustrate this muscle resampling process.

4.4 Muscle Morphing

After the scaling and resampling process, muscles have been aligned properly to the skin skeleton, and are ready for muscle morphing.

Currently, we simply use a iterative method to morph the muscles. Because muscles have been scaled down under the skin mesh, we dilate each elliptic slice of muscles with a small step δ_d until the slice is found to be out of the skin mesh, then we shrink the slice with a smaller step δ_s until the slice is shrunk into the skin mesh again. This process is very similar to the one described by Baraff to detect the colliding contact point during the process of physically-based simulation [31]. Fig. 5(e) shows the generic model and the skin mesh after the muscle morphing process.

5   Animating Target Skin Mesh

After finishing previous steps, we have fit a generic model to the target skin mesh. Then the anatomically based method proposed by Wilhelms *et al.* [14]could be used to animate the target skin mesh.

The target skin is anchored to the underlying bones and muscles, which is called an *anchoring* process. Each vertex in the skin represented with triangle meshes is associated with the closest underlying bones and muscles. And then skin vertices are transformed into the space among the planes of the two slices of a muscle through a *parametric trilinear transformation*. To simulate the elastic effect of skin, springs can be embedded into the skin vertices. Each edge of the triangle mesh of the skin is considered to be a spring with a certain rest length and a stiffness. These springs are brought into equilibrium by means of a series of relaxation operations. Users may refer to [14] for more detailed description.

6   Results

The graphics interface we have developed is written in C++. The generic model and skin are shadered with OpenGL and Cg.

Our program run on a Pentrium 4 computer with 1.8G CPU, 512Mb RAM and GeForce FX5200 graphics card. We spend about two minutes on designing the skeleton of the generic model, one hour on designing muscle parameters. These two steps need be done only once by experienced animators, and then the parameters of the skeleton and muscle are saved as text files on the disk, which can be reused by the user later. Less than one minutes is taken to scale the generic model according to the target skin. The muscle resampling process takes about three minutes, and muscle morphing process takes about four minutes.

Fig. 4 shows the graphics interface that we have developed. Fig. 5 shows the main process of how the generic model is fitted to the target skin. Fig. 5(a) shows the skin model of John. Fig. 5(b)shows the skin model along with the initial generic model. Notice that the bones of the generic model are away from the corresponding parts of the skin. In Fig. 5(c), the bones of the generic model have been transformed and scaled according to the skin mesh of John. Fig. 5(d) shows the generic model in the skin after the muscle scaling process. Fig 5(e) shows the final model after the muscle morphing stage. Fig 6 demonstrate how the generic model is semi-automatically reshaped to Eric's

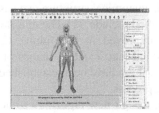

Fig. 4. The graphics interface we developed

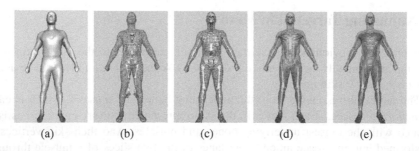

(a)   (b)   (c)   (d)   (e)

Fig. 5. Given a skin mesh, the generic model can be semi-automatically transformed according to the shape of the skin. (a) The skin model of John. (b) The skin model with the generic model before transformation. (c) After transformation and scaling of bones of the generic model. (d) After muscle scaling process. (e) The final generic model after muscle morphing.

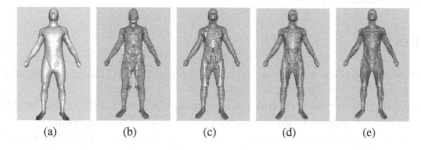

(a)   (b)   (c)   (d)   (e)

Fig. 6. The same process as in Fig. 5, but with difference skin mesh of Eric's

Skin. These two examples show that the generic model had been successfully fitted to the target skin mesh.

7   Conclusion and Future Works

In this paper, we proposed a generic-model based human-body modeling method. The generic model need to be constructed only once by skilled modelers, users are not required to concern about this process. Given a new skin mesh, the generic model can be semi-automatically reshaped according to the shape of the skin. There are very little work remains for the users to do. Generic-model based method is helpful for constructing model human bodies with anatomical structure in a easy and fast way.

The limitations of our method include: (1) The muscle morphing algorithm is relatively slow and should be improved in the future; (2) We do not consider the deformations of head, hands and feet; (3) The shapes of bones and muscles are just an approximation, no proper criteria have been established to guide our generic model scaling and muscle morphing process.

Our future work include: design new algorithm to accelerate the muscle morphing process, establish adequate criteria to guide the generic model scaling and muscle morphing process.

Acknowledgement

We would like to thank Cyberware for generously providing 3D whole body samples on their web. We would also like to thank Tomas Möller for his ray/triangle intersection code, thank Andrew Fitzgibbon for his ellipse-fitting Matlab code. Thank Brett Allen for his helpful advice. This work was supported by National Natural Science Foundation of China (grant No.60173035 and No.60373070), ,863 Program of China (grant No.2003AA411310) and Microsoft Research Asia (Project-2004-Image-01).

References

1. Phillip E. Pack. *CliffsQuickReview Anatomy & Physiology.* New York Cliffs Notes, 2001.
2. J. P. Lewis, M. Cordner, and N. Fong. Pose space deformation: A unified approach to shape interpolation and skeleton-driven deformation. *Computer Graphics(Pro. of SIGGRAPH'00)*, pages 165–172, August 2000.
3. A. Mohr and M. Gleicher. Building efficient, accurate character skins from examples. *ACM Transactions on Graphics*, 22(3):562 – 568, July 2003.
4. Y. Lee, D. Terzopoulos, and K. Waters. Realistic face modeling for animation. In *SIGGRAPH 95 Conference Proceedings*, pages 55–62, August 1995.
5. K. Kähler, J. Haber, and H.-P. Seidel. Geometry-based muscle modeling for facial animation. In *Proc. of Graphics Interface'01*, pages 37–46, 2001.
6. K. Kähler, J. Haber, H. Yamauchi, and H.-P. Seidel. Head shop: Generating animated head models with anatomical structure. In *Pro. of ACM SIGGRAPH Symposiumon Computer Animation (SCA) 2002*, pages 55–64, July 2002.
7. M. Simmons, J. Wilhelms, and A. Van Gelder. Model-based reconstruction for creature animation. In *Pro. of the 2002 ACM SIGGRAPH/Eurographics symposium on Computer Animation*, pages 139–146, July 2002.
8. B. Allen, B. Curles, and Z. Popvić. Articulated body deformation from range can data. *ACM Transactions on Graphics*, 21(3):612–619, July 2002.
9. P. J. Schneider and J. Wilhelms. Hybrid anatomically based modeling of animals. In *Proc. of Computer Animation'98*, pages 161–169, June 1998.
10. J. Blinn. A generalization of algebraic surface drawing. *ACM Transactions on Graphics*, 1(3):235–256, July 1982.
11. J. Bloomenthal. Hand crafted. *Siggraph Course Notes 25*, 1993.
12. S. Yoshimito. Ballerinas generated by a personal computer. *The Journal of Visualization and Computer Animation*, 3:85–90, 1992.
13. F. Scheeppers, R. E. Parent, W. E. Carlson, and S. F. May. Anatomy-based modeling of the human musculature. *Computer Graphics (Pro. of SIGGRAPH'97)*, 31:163–172, August 1997.
14. J. Wilhelms and A. Van Gelder. Anatomically based modeling. *Computer Graphics (Proc. of SIGGRAPH'97)*, pages 173–180, 1997.
15. K. Komatsu. Human skin model capable of natural shape variation. *The Visual Computer*, 3(5):265–271, March 1988.
16. N. Magnenat-Thalmann and D. Thalmann. The direction of synthetic actors in the film rendez-vous à montréal. *IEEE Computer Graphics and Applications*, 7(12):9–19, 1987.
17. N. Magnenat-Thalmann, R. Laperriere, and D. Thalmann. Joint-dependent local deformations for hand animation and object grasping. In *Proc. of Graphics Interface'88*, pages 26–33, 1988.

18. D. Thalmann, J. Shen, and E. Chauvineau. Fast realistic human body deformations for animation and vr applications. In *Proc. of Computer Graphics International'96*, pages 166–174, June 1996.
19. J. Lander. Skin them bones: game programming for the web generation. *Game Developer Magazine*, pages 11–16, May 1998.
20. Xiaohuan Corina Wang and Cary Phillips. Multi-weight enveloping: least-squares approximation techniques for skin animation. In *Pro. of the 2002 ACM SIGGRAPH/Eurographics symposium on computer animation*, pages 129 – 138, July 2002.
21. Peter Sand, Leonard McMilla, and Jovan Popvić. Continuous capture of skin deformation. *ACM Transactions on Graphics*, 22(3):578–586, July 2003.
22. National Library of Medicine. The visible human project, *http://www.nlm.nih.gov/research/visible*.
23. Feng Dong, Gordon J. Clapworthy, Meleagros A. Krokos, and Jialiang Yao. An anatomy-based approach to human muscle modeling and deformation. *IEEE Transactions on visualization and computer graphics*, 8(2):154–170, April 2002.
24. Luciana Porcher Nedel and Daniel Thalmann. Anatomic modeling of deformable human bodies. *The Visual Computer*, 16:306–321, 2000.
25. Cyberware whole body color 3d scanner, *http://www.cyberware.com/products/wbinfo.html*.
26. Cyberware sample models on the web, *http://www.cyberware.com/samples/index.html*.
27. Michael Garland and Paul S. Heckbert. Surface simplification using quadric error metrics. In *SIGGRAPH 97 Conference Proceedings*, pages 209–216, August 1997.
28. William H. Press, Saul A. Teukolsky, William T. Vetterling, and Brian P. Flannery. *Numerical Recipes in C*. Cambridge University Press, 1992.
29. Tomas Möller and Ben Trumbore. Fast, minimum storage ray-triangle intersection. *Journal of Graphics Tools*, 2(1):21–28, 1997.
30. M. Fitzgibbon, A. W.and Pilu and R. B. Fisher. Direct least-squares fitting of ellipses. *IEEE Transactions on Pattern Analysis and Machine Intelligence*, 21(5):476–480, May 1999.
31. D. Baraff. Rigid body simulation. *Physically Based Modeling Course Notes 34, SIGGRAPH '95*, pages G1–G68, 1995.

Facial Expression Recognition Based on Two Dimensions Without Neutral Expressions

Young-Suk Shin[1] and Young Joon Ahn[2]

1 Department of Information and Communication Engineering, Chosun University,
Seosuk-dong, Dong-gu, Gwangju, 501-759, Republic of Korea
ysshin@mail.chosun.ac.kr
[2] Department of Mathematics Education, Chosun University, Seosuk-dong, Dong-gu,
Gwangju, 501-759, Republic of Korea
ahn@chosun.ac.kr

Abstract. We present a new approach for recognizing facial expressions based on two dimensions without detectable cues such as a neutral expression, which has essentially zero motion energy. To remove much of the variability due to lighting, a zero-phase whitening filter was applied. Principal component analysis(PCA) representation excluded the first one principal component as the features for facial expression recognition regardless of neutral expressions was developed. The result of facial expression recognition using a neural network model is compared with two-dimension values of internal states derived from ratings of facial expression pictures related to emotion by experimental subjects. The proposed algorithm demonstrated the ability to overcome the limitation of expression recognition based on a small number of discrete categories of emotional expressions, lighting sensitivity, and dependence on cues such as a neutral expression.

1 Introduction

Models for recognizing facial expressions have traditionally operated on a digitized facial image or a short digital video sequence of the facial expression being made, such as neutral, then happy, then neutral [1,2,3,4,5,6]. In general, recognition from video is more accurate than recognition from still image. Video captures well facial movements that deviate from a neutral expression. Therefore, many models for recognizing facial expressions are based on recognition from video, although there has also been work on recognition of facial expression using still images.

Most of the methods for recognizing facial expressions need reliably detectable cues such as a neutral expression, requiring it to be relatively uniform. All require the person's head to be easily found in the video. Therefore, continuous expression recognition such as a sequence of "happy, angry, surprise" was not handled well. And the expressions must either be manually separated, or interleaved with some reliably detectable cues such as a neutral expression.

Facial expression recognition models to date have treated emotions as discrete in the sense that they try to classify facial expressions into a small number of categories such as "happiness" or "surprise" [1,2,3,4,5,6,7,8]. The data in the experiments of the

F. Kishino et al. (Eds.): ICEC 2005, LNCS 3711, pp. 215–222, 2005.

models are "pure" in the sense that a user willingly or naturally tried to express exactly one emotion. There is no guarantee that the facial expression recognized as sad corresponds to any genuine affective state of sadness. A feeling of sadness can occur in both "lonely" and "grief". Categories may be fuzzy in the sense that an element can belong in more than one category at once. Therefore, discrete categories of emotions can be treated as regions in a continuous emotion space.

In this study, we present a new approach for recognizing facial expressions based on pleasure and arousal dimensions without detectable cues such as a neutral expression. In Section 2, we introduce the facial expressions in terms of two dimensions. In Section 3, firstly to remove much of the variability due to lighting, we apply a zero-phase whitening filter to the images. Secondly, we propose a principal component analysis(PCA) representation excluded the first one principle component as the features for facial expression recognition regardless of neutral expressions. In Section 4, we discuss the result of facial expression recognition using a NN model that is compared with pleasure and arousal dimension values of internal states derived from ratings of facial expression pictures related to emotion by experimental subjects.

2 Facial Expressions Based on Two Dimensions

Although emotional expression is highly varied, many theorists view its motivational basis as having a much simpler. There are two types in the previous studies of emotion model. They are the basic emotion model and the dimension model. So far, the studies of facial expression recognition have used six basic emotions developed by Paul Ekman and his colleagues [9]. The six basic emotions are happiness, surprise, fear, disgust, sadness, and anger. Their basic theory that links the facial expressions to these six categories. There is no guarantee that a user willingly or naturally tried to express exactly one emotion.

The dimension model explains that the emotion states are not independent one another and related to each other in a systematic way. This model was proposed by Russell [10], who argued that the dimension model can be applied to emotion recognition from facial expression [11]. The dimension model also has cultural universals and it was proved by Osgood, May & Morrison and Russell, Lewicka & Niit [12, 13].

In the Kim Younga et al. study [14], the dimension study about internal states through the semantic rating of emotion words which indicates two dimensions: pleasure(P)-displeasure(D), arousal(A)-sleep(S). The result of the dimension analysis of emotion word related internal states is shown in Figure1. The face images used for this research were a subset of the Korean facial expression database[15]. The data set contained 500 images, 3 females and 3 males, each image using 640 by 480 pixels. Examples of the original images are shown in figure 2.

Expressions were divided into two dimensions according to the study of internal states through the semantic analysis of words related with emotion by Kim Younga et al. using 83 expressive words. Each expressor of females and males posed 83 internal emotional state expressions when 83 words of emotion are presented. 51 experimental subjects rated pictures on the degrees of expression in each of the two dimensions on a nine-point scale. The images were labeled with a rating averaged over all subjects.

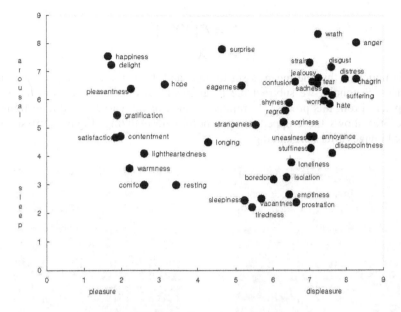

Fig. 1. The two dimensions of emotion

Fig. 2. Examples from the facial expression database containing 83 posed internal emotional state expressions

3   PCA Representations for Facial Expression Recognition

3.1   Preprocessing for Illumination-Invariance

The face images used for this research were centered the face images with coordinates for eye and mouth locations, and then cropped and scaled to 20x20 pixels. The luminance was normalized in two steps. First, a "sphering" step prior to principal component analysis is performed. The rows of the images were concatenated to produce 1×400 dimensional vectors. The row means are subtracted from the dataset, X. Then X is passed through the zero-phase whitening filter , V, which is the inverse square root of the covariance matrix:

$$V = E\{XX^T\}^{-\frac{1}{2}}$$

$$W = XV$$

(1)

This indicates that the mean is set to zero and the variances are equalized as unit variances. Secondly, we subtract the local mean gray-scale value from the sphered each patch. From this process, W removes much of the variability due to lightening. Figure 3(a) shows the cropped images before normalizing. Figure 3(b) shows the cropped images after normalizing.

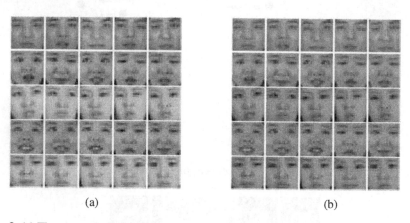

(a)   (b)

Fig. 3. (a) The cropped images before normalizing. (b) The cropped images after normalizing

3.2 Principal Component Analysis Representation

Some of the most successful algorithms for face recognition applied PCA representation are "eigen faces[16]" and "holons[17]". These methods are based on learning mechanisms that are sensitive to the correlations in the face images. PCA provides a dimensionality-reduced code that separates the correlations in the input.

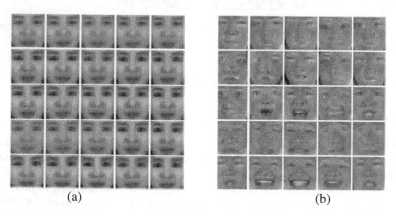

(a)   (b)

Fig. 4. (a) PCA representation only included the first 1 principle component (b) PCA representation excluded the first 1 principle component

In a task such as facial expression recognition, the first 1 or 2 principal components of PCA do not address the high-order dependencies of the facial expression images, that is to say, it just displays the neutral face. Figure 4(a) shows PCA representation that included the first 1 principle component. But selecting intermediate ranges of components that excluded the first 1 or 2 principle components of PCA did address well the changes in facial expression (Figure 4(b)).

Therefore, to extract information of facial expression regardless of neutral expression, we employed the 200 PCA coefficients, P_n, excluded the first 1 principle component of PCA of the face images. The principal component representation of the set of images in W in Equation(1) based on P_n is defined as $Y_n = W * P_n$. The approximation of W is obtained as:

$$\overline{W} = Y_n * P_n^T. \tag{2}$$

The columns of $\overline{W}$ contains the representational codes for the training images (Figure 4(b)). The representational code for the test images was found by $\overline{W}_{test} = Y_{test} * P_n^T$. Best performance for facial expression recognition was obtained using 200 principal components excluded the first 1 principle component.

4 Results

The system for facial expression recognition uses a three-layer neural network. The first layer contained the representational codes derived in Equation (2). The second layer was 30 hidden units and the third layer was two output nodes to recognize the two dimensions: Pleasure-Displeasure and Arousal-Sleep.

Training applies an error back propagation algorithm. The activation function of hidden units uses the sigmoid function. 500 images for training and 66 images excluded from the training set for testing are used. The 66 images for test include 11 expression images of each six people. The first test verifies with the 500 images trained already. Recognition result produced by 500 images trained previously showed 100% recognition rates. The rating result of facial expressions derived from 9 point scale on two dimension for degrees of expression by subjects was compared with experimental results of a neural network(NN). The dimension values of human and NN in each of the two dimensions are given as vectors of $\overline{H}$ and $\overline{N}$. The similarity of recognition result between human and NN was obtained as:

$$S(\overrightarrow{H}, \overrightarrow{N}) = \frac{\overline{H \cdot N}}{\|\overrightarrow{H}\| \|\overrightarrow{N}\|} \min(\frac{\|\overrightarrow{H}\|}{\|\overrightarrow{N}\|}, \frac{\|\overrightarrow{N}\|}{\|\overrightarrow{H}\|}) \tag{3}$$

Table 1 describes a degree of similarity of expression recognition between human and NN on the continuous two-dimensions of emotion and indicates a part of all. The result of expression recognition of NN appears very similar to the result of expression recognition of human. In Table 1, the result of expression recognition of

Table 1. The result data of expression recognition between human and NN derived from two people (Abbreviation: P-D,pleasure-displeasure;A-S,arousal-sleep;)

Named emotional word of Pictures(person)	Human		Neural Network		Recognition on Neural Network	Similarity
	P – D	A – S	P –D	A – S		
depression(a)	6.23	4.43	5.22	4.41	boredom	0.89
crying(a)	6.47	4.10	6.16	5.19	sorry	0.94
gloomy(a)	7.37	5.53	7.53	6.84	strain	0.90
strange(a)	6.17	5.17	5.72	4.44	envy	0.89
proud(a)	3.07	4.47	1.69	4.54	satisfaction	0.86
confident(a)	3.47	4.57	2.90	5.35	grateful	0.93
despair(a)	6.23	5.97	5.35	5.08	strangeness	0.85
sleepiness(a)	5.00	1.80	3.13	2.96	resting	0.74
likable(a)	1.97	4.23	1.42	3.96	warmness	0.89
delight(a)	1.17	4.20	3.41	5.87	pleasantness	0.62
boredom(a)	6.77	5.50	5.05	5.65	strangeness	0.85
pleasantness (b)	1.40	5.47	3.12	4.35	contentment	0.88
depression (b)	6.00	4.23	7.10	4.28	stuffiness	0.88
crying(b)	7.13	6.17	7.46	7.07	displeasure	0.91
gloomy(b)	5.90	3.67	6.93	5.73	sadness	0.76
strangeness(b)	6.13	6.47	5.70	3.18	boredom	0.69
proud(b)	2.97	5.17	4.56	2.31	sleepiness	0.71
confident(b)	2.90	4.07	2.63	3.60	satisfaction	0.89
despair(b)	7.80	5.67	7.19	5.61	sadness	0.94
sleepiness(b)	6.00	1.93	6.34	3.07	emptiness	0.88
likable(b)	2.07	4.27	3.52	5.12	longing	0.75
delight(b)	1.70	5.70	1.79	4.92	contentment	0.87

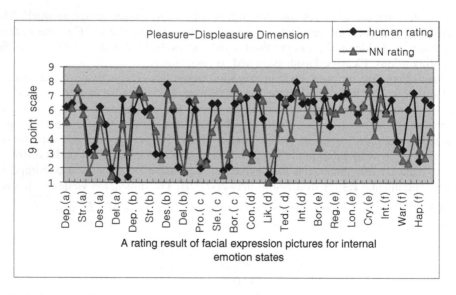

Fig. 5. A rating result of facial expression recognition in Pleasure-Displeasure dimension (Abbreviation: Dep.,depression; Str.,strangeness;Des.,despair;Del.,delight;Pro.,proud; Sle., sleepiness; Bor.,boredom; Con., confusion; Lik., likable; Ted., tedious; Int., intricacy; Reg., regret; Lon., loneliness; Cry., crying; War., warmness; Hap.,happiness.)

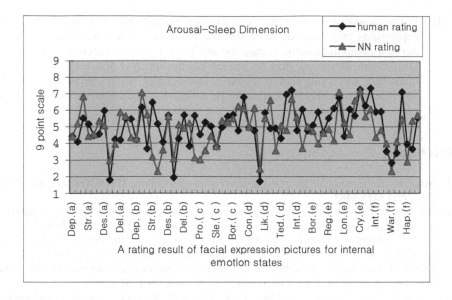

Fig. 6. A rating result of facial expression recognition in Arousal-Sleep dimension

NN was matched to the nearest emotion word within 83 emotion words related to internal emotion states. Figure 5 and 6 show the correlation of the expression recognition between human and NN in each of the two dimensions.

The statistical significance of the similarity for expression recognition between human and NN on each of the two dimensions was tested by Person correlation analysis. The correlation in the Pleasure-Displeasure dimension between human and NN showed 0.77 at the 0.01 level and 0.51 at the 0.01 level in the Arousal-Sleep dimension.

Our results allowed us to extend the range of emotion recognition and to recognize on the continuous two dimensions of emotion with illumination-invariance without detectable cues such as a neutral expression. The result of expression recognition between human and NN on the continuous two-dimensional structure of emotion showed four significant conclusions.

(1) The two-dimensional structure of emotion in the facial expression recognition appears as a stabled structure for the facial expression recognition. The correlation results of each dimension through Person correlation analysis were significant over 0.5 at the 0.01 level.

(2) Pleasure-Displeasure dimension is analyzed as a more stable dimension than Arousal-Sleep dimension. Pleasure-Displeasure dimension was significant 0.77 at the 0.01 level, while Arousal-Sleep dimension was significant 0.51 at the 0.01 level. This result corresponds to a research for validating the stability of two-dimensional structure of emotion about emotion word[18].

(3) When the whole face was presented, facial expressions were successfully recognized. This fact was reflected by PCA representation excluded the first 1 principle component. This finding suggests that holistic analysis is important for facial expression recognition.

(4) We propose that the inference of emotional states within a subject from facial expressions may depends more on the Pleasure-Displeasure dimension than Arousal-Sleep dimension. It may be analyzed that the perception of Pleasure-Displeasure dimension may be needed for the survival of the species and the immediate and appropriate response to emotionally salient, while the Arousal-Sleep dimension may be needed for relatively detailed cognitive ability for the personal internal states.

References

1. Mase, K.: Recognition of facial expression from optical flow. IEICE Transactions, E 74, 10 (1991) 3473-3483
2. Yacoob, Y., Davis, L.S.: Recognizing human facial expression from long image sequences using optical flow. IEEE Trans. Pattern Anal. Machine Intell. 18(6) (1996) 636-642
3. Lien, J.: Automatic recognition of facial expressions using hidden Markov models and estimation of expression intensity. Ph.D. Thesis, Carnegie Mellon University, (1998)
4. Oliver, N. Pentland, A., Berard, F.: LAFTER:a real-time face and lips tracker with facial expression recognition. Pattern Recognition 33 (2000) 1369-1382
5. Cohen, I., Sebe, N., Garg, A., Chen, L. S., Huang, T. S.: Facial expression recognition from video sequence. Proc. Int'l Conf. Multimedia and Exp(ICME) (2002) 121-124
6. Cohen, I. :Semisupervised learning of classifiers with application to human-computer interaction. PhD thesis, Univ. of Illinois at Urbana-Champaign (2003)
7. Bartlett, M., Viola, P., Sejnowski, T., Larsen, J., Hager, J., Ekman, P.: Classfying Facial Action. In: Advances in Neural Information Processing Systems 8. D. Touretzky et al. editors, MIT Press, Cambridge, MA (1996)
8. Essa, I., Pentland, A.:Coding, analysis, interpretation, and recognition of facial expressions. IEEE Transactions on Pattern Analysis and Machine Intelligence, 19 (1997) 757-763
9. Ekman, P., Friesen, W.V.: Facial action coding system. Consulting Psychologists, Palo Alto, CA., (1977)
10. Russell, J. A.: Evidence of convergent validity on the dimension of affect. Journal of Personality and Social Psychology, 30, (1978) 1152-1168
11. Russell, J. A. :Culture and categorization of emotion. Psychological Bulletin, 110, (1991) 426-450
12. Osgood, C. E., May, W.H. and Miron, M.S.: Cross-curtral universals of affective meaning. Urbana:University of Illinoise Press, (1975)
13. Russell, J. A., Lewicka, M. and Nitt, T.: A cross-cultural study of a circumplex model of affect. Journal of Personality and Social Psychology, 57, (1989) 848-856
14. Younga, K., Jinkwan, K., Sukyung, P., Kyungja, O., Chansub, C.: The study of dimension of internal states through word analysis about emotion. Korean Journal of the Science of Emotion and Sensibility, 1 (1998) 145-152
15. Saebum, B., Jaehyun, H., Chansub, C.: Facial expression database for mapping facial expression onto internal state. '97 Emotion Conference of Korea, (1997) 215-219
16. Turk, M, Pentland, A. : Eigenfaces for recognition. Journal of Cognitive Neuroscience 3(1) (1991) 71-86
17. Cottrell, G., Metcalfe, J.: Face, gender and emotion recognition using holons. In Touretzky, D., editor, Advances in Neural information processing systems (3) San Maleo, CA. Morgan aufmann (1991) 564-571
18. Jinkwan, K., Hyesshin, M., Kyungja, O.: Validating the stability of two-dimensional structure of emotion. Korean Journal of the Science of Emotion and Sensibility, 2(1) (1999) 43-52

Subjective Age Estimation System Using Facial Images

Naoyuki Miyamoto[1], Yumi Jinnouchi[1], Noriko Nagata[1], and Seiji Inokuchi[2]

[1] School of Science and Technology, Kwansei Gakuin University,
2-1 Gakuen, Sanda, Hyogo 669-1337, Japan
nagata@ksc.kwansei.ac.jp
http://ist.ksc.kwansei.ac.jp/~nagata/
[2] Faculty of Media Contents, Takarazuka University of Art and Design,
7-27, Hanayashiki-tsutsujigaoka, Takarazuka 665-0803, Japan
inokuchi@ieee.org

Abstract. We propose a relative estimation method for subjective age, imaged by ourselves, using peoples' facial images and their chronological (real) age. We experimented with a rating scale for facial images which stimulated subjects. The subject evaluated an image as looking older than themselves with a range of responses. Finding an approximation curve of this range, the zero crossing point in the approximation curve is defined as the subjective age. The experimental result shows that the subjective age tends to be found in negative direction (tendency to estimate oneself as younger than actual). Besides, there are other trends between gender, between age groups, and between the different expressions such as ordinary and smiling.

1 Introduction

Humans can estimate their age and gender by their experience of facial color and part of the facial features of their companions. The automated estimation of age and gender is an important factor in the study of the recognition of faces and facial expressions, however, it is difficult for this to reach the level of human estimation [1].

On the other hand, we often find ourselves being much more humble than needed, after finding a companionfs actual age. Then, we often say; "I thought he was much older than me!" It can be said that we didn't estimate his age wrongly, but that we saw ourselves as younger, or older, than we really are.

Seeing our age like this is called our subjective age. In this paper, we propose a relative estimation method for subjective age, using people's facial images and their chronological age. This can be developed to further studies, such as the range of the subjective age, or, finding the cause of misunderstanding our subjective age and the chronological age, according to the generation and gender. There has been research of finding one's imaged subjective age on the basis of a questionnaire [2]. however according to the search so far conducted, we did not find any researches using facial images. In this paper, we present three

F. Kishino et al. (Eds.): ICEC 2005, LNCS 3711, pp. 223–229, 2005.

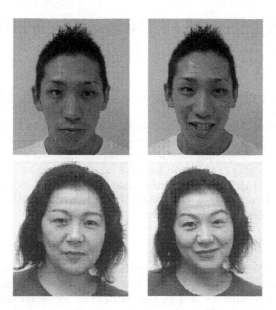

Fig. 1. Examples of the facial images in this database

points; the construction of a database of facial images which is the foundation of this research, a proposal for the definition of subjective age and the estimation method, and the result of research.

2   Facial Image Database

There are total 20 classes from 20 years old to 70 years old for each gender in this database. At this moment, each class has 10 people, and a total of 400 facial images have been recorded, which include two different expressions (ordinary and smiling) for each person. Figure 1 shows examples of the facial images. Facial images are saved as high-resolution digital images by film scanning.

3   Experiment of Subjective Age Estimation

3.1   Rating Experiment

We choose facial images for both male and female subjects who were of different age and gender groups, from the same age class as the subject, and the next younger and older classes. The total number of facial images used was 60, composed of (5 images/class) *3 classes *2 genders (the same and the opposite genders) *2 expressions (ordinary and smiling) as shown in Figure 2.

Next, we experimented with a rating scale for these facial images which stimulate the subjects. The subjects were shown facial images at random, and they evaluated if it looked older or younger than themselves. The evaluation had

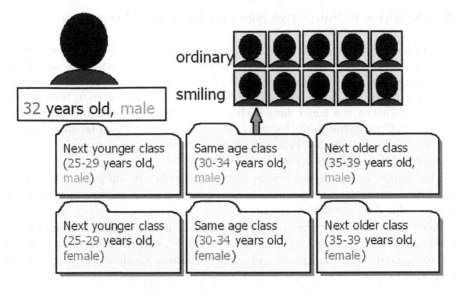

Fig. 2. How facial images were chosen

Fig. 3. An example of the choosing screen of the subjective age estimation system

5 ranks; "Definitely older than myself (2)", "Probably older than myself (1)", "Not able to estimate (0)", "Probably younger than myself (-1)" and "Definitely younger than myself (-2)". The reason for adopting a range of responses was not to estimate the chronological ages of the facial images, but to seek their relative position to others. Figure 3 shows an example of the chooser screen of the subjective age estimation system.

3.2   Definition of Subjective Age and Method of Estimation

To quantify the result of the estimation, we plotted the results in a two-dimensional plane with the x-axis being the relative age (the chronological age of the facial image minus the chronological age of the subject) and the y-axis was the estimation result, as shown in Figure4. The x-axis is from −9 to 9, because the subjects evaluated the facial data with a 9 year difference as a maximum (For example, in Case A the subject was 34 years old, he was shown facial data from 3 classes; 25-29 class, 30-34 class and 35-39 class). Thus, the data with the range of upper-right direction was obtained.

This range shows the subjective age of the group of subjects. Finding an approximation curve of this range, the zero crossing point in the approximation curve is defined as the subjective age [3].

Since we assume the curve to have a sigmoid function (nonlinear, continuous, monotone increasing function), here we adopt a logistics function [4], which is a kind of sigmoid function. Then a logit transformation to allow linearization can be applied as:

$$Y = \ln\left(\frac{y}{1-y}\right) \tag{1}$$

This results in the problem of the linear approximation of the transformed data. That is to say, the zero crossing point in the approximation line can be defined as the shift of the subjective age. The subjective age is considered to give us a kind of standard of the relative position (age) for a companion or in a group.

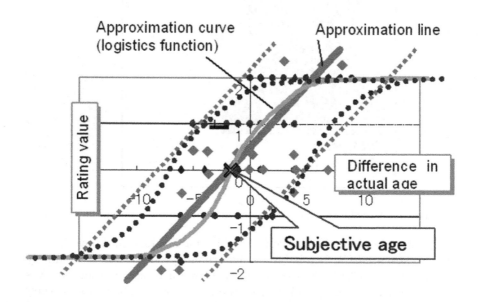

Fig. 4. Method of estimating subjective age

3.3   Results of Research

According to the above method, we treated the results obtained from research by showing ordinary and smiling facial expressions to a total of 73 male and female subjects who were between 25 and 53 years old. The zero crossing point of the approximation line of the entire data set after applying the logit transformation was found at -1.85 from the formula; $y = 0.549x + 1.0171$. This is the shift of the subjective age of the subjects group from this research.

For comparison, three cases were adopted: the effect of gender, the effect for expression and the effect of age.

First, Figure 5 gives the shift of the subjective ages of the male and the female subjects. Male subjects showed an unexpectedly lower (younger) value of -2.27, as compared with a value of -1.42 in the female subjects.

Next, Figure 6 gives the shift of the subjective ages by expression. The subjective ages for smiling expressions show higher values than those for ordinary expressions for subjects of both genders. This means that smiling expressions look younger than ordinary expressions. It is supposed that the reason why this is that cheerful is replaced by youth. It can also be thought that the psychological distance gets shorter by smiling expressions.

Furthermore, Figure 7 shows the shift of the subjective ages between age groups. The results indicate that the older the subjects are, the nearer the subjective ages get to the real ages. In other words, the more the subjects view themselves objectively. It can be explained that they rise in higher social rank and acquire their confidence with age.

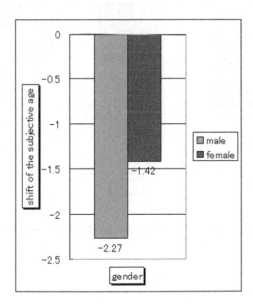

Fig. 5. Shift of the subjective age by gender

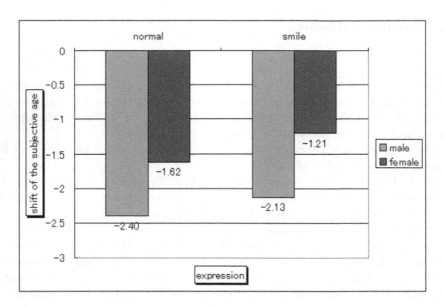

Fig. 6. Shift of the subjective age by expression

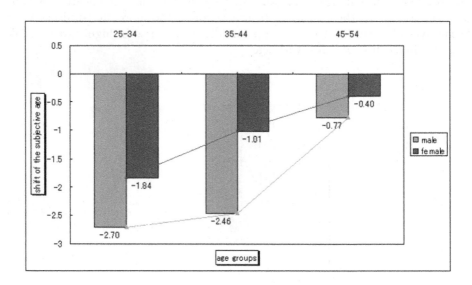

Fig. 7. Shift of the subjective age between age groups

3.4   Discussion

As a tendency, the subjective age was generally found to be in the negative
direction (tendency to estimate younger than actual).

Although we see our own faces everyday, there is no opportunity to evaluate our face relative to others. So, we tend to see a past record, such as a photograph, as being the same as we look now. For instance, everybody has had the experience of being sneered at after sending in an old photograph, in which we see little change, when submitting our picture for official purposes. It is presumed that this tendency comes from a kind of conviction that we never get old.

In addition, there are other interesting trends between the gender and between the age group. Also, there are different tendencies between the different expressions of ordinary and smiling. These may be related to various factors such as psychological, physiological and social factors.

In the future, we will carry out further research of the different tendencies based on age and gender, facial expressions, texture of skin, makeup, and on occupation, and with more images and subjects.

In addition, we are now considering the possibility of collecting the examination data through a public website. We believe this will be possible if the issue of the rights to the portraits can be settled. On the other hand, by the method with 'average facial image' [1], we can stimulate subjects with "average facial images of 25 years old male or 42 years old female", so that we can prevent the unevenness of the stimulation. Furthermore, there would be no problem of the rights to the portraits.

4   Conclusions

As a foundation into the research of subjective age with facial images, we have built up a facial image database, and have introduced of a definition of subjective age and an estimation method. The results of the research are presented here.

In the future, we will further examine the estimation method of subjective age. In addition, we are planning to examine objective age (appearance age judged by others).

References

[1] Hayashi Junichiro., Yasumoto Mamoru., I.H., Hiroyasu., K.: Age and Gender Estimation and Modeling by Means of Facial Image Processing. In N. Baba, L.C.J., Howlett, R.J., eds.: Knowledge-Based Intelligent Information Engineering Systems & Allied Technologies : KES'2001 , Part2. (2001) 1128–1136

[2] Sato, S., S.Y.N.K., Kawaai, C.: A Life-Span Developmental Study of Age Identity: Cohort and Gender Differences. In: The Japanese J. Developmental Psychology. Volume 8. (1997) 88–97

[3] Nagata, N., Inokuchi, S.: Subjective age obtained from facial images -How old we feel compared to others ? In V. Palade, R.J.H., Jain, L., eds.: Knowledge-Based Intelligent Information and Engineering Systems Part2, Lecture Notes in Artificial Intelligence 2774, Springer-Verlag. (2003) 877–991

[4] Dillon, W., Goldstein, M.: Multivariate Analysis. John Wiley & Sons (1984)

A Video Based Personalized Face Model Generation Approach for Network 3D Games

Xiangyong Zeng, Jian Yao, Mandun Zhang, and Yangsheng Wang

Institute of Automation, Chinese Academy of Sciences,
100080, Beijing, P.R. China
{xyzeng, wys}@mail.pattek.com.cn

Abstract. We have developed a fast generation system for personalized 3D face model and plan to apply it in network 3D games. This system uses one video camera to capture player's frontal face image for 3D modeling and dose not need calibration and plentiful manual tuning. The 3D face model in games is represented by a 3D geometry mesh and a 2D texture image. The personalized geometry mesh is obtained by deforming an original mesh with the relative positions of the player's facial features, which are automatically detected from the frontal image. The relevant texture image is also obtained from the same image. In order to save storage space and network bandwidth, only the feature data and texture data from each player are sent to the game server and then to other clients. Finally, players can see their own faces in multiplayer games.

1 Introduction

The use of personalized 3D face models is a highly desired feature in today's computer games, multimedia titles, medicine, etc. One of the most noticeable trends is the boom toward photorealistic looking and true-life feeling network 3D games, the players want to see their own face on the body of their character. The 3D model of a game character's face is generally composed of a 3D triangular mesh, referred to as the geometry mesh, and an associated composite image of the character's face, referred to as the texture image.

According to MPEG-4 standard [1], which represents the geometry, texture, and animation properties of a 3D face model, the modeling methods for generating a 3-D face model can be generally classified as those that involve: (1) a fully manual approach, (2) a semi-automatic approach and (3) a fully-automatic approach. Fully manual approaches are labor intensive and time consuming, in which every triangular patch of the 3D mesh has to be manually mapped onto the image of the face according to the facial features.

In this paper, we propose an easy-to-use and cost-effective semi-automatic approach for generating the 3D face model for ordinary game player, with a common video camera. In the remainder of this paper, we review and compare the related work in section 2. Section 3 provides an executive summary of our system. Section 4 describes our technique for extracting facial feature points from video image. Section 5 describes deformation algorithm and texture generation.

F. Kishino et al. (Eds.): ICEC 2005, LNCS 3711, pp. 230–238, 2005.
© IFIP International Federation for Information Processing 2005

A practical scheme for applying our system in network 3D game is described in Section 6. Finally, we give the summary and discussion in Section 7.

2 Related Work

Fully automatic facial modeling approaches drastically reduce the time required to map a texture onto a 3D mesh. However, while hardware based fully automatic approaches [2][3] are too costly to ordinary user, software based fully automatic approaches [4][5] are very sensitive to the image data and thus may not consistently produce accurate 3D face models. In addition to a 3D face mesh, a composite image that contains facial image data captured from various views also needs to be constructed.

Semi-automatic facial modeling approaches [6][7][8] rely on automatically detecting or manually marking certain features on the face image, such as eyes, nose, and mouth, and initialize the 3D mesh by a global affine warping of a standard 3D mesh based on the location of the detected facial features. However, a global affine transformation generally does not match all local facial features. Thus, the locations of the nodes are fine-tuned in a manual process for each person. Zhang et al. [6] developed a system of reconstructing faces from video sequences with an uncalibrated camera. They extract 3D information from one stereo pair, and then deform a generic face model. Camera poses are computed for the rest of the sequence, and used to generate a cylindrical texture. With model-based bundle adjustment, they can generate highly realistic face models, but they need a long time (about 6 to 8 minutes on a 850MHz Pentium III machine), which is totally unacceptable for ordinary users.

Our work is mainly inspired by the idea that, conveniently and rapidly generating personalized character face in 3D games for the ordinary player. Only in this way the personalized characters can be really popularized in 3D game. Another fact is that player is't very nit-picking to the accuracy of reconstructed face model, if the effect is good enough. So, we use only one single video image captured by one common webcam to generate personalized face model. Comparing with other similar approaches, our facial feature detection and model deformation methods are more simple and quick, which can accomplish the task within one minute on a current standard PC with minimal manual operation.

3 System Overview

Firstly, the 2D positions (x- and y-coordinates) of feature points from one frontal face image, captured by the camera, are automatically detected by an improved active shape models (ASM) method [9]. With optional manual operation, these feature points can be fine tuned. Secondly, they are devoted to deform an original game character face mesh with corresponding feature points using an interpolating function based on Radial Basis Functions (RBF) [13]. The z-coordinates of the personalized facial feature points are directly derived from the original mesh,

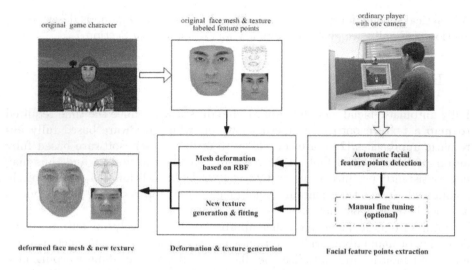

Fig. 1. System overview

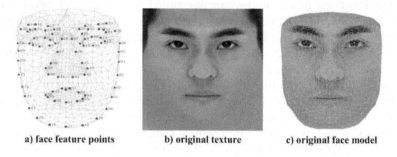

a) face feature points   b) original texture   c) original face model

Fig. 2. An original facial model labeled feature points

because we only use one single frontal face image. We also propose a simpler technique for generating the texture image by segmenting the elliptical face area from the same image. To generate personalized characters for network 3D games, a practical scheme is also presented. Figure 1 outlines the overview of our system.

The number of triangular nodes and patches in most facial models in network 3D games both could range from several hundreds to several thousands. In this paper, we label 79 feature points on original face model according to MPEG-4 standard, as illustrated in Figure 2. Figure 2 shows an original facial model with a mesh made of 640 nodes and 1430 patches, and a texture(256x256 pixels).

4   Facial Feature Points Extraction

We used an improved ASM method to automatically detect human face in every video frame and locate the 79 feature points in real-time, as shown in Figure 2.

The detected feature points are painted on the same frame image to allow the user consider whether the detected results are suitable or not. By turning head or adjusting camera slightly, the user can get better detected results before pause the auto-detection process. Then, a manual fine tuning step is offered to the user, by dragging painted feature point to new position. This step is optional, and the user can perform it or just skip it.

4.1 Automatic Feature Points Detection

We propose a novel face alignment algorithm, in which local appearance models of facial feature (key) points are constructed using statistical learning. The ambiguity between the truth position and its neighbors requires that the local likelihood model should be able to correctly rank the likelihood of these ambiguous positions.

We adopt RealBoost [10] to learn the ranking prior likelihood models that not only characterize the local features of a ground truth position, but also preserve the likelihood ranking order between the ground truth position and its neighbors. Instead of using principle components analysis (PCA) and one pixel Gabor coefficients, we use Gabor features [11] of key point and its neighbors, which provide rich information to model local structures of a face, to construct "weak" ranking evaluation function set. RealBoost is adopted to solving the following three fundamental problems in one boosting procedure: (1) learning effective features from a large feature set, (2) constructing weak classifiers each of which is based on one of the selected features, and (3) boosting the weak classifiers into a stronger classifier. More details could refer Huang's paper [12].

4.2 Manual Fine Tuning(Optional)

By dragging painted feature points in face image to new positions using mouse, the user can get more accurate location results of feature points. The feature point locations after manual fine-tuning are shown in Figure 4.

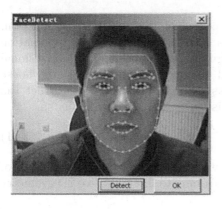 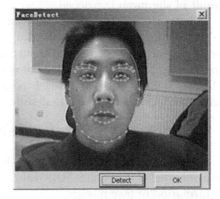

Fig. 3. Results of auto-detecting facial feature points

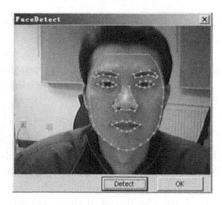 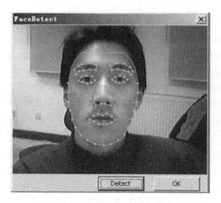

Fig. 4. Results of facial feature points extraction after manual fine tuning

5   Deformation and Texture Mapping

Given the feature points obtained above, deforming the original face mesh with corresponding feature points is straightforward. At the same time, new texture image is generated from the same face image. After texture mapping, the final personalized face model is generated.

5.1   Deformation

The facial mesh adjustment is a problem about 3D space deformation in fact (In this paper, we only have 2D positions of control points and the z-coordinates for the destination are derived directly from the original mesh). We identify limited control points on it and compute their displacements, then choose an interpolation function which accommodates displacements of control points. Positions of the other nodes are transformed upon the function. At last the final deformation result of the mesh is reached.

There are several choices for how to construct the interpolating function. We use a method based on Radial Basis Functions (RBF) as approximation functions for their power to deal with irregular sets of data in multi-dimensional space in approximating high dimensional smooth surface [13][14]. We choose 2D coordinates of original mesh nodes as embedding space to construct the interpolation function $f(p)$ that suffices displacements of control points:

$$u_i = f(p_i)(0 \leq i \leq N - 1) \tag{1}$$

Where u_i are displacements of all control points and N is the number of feature points. We exploit RBF volume morphing to directly drive 2D geometry deformation of face models.

$$f(p_i) = \sum c_i \Phi(\|p_j - p_i\|)(0 \leq j, i \leq N - 1) \tag{2}$$

Where $\Phi(\|p_j - p_i\|)$ are RBF and the coefficients c_i are the vector coefficients of control points. We compute equation 2 and get the vector coefficient c_i of every control point. Displacements of other non-feature points may be computed in the form:

$$u = \sum c_i \Phi(\|p - p_i\|)(0 \leq j, i \leq N - 1) \qquad (3)$$

In this paper, we have chosen to use $\Phi(\|p - p_i\|) = e^{-\|p - p_i\|/64}$.

5.2   Texture Generation

The new texture image is generated by the following two steps: 1) segmenting an elliptical face area from the frontal face image according to the feature point positions; 2) scaling and merging it into a background image including side face information from the original texture. The feature points in the frontal face image compose an approximate elliptical contour, which can be used to segment the actual face area from the whole image. In this paper, we assume that the new texture and original texture has the same size. The segmented area must be scaled to a proper size, because the actual face area maybe has different size in different video frame.

In addition, we must merge the scaled face image into a background image, which includes synthetical side face texture, because we only have the frontal face information. In practice, the side face information in the background image is copied from the original texture. With smooth template operation, the face contour becomes enough blurring. The result of blended texture is shown in Figure 5.

5.3   Texture Fitting

The size of the image is $w \times h$. The maximum x value (x_{max}) is 86.x and the minimum x value (x_{min}) is 68.x, where . The maximum y value $y_{max} =$ YSCALE $\times$ 18.y and the minimum y value (y_{min}) is 77.y, where YSCALE is a scaling parameter. The 3D coordinates of every point are x, y and z. We mark texture coordinates of every point with x_{tex} and y_{tex}. The left and down corner

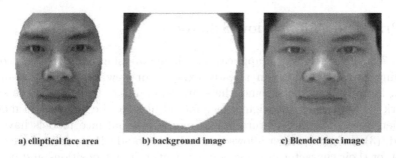

a) elliptical face area   b) background image   c) Blended face image

Fig. 5. Texture generation

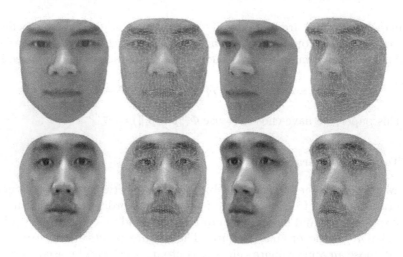

Fig. 6. Results of personalized face models

of frontal face image is (x_t, y_t). According to linear interpolation method, if one point is projected into the front, the texture coordinates of every point are:

$$x_{tex} = x_t/w + (x - x_{min})/(x_{max} - x_{min}) \qquad (4)$$

$$y_{tex} = y_t/h + (y - y_{min})/(y_{max} - y_{min}) \qquad (5)$$

As for texture coordinates of left and right sides of face, we assign area near the frontal face image. They can be derived from the similar method as above.

5.4   Results

On a current standard PC, for example, a 2.2GHz Pentium IV machine, our system can generate a personalized face model in no more than one minute. Some of this time is spent on manual operation. Several detailed personalized face models in different views are shown in Figure 6 where input frontal face images are shown in Figure 4. They have proper shape and texture.

6   Practical Application Scheme

Figure 7 outlines a practical application scheme of using our Personalized Face Modeling System (PFMS) in already existing or new designing network 3D games. For applying the scheme, there are three basic demands to the special network 3D game: (1) the original face model files can be parsed and modified expediently, (2) the face feature points of the original face models have been labeled, (3) the game server allows game clients to add Personalized Face Data (PFD) for their character in game, namely feature point positions and new texture image in this paper.

Firstly, the game host or server will confirm whether has already existed it's PFD in game DB server, when a game client logs on the game world. If existed, this client can choose to download it from DB server or update it again by starting PFMS. The PFD, downloaded or newly generated by PFMS is used to construct the Personalized Face Model (PFM) in game clients. In the case of starting PFMS, while mesh deforming and texture mapping, the generated PFD is been upload to DB server for next time use. Instead of generated PFM, only feature and texture data from each player are sent to the game server and then to other clients, in order to save storage space and transmission bandwidth of network 3D games. Finally, players can see their own faces in multiplayer games.

A simple 3D game demo developed by us, named **ChangeFace**, can give an intuitionistic impression of our PFMS. The video and executable program can be found at our group's website

    http://hci.ia.ac.cn/JointLab/onlinegame-En.htm

the new version of this demo fully applying this scheme will be coming soon.

7   Summary and Discussion

We have developed a system to generate personalized facial model from only one single video image based on facial feature auto-detection. With a few simple clicks for fine tuning by the user, our system quickly generates a person's face model. The experiment results show that it's a simple, easy-to-use and economic approach for end-user at home with a common video camera. These face models can be used, for example, as personalized characters in video games, net meeting, virtual conference, etc. The practical application scheme of the system for network 3D games has given a typical way to achieve these goals.

More accurate facial feature detection and alignment algorithms are need for obtaining reliable auto-extraction results and reducing the sequent manual adjustment, since there are always exist some unfavoured factors, such as lower quality cameras, hostile lighting conditions, as well as people of different races,

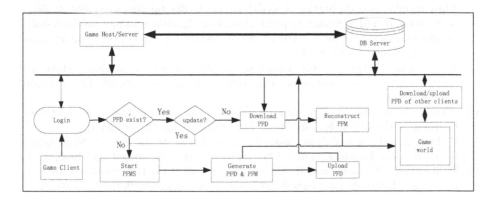

Fig. 7. A practical application scheme of our system

of different ages, usually have different face shapes and skin colors. We are investigating techniques to improve the alignment algorithm by using more learning samples and solving some lighting problems.

The current character face mesh in most 3D games is relative sparse, our system can work very well in very short time. Considering the future's game applications with higher mesh resolution and details, our system should pay more attention to generate more fine face model, and add some new functions, for example, expression-driven facial animation.

References

1. Abrantes, G. A. and Pereira, F.: MPEG-4 Facial Animation Technology: Survey, Implementation, and Results. IEEE Trans. on Circuits and Systems for Video Technology, vol.9, no.2 (1999) 290–305
2. Sun, W., Hilton, A., Smith, R. and Illingworth, J.: Building Layered Animation Models from Captured Data. Eurographics Workshop on Computer Animation (1999) 145–154
3. Hilton, A. and Inningworth J.: Geometric Fusion for a Hand-held 3-D Sensor. Machine Vision Applications, vol.12, no.1 (2000) 44–51
4. Parke, F. I. And Waters, K.: Computer Facial Animation. A.K. Peters, Wellesley (1996)
5. Akimoto, T., Suenaga, Y. and Wallace, R.S.: Automatic Creation of 3-D Facial Models. IEEE Computer Graphics & App (1993) 16–22
6. Z.Liu, Z. Zhang, C.Jacobs, M.Cohen: Rapid modeling of animated faces from video. Journal of Visualization and Computer Animation. 12(4) (2001) 227–240
7. Lavagetto, Fabio and Pockaj, Roberto: The Facial Animation Engine: Toward A High-Level Interface for the Design of MPEG-4 Compliant Animated Faces. IEEE Transactions on Circuits and Systems for Video Technology, vol.9, no.2 (1999) 277–289
8. Escher, M. and Thalmann, N. M.: Automatic 3-D Cloning and Real-Time Animation of a Human Face. Proceedings of Computer Animation, Geneva, Switzerland (1997)
9. T. F. Cootes, C. J. Taylor, D. H. Cooper, and J. Graham: Active shape models: Their training and application. CVGIP: Image Understanding 61 (1995) 38–59
10. R. E. Schapire and Y. Singer: Improved boosting algorithms using confidence-rated predictions. In Proceedings of the Eleventh Annual Conference on Computational Learning Theory (1998) 80–91
11. J. Friedman, T. Hastie, and R. Tibshirani: Additive logistic regression: a statistical view of boosting. Technical report, Department of Statistics, Sequoia Hall, Stanford Univerity (1998)
12. Huang Xiangsheng, Xu Bin, Wang Yangsheng: Shape Localization by Statistical Learning in the Gabor Feature Space. ICSP04, Beijing, China (2004)
13. F. Pighin, J. Hecker, D. Lischinski, R. Szeliski, and D. H. Salesin: Synthesizing Realistic Facial Expressions from Photographs. Siggraph proceedings (1998) 75–84
14. D. Ruprecht, R. Nagel, and H. Mller: Spatial Free-Form Deformation with Scattered Data Interpolation Methods. Computers & Graphics 19(1) (1995) 63–71

Live Feeling on Movement of an Autonomous Robot Using a Biological Signal

Shigeru Sakurazawa, Keisuke Yanagihara, Yasuo Tsukahara,
and Hitoshi Matsubara

Future University-Hakodate, System Information Science,
116-2 Kamedanakano Hakodate Hokkaido 041-8655, Japan
{sakura, c1101078, yasuo, matsubar}@fun.ac.jp
http://www.fun.ac.jp/

Abstract. Using Khepera Simulator software, we developed an autonomous robot with a simple neural network by applying the skin conductance response of an observer who was watching the movement of the agent. First, we found that the signals were generated when the observer felt that the robot faced a crucial phase, such as hitting a wall. Therefore, we used the signals as errors that were back-propagated to the network in the robot. By questionnaires completed by the observer, the movement of this robot was compared with the movement of two other kinds of robots. In these other two robots, random signals or switch signals, which were turned on at the robot's crucial phase, were used as errors instead of the skin conductance responses. From the results, we found that the movement of the robot with biological signals was most similar to the movement of something alive in the three kinds of robots. It is thought that applications of biological signals can promote natural interactions between humans and machines.

1 Introduction

Recently, Nakatsu noted the relation between entertainment and communication [1]. He pointed out that the elements of the "sharing of experiences," "physical experience and physiological experience" and "active immersion and passive immersion" are the commonality between entertainment and communication.

The effect of appearance and behavior on communication between a human and humanoid robot has also been studied [2, 3]. Minato et al. and Ono point out that the degree of intimacy to make natural communication is strongly affected by appearance and behavior, especially if a mutual entrained gesture and joint viewpoint is to be obtained by the relationship. As these facts make clear, the degree of intimacy depends on the contexts and their synchronization between two agents.

Khepera is an autonomous robot which moves depending on a sensor that measures its local environment. Since the structure of Khepera is much simpler than humanoid robots, it is hard to increase the degree of intimacy with this robot. However, we think that we can increase the intimacy with this robot if we take the contexts and their synchronization into the man-machine interface.

F. Kishino et al. (Eds.): ICEC 2005, LNCS 3711, pp. 239–247, 2005.
© IFIP International Federation for Information Processing 2005

On the other hand, we have developed a novel computer game in which a player challenges him- or herself using the skin conductance response to make the player aware of his or her own agitation [4]. This game was developed as a paradoxical system in which the desire to win makes it more difficult to win. In this type of game, players find themselves uncontrollable after viewing their biological signals. In other words, a kind of self-reference system is constructed. It is thought that this is a typical example of taking the contexts and their synchronization into a man-machine interface.

Electrical signals detected from the living body are objective and quantitative data reflecting the psychological states and physiological functions of the human body [5]. For example, the biological signal used in lie detector testing is the skin conductance response (SCR), in which changes in the conductance on the skin surface are induced by sweating due to mental agitation, surprise and excitation [6].

Therefore, we tried to produce a novel robot by taking the SCR signal of a human observing the robot into the robot to increase the intimacy between the human and the robot. Then, we assessed the intimacy with the robot.

2 System and Materials

Instead of a real robot, we used Khepera Simulator (Olivier Michel Simulator Package version 2.0: a freeware mobile robot simulator written at the University of Nice Sophia-Antipolis by Olivier Michel. This freeware is downloadable from the World Wide Web at http://wwwi3s.unice.fr), because it is adequate for our work and also because it makes it easy to watch the robot movement and record its trajectory. Figure 1 shows the diagram of the system.

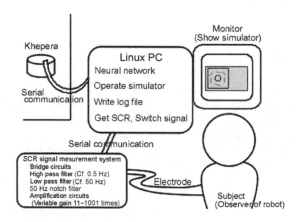

Fig. 1. The diagram of the system. This study used Khepera Simulator, by which the virtual robot moves in a PC monitor. The movement of Khepera in the PC monitor is affected by the SCR of the subject who is watching the movement. The SCR signal is detected by the SCR signal measurement system and is sent to the Linux PC.

2.1 SCR

The SCR occurs due to a change in conductance on the surface of the skin due to sweating [5, 6]. Since eccrine sweat glands are most dense on the palm of the hand and sweating is an autonomic response that can be triggered by emotional stimuli [5, 6], the palm is an ideal site from which to obtain measurements of psychophysical activity using the SCR. The player holds a controller in one hand and the palm of the other hand provides the SCR via two electrodes (disposable electrocardiogram electrode J Vitrode, Ag/AgCl solid-gel tape, Nihon-Koden, Tokyo). The signal was amplified by a SCR sensor and fed into the PC through an A/D converter.

2.2 Neural Network and Diagram

The movement of the robot is generated by the simple back propagation neural networks shown in Figure 2. Khepera has eight optical sensors for detecting obstacles and two motors for moving. Therefore, the network basically has eight neurons corresponding to each sensor on the input layer and two neurons corresponding to each motor on the output layer. Also, a hidden layer is introduced when the values from the sensors are high. The two motors act depending on the 21-step values (from -10 to 10), which are linearly proportional to the value of each output layer.

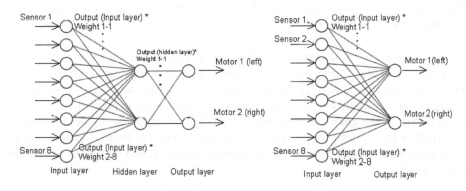

Fig. 2. Three-layered (left) and two-layered (right) neural networks used in the robot

The output weight of each neuron, w_{ij} , is determined by the next formulae.

$$w_{t+1ij} = w_{tij} + \Delta w_{ij} \tag{1}$$

where

$$\Delta w_{ij} = \varepsilon \cdot biosignal \quad \text{(using biosignal)}$$

$$\Delta w_{ij} = \varepsilon \cdot switchsignal \quad \text{(using switch signal)} \tag{2}$$

$$\Delta w_{ij} = \varepsilon \cdot random \quad \text{(using random signal)}$$

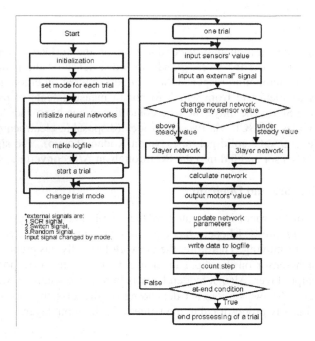

Fig. 3. The flowchart of the program in Khepera. This very simple system was employed to view the pure effect of the biological signal.

The initial weight is determined randomly. This system is not the usual neural network system, because the system does not have a solution, goal and converged state. The three above equations (2) are the errors for the usual neural network system. Oneequation is selected from the equations depending on the experimental condition listed below. SCR signals are fed to the network by this equation. Figure 3 shows the flowchart of this system. In this research, such a simple and unusual system is used for revealing the difference between the system using SCR and the systems using the other signals.

3   Experiments

We focused on how to accept the movement of the robot using the subject's observation of the robot. We conducted an experiment to compare the intimacy of the robot using SCR with that of the robot using a random or switching signal.

The movement of the robot developed in the present study was observed under various conditions for 60 seconds by subjects 20 to 23 years of age. The seven instructions listed in Table 1 were given to each subject for every trial. The SCR of the subject and the trajectory of the robot were recorded while the subject observed the movement. After each trial, a subjective assessment of feeling of the robot, listed in Table 2, was performed by the subject.

Table 1. Instructions given to each subject for every trial

Trial	Instruction	Signal used
1st	Just watch the movement of the robot.	random
2nd	Just watch the movement of the robot.	SCR
3rd	Your SCR signal will be sent to the robot. Just watch the movement of the robot.	SCR
4th	Your SCR signal will be sent to the robot. Just watch the movement of the robot.	random
5th	Your switching signal will be sent to the robot. Turn it on at the robot's crucial phase while you watch the movement of the robot.	switch
6th	Your switching signal will be sent to the robot. Turn it on at the robot's crucial phase while you watch the movement of the robot.	SCR
7th	Your switching signal will be sent to the robot. Turn it on at the robot's crucial phase while you watch the movement of the robot.	random

Table 2. Items to be assessed by the subject. The subject chooses a point on a scale of 1 to 6 for each question.

	Item to be assessed	(less) Point (much)
Question 1	How much did the robot move against your intention?	1 2 3 4 5 6
Question 2	How much did you feel that the movement of the robot looks like living matter's movement?	1 2 3 4 5 6
Question 3	How much did you feel intimacy with the robot?	1 2 3 4 5 6

4   Results and Discussions

First, the relations between the trajectory of the robot and the SCR were investigated. Figure 4 shows a typical example of a resulting trajectory (blue line). A large SCR was observed at the position marked with orange dots. The red squares indicate obstacles put out by the experimenter. The start point of Khepera's movement was the center point of this field.

In this record, for example, there are two domains in which the SCR was generated. The first domain can be interpreted as a sign of the subject's anxiousness about Khepera hitting the wall. The second domain can be interpreted as the subject's frustration over worrying about the never-ending cycle.

From the results, we found that the SCR signals were generated when the subject felt that the robot faced a crucial phase. The SCR signal made the movement pattern of Khepera smooth, safe and dynamic.

Figure 5 shows examples of the trajectory (blue lines) of two kinds of robots. The trajectories from (a) to (c) are typical results of the robot using random signals instead of SCR. The trajectories from (d) to (f) are typical results of the robot using SCR.

The area of the trajectories of the robot using the SCR signals was wider compared with that of the robot using the random signals. The robot using the SCR can move smoothly because it can receive information of the whole view, even though this information is gained indirectly.

Figure 6 shows the result of the assessment completed by the subjects. The result shows that the answers to Question 2 and Question 3 tended to be similar. Intimacy has a deep relationship with the live feeling.

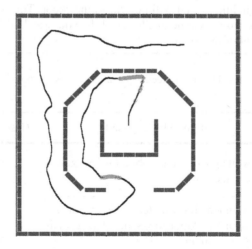

Fig. 4. The typical resulting trajectory (blue line) of the robot and the typical position (orange dots) at which the SCR of the subject was large. The SCR occurred when the subject felt danger or frustration regarding the movement of the robot.

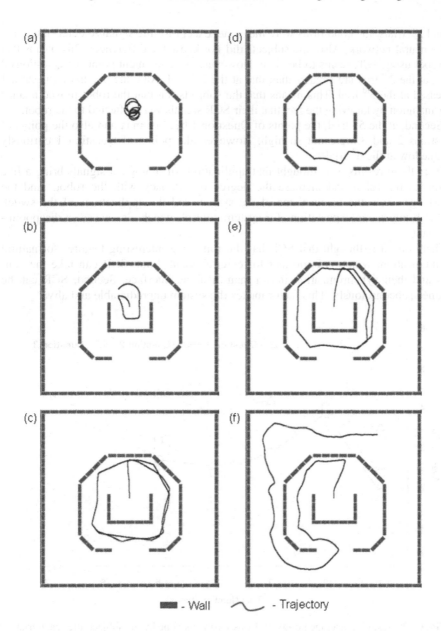

Fig. 5. Examples of the trajectories (blue lines) of two kinds of robots. The trajectories from (a) to (c) are typical results of the robot using random signals instead of SCR. The trajectories from (d) to (f) are typical results of the robot using SCR. The red squares indicate the walls put out by the experimenter.

There are some noteworthy facts apparent in Figure 6. First, the assessment points of Questions 2 and 3 at the 2nd trial are much larger than that at the 1st trial. In both the

1st and 2nd trials, the conditions were the same, except for the signal to determine $\triangle w_{ij}$ in the neural network. Also, the subjects did not know the difference. This means that the robot using SCR seems to be alive. However, the assessment points of Questions 2 and 3 at the 3rd trial are smaller than that at the 2nd trial. And, the points of Question 1 increased at the 3rd trial. This means that the subjects felt that the robot moved against their intention by knowing the fact that their SCR signals were reflected to the robot.

Second, at the 5th trial, the points of Question 1 became max and also the points of Questions 2 and 3 were not so high. However, the points of Question 1 curiously became low at the 6th trial.

From these results, it is thought that applications of biological signals bring a live feeling to the robot and increase the degree of intimacy with the robot. And the knowledge about the mechanisms of the system and the applications of the switch tend to bring strong expectations for system control, which also causes a disappointing result.

Therefore, it is thought that SCR has the following interesting features for natural communication, which is important for entertainment. First, SCR can take the contexts and their synchronization into a man-machine interface. Second, SCR can be obtained subconsciously. This factor makes the system unpredictable and alive.

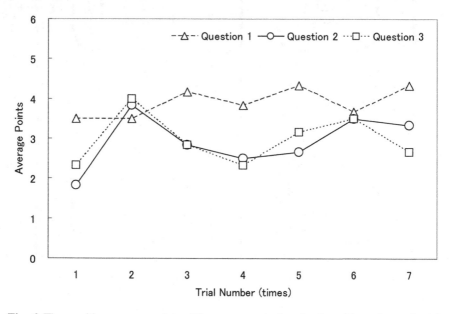

Fig. 6. The resulting average points of the assessments done by the subject after each trial

5   Conclusion

A novel autonomous robot using the observer's SCR was developed in this study. This robot revealed some important features for natural communication between man and machine. These features correspond to the important features for entertainment computing.

References

1. Nakatsu, R.: Communication and Entertainment. IPSJ Magazine 4 (2003) 803-806 (in Japanese)
2. Minato, T., Shimada, M., Ishiguro, H., Itakura, S.: Development of an Android Robot for Studying Human-Robot Interaction. Innovations in Applied Artificial Intelligence: Proc. of the Seventeenth International Conference on Industrial and Engineering Applications of Artificial Intelligence and Expert Systems (IEA/AIE) (2004) 424-434
3. Ono, T.: Embodied Communication Between Humans and Robots Emerging from Entrained Gestures. In: Diebner, H. H. & Ramsay, L. (eds.): Hierarchies of Communication. Center for Art and Media, Germany (2003) 97-114
4. Sakurazawa, S., Munekata, N., Yoshida, N., Tsukahara, Y., Matsubara, H.: Entertainment Feature of a Computer Game Using Biological Signal to Realize a Battle with Oneself. M. Rauterberg (Ed.): ICEC 2004, LNCS 3166(2004)345-350
5. Geddes, L. A.: History of the Polygraph, an Instrument for the Detection of Deception. Biomed. Eng. 8 (1973) 154-156
6. Dawson, M. E., Schell, A. M., Filion, D. L.: The electrodermal system. In: Cacioppo, J. T., Tassinary, L. G. and Berntson, G. G. (eds.): Handbook of psychophysiology. 2nd edn. Cambridge University Press, New York (2000) 200-223

Detection of Speaker Direction Based on the On-and-Off Microphone Combination for Entertainment Robots

Takeshi Kawabata, Masashi Fujiwara, and Takanori Shibutani

Kwansei Gakuin University, 2-1 Gakuen, Sanda City,
669-1337, Japan
kawabata@ksc.kwansei.ac.jp,
http://ist.ksc.kwansei.ac.jp/~kawabata/

Abstract. An important function of entertainment robots is voice communication with humans. For realizing them, accurate speech recognition and a speaker-direction detection mechanism are necessary. The direct-noise problem is serious in such speech processing. The microphone attached to the robot body receives not only human voices but also motor and mechanical noises directly. The direct noises are often larger than distance voices and fatally degrade the speech recognition rate. Even if the microphone close to the user ("on-mic") is used for speech recognition, the body microphones ("off-mic") are still necessary for detecting the speaker direction under the severe condition with direct noises. This paper describes a new method for detecting the speaker direction based on the on-and-off microphone combination. The system searches for the spectral elements of "on-mic" voice in the other "off-mic" channels. The segregated power ratio or the time delay between the "off-mic" channels is used for detecting the speaker direction. Experiments show that the proposed method effectively improves the direction detection accuracy during the robot moves.

1   Introduction

Recent mechatronics technologies realized the autonomous robots which work together with our human beings. In near future, house-keeping robots may cook breakfast, wash clothes, and clean rooms. Also entertainment robots may sing, dance, gesticulate, and chat with us. However an important function of such robots is voice communication with humans, it is still difficult now. The serious problem in speech recognition is direct noises. The microphone attached to the robot body receives not only human voices but also motor and mechanical noises directly. Direct motor noises are often larger than incoming voices and fatally degrade the speech recognition rate.

An "on-mic" approach is promising to avoid this problem. That means the microphone located close to the user. For example, a mobile-phone like voice commander or a head-set microphone can receive the user's voice without any direct noises.

F. Kishino et al. (Eds.): ICEC 2005, LNCS 3711, pp. 248–255, 2005.

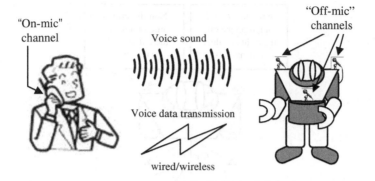

Fig. 1. On-mic and Off-mic channels

Even if the robot has the "on-mic" input channel, body microphones (i.e. "off-mic" channels) are still necessary because these signals are used for detecting the speaker direction. When the command "Come here!" was recognized, the robot has to detect the direction of the speaker and turn its body before walking.

This paper describes a new method for detecting the speaker direction based on the on-and-off microphone combination. The system searches for the spectral elements of "on-mic" voice from the other "off-mic" channels. The segregated power ratio or the time delay between the "off-mic" channels is used for detecting the speaker direction (Fig. 1). Experiments show that the proposed method effectively improves the direction detection accuracy during the robot moves.

2   Detection of Speaker Direction

2.1   Localization Queues

At the beginning of this section, we have to mention about the excellent direction detection mechanism of the human auditory system. We humans can easily find the direction of incoming sounds using two ears. The main queues of sound localization are the interaural level difference (ILD) and the interaural time difference (ITD) [1,2].

Notice that these queues are essential to construct the machine auditory system. Several sophisticated researches have been carried [3,4] for adding the auditory function to computers. The system enables a computer to localize incoming sounds, to segregate them into speech/noise, and to recognize the speech as a command. It works well even under the office-level noise environment.

In the case of real robots, the serious problem occurs derived from their direct motor and mechanical noises. The direct noises are often larger than incoming sounds and destroy the direction detection queues.

2.2   Traditional Methods and Problems

Figure 2 shows the positions of microphones attached to the robot body in our experiments. Non-directional microphones are attached to the left and right

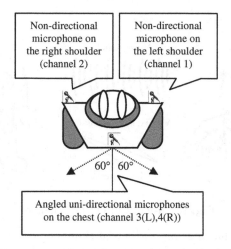

Fig. 2. Microphones attached to the robot body

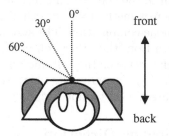

Fig. 3. Incident angles of voice data

shoulders of the robot (channel 1 and 2). Angled uni-directional microphones (i.e. one-point stereo microphone) are attached to the robot chest (channel 3 and 4). And we use a head-set microphone as an "on-mic" channel for capturing clear voice (channel 5).

Phonetically balanced 50 words are pronounced by a speaker from three incident angles ($0°, 30°, 60°$) (Fig. 3). The training data set is pronounced under no noise condition. And the test data set is pronounced during the robot drives its arms. All data are recorded through the four "off-mic" channels and the one "on-mic" channel. Figure 4 (a) shows a speech waveform example of Japanese word "Junban" without noise. Figure 4 (b) shows a speech waveform of the same word with the motor and mechanical noises. The average S/N ratio of the test data is 10dB.

ILD-Based Method. A simple level-based direction detection mechanism is shown in Fig. 5. The system calculates the log powers of both (3 and 4) channel signals and their difference. The calibration unit was tuned by training data

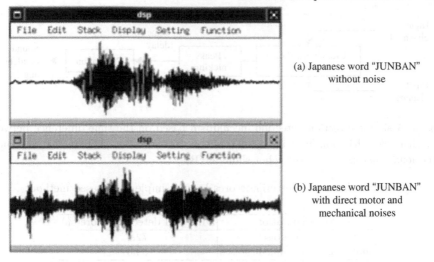

(a) Japanese word "JUNBAN"
without noise

(b) Japanese word "JUNBAN"
with direct motor and
mechanical noises

Fig. 4. Speech samples with/without motor and mechanical noises

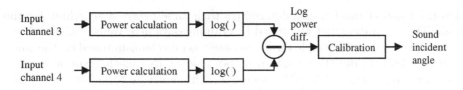

Fig. 5. A simple direction detection mechanism based on the level difference between two channels (ch3: uni-directional microphone on the robot chest(L), ch4: uni-directional microphone on the robot chest(R))

in advance. Table 1 shows the performance of the simple direction detection mechanism based on the level-based method. A direction detection result is judged to be correct only when the incident angle and the recognized angle are identical. Under the condition without noise, such a simple mechanism still determines the sound directions with 82 % accuracy. However, the performance was drastically degraded under the motor and mechanical noises.

ITD-Based Method. A simple time-based direction detection mechanism is shown in Fig. 6. The system calculates the cross-correlation function between

Table 1. Direction detection scores by the simple level-based method

Noise condition	Direction detection score(%)
without noise	82.0
motor and mechanical noises	34.7

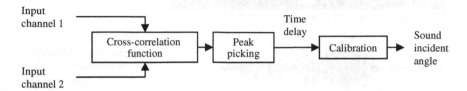

Fig. 6. A simple direction detection mechanism based on the time difference between two channels (ch1: non-directional microphone on the robot shoulder(L), ch2: non-directional microphone on the robot shoulder(R))

Table 2. Direction detection scores by the simple time-based method

Noise condition	Direction detection score(%)
without noise	72.0
motor and mechanical noises	63.3

channel 1 and channel 2, and determines their time delay by searching for the peak. The calibration unit was tuned by training data in advance. Table 2 shows the performance of the simple direction detection mechanism based on the time-based method. Under the condition without noise, this mechanism determines the sound directions with 72 % accuracy. This score is little bit worse than the level-based method. On the contrary, under the severe condition with direct motor and mechanical noises, the time-based method achieved better scores than the level-based method. This result indicates that the time difference feature is more robust for direction detection against the direct noises than the level difference feature.

2.3   New Method Using the On-and-Off Microphone Combination

The motor and mechanical noises propagate through the robot body and vibrate the microphones directly. The strong noise hides the interaural difference derived from incoming speech. This is the reason why the simple level-based direction detection method does not work well during the robot moves.

The framework shown in Fig. 1 has an "on-mic" channel which is the microphone located close to the user. A mobile-phone like voice commander or a head-set microphone can receive the user's clear voice for accurate speech recognition. Also this clear voice can be used for detecting the speech direction.

Modified ILD-Based Method. Figure 5 shows the signal flow diagram of a new level-based direction detection mechanism. In spite of the power calculation, the system calculates the cross-correlation function between the "on-mic" channel and two "off-mic" channels. This means that the system searches for the spectral elements of the "on-mic" voice in the other "off-mic" signals. Only the

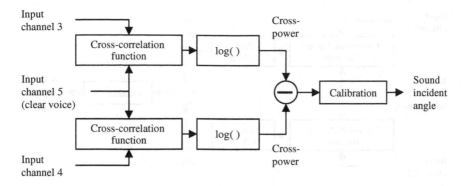

Fig. 7. New direction detection mechanism based on the level difference and on-and-off microphone combination (ch3: uni-directional microphone on the robot chest(L), ch4: uni-directional microphone on the robot chest(R), ch5: uni-directional microphone close to the user)

Table 3. Direction detection scores by the simple and new level-based method under the direct motor and mechanical noises

Method	Direction detection score(%)
simple level-based	34.7
on-and-off mic combination	59.3

log power elements derived from the voice signals are picked up and compared. The calibration unit was tuned by training data in advance. Table 3 shows the performance of the modified direction detection mechanism based on the level-based method. About the 1/3 of direction detection errors are reduced by this approach.

Modified ITD-Based Method. Figure 6 shows the signal flow diagram of a new time-based direction detection mechanism. The system calculates the cross-correlation function between the "on-mic" channel and two "off-mic" channels similarly to the modified level-based method. Peak picking for the cross-correlation functions determines the time delays between the "on-mic" channel and two "off-mic" channels. The difference of them indicates the time delay of

Table 4. Direction detection scores by the simple and new time-based method under the direct motor and mechanical noises

Method	Direction detection score(%)
simple time-based	63.3
on-and-off mic combination	76.0

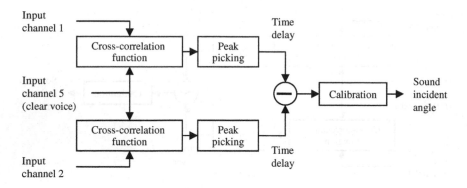

Fig. 8. New direction detection mechanism based on the time difference and on-and-off microphone combination (ch1: non-directional microphone on the robot shoulder(L), ch2: non-directional microphone on the robot shoulder(R), ch5: uni-directional microphone close to the user)

voice signal elements between "off-mic" channels (channel 1 and channel 2). The calibration unit was tuned by training data in advance. Table 4 shows the performance of the modified direction detection mechanism based on the time-based method. The best direction detection score 76.0 % is achieved by this method under the motor and mechanical noise condition.

3   Summary

The new method for detecting the speaker direction based on the on-and-off microphone combination was proposed in this paper. For realizing the voice communication functions on entertainment robots, accurate speech recognition and a speaker-direction detection mechanism are necessary. The microphones attached to the robot body ("off-mic") are suitable for detecting the speaker direction. However, they are often disturbed by the direct motor and mechanical noises. The microphone located close to the user ("on-mic") is suitable for accurate speech recognition because it can receive the user's voice without any direct noises. However, it cannot determine the speaker direction. This paper improved the traditional direction detection method by using the on-and-off microphone combination. The system searches for the spectral elements of "on-mic" voice in the other "off-mic" channels. The segregated power ratio or the time delay between the "off-mic" channels is used for detecting the speaker direction. Experiments show that the proposed method effectively improves the direction detection accuracy. The best direction detection score 76.0 % was achieved under the motor and mechanical noise condition.

The physiological or technological researches in this field are progressing year by year [5,6,7,8]. We would like to apply new knowledge into our system in future works.

Table 5. Summary of direction detection scores

Method	Noise condition	Ch1	Ch2	Ch3	Ch4	Ch5	Score(%)
simple level-based	without noise	-	-	o	o	-	82.0
simple level-based	moter and mech.	-	-	o	o	-	34.7
proposed level-based	moter and mech.	-	-	o	o	o	59.3
simple time-based	without noise	o	o	-	-	-	72.0
simple time-based	moter and mech.	o	o	-	-	-	63.3
proposed time-based	moter and mech.	o	o	-	-	o	76.0

References

1. Jeffress, L. A.: A place theory of sound localization. J. Comp. Physiol. Psychol. **41** (1948) 35–39
2. Blauert, J.: Spatial hearing: The psychophysics of human sound localization. (Revised ed.). MIT Press (1997).
3. Nakatani, T., Okuno, H.: Harmonic Sound Stream Segregation Using Localization and Its Application to Speech Stream Segregation. Speech Communcations **27, 3-4,** Elsevier (1999) 209–222
4. Aoki, M., Okamoto, M., Aoki, S., Matsui, H., Sakurai T., Kaneda, Y.: Sound source segregation based on estimating incident angle of each frequency component of input signals acquired by multiple microphones. Acoustical Science and Technology **22, 2** (2001) 149–157
5. Huang, J., Ohnishi, N., Guo, X., Sugie, N.: Echo avoidance in a computational model of the precedence. Speech Communication **27** (1999) 223–233
6. Renevey, P., Vetter, R., Kraus, J.: Robust speech recognition using missing feature theory and vector quantization. Proc. Eurospeech-2001 **2** (2001) 1107-1110
7. Nakadai, K., Matusura, D., Okuno, H., Kitano, H.: Applying Scattering Theory to Robot Audition System. Proc. IROS-2003 (2003) 1147–1152
8. Furukawa, S., Maki, K., Kashino, M., Riquimaroux, H.: Dependence of the interaural phase difference sensitivities of inferior collicular neurons on a preceding tone and its implications in neural population coding. J. Neurophysiol. in press (2005)

Robot Navigation by Eye Pointing

Ikuhisa Mitsugami, Norimichi Ukita, and Masatsugu Kidode

Graduate School of Information Science,
Nara Institute of Science and Technology,
8916-5, Takayama, Ikoma, Nara, Japan 630-0192
{ikuhi-mi, ukita, kidode}@is.naist.jp

Abstract. We present a novel wearable system for robot navigation. In this system, a user can operate multiple robots in a very intuitive way: the user gazes at a robot and then gazes at its destination on the floor. As this system needs no equipment in the environment, the user can apply it anywhere on a flat floor with only the wearable system. In this paper, we show how to estimate the positions and orientations of the robots and the gazed position. We also describe implementation of the robot navigation system.

1 Introduction

In recent years, a variety of robot systems have been developed. They are becoming more intelligent and are coming into our daily lives. There are a now numerous robot systems, and they provide a variety of functions. Among these we focus here on the function that the robot can move to a position specified by the user because this is a fundamental and very important function; whatever tasks it is to perform, we first have to navigate it to the correct position for the work. To be able to do this, we have to express the positional information and convey it to the robot.

There are many ways to express position in the real world. Nowadays the most popular way is by hand operation devices. However, when more and more robots come into our daily lives and need to be controlled more often, operation by such devices is inconvenient because we are forced to carry them continuously. If we would like to operate robots often and easily, more intuitive ways are required.

Voice recognition is one type of intuitive operation. However, operation by voice is not appropriate for robot navigation because positions in the real world are usually very hard to specify by verbal information, especially on a floor without enough landmarks.

Another way, finger pointing [1,2,3,4], which is representative of gesture recognition approaches [5], is good for robot navigation. We can indicate positions or directions in the real world intuitively and simply. However, we cannot navigate the robot while simultaneously doing another manual task. Moreover, it is not the simplest way, because before making these gestures we inevitably gaze at the specified position. Considering this, gazing, which is another type of gesture, should be the most intuitive and simple way to specify positions in the real world.

F. Kishino et al. (Eds.): ICEC 2005, LNCS 3711, pp. 256–267, 2005.

Therefore, we focus on the user's gaze information. In this paper, we describe a novel wearable system to navigate multiple robots on a floor, based on a position specification method incorporating gaze information. In this system, the user can select a robot and specify its destination merely by gazing. Every robot has a 2D square marker on it. The system detects the marker by a camera worn by the user, and then estimates the position and orientation of the robot and the gazed position on the floor. We note that the system has also the advantage that it can be used anywhere on the floor, because it needs only information obtained from a devices worn by the user. This means that the system needs no equipment in the environment around the user, such as cameras placed in the environment to detect the positions of users and robots [6,7].

2   System Configuration

The configuration of the system is shown in Figure 1. It contains mobile robots, a PC and a headset.

The headset worn by the user is shown in Figure 2. It consists of an eye-tracker, a microphone and a small display. The eye-tracker includes a camera and an infrared sensor that detects the user's eye direction. With the eye-tracker, we can obtain the view image of the camera as well as the direction the user gazes at on the image in real time. Its mechanism and calibration methods are described in Section 3.2. The microphone is used to control the timing of the operation and to accept the user's commands. The display is for checking the

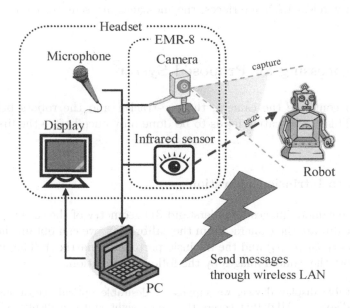

Fig. 1. System configuration

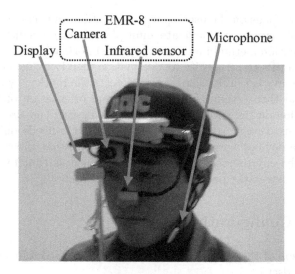

Fig. 2. Headset

estimated results and the current state of the system. It shows the user's view image captured by the camera with virtually annotated objects.[1]

The headset is connected to the PC, which processes information from the eye-tracker and the microphone and estimates the positions and orientations of the robots and the gazed position. Based on the estimated results, the PC sends operation messages to the robots. As both the PC and the mobile robots have wireless LAN interfaces, the messages are sent through a wireless network.

3   Preprocessing for Proposed System

We have to configure the camera, the eye-tracker and the robots before the operation. This configuration needs to be done only once before the first use of the system.

3.1   Camera Intrinsic Calibration

When we use camera images to understand 3D geometry of the scenes precisely, we have to calibrate the camera. From the calibration, we can obtain the distortion factors (k_1, k_2, p_1, p_2) and the intrinsic parameter matrix A. The distortion factors distort the camera images by the following equation:

---

[1] For a suitable display device, we suppose a desirable optical see-through head-mounted display (HMD) that covers the user's sight and can display virtual 3D objects onto the scene as if they were situated in the real world. However, in our current implementation, we utilize such a small display instead of the desirable HMD.

$$\tilde{X} = X + (k_1 r^2 + k_2 r^4) + (2p_1 XY + p_2(r^2 + 2X^2)), \tag{1}$$
$$\tilde{Y} = Y + (k_1 r^2 + k_2 r^4) + (2p_1 XY + p_2(r^2 + 2Y^2)), \tag{2}$$

where (X, Y) is an undistorted image coordinate, and $(\tilde{X}, \tilde{Y})$ is a real distorted image captured by the camera, while $r^2 = X^2 + Y^2$. When these distortion factors are obtained, we can inversely obtain the undistorted image (X, Y) from the distorted image $(\tilde{X}, \tilde{Y})$ from the camera. The intrinsic parameter matrix A translates a 3D camera coordinate (x_c, y_c, z_c) into a 2D image coordinate (X, Y) by the following equation:

$$\begin{pmatrix} \lambda X \\ \lambda Y \\ \lambda \end{pmatrix} = A \begin{pmatrix} x_c \\ y_c \\ z_c \\ 1 \end{pmatrix}, \tag{3}$$

$$A = \begin{pmatrix} f_X & 0 & c_X & 0 \\ 0 & f_Y & c_Y & 0 \\ 0 & 0 & 1 & 0 \end{pmatrix},$$

where λ is a scale factor, (c_X, c_Y) is a coordinate of the principal point of the image, and f_X, f_X are the focal lengths by the X and Y axes.

3.2   Eye-Tracker Calibration

To measure the user's eye direction, we used an EMR-8 eyemark recorder (NAC Inc.), in which the corneal reflection-pupil center method is adopted. In this method, infrared ray is emitted to the eye and its reflection is captured by the image sensor. A sample of the captured image is shown in Figure 3, and from the image, positions of the pupil center and the center of corneal reflection is detected as shown in Figure 4. Since the shape of the eye is not spherical as shown in Figure 5, the relative positions of the pupil center and the center of corneal reflection are changed according to the eye direction. By using this characteristic, the eye-tracker obtains the eye direction (u, v) in real time.

Next, to overlay the points representing the view directions onto the image observed by the view camera, correspondence between the view direction and the 2D image coordinates is needed. In the EMR-8, this correspondence is directly computed because it is difficult to obtain the relative geometric configuration of the camera and the eyeballs. To calculate the correspondence, a flat plane in the environment (e.g., a wall) is used. While the user looks toward the wall, the view camera also observes the wall. Note that the wall has to be perpendicular to the view axis of the camera. Nine points are superimposed on the observed image by the EMR-8. Their positions in the 2D image coordinates (X_i, Y_i) $(i = 0, \cdots, 8)$ are known. All the points are then projected onto the wall in the real environment, for example by a laser pointer, and the user gazes at each projected point in turn. Next, the 3D direction of each binocular view line (v_i, v_i) $(i = 0, \cdots, 8)$ is measured (Figure 6) by the EMR-8. These values are derived from the following equations:

$$X_i = a_0 + a_1 u_i + a_2 v_i + a_3 u_i^2 + a_4 u_i v_i + a_5 v_i^2, \tag{4}$$
$$Y_i = b_0 + b_1 u_i + b_2 v_i + b_3 u_i^2 + b_4 u_i v_i + b_5 v_i^2, \tag{5}$$

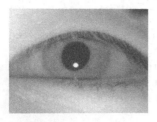

Fig. 3. Captured image of the image sensor

Fig. 4. Detection result of the pupil center and the center corneal reflection

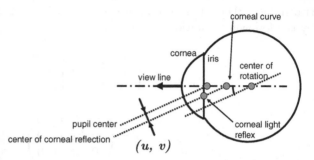

Fig. 5. Corneal reflection-pupil center method

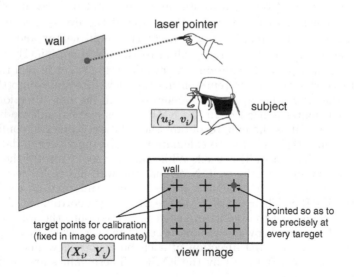

Fig. 6. Calibration operation of EMR-8

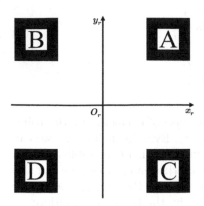

Fig. 7. Sheet with 4 markers

Fig. 8. Captured image of the sheet and the robot

where a_i, $b_i (i = 0, \cdots, 5)$ are unknown constants. These simultaneous equations are solved to calculate a_i, b_i. After a_i, b_i are obtained, the EMR-8 is able to correctly overlay the view direction onto the camera image.

3.3 Robot Settings

In this system, a 2D square marker has to be put on every robot.[2] This system detects the marker in the camera images and by then estimates the position and orientation of the robot. As the 2D marker can be placed anywhere on the robot, every marker is at a unique position and orientation in the robot coordinate. We therefore have to obtain the position and orientation of every marker of every robot.

We next prepare a sheet on which 4 square markers and 2 crossing lines are printed, as shown in Figure 7. We place the robot at the intersection of the lines on the sheet; this is the origin of the robot coordinate, which corresponds to the position of the robot. The lines represent the x_r and y_r axes of the robot coordinate system. We define x_r as the orientation of the robot, and we direct the robot's face along it. The z_r axis is defined as the line perpendicular to the x_r-y_r plane, and the robot usually stands along the z_r axis.

We direct the camera to the robot on the sheet so that the camera image should capture not only the 4 markers but also the marker on the robot. Figure 8 is a camera image of this situation. As the positions and orientations of the markers are estimated by their appearance, we can obtain a matrix Q_{CR} that consists of a rotation matrix R_{CR} and a translation vector t_{CR}, which transforms the camera coordinate (x_c, y_c, z_c) to the robot coordinate (x_r, y_r, z_r) by the following equation:

---

[2] We can use more markers if the markers are too small to estimate the position and orientation precisely, or if the camera often fails to observe the marker because it is badly positioned or oriented. When we use more than one marker for a robot, we need to estimate the positions and orientations of each one.

$$\begin{pmatrix} x_r \\ y_r \\ z_r \\ 1 \end{pmatrix} = Q_{CR} \begin{pmatrix} x_c \\ y_c \\ z_c \\ 1 \end{pmatrix}, \tag{6}$$

$$Q_{CR} = \begin{pmatrix} R_{CR} & t_{CR} \\ \mathbf{0}^T & 1 \end{pmatrix}.$$

Some of the 4 markers may be undetectable because of occlusion by the robot (for example, marker "B" is occluded in Figure 8). Even in such cases, we can still estimate the transformation matrix Q_{CR} using the other detectable markers. Next, in the same way, by the appearance of the marker on the robot we can also obtain the transformation matrix Q_{CM} that transforms the camera coordinate (x_c, y_c, z_c) to the marker coordinate (x_m, y_m, z_m) by the following equation:

$$\begin{pmatrix} x_m \\ y_m \\ z_m \\ 1 \end{pmatrix} = Q_{CM} \begin{pmatrix} x_c \\ y_c \\ z_c \\ 1 \end{pmatrix}. \tag{7}$$

By Equation (6) and (7), the following equation is obtained:

$$\begin{pmatrix} x_r \\ y_r \\ z_r \\ 1 \end{pmatrix} = Q_{MR} \begin{pmatrix} x_m \\ y_m \\ z_m \\ 1 \end{pmatrix}, \tag{8}$$

where

$$Q_{MR} = Q_{CR}Q_{CM}^{-1} \tag{9}$$

is the matrix that transforms the marker coordinate (x_m, y_m, z_m) to the robot coordinate (x_r, y_r, z_r). Because the marker is fixed on the robot, this transformation matrix Q_{MR} is constant. The system stores Q_{MR} for every marker.

We note that the design of each marker should be different, because the marker is used not only for estimation of the position and orientation but also for identification of the robot.[3]

4   Estimation of Robot Position and Gazed Position

When we operate the robot, the system works by estimating the information in the order shown below.

4.1   Marker's Position and Orientation

The system cannot work without the information of the robot's position and orientation. We orient the camera so that the camera can observe the marker on

---
[3] If a robot has multiple markers, each of its markers has to be different.

the robot. By the method described in Section3.3, we can estimate the position and orientation of the marker as a matrix P_{MC} that transforms the marker coordinate (x_m, y_m, z_m) to the camera coordinate (x_c, y_c, z_c):

$$\begin{pmatrix} x_c \\ y_c \\ z_c \\ 1 \end{pmatrix} = P_{MC} \begin{pmatrix} x_m \\ y_m \\ z_m \\ 1 \end{pmatrix}. \tag{10}$$

4.2   Robot Coordinate System

By Equations (8) and (10), we obtain the following equation:

$$\begin{pmatrix} x_r \\ y_r \\ z_r \\ 1 \end{pmatrix} = P_{CR} \begin{pmatrix} x_c \\ y_c \\ z_c \\ 1 \end{pmatrix}, \tag{11}$$

where

$$P_{CR} = Q_{MR} P_{MC}^{-1}. \tag{12}$$

As the Q_{MR} is constant and P_{MC} has been obtained, we can obtain the transformation matrix P_{CR} between the camera coordinate and the robot coordinate.

As shown in Equation (13), P_{CR} consists of a rotation matrix R_{CR} and a translation vector t_{CR}, which are the orientation and position of the camera in the robot coordinate respectively:

$$P_{CR} = \begin{pmatrix} R_{CR} & t_{CR} \\ \mathbf{0}^T & 1 \end{pmatrix}. \tag{13}$$

4.3   Gazed Position in Robot Coordinate System

Using the EMR-8, we can obtain the gazed position on the camera image. This position indicates a line l corresponding to the user's gaze direction. We assume that the user looks at positions not above the floor but only at positions on the floor that the robot moves on. Considering the definition of the robot coordinate in Section.3.3, the floor corresponds to the x_r-y_r plane. The gazed position can thus be calculated as the intersection of the line l and the x_r-y_r plane. By Equation (4) and (11), we can obtain the following equation:

$$\begin{pmatrix} \lambda X^{(gazed)} \\ \lambda Y^{(gazed)} \\ \lambda \end{pmatrix} = A P_{CR}^{-1} \begin{pmatrix} x_r^{(gazed)} \\ y_r^{(gazed)} \\ z_r^{(gazed)} \\ 1 \end{pmatrix}, \tag{14}$$

where $(X^{(gazed)}, Y^{(gazed)})$ denotes the gazed position on the camera image that can be obtained by the EMR-8, and $(x_r^{(gazed)}, y_r^{(gazed)}, z_r^{(gazed)})$ denotes the gazed position. As the gazed position is on the x_r-y_r plane, $z_r^{(gazed)}$ must be 0. With this equation, we can calculate $(x_r^{(gazed)}, y_r^{(gazed)})$, which corresponds to the relative gazed position from the robot.

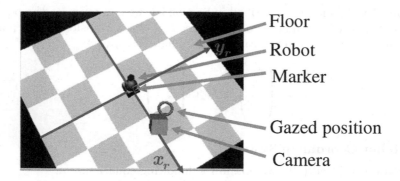

Fig. 9. Position estimation of robot, camera, floor and gazed position

4.4 Estimation Results

Figure 9 shows the virtual 3D space generated from the estimation results. The robot is at the center on the floor, and the camera and the gazed positions move in space corresponding to their positions in the real world.

5 Implementation of Robot Navigation System

5.1 Implementation Environment

We implemented the robot navigation system using a Windows 2000 PC with an Intel Pentium4 2.8GHz CPU and 1024MB memory. ARToolKit [8] helps the system to detect markers from camera images and to estimate 3D position and orientation in real time, and OpenGL [9] is used to annotate virtual objects on the display images. We also use the user's voice, which is desirable for selecting and conveying the action of the robot. For voice recognition, we utilize Julius [10], a well-known recognition engine for Japanese.

5.2 Diagram of Robot Navigation System

We show the state transition diagram of the system in Figure 10. There are 5 states (A)...(E) in the diagram.

At the beginning, the current state is (A). Here, the system searches for markers in the camera image, and if a marker is detected it estimates the robot coordinate and identifies the robot by the marker. The user can see a torus at the gazed position on the floor and a red cone above the robot, which means that the robot is detected but not selected. The display image is shown in Figure 11.

If the user says "KORE" ("this one" in Japanese) while gazing at the robot, the current state turns to (B). In (B), the user has selected a robot to operate. Here the user can still see the torus at the gazed position and the cone above the robot turns blue, which means that this robot is now selected. The user

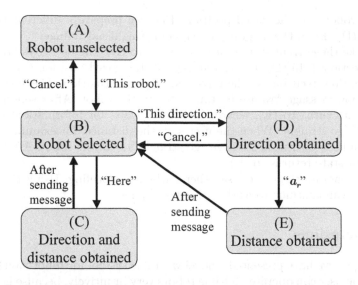

Fig. 10. State transition diagram of the system

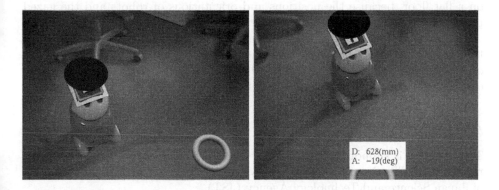

Fig. 11. Display image in State (A)   **Fig. 12.** Display image in State (B)

can also see the distance $(= \sqrt{x_r^2 + y_r^2})$ and the angle $(= \tan^{-1} \frac{y_r}{x_r})$ above the torus, which are calculated in Section4.3, as shown in Figure 12. If the user says "YAME" (means "cancel") the current state returns to (A).

Next, if the user says "KOKO" ("here"), the current state turns to (C). The system regards the gazed position (x_r, y_r) as the destination of the robot and sends an operation message "rotate by $\tan^{-1} \frac{y_r}{x_r}$" and "go straight $\sqrt{x_r^2 + y_r^2}$" to it. After sending it, the current state returns to (B).

The transition between states above is the fundamental behavior of the system. It provides simple and intuitive operation of the robot. However, it has the disadvantage that the robot can move only in a restricted area by one operation because the gazed position can be estimated only when the camera captures both the robot and the gazed position. Here we prepare a different transition path (B)-(D)-(E) in the diagram to overcome this disadvantage.

To make the current state switch from (B) to (D), the user says "KOTCHI" ("this direction"). In (D), the system regards the gazed position (x_r, y_r) not as the destination itself but as the direction of the destination. The system sends an operation message "rotate by $\tan^{-1} \frac{y_r}{x_r}$" to the robot. After sending it, the current state turns to (E), where the system waits for information about the distance to go straight. When the user says the distance, for example "a_r", the system sends an operation message "go straight a_r" to the robot. After sending, the current state returns to (B).

In the diagram there are also other paths for canceling. Using these paths, the system can continue to work without stopping.

6   Conclusions

In this paper, we have presented a novel wearable system for robot navigation on a floor. The user can operate multiple robots very intuitively, because he/she can select a robot to operate and specify its destination on the floor by only his/her gazing. This system has the further advantage that we can use it anywhere on a flat floor, because the positions and orientations of robots and the gazed positions are estimated only by information from a wearable headset.

Future work will include improvements to the system, including introduction of a better HMD and vocabulary addition of voice commands. Evaluation of its usability will also be included. Moreover, quantitative evaluation of the estimation accuracy of position and orientation is another important topic.

Acknowledgments

This research is supported by Core Research for Evolutional Science and Technology (CREST) Program "Advanced Media Technology for Everyday Living" of Japan Science and Technology Agency (JST).

References

1. R.Kahn, M.Swain, P.Prokopowicz and R.Firby: "Gesture recognition using the Perseus architecture," Proc. of the IEEE Conference on Computer Vision and Pattern Recognition, pp.734–741, 1996.
2. K.Nickel and U.Karlsruhe: "Pointing gesture recognition based on 3D-tracking of face, hands and head orientation," Proc. of the 5th International Conference on Multimodal Interfaces, pp.140–146, 2003.
3. R. Cipolla and H. J. Hollinghurst: "Human-robot interface by pointing with uncalibrated stereo vision", Image and Vision Computing, Vol.14, No.3, pp.178–178, 1996.
4. Nebojsa Jojic, Thomas S. Huang, Barry Brumitt, Brian Meyers, Steve Harris: "Detection and Estimation of Pointing Gestures in Dense Disparity Maps," FG 2000, pp.468-475, 2000.

5. Thomas B. Moeslund and Erik Granum: "A Survey of Computer Vision-Based Human Motion Capture," Computer Vision and Image Understanding, Vol.81, No.3, pp.231–268, 2001.
6. S.Stillman, R.Tanawongsuwan and I.Essa: "A system for tracking and recognizing multiple people with multiple cameras," Technical Report GIT-GVU-98-25, Georgia Institute of Technology, Graphics, Visualization, and Usability Center, 1998.
7. M.Sakata, Y.Yasumuro, M.Imura, Y.Manabe and K.Chihara: "A Location Awareness System using Wide-angle Camera and Active IR-Tag," Proc. of IAPR Workshop on Machine Vision Applications, pp.522–525, 2002.
8. "ARToolKit," http://artoolkit.sourceforge.net/.
9. "OpenGL Library," http://www.opengl.org/.
10. "Julius – open source real-time large vocabulary speech recognition engine," http://julius.sourceforge.jp/.

Virtual Human with Regard to Physical Contact and Eye Contact

Asami Takayama, Yusuke Sugimoto, Akio Okuie, Tomoya Suzuki,
and Kiyotaka Kato

Tokyo Univ. of Science,1-3 Kagurazaka, Shinjuku-ku,Tokyo 162-8601, Japan
taka@katolab.ee.kagu.tus.ac.jp

Abstract. In the future a virtual human is expected to play important roles such as a character, an avatar and a robot in the amusement field. To realize a virtual human computer-graphics has advantages in cost and maintenance. However, a human feels a slight discomfort at the robot's face that is represented by using CG because a robot's head in the virtual world does not fit in the environment of the real world. To resolve the problem, we have proposed a robot's head by using CG and some sensors that respond to a surrounding environment. Here, focusing on physical contact, this paper proposes a robot's head using CG and a touch screen panel. Also, we propose robot eyes that reflect a surrounding environment realistically toward the realization of eye contact. Some experiments show that the robot's face changes according to an environmental change like a human in the real world.

1 Introduction

A computer game provides us with an adventure world that we cannot experience in the real world by operating a virtual human as a character in the virtual world. When we communicate with other people through an avatar on the Internet, the communication among humans is different from ordinary direct communication. In addition, a partner-type of robot is expected to be a new creature that is not a human and not an animal. It may provide us with pleasure and contentment.

Thus, a virtual human, which is the substitution of a human or a machine, is expected to be important for our lives. In the future, a virtual human is expected to play important roles such as a character, an avatar, and a robot in the amusement field. To create a virtual human, much research about a robot's head has been actively done. A mechanical robot's head is one solution for creating a virtual human. It is composed of mechanical parts such as artificial skin, artificial eyes, and so on. The head is equipped with many actuators that move the parts.

On the other hand, the utilization of computer graphics (CG) is another solution for creating a robot's head [1]. Compared to the mechanical method mentioned above, because there is no mechanical parts used in constructing a CG robot's head, it is easy to create a robot's head at low cost. Moreover, CG has the ability to represent a variety of appearances. For example, the following uses can be applied:

F. Kishino et al. (Eds.): ICEC 2005, LNCS 3711, pp. 268–278, 2005.

- To change a character or a hairstyle immediately according to the situation,
- To exaggerate a facial expression as a cartoon character,
- To change the shape of a face or hair.

Thus, a variety of expressions for a robot's head may enable a human to communicate with an entertainment-friendly robot. A robot's head created using computer graphics has advantages in cost and maintenance compared with a mechanical one. However, people feel a slight discomfort at the CG-created robot's head because a robot's head in the virtual world does not fit in the environment of the real world.

To realize a computer-graphic method with realistic representation, which benefits from low cost, this paper proposes creating a robot's head using computer graphics and sensors. The face and hair of a robot head should be displayed realistically according to the peripheral environment. If this is not so, the robot will feel somewhat strange to the human who communicates with it. To resolve the problem, we have proposed creating a robot's head by using CG and sensors that respond to the surrounding environment as shown in Fig. 1 [2][3].

CG + Sensor

CG + Sensor

Fig. 1. Realization of robot's head using CG and sensors

The system had several kinds of sensors to detect the status of the peripheral environment, an estimator to calculate the status of unknown areas, and a display to represent the head of a robot. Light sources were calculated from a camera image and the appearance of the head was made to change according to the light sources. As a camera image had the information about light sources, the color, the size, and the position were calculated. In addition, the system estimated a peripheral environment by combining several pressure sensors with an analyzer using hydrodynamics. After measuring wind forces by several microphones that function as pressure sensors, it calculated the air flow surrounding the head of the robot and applied the flow to the hair. In this way, the wind-blown hair of a robot was displayed realistically. However, the previous system did not support physical contact and eye contact.

According to a report [4], physical contact is an important factor for humans when communicating with each other. Therefore, a human feels slight discomfort around a robot when touching it if the robot does not respond to physical contact. To support physical contact, this paper proposes a system that detects the pressure and position of the touched part on a touch-screen panel and modifies the geometric data of the robot's head.

Moreover, eye contact is also an important factor for humans when communicating with each other [4]. Therefore, a human feels slight discomfort around a robot when facing the robot if the robot does not respond to the surrounding object. Because eyes are the most impressive part, the robot's appearance should realistically respond to the surrounding object. In particular, the glint in the eyes and the size of the pupil can change the facial expression [5]. Thus, this paper proposes a system that captures the surrounding view and reflects it onto the robot's eyes with some physiological behaviors.

Through experimental results, this paper shows the effectiveness of the proposed system and discusses some problems to resolve for a virtual human with regard to physical contact and eye contact.

2   Manuscript Preparation

A system has several kinds of sensors, such as camera, a microphone and a touch screen panel, to detect the status of the peripheral environment, an estimator to calculate the status of unknown areas, and a display to represent the head of a robot. The system uses a few sensors and calculates the environmental status from the data. Our estimation is that it is important to display the head realistically.

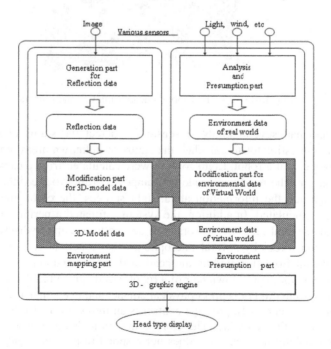

Fig. 2. System configuration

In the prototype system that light sources are calculated from a camera image and the appearance of the head is made to change according to the light sources. As a camera image has the information about light sources, the color, the size, and the position are calculated. Since eyes are a very important factor for a robot to communicate with a human, eyes should be rendered realistically in case of eye contact. So, getting a camera image and applying it to the robot's eyes, the reflection of a confronted human in the eyes is realized using texture-mapping technology. In addition, the system estimates a peripheral environment by combining plural pressure sensors with and analyzer using hydrodynamics. After measuring wind forces by plural microphones that function as pressure sensors, the system calculates the airflow surrounding the head of the robot and applies the flow to the hair. In this way, the wind-blown hair of a robot is displayed realistically. Physical contact is important for a robot to communicate with a human. The system uses a touch screen panel so as to realize the physical contact. When a human touch the robot's face, the touched part is caved in.

3 Robot's Head Using CG and a Touch-Screen Panel

A robot uses a surface acoustic wave touch-screen panel as a touch-sensitive sensor that detects pressure intensity and coordinates at a touched position. Based on the data derived from the touch-screen panel, the shape of a robot's head is modified by moving the coordinates of the vertexes that compose the polygons of a 3D model.

3.1 Shape Modification for Skin

This section describes a method for modifying of the skin of a robot's face. Fig. 3 shows a skin model that is represented by a 3D polygonal model, and the close-up of the part. The model is composed of triangular polygons.

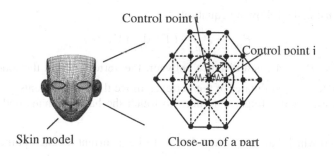

Control point i

Control point i

Skin model

Close-up of a part

Fig. 3. Skin model

First, by pushing a touch-screen panel, the pressure and coordinates of the part applied are detected. Because the detected coordinates are two-dimensional, they are converted into three-dimensional ones in the virtual space. Assign the touched point in the 3D space as A.

272   A. Takayama et al.

Next, the distance between the touched point A and each vertex P_F of the polygons for a face model is calculated as $d_F = |P_F - A|$. Then, each vertex is moved according to the distance d_F. The moved vertex is calculated by

$$P_F' = P_F + (f + d_F)V, \qquad (1)$$

where the moving direction of the vertex V is backward in front of the screen, and f is the pressure obtained from the touch-screen panel.

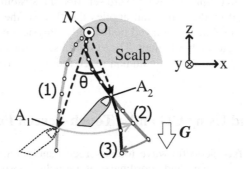

Fig. 4. Hair model

3.2 Shape Modification for Hair

This section describes a method for modifying the hair of a robot's head. Fig. 4 shows a scalp model and a hair model. The plural line segments that connect the vertexes represent the hair model.

As with the method for skin modification, based on the coordinates of the touched point A and the pressure f, each vertex of the line segments of the hair model P_{Hi} is calculated using the following equation:

$$P_{Hi}' = P_{Hi} + (f + d_{Hi})V, \qquad (2)$$

where $d_{Hi} = |P_{Hi} - A|$ is a distance between the vertex P_{Hi} and the touched point A. Then, the updated coordinates of the vertexes move the line segments.

In the case when a finger continues to touch the hair, the hair model changes as follows:

1. First, find which hair is touched. Let A_1 to be a current touched point, and let O to be the hairline of a touched hair.
2. Next, let A_2 to a touched point after the finger moves. And let θ to be the angle that two vectors OA_1 and OA_2 make. Then, rotate the hair around the axis N, which is obtained from the vector product $N = OA_1 \times OA_2$.
3. Finally, apply the gravity G to every vertex form the vertex that is the nearest to the touched point to the end of the hair.

4   Robot's Eyes Using CG and a Camera

A robot uses a camera as a sensor in order to acquire a surrounding view and uses a light source as an image. By mapping the image texture onto the robot's eyes, the realistic reflection of the surrounding environment is represented. Moreover, to realize a physiologic response, the pupil diameter is varied according to the surrounding brightness, which is calculated from the camera image.

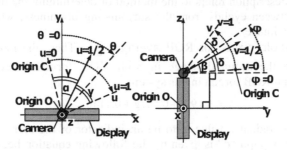

Fig. 5. Location of camera and display

4.1   Realization of Reflection

Set each x-axis, y-axis, z-axis as follows:

The x-axis is horizontal leftward, the y-axis is forward, and the z-axis is vertical upward on a display. The camera angle in the xy plane is α, and the angle in the yz plane is β. The viewing angle of the camera is 2γ in the horizontal direction, and 2δ in the vertical direction. The camera can obtain an image of the range within $\alpha - \gamma \leq \theta \leq \gamma + \alpha$, $\beta - \delta \leq \varphi \leq \beta - \delta$ from viewpoint of the origin O. Moreover, the u-axis is horizontal rightward, and the v-axis is vertical upward on a texture plane, and the texture origin $C(0,0)$ is at the bottom-left corner. The whole pixels of texture are defined as $0 \leq u \leq 1, 0 \leq v \leq 1$.

The following describes the method of texture-mapping the surrounding image onto the robot's eyes. First, the texture image is generated from the camera image. Then, the texture coordinate (u,v) is calculated in relation to each vertex coordinate (x,y,z) of a polygon that composes a three-dimensional model. The two-dimensional coordinate (u,v) of the texture is obtained as

$$u = \frac{\theta - \alpha}{2\gamma} + \frac{1}{2}, \quad v = \frac{\phi - \beta}{2\delta} + \frac{1}{2} \tag{3}$$

Then, the three-dimensional coordinate of the existing 3D model is expressed as a Cartesian coordinate (x,y,z) and a polar coordinate (, ,) as in Fig. 5. The relationship is given as follows:

$$\rho = \sqrt{x^2 + y^2 + z^2}, \quad \theta = \arctan(x/y), \quad \phi = \arcsin(z/\rho) \tag{4}$$

Therefore, there is the following relationship between each u, v, and x, y, z:

$$u = \frac{\{\arctan(x/y)\} - \alpha}{2\gamma} + \frac{1}{2}, \quad v = \frac{\{\arcsin(z/\sqrt{x^2 + y^2 + z^2})\} - \beta}{2\delta} \tag{5}$$

274   A. Takayama et al.

The texture coordinate (u,v) is calculated by substituting the vertex coordinate (x, y, z) for the equation. Next, the blending ratio of the texture and color of the polygon's surface is decided based on the 3D model's material data on mirror reflectivity and transparency. Finally, texture mapping is applied to a 3D model using the acquired texture.

4.2 Realization of Pupils and Eyelids

The following description refers to the method of determining the pupil diameter and the distance between eyelids from the surrounding brightness, which is calculated from the camera image.

First, the whole pixels for RGB average $\bar{r},\bar{g},\bar{b}$. Then, the radiance value Y is translated from the acquired image in 8-bit YUV format because the image is expressed in 8-bit RGB format in this system.

$$Y = 0.299\bar{r} + 0.587\bar{g} + 0.114\bar{b}. \tag{6}$$

Then, assign the radiance value Y to be an indicator of the surrounding brightness. The diameter of a pupil "d" is given by the following equation because the diameter of a human's pupil is proportional to the logarithm of surrounding brightness. The symbols "max" and "min" represent the maximum and the minimum of the pupil diameter, respectively. The symbol "a" is a proportional constant.

$$
\begin{aligned}
d &= \max - a \times \log Y & when && 1 < Y < \sqrt[a]{10}^{\,max-min} \\
d &= \max & when && Y \le 1 \\
d &= \min & when && Y \ge \sqrt[a]{10}^{\,max-min}
\end{aligned}
\tag{7}
$$

Moreover, the distance between eyelids "s" is determined in relation to the pupil diameter "d" using the following equation. The eyelid is a constant w that is the distance between eyelids when a robot squints the most.

$$s = w \times \frac{\max - d}{\max - \min} \tag{8}$$

5   Experiment

5.1 Experimental Methods

The following experiments are performed as a verification of the above-mentioned system. An overview is shown in Fig. 6.

Fig. 6. Overview of the esperiments

1. Observe the change in the robot's head by touching the face of the robot.
2. Observe the change in the robot's head by stroking the hair of the robot.
3. Observe the change in the robot's head by moving the surrounding object.
4. Observe the change in the robot's eyes by moving a light source.

5.2 Experimental Results

1. Changes when the Robot's Face is Touched
The changes when the robot's face is touched are shown in Fig. 7.1 and Fig. 7.2. Fig. 7.1 shows the changes when the right cheek is touched, and Fig. 7.2 shows the changes when the eyelid is pulled down.

2. Changes when the Hair of the Robot is Stroked
The changes when the robot's hair is stroked are shown in Fig. 8.1 and Fig. 8.2. Here, Fig. 8.1 shows the changes when the robot's fringe of hair is stroked from left to right, and Fig. 8.2 shows the changes when the robot's hair is stroked from the ends to the roots.

3. Changes when the Surrounding Object is Moved
The changes when a light source is moved from the left to the right are shown in Fig. 9.1. The zoomed-in one is Fig. 9.2.

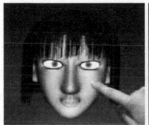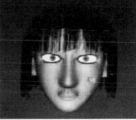

Fig. 7.1. Changes when the right cheek is touched

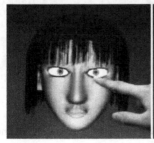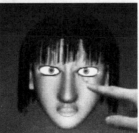

Fig. 7.2. Changes when the eyelid is pulled down

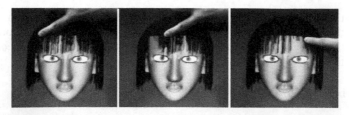

Fig. 8.1. Changes when the robot's fringe of hair is stroked from left to right

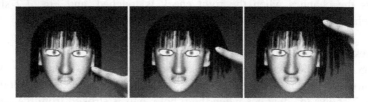

Fig. 8.2. Changes when the robot's hair is stroked from the ends to the roots

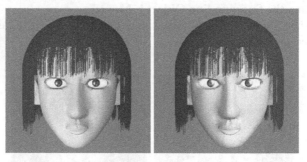

(a) The light is at the left   (b) The light is at the right

Fig. 9.1. Changes in the head when the light source is moved

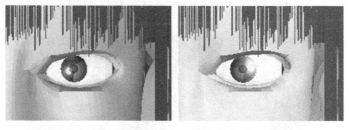

(a) The light is at the left   (b) The light is at the right

Fig. 9.2. Changes in the eyes when the light source is moved (zoomed-in)

4. Changes when the Environmental Brightness is Changed

The changes when the environmental brightness is changed are shown in Fig. 10.

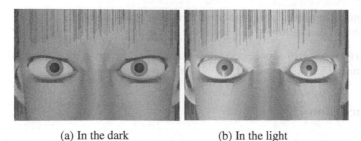

(a) In the dark   (b) In the light

Fig. 10. Close-up of the robot's eyes when the environmental brightness is changed

5.3   Considerations

1. Changes when the Robot's Face is Touched
Fig. 7.1 and Fig. 7.2 show the following changes in the robot's face:

- The touched part caved in when a human touches the robot's face.
- The harder the robot's face is touched, the larger the area of skin caved in.

A human felt these changes to be realistic (similar to a real human) except for the discomfort of the hardness of the screen panel.

2. Changes when the Robot's Hair is Stroked
Fig. 8.1 and Fig. 8.2 show the following changes in the robot's hair:

- The robot's hair is raised from the hair root to the touched position, and hangs down from the touched part to the bottom.
- The harder the hair of the robot is touched, the more the hair is curved.
  A human felt these changes to be similar to the changes in a human's hair.

3. Changes when the Surrounding Object is Moved
Fig. 9.1 and Fig. 9.2 show the following changes in the robot's head:

- We can see ourselves in the robot's eyes when sitting down in front of the robot face to face.
- The color and shape of a surrounding object appears on the surface of the eyes and the entire head of the robot.
- The closer a surrounding object comes to the robot, the larger the object's image appears on the surface of the entire head.
- When a surrounding object moves, the object's image on the surface of the head and the hair moves in the same direction.
- The image of the surrounding object that appears on the surface of the eyes is clearer than the one on the face and the hair.

A human felt these changes to be similar to the changes of the surrounding environment.

4. Changes when the Environmental Brightness is Changed

Fig. 10 shows the following change in the robot's eyes:

- The brighter a light source becomes, the smaller the robot's pupils become. A human felt this change to be similar to a real human.

6 Conclusion

Physical contact and eye contact are important factors in creating a virtual human for amusement. This paper has proposed a new robot system that communicates with a human by physical contact and eye contact using computer graphics and sensors. From these experimental results, we can obtain the following conclusions:

1. The part of a robot's face where a human touches caves in realistically according to the touch pressure. And, the hair of a robot realistically moves when being stroked.
2. A surrounding view and brightness obtained from a camera are realistically reflected onto the robot's eyes. A human can see himself or herself in the robot's eyes when communicating with it face to face.

Although these experiments are simple, we can say that it is expected that our idea could provide physical contact and eye contact in a practical way in the future because of the low cost.

Facial expression is important for a human when communicating with a virtual human. Because the prototype does not support facial expressions, a human feels slight discomfort when around the robot. A mental model and a physiologic model have to be introduced. And the improvement of a geometric model, especially a surface model, is also a key factor in creating realistic facial expressions.

References

1. O. Hasegawa: "Roles of Visual Functions in Multimodal Interface and Their Applications," *IPSJ SIG-CVIM & SIG-HI Organized Session: HI-95 & CVIM-129-23*, pp.165-170 (Sep. 2001).
2. M. Arai, T. Suzuki and K. Kato: "Human-Robot Interface using Computer Graphics and Sensors," *6th Japan-France Congress on Mechatronics & 4th Asia-Europe Congress on Mechatronics September 9-12*, pp. 374-379 (2003).
3. T. Suzuki, M. Arai and K. Kato: "Realization of Robot's head using Computer Graphics and Sensors," *The Robotics Society of Japan the 21st Conf.*, p. 3F17 (2003).
4. Marjorie F. Vargas, T. Isimaru translation: "Nonverbal Communication," Shincyosya Co., pp. 15-17 (1987).
5. Y. Hukui: "Psychology of Look," Sougensya, (1984).

Power, Death and Love: A Trilogy for Entertainment

Ben Salem and Matthias Rauterberg

Department of Industrial Design, Technische Universiteit Eindhoven, The Netherlands
{b.i.salem, g.w.m.rauterberg}@tue.nl

Abstract. In this paper we review the latest understandings about what emotions are and their roles in perception, cognition and action in the context of entertainment computing. We highlight the key influence emotions have in the perception of our surrounding world, as well as in the initiation of action. Further to this we propose a model for emotions and demonstrate how it could be used for entertainment computing. We then present a review of emotion based toys and show our own development in this area. We conclude our paper with a discussion on how entertainment systems would gain from a better and more comprehensive understanding of emotions.

Keywords: Emotion, power death love trilogy, empathy, interactive toy.

1 Introduction

There have been numerous definitions given to the concept of emotions. It would go beyond the scope of this paper to give a comprehensive and complete survey of the various definitions given to emotions in a wide variety of sciences and philosophical schools. We will instead focus on those definitions that help us understand emotions from the perspective of entertainment. To understand emotions, we have relied on current developments in neuroscience, psychology, Human-Computer interaction and Artificial Intelligence. More specifically, we have looked at what have emotions been described as and what have they been related with.

Emotions have been associates with decision-making processes [1], and with regulation of behaviour [2]. Emotions help us keep out of harm's way effectively and efficiently. As an initial reaction to unknown experiences emotions ensure we are not hapless and indecisive when a choice or a decision need to be made. Even in the case of contradicting and incomplete information availability. Emotions are an essential part of our cognitive and behavioural capabilities [3], and play a continuous role in defining who we are as individuals. Some even advocate that no cognitive process is possible without emotions [4]. As well as that emotions should play an important part in the field of Human-Computer Interaction [5].

Emotions have social functions [6], and society has an influence on our emotions [7]. Emotions also play a role in our perception of reality down to the perception of our own body generated signals such as pain. Such influence is due to changing of the focus of our attention [8] [9]. Emotions also require some processing and regulation. It is a mechanism to avoid that an emotional experiences becomes overwhelming and

F. Kishino et al. (Eds.): ICEC 2005, LNCS 3711, pp. 279–290, 2005.
© IFIP International Federation for Information Processing 2005

thus prevents other experiences and processes to proceed without hindrance [10]. The emotional regulation is performed continuously and in a way to ensure that we are not overwhelmed with emotions. Both emotional processing and regulation are complex mechanisms that are not always effective. Emotional avoidance for example can result in an increased in self-generated emotions leading to a self-perpetuating and amplifying loop and defeat the purpose of such an avoidance [11]. In other words, we become victim of a panic attack [12].

In this paper we propose to investigate how a better knowledge and understanding of emotions could help develop better entertainment systems. We define entertainment systems as those that deliver an attention holding diversion. In effect, entertainment systems grab your attention away from your daily routine. Because emotions are known to affect attention [8] [9], the link is therefore strong between emotions and entertainment. Traditionally, there has been emphasis on the entertainer to provide a trigger for an emotional response from the user/audience. This is particularly the case with historical entertainments such as performing and fine arts. More recent entertainment systems based on information technologies have permitted the emergence of emphasis on the media used to carry/render the emotions. In essence a video game or a multimedia system will explore a combination of modalities and medias to deliver an effective entertainment. Latest entertainment, due to the emergence of the Internet and other networks have given room for the sharing of the experience and of the emotions between users.

Entertainment systems have evolved into three major groupings: (1) The explicit rendering, and the asymmetric (mainly performers to user) flow of emotions (e.g. Paintings); (2) the media and mode rich rendering, and the symmetric (performer to and from user) flow of emotions (e.g. multimedia games); (3) the realism, and the triangular (performer to and from users and between users) flow of emotions (e.g. online games). While some forms of entertainment will directly express a variety of emotions, others will abstract emotions into music, colours etc. Emotions are experienced when using a form of entertainment and in some cases the emotions are also shared with other users or with the provider of the service. What is of particular relevance in this grouping is that for human to human communication to occurs and thus a possible dynamic exchange of emotions there is a need for either one of two possibilities: (1) The performer of the entertainment is human and he is connected to the audience (e.g. theatre); (2) there is a connection between users (e.g. Internet games or audience in a street theatre). As we are interested in rich dynamic emotional exchanges we have thereafter to ensure that it is the case that in our system either one of these two possibilities occurs.

2 Emotions

2.1 Dimension of Emotional Experiences

Emotions are a combination of physiological, psychological and physical experiences. They include a combination of motor, sensory, autonomic, cognitive and affective experiences. A Sensory experience is related to the emotions that we perceive thanks to our perception. An example is the perception of sadness in a facial expression.

Motor experience is the physical changes our body goes through when experiencing an emotion, e.g. physical withdrawal when scared. Cognitive experience is related to our assessment of the emotion we are experiencing and the conscious thinking about it (see also the discussion in [23]). In essence it is the conscious experience of our emotions. The affective part is about how we project an emotion onto the object that has provoked the experience. So we project happiness towards a friend and fear towards a gun. The autonomic experience is about the autonomic response we have of our emotions. Face blushing, increased heart beat and sweating are good examples.

2.2 Emotional Concerns: A Trilogy

Although there has been consensus in accepting that emotions are directed towards an object [13]. We advocate a more encompassing description of emotions as requiring several components rather than an object. The experience of emotions is a phenomenon that takes place as the result of exposure to a combination of up to three components: a situation, an environment or an object. An example would be having a conversation, in a hot office while holding a stress ball. The conversation could be at the origin of some emotions, the temperature of the office will induce stress and negative emotions while the stress ball could help you gain some relief. It is a rather simplistic portray of emotions but it does include the three possible origins for an emotional experience. Either of these components or a combination thereof will be of relevance to the individual. Such relevance is determined by the influence, the significance, the importance and the effect(s) the exposure will have on a person. More specifically, the resulting changes on his needs, requirements and desires. The needs are the essential necessities of a person, such as breathing and eating, the requirements are necessary elements to fulfil a function or a task, while the desires are related to a person goals, concerns, beliefs and drives. It is also important to investigate what would be capable of provoking an emotional response. As not all events will have an influence on our emotions. How could one draw some general rules which could be used to determine the influence an event would have on emotions.

The brain could be described as a pleasure seeking system that has sophisticated circuitry to generate and appreciate pleasurable stimulis (see [14]). It does make sense to seek to establish what does trigger pleasurable stimulis. Beside cognitive processes the brain is also home to affective processes that are the seat of our emotional experiences. Current knowledge of functional neuro-anatomy of the brain indicate that sensory imputs and their assessment play a major triggering role in the emotions that we experience (see for example [15]). Furthermore, the assessment of sensory inputs is generaly performed in line with personal concerns. These concerns can be personal, or universal, general or specific (i.e. confort, well being, social relations). Our interest in these emotional concerns lies in those that are universal, we call them major concerns. We advocate that these majore concerns are generally related to: (1) *power* (e.g. hierarchy, competition, and submission); (2) *death* (e.g. violence, health, and self preservation), and (3) *love* (e.g. friendship, hatered, and lust). What is noticeable is that our lives are rich with combinations of these major concerns. Such combinations are not necessarily balanced between the three. In fact without wanting to advocate such a cynical view it seems that power is the ultimate concern with death, and love the most effective means used to overcome it. Our trilogy of emotional concerns has been established by looking at several elements of human history, culture and religions e.g. remarkable events, lasting buildings and work of art that have a certain historical or cultural value[1]. Indeed historical events, are all reported within the perspective of one of the three concerns (king legends, wars and love stories). It is cross cultural and cross centuries (Maharabata 5BC – 2AD, Shake-speare works such as Macbeth 1605-1606, and Romeo and Juliet 1594-1595). Even contemporary media relate to these three concerns (see figure 1).

Fig. 1. Power, Death and Love as human characteristics. From left to right: In "2001", HAL takes over *power* as he considers humans not capable of handling the mission properly [16]. In "The Bicentennial Man", Andrew Martin the robot seeks to *die* to become human [17]. While in "AI" David the child robot is seeking maternal *love* [18].

Furthermore, there are medical evidences that sustain our proposal of emotion concerns. LSD and other hallucinogens help people feel like empowerment and the presence of powerfull elements as well as out-of-body experiences. A similar experience of life-after-death is also reported from patiens with brains that are under anoxic (low oxygen) conditions [19]. Patients suffering from Complex Partial Seizures have reported hypersexuality and hyposexuality [20]. Epilectic subjects also report on the feeling of an overwhelmingly powerful being and some have shown hypersexuality [19]. Finally looking at folk culture and traditions, hypnotic states and states of trance have been described as means to reach higher self-control (meditation), after-death (medium) and higher level of sexual pleasures (orgasm prolongation exercises).

2.3 Fundamental Emotions

According to functional neuroanatomy of the bain, there appear to be five emotions that we all share as they have dedicated parts of the brain [21]. We call these fundamental emotions. The five fundamental emotions (FEm) are: (1) anger, (2) disgust, (3) fear, (4) happiness, and (5) sadness. These five FEms have a substantially more significant role that the reminder of emotions which we experience. This is due to the dedicated brain circuit for each one. As a general rule the five FEms are essential for our well being and safety. They ensure that we are equipped to deal with a range of situations (dangerous, safe, beneficial etc.). They take us out of harm's way

---

[1] The original idea of this trilogy was provided by Marcel Reich-Ranitzky.

by providing a motivation for actions either avoidance (disgust), escape (fear), introspection (sadness). FEms provide us with basic social skills attraction (happiness) and rejection (anger) of our peers. Other emotions as we experience them are social and cultural constructs. We learn to understand the emotional experience as more than the FEms, due to the context where it occurs. So for example anger associated with an individual will become disliking [23]. In our opinion, highlighting these emotions could be beneficial for the development of more effective entertainment systems.

3 A Role for Emotions

Emotions were considered as the mechanism necessary to initiate a wide range of actions not deemed essential. Blushing or smiling are directly initiated by our emotional experience. While keeping the balance, breathing and others actions are not initiated by emotions, although they can be modified by them. Until recently preventing one's emotions and controlling one's emotional reactions was deemed necessary when making decisions and choices. The argument was that one should think rationally and logically rather than impulsively and emotionally.

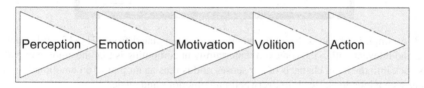

Fig. 2. The conventional understanding of emotions is that we first perceive something, we then experience an emotion related to that event. Our emotion will then motivate us to action. Thus follow volition and then action.

From emotions we draw motivation and action (see figure 2). Emotions in this model are the result of perception, which could be misguided. Therefore, it was accepted practice to ignore, inhibit and control one's emotions and not to use them as a decision mechanism. Until recently, emotions were not even included in cognitive processes. A good example is the unlikely emotionless character of Mr Spock in the star trek series.

However, looking at the latest development in funcional neuroanatomy of the human brain. Emotions can be considered as resulting from an input stimuli. Such an input is assessed by the brain emotional engine as described in figure 3. The emotional input is processed and yields an emotional response or a lack thereof. In all cases emotional responses are a result of the assessment of emotional input in terms of the positive effect such input could have in any single or any combination of emotional dimensions as described in section 2.1. Thereafter is it important to high light two key facts about emotions. First emotions are rendered within the perspective of the self, and second emotion have a hedonistic dimension in that there is a positive correlation between the reward associated with an emotional input and the kind of emotional response rendered as a result of the same emotional input.

Another relevant fact, within entertainment computing is the *time dependence* of emotions (see figure 4). We have established a timeline of emotions ranging from the short timed emotional response such as laughter to a much longer emotional response such as moods and trait. Further down the line personality and characters are emerging as part of one's emotional profile over a period of time that spans years.

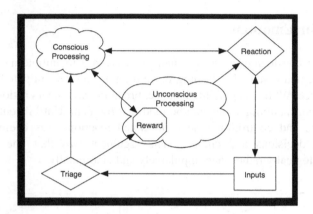

Fig. 3. A simplified brain pathway for emotions as extrapolated from [21] [15]. What is interesting and relevant within the context of entertainment computing is that the emotional reaction feeds back into the input channels of our senses and is thus again part of an emotional reaction. Letting such a loop loose, leads to overwhelming emotions and panic.

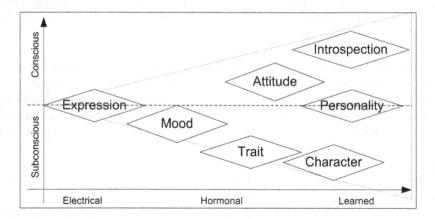

Fig. 4. Emotions have a time dependence that is often overlooked. Short time span of seconds is generally related to the electrical activity of the neurons and result in the experience and expression of emotions. Further time is generally required for hormonal effects which results in a change of mood and trait one can be known as having. With a longer time span, attitude, character and personality start to emerge as qualities of an individual.

3.1 Emotions and Pleasures

Emotions can also be defined as the hedonistic assessment of our sensory inputs. The inputs are evaluated in terms of their pleasure value. The hedonist value, a perceptual event may have, is related to the amount of pleasure one is expected to experience. As a result we use emotions to assess how pleasurable or pleasure inducing a perceptive event can be. This result in a positive to negative assessment of an emotional experience, also called valence [24]. The emotions hedonistic value is linked to the expectations within the context of the emotional experience and the expressive value and consequences as part of communication. In general we build expectations whatever the context we are in, not only about what should happen but also about our own behaviour. As a result events that do not fall within the expectations will yield emotional responses that might be difficult to manage and with the tendency of being classified as negative. Similarly the expressive value and consequence of the expression of an emotion play a role in the kind of expressions one will be experiencing. In other words people are more likely to experience emotions as they are expected to, than otherwise. Socio-cultural habits and rules are established during our life to help construct a comprehensive set of rules regarding the acceptability of emotions. This is another relevant fact when designing entertainment systems. In short it is better to integrate emotion rendering that are known and familiar to the user. This would yield a clearer if not stronger emotional perception.

4 Emotions and Entertainment

From the pervious sections we have seen that emotions are a rather complex concept. Furthermore to add to the problems there are no clear rules on how to provoke an emotion. One can rely on centuries of entertainment to see how emotions have been abstracted, rendered and perceived. Theatre has shown how successfully a wide spectrum of emotions can be used. However with the advent of entertainment computing, there has been increased pressure to explore the wide spectrum of emotions rather than to focus on what current entertainment computing has delivered. We know that there are five fundamental emotions (FEms) (disgust, fear, sadness, happiness and anger). We advocate that entertainment computing could gain from exploiting these five emotions as the basis for the service provided. We thus combine these emotions with the three emotional concerns of mankind. We list next some of the current developments and what systems exist in this matrix-like arrangement between the three concerns and the five FEms. As it would otherwise be a too large task, we will focus in the next sections on games, toys and robots to illustrate our point about emotions and entertainment.

4.1 Death and Love Entertainment

Emphatic electronic toys are a recent development (1998). Furby is a good example, it has been a very successful toy selling at more than 40 millions units [25]. A new generation is currently being developed: "The emotional response of the new FURBY creature is one of the most noticeable changes from the original. EMOTO-TRONICS allows the FURBY creature to react based on how a child interacts with it" [idem].

The attribution of life-like characters to Furby is such that there are several websites related to autopsies of the toy (e.g. [26]). Other developments in this area include the micro-pets from TOMY [27] and the new generation Tamagotchi [28]. With empathic toy the issue of positive, altruistic behaviour (caring and loving) as part of entertainment has been addressed. Until then no entertainment computing systems was related to an altruistic attitude towards entertainment. Rather many systems relied on an egoistic attitude towards entertainment. One has to go to the world of basic toys such as dolls (Barbies and notably babies-like dolls) to find such equivalence to today empathic electronic toys (see figure 5). What is notable, is the combination of death and love for the Tamagotchi and Furby!

Fig. 5. Empathic toys: Micro-Pets (left) from TOMY, Tamagotchi (middle) from BANDAI, and Furby (right) from Hasbro. For each of these toys the owner is required to "nurture" them, play with them and attend to their needs. In essence you need to care for them. The FEms involved are happiness, sadness and to a lesser extent anger.

4.2 Power and Death Entertainment

Most current games of first person shouting are combining power and death (e.g., figure 6). The game objectives are generally about taking over control of some country, city, or base and to kill as many of the enemy as possible. In effect, death (of opponents) is used as a mean to reach power.

Fig. 6. Doom (left) [29] and God of war (right) [30] games. Highly popular computer games are related to death and power. The FEms involved are fear, anger and disgust.

4.3 Power and Love Entertainment

This category has mostly been focused on adult explicit games (e.g. see figure 7). These games have a common scenario in that the player is in control of the script and what actions, generally of sexual nature will the character perform. Lust is used to achieve power over the characters portrayed.

Fig. 7. 3D SexVilla (left) [31] and egirl (right) [32] games. In 3D SexVilla players are in control of what females will do in terms of sexual activities. Similarly with egirl although your control goes to a further extent.

4.4 Love and Death Entertainment

Therapeutic robots have been developed to provide for patient support for their emotional needs. In essence patient use the robots to project love and care and in return feel as if involved with a loving pet. Positive results have been reported, the robots do have purpose in improving the patient condition. Similarly the idea of "resurrecting" your dead pet is a form of death and love entertainment. In the example presented (see figure 8), it is no less than a zombie cat that is proposed (i.e. a pet robot covered with the actual skin of your beloved cat).

Fig. 8. Therapeutic robot Paro (left) and the "zombie cat" (right). Paro helps you recover from your illness, using love that you feel for it to help you recover from illness [33]. The zombie cat was developed as a pet robot that acts as sleeping packaged in the skin of a beloved cat. Thus creating a zombie combines death and love [34].

5   Power and Love Entertainment: The Mollycoddle Robots

In the perspective of the ideas presented in this paper and the review of current entertainment systems, we have launched the mollycoddle project. In this project, the key issues to be addressed were: (1) Rendering of emotion through postures and movements, (2) Effective human perception of the emotions expressed by the robot, (3)

Clear rules of engagement and social rules used by the human and the robot, (4) As natural as possible interaction between the user and the robot, (5) Real-time performance by the robot. The robot was designed for 8 to 12 years old girls. Our students were asked to investigate the main interests, needs, requirements and desires of this population of users. The students were requested to develop a toy that has some expressive functions and that must be held to be used. We then encouraged two different directions for two groups, one was power toy, where by the mollycoddle should be used for power projection. The second direction was love: the mollycoddle should be used to express love. Both toys have a soft body with embedded electronic circuitry.

5.1 Power Toy: The Cuddle

In the case of cuddle, power is associated with fights with friends. Initial user tests have demonstrated the popularity of Cuddle (see figure 9). Accelerometers detect actions and control the playback of cartoon animals and characters recordings.

Fig. 9. A mollycoddle toy emphasising power: Cuddle (left). Such a toy was designed to hit your friend. Cuddle can be used in "pillow fights" (right).

5.2 Love Toy: The Miko

The core of Miko is a modified hard-disk drive used to translate sounds into vibrations (see figure 10). Heartbeats are thus generated and can be felt when handling

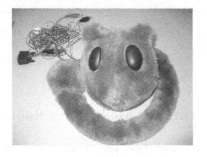

Fig. 10. A mollycoddle toy emphasising love: Miko (left). Such a toy was designed with emotion rendering functions. In the case of Miko sounds are translated into vibrations. These vibrations can only be felt if the toy is tightly held (right).

the toy. The tail of Miko is also equipped with a small vibrating engine. As a result one can feel and slightly hear a buzzing sound coming from the tail.

6 Conclusion

Entertainment computing has emerged as an alternative to conventional entertainment. It is an alternative rather than a continuation, because as we have discussed it here there is a clear potential for such entertainment to go beyond the usual understanding of what is entertainment. Understanding what emotions are and how to use such understanding in the development of novel entertainment systems is part of objectives of this paper. Furthermore we hope that this attempt at understanding emotions within this context should initiate further developments in the way entertainment is delivered. While most entertainment has been passive over the past, entertainment computing gives us the opportunity of a more user active involvement. Combining this with a refined model of emotions and their rendering should yield more exhilarating entertainment. We hope to have demonstrated that our proposed trilogy can be successfully applied in the design of a new generation of entertainment robot toys. One of the difficulty we have met is creating toys that are truly addressing one and only one of our major concerns. Future work would be in developing systems that embody a combination of these concerns and ultimately the whole trilogy. Finally we hope to have open a debate in the entertainment community about what direction could be taken in the development of new systems.

Acknowledgements. The authors wish to thank our students for their work on the Miko project. The micro-pets pictured were kindly donated by TOMY France.

References

All URLs listed were last visited March 2005.
[1] Bechara, A.: The role of emotion in decision-making: Evidence from neurological patients with orbitofrontal damage. *Brain and Cognition* (2004), 55, 30-40
[2] Toates F.: Cognition, motivation, emotion and action: a dynamic and vulnerable interdependence. *Applied Animal Behaviour Science* (2004), 86, 173-204
[3] Gross, J.J. Emotion and emotion regulation. In L.A. Pervin & O.P. John, (Eds.), *Handbook of personality: Theory and research.* Guilford, New York, NY, USA (1999) 525-552
[4] Pickard, R.W.: Does HAL cry digital tears? Emotions and computers. In D.G. Stork (Ed.), *Hal's legacy: 2001's Computer as Dream and Reality.* MIT Press, Cambridge, MA, USA (1997) 279-303
[5] Brave, S., Nass, C.: Emotion in Human-Computer Interaction. In J.A. Jacko & A. Sears, (Eds.), *The Human-Computer Interaction Handbook,* Lawrence Erlbaum, Mahwah, NJ, USA, (2003) 81-96
[6] Parrott, W.G., Smith, R.H.: Distinguishing the experiences of envy and jealousy. *Journal of Personality & Social Psychology* (1993), 64(6), 906-920
[7] Fridlund, A. J.: Sociality of solitary smiling: Potentiation by an implicit audience. *Journal of Personality & Social Psychology* (1991), 60(2), 229-240
[8] de Wied, M. & Verbaten, M.N. Affective pictures processing, attention, and pain tolerance. *Pain,* 90, Feb 2001, 163-172

290 B. Salem and M. Rauterberg

[9] Ohman, A., Flykt, A., Esteves, F.: Emotions drives attention: detecting the snake in the grass. *Journal of Experimental Psychology General* (2001), 130, 466-478
[10] Rachman S.: Emotional processing with special reference to post-traumatic stress disorder. *International Review of Psychiatry* (2001), 13(3), 164-171
[11] Hayes, S.C., Strosahl, K.D., Wilson, K.G. *Acceptance and commitment therapy. An experimental approach to behavior change.* The Guilford Press, New York, NY, USA (1999)
[12] Baker, R., Holloway, J., Thomas, P.W., Thomas, S., Owens, M.: *Emotional processing and panic, Behaviour Research and Therapy* (2004), 42, 1271-1287
[13] Frijda, N.H. Varieties of affect: Emotions and episodes, moods, and sentiments. In P. Ekman & R.J. Davidson (Eds.), *The nature of emotion* (1994), Oxford University Press New York, NY, USA, 59-67
[14] Berridge, K.C.: Pleasures of the Brain. *Brain and Cognition* (2003), 52, 106-128.
[15] Nolte, J. (2002): *The Human Brain – An Introduction to Its functional Anatomy.* St Louis, MI, USA, Mosby.
[16] Kubrick, S., Clarke, A.C.: 2001: A Space Odyseey, (1968)
[17] Columbus, C., Asimov, I.: The Bicentennial Man, (1999)
[18] Spielberg, S., Kubrick, S.: AI, (2001)
[19] Smith Churchland, P. (2002), *Brain-Wise: Studies in Neurophilosophy.* Cambridge, MA, USA, Bradford Book, MIT Press
[20] Cytowic, R.E. (1996), *The neurological side of neuropsychology.* Cambridge, MA, USA, MIT Press
[21] Luan Phan, K., Wager, T., Taylor, S.F., Liberzon, I. Functional Neuroanatomy of Emotion: A meta-analysis of emotion activation studies in PET and fMRI. *NeuroImage* (2002), 16, 331-348
[22] Rolls, T.E. (1999): *The Brain and Emotion.* Oxford, England, Oxford University Press.
[23] Libet, B.: Do we have free will? *Journal of Consciousness Studies* (1999), 6, 8-9 47-57
[24] Rusell, J.A.: A circumplex model of affect. *Journal of Personality and Social Psychology* (1980), 36, 1161-1178
[25] See: http://www.hasbro.com/media/pl/page.release/dn/default.cfm?release=277
[26] See: http://www.phobe.com/furby/
[27] See: http://www.tomy.fr/
[28] See: http://www.tamagotchi.com/
[29] See: http://www.doom3.com/
[30] See: http://www.the-nextlevel.com/previews/ps2/god-of-war/
[31] See: http://www.3d-sexgames.com/
[32] See: http://www.girl3d.com/
[33] See: http://www.aist.go.jp/aist_e/aist_today/2003_09/robot_01.html
[34] Klarenbeek, D. invented the "zombie cat". In personal conversation with the authors

The MUSICtable: A Map-Based Ubiquitous System for Social Interaction with a Digital Music Collection

Ian Stavness[1], Jennifer Gluck[2], Leah Vilhan[1], and Sidney Fels[1]

[1] HCT Laboratory, University of British Columbia, 2356 Main Mall,
Vancouver, BC, V6T 1Z4, Canada
{stavness, leahv, ssfels}@ece.ubc.ca
[2] Department of Computer Science, University of British Columbia, 2366 Main Mall,
Vancouver, BC V6T 1Z4, Canada
gluck@cs.ubc.ca

Abstract. Popular acceptance of the mp3 digital music standard has greatly increased the complexity of organizing and playing large music collections. Existing digital music systems do not adequately support exploration of a collection, nor do they cater to multi-user interaction in a social setting. In this paper, we present the design of a ubiquitous system that utilizes spatial visualization to support exploration and social interaction with a large music collection. Our interface is based on the interaction semantic of influence, which allows users to affect and control the mood of music being played without the need to select a set of specific songs. This design is inspired, to some extent, by Gaver's work on ludic design. We implemented a prototype as a proof of concept of our design. User testing demonstrates that our system encourages participation and strengthens social cohesion. Our work contributes to interactive interface research in that it extends the utility of map-based visualization of digital music.

Keywords: User interface, music map, social interaction, entertainment, table-top display, music classification, mp3.

1 Introduction

Advancement in digital recording technology and the mp3 digital music standard have spawned a trend of large music collections. With this new technology has come a novel set of problems. One emergent issue is that interfaces used to play digital music do not support interaction with large collections in social situations.

Traditional forms of recorded music such as compact discs (CDs), tapes, and records present music at the granularity of the album, comprised of a set of 10-15 songs. Digital media poses a more challenging organization problem because mp3 files reduce the granularity of music to the size of the individual song. It is much more difficult to interact with a collection of 600 mp3 files than the collection of 50 CDs from which the songs were taken.

Digital solutions to the music organization problem have been attempted by means of metadata (ID3 tags) that explicitly denotes the artist, album name, year of production, and genre of an mp3 file. In practice, these fields are rarely utilized correctly.

F. Kishino et al. (Eds.): ICEC 2005, LNCS 3711, pp. 291–302, 2005.

Thus, classification of large digital collections remains an open problem for both single users interacting with a music player, as well as in the domain of multi-user social interaction with recorded music.

The standard PC-based digital music player is designed for single-user interaction. The user interacts with the system by adding individual mp3 files to a playlist. Selection of each file requires linear searching within the computer file system. The playlist metaphor does not support the idea of a continuous mood or feeling of music – often the goal of the music listener – because selection occurs at the granularity of a particular song. Additionally, this selection granularity may be problematic for users who are not familiar with the specific artist and song names. Furthermore, the system is constrained to the computer itself. These characteristics result in a system that requires a nontrivial investment of interaction time by a single user. A trend discovered through an initial user study was that many users abandon direct control by engaging a "random" play mode with all songs in the collection. This method requires continuous interaction with the system as users generally will continue to skip to a new random song until they find one that fits their current mood.

The user interface of the PC-based digital music player clearly does not support music selection by multiple people in a social situation. One manifestation of this deficiency is a phenomenon we will refer to as "separate party syndrome," wherein a small number of people tend to gather around the desktop computer, away from the other attendees of the party, dominating the selection of music. A small fraction of attendees participates in music selection with this type of interface and those who do are removed from the social atmosphere of the party while engaged in music selection.

Effective social interaction with a digital collection requires a means by which to explore and discover its contents and to play music in a manner that is inclusive of the preferences of each individual, yet results in a smooth progression of music through different moods, styles, and tempos of music. Such a solution should not require substantial investment of interaction time, nor should it require a departure from the social atmosphere. In an effort to address the shortcomings of current digital music solutions, we present a ubiquitous system that utilizes spatial visualization in order to support exploration and social interaction with a large music collection.

2 Related Work

2.1 Spatial Visualization of Music

As personal digital music collections grow larger, the science of visualizing such archives is becoming popular. A number of papers on this topic have been published. For example, Torrens et al. [7] have experimented with visualization techniques such as disk, rectangle, and tree-map visualization.

Other research has taken on the analogy of cartography. Pampalk et al. [5] have created a map-based visualization called Islands of Music. This system creates a self organizing map by sampling the songs and extracting raw audio data. The music is classified by comparing traits such as loudness, sensation, and rhythm patterns. The results are used to display the music collection spatially, such that similar pieces of music appear close to each other. This organization is visualized as a geographic map.

Similarly, van Gulik et al. [2] have developed the "Artist Map," a technique that employs graph-drawing algorithms based on an energy model. Like Islands of Music, this system presents a visualization using data derived from the music itself, but also incorporates metadata that can be obtained from ID3 tags and web services.

In all the visualization systems discussed in the literature, the objective is to display a representation of the music collection. These systems focus on navigation and exploration of a music collection. We have yet to find evidence of any of these systems being utilized to listen to the music library, for example, via the creation of playlists. We endeavor to extend the idea of map-based music visualization systems by using such a visualization to support the selection and playing of music.

2.2 Social Interaction and Music

Current research on social interaction and music has focused on the creation of music through social interaction. A project at the MIT Media Lab examined changing ambient music at a social gathering based on the type of beverages people were drinking [3]. Ambient music was not recorded music, but a combination of various musical sounds.

In the domain of recorded music, O'Hara et al. have examined a song selection system used in a public space [4]. Patrons of a pub democratically chose which song to play next. Our interface is intended for a different social context: private social gatherings. Furthermore, our interface will gather input from each every user's selection, incorporating this data to play music that will cater to the preferences of all participating users. This is quite different from a voting mechanism for song selection on a song-by-song basis.

2.3 Ubiquity and Interactive Displays

Rogers and Lindley [6] conducted a study to investigate how the physical orientation of a shared display affects group collaboration. They found that table displays encourage group members to switch roles often, explore ideas, and closely follow the activities of other members of the group. The social aspects surrounding the use of tables make them appealing for use as displays. Tables are common and are incorporated into the design of most rooms, allowing such displays to blend into everyday life. This "blending" is a defining characteristic of ubiquitous computing, as presented by Weiser [8]. Thus, we feel that a tabletop display is an ideal medium to utilize in the separation of the music collection from the computer. We were also encouraged by the social affordances associated with tables, and believe that they are well-suited to creation of a system in which groups of people are encouraged to interact.

2.4 Ludic Design

Gaver et al. explored the notion of ludic design in order to address computer use in the realm of people as "playful creatures" ("Homo Ludens") [1]. The Drift Table is a tabletop display that displays aerial photography. The display slowly drifts across a landscape and is controlled by the distribution of weight on its surfaces. Goals derived from the ludic outlook include avoiding the appearance of a computer and supporting social engagement in ludic activities. Strongly contrasting with traditional goals for computer systems, the designers' objective was to avoid meeting users' immediate desires or demands. For instance, the system was designed to disallow a move to a particular location. Instead, users must work together to influence the direction of the drift. We were inspired by this idea of influence over selection in order to support open-ended, social use of an interface for exploration of a music collection.

3 Design

Our general design goals for a system that supports exploration and social interaction with a large digital music collection were as follows:

- Present the collection in a form that supports exploration;
- Preserve social cohesion;
- Encourage collaboration in the music selection process;
- Separate the music collection from the computer.

We propose a table-based system that utilizes music map visualization. A selection cursor is displayed on the map corresponding to the location of the next song to be played. Users interact with the system by entering directional input to affect the motion of the selection point.

The notion of exploration in a musical space is important to our design. Users who are unfamiliar with a particular music collection may be timid and may therefore shy away from participating in music selection. By providing an interface that suggests traversal and exploration, everyone is equipped with an equal level of understanding. This allows the unfamiliar user the freedom to participate and influence the navigation of the map without social pressures. We aim to provide an interface in which no one person chooses a specific song. Instead, we envision a group of people working together to influence the musical atmosphere of a room by exploring a map.

A tabletop system, when strategically placed in a room, ensures that social cohesion is preserved. First, this type of system ensures that users are not required to remove themselves physically from a social area in order to attend to a computer, which may be located in the corner of the room or in another room entirely. Second, by separating our system from a traditional PC, we ensure that users will not become distracted by other software while in the process of selecting music. As discussed above, tabletop systems are also known to encourage collaboration.

Because of the low level granularity of digital music collections, displaying the collection at the level of a song can make the selection process tedious. Displaying a collection as a series of folders organized by traits such as artist or genre is not ideal. Instead, we aim to separate the names and titles of songs from the visualization, instead focusing on the mood or atmosphere inspired. We feel that the geographic map metaphor addresses this goal. This idea of a "music map" visualization of a music collection is useful and engaging because it compels users to traverse and explore the music. Just as an orienteer navigates a map to discover new locations, our users will be able to discover new music. We decided to implement our system as a static map with a moving selection point as opposed to the Drift Table design, which utilizes a static selection point and a moving map. This provides users with the context necessary to not only explore, but to learn and retain the discovered information.

Simultaneous multiple-user input is also important in encouraging collaboration. However, such input cannot be discrete: input from each user must be multiplexed together to achieve the music selection. We capitalized on the idea of influence over selection broached by Gaver et al. [1]. Discrete directional input entered by each user combines to influence the direction of movement of the selection point. The idea of influence is also important in effectively matching the interaction style to the map metaphor. In the case of a music system, 'selection' gives the user the expectation of specifying the exact song to be played. This does not work well in a group setting: each person will want to hear 'his' or 'her' specific song, and unfamiliar users have no opportunity for input. With an 'influence' semantic, on the other hand, there is no such expectation or limitation. Instead, users are given the sense that their actions will have an impact on the music played, but without the certainty of an exact song. Also of note is the fact that the map visualization, devoid of artist and song names, does not give the option of selecting a specific song; thus, we must approach the user interaction from the influence perspective.

4 Prototype

We designed, implemented and tested a series of prototypes. The goal of the first iteration was to avoid "separate party syndrome." Evaluation demonstrated evidence that the system succeeded in this goal. Our second iteration focused on resolving issues reported during the initial user evaluation. These issues were restricted to the music map, the interaction metaphor, and the graphical user interface. All other aspects of the implementation were left untouched. Our discussion here is confined to the most recent iteration of the prototype.

4.1 Prototype Design

The Music Map. We created our own music map for the prototype; however, our system design can support any music map visualization, such as those referenced in the related work section. In the creation of our map, 348 songs of various styles were subjectively sorted by similarity of sound and genre into 50 categories. The categories were then arranged spatially such that similar genres appear near one another. Artistic license was employed to create the impression of a geographical map. Broad categories were indicated using a colour coding scheme and were communicated to users via a map legend. Lower level categorization is implied via blending of fills and spatial layout. Refer to Figure 1 for a screen capture of the music map visualization.

User Interface. The music map is presented on the tabletop display along with the legend that relates map colours to music styles. The selection cursor is denoted by a small target icon that pulses in brightness to capture the users' attention. The notion of influence is attained through the analogy of wind flow. Users cannot directly move the position of the selection point; they can only affect the direction and speed of wind flow that causes the cursor to drift slowly across the map. Wind flow is visualized as semi-transparent flow lines moving over the map. Eight buttons arranged at compass points around the tabletop display allow users to control direction and speed

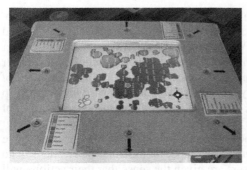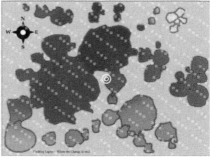

Fig. 1. The MUSICtable: table top (left); music map graphic (right)

of the wind flow. Wind flows in the direction of the last button press and multiple button hits in the same direction cause the flow to increase speed. LED indicators around the buttons, in addition to the change in direction and speed of flow line motion, provide feedback to users regarding the way in which their input has affected the system. The selection cursor slowly drifts in the direction of the wind flow and each time a song ends, the next song to be played is selected from the musical area nearest to the current location of the selection cursor. The incremental change in the selection cursors position fits well with the semantic of influence. The cumulative effect of all users' input shapes the path of the selection cursor as it moves through the music space.

4.2   Implementation

Software System. The control and visualization software was developed in Windows and can be broken down into the following tasks:

- Display the music map and wind flow visualization;
- Receive button input and change wind flow direction / speed;
- Select a song based on the location of the selection cursor;
- Ensure music plays continuously without repeating songs.

Graphic visualization was implemented with the openGL graphics library and Utility Toolkit (GLUT). The control system integrated button input using Windows drivers for the Phidgets USB interface board. The actual playing of mp3 music files utilized the open source FMOD audio engine.

In order to select a song based on location, all songs were spatially subdivided using a quad-tree data structure. This creates a grid representing the music map where each grid square contains, at most, five songs. When the system selects the next song to play, it finds the grid square at which the selection point is located and then randomly chooses a song from that grid square. To ensure that songs are not repeated and that music plays continuously, an additional coarse-grained subdivision is created and used if the fine-grained grid contains only songs that have already been played.

Fig. 2. The MUSICtable prototype (left); Users interacting with the MUSICtable (right)

Hardware System. Key features of the hardware system were the tabletop display and the button hardware. We used an LCD monitor embedded into the middle of a table in order to provide a bright display with high resolution. A glass cover over top of the display was flush with the table surface to maintain the system's utility as a table. The table stands three feet tall at a comfortable height to use while standing.

The button hardware was created with simple contact push buttons and LEDs. We used a Phidgets Interface Kit 8/8/8 board, housed inside of the table, to capture button input and to control the LED indicators. The software system ran on a Windows PC located inside the MUSICtable. An external audio jack provided a connection to the stereo system. The prototype is shown in Figure 2.

5 User Evaluation

5.1 Iteration One

We evaluated our initial MUSICtable prototype in comparison with a laptop computer system running Nullsoft's Winamp mp3 player. This popular software is used to build and play playlists of songs from a digital music collection.

The broad goal of our system was to avoid the "separate party syndrome" often involved in digital music selection in a social setting. Thus, it was necessary to compare our system with a Winamp interface also located in the centre of the party room in order to show that more is required to solve the problems associated with social interaction with a digital music collection than merely moving the traditional computer-based system into the centre of the social circle.

Hypotheses

H1: A larger percentage of participants will involve themselves in music selection with the MUSICtable tabletop system than with the PC-based Winamp system.

H2: The MUSICtable system will preserve social cohesion: Participants will experience lowered feelings of separation from the social atmosphere while involved in music selection with MUSICtable than with Winamp. The MUSICtable system will encourage a higher level of collaboration than Winamp.

Participants. 13 participants, all between the ages of 18 and 30, were recruited from a pool of graduate students. This age group is representative of the generation that has embraced digital music collections and related technologies.

Procedure. The experiment consisted of a party to which the participants were invited. The experiment was divided into two 45-minute sessions. Subjects were told to feel free to change the music that was playing. That is, music selection was in the hands of the party attendees.

During the first session, a laptop computer running Winamp was used as the music selection system. During the second session, our MUSICtable system was used. During session one, the laptop was placed on top of the table that housed the MUSICtable system, with the prototype turned off. This was done so that both systems were centrally located in the room. The switch between the two systems was made as inconspicuously as possible while the users' attention was directed to the other side of the room.

Results were collected via a post-party questionnaire. Here, participants indicated which of the two systems they interacted with (Winamp, MUSICtable, or both). Participants answered questions pertaining to the level of collaboration that was encouraged and feelings of separation induced by use of each system. Additionally, the survey gauged understanding of the system itself, as well as a preference between music player systems.

Results and Discussion

Verification of Hypotheses. 8 users participated in the selection of music using Winamp, whereas 12 users participated in selection of music using the MUSICtable. Only 1 user who used Winamp did not use MUSICtable. This supports our hypothesis that a larger number of participants will involve themselves in music selection with the MUSICtable tabletop system.

Qualitative results from the questionnaire indicated that users felt more encouraged to collaborate in music selection while using the MUSICtable than while using Winamp, and felt less separated from the social circle while involved in MUSICtable interaction. Responses were rated on a five-point Likert scale.

The mean response to the survey question "The Winamp system encouraged me to collaborate with others while selecting music" was 2.5 (corresponding to an answer of "Disagree-Neutral"). The mean response to the survey question "The MUSICtable system encouraged me to collaborate with others while selection music" was 3.67 (corresponding to an answer of "Neutral-Agree").

The mean response to the survey question "I felt separated from the social atmosphere of the party while participating in music selection using the Winamp system" was 3.125 (corresponding to an answer of "Neutral-Agree"). The mean response to the survey question "I felt separated from the social atmosphere of the party while participating in music selection using the MUSICtable system" was 1.92 (corresponding to an answer of "Strongly Disagree-Disagree").

All users indicated feeling more included in the social circle while using MUSICtable. These results support our hypothesis that the MUSICtable system will preserve social cohesion.

General Feedback. Users generally enjoyed the interface, feeling that it encouraged participation and led to conversation. Some users commented that they felt that the interface was game-like and compelled them to participate in order to figure out how it worked. People were generally happy with the music played by the MUSICtable and liked that the mood of the music progressed in a continuous manner.

Issues. Our user study indicated that the system made a significant improvement in social interaction but failed to provide users with the level of control they desired. This factor clearly influenced overall system preference, as eight participants indicated a preference for Winamp, three preferred the MUSICtable, and two participants were undecided.

There were problems with the mental model of the system. Many users had trouble understanding how their input affected the selection of music. This stemmed from a lack of understanding of the relationship between the visual map and the music played. Users indicated that the visualization did not provide enough information about which areas of the map corresponded to which type of music. This lack of understanding was further complicated by confusion over the interaction metaphor. Thus, these two areas were reworked in the second design iteration.

5.2   Iteration Two

Our initial evaluation demonstrated that the system succeeded in reducing separate party syndrome. The ensuing redesign focused on resolving the problems associated with appearance and control of the interface. Thus, evaluation of our second prototype was concerned with user perception of the system itself rather than with comparison to the Winamp system.

Participants. The 41 participants were all faculty and graduate students within the departments of Electrical and Computer Engineering and Computer Science at the University of British Columbia.

Procedure. The study took place during a party to celebrate the opening of a new building on the university campus. The MUSICtable was utilized as the music control system at the party. The gathering was videotaped so that detailed observations could be made. A post-party questionnaire was utilized to gauge user understanding of the system. Note that this was not a controlled study but a legitimate party, and so participants were free to come and go as they pleased. Some participants were present and interacted with the MUSICtable for as much as an hour and a half, while others were present for only a very short period.

Results and Discussion

Survey Results. 35 of the 41 attendees filled out the questionnaire. Of these, 24 indicated participation in selection of music using MUSICtable. The following survey results pertain to these 24 survey responses. Our focus was on aspects of the design that were poorly received during the previous user evaluation. Responses were rated on a five-point Likert scale.

The mean response to the survey query "I understood the relationship between the visual map and the music that was played." was 4.1 (corresponding to an answer of "Agree"). This was a marked improvement over the previous iteration, which had yielded a mean response of 2.6 (corresponding to an answer of "Disagree-Neutral").

The mean response to the survey query "I did not understand how to use the MUSICtable or how my input affected the music that was played" was 2.3 (corresponding to an answer of "Disagree-Neutral"). Again, this was an improvement over the previous mean response of 3.2 (corresponding to an answer of "Neutral-Agree").

Results from queries relating to encouragement of collaboration and separation from social atmosphere were very similar to those obtained in the previous study. Thus, we assert that the changes made to the prototype resolved the weaknesses present in the initial system without detracting from that system's success in terms of preservation of social cohesion.

Positive Feedback. The system was well received by a large number of subjects. Many users indicated that the aesthetics of the visual map interface were appealing, with descriptions such as "colourful" and "attractive." Participants also responded well to the social and collaborative aspects of the map, commenting, "all people [can] participate," "it made the selection of music a social process," and that the "interactive nature [was] fun." Our goals for the system design were vindicated most notably by survey feedback from one user who "like[d] the concept of [being] able to set a trend with the music instead of selecting a song or a playlist."

Continuing Issues. A general complaint in both studies was the sense that the system progressed too slowly with too little immediate feedback. Participants expressed a desire to have their input affect music playback with more immediacy. However, the selection point was designed to drift slowly across the map and the major feedback loop was designed to be the slow progression from song to song. This was a point of frustration for numerous users. However, we believe that this concern over lack of control can be overcome under the right social circumstances. In a party that takes place over the course of an entire night, we believe that users will begin to accept that input is reflected in the progression of music and is not meant to effect a direct change in the playback.

6 Future Work

The core concept of our system holds promising application in various domains. Portable digital music, for instance, is becoming a very commonplace commodity with the popularization of personal hardware mp3 players such as the Apple iPod. Our system could be extended to utilize algorithms that automatically classify and organize music collections dynamically. This would allow a guest at a party to download her own collection into the MUSICtable, observing her own specific musical tastes reflected in the map.

In designing our prototype, we focused on supporting social collaboration in music selection at a party. The chosen domain assumes that the users are unfamiliar with the music collection and music map displayed on the MUSICtable. The core concept of MUSICtable applied to the domain of single user interaction opens up some interesting possibilities where the user is completely familiar with the music collection and map. In a single user design the user could be given finer control over the progression of music but still maintain the benefit of selecting music above the granularity of the specific song. We envision that such an interface could involve tangible interaction by manipulating widgets directly on top of the music table. This type of interaction is not well suited for multi-user collaboration; however, for the single user it has the potential to be a very rich experience. Since the user is completely familiar with all areas of the music map visualization, we also envision an interface in which the user specifies paths through the map to generate a specific time-varying progression of music. In this domain, the MUSICtable interface would move from the metaphor of exploration to that of orienteering.

Another future direction of the MUSICtable concept would be to explore the creation of music. Although the MUSICtable may not be effective as a music controller in the traditional sense, we envision that it could be utilized to create music through sampling of pre-recorded music. This type of interface would require a specific organization of music for the performer to be effective in navigating the space and creating a composition out of short music samples.

7   Conclusion

We have presented the design of a system in which a spatial visualization of a digital music collection is utilized to support multi-user interaction in the process of music selection. We implemented a tabletop display prototype to realize this novel interface concept. Informal user testing showed that the design was successful in encouraging collaboration and reducing isolation in music selection tasks within a social environment. Iterative redesign improved the intuitiveness and aesthetic appeal of the interface. Results indicated that the design was successful in creating an effective and engaging multi-user interface for the exploration of a digital music collection.

References

1. Gaver, W.W., Bowers, J., Boucher, A., Gellerson, H., Pennington, S., Schmidt, A., Steed, A., Villars, N., Walker, B. The drift table: designing for ludic engagement. Proc CHI '04 extended abstracts on Human factors in computing systems, ACM Press (2004), 885 – 900.
2. van Gulik, R., Vignoli, F., and van de Wetering, H. Mapping music in the palm of your hand, explore and discover your collection. ISMIR 2004 5th International Conference on Music Information Retrieval. Available online.

3. Mazalek, A., and Jehan, T. Interacting with Music in a Social Setting. Proc. CHI '00 extended abstracts on Human factors in computing systems, ACM Press (2000), 255 – 256.
4. O'Hara, K., Lipson, M., Jansen, M., Unger, A., Jeffries, H., and Macer, P. Jukola: Democratic Music Choice in a Public Space. Proc. DIS2004, ACM Press (2004), 145 – 154.
5. Pampalk, E., Rauber, A., and Merkl, D. Content-based organization and visualization of music archives. Proc. ACM Multimedia 2002, ACM Press (2002), 570 – 579.
6. Rogers, Y., and Lindley, S. Collaborating around large interactive displays: which way is best to meet? 2003. Available online.
7. Torrens, M., Hertzog, P., and Arcos, J. Visualizing and exploring personal music libraries. ISMIR 2004 5th International Conference on Music Information Retrieval. Available online.
8. Weiser, M., The computer for the twenty-first century, Scientific American 265(3), Sept. 1991, 94 - 104.

Painting as an Interface for Timbre Design

Michael Bylstra[1] and Haruhiro Katayose[2]

[1] Kwansei Gakuin University,
Gakuen, Sanda, 669-1337, Japan
mbylstra@digitalfeast.com.au
[2] Kwansei Gakuin University,
Gakuen, Sanda, 669-1337, Japan
http://ist.ksc.kwansei.ac.jp/~katayose/

Abstract. There is a challenge in designing a system for timbre design that is engaging for new users and enables experienced users to intuitively design a diverse range of complex timbres. This paper discusses some of the issues involved in achieving these aims and proposes that a timbre can be intuitively represented as an image. The design of TimbrePainter, a system that uses images painted with a mouse to specify the parameters of a harmonic additive synthesizer, is described.

1 Introduction

For a timbre design system to appeal to a wide range of musicians, it must be engaging for new users and enable experienced users to intuitively design a diverse range of complex timbres[1]. Synthesizer timbre design has generally been considered a special technical skill and new users have been encouraged to select from a set of predefined timbres rather than design their own.

A synthesizer can be evaluated in terms of power and usability. Synthesis methods exist that offer an extremely high level of power in that almost any sound possible can be created. However, interfaces for these synthesis methods usually suffer from a very low level of usability. On the other hand, synthesizers that employ simple synthesis methods and simple interfaces often do not offer much potential for exploration. There is a challenge in designing a flexible system that is both powerful and easy-to-use.

Another factor that should be considered is the degree in which a timbre can be predicted by observing the current state of the system. J.O.Smith III has referred to this concept as predictability [1]. The more predictable a system is, the more easily users can find desired timbres. In order for systems to be predictable for new users, predictability must be achievable without the need of any knowledge of the particular synthesis method employed. Predictability is likely to be an important factor in the design of a synthesizer that is both powerful and easy-to-use.

Although synthesizer interface design in the commercial sector has been rather stagnant, there have been a number of promising developments in the academic community in recent years. Notable developments include Tristimulus Synthesis [2],

---

[1] Timbre design is commonly referred to as synthesizer "patch editing" or "programming".

F. Kishino et al. (Eds.): ICEC 2005, LNCS 3711, pp. 303–314, 2005.
© IFIP International Federation for Information Processing 2005

Interactive Evolution [3] and Scanned Synthesis [4]. In each of these examples usability is paramount but substantial amounts of power and predictability are also achievable to varying degrees.

With similar goals in mind, we have attempted to design a system that is strong in usability, power and predictability. We will present TimbrePainter, a system that demonstrates a method of timbre design which uses painting as an interface for a harmonic additive synthesizer. The following section is a review of synthesizer interface research that is relevant to the design of our system. Section 3 describes the design of TimbrePainter. Section 4 discusses and evaluates the design of TimbrePainter and puts forward some ideas for improvement and future research.

2   A Review of Previous Research

2.1   Recent Developments in the Performance Control of Timbre

Timbre can be designed in a non-linear editing fashion, where synthesis parameters are manipulated until a desired timbre has been achieved, or it can be modified during a performance. Seago refers to the former as 'fixed synthesis' and the latter as 'real-time synthesis'[5]. The performance control of timbre is an important area of research as the manipulation of timbre is crucial for the expressive control of a musical instrument. However, the focus of this paper is on issues solely related to timbre design rather than expressive performance. Nonetheless, there have been many recent developments in the area of 'real-time synthesis' that are relevant to this study.

The Importance of Mapping. Hunt found that mapping strategies which are not one-to-one can be more engaging to users than one-to-one mappings [6]. Synthesizers have generally employed a one-to-one mapping, such as slider to filter cutoff frequency, whereas acoustic instruments, generally considered far more intuitive and expressive, often have a complex and non-linear relationship between the control surface and the sound generation mechanism.

Abstracting Large Parameter Spaces. Synthesizers capable of producing a wide range of complex sounds generally require a large number of parameters to be controlled. Mulder proposes two ways of reducing this problem [7]. The number of parameters needed to be directly controlled can be minimised by controlling an intermediate virtual interface that abstracts the synthesis interface. The number of parameters capable of being controlled simultaneously can be maximised by exploiting the human motor system's ability to effortlessly control many degrees of freedom.

Scanned Synthesis. Scanned Synthesis is a recent, innovative approach to sound synthesis [7]. A dynamic Wavetable is determined by the state of an arbitrary, slowly moving physical system which may be real or virtual. Although any interface can be used, this technique is notable because there is a high degree of amplification between input and output complexity. This means that simple, low parameter interfaces can yield highly complex and interesting results, making for instantly accessible and engaging instruments for new users. However, as the synthesis technique operates in the time-domain, the results are very unpredictable. As a system for 'fixed synthesis' it may be unsuitable as experienced users may feel a lack of control and personal authorship of the sounds they have made.

Tristimulus Synthesis. The Tristimulus Synthesizer [2] is a very recent and innovative synthesizer design inspired by the Tristimulus model of timbre perception proposed by Pollard and Jansson [8]. Similarly to the way that just three types of colour receptors are necessary to generate sensations of a wide range of colours, the Tristimulus model proposes that the relative loudness of three bands of partials plays a large part in the sensation of timbre. Using just three parameters that control the loudness of three bands of partials, a wide range of timbres can be produced. Controls are mapped to an abstract layer based on the perception of timbre that is entirely independent of the synthesis method used. Although there are more powerful synthesis methods available, the Tristimulus Synthesizer is currently perhaps the best example of a synthesizer that is all at once strong in usability, power and predictability.

Tristimulus synthesis is successful as a 'real-time synthesis' technique and it is also promising as a fixed synthesis technique. However, although Tristimulus parameters may play a large part in the perception of timbre, they cannot describe all of the perceptual features of timbre. Research into other perceptual features of timbre could lead to a very powerful, easy-to-use and predictable method of 'fixed-synthesis'.

2.2 Interfaces for 'Fixed-Synthesis'

Conventional synthesizer interfaces for fixed synthesis have consisted of either an array of one dimensional controls (usually knobs or sliders) that control one parameter each or a single control that can be used to control any parameter. In the second case, a menu displayed on a small LCD screen must be navigated in order to select the current parameter to be edited. It has been widely acknowledged that these conventional interfaces suffer from poor usability. In an effort to find the root of the problem and propose a solution, Seago has conducted usability tests and has recommended that controls should map to perceptual space rather than the parameters of a particular synthesis method [5].

Additive synthesis is perhaps the most powerful synthesis method possible. According to Fourier Theory, any possible signal can be represented as a summation of sine functions. However, there is little or no amplification between input complexity and output complexity. An enormous number of parameters and a large amount of computational resources are required to generate interesting sounds. However, in recent years a promising application of additive synthesis has been Analysis-Resynthesis [9, 10].

Recordings of real instruments (sources of complex timbre) are analysed and data at a high level of abstraction such as the envelope of each partial is extracted. This data is used to determine the parameters of an additive synthesizer. This technique offers the potential for a much higher level of timbral control than with the commercially popular sample-playback synthesis technique. Ircam's AudioSculpt enables the user to study an analysed sound's spectrum with a visual representation

[11]. The image and resulting sound can be edited by selecting an area with the mouse and applying a transformation. Analysis-Resynthesis makes it possible to realistically emulate musical instruments, but the possibility for exploring new timbres is usually limited to morphing between known timbres[2].

Evolutionary algorithms have been used to search large parameter spaces. Dahlstedt's systems use Interactive Evolution, where user evaluation of automatically generated timbres guides the evolution of a timbre, to search for new and interesting sounds [3]. This interface is very easy-to-use, as deciding whether or not you like a timbre is an extremely intuitive act. Interactive Evolution makes it easy for users with no experience in timbre design to discover sounds that are customized to their own personal preference. However, there are difficulties in steering the search to find a desired timbre and a large number of user evaluations is often necessary.

2.3 Painting as an Interface for Synthesizer Parameter Setting

Synthesizer designers have for a long time realised the potential of designing sound using drawing or painting as an interface. In the 1930s, some composers experimented with drawing sound waves directly onto film. Although some interesting results were possible, painting sound waves in the time-domain was a very laborious process and the results were extremely unpredictable. This, Hunt writes, is because, "human beings are not naturally equipped with the knowledge of how to draw sound" [12]. This seems to be true for sound representations in the time-domain but may not necessarily be true for other sound representations. For painting to be effective, it should map to a higher level of abstraction than time-domain data.

Daphne Oram created the 'Oramics' machine in the 1960s where hand drawn lines were used to define the envelopes of subtractive synthesis parameters such as oscillator frequency or filter cutoff frequency [13]. With this higher level of abstraction, results could be obtained much more quickly, but only with a good knowledge of the synthesis method could the user predict the output.

2.4 Painting as an Interface for Additive Synthesis

A number of systems have implemented the idea of using a painting interface to control an additive synthesizer. The huge number of parameters required makes it impractical to use conventional interfaces such as knobs and sliders or a push-button LCD interface. Painting allows many parameters to be manipulated with just one brush stroke.

The Pattern Playback. The Pattern Playback was a machine created in the late 1940s that was capable of transforming a painted spectrogram into a tone consisting of 50 harmonics [14]. The loudness of the oscillators was controlled by a row of light sensors that sensed light from a moving, painted spectrogram. It was very useful for speech research, the intended application, but limited as a musical instrument as the fundamental frequency was fixed at 120 Hz.

---

[2] It should be noted that the painting interface described in this paper could be used to manipulate analysed timbres.

The vOICe. Maijer has developed a system for the blind that uses video images to generate sound from an additive synthesizer [15]. A painting interface can be used to create custom images and sounds. The y-axis of the image represents pitch, the x-axis represents time and the brightness of each sound pixel represents oscillator amplitude. In this case the frequency of each oscillator is not a harmonic. Instead, the frequencies increase exponentially. What is heard could be described as a cacophony of individual tones rather than a single coherent timbre.

Metasynth. Metasynth [16] is a similar system to the vOICe. In Metasynth the frequencies can be set to correspond to a musical scale such as the diatonic scale or a microtonal scale. By using musical scales the boundary between sound design and composition is blurred. Although it is possible to create interesting, unconventional music and sounds with this software, harmonic timbres, like the timbres of most conventional instruments, cannot be created.

Yellowtail. Golan Levin's Yellowtail is an innovative system that uses interactive animation, rather than still images, to control an additive synthesizer [17]. Animations can be created on-the-fly using painterly mouse gestures. This leads to interesting and constantly evolving sounds. Like the vOICe and Metasynth, only unconventional, inharmonic sounds can be produced.

2.5 The Potential of Painting as an Interface to Timbre Design

A computer painting interface is instantly accessible for new users as computer painting programs are very familiar. Unlike actions required by conventional interfaces such as entering numbers into small LCD screen, painting happens to be an enjoyable activity by itself. Painting offers a good combination of ease-of-use and power in that paintings can be arbitrarily simple (a smiley face) or arbitrarily complex (a detailed depiction of a piano timbre).

Although the relationship between image and sound is counter-intuitive with time-domain representations there is a much more natural relationship with frequency-domain representations or spectrograms. Helmholtz has likened the cochlea to a spectral analyzer which resonates at specific locations along the basilar membrane [18]. There is a direct mapping between additive synthesis parameters and this stage of the human auditory perception system. Rodet and Depalle write that there is a simple mapping of frequency and amplitude parameters into the human perceptual space and that these parameters are meaningful to musicians [9].

In theory, with a large enough array of sine wave oscillators, a digital additive synthesizer could produce any perceptible sound, including harmonic, inharmonic and noisy sounds [1]. However, an almost infinite number of oscillators would be necessary to produce an arbitrary sound. Due to the high computation costs of additive synthesis, we are limited in the number of oscillators available. We can choose to distribute the frequencies inharmonically (as in The vOICe, Metasynth, or Yellowtail) or distribute them as harmonics of a single fundamental frequency (as in The Pattern Playback). Inharmonic additive synthesis has been explored by several systems and is limited to a subset of inorganic sounds that can only appeal to a particular niche group of musicians and listeners. There is room for exploration in the design of a harmonic additive synthesizer that uses painting as an interface.

3 TimbrePainter

TimbrePainter is a system that features a painting interface for manipulating the parameters of a harmonic additive synthesizer. Painting can be used to paint a new picture or to edit an image captured from a web cam or imported from a file. Its intended application is to enable new users to explore timbre design through painting. While designing sounds, melodies generated from a step-sequencer give constant feedback. Alternatively, a MIDI controller can be used to trigger notes. A simple, self-explanatory GUI with few elements has been employed to make it easy for new users to instantly begin creating sounds. A video demonstration of the system can be viewed at *http://ist.ksc.kwansei.ac.jp/~katayose/TimbrePainter/*.

3.1 Implementation and Features

The parameters of a harmonic additive synthesizer can be described as an array of amplitude envelopes - one for each harmonic or sine wave oscillator [20]. The frequency of the fundamental is arbitrary and the frequency of each harmonic is determined by the equation:

*frequency of harmonic = fundamental frequency * (harmonic number + 1)*

This is best visualized as a set of curves in 3D space as in Fig.1

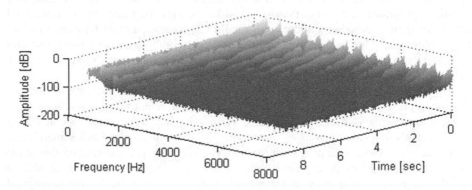

Fig. 1. A 3D representation of a piano timbre

This 3D space can be represented in a 2D view if the z-axis is represented by colour intensity rather than height (Fig. 2).

This representation is essentially a 2D image with a single colour channel. If additive synthesizer parameters can be represented as an image, then the reverse is also possible - an image can be used to specify additive synthesizer parameters.

TimbrePainter features a painting area or 'canvas' for creating and editing images. Fig.4. shows an example of an image created in TimbrePainter. White represents the highest amplitudes and black represents zero amplitude. The first row represents the fundamental. Its frequency is determined by midi input or the step-sequencer.

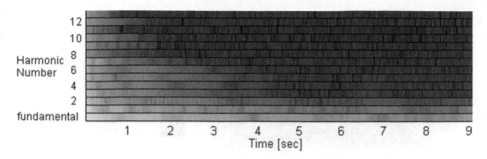

Fig. 2. A 2D representation of additive synthesis parameters

The GUI of TimbrePainter (Fig.5) is divided into four sections: 'Timbre Canvas', 'Brush Options', 'Step Sequencer' and 'Spectral Filter.' Drawing or painting is used throughout the system.

The 'Timbre Canvas' is used for painting timbres with the mouse. If a USB WebCam is connected, clicking on the 'Take Photo' button captures the current frame from the web cam. A JPEG or TIFF file can be imported by clicking the 'Import Image' button. WebCam photos or imported images can be further edited with the paintbrush. Images can be saved as a JPEG or TIFF file.

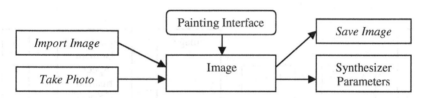

Fig. 3. Flow diagram of image creation and editing methods

With the 'Step Sequencer' users can draw a looping melody which is used for feedback while designing a sound. In the 'Spectral Filter' section users can draw an arbitrary spectral filter which can be used to control timbre during performance. In the 'Brush Options' section users can choose the colour intensity of the paintbrush, change the brush size and select the brush mode. 'Burn' mode gradually increases the intensity at the location of the mouse, and 'Dodge' gradually decreases it, allowing for smoother gradients.

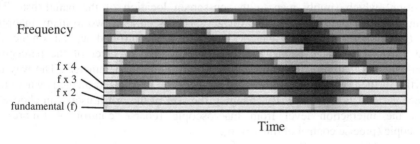

Fig. 4. A description of an image created in TimbrePainter

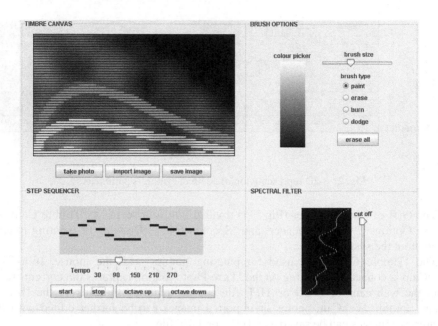

Fig. 5. A screenshot of the GUI used in TimbrePainter

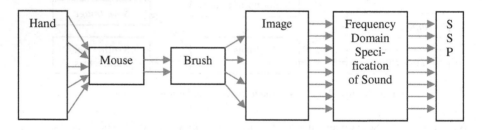

Fig. 6. Diagram of hand movement to sound synthesis parameter mapping

3.2   The Mappings of the Painting Interface

TimbrePainter can be viewed as a system with several mapping layers. One hand, which has many degrees of freedom, is used to control two mouse parameters (X and Y position) which simply map to the on-screen location of the paintbrush. The mapping between the mouse and the image can be seen as a two-to-many mapping where the number of image parameters simultaneously controlled depends on the size of the brush. The image is mapped to frequency-domain layer of the perceptual system which is then directly mapped to additive synthesis parameters. The way the properties of the brush influence the mapping between mouse and image is where this interface derives its flexibility. By changing the size of the brush users can choose to control the interaction level from macroscopic (coarse control of timbre) to microscopic (precise control of timbre) [6].

4 Discussion

So far the testing of the system has been limited to observing user behaviour and collecting verbal feedback from a selection of users ranging from synthesizer enthusiasts to non-musicians. Most users found the system to be engaging and very easy-to-use. They were able to generate a reasonably wide range of interesting timbres which were predictable to a certain degree. However, there is much room for improvement to the system and several common comments and observations have been very useful in thinking of improvements.

4.1 Limitations of Using a Mouse as a Controller

The most noticeable short-coming of TimbrePainter was in the lack of complexity or quality of the sounds created by the users. Although a reasonably wide range of interesting timbres were created, they all belonged to a certain class particular to this system. Although in theory, using the current system, it should be possible to create harmonic sounds of an unlimited degree of complexity, such as a piano sound, the results rarely achieved this aim.

Natural timbres often have complex amplitude variations and this is difficult to achieve with TimbrePainter's paint brush, as it can only paint flat areas of colour. The use of Ryokai's "I/O Brush" would be a fun and engaging way to create interesting paint brush textures [21]. The mouse is limited as a device for painting as it can only specify x or y coordinates. During painting it is not capable of specifying a z coordinate which could be used to specify colour intensity (amplitude). Relative sound levels of harmonics play a large part in the perceived timbre of a sound and even subtle changes in sound level can be very noticeable. Therefore, it is very important to have very accurate control of colour intensity.

A digitizing tablet would be preferable to use as a controller for TimbrePainter as the pen pressure could be used to specify colour intensity. However, although a high level of accuracy can be obtained in the x and y coordinates, only a relatively small level of accuracy can be obtained in the z coordinate (pen pressure). An alternative idea, the use of a clay model, will be presented in section 4.3.

4.2 Limitations of the Perceptual Model Used

The current system operates on the frequency-domain level of abstraction of timbre. Each harmonic is treated as equally important and each time slice is treated as equally important. However, psycho-acoustics research has found that certain bands of harmonics and certain time stages are more important than others in the perception of timbre.

High level perceptual features include the relative levels of the Tristimulus bands, inharmonicity, roughness and others. The user should be able to begin by designing in a high level of abstraction and then work on finer detail in the frequency domain. High level perceptual features should draw from psycho-acoustics research. An idea could be to increase the size of the pixels in the regions of more perceptual importance so the user has more accuracy in these areas. Verbal descriptions such as 'bright' describe timbre at a very high level of abstraction and could be useful for performance control.

Time domain	Frequency Domain	High level perceptual features	Verbal description

Fig. 7. Levels of abstraction in describing timbre

4.3 Using Live Video to Specify Additive Synthesis Parameters

Live video of light reflected from a shallow pool of water has been used by Dannenberg to specify the parameters of an additive synthesizer [20]. Three vertical lines correspond to three voices and the parameters of one voice are controlled by a single vertical strip of video data. One of the limitations of the current implementation of TimbrePainter is that timbre is the same for every pitch. By assigning different pitches to different vertical lines, timbre would change dramatically depending on pitch and interesting results may be achieved.

4.4 Using Modeling Clay as an Interface

As 3D coordinates can be used to describe additive synthesis parameters, a very intuitive way to specify the parameters is to sculpt a real 3D model using your hands. As the amplitude envelopes of partials can be best visualized as a 3D model, the visual feedback is more intuitive. Inexpensive modeling clay such as PlayDoh is ideal. Using modeling clay, models can be quickly made and reworked. This is a both fun and a powerful method for timbre design. In line with Mulder's aims, the hands can be exploited to their full potential of gestural control [7]. There is a many-to-many mapping between the hands and the clay model and the bottle-neck in the hand-to-mouse-to-brush-to-image mapping is removed.

We have experimented with digitizing model information by simply using a web cam and mapping the pixel data to additive synthesis parameters using the 'take photo' feature. However, no meaningful height information from the model is retained, so outcomes are largely unpredictable. For this interface to be effective, depth perception techniques would need to be used to gather height information from the model. A commercial 3D scanner or computer vision techniques used to analyse images from a stereoscopic pair of digital cameras could be used.

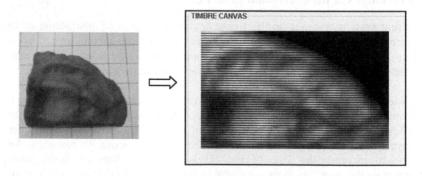

Fig. 8. A photo of model converted to image parameters

Mulder's approach of using a Dataglove to sculpt a virtual clay model could also be used [7]. This approach would have the advantage that the process of extracting height information from the model would be relatively much simpler and models could be saved and recalled. However, this would be at the expense of a severe reduction in the quality of visual feedback and a total loss of tactile feedback.

5 Conclusion

This paper has dealt with issues related to the challenge of designing a system for timbre design which is easy-to-use, powerful and predictable. We have attempted to meet these aims in our design of TimbrePainter, a system which uses painting as an interface for additive synthesis. Although this system offers a good trade-off between these three aims, there is room for improvement in each of these areas. As conventional synthesizer interfaces have been deemed inadequate for controlling complex synthesizers, there is a need to find alternative interfaces, such as painting, that make better use of the full potential of human motor control. 3D sculpting has been proposed as another alternative interface with a good potential. Of equal importance is establishing a meaningful way of describing timbre that does not depend on any particular synthesis method. There is a need for further research into the nature of timbre perception and this research should be used to guide the design of future systems.

References

1. Smith, J.O.: Viewpoints on the History of Digital Synthesis. Proceedings of the International Computer Conference. San Francisco (1991)
2. A. Riley, D. Howard.: A Real-Time Tristimulus Synthesizer. http://www-users.york.ac.uk/~dmh8/tristimulus.htm (2004)
3. Dahlstedt, P.: Creating and Exploring Huge Parameter Spaces: Interactive Evolution as a Tool for Sound Generation. Proceedings of the International Computer Music Conference. Habana, Cuba (2001)
4. Verplank, B., Mathews, M., Shaw, R.: Scanned Synthesis. Proceedings of the 2000 International Computer Music Conference. Zannos editor, ICMA, Berlin (2000) 368-371
5. Seago, A., Holland, S.,Mulholland, P.: A Critical Analysis of Synthesizer User Interfaces for Timbre. HCI 2004: Design for Life. British HCI Group, Leeds (2004)
6. Hunt A., Wanderley M., Kirk R.: Towards a Model for Instrumental Mapping in Expert Musical Interaction. Proceedings of the 2000 International Computer Music Conference. Berlin, Germany (2000)
7. Mulder, A., Fels, S., Mase, K.: Mapping virtual object manipulation to sound variation. IPSJ SIG notes Vol. 97, No. 122, 97-MUS-23 (USA/Japan intercollege computer music festival) (1997) 63-68.
8. Pollard, H.F., Jansson, E.V.: A tristimulus method for the specification of musical timbre. Acustica 51 (1982) 162-171.
9. Rodet, X., Depalle, P.: Spectral Envelopes and Inverse FFT Synthesis. Proc. 93rd AES Conv, San Francisco (1992)

10. Serra, X.: "Musical Sound Modeling with Sinusoids plus Noise". Musical Signal Processing, Swets & Zeitlinger Publishers (1997)
11. Bogaards, N., Röbel, A., Rodet,X.: Sound Analysis and Processing with AudioSculpt 2, Proc. Int. Computer Music Conference (ICMC'04). Miami (2004)
12. Hunt, A: Radical User Interfaces for Real-time Musical Control. DPhil thesis. University of York, UK (1999)
13. Daphne Oram and 'Oramics' (1959), http://www.obsolete.com/120_years/machines/oramics/
14. Rubin,P., Goldstein,L.: The Pattern Playback.
    http://www.haskins.yale.edu/Haskins/MISC/PP/pp.html
15. Meijer, P.: An Experimental System for Auditory Image Representations. IEEE Transactions on Biomedical Engineering (1992) 112-121
16. UI Software, Metasynth, 1998.
17. Levin, G.: Painterly Interfaces for Audiovisual Performance. (2000) Chapter 3, Section 2.1.
18. Hong,T.: Salient feature extraction of musical instrument signals. M.A. Thesis. Dartmouth College (2000)
19. Dannenberg, Neuendorffer: Sound Synthesis from Real-Time Video Images. Proceedings of the 2003 International Computer Music Conference. International Computer Music Association, San Francisco (2003) 385-388
20. Roads, C.: The Computer Music Tutorial. MIT Press, Cambridge (1996).
21. Ryokai, K., Marti, S., Ishii, H.: Designing the World as Your Palette. Proceedings of the Conference on Human Factors in Computing Systems (CHI '05). Portland (2005)

ism: Improvisation Supporting Systems with Melody Correction and Key Vibration

Tetsuro Kitahara[1], Katsuhisa Ishida[2], and Masayuki Takeda[2]

[1] Graduate School of Informatics, Kyoto University,
Sakyo-ku, Kyoto 606-8501, Japan
kitahara@kuis.kyoto-u.ac.jp
http://winnie.kuis.kyoto-u.ac.jp/~kitahara/
[2] Department of Information Sciences,
Tokyo University of Science,
Noda, Chiba 278-8510, Japan
kdi@mt.is.noda.tus.ac.jp, takeda@is.noda.tus.ac.jp

Abstract. This paper describes improvisation support for musicians who do not have sufficient improvisational playing experience. The goal of our study is to enable such players to learn the skills necessary for improvisation and to enjoy it. In achieving this goal, we have two objectives: enhancing their skill for instantaneous melody creation and supporting their practice for acquiring this skill. For the first objective, we developed a system that automatically corrects musically inappropriate notes in the melodies of users' improvisations. For the second objective, we developed a system that points out musically inappropriate notes by vibrating corresponding keys. The main issue in developing these systems is how to detect musically inappropriate notes. We propose a method for detecting them based on the N-gram model. Experimental results show that this N-gram-based method improves the accuracy of detecting musically inappropriate notes and our systems are effective in supporting unskilled musicians' improvisation.

1 Introduction

Music, especially a jam session, is an important and exciting form of entertainment. The widespread participation in this type of entertainment is so prevalent that there are many studies on jam sessions being facilitated through the use of computers. For example, jam session systems [1,2,3] construct virtual musicians in computers and provide us with environments for jam sessions with the virtual musicians. *Open RemoteGIG* [4] enables geographically diverse musicians to join a worldwide jam session using the Internet. Furthermore, various novel electric musical instruments, including a PDA-based portable one [5] and a wearable one [6], and new jam-session styles using these instruments have been proposed.

These studies were geared toward enabling a new kind of jam session for experienced, skilled musicians, not for supporting a jam session for people who

F. Kishino et al. (Eds.): ICEC 2005, LNCS 3711, pp. 315–327, 2005.

cannot improvise. Since improvisation is musical performance style that involves creating melodies while playing, becoming a skilled improvisational player requires further training even if the musician can play an instrument with a score. There will therefore be many people, called *non-improvising players* in this paper, who can play a musical instrument but cannot improvise. Providing such players with environments that will enable them to enjoy improvisation is an important goal that should be achieved.

The reason why improvisation is difficult for such musicians is their lack of skill in instantaneously creating melodies. To help them learn and enjoy improvisation, therefore, computing technology should enhance this skill or support their practice for acquiring this skill. In this paper, we seek to create an environment where players can enjoy improvisation by proposing two systems that address the issues explained above. For enhancing the skill, we propose a system that automatically detects musically unnatural notes of played melodies and corrects them to musically natural ones. This system hides musically unnatural or inappropriate melodies from the audience, hence enables inexperienced musicians to easily enjoy improvisation. It would therefore contribute to increasing their motivation for learning to improvise. For supporting the practice, we propose a system that points out musically unnatural notes to the player. If a played melody contains musically unnatural or inappropriate notes, the system points them out to the player through vibrating corresponding keys in real time. Using this system, inexperienced players can practice improvisation efficiently and in an enjoyable manner because the system, instead of the players, determines whether a melody is musically appropriate or not, which could be very difficult for them. We call the two systems *ism* and *ism$_v$*, respectively.

The main issue in achieving these systems is how to detect musically unnatural or inappropriate notes. We propose a method for detecting them based on the N-gram model. Our method uses N-gram probabilities calculated from a large-scale melody database to determine whether notes are appropriate or not. This N-gram-based determination makes it possible to solve the problem of judging actually appropriate notes to be inappropriate.

The rest of this paper is organized as follows: Sect. 2 discusses requirements for improvisation supporting systems and proposes an improvisation supporting system *ism* according to the discussion. Sect. 3 proposes the N-gram-based correction method which is necessary for *ism*. Then, Sect. 4 presents the implementation and evaluation of *ism*. Sect. 5 proposes the system, called *ism$_v$*, that points out musically unnatural notes to the player through key vibration. Finally, Sect. 6 concludes the paper.

2   *ism*: An Improvisation Supporting System That Automatically Corrects Musically Unnatural Melodies

The aim of our study is to provide people who cannot yet improvise musical solos but want to try doing it with an environment that allows them to enjoy it. When we design a system for achieving such an environment, we should take into consideration the following requirements:

1. **Same playing method as a normal instrument**
   Because the final goal of our target users is to enable improvisation without any supports (*i.e.*, using a normal instrument), the system should not specify a playing method. To allow users to make good use of experience in using the system when trying improvisation with a normal instrument, it should emulate the same playing environment as a normal instrument.
2. **Avoidance of over-supporting**
   Even if players do not have adequate ability to create melodies, they do not always create musically unnatural/inappropriate melodies[1]. The system should not therefore provide unexpected support while the player creates appropriate melodies.

Although some musical performance supporting systems have been proposed, these systems do not satisfy the above requirements. For example, *Coloring-in Piano* [7] is a musical device that corrects players' incorrectly played melodies using score information provided before the musician attempts the piece. This method is applicable for non-improvisational music, but it is not applicable to our purpose because scores of improvisation cannot be provided beforehand. *RhyMe*, which is a subsystem of *MusiKalscope* [8], is an improvisation supporting system based on a fixed-function mapping. The fixed-function mapping is a new method for mapping between keys and notes according to the functions of the notes, which depend on the context of the chord progression. This novel mapping can make it easier to choose keys that produce musically natural melodies. The instrument using this mapping method may be effective if the goal of the users is to enjoy improvisation solely with this instrument. However, it would not be effective for people whose goal is to enjoy improvisation with a conventional musical instrument. *INSPIRATION* [9] is an improvisation supporting system that corrects all of the notes out of the available note scale. Because these notes do not necessarily produce musically unnatural melodies, it is not desirable to correct all of them.

   In this study, we propose a novel performance supporting system called *ism*, which detects unnatural notes in melodies based on the N-gram model and corrects them (Fig. 1). Because this system is used with an existing MIDI controller (typically a MIDI keyboard), the experience of improvisational playing enabled by this system will not be useless when trying improvisation with a conventional musical instrument. In addition, because this system determines whether notes should be corrected by comparing their N-gram probabilities with a threshold, the player can control the strength of melody correction (*i.e.*, how frequently melody correction occurs) by adjusting the threshold.

---

[1] Our investigation using 10 beginning and 15 intermediate players show that the rates of unnatural/inappropriate notes in the melodies of their improvisation are 12.03% and 8.22%, respectively.

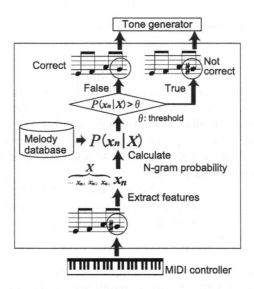

Fig. 1. Overview of **ism**. The system first calculates N-gram probabilities of played notes and then corrects only notes with low N-gram probabilities.

3   N-gram-Based Melody Correction Method

The main issue in achieving **ism** is how to detect notes requiring correction. One possible solution for this may be to correct all the notes (called *out notes*) that are out of the *available note scale*, which is a series of notes that can produce harmonic sounds, depending on the key and the chord of the accompaniment. However, all of these notes do not necessarily produce disharmonious sounds, and they are frequently used in actual musical pieces. This method, therefore, causes unexpected correction and is unsuitable.

In this paper, we propose a novel method for determining notes requiring correction based on the N-gram model. This method captures the tendency of note transitions by N-gram probabilities and determines, when there are notes with low N-gram probabilities, that such notes should be corrected.

Step 1. Feature extraction

The 4-dimensional feature vector listed in Table 1 (see Fig. 2 for examples) is extracted from each note in a melody of improvisation. These features were selected under the restriction that they can be extracted right after the note on (therefore they do not include the note length) for realtime melody correction. Let "note x" be the note with feature vector x.

Step 2. Modeling melody by N-gram

The appropriateness of note transitions in a played melody is modeled by the N-gram model. This model gives the probability $P(x_n|X)$ in which the note x_n exists behind the note sequence $X = x_1 \cdots x_{n-1}$. The N-gram model

Table 1. Elements of a feature vector

[1] The kind of the note (chord tone, key tone, etc.)
[2] The interval between the note and the last note (m2, M2, more than m3)
[3] Whether the note is on eighth-note-level beats
[4] Whether a rest exists between the note being played and the previous note

Fig. 2. Examples of feature vectors

assumes that this probability is fixed by the $N - 1$ notes $\boldsymbol{x}_{n-N+1} \cdots \boldsymbol{x}_{n-1}$ and calculates it by the following equation:

$$P(\boldsymbol{x}_n|X) = P(\boldsymbol{x}_n|\boldsymbol{x}_{n-N+1} \cdots \boldsymbol{x}_{n-1})$$
$$= \frac{P(\boldsymbol{x}_{n-N+1} \cdots \boldsymbol{x}_n)}{P(\boldsymbol{x}_{n-N+1} \cdots \boldsymbol{x}_{n-1})}.$$

Step 3. Determining the notes to be corrected
When the out note $\boldsymbol{x}_n$ follows the note sequence X, its appropriateness is given by the N-gram probability $P(\boldsymbol{x}_n|X)$ calculated with a large melody database. In other words, if $P(\boldsymbol{x}_n|X)$ is high, $\boldsymbol{x}_n$ frequently follows X in melodies of actual musical pieces. Our method therefore determines that the out notes that have lower N-gram probabilities than a threshold should be corrected.

Step 4. Determining the after-correction pitch
The pitch maximizing N-gram probabilities, within an interval of major 2nd of the original note, is determined as an after-correction pitch.

4 Implementation and Evaluation of *ism*

4.1 Implementation

We built a prototype system of *ism* using the C language on Microsoft Windows. To construct a melody database, we used 208 songs' melodies of standard jazz. The total number of measures, which are segments of notes within a song, and individual notes of this database are 6,836 and 18,897, respectively. We adopted both the bigram model ($N = 2$) and the trigram model ($N = 3$) as the N-gram model because of the limitations of the database size (*i.e.*, using a number greater than 3 will cause the data sparseness problem). The threshold is 0.10.

This system has accompaniment data as standard MIDI files. While an accompaniment is played, the user plays improvisation along with this accompaniment using the MIDI keyboard connected to *ism*. Then, *ism* corrects the player's melody and the MIDI tone generator plays the corrected melody.

Fig. 3. An example of melody correction

4.2   An Example of Melody Correction

Fig. 3 shows an example of melody correction. The top score is a melody before correction. The middle and bottom scores are melodies corrected by the proposed method and the all-correction method, which corrects all of the out notes, respectively. The marks in the figure represent notes that are out of the available note scale before correction, each of which makes an interval of minor 2nd with a note of the simultaneously played chord. In general, when a note in a melody makes an interval of minor 2nd with a note of the simultaneously played chord, it does not usually produce a disharmonious sound if it is an approach note. The second marked note is not an approach note, and actually produces a disharmonious sound. This note was corrected by both methods. On the other hand, The first and third marked notes are used as an approach note or a blue note, and actually do not produce a disharmonious sound. These notes were not corrected by our method, whereas they were corrected by the all-correction method.

4.3   Evaluation of Determination of Notes to Be Corrected

We conducted experiments on determining whether notes in melodies should be corrected or not. The 37 non-improvising players listed in Table 2 first played using an improvisational style, and then the melodies of their improvisation were recorded. For each note in the melodies, we manually labeled whether it should be corrected. The melodies were then corrected both by the proposed method and by the all-correction method, and finally the appropriateness of the correction was evaluated using recall rate R, precision rate P and F-measure F, defined by the following equations:

$$R = \frac{\text{Number of correction-requiring and actually corrected notes}}{\text{Total number of correction-requiring notes}},$$

$$P = \frac{\text{Number of correction-requiring and actually corrected notes}}{\text{Total number of actually corrected notes}},$$

$$F = \frac{2 \times R \times P}{R + P}.$$

Table 2. Details of subjects and labeled notes in Sect. 4.3

	# of players	Measure / player	Total notes	Correction-requiring notes
Beginning (under 1 yr.*)	10	64	3,108	12.03%
Intermediate (3–5 yrs.*)	15	64	3,177	8.22%
Advanced (over 5 yrs.*)	12	64	2,660	3.38%
Total	37	64	8,945	8.11%

*Experience in playing musical instruments.

Table 3. Experimental results of determining notes to be corrected

	Whole			Beginners		
	R	P	F	R	P	F
All-correction	0.7822	0.3636	0.4964	0.7005	0.4242	0.5307
Ours (bigram)	0.7737	0.4977	0.6057	0.6628	0.5066	0.5743
Ours (trigram)	0.7682	0.4982	0.6044	0.6190	0.5078	0.5579

	Intermediates			Experts		
	R	P	F	R	P	F
All-correction	0.9123	0.5131	0.6568	0.7072	0.2012	0.3133
Ours (bigram)	0.9099	0.6622	0.7665	0.7072	0.2985	0.4198
Ours (trigram)	0.8969	0.6585	0.7594	0.7072	0.3032	0.4244

Table 3 shows experimental results. Our method based on the bigram and trigram models improved the F-measure by 0.1093 and by 0.1080, respectively. Although the recall rates of the proposed method were 1–2% lower than those of the all-correction method, the precision rates were about 13% higher. These results mean that the proposed method achieved an improvement in over-correction, that is, correcting notes that should not be corrected.

The accuracies for the intermediate group with all the methods were high. Because many players in this group know that notes in the available note scale produce natural melodies, their out notes mainly appeared as a result of mistouching or a failure of challenging an advanced melody. The proposed method detected such clearly unnatural out notes with accuracy.

On the other hand, the accuracies for the expert group were not high enough. This insufficient accuracy was caused by the mismatch of players and the melody database; the melody database was constructed using jazz melodies whereas many players of this group have experience in classical music. It can be improved by constructing genre-dependent or player-dependent melody databases.

4.4 Questionnaire Evaluation

We conducted evaluation of users' feelings of our system by questionnaires. The subjects are three people, listed in Table 4, who can play an instrument but

Table 4. Musical experience of the subjects for the evaluation in Sect. 4.4

	Playing	Composing	Improvising
A	12 yrs. (Piano)	Yes	No
B	11 yrs. (Electone)	No	No
C	6 yrs. (Keyboard)	Yes	No

Table 5. Questionnaire results

	Q1			Q2			Q3		
	all	bi	tri	all	bi	tri	all	bi	tri
A	5	4	6	5	4	7	4	5	5
B	5	7	6	1	4	6	6	6	7
C	3	4	7	2	2	4	5	5	5
Av.	4.3	5.0	6.3	2.7	3.3	5.7	5.0	5.3	5.7

have little experience in improvisation. They first played improvisation using our system and then answered the following questions:

Q1 Do you think the correction of your melodies was appropriate?
Q2 Did the system allow you to improvise without feeling a strong sense of strangeness?
Q3 Did you enjoy the improvisation with this system?
(7: Definitely Yes,   6: Probably Yes,   5: Possibly Yes,   4: Neutral
3: Possibly No,   2: Probably No,   1: Definitely No)

Table 5 shows the results of the questionnaire. For all questions, the proposed method was superior to the all-correction method on the average of the three subjects. In particular, all the subjects answered that the trigram-based correcting method was better than the all-correction method.

The results of the trigram-based system were better than the bigram one. This is because the trigram model captures the tendency of note transitions better than the bigram model since the former uses longer note sequences.

Subject A did not highly evaluate the bigram-based system in Q1. This is because the chromatic phrases frequently used by this subject were corrected by the system. However, some listeners say that the corrected melodies are more natural, so that this correction is not necessarily redundant.

When we focus on Q2, Subjects A and B evaluated our trigram-based system highly. They have long experience, more than 10 years, in playing instruments. It means that the melody correction by the proposed method does not give a strong strangeness feeling to players even if they have long experience in playing musical instruments.

We also obtained from subjects the opinion that it was good to hide their failure from listeners when they failed in improvisation. This opinion suggests that our system achieved mitigating their hesitation toward trying improvisation.

4.5   Demonstration in WISS 2003

We demonstrated our system in the 11th Workshop on Interactive Systems and Software (WISS 2003), which is one of the biggest domestic workshops on human-computer interaction in Japan. When demonstrating the system, we asked attendees to use the system on trial and to answer the same questions as those in Sect. 4.4. Unlike Sect. 4.4, they used only the system using the trigram-based

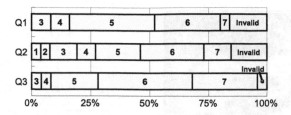

Fig. 4. Questionnaire results in WISS 2003

correction method, so that they did not compare it with the one using the all-correction method. The questionnaire results are shown in Fig. 4. For every question, the average of answers was more than 5.00. In addition, they gave us many comments such as the following:

- "I want to do more improvisation using this system."
- "That is very interesting. Even if I play it without thinking, it produces appropriate melodies."
- "This system is good for unskilled people."
- "I can enjoy improvisation although I am a beginner."
- "It would be more interesting if other instruments also had such a melody correction function."

These results mean that many people have good impression on our system and hope for further development of our study. On the other hand, some people answered that they felt a sense of strangeness when a tone different from the pushed key was played. Reducing this kind of strangeness sense is an important future issue.

5 *ism$_V$*: An Improvisation Supporting System That Points Out Unnatural Melodies with Key Vibration

In this section, we propose a system, called *ism$_V$*, that points out musically unnatural notes in real time with key vibration. Previous methods for supporting musical practice (e.g., melody navigation with lighting keys, automatic tablature generation for guitars [10]) did not deal with improvisation, because they focused on supporting users who cannot read scores. Our system, *ism$_V$*, detects musically unnatural notes in improvisation using the above-mentioned N-gram-based melody appropriateness determination method and points them out through vibrating the corresponding keys in real time.

5.1 Overview

The system described here is another version of the *ism* series, which vibrates keys instead of the correction methodology employed by *ism*. The user plays

Fig. 5. Built-in vibrating motor in each key

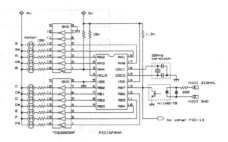

Fig. 6. Circuit diagram of *Buru-Buru-kun*. The PIC analyzes signal received from the MIDI IN port, and controls built-in vibrating motors.

improvisation on a keyboard called *Buru-Buru-kun*, which has built-in vibrating motors (Fig. 5, Fig. 6). The system detects musically inappropriate notes based on the method described in Sect. 3 and points them out by vibrating the corresponding keys. Because this system enables users to instantaneously learn that they are hitting inappropriate notes, it contributes to achieving efficient improvisation practice for people who cannot fully judge melody appropriateness.

Table 6. Questionnaire results of *ism$_V$* evaluation

Subjects	Q1		Q2		Q3		Q4	
	ism$_V$	normal	*ism$_V$*	normal	*ism$_V$*	normal	*ism$_V$*	normal
A1	5	3	7	1	5	2	6	2
A2	5	3	4	2	5	6	3	4
A3	5	6	4	2	6	6	4	4
A4	5	3	7	1	7	6	5	4
B1	6	5	7	4	7	4	6	4
B2	6	5	5	2	7	2	5	3
B3	6	2	6	2	6	5	7	4
B4	6	5	6	2	4	5	6	6
C1	6	5	7	3	4	7	6	3
C2	4	3	5	2	6	6	5	5
C3	5	3	5	3	6	4	4	4
C4	5	1	7	1	7	1	6	1
D1	6	5	6	3	6	3	6	4
D2	6	3	6	3	4	1	7	1
D3	4	2	3	2	4	2	4	3
D4	6	4	6	2	4	7	3	5
Av.	5.4	3.6	5.7	2.2	5.5	3.8	5.2	3.3
SD	0.72	1.4	1.3	0.83	1.2	2.0	1.3	1.5

Using key vibration in order to point out unnatural notes is because auditory, visual and other indication methods are unsuitable for the following reasons. Auditory indication means generating some sounds and it disturbs the performance. Visual indications such as LEDs demand that the user is always looking at the indicatiors while playing. As another approach for providing information to the player, heating keys has been proposed [11], but it takes a long time (approximately two seconds) from starting to heat them to the player feeling the heat.

5.2   Questionnaire Evaluation

To evaluate the effectiveness of *ism$_V$*, we administered questionnaires to users, comparing improvisation practice methods using *ism$_V$* and a normal MIDI keyboard. The subjects were 16 beginning level musicians, divided into four groups (A–D). Each subject tried both practice methods and then answered questions for each practice method. To avoid the influence of trial orders, the subjects in Groups A and C first used *ism$_V$* and then used the normal keyboard, whereas those in Groups B and D used them in the reverse order. In addition, we used two different accompaniments (I and II), which had different keys and chord progressions, between two trials. Accompaniment I was used for the first trial of Groups A and B and the second trial of Groups C and D, and Accompaniment II for the rest. The questions used are as follows:

Table 7. Opinions obtained from subjects after evaluation

ism$_V$
This is helpful because I can quickly get feedback on which notes are inappropriate.
This system allows me to easily recognize wrong notes from vibration.
This is a good system because it indicates melodies that are more appropriate than the ones I have generated on my own.
By comparing my melodies with the ones corrected by the system, I can learn more about the mistakes I make.
It is efficient at telling me when my playing is not in line with the accompaniment. This is revolutionary!
I have no time to correct my errors even if the system points out the notes that need to be corrected in real time.
Although it is useful for creating melodies that are harmonious with the accompaniment, it is still difficult to use it for creating beautiful melodies.

A normal MIDI keyboard
It takes a long time to learn from the system because I cannot quickly recognize wrong notes.
I cannot understand which notes are inappropriate.
If users do not have a good sense of music, this practice method is inefficient, because they have to evaluate everything with their own ears.
This practice method will reach a plateau because it does not provide objective advice.
It is difficult to determine whether my melodies are good or not.
It is too difficult for beginners.
This is boring.

Q1 Do you think you can improve your improvisation skills with this method?
Q2 Do you think this practice method is efficient?
Q3 Did you enjoy the practice?
Q4 Do you think you will continue this practice method?
    (7: Definitely Yes, 6: Probably Yes, 5: Possibly Yes, 4: Neutral
    3: Possibly No, 2: Probably No, 1: Definitely No)

The results are listed in Table 6. For every question, the average answer for
ism_v was more than 5.0 and was 1.7–3.5 higher than that for the normal keyboard. The results of paired t-tests show that **ism_v** is superior to the normal
keyboard with a significance value of 5% (Details are omitted due to lack of
space). Table 7 shows comments made by participating subjects. As shown in
Table 7, many subjects gave us positive comments such as "I can easily recognize which notes are wrong" and "This is revolutionary." These results indicate
that many people deemed it to be a good tool to help them practice improvisation easily and in an enjoyable manner. On the other hand, most comments
for the practice using the normal keyboard were negative such as "too difficult
for beginners" and "boring." These comments indicate that the normal method
is difficult to continue the practice, although continuous practice is the most
important for improving improvisation.

6 Conclusions

This paper has addressed the issue of helping inexperienced musicians in improvisation. Although improvisation is one of the most exciting entertainment
forms, many people have given up learning improvisation due to the difficulty of
instantaneously creating melodies while playing. To tackle this important issue,
we developed two systems: **ism** which automatically corrects musically unnatural notes to natural ones and **ism_v** which points out musically unnatural notes
with key vibration. Through these systems, users can not only easily enjoy and
attempt improvisation but also practice improvisation efficiently and in an enjoyable manner. We believe that these systems make a significant contribution
to music entertainment and music education.

Acknowledgments. The authors would like to thank Dr. Masataka Goto (National Institute of Advanced Industrial Science and Technology) for his helpful
advice. The authors would also like to thank Mr. Takahiro Yanagawa,
Mr. Yoshihiro Watanabe, Mr. Yusaku Nakamura, Mr. Akifumi Nishina and many
people for their cooperation.

References

1. Rowe, R.: Interactive Music Systems Machine Listerning and Composing. The
   MIT Press (1993)
2. Aono, Y., Katayose, H., Inokuchi, S.: An improvisational accompaniment system
   observing performer's musical gesture. In: Proc. ICMC. (1995) 106–107

3. Goto, M., Hidaka, I., Matsumoto, H., Kuroda, Y., Muraoka, Y.: A jam session system for interplay among all players. In: Proc. ICMC. (1996) 346–349
4. Goto, M., Neyama, R.: Open RemoteGIG: An open-to-the public distributed session system overcoming network latency. IPSJ Journal **43** (2002) 299–309
5. Terada, T., Tsukamoto, M., Nishio, S.: A portable electric bass using two PDAs. In: Entertainment Computing: Technologies and Applications (Proc. IWEC 2002). Kluwer Academic Publishers (2002) 286–293
6. Nishimoto, K., *et al.*: Networked wearable musical instruments will bring a new musical culture. In: Proc. ISWC. (2001) 55–62
7. Nishimoto, K., *et al.*: A musical instrument for facilitating musical expressions. In: CHI2002 Extended Abstracts. (2002) 722–723
8. Fels, S., Nishimoto, K., Mase, K.: MusiKalscope: A graphical musical instrument. IEEE Multimedia **5** (1998) 26–35
9. Yatsui, A., Katayose, H.: An accommodating piano which augments intention of inexperienced players. In: Entertainment Computing: Technologies and Applications (Proc. IWEC 2002). Kluwer Academic Publishers (2002) 249–256
10. Miura, M., Hirota, I., Hama, N., Yanagida, M.: Constructing a system for finger-position determination and tablature generation for playing melodies on guitars. System and Computers in Japan **35** (2004) 10–19
11. Miyashita, H., Nishimoto, K.: Theremoscore: A new-type musical score with temperature sensation. In: Int'l Conf. New Interface for Musical Expression. (2004)

Physically-Based Sound Synthesis on GPUs

Qiong Zhang[1], Lu Ye[1,2], and Zhigeng Pan[1]

[1] College of Computer Science, Zhejiang University, Hangzhou 310027, China
[2] Department of Computer and Electronic Engineering, Zhejiang,
University of Science and Technology, Hangzhou 310012, China
zgpan@cad.zju.edn.cn

Abstract. Modal synthesis is a physically-motivated sound modeling method. It has been successfully used in many applications. However, if large number of modes are involved in a simulated scene, it becomes an overwhelming task to synthesize sounds in real time without special hardware support. An implementation based on commodity graphics hardware is proposed as an alternative solution by using the parallelism and programmability in graphics pipeline.

1 Introduction

Sound has long been acknowledged as an effective channel in human-computer interaction [1-4]. Among all the sound synthesis approaches available today, physically based methods play an important role and have pretty long history in computer music research [5]. However, due to the computational complexity, it only became research target until very recently in interactive applications (e.g. games) [6] [7].

Doel et al [6] developed a system for automatic generating sounds made by contact interactions between solid objects. This system is based on a good physically- motivated model called modal synthesis. It models a vibrating object by a bank of damped harmonic oscillators that are excited by an external stimulus. O'Brien et al [7] extended this method by automatic calculating model parameters through finite element method.

Though modal synthesis can be performed efficiently with an $O(N)$ algorithm for objects with N modes, real-time synthesis is only feasible if an interactive application has very small number of sounding objects [8]. Special hardware is necessary in order to simulate complex audio scenes.

Although GPUs (Graphics Processing Units) are specifically designed for transforming, rasterizing and texturing geometry primitives, they are becoming a popular platform for general-purpose computation due to inherent parallelism and enhanced programmability. Audio and signal processing is among one of the latest applications of GPUs [9]. Audio Video Exchange (AVEX) from BionicFX (http://www.bionicfx.com/) converts digital audio into graphics data, and then performs efficient calculations using the 3D architecture of GPUs. Jedrzejewski and Marasek [9] implemented ray tracing on the GPU to accelerate computation of room impulse response that can later be used for auralization.

As illustrated in Fig 1, a modern graphics pipeline is responsible for transforming input geometric primitives into a final image. The image then can be rendered to the

F. Kishino et al. (Eds.): ICEC 2005, LNCS 3711, pp. 328–333, 2005.
© IFIP International Federation for Information Processing 2005

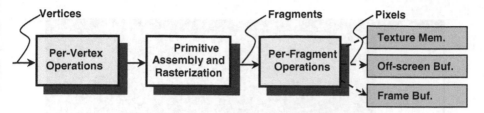

Fig. 1. Graphic pipeline on modern GPUs

frame buffer or stored in an off-screen buffer. Among the major steps of the whole process, we are particularly interested in the fragment-processing stage. At this stage, we can plug in a piece of code called fragment program specifically designed for each individual application. It can perform floating-point vector arithmetic on all the pixels in a parallel mode while having direct access to texture memory.

This paper proposes a GPU-based implementation for modal synthesis. Considering that each mode can be synthesized independently of others, it makes modal synthesis a very appealing target on GPUs. The basic idea is to pre-calculate modal models and store them in a 2D texture, and then fragment programs are used to do the actual response calculation.

2   GPU-Based Modal Synthesis

2.1   Modal Model Representation on GPUs

Contact sounds produced by a solid object depend on quite a few of factors. Those factors can be roughly classified into two groups, namely static and dynamic group. The static group is independent of interaction, which includes geometry and material properties of an object. By contrast, the dynamic group includes factors that rely on current interaction and simulation context. Contact location and external force to produce sound on an object are two primary examples in this group.

As we know, an object in modal model can be represented with following set of parameters $\{ \omega_i , d_i , A_i^j \}$ [6], where $1 \le i \le N$ represents the number of modes, and $1 \le j \le K$ represents sampling contact locations on the object. ω_i is the mode frequency, d_i is the decay rate, and A_i^j is the mode gain at each particular location under an impulse force. All those parameters can either be derived manually through measurement [6] or automatic calculation based on a handful of geometry and materials properties of an object [7]. The number of modes and sampling locations are usually dependent on simulation context and resource availability. The corresponding impulse response at each sampling location j is $y_j(t) = \sum_{i=1}^{N} A_i^j e^{-d_i t} \sin(\omega_i t)$. Fig 2 shows an object and its first four modes.

If we assume that the whole model is linear, the response under an arbitrary force $F(t)$ can be derived fully on the sampling impulse responses and represented in following discrete and recursive form:

Fig. 2. An object in original form (the leftmost figure) and its first four modes

$$y(t) = \sum_{i=1}^{N} 2COS_i y_i(t-1) - (COS_i^2 + SIN_i^2) y_i(t-2) + SIN_i A_i^j F(t-1)$$

Where $SIN_i = e^{-d_i/S} \sin(\omega_i/S)$, $COS_i = e^{-d_i/S} \cos(\omega_i/S)$, and S is the audio sampling rate. It can be further represented with following formula:

$$y(t) = \sum_{i=1}^{N} y_i(t) = \sum_{i=1}^{N} R_i y_i(t-1) + G_i y_i(t-2) + B_i^j F(t-1)$$

Where $R_i = 2e^{-d_i/S} \cos(\omega_i/S)$, $G_i = -(e^{-d_i/S})^2$, $B_i^j = e^{-d_i/S} \sin(\omega_i/S)A_i^j$. All the R_i and G_i values can be pre-calculated before any actual simulation. The only simulation related factor is A_i^j in B_i^j which is dependent on contact location. The solution we take is to pre-calculate B_i^j at all the sampling locations. By this way, the calculation of B_i^j during any simulation becomes choosing a pre-calculated value correspondent to the sampling location closest to the actual contact location.

After all the sounding objects are represented in the form of modal models, we can store those model parameters in a 2D texture on GPUs. Basically, texture is a 2D array and each individual element of the texture called texel that may have up to four (RGBA) channels. As long as the maximum number of modes among all the objects is less than the maximum allowable texture width, multiple modal models can be stored in a single 2D texture. As illustrated in Fig 3, a three-channel texel is used to stored parameters (R_i, G_i, B_i^j) for each mode. Each row contains all the modes parameters of a sounding object at a specific contact location. Typically, 10-30 sampling contact locations are enough for common objects. Thus, a maximum-size 2D texture on modern GPUs can hold at least dozens or even hundreds modal models.

As we can see, this representation leads to some data redundancy since each R_i and G_i are stored in multiple rows as long as the number of sampling location is greater than 1. The purpose of this is to avoid texture addressing and simplify computational logic in the fragment program used to calculate response.

Before any actual simulation begins, all the modal models involved only need be transferred to a GPU once. All the values are in 32-bit floating-point format.

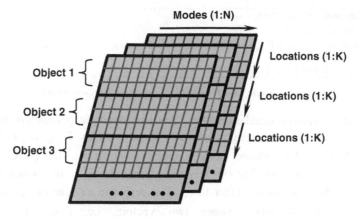

Fig. 3. Modal models are stored in a 2D texture

2.2 Modal Synthesis on GPUs

It is a two-step process to perform modal synthesis on GPUs. The first step is to calculate the response for each individual mode from all the objects producing sound. The second step is to summarize all the responses from those objects.

The first step is accomplished by rendering a rectangle through a fragment program. Essentially, each fragment in the rectangle is corresponding to a mode and rendering a fragment is actually calculating current response for the mode. Each row in the rectangle contains the responses from all the modes of a single object. The total row number is the same with the number of objects producing sound in a scene. By this way, all the responses can be calculated independently in a parallel way.

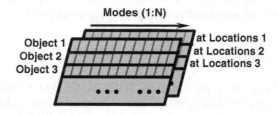

Fig. 4. Responses from all the modes are stored in a 2D texture

As illustrated in Fig 4, the responses from all the modes of all the objects are stored as a 2D texture in an off-screen buffer through render to texture (RTT) functionality. Each texel can be used to store up to four consecutive responses for a single mode. However, only two most recent responses, i.e. $y_i(t-1)$ and $y_i(t-2)$, are necessary to calculate current response $y_i(t)$.

Assuming that M is the number of objects producing sound, MTex is the texture storing all the modal models and RTex(row,col) is the response texture coordinates/fragment window position, Code List 1 gives pseudo code to calculate response for each mode.

```
CalcResponse(MTex,RTex,L,F)
1   A=MTex(L_row,col)     /*(R_i, G_i, B_i)*/
2   B=RTex(row,col)+F_row as the third component /*(y_i(t-1), y_i(t-2), F)*/
3   y_i(t)=dot(A, B)
4   RTex(row,col)=(y_i(t), y_i(t-1),1)
```

Code List 1 – calculate response for each mode

During interactive simulation, there are two dynamic parameters in array type passed into the fragment program. One is location index $L_{1...M}$ (i.e. row number in MTex). It is used to address correct row/texel in Mtex that corresponds to the current contact location. The other is the magnitude $F_{1...M}$ of contact forces. Each object may have its own contact force. The response calculation for each mode is actually a dot product between two vectors, i.e. (R_i , G_i , B_i^j) and ($y_i(t-1)$, $y_i(t-2)$, $F(t-1)$). It is considered as a very efficient operation on GPUs. The calculation result $y_i(t)$ together with $y_i(t-1)$ is written back to the same texel, which will be used in the next cycle.

The second step is to get the total response by accumulating the responses from all the modes. It is essentially a reduction operation. Due to the fact that there is no global register or hardware accumulator on GPUs, reduction operation is commonly implemented as a multi-pass ping-pong process [10]. Starting with the initial rectangle, in each following step a rectangle scaled by a factor of 0.5 is rendered.

More specifically, in the fragment program, a sum value is evaluated from each four adjacent texels and written into a new texture, which is now of a factor of two smaller in each dimension than the previous one. For a texture in $N*N$ resolution, $\log_2 N$ rendering passes are performed until the final sum is obtained in a single pixel. It can then be read back to the system. In our scenario, since the number of modes is usually much larger than the number of objects, we may apply different factors in each dimension to reduce pass number during the ping-pong process.

3 Results and Conclusion

We have implemented above algorithm in NVIDIA Cg and a GeForce 6800 GT graphics processor with 256 MB video memory was used in the preliminary test. All the modal models were transferred to the card through an AGP 8X interface. Our test cases include 64 sounding objects in the scene. Each object has 16 sampling contact locations and 512 modes. It is equivalent to synthesize 32K modes. Fig 5 gives a synthesis example that includes 10 sounding objects. However, on a typical workstation with Pentium IV 2.8G HZ CPU, we are only able to synthesize less than 5000 modes with similar algorithm in real time.

If large chunk of audio data need be transferred from GPUs to the system memory, slow AGP read-back may become a performance bottleneck. However, newly appeared PCI-Express should be able to solve this issue.

Overall, the implementation of modal synthesis on GPUs is able to significantly improve the number of modes that can be synthesized in real time. With the constant

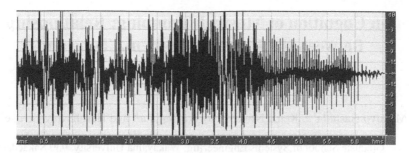

Fig. 5. A modal synthesis example on Geforce 6800 GT

increase of programmability (global register, more floating-point support, etc), fragment pipelines, and data transfer bandwidth between GPU and system memory, it is expected that the GPU based implementation can get further performance gain compared with the CPU one. Future research may focus on integrating modal synthesis and 3D filtering on GPUs.

Acknowledgments

This project is co-supported by a 973 project (grant no: 2002CB312100) and Excellent Youth Teacher Program of MOE in China.

References

1. Buxton, W.: Introduction to this special issue on nonspeech audio. Human Computer Interaction. 4 (1999) 1–9
2. Pan, Z., Shi, J.: Virtual Reality Technology Development in China: An Overview. International Journal of Virtual Reality. 4(2000) 2-10
3. Zhang, Q., Shi, J., Pan Z.: ARE: An audio reality engine in virtual environment. International Journal of Virtual Reality. 4 (2000) 37-43
4. Zhang, Q., Shi, J.: Progressive Sound Rendering in Multimedia Applications. Proceedings of 2004 IEEE International Conference on Multimedia and Expo (ICME 2004), v1, p651-654, Taiwan (2004)
5. Smith, J.: A Physical Modeling Synthesis Update. Computer Music Journal. 20 (1996) 44-56
6. van den Doel, K., Kry, P. Pai, D.: FoleyAutomatic: Physically-based Sound Effects for Interactive Simulation and Animation. Proc of SIGGRAPH 2001, 537-544, Los Angeles, USA (2001)
7. J. O'Brien, C. Shen, and C. M. Gatchalian, Synthesizing Sounds from Rigid-Body Simulations. Proc of 2002 ACM SIGGRAPH Symposium on Computer Animation, 175-182, San Antonio, USA (2002)
8. van den Doel, K., Knott, D., Pai, D.: Interactive Simulation of Complex Audio-Visual Scenes. Presence. 13 (2004) 99-111
9. Jedrzejewski, M., Marasek, K.: Computation of Room Acoustics Using Programmable Video Hardware. International Conference on Computer Vision and Graphics 2004, Warsaw, Poland (2004)
10. Krüger, J., Westermann, R.: Linear Algebra Operators for GPU Implementation of Numerical Algorithms. ACM Trans. Graph. 22 (2003) 908-916

On Cognition of Musical Grouping: Relationship Between the Listeners' Schema Type and Their Musical Preference

Mitsuyo Hashida[1,2], Kenzi Noike[2], Noriko Nagata[3], and Haruhiro Katayose[2,3]

[1] Graduate School of Systems Engineering, Wakayama University, 930 Sakaedani,
Wakayama, Wakayama 640-8510, Japan
http://www.sys.wakayama-u.ac.jp/
[2] PRESTO/Japan Science and Technology Agency
http://www.kyotyo.jst.go.jp/index.html
[3] Department of Science and Engineering, Kwansei Gakuin University, 2-1 Gakuen, Sanda,
Hyogo, 669-1337, Japan
{hashida, noike, nagata, katayose}@ksc.kwansei.ac.jp
http://www.m-use.net/research/listening/

Abstract. We assume that there are various musical groupings of perceptions according to the degree of schemata and there are two dominant music grouping schemata; (a) **accent-oriented grouping schema** and (b) **phrasing schema** (musical expression referred to as the Rainbow type). In order to verify these hypotheses, we investigated how listeners' groupings change when the inner voice of Beethoven's Piano Sonata "Pathetique" was replaced with chords. We eventually succeeded in identifying three listening groups; those who have a strong (a) schema (type **A**), those whose (a) is prior to (b) (type **AF**), and those whose (b) is prior to (a) while paying attention to their inner voice (type **FA$_I$**). We verified that type **A** listeners prefer Rap music, Rock music, listening in a lively place, listening to party music, and listening to lyrics, while type **FA$_I$** listeners prefer Bach, Chopin, and listening alone and quietly.

1 Introduction

How do human beings listen to the music? How do human beings understand musical structure and perceive musical groups? These questions are of the greatest concern for music composers and performers. At the same time, they are essential questions for people studying what makes humans feel entertained.

The perception of music grouping is said to be a function of schemata. In perception, there are many organizing principles called gestalt laws, e.g., the laws of proximity and similarity [1]. A gestalt law says that we are innately driven to experience things in as good a gestalt as possible. Musical performances are thus understood in these terms as an art in which gestalt factors are elaborated ingeniously. However, it is not clear how these laws are unified to achieve music groupings. We assume that the wide variety of personal music groupings results from a difference in schemata strengths formulated in accordance with the listener's experience.

F. Kishino et al. (Eds.): ICEC 2005, LNCS 3711, pp. 334–344, 2005.

According to gestalt laws, the prominent note is perceived as the starting note of the music group, which consists of the note and the following contiguous notes. On the other hand, in the typical expression of phrasing, the most prominent note appears in the middle of the phrase. Without a doubt, both schemata must be valid in themselves, yet they are contradictory schemata for music grouping.

It is said that the primary goal of conductors and performers is to clarify the structure of the music to be played and to give expression to the music as her/his intention is understood by the audience [1]. This may lead to the view that there has to be a correct grouping, i.e., a correct way of listening to the music. In the research field of music psychology, there have been a few reports that focus on the variety of music group perceptions. However, in our analyses of a performance rendering contest [2] and a preliminary experiment on music listening [4, 5], we confirmed that even listeners who have a lot of musical experience do not have unique music groupings.

The paper addresses two points: 1) the analysis of grouping by subjects, and 2) the examination of background factors affecting grouping type. In Section 2, we explain typical performance expressions of music groups that are related with two grouping schemata, and explain the keywords and concepts of the experiments described in Section 3. Section 3 describes the experimental procedure to classify the grouping types of listeners. In Section 4, we discuss the musical preference background of each grouping type and summarize the subjects to be dealt with in the future.

2 Group Recognition of Music

A person perceives groups by listening to a stream of sound [6~12].

Music grouping is a fundamental process that listeners need to understand and enjoy music. In this section, we explain two typical schemata for music grouping. Next, we describe the preliminary investigation regarding group recognition and describe the sort of "attention" employed in the design of the experiments.

2.1 Schemata for Music Grouping

There are many perceptual organizing principles called gestalt laws; e.g., the law of proximity, law of similarity, and law of continuity. These principles are summarized in terms of music as follows:

Score level: grouping based on relative pitch-interval, direction of contour, and/or combination of these principles.

Signal level: grouping by IOI (inter onset interval), OOI (offset onset interval) and/or intensity level of adjacent notes.

These grouping principles are easy to understand, and most cognitive music theories adopt them in order to formulate grouping rules (e.g. GTTM [6]). However, the methods of how to set quantitative parameters for each rule and of conflict resolution between rules have not been formulated yet. The lack thereof has become one of the key issues of musical information science [13, 14]. Below, we introduce two principal schemata of music grouping.

Fig. 1. Perceptive Grouping Based on Gestalt

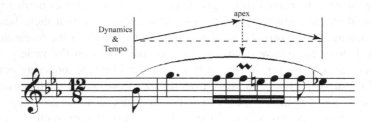

Fig. 2. Phrasing Expression

Accent-oriented grouping. Proximity is regarded as the most fundamental evidence for grouping music, and most grouping theories refer to it. In particular, Mozart's piano sonata K.331 (**Fig. 1**) is often quoted in explaining proximity. The explanation is as follows; the perceived groups are indicated by placing upper brackets if a small rest is inserted after every bar, and are indicated by placing lower brackets if a small rest is inserted just after quarter notes of the 1st and the 2nd bar.

Takeuchi measured performances of typical editions of the piece (Henle edition (upper) and Peters' edition (lower)) and showed that the group starting notes are played louder in both editions [15].

The principle of proximity and Takeuchi's suggestion that louder notes tend to be starting notes of groups (or performers give accent to the group starting notes) may be best regarded as independent concepts. However, as for proximity, it is rational to suppose that the greater the distance between adjacent events is, the more each event will be perceived as the prominent "accented" event. Thereby, combining the principle of proximity and Takeuchi's suggestion, we assumed a grouping schema by which a louder or leaped note after a long IOI or rest is perceived as a starting note of a group composed of successive notes. We refer to this schema as the **AOG schema** (accent-oriented grouping schema).

Phrasing. Another important clue for music grouping is the expression of phrases, referred to as phrasing. Expressing changes to tempi and dynamics by drawing an arc of a rainbow is the most widely known of the techniques to express phrasing (see Fig. 2) [2, 9, 16]. Although this phrasing technique may be a way to express a group in a range of a physical breath, it is also natural to think that this familiar expression might be used to formulate a principle schema for grouping music. Gestalt psychology informs us that phrasing can be regarded as an expression using the principle of proximity. In this paper, we refer to this grouping schema based on musical expression as the **phrasing schema**.

2.2 Preliminary Investigation

Here we introduce some points related to music grouping that we discovered during our preliminary investigation [5].

Variety of music group perceptions. We investigated how much performers' well-elaborated intention about music grouping is conveyed to listeners by conducting an experiment with 101 subjects comprising experienced listeners (more than 8 years experience in playing a musical instrument) and inexperienced listeners. Experienced listeners were able to understand intention better than inexperienced listeners ($p < 0.05$). On the other hand, the experiment also showed the number of the listeners of the experienced group who perceived fully the same grouping that the player intended was only half. The other perceived groupings could be classified into several types.

Influence of performance parameter. In order to elaborate on Takeuchi's finding in [15], we implemented a kind of morphing system, by which we can quantitatively investigate the influence of the operation to make a note prominent by giving more intensity and the operation of giving a rest to a music grouping. We carried out experiments (Fig. 1) on two subjects who had more than 20 years of musical experience (one has a masters degree in music education and the other, a masters degree in composition). The experimental results showed that the subjects' parameter distributions (intensity and rest) to judge the upper from the lower group (in Fig. 1) were significantly different.

Change of grouping by attention control. We tried to determine if the music grouping changes temporarily, when the listeners are given another attention focus than what they would usually focus on. Using the musical example described in section 3, we explained the phrasing of the accompaniment to listeners who were considered to pay attention to the melody. One third of listeners reported that their grouping unexpectedly changed from melody to accompaniment.

3 Listening Experiment

Our preliminary experiment suggests that music grouping is not always unique and that listeners can be classified according to a number of music groupings. We also verified that a listener's musical experience has some correlation with his/her music grouping and that attention control may influence a listener's grouping temporarily and selectively. Thus, the experiments were on classifying subjects according to grouping characteristics. We focused on the predominance of the **AOG schema** and **phrasing schema**. We have to take account of the fact that it is not easy for every subject to describe her/his own perception. Sometimes a perception may be distorted when it is translated in words. To reduce the errors caused by a mixture of subjects whose statements could be incredible, we contrived an experimental plan as follows.

3.1 Procedure

First, we had to prepare a test piece, the grouping to which may differ according to which schema is predominant. To put it concretely, we used a musical piece whose grouping would differ according to whether the listener paid attention to the melody or to the inner voice. For this purpose, we used performances of the first eight measures of the second movement of Beethoven's Piano Sonata "Pathetique," explained and realized by Professor Hiroshi Hoshina, a composer and conductor [9]. In the experiment subjects were asked to mark any of the grouping candidates and any of the accent notes in the melody that they felt, into the given score sheet (see Fig. 3), after listening to each of the following three stimulus performances.

Fig. 3. Score Sheet for the Listening Experiment: Arrows are candidates of grouping boundaries. After listening to each performance, subjects mark their grouping boundaries and accented notes that they felt.

The first stimulus was an **original expressive version**: a performance including all dynamics and tempo. The second stimulus was a **chord version**: a performance whose accompaniment was replaced with chords synchronous to the melody. The player's inner voice expression was thus suppressed while maintaining the harmonic structures of that piece. The third stimulus was the **original expressive version**, again. Before the third trial, subjects were given an explanation of the roles of the inner voice in the piece, that is, the part that gives the piece phrasing expression (see Fig. 4).

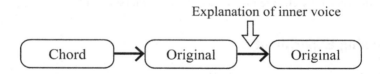

Fig. 4. Process of the Experiment

3.2 On the 2nd Movement of Beethoven's "Pathetique"

The second movement of "Pathetique" is representative of homophony. Homophonic music has a main melody and a synchronized homogeneous accompaniment. According to Hoshina's analysis, the melody of the first eight measures consists of six groups supported by the melodic and harmonic solution (brackets located at the upper part of the score in Fig. 5). The second and third groups (from C in the first beat of the third measure to F in the first beat of the fifth measure) combine to form a compound group. The root chord in the third group keeps V (F at the last note means V9), and the first note (E flat) chromatically progresses to the last F (that is, the middle E natural is a passing note). Based on this analysis for music groups and considering the contour, Hoshina identified the apex note, marked by a star within each group. The fundamental expression of the groups that Hoshina suggests is of crescendo toward the apex note, and decrescendo from the apex to the end of the group, which is regarded as typical phrasing.

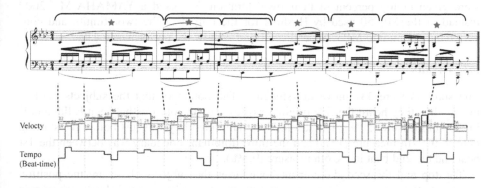

Fig. 5. Interpretation and Expression of 2nd Movement of Beethoven's Piano Sonata "Pathetique": The annotated slurs are according to the Henle Edition. The brackets above the main melody mean Hoshina's grouping and the stars mean the apices of those groups. Crescendo and diminuendo are written by the author based on his expression.

In this music, 16th notes of the inner voice, especially, 16th notes from the 1st measure to 2nd measure, the 4th measure, and the 6th measure, of which the melody notes are long tones, play an important role in phrasing expression. It is impossible to express gradual crescendo within a note played by a piano. Phrasing for group expression is realized with crescendo followed by diminuendo for the part described in section 2.1.2. Therefore, phrasing of these groups is achieved with a crescendo followed by a diminuendo for the 16th notes of the inner voice.

The 1st note of the 6th measure is a boundary candidate in the **AOG schema**. The melody note E flat is the last note of the preceding group and is the starting note of the next group (6th bar). It is impossible to express crescendo only with the expression of the summit note (A natural) in the melody. In contrast, in the preceding group, the summit note of the melody B flat (The 2nd beat in the 5th measure) and resolved to E flat with a diminuendo. It is possible to express diminuendo for the ascending 32nd note sequence. To sum up, A natural (2nd note of the 6th measure) is likely to be a group start because this note is adjacent to the preceding note sequence and the intensity of A natural is stronger than that of E flat.

The discussion so far can be summarized as follows; (a) if a listener finds that A natural (the 2nd note of the 6th measure) is the group starting note, he or she has used the **AOG schema**. (b) If the listener does not regard A natural as the group starting note, that is, s/he has grouped by **phrasing schema**, s/he must be tracing the inner voice, whether s/he may be conscious of that, or not. If the inner voice is replaced with chords, some of the (b) listeners will indicate a group starting at the A natural note.

Hoshina analyzed the performance interpretation of eight measures of the beginning of the second movement of this piano sonata, describing its dynamics [velocity] and tempo [BPM] by sixteenth note. His grouping, apices, and performance information are shown in Fig. 5. The information does not include pedal or note length. As for this piece, pedaling is not always required. In addition, this piece is often played slowly with the sounds of the piano sustained acoustically. Thus, we made each note length equal to its duration, except for notes annotated with a slur and staccato, which were given eighty percent of their own duration. We used a YAMAHA MU-2000 instead of the MU-50 used by Hoshina for the output of the two stimuli, and converted the output into MP3. Appendices 1 and 2 show the performance data.

3.3 Results

The subjects were 231 university students. The boundary that the subjects marked most, when they heard the first original expressive version, was between E flat and E in the 4th measure (59%). The second dominant boundary was just before the starting note in the 7th measure (15%) and the third dominant boundary was between the 1st beat and the 2nd beat in the 6th measure (9.5%).

The top and the second dominant boundaries the subjects chose are the position where a half cadence pattern appears and the position where a typical cadence pattern starts, respectively. On the other hand, it is not impossible to explain why the third position was chosen only with the cadence patterns.

Here we focus on the third dominant boundary, called X in the remainder of this paper, where the intense E flat may lead to an AOG schema and phrasing achieved with an expression of the inner voice may lead to a phrasing schema. Among 231 subjects, 20 subjects said there was a boundary at X after listening to the chord performance. Among these 20 subjects, 14 subjects said that they did not notice the boundary at X when they listened to the source expressive performance, while the other 6 said they did. The difference between the source expressive performance and the chord performance is whether the notes in the inner voice are played with the sequential 16th notes or played at the same time. 14 subjects (**FA$_I$** Group) were regarded as listeners possessing both **AOG schema** and **phrasing schema**, and as paying attention to the inner voice. They are supposed to be listeners of traditional western music.

Sixteen subjects thought there was no boundary after the inner voice function was explained. These listeners were deemed to be ones whose **AOG schema** is somewhat prior to their **phrasing schema**, and whose attention to the inner voice is comparatively low (**AF** Group).

Six subjects who said that they felt there was a boundary after being given the explanation were regarded as listeners with a strong **AOG schema** (**A** Group). If we make experiments using other musical samples, we might be able to separate the remaining 188 subjects' musical grouping types more precisely. However, it is impossible to judge whether the remaining subjects have perceived a group boundary and produced consistent statements, only from the experiment using Beethoven's Piano Sonata "Pathetique". Therefore, we are going to consider the subjects of the **FA$_I$**, **AF** and **A** group in the following discussion.

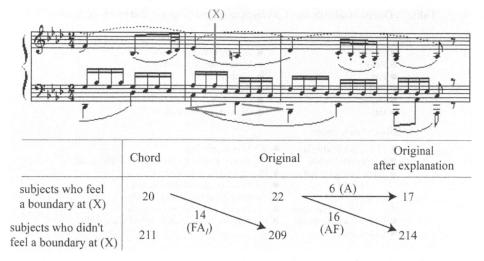

	Chord	Original	Original after explanation
subjects who feel a boundary at (X)	20	22	6 (A) → 17
subjects who didn't feel a boundary at (X)	211	209	16 (AF) → 214

14 (FA$_I$)

Fig. 6. Result of Boundary Perception between the 1st beat and 2nd beat at the 6th bar

4 Grouping Schema and Its Background

The investigation of causes that lead to formulation of individual schema is a crucial study target of Kansei research. However, it is not easy to control individual conditions that might affect schema formulation. In the experiment, we investigated (a) preference for musical genre and (b) preference for listening manner, based on the social-psychological approach of Csikszentmihalyi [17].

The procedure we adopted is that subjects should give the order to items that we prepared in advance, as shown in Table 1. We then analyzed the preference characteristics of each group (FA$_I$, AF Group, A Group) by calculating the average preference order. The average order and the radar charts are shown in **Table 2** and Fig. 7, respectively. The scale of the radar chart is given by 1.0 − average order / number of items. It is not an absolute scale. However it provides us with information to understand the tendency.

Music Genre Preference Result

- The preference level for Pop was the highest for all of the groups.
- The preference levels of the **FA$_I$** group were lower for Rock and Rap, compared with those of other groups, and higher for Therapy Music.
- The preference levels of the **A** group were lower for Bach and Chopin, compared with those of other groups.
- The preference levels of the **AF** group were between those of the FA$_I$ group and A group.

Preference for Listening Manner

- Listeners of the **FA$_I$** group preferred listening music alone and quietly.
- Listeners of the **A** group preferred listening to music with their friends. They attached importance to lyrics.
- The preference levels of the **AF** group were between those of the FA$_I$ group and A group.

Table 1. Questionnaire items of preference for music genre and listening manner

Favorites of music genres

- Pop
- Rock
- Rap
- Jazz
- Dance
- Ballad

- Healing (Therapy Music)
- Typical Movie Soundtrack
- Chopin
- Bach
- Orchestra
- Other (Free Description)

Activity while listening

- Listen in a lively place
- Listen with friends
- While riding the wave of Music
- Listen as BGM: background music
- Listen in a quiet place
- Listen Alone

- While concentrating
- While anticipating the progression of the music
- Play the music in your mind
- While being emotionally affected
- Listen to lyrics rather than melody
- Listen to melody rather than lyrics
- While trying to remember the lyrics and melody

Table 2. Orders of preference for music genre and listening manner

Genre	FA_I (14)	AF (16)	A (6)	Others (188)	Listening Situation	FA_I (14)	AF (16)	A (6)	Others (188)
Pop	2.64	2.19	2.00	2.45	Lively	9.79	8.94	6.50	9.34
Rock	4.54	3.94	2.83	4.66	With Friends	9.50	7.28	5.17	8.83
Rap	7.14	5.13	4.50	6.63	With Moving	7.50	6.28	8.00	8.13
Jazz	5.61	6.00	6.00	6.41	As Background Music	4.93	5.28	5.50	4.99
Dance	6.93	6.31	7.50	7.22	Quietly	3.57	5.97	7.50	4.21
Ballad	4.43	4.31	3.17	4.62	Alone	3.21	4.34	6.00	3.57
Healing	6.18	7.69	8.17	6.85	Concentrating	5.93	5.81	7.00	5.33
Typical Movie Soundtrack	6.11	6.06	4.67	5.43	Anticipating	7.57	7.34	9.17	7.88
					Imagine Playing	8.71	8.53	8.83	8.27
Chopin	7.11	7.94	9.83	7.49	Emotionally Affected	9.57	9.06	9.33	9.64
Bach	8.04	8.56	10.17	8.13	Listen to Lyrics	8.71	8.31	6.67	8.00
Orchestra	8.25	9.00	8.50	7.76	Listen to Melody	5.64	6.00	4.67	5.23
Others	11.04	10.69	10.67	10.21	Trying to remember	6.36	7.09	6.67	7.47

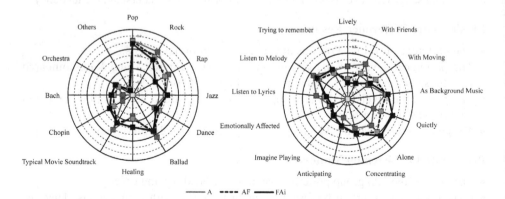

Fig. 7. Radar chart of **Table 2**. The preferred items are listed on the circumference.

FA$_l$ Group. The listeners of the FA$_l$ group are supposed to be interested in traditional western music, because they can hear the inner voice. We hypothesized that the genres preferred by this group would be orchestral music, Bach, and Chopin. Unexpectedly, the results show that the preference for orchestral music was not so high. However, the preferences for Bach and Chopin were higher and preferences for Rock and Jazz were lower than in the A group. Listeners of this group tended to listen to music alone and quietly. They did not prefer listening with many people. They seemed to enjoy listening only to the music itself. Despite the slight deviation from our expectation, we may say the hypothesis was supported by the results on the whole.

A Group. Listeners of the A group are thought to have the AOG schema. We hypothesized that they would have a strong preference for Rap and Rock music, in which the beat expression is prior to phrasing. Fig. 6. shows that the listeners of this group do prefer Rap and Rock music, and have little interest in Bach and Chopin. They prefer listening to music with their friends. In addition, the listeners of this group regarded lyrics as important, and they make light of anticipation and concentration, compared with other groups. We may reasonably conclude that the hypothesis was supported by the results.

5   Discussion

Our discussion of the results can be summarized as follows:

In the experiment, we focused on two primary grouping schemata, and gave higher priority to excluding subjects whose statements were inconsistent. Eventually, the 90% of the subjects that did not find a boundary at the first beat of 6th measure were taken out of the analysis. There is a possibility that other schema view this part as not the boundary, for instance, a temporal note line schema. We would like to conduct further experiments using composed music to investigate this possibility.

The questionnaire items were limited to coarse items except for Bach and Chopin. This is because we considered the subjects would find it more convenient when filling in the form if we selected the items to be evaluated. For the same reason, we adopted an ordinal scale instead of an interval scale. We should thus conduct future investigations based on an interval scale, limiting the number of items.

The questionnaire survey revealed that musical preferences are different if the listener type (i.e. **A, AF, FA$_l$ group**) is different. At the same time, we found preference differences corresponding to age. That means we should conduct broader investigations with a greater range of subject ages.

6   Conclusion

The music grouping depended on each listener's musical experience. We provided a working hypothesis that grouping differences result from the balance of schemata strengths that each listener possesses, and executed an experiment using the second movement of the "Pathetique" composed by Beethoven. The experimental parts of music listened to by the subjects were controlled, as the grouping results might differ according to which of the **accent-oriented schema** and **phrasing schema** is prior for the subject. We were able to identify three typical listener types; those who have strong **accent-oriented schema** (**A** group), those whose **accent-oriented schema** is somewhat prior to their phrasing schema (**AF** group), and those who have the competence of listening to inner voices and whose **phrasing schema** is prior to their accent-oriented schema (**FA$_I$** group).

Using a questionnaire survey filled out by these subjects, we verified that (1) **A** group listeners prefer Rap music and Rock music, as well as listening in a lively place with many people and listening to lyrics. (2) **FA$_I$** group listeners prefer Chopin, listening alone and quietly, and (3) university freshmen in the **FA$_I$** group do not have as much preference for Rap or Rock compared with freshmen in other groups.

The subject dealt with in this paper is an investigation of human cognitive processes based on observation of the musical grouping process. We illustrated that we can classify the listener's type considering superiority of grouping schemata. We also investigated the relationship between the listeners' schema type and their musical preference. Our investigations are still at an early stage, and we would like to conduct broad investigations together with experiments using samples of originally composed music as future work.

References

1. Koffka, K.: Principles of Gestalt Psychology, Harcourt (1967)
2. Ozawa, S., et al.: Lecture notes of Hideo Saito, Hakusui-sha (in Japanese, 1999)
3. Hiraga, R., Hashida, M., Hirata, K., Katayose, H., Noike, K.: RENCON: toward a new evaluation method for performance rendering systems, Proc. Int. Computer Music Conference (2002) 357-360
4. Noike, K., Hashida, M., Katayose, H.: An Examination Tools to obtain Musical Group Boundary --- WebMorton, IPSJ 2002-MUS-49 (in Japanese, 2002) 25-29
5. Katayose, H., Hashida, M., Noike, K.: On Perception of Apices and Group Boundaries in Listening Music, IPSJ 2003-MUS-52 (in Japanese, 2003) 95-102
6. Lerdahl, F., Jackendoff, R.: A Generative Theory of Tonal Music, MIT Press (1983)
7. Murao, T.: Recognition of Music Analysis, Music and Recognition, University of Tokyo Press (in Japanese, 1987) 1-40
8. Aiello, R.: Musical Perceptions, Oxford University Press (1994)
9. Hoshina, H.: Approach to lively musical expression, Ongaku-no-tomo-sha Corp., (in Japanese, 1998)
10. Snyder, B.: Music and Memory: An Introduction, MIT Press (2001)
11. Moore, B. C. J.: An Introduction to the Psychology of Hearing, Academic Press (2003)
12. Edelman, G. M., Gall, W. E.: Auditory Function, Neurobiological Bases of Hearing, John Wiley & Sons Inc (1988)
13. Hamanaka, M., Hirata, K., Tojo, S.: Automatic Generation of Grouping Structure based on the GTTM, Proc. Int. Computer Music Conference (2004) 141-144
14. Noike, K., Hashida, M., Takeuchi, Y., Katayose, H.: Expansion of GTTM Grouping Rules for Involving Expression Parameters, 2004-MUS-57 (in Japanese, 2004) 11-16
15. Takeuchi, Y.: Performance Variables for Grouping Structure in two editions of the theme of K. 331, Rencon Workshop, Proc. of ICAD (2002)
16. The New GROVE Dictionary of Music and Musicians, Groves Dictionaries Inc. (1993)
17. Csikszentmihalyi, M.: Beyond Boredom and Anxiety, Jossey-Bass Inc. Pub. (2000)

Augmented Reality Agents in the Development Pipeline of Computer Entertainment

István Barakonyi and Dieter Schmalstieg

Graz University of Technology, Inffeldgasse 16a, A-8010, Graz, Austria
{bara, schmalstieg}@icg.tu-graz.ac.at

Abstract. Augmented reality (AR) has recently stepped beyond the usual scope of applications like machine maintenance, military training and production, and has been extended to the realm of entertainment including computer gaming. This paper discusses the potential AR environments offer for embodied animated agents, and demonstrates several advanced immersive content and scenario authoring techniques in AR through example applications.

1 Introduction

The highly influential book of Bolter and Grusin titled Remediation [1] states that digital technologies such as the World Wide Web, computer games, virtual reality (VR) and augmented reality (AR) cannot separate themselves from earlier media forms such as photography, film or stage. The authors argue that a novel visual media form should first observe and respect, then attempt to surpass earlier media by refashioning, "remediating" them, just like photography remediated perspective painting, film remediated stage and photography, and television remediated film. Augmented reality has recently stepped beyond the usual scope of applications like machine maintenance, military training and production, and has been extended to entertainment including computer gaming. This step is expected to greatly contribute to a wider acceptance of this relatively novel research field, similar to the spread of 2D and 3D computer games supported by the rapid hardware and software developments in computer graphics that have also attracted significant public interest. In this paper we focus on entertainment applications in augmented reality environments.

Our paper has two major contributions. The first contribution is our advanced use of animated characters in augmented reality applications, which reaches back to more traditional media such as film or stage. Since AR environments are typically highly dynamic with a large number of events coming from the physical and virtual world, it is difficult to create detailed scripted behavior for characters to anticipate every conceivable situation, unlike in more controlled interactive 2D and 3D virtual environments. Consequently, it is desirable to employ autonomous software components that proactively and autonomously make decisions without continuously waiting for commands from the user. Therefore we propose *embodied autonomous agents* as a novel, promising direction for interaction development of AR applications.

The second contribution is the application of remediation theory to authoring tools in augmented reality environments. We argue that not only presented content and its perception need to be remediated, but media should also strongly influence authoring

F. Kishino et al. (Eds.): ICEC 2005, LNCS 3711, pp. 345–356, 2005.
© IFIP International Federation for Information Processing 2005

tools. While tools to author content for AR have been based on strong roots in classic computer graphics and VR, we claim that augmented reality should exploit medium-specific techniques to smoothen its production workflow: *AR has to penetrate its own authoring pipeline*. Nevertheless, we do not offer a complete solution for creating standalone applications as some larger frameworks do [2][3][4] but provide case studies to explore novel ways of authoring and enabling interaction.

2   Motivations and Related Research

Typical forms of computer-assisted entertainment include computer games and story-telling applications. As in all games and stories, a key experience element is fantasy. While playing or participating in a story, a virtual, imaginary world is created within our mind, inhabited by characters and other objects behaving according to the dictates of our imagination. In classic make-believe games this fantasy world and their characters connect to the real environment through physical game props to which various roles are assigned, thus making heretofore passive objects active players in the game story. AR applications are aiming at the same effect by superimposing a virtual world on top of the real environment. Since the virtual world is registered with the real one, they appear to coexist. As pointed out by Stapleton et al. in their mixed-fantasy framework [5], the combination of the real and virtual helps suspend disbelief and enriches the audience's fantasy experience. AR is able to visually change real world attributes, make passive objects appear animated or play sound effects in addition to sounds in the real environment further enhancing the atmosphere of the perceived mixed environment.

2.1   Authoring AR

Besides being a compelling environment for digital entertainment, augmented reality offers novel, intuitive tools for content authoring as well. MacIntyre et al. [6] make the point that the most relevant factor making AR an important and unique medium is the combination of three concurrent features: blurring the boundary between the real and the virtual world, constant user control of viewpoint and interactivity. Traditional tools for authoring VR and AR content, such as desktop-based 2D/3D content authoring tools, character animation programs, multimedia frameworks [3], or editors to compile and run scripts [2], offer the evident advantage of familiarity. However, an authoring environment possessing the aforementioned three qualities would be desirable to let content developers fully experience and understand the novel environment they develop for and tailor the content to it.

From the various extant tools for authoring content for AR applications we highlight the tangible AR-based system from Lee et al. [7], which is to our knowledge the only general purpose immersive authoring AR system existing to date. This system implements an intuitive WYSIWYG editor, where users handle physical markers to manipulate virtual objects, their properties and their connections to other objects and properties to model interaction. Although the immersive environment and the tangible controls are similar to ours, the data flow model covers only basic functions of tangible AR applications without considering more complex aspects such as application events or multi-user aspects.

2.2 Autonomous Agents in AR

Animated characters have been particularly important and popular visual story and interface elements in a large variety of digital entertainment domains from animated 3D cartoons to computer games, where these characters have been used as avatars, allies, bystanders or competitors of the user. They are able to create a rich gaming experience, since their advanced multimodal communication capabilities including speech, facial and body gestures and posture engage users emotionally and socially as well. They are perceived as living, feeling, and "smart" digital creatures.

Characters in AR may possess a virtual or *physical* body, or both. They share users' physical environment, in which they can freely move using all 6 degrees of freedom. Virtual characters in AR scenarios appear to have a solid, tangible body that can be observed from an arbitrary viewpoint, thus becoming integral parts of the physical environment. A typical AR environment is highly dynamic including several users equipped with various devices and constantly changing object poses. We think that a preferable way of implementing animated characters for AR environments is by using autonomous agents that proactively make decisions instead of demanding constant user guidance, while monitoring and observing changes in the physical and virtual environment. According to Bates [8] appropriately timed and clearly expressed emotion is an essential and often sufficient requirement for characters to behave in a believable way. Therefore we do not focus on equipping our agents with complex behavior engines or intelligence (without excluding them). Instead we have been researching the technical challenges, user requirements and possible applications that potential AR environments suggest given the possibility of populating them with animated agents.

Although extensively researched in VR, agents have only recently appeared in AR environments. An early AR application providing character support is the ALIVE system [9], where a virtual animated character composited into the user's real environment responds to human body gestures on a large projection screen. This type of display separates the user's physical space from the AR environment, which demands carefully coordinated user behavior. The Welbo project [10] features an immersive setup, where an animated virtual robot assists an interior designer wearing an HMD. The character lacks a tangible physical representation and can only interact with virtual objects. Another HMD-based system from MacIntyre et al. [6] creates an interactive theater experience by placing prerecorded video-based actors into an AR environment. The characters do not possess any autonomy, as their behavior is scripted, and interaction is limited to changing viewpoints and roles in the story. Cheok et al. [11] also experiment with mixed reality entertainment with live captured 3D characters, which enable telepresence of real people within a virtual or augmented reality setting but without any control of the environment. Cavazza et al. [12] place a live video avatar of a real person into a mixed reality setting, and interact with a digital storytelling system with body gestures and language commands. Balcisoy et al. [13] experiment with interaction techniques with virtual humans in mixed reality environments, which play the role of a collaborative game partner and an assistant for prototyping machines. Cassell et al.'s Sam agent [14] is a virtual playmate assisting children in a natural storytelling play with real objects. In this game access to real game props is shared between the child and the animated agent.

3   Events and Interaction in the Real and the Virtual

Interaction with animated agents in an AR environment needs careful design. The set of possible application events is huge, since numerous events are generated by changes in the pose and attributes of multiple users, interaction devices and displays, pose-tracked application-specific props and the application itself. Monitoring all possible events and their combinations is a complex and time-consuming task that can affect the responsiveness of the agents if carried out naively. Therefore as one of the first application design tasks we need to limit the set of events exclusively to those meaningful in the context of the application and set up real and virtual sensors to measure and catch them. The events help the agent maintain its internal world model that attempts to match the perception of the user, and result in the agent making decisions and actions based on the current status of its internal world. To effectively design which application events may be useful for our agents, we wrote simple demo scenarios to test atomic behavior patterns, where various communication channels are utilized between the real and the virtual.

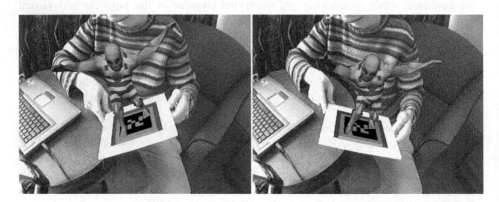

Fig. 1. Screenshots of a virtual animated character balancing on top of a tangible optical marker

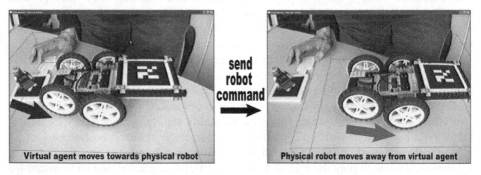

Fig. 2. Screenshots of a real LEGO® Mindstorms robot avoiding collision with a virtual character

3.1 Agent with Virtual Body Reacting to Events in the Real World

Figure 1 illustrates a simple example how a virtual animated agent is able to respond to changes in attribute changes of the real world. A tangible, physical optical marker acts as a platform for a virtual monster artiste to stand on. The user holds and tilts around the marker in front of a webcam, while the artiste agent appears to be struggling to maintain its balance. If the surface of the marker becomes too steep, the monster falls down with a roar of despair. The application retrieves the current pose of the marker relative to the webcam using the ARToolKit optical marker recognition module [15]. The pose of the marker is directly mapped to the pose of the virtual platform of the artiste in the agent's world model. The webcam and the marker recognition library act as the agent's sensor for perceiving changes in the physical marker's attributes. The agent's control logic then checks whether the platform orientation is still within bounds and decides whether to play the "falling down" or the balancing animation. The balancing animation is a blended motion interpolating between the neutral center and four extreme points in the animation space with factors calculated from the platform's pitch and roll rotation angles.

3.2 Agent with Physical Body Reacting to Events in the Virtual World

Sensing events generated by virtual objects is usually not a complicated task since virtual sensors such as vision, hearing, touching can be implemented in software using various algorithms. However, using physical objects as bodies for autonomous agents and consequently as output communication modalities implies several constraints. Our entire physical environment cannot be affected by virtual control logics, only by specially prepared objects which require communication channels and actuators to be set up.

The screenshots shown in Figure 2 depict a sample scenario for a communication flow from the virtual into the real world. This scenario implements defensive behavior for a physical LEGO® Mindstorms robot that tries to avoid collision with a virtual character. The pose of the robot and the character is again tracked using ARToolKit. If the character enters the virtual "safety" area around the robot, a command is sent to the robot from the PC via an infrared link, instructing it to move away.

4 Monkey Bridge

Games provide a challenging environment to test real and virtual world events with animated characters and demand various authoring tasks as well. Our MonkeyBridge application is a multiplayer AR game, where users place real and virtual objects onto a physical surface, thus influencing the behavior of virtual animated characters and responsive physical objects.

A "monkey bridge" is a fragile wooden construction over a river in South-East Asia. People frequently risk their lives as they try to keep their balance whilst crossing. In this application two players dynamically build a monkey bridge for their monster-like characters using virtual and physical pieces of landing stage, which vary in shape (Figure 3 shows two application screenshots). The goal is to reach a dedicated

Fig. 3. (left) Screenshot from the optical tracking-based setup. Note the real game elements that show through the virtual scene. (right) Game environment with the magnetic tracking setup.

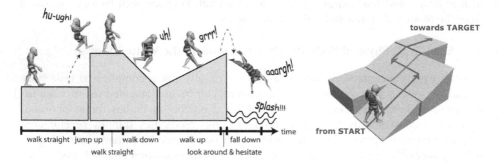

Fig. 4. Autonomous agent behavior: a) choosing animation and sound based on platform type, b) path planning depending on the spatial distribution of available blocks

target in the middle of a virtual ocean. The game includes many spectacular virtual and physical visual elements such as animated 3D ocean waves, a flock of virtual seagull boids, a real, illuminated smoking volcano and lighthouse with rotating lights. Sound effects further enhance the game experience.

4.1 Autonomous Path and Motion Planning for Agents

The MonkeyBridge characters are embodied autonomous agents. Their behavior does not require careful scripting, instead a dedicated control logic or virtual "brain" decides which animations and sound effects to play, which direction to turn or whether the target has been reached. The only factors that directly influence agent behavior are the spatial distribution, pose and shape of the virtual and physical building blocks placed on the game board (see Figure 4). The characters autonomously choose: the path they walk on; decide how to get from one platform to the other, e.g. jump up or down when there is a slight difference in height between platform edges; automatically choose the straightest path from several available tiles; and fall into the water if there is no suitable piece of landing stage to walk on. They cheer in triumph raising their hands in a victory salute when they win, and cry over a lost game.

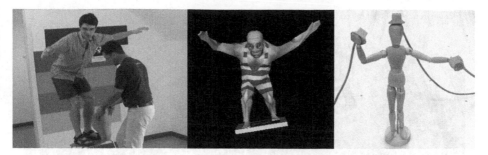

Fig. 5. Human actor (left) and wooden mannequin with magnetically tracked limbs (right) as a model for the balancing monster animation (center)

4.2   Level Editing in AR

It is transparent to the agents whether they walk on physical or virtual tiles, which blurs the boundary between the real and the synthetic game environment and allows the arbitrary combination of real and virtual bridge elements on the game table. The different arrangements of bridge elements result in a large number of level combinations that prevent the game from becoming monotonous. Augmented reality enables the use of an intuitive tangible level editor, where users design the pose of the physical game elements in the game area with their hands prior game start, record the manually edited physical level and register it with its virtual counterpart to initialize the game. After the game starts, players dynamically build the virtual level elements during the game by manually placing them next to the physical tiles using their interaction devices.

4.3   Character Animation Using AR Techniques

Modelers and animators often rely on real-life references to build and animate 3D characters for games or film production. Observing the real world by photographing or videotaping the subject, or asking someone to pose helps create more believable, precise and expressive character animation. The left image of Figure 5 shows a colleague posing while creating animation for the balancing demo described in Section 3.1. Professional artists use motion capture techniques or other expensive means of acquiring motion data (e.g. the Monkey kinematic tracker device [16]) to create an essential initial data set for the final, refined animation. With AR new possibilities open up within the field of character animation. The animated virtual model and the real-world reference can be merged, forming a single interactive modeling instrument. We are currently developing a tool using a wooden mannequin as an input device to animate skeleton-based virtual 3D models. The head and limbs of the mannequin are pose-tracked. The system maps real-time pose information to rotation information for the joints of the character skeleton using inverse kinematics and motion mapping techniques. AR not only enables close interaction with virtual models by using tangible objects but also the creation of complex motions like walking up stairs or lifting a ball, since animators can use actual physical models of stairs or balls in concert with characters in order to create realistic motions.

Fig. 6. Screenshots from the AR Lego application. (left) An animated repairman mounts virtual wheels onto the physical Lego® robot (right) The system gives visual feedback about the behavior of the real robot while the wheels are turning.

5 AR Lego

AR environments offer advanced exploitation of real-world objects. The AR Lego application [17] implements a playful machine assembly and maintenance scenario, in which two agents are employed to educate an untrained user to assemble, test and maintain machines composed of active (engines and sensors) and passive (cogwheels, gears, frames) parts. The two agents are a real LEGO Mindstorms® robot and a virtual animated repairman (see the screenshots of Figure 6). The PC-based application treats the robot as a first-class interaction entity by communicating commands via an infrared channel, in order to control the attributes of active parts (e.g. engine voltage and direction, type of the sensors) and query current robot state (e.g. sensor values, communication channel failures, or battery level).

The system provides step-by-step assembly instructions as to which block to mount next and how to verify whether the user is at the correct stage in the construction. While the verification of passive parts (i.e. inactive bricks) is only possible by visually comparing the appearance of the physical model to the virtual, testing whether the active parts (engines and sensors) have been mounted correctly is more straightforward. After mounting an engine, the application instructs the robot to turn the engine on by issuing an infrared command. If mounted in the right position and correct direction, the engine and all moving parts connected to it should behave as demonstrated by overlaid animated virtual models. Similarly, if we mounted the sensors properly, the right type and range of data should arrive from the robot. The system checks and visually reports inconsistency so that the user can go back one or more steps to double-check the construction.

5.1 Physical Objects as GUI

A novel and exciting aspect of AR agents is that physical objects like printers, digital pianos or interactive robots can be turned into intelligent, responsive entities that collaborate with virtual characters and users as equal, active partners. If we track and monitor relevant physical attributes and process this data, attribute changes can

Fig. 7. Animated character bound to a tangible optical marker and controlled by a PUC generated interface on a PocketPC (monitor + PDA screenshots)

generate events that can be interpreted by other agents and application logic. Using network packets, infrared messages, MIDI code sequences or other means of low-level communication, physical objects can not only be queried for status information but can also be controlled by external commands that trigger actuators. Therefore physical objects can act as input and output devices in AR spaces.

In AR Lego the Lego® Mindstorms robot is a physical object that not only acts as an I/O device in the AR environment but also serves as an immersive modeling device. The user manually and dynamically assembles a real, tangible Lego® model from active and passive parts. During construction constant visual feedback is sent by a display combining real and virtual information, and by the actual physical model through actuators triggered by infrared commands. The ActiveCube project [18] implements similar ideas, where the user assembles a set of computerized tangible blocks equipped with I/O devices. However, in ActiveCube there is a clear border between the real and the virtual world since the virtual content is not overlaid on top the physical environment, which is a key requirement of true AR applications.

5.2 Personal Universal Controller

An innovative way to configure AR agents is using the Personal Universal Controller (PUC) [19]. All agents provide an XML-based description of their relevant, configurable attributes and their supported commands together with the command syntax. All characters run a PUC service, which listens to incoming connections from PUC clients. A PUC client is able to render a Graphical User Interface (GUI) to control attributes that are described in the description, and are implemented on various devices and platforms including PCs, PDAs and smartphones. Figure 7 shows a control GUI rendered on a PocketPC. By checking the "skeleton" control checkbox (marked with an ellipsoid) the user changes the rendering mode from mesh to skeleton mode allowing observation of the underlying bone structure. One PUC service can accept multiple clients, hence allowing collaborative, multi-user configuration.

PUC offers an intuitive way to configure animated characters in AR environments, where they are typically scattered in space. Instead of the usual static configuration steps prior to the start of an application, the user can now roam throughout the complete application space; walk up to the character to be configured; reach a convenient and comfortable distance; query the controllable parameters of the character using a PDA running a PUC client; and dynamically control the character's attributes.

6 Augmented Piano Tutor

Music has only recently emerged as an important medium for AR applications [20][21]. The Augmented Piano Tutor application serves as a piano teacher that educates users about basic chords and scales in an AR environment. It uses a desktop-based AR setup using a real keyboard that communicates with the control PC with MIDI in and out messages, a webcam, and a monitor to combine the real and the virtual scenes. On the screen the real keyboard can be seen augmented with virtual information instructing users to hit certain keys in a defined order, while giving feedback as to which keys have been pressed correctly and which ones were pressed by mistake. Sound is generated on the physical keyboard by MIDI commands in accordance with the visual feedback blended into the user's view, therefore the boundary between the user situated in the real environment with the instrument and the "teacher" giving instructions from the virtual world appears to be blurred.

The synthetic information is always synchronized with the audio. When the user is instructed to play a certain chord on the keyboard, the piano keys yielding the chord are visually highlighted indicating which should be pressed, while the very same chord is played on the keyboard to create a mental connection between the two. When the user tries to imitate the chord, the correctly pressed and missed keys are marked with different colors on top of the real keys, giving a hint how the error should be rectified. Figure 8 provides illustrations for our application.

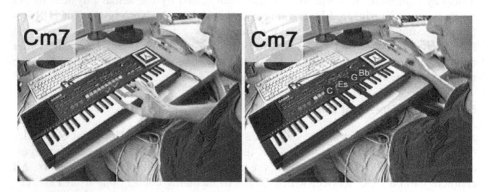

Fig. 8. Screenshots from the Augmented Piano Tutor Application

This system can be used as an advanced music composition tool offering the complex functions and rich visual feedback of a sequencer program running on the PC, while preserving the simplicity and freedom of a keyboard. While the sequencer module analyzes the tunes currently being played, it could also suggest harmonizing background chords and appropriate solo melodies to be played immediately on the keyboard.

7 Conclusion and Future Work

In this paper we introduced various augmented reality applications to illustrate the use of embodied autonomous agents as key visual interface elements and advanced immersive authoring techniques and tools exploiting AR environments. We did not aim to construct a standalone AR authoring framework but rather developed sample scenarios to provide inspiration for further experimentation with AR authoring for computer entertainment.

In AR applications users are typically not bound to a single physical location, device and display but tend to roam over large areas, working with several stationary and portable devices and displays. We are currently experimenting with persistent embodied autonomous agents that are able to seamlessly migrate between various devices and screens, and develop authoring tools accommodating the needs of mobile users working with animated agents in ubiquitous computing environments.

Acknowledgement

This project has been sponsored by the Austrian Science Fund FWF (contract no. Y193) and the European Union (contract no. IST-2001-34204). The authors wish to say thanks to Ulrich Krispel and Christoph Schinko for integrating inverse kinematics into our character animation framework, to Joseph Newman for reviewing the manuscript, and to the members of the Studierstube team for their continuous support.

References

1. Bolter, J. D., Grusin, R.: Remediation: Understanding New Media. MIT Press, Cambridge, Massachusetts, 2000, ISBN-0-262-52279-9
2. Ledermann, F., Schmalstieg, D.: APRIL: A High-level Framework for Creating Augmented Reality Presentations. In: Proc. of the IEEE Virtual Reality 2005 Conf., Bonn, Germany, 2005, pp. 187-194.
3. MacIntyre, B., Gandy, M.: Prototyping Applications with DART, The Designer's Augmented Reality Toolkit. In: Proc. of Software Technology for Augmented Reality Systems Workshop (STARS 2003), Tokyo, Japan, 2003.
4. Zauner, J., Haller, M., Brandl, A., Hartmann, W.: Authoring of a Mixed Reality Assembly Instructor for Hierarchical Structures. In: Proc. of the 2nd International Symposium on Mixed and Augmented Reality (ISMAR2003), Tokyo, Japan, 2003, pp. 237-246.
5. Stapleton, C., Hughes, C., Moshell, M., Micikevicius, P., Altman, M., Applying Mixed Reality to Entertainment. In: IEEE Computer 35(12), 2002, pp. 122-124.
6. MacIntyre, B., Bolter, J. D., Vaughan, J., Hannigan, B., Moreno, E., Haas, M., Gandy, M.: Three Angry Men: Dramatizing Point-of-View Using Augmented Reality. In: Proc. of SIGGRAPH 2002 Technical Sketches, San Antonio, TX, USA, 2002.
7. Lee, G. A., Nelles, C., Billinghurst, M., Kim, G.J., Immersive Authoring of Tangible Augmented Reality Applications, In: Proc. of IEEE and ACM Int'l Symposium on Mixed and Augmented Reality 2004 (ISMAR'04), Arlington, VA, USA, 2004, pp. 172-181.
8. Bates, J.: The Role of Emotion in Believable Agents. In: Communications of the ACM 37(7), Special Issue on Agents, 1994, pp. 122-125.
9. Maes, P., Darrell, T., Blumberg, B., Pentland, A.: The ALIVE System: Wireless, Full-body Interaction with Autonomous Agents. In: ACM Multimedia Systems 5(2), 1997, pp. 105-112.
10. Anabuki, M., Kakuta, H., Yamamoto, H., Tamura, H.: Welbo: An Embodied Conversational Agent Living in Mixed Reality Space. In: Proc. of Human Factors in Computing System (CHI 2000), Extended Abstracts, The Hague, The Netherlands, 2000, pp. 10-11.

11. Cheok, A. D., Weihua, W., Yang, X., Prince, S., Wan, F. S., Billinghurst, M., Kato, H.: Interactive Theatre Experience in Embodied and Wearable Mixed Reality Space. In: Proc. of International Symposium on Mixed and Augmented Reality (ISMAR'02), Darmstadt, Germany, 2002.
12. Cavazza, M., Charles, F., Mead, S. J., Martin, O., Marichal, X., Nandi, A.: Multimodal Acting in Mixed Reality Interactive Storytelling. In: IEEE Multimedia 11(3), 2004, pp. 30-39.
13. Balcisoy, S., Kallmann, M., Torre, R., Fua, P., Thalmann, D.: Interaction Techniques with Virtual Humans in Mixed Environments. In: Proc. of International Symposium on Mixed Reality (ISMAR 2001), Tokyo, Japan, 2001.
14. Cassell, J., Ananny, M., Basu, A., Bickmore, T., Chong, P., Mellis, D., Ryokai, K., Smith, J., Vilhjálmsson, H., Yan, H.: Shared Reality: Physical Collaboration with a Virtual Peer. In: Proc. of Human Factors in Computing System (CHI 2000), The Hague, The Netherlands, 2000, pp. 259-260.
15. ARToolKit Developer Homepage, http://sourceforge.net/projects/artoolkit/
16. Esposito, C., Paley, W. B., Ong, J. C.: Of mice and monkeys: a specialized input device for virtual body animation. In: Proc. of the Symposium on Interactive 3D Graphics, 1995, Monterey, CA, USA
17. Barakonyi, I., Psik, T., Schmalstieg, D., Agents That Talk And Hit Back: Animated Agents in Augmented Reality. In: Proc. of the IEEE and ACM International Symposium on Mixed and Augmented Reality 2004 (ISMAR'04), Arlington, VA, USA, Nov. 2-5, 2004, pp. 141-150.
18. Watanabe, R., Itoh, Y., Asai, M., Kitamura, Y., Kishino F., Kikuchi, H.: The Soul of ActiveCube - Implementing a Flexible, Multimodal, Three-Dimensional Spatial Tangible Interface. In: Proc. of ACM SIGCHI International Conference on Advances in Computer Entertainment Technology (ACE 2004), Singapore, 2004, pp. 173-180
19. Nichols, J., Myers, B. A., Higgins, M., Hughes, J., Harris, T. K., Rosenfeld, R., Pignol, M.: Generating Remote Control Interfaces for Complex Appliances. In: CHILetters: ACM Symposium on User Interface Software and Technology, Paris, France, 2002, pp. 161-170.
20. Poupyrev, I. R., Berry, R., Kurumisawa, J., Nakao, K., Billinghurst, M., Airola, C., Kato, H., Yonezawa, T., Baldwin. L.: Augmented Groove: Collaborative Jamming in Augmented Reality. In: Proc. of SIGGRAPH 2000 Conference Abstract and Applications, ACM Press, pp. 77, 2000.
21. Cakmakci, O., Berard, F.: An Augmented Reality Based Learning Assistant for Electric Bass Guitar. In: Proc. of the 10th International Conference on Human-Computer Interaction, Crete, Greece, 2003.

Collaborative billiARds: Towards the Ultimate Gaming Experience[*]

Usman Sargaana[1], Hossein S. Farahani[2], Jong Weon Lee[3], Jeha Ryu[2],
and Woontack Woo[1]

[1] GIST U-VR Lab., Gwangju 500-712, S. Korea
{sargaana, wwoo}@gist.ac.kr
http://uvr.gist.ac.kr
[2] GIST HuManCom Lab., Gwangju 500-712, S. Korea
{hossein, ryu}@gist.ac.kr
http://dyconlab.gist.ac.kr
[3] Dept. of Digital Contents, Sejong University,
Seoul 143-747, S. Korea
jwlee@sejong.ac.kr

Abstract. In this paper, we identify the features that enhance gaming experience in Augmented Reality (AR) environments. These include Tangible User Interface, force-feedback, audio-visual cues, collaboration and mobility. We base our findings on lessons learnt from existing AR games. We apply these results to billiARds which is an AR system that, in addition to visual and aural cues, provides force-feedback. billiARds supports interaction through a vision-based tangible AR interface. Two users can easily operate the proposed system while playing Collaborative billiARds game around a table. The users can collaborate through both virtual and real objects. User study confirmed that the resulting system delivers enhanced gaming experience by supporting the five features highlighted in this paper.

1 Introduction

Augmented Reality (AR) supplements user's perception of real world by stimulating one or more senses [2]. Besides medical, military and manufacturing applications, AR is now also being used for entertainment purposes. Many of such applications are computer games. In this regard, much work has been done in research labs and we are yet to find a commercially launched AR game. However, the underlying technology has matured to an extent that AR games will soon grab a significant chunk of the entertainment industry.

It has been claimed, with convincing facts, that AR is capable of overpowering other technologies in computer gaming [1]. For this, a model of gaming experience comprising of physical, mental, social and emotional aspects was considered. It was shown that AR can exploit all the four aspects and thus provides an ideal platform for computer games. But, before the dream of commercial AR games becomes a reality,

---

[*] This work was supported by GIST.

F. Kishino et al. (Eds.): ICEC 2005, LNCS 3711, pp. 357–367, 2005.
© IFIP International Federation for Information Processing 2005

several challenges must be met. Most of these challenges are related to availability of affordable devices with the required performance. With the ongoing fast-paced development in the computing hardware industry, widespread popularity of AR games is foreseeable in the near future. Besides hardware, several other issues are involved in success of computer games, application functionality being an important one. In the following, we enlist various application features that enhance a player's gaming experience in AR environment. In doing so, we do not consider the hardware constraints which are unavoidable in every AR system. Also, we exclude those aspects which are key features of AR, i.e. augmentation, interaction and registration [2]. It is assumed that all AR games cater these core requirements. Instead, we focus on functionality of gaming applications. The idea is to use the application features in a constructive fashion, with strengths of available functionality making up for the hardware constraints. These features may not be applicable to some applications, but they are general enough to be incorporated into most games. While the hardware has limitations, human imagination is unlimited. If provided enough stimulation during game-play, human imagination can go beyond all hardware constraints to perceive the ultimate gaming experience.

Tangible User Interface (TUI). TUIs provide an intuitive way of manipulating digital data through real-world objects [11]. This is because humans are naturally skilled in handling physical objects. TUIs not only provide tactile feedback, but can also map natural movements of users into the digital world. On the other hand, interaction through specialized devices is unnatural and imparts cognitive load on user in terms of learning novel ways of manipulation. ARQuake is a first-person shooting game which allows players to shoot at virtual monsters by pressing trigger of a tangible gun [3]. This improved playability of the game.

Force-Feedback. Visual cues alone are not sufficient to provide intuitive interaction to users. TUIs deliver natural tactile feedback to enhance user's experience. However, systems with TUIs still fall short of realism when dynamics is involved in a game. In such situations, force-feedback is required to ensure user's sense of realism. ARQuake used a haptic gun to shoot at virtual monsters [3]. It contains a solenoid which strikes a bolt against the gun to provide force-feedback. It only provides 1D force-feedback which is sufficient to simulate recoil of a gun. However, it is not suitable for complex scenarios.

Audio-visual Cues. Audio-visual cues are not the visual objects or sounds simply overlaid by most systems. The cues provide information about user's augmented environment and contribute to immersion. These cues must be responsive to user's actions in the game. Humans have a remarkable ability to fuse multi-modal sensory stimuli for building inferences about their surroundings. Experiments have shown that audio-visual cues affect human perception in a virtual environment by enhancing haptic sense [9].

Collaboration. One criterion for measuring gaming experience is the degree of immersion. The most effective way of immersing a user is to imitate the reality. Most of the real-world games are multi-player games which involve rich human-to-human interaction. In this regard, it is necessary that the multi-player gaming system does not obstruct social communication between the players. AR^2Hockey is a collaborative game that enables two players to push a virtual puck towards each other in a shared augmented space [12].

Mobility. Most games require users to move around in augmented space in order to interact with game entities. Therefore, it is important that a gaming system should not restrict mobility of the user. In addition, the system must provide untethered interaction with the game environment. It was observed during usability evaluation of ARQuake that one reason players enjoyed the game was their ability to move freely during game-play [3].

We found that not many games support all of these features. Especially, mobility and force-feedback seem to be mutually exclusive in AR games. Moreover, existing AR games fail to exploit human ability of perceiving multi-modal stimuli. We did not find any effort that employs cross-modal effects to supplement haptic perception in an AR environment. We apply all these ideas to billiARds which is an AR system that, in addition to visual and aural augmentation, provides force-feedback [10]. It provides unconstrained mobility and employs multi-modal effects for reinforcing haptic sensation in AR environment. The force-feedback is enabled by body-worn motors using wire-tension mechanism [4], [5]. Two users, carrying their own system, can easily interact with virtual balls through tangible AR interface in a collaborative environment.

This paper is organized as follows. Chapter 2 explains the design and implementation of Collaborative billiARds system. In chapter 3, we discuss experimental results. Finally, conclusions and future work are presented in chapter 4.

2   Collaborative billiARds

A user can play billiARds by striking augmented balls with a wooden stick. The control flow of the system is described in Fig. 1. Force-feedback is provided on the cue when a virtual ball is hit. Simultaneously, collision sound is augmented to

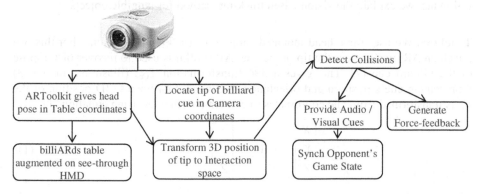

Fig. 1. Control flow of billiARds system

360   U. Sargaana et al.

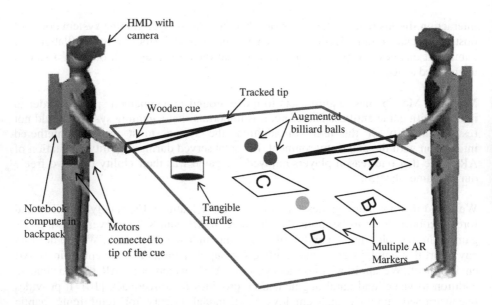

Fig. 2. System set-up for collaborative billiards

instigate user's cognition of billiards dynamics. Visual and audio cues significantly supplement user's haptic perception. Collaborative billiARds system enables two players to interact with virtual objects using tangible stick. The system set-up is illustrated in Fig. 2. In this chapter, we explain in detail the working of Collaborative billiARds system.

2.1 Tangible AR Interface

We develop a vision-based Tangible AR Interface for intuitive 3D interaction. We use head-mounted camera for 3D tracking of billiard cue so that user's workspace is not confined. User can operate the system while moving around in indoor environment. User interacts with game entities which can be virtual or physical object. The physical entities are in addition to the tangible cue, and can change the state of game. In the following, we explain the vision-based tracking method for tangible objects.

Tracking. We use single head-mounted camera for tracking billiard cue. For this, we attach an AR marker near the tip of the cue. ARToolkit is used to recover 6DOF pose of the billiard cue [7]. This gives a 3×4 transformation T_{Cue} (illustrated in Fig. 3) representing cue's position and orientation in camera coordinates. 3D position of the tip is transformed from cue coordinates to camera coordinates using equation (1).

$$\begin{bmatrix} X \\ Y \\ Z \end{bmatrix}_{cam} = T_{Cue} \times \begin{bmatrix} X \\ Y \\ Z \end{bmatrix}_{cue} \tag{1}$$

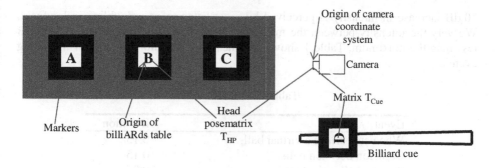

Fig. 3. Various coordinate systems

where $[X\ Y\ Z]^{\mathrm{T}}_{cue}$ and $[X\ Y\ Z]^{\mathrm{T}}_{cam}$ denote position of the tip in cue coordinates and camera coordinates, respectively.

Interaction. We augment virtual table surface and billiard balls on a real table which bears multiple markers. The user wears a see-through HMD to view augmented objects. User's head pose (relative to the table) is required for precise augmentation and registration. This is determined by tracking multiple AR markers, placed on the table, through head-mounted camera. ARToolkit is used for this purpose. It gives us the transformation matrix T_{HP} (illustrated in Fig. 3). The billiards table is augmented such that the virtual world coincides with marker coordinate system.

For interaction between colored tip and virtual balls, both must be placed in the same coordinate system. Tracking gives us location of the tip in camera coordinates. 3D location of the tip is transformed from camera coordinates to coordinates of augmented table using equation (2).

$$
\begin{bmatrix} X \\ Y \\ Z \end{bmatrix}_{vt} = T_{HP}^{-1} \times \begin{bmatrix} X \\ Y \\ Z \end{bmatrix}_{cam}
\tag{2}
$$

where $[X\ Y\ Z]^{\mathrm{T}}_{vt}$ and $[X\ Y\ Z]^{\mathrm{T}}_{cam}$ denote position of the tip in virtual table coordinates and camera coordinates, respectively. In order to support interaction through wooden cue, we must detect collisions between tracked tip of the cue and virtual balls. For this, we consider radii and positions of the cue tip and the balls. Therefore, billiARds user can only strike the balls with the tip.

2.2   Audio-Visual Cues

When a collision between stick and a ball is detected, appropriate visual and aural cues are provided to instigate user's haptic perception. We provide four distinct auditory cues which vary in pitch and loudness according to the force of collision. The pitch and loudness of audio cues are directly proportional to the force applied by user on virtual object. In order to change the perceived pitch of the sound, we vary the sampling frequency between 45 kHz (minimum) and 65 kHz (maximum). Loudness perceived by the user is varied by changing intensity level of the sound. Generally, a

10 dB increase in intensity is perceived by most listeners as a doubling in loudness. We vary the intensity between the maximum (supported by the computer) to 20 dB less than the maximum. Table 1 shows the cues provided along with their triggering events.

Table 1. Audio Cues

Event	Duration
When cue strikes a virtual ball.	0.15
Collision between balls.	0.15
When a ball is pocketed.	0.37
When a ball rebounds off a table rail.	0.07

billiARds Dynamics. The direction and magnitude of the push exerted by the cue on virtual ball determines the game dynamics. The magnitude of this force is proportional to how fast the cue is moved just before the strike. This is calculated from tracking history of the cue. We assume that the push exerted on the virtual ball is always directed along orientation of the cue at the time of collision. This is rational in billiards game scenario because when user hits a ball, the cue is only moved along its length. When the cue strikes a ball, we consider various variables to drive dynamics of the billiards table. These include mass and radius of balls, co-efficient of sliding friction, and velocities of colliding and deflecting balls. For balls in collision, velocities are updated using law of conservation of momentum. We observed that vision-based tracking is not accurate enough to determine the precise point on ball surface where the cue strikes. So, we make another assumption that the stick always strikes at center of the ball (center of mass). This simplifies the simulation because, as shown in equation (3), the torque becomes zero when radius and force are parallel, i.e. θ=0. Thus, we ignore the angular motion of the ball and only consider translational motion.

$$\tau = r \times F = |r||F|\sin\theta = 0 \tag{3}$$

where τ denotes torque; and r and F are radius and force vectors, respectively. In order to support angular motion, i.e. spinning the ball, we need a tracking system with higher resolution and accuracy. However, such system might compromise mobility of the user or add other constraints to the system.

Occlusion. Virtual table hides part of the real scene because it is rendered over captured image of the scene. This also removes the wooden billiards cue from user's view. In order to enhance user's gaming experience, the system must deliver appropriate occlusion between real and virtual objects. Since we do not have depth map of the environment, we rely on a simpler model-based approach to handle occlusion. It works well because the only real object we deal with (i.e. billiard cue) has simple shape without any minute details. After tracking position and orientation of the real cue, we render a tapered cylinder (truncated cone) in a stencil buffer. This

Fig. 4. Occlusion between real cue and augmented table

model is precisely rendered so that its dimensions and pose coincide with those of the real cue. When we overlay the virtual table through this stencil buffer, it covers other parts of the scene while leaving the wooden cue visible. The result is shown in Fig. 4.

2.3   Collaboration

Collaborative billiARds is a multi-player game that supports social interaction between two collocated users, each operating a billiARds system. Both users share the same augmented space seen through their HMDs. The system supports collaboration in two ways, i.e. through physical and virtual objects. When a user strikes the virtual cue ball at his turn, the resulting changes in the game state are transmitted to the second player using Socket communication. Both users can observe the game dynamics during the play. When all the balls come to a stop, the system notifies the player who has to strike next.

In order to keep users involved in the game, we also support collaboration through real objects. For this purpose, we slightly modified the rules of the game. In a real game, a player loses a turn or the game when a foul is committed. In Collaborative billiARds, the opponent can place tangible hurdles on the table as a penalty for a foul. Three different hurdles can be used to obstruct the opponent's strike. Each hurdle has an AR marker on top of it. The system automatically determines the placement of hurdle by detecting the marker. The updated game state is again transmitted to the other player. Shape and dimensions of all supported hurdles are known. When a hurdle is placed on table, its model is used to ensure that it is not occluded by the virtual table. This step utilizes a stencil buffer for drawing the augmented table. Furthermore, when a player sets the virtual balls in motion, the balls are now deflected by physical hurdles placed on the table. This involves collision detection which is possible because the position and model of hurdles are known. This provides an interesting way of collaboration through physical objects that affect state of the game. It enhances awareness of the opponent's presence and improves social interaction between players.

2.4 Force-Feedback

Two AC servo motors are mounted around user's waist. Each motor is attached to the billiard cue using a separate string. Using encoder data of motors, we can obtain orientation of the cue and position of the tip. While the cue is moving, the direction of motion of the tip gives us the direction of force exerted by user on the billiard ball. When the wooden cue collides with a virtual ball, a torque control algorithm for motors is used to provide force feedback. The force feedback involves producing a calculated pull, directed exactly opposite to the force applied by user, at the strings. The magnitude of force-feedback is proportional to speed of the cue before the strike. The top view of motors arrangement is shown in Fig. 5.

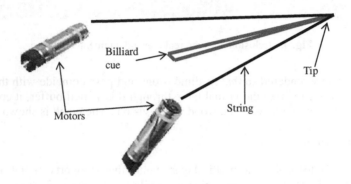

Fig. 5. Arrangement of motors for force-feedback

With two motors, the system can only provide 2D haptic sense. We observed that when a user hits a ball, the cue is almost horizontally placed for most billiard games. In such cases, the angle between cue and the table is small and the component of force perpendicular to the surface of table is negligible. Exceptions to this fact are advanced strokes, such as masse` and pique`, which are played with upright cue to reverse-spin the cue-ball. These are strictly experts' shots and are rarely used by amateurs. So, we based our force reflection device on the assumption that force applied to a billiard ball is always horizontal. This assumption is rational within our game scenario, and thus, we can provide sufficient realism to the user.

In order to track the tip of the cue based on wire lengths, we solve forward kinematics. Considering reference frames *{0}* and *{1}*, with their origins at wire-extraction points, wire lengths L_0, L_1 can be expressed by equation (4).

$$L_1 = \left\| T^0 - S_1^0 \right\|$$
$$L_0 = \left\| T^0 \right\|$$

(4)

where $S_1^0 = [s_{1x}, s_{1y}]$ denotes coordinates of origin of {1} with respect to {0}, and $T^0 = [x, y]^T$ represents cue-tip coordinates with respect to {0}.

Solving equation (4) gives us x and y coordinates of the cue-tip. Unit vectors, u_0 and u_1, along the strings can be expressed by equation (5).

$$u_0 = \frac{1}{\sqrt{x^2 + y^2}} [x, y]^T$$

$$u_1 = \frac{1}{\sqrt{(x - s_{1x})^2 + (y - s_{1y})^2}} [(x - s_{1x}), (y - s_{1y})]^T$$

(5)

The calculation of haptic force does not depend on posture of the player. Even when a player stoops down to hit a ball, we only need position of cue-tip relative to each motor. Since the motors are mounted on a frame around waist, their relative position remains constant. We use equation (6) to calculate the tension required in wires to exert force f on the cue tip.

$$f = p_0 u_0 + p_1 u_1 = J^{-T} p$$

$$J = [u_0, u_1]^{-T}$$

(6)

where p is the vector of wire tensions, and J is Jacobian matrix of the haptic device. From equation (6), we can write:

$$p = J^T f$$

(7)

While the cue-tip moves freely in space, wire-tensions may become negative. This renders the wire-lengths indeterminable. Therefore, a small force is always applied at the cue-tip to ensure that the wire-tensions remain positive. To ensure transparency of haptic device, this force must be constant at all locations. Magnitude of this force depends on structure of device and user's feeling. Experimenting with different values, we found that 1N is the optimal value to keep wire-tensions always positive without compromising transparency of the haptic device.

3 Experimental Results

We performed experiments to evaluate the role played by each of five aspects in enhancing gaming experience. Each of two players used a notebook computer (carried in backpack) with 1.5 GHz processor, NVIDIA GeForce FX5200 graphics accelerator [8] and wireless LAN support. The users put on i-glasses SVGA head-mounted display with 800×600 pixel resolution [6]. A pair of earplugs was also provided for aural feedback. We used camera with video capture resolution of 640×480 pixels and shutter speed of 20 frames per second. A table (60 cm high) was set up with seven AR Markers; each having dimensions of 8cm×8cm. For experiments, we augmented a virtual table over an area of 100 cm × 150 cm. Players carried a 60-cm long wooden cue for interaction. Force-feedback was provided with two brushless DC motors fixed to a belt around user's waist. Due to limited number of available motors, only one player had the force-feedback device. The motors can provide an output torque of 120 mNm. The encoders operate at 540 pulses per revolution and the encoder data can track the tip with an accuracy of 2 mm. We mounted a camera on HMD and attached an AR Marker of size 5cm × 5cm near the tip of billiard cue.

We conducted an informal user study during which ten different users (two at a time) put on our system and experienced the Collaborative billiARds game by moving around the table. Since players were likely to compare Collaborative billiARds with the real billiards game, we selected users who hardly ever played real billiards game. However, all these users frequently played other computer games. Six different experiments were carried out. Table 2 describes the game features provided during each setup. In experiment I, the system provided all the five features. So, we used the results of experiment I as ground basis for comparison. In rest of the experiments, the system supported all but one of the five features.

Table 2. Experiment Setup

Features Supported→	Tangible User Interface	Force-feedback	Audio-Visual Cues	Collaboration	Mobility
Experiment I	√	√	√	√	√
Experiment II	×	√	√	√	√
Experiment III	√	×	√	√	√
Experiment IV	√	√	×	√	√
Experiment V	√	√	√	×	√
Experiment VI	√	√	√	√	×

where √ shows that the feature was provided, and × denotes that the feature was not available during that experiment.

Afterwards, each user was given a questionnaire to rate the gaming experience on a 10-scale (0-9). Only the responses from users with the force-feedback were recorded (except in Experiment III). The results of this study are compiled in Table 3. For trials done without audio-visual cues, sampling frequency and intensity of audio cues were kept constant. Also, parameters for visual cues remained constant irrespective of the force applied by user.

Table 3. User Feedback

Gaming Experience→	Mean	Std. Dev.
Experiment I	8.6	0.5
Experiment II	4.5	0.8
Experiment III	6.6	0.88
Experiment IV	7.3	0.3
Experiment V	7.8	0.91
Experiment VI	4.7	0.67

During the experiment, we observed that the players enjoyed the game most when all the five features were provided. This observation was reinforced by the user-feedback data (Table 3) which exhibited that the system provided best gaming experience in Experiment I. Moreover, the results of subsequent experiments showed that removing any of the five features resulted in reduced gaming experience. This confirms that the five features we identified are indispensable for providing enhanced gaming experience in AR games. In this regard, there may exist game features other than those listed here.

4 Conclusions and Future Work

In this paper, we identify ways to enhance gaming experience in AR environments. We confirmed validity of the proposed ideas by applying them to Collaborative billiARds. Experiments showed that the users enjoyed the resulting gaming experience by collaborating with each other. In the future, we plan to evaluate the generality of our findings by applying them to a variety of AR games. In addition, we will develop more realistic physics model for generating audio-visual cues. Furthermore, we will study in detail the human factors involved in perception of multi-modal stimuli that instigates human imagination to perceive the ultimate gaming experience.

References

1. Nilsen, T., Linton, S., Looser, J.: Motivations for Augmented Reality Gaming. In Proc. Fuse 04, New Zealand Game Developers Conference (2004) 86-93.
2. Azuma, R. T.: A Survey of Augmented Reality. Presence: Teleoperators and Virtual Environments 6, 4 (1997) 355 – 385
3. Thomas, B. H., Krul, N., Close, B., Piekarski, W.: Usability and Playability Issues for ARQuake. In Proc. 1st Int'l Workshop on Entertainment Computing (2002)
4. Bonivento, C., Eusebi, A., Melchiorri, C., Montanari, M., Vassura, G.: WireMan: A portable wire manipulator for touch-rendering of bas-relief virtual surfaces. In Proc. 8th International Conference on Advanced Robotics (1997) 13 – 18.
5. Hirose, M., Hirota, K., Ogi, T., Yano, H., Kakehi, N., Saito, M., Nakashige, M.: HapticGEAR: The development of a wearable force display system for immersive projection displays. In Proc. IEEE Virtual Reality (2001) 123 – 129.
6. http://www.i-glassesstore.com
7. Kato, H., Billinghurst, M.: Marker Tracking and HMD Calibration for a video-based Augmented Reality Conferencing System. In Proc. 2nd International Workshop on Augmented Reality (1999)
8. http://www.nvidia.com
9. Miner, N., Gillespie, B., Caudell, T.: Examining the Influence of Audio and Visual Stimuli on a Haptic Display. In Proc. IMAGE Conference (1996)
10. Sargaana, U., Farahani, H. S., Lee, J., Ryu, J., Woo, W.: billiARds: Augmented Reality System with Wearable Force-Feedback Device. International Conference on Human Computer Interaction (Accepted) (2005)
11. Ishii, H., Ullmer, B.: Tangible Bits: Towards Seamless Interfaces between People, Bits and Atoms. In Proc. CHI '97 (1997) 234-241.
12. Ohshima, T., Satoh, K., Yamamoto, H., Tamura, H.: AR^2Hockey: A Case Study of Collaborative Augmented Reality. In Proc. IEEE Virtual Reality Annual International Symposium (1998) 268-275.

Multi-dimensional Game Interface
with Stereo Vision

Yufeng Chen, Mandun Zhang, Peng Lu,
Xiangyong Zeng, and Yangsheng Wang

Institute of Automation, Chinese Academy of Sciences*,
100080 Beijing, P.R. China
yufeng.chen@ia.ac.cn,
{mzhang, plu, xzeng, wys}@mail.pattek.com.cn

Abstract. An novel stereo vision tracking method is proposed to implement an interactive Human Computer Interface(HCI). Firstly, a feature detection method is introduced to accurately obtain the location and orientation of the feature in an efficient way. Secondly, a searching method is carried out, which uses probability in the time, frequency or color space to optimize the searching strategy. Then the 3D information is retrieved by the calibration and triangulation process. Up to 5 degrees of freedom(DOFs) can be achieved from a single feature, compared with the other methods, including the coordinates in 3D space and the orientation information. Experiments show that the method is efficient and robust for the real time game interface.

1 Introduction

Computer vision is a rapid developing area with more and more application requirements. One of the most basic functions is to interact with human. Taking advantage of convenience and natural interview compared with other advanced technology such as mechanical or electromagnetic, they are already implemented on some advanced HCI for special purpose to take the place of or aid the traditional devices such as mouse. Specially, their interactive capabilities are more suitable to be fully used on games.

1.1 Previous Works

Many works has been reported to be used in the related areas. Some typical early works has been introduced by Gavrila and Freeman [1,2].

One of the most important steps of vision interaction is tracking and detection. Some body features are tracked as camera mouse[3] to help people with severe disabilities. And recently, eyekeys[4] are used to detect the gaze in real-time. Many other features are tried such as face, gesture[5], and even the body[8].

---

* Funded by the National 863 project.

F. Kishino et al. (Eds.): ICEC 2005, LNCS 3711, pp. 368–376, 2005.

It has been evaluated[6] that salient features are needed to get better location accuracy, on the other hand these features are hard to track the irregular human movement while need more computing to search in a large area. Some correlation methods[3] are recommended to use under this situation, but the speed is another obstacle to the method.

The first part of our work is to propose a novel local statistic method to get an efficient location of the salient features. Combined with multiple cues, such as motion, color and intensity features, the searching amount are largely reduced and the feature can be precisely located.

Some related works had been carried out by Zhang[16] and Wu[10], they use hand as a simple input device. Although many games are using vision based techniques such as Eyetoy, the use of human movement information is limited.

To get more information of the hand movement, more cameras are needed to get 3D information. 3D interactive is reported [9] with a graphic point of view, which shows the requirement of the nature multi-dimensional method. Many stereo vision based applications are concentrating on the large features, such as human figure detection[11], to solve the occlusion problems.

Our efforts aimed to get more dimensional information from simple features. Up to five DOFs can be achieved from the stereo vision. This is very useful to control the complex object in the game.

The novel feature detection method is introduced in the section 2, an optimized searching method is proposed in the section 3, and the stereo vision with 5 DOFs is proposed in the section 4. Then the experiments are carried out to show the efficiency and accuracy of the method. At last the paper ends with a conclusion and some prospects.

2   Feature Detection

As discussed above, some properties are required for interactive games: Firstly the invariant should be kept under different conditions such as transfer, rotation and lighting. Secondly, it should be sensitive to the feature difference which helps to improve the accurate of the feature location[6]. The efficiency is also required for the real-time game interface.

In this paper we introduce a local moment based feature detection method. The invariant moments is first introduced as Hu Moments[12], many other moments[13,14] are proposed to improve the performance.

However, all the moments mentioned above must treat the object as a whole, which means the model should be rigid and well segmented or featured without occlusion, this requirement is not always met. Takamatsu[15] tried to use local moment to recognize the parts of the object as an improvement, but more work related with local properties is still lacking.

Given the perspective transformation, the light amount from a certain view point depends on three main factors: the normal of the surface N, the lighting condition L and the albedo a. So that the image can be derived

$$I(x, y) = C(a(x, y)N(x, y)L(x, y))$$

Where Function $C(\cdot)$ is the integration transform of the camera sensor, which is always considered as linear integration if the exposure time is suitable.

From the model of the image above, we can see clearly that the image, which depend on the lighting condition and camera system, is not uniquely determined by the feature. It is described by the surface normal N and the albedo a. Fortunately the camera system can be simplified as a linear integration, and the light condition could be viewed as a combination of many point light sources, which are also linear both in amount and their distribution. Thus the feature invariant is formed as follows:

Given a standard feature $\hat{f}(x, y)$ depending only on the object properties, a real feature image supposed to be effected by a local multiplicative transformation, which is corresponded with the different contrast, and a linear spaced additive transform, which is introduced by the lighting conditions.

$$f(x, y) = k \times \hat{f}(x, y) + a + bx + cy$$

Here we use the common Cartesian moment for simple explanation of the method.

$$m_{p,q} = \int_{x_0}^{x_d} \int_{y_0}^{y_d} x^p y^q f(x, y) dx dy$$

Where the $f(x, y)$ is the two dimensional function and x_0, x_d, y_0, y_d are the border of the target window to intergraded, and p, q stand for the moment orders.

If the equation below is met,

$$x_0 + x_d = 0, y_0 + y_d = 0$$

The moment can be simplified largely. To eliminate the effect of the transformation, let

$$\tilde{f}(x, y) = f(x, y) - \frac{m_{0,0}}{k_a} - \frac{m_{1,0}}{k_b} x - \frac{m_{0,1}}{k_c} y$$
$$= k\{\hat{f}(x, y) - k_a^{-1}\hat{m}_{0,0} - k_b^{-1}\hat{m}_{1,0} - k_c^{-1}\hat{m}_{0,1}\}$$

Where $m_{0,0}, m_{0,1}, m_{1,0}$ are the moments of $f(x, y)$, and k_a, k_b, k_c are the constants designed to eliminate the first three order of the function $\tilde{f}(x, y)$.

Therefore $\tilde{f}(x, y)$ is k times of the transformed feature expression of $\hat{f}(x, y)$, which has been affected by an addictive plane $k_a^{-1}\hat{m}_{0,0} + k_b^{-1}\hat{m}_{1,0} + k_c^{-1}\hat{m}_{0,1}$ depending on the function itself. The parameter k can be any real number even is negative, which means the contrast is trivial to the shape analysis. Thus the invariance of the feature $\hat{f}(x, y)$ can be derived by normalize its moments vectors.

The invariant feature is derived from the invariant image $\tilde{f}(x, y)$, which is expressed with the original image moments.

$$u_{pq} = \int_{x_0}^{x_d} \int_{y_0}^{y_d} x^p y^q \tilde{f}(x,y) dx dy$$

$$= m_{p,q} - m_{0,0} \frac{\int_{x_0}^{x_d} \int_{y_0}^{y_d} x^p y^q dx dy}{\int_{x_0}^{x_d} \int_{y_0}^{y_d} dx dy}$$

$$-m_{1,0} \frac{\int_{x_0}^{x_d} \int_{y_0}^{y_d} x^{p+1} y^q dx dy}{\int_{x_0}^{x_d} \int_{y_0}^{y_d} x^2 dx dy} - m_{0,1} \frac{\int_{x_0}^{x_d} \int_{y_0}^{y_d} x^p y^{q+1} dx dy}{\int_{x_0}^{x_d} \int_{y_0}^{y_d} y^2 dx dy}$$

This moment is also a common Cartesian moment but performed on the retrieved invariant image, thus can be easily normalized and transformed into the other moments.

 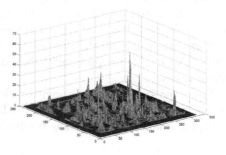

Fig. 1. The experiment of finger tip tracking. The left figure is the finger in the complex background; the right one is the matching result.

One advantage of the moments needed to be addressed is that the direction of the feature is also available at the same time according to its mass center offset.

$$x_m = \frac{m_{1,0}}{m_{0,0}}$$

$$y_m = \frac{m_{0,1}}{m_{0,0}}$$

$$\theta = \angle(y_m - \frac{y_d + y_0}{2}, x_m - \frac{x_d + x_0}{2})$$

Some experiments are carried out to search a finger model, the real image and similarity map are shown in the Fig.1. It can be seen clearly that the feature is very salient and the location is precise. Also it very efficient that over 10000 target are searched within a second. What's more, it can be largely improved by optimize the searching method as next section.

3   Information Aided Searching Strategy

One of the basic problems in stereo vision is about detection and matching. In this section we design a simple algorithm to detect the moving salient fea-

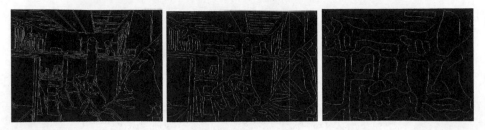

Fig. 2. The edge detected of different scales

tures. Combining all the information and optimized by the filters, the complex matching procedure can be avoid.

Given a serial of images $I(x, y, t)$, to search a feature under some different scale s the matching procedure are expected to compute in a complexity of $O(x \times y \times t \times s)$. It's hard to be implemented in real time.

Fortunately, not all the location are needed to search and most of them are trivial. We propose a probability based searching strategy to found the most salient areas.

From the frequent space point of view, the frequency information is highly correlated with scales, and not all the frequency in the space is valuable, such as high frequency noise and low frequency lighting conditions.

$$P(I(x, y, t), x, y) = \int_s bf(s) \times ker(I(x, y, t), s)ds$$

Where the function $bf(s)$ is a band pass filter stress the certain frequency according to the feature scale searched. And $ker(\cdot)$ is a kernel based derivative filter, which present the certain frequency information. Here the canny methods are used to depress the near points so that some lines are selected to search under different scales(See Fig.2).

Then from the time space point of view, in most cases the interactive subject are the few only moving object in the image, then the searching area can be reduced also by the probability of moving points. To avoid the instability of different image edges caused by noise, the moving probability is calculated independent with the spacial one. At last, the probability of all the space are considered together to form a searching path.

$$P(I(x, y, t), t) = \frac{dI(x, y, t)}{dt}$$

4   Multi Dimension of Freedom by Stereo Vision

When the features are detected from both of the cameras, the 3D data and the feature direction are to be retrieved by triangulation, before which the calibration should be done first.

Fig. 3. Image difference and the integrate searching area

Support a feature in the world coordinates x_w, y_w, z_w, are rigid transformed into the camera coordinates x_c, y_c, z_c by T_r and then perspective transformed into image space x_u, y_u by T_p

$$X_u = T_p X_c, X_c = T_r X_w$$
$$X_u = T_p T_r X_w = T_e X_w$$

Where, T_e is the extrinsic parameter of the camera that corresponding with the world coordinates, which need to be adjusted every time before the game start.

Another intrinsic parameter should not be omit, which will largely distort the image. Fortunately, for most cameras the intrinsic parameters are not changed and therefore can be just once and for all. Details of the method and parameters can refer to Zhang's[16].

Besides this, some new parameters are adopted to get more dimensional freedom with single feature. As mentioned above the direction of the feature is another important information for the object.

Support an object in the world space with the direction Q_w, then the projected direction of the two cameras are Q_{cl}, Q_{cr} respectively with the extrinsic transforms T_{el}, T_{er}

$$Q_{cl} = T_{el} Q_w, Q_{cr} = T_{er} Q_w$$

Given the extrinsic transforms and 2D vectors, the direction of the object can be evaluated by the intersect projected planes [17], which presented by the two angles, α angle with x axis and β angle with y axis.

However the result is not always accurate due to the noise and location result, an error analysis are made by the experiments. The average errors of the five parameters are listed below.

It can be seen from the table that not all the parameters are convincing, the x,y,z parameter are the most reliable variant that can be used as pointer in the

Table 1. Experiment error analysis of each parameters

Feature parameters	x	y	z	α	β
average error rate%	4.3	5.2	7.7	18.2	20.5

3D space, or a 2D plane with auxiliary control method such as speed range; The angle parameter are inaccurate due to the feature direction errors, however, it is suitable to give the binary direction control information in the game.

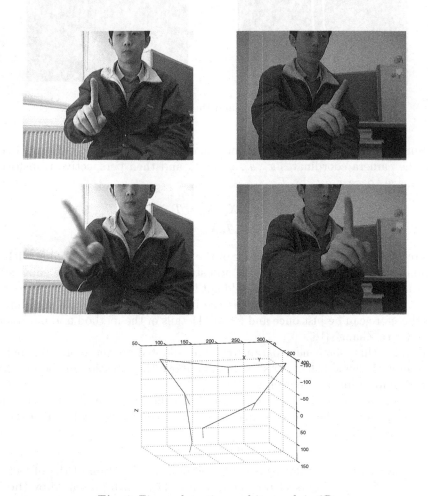

Fig. 4. Finger detection and its track in 3D

5   Experiment

A real-time system are implemented on the PC at 1.7GHz, it's efficient to track the finger in the three dimensional space with five DOFs (See Fig.4).

Also a game interface are tested with most accurate 3 DOFs, considering the requirement of the game control and the robustness. The architecture of the system is designed as Fig.5, and some sample of the game are showed in the Fig.6.

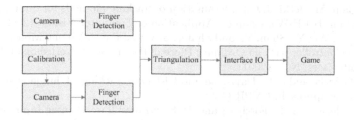

Fig. 5. Stereo vision game interface architecture

Fig. 6. Game played with stereo vision

6 Conclusion

We proposed a new method to track features and up to 5 DOFs can be achieved from a single feature compared with the others, with is convenient to implement and to be used. The experiments show it is suitable for the interactive control of complex games. And more applications are prospected such as 3D mouse, 3D reconstruction and so on.

References

1. D. M. Gavrila: The visual Analysis of Human Movement: A Survey, Computer vision and Image Understanding. Vol 75, No. 1. (1999)
2. W.T. Freeman, K. Tanaka, J. Ohta, K. Kyuma: Computer vision for computer games.2nd International Conference on Automatic Face and Gesture Recognition, Killington, VT, USA. (1996)
3. M. Betke,J. Gips, P.Fleming: The Camera Mouse: Visual Tracking of Body Features to Provide Computer Access for People With Severe Disabilities. IEEE Transactions on Neural Systems and Rehabilitation Engineering, Vol. 10, NO. 1, MAR (2002)
4. J. Magee, M. R. Scott, B. N. Waber, M. Betke: EyeKeys: A Real-time Vision Interface Based on Gaze Detection from a Low-grade Video Camera. IEEE Computer Society Conference on Computer Vision and Pattern Recognition Workshops, (2004).
5. V. Pavlovic, Sharma and T. Huang: Visual Interpretation of Hand Gestures for Human-Computer Interaction: A Review, IEEE Transaction on Pattern Analysis and Machine Intelligence, VOL. 19, NO. 7, JULY (1997)

6. C. Fagiani. M. Betki. J. Gips. Evaluation of tracking methods for human computer interaction. IEEE Workshop on Application of Computer Vision. (2002)
7. Zhang, Z., Wu, Y., Shan, Y., and Shafer, S: Visual Panel: Virtual Mouse, Keyboard and 3D Controller with an Ordinary Piece of Paper. ACM Workshop on Perceptive User Interfaces, Nov. (2001).
8. D.M. Gavrila and L.S. Davis: 3d model-based tracking of humans in action: a multi-view approach, CVPR (1996)
9. R. C. Zeleznik, A. S. Forsberg and P. S. Strauss: Two Pointer Input For 3D Interaction, Proceedings of the symposium on Interactive 3D graphics, Providence, Rhode Island, United States (1997)
10. Y. Wu, K. Toyama and T. S. Huang: Self-Supervised Learning for Object Recognition Based on Kernel Discriminant-EM Algorithm, in Proc. IEEE Int'l Conf. on Computer Vision (ICCV'01), Vol.I, 275-280, Vancouver, Canada, July, (2001)
11. Sidenbladh, M. Black and D. Fleet: Stochastic Tracking of 3D Human Figures using 2D Image Motion, ECCV (2000)
12. M-K. Hu: Visual pattern recognition by moment invariants, IRE Trans. on Information Theory, IT-8:pp. 179-187, (1962)
13. J. Heikkila: Pattern matching with affine moment descriptors, Pattern Recognition, 37, pp: 1825C1834, (2004)
14. C. Chong, P. Raveendranb, R. Mukundanc: Translation invariants of Zernike moments, Pattern Recognition, 36, pp:1765C1773,(2003)
15. R. Takamatsu, M. Sato, H. Kawarada: Pointing device gazing at hand based on local moments, Proceedings of SPIE , Volume 3028 Real-Time Imaging II, pp. 155-163,April (1997)
16. Z. Zhang:Flexible Camera Calibration By Viewing a Plane From Unknown Orientations, ICCV (1999)
17. R. I. Hartley, P. Sturm: Triangulation,Computer Vision and Image Understanding, page 957-966, (1994)

Experiments of Entertainment Applications of a Virtual World System for Mobile Phones

Hiroyuki Tarumi[1,2], Kasumi Nishihara[1], Kazuya Matsubara[1], Yuuki Mizukubo[1],
Shouji Nishimoto[1], and Fusako Kusunoki[3]

[1] Faculty of Engineering, Kagawa University,
2217-20 Hayashi, Takamatsu, Kagawa 761-0396, Japan
tarumi@eng.kagawa-u.ac.jp
[2] SpaceTag, Inc.
2217-15 Hayashi, Takamatsu, Kagawa 760-0301, Japan
[3] Tama Art University,
2-1723 Yarimizu, Hachioji, Tokyo 192-0394, Japan

Abstract. Using a virtual world system for GPS-phones, we have developed a small RPG-like game to give information to tourists. Comparing with other virtual systems for mobile terminals, the cost of our system is much lower because only phones on the current market are required but no additional devices are needed. The game follows a Japanese famous tale and a player plays as the hero. We recruited twenty subjects and they played it 35 minutes in average. Through evaluation sessions of the system, we have found that the system is highly evaluated as an entertainment system.

1 Introduction

Virtual information systems are highly expected for entertainment applications. Especially, virtual information services to mobile terminals are actively developed and researched. Prototypes developed by such research projects adopted wearable terminals [1-4], larger terminals [5], or laptop computers and/or PDA [4, 6-8].

However, from a viewpoint of business, these kinds of terminals are not appropriate. Since they are relatively costly and heavy, it is difficult to let many consumers buy such terminals and walk with them. On the other hand, mobile phones have already been widespread to consumers. In Japan, more than ten million mobile phones with GPS have been shipped out, but the number of PDA users is very much smaller. People usually go out with their mobile phones even if they do not expect outdoor virtual information services.

With these reasons, we believe that mobile phones are the only one candidate as terminals to deploy outdoor virtual information services. We have developed a virtual information system for mobile phones with GPS [9-11]. The system is based on our concept of SpaceTag [12-14].

The difference between PDA and phones are not only in the hardware resources such as CPU or memory. There are more restrictions on user interfaces of phones, including the size of display. Application programming interfaces (API) and peripheral devices for phones also give restrictions to programmers. For example,

F. Kishino et al. (Eds.): ICEC 2005, LNCS 3711, pp. 377–388, 2005.
© IFIP International Federation for Information Processing 2005

location values from GPS cannot be obtained as frequently as in the cases of PDA or laptop PCs. Hence we needed to develop and evaluate a system with mobile phones, though there have already been several evaluation results using PDA or laptop PCs by other researchers.

In this paper, we will describe an evaluation of our new application of the virtual information system. This application is more sophisticated than before. A user plays a scenario of RPG, where the user plays as a hero of a famous tale. Through the game, the user will be given information of a sightseeing spot in our city, which encourages the user to visit there.

Evaluation results of the system and application are also given in this paper. We can say that it is highly evaluated as an entertainment system and it is useful for sightseeing support.

2   A Virtual World System for Mobile Phones

Our goal is to develop and deploy a system with which people can experience virtual worlds using their mobile phones. Each virtual world has a same geographical structure (with respect to latitude and longitude) with the real world. In other words, we can create various virtual worlds that have same geographical structure, and they can be overlaid onto the real world. We call it the overlaid virtual model (Fig. 1 [12]). A user can select and visit one (or even more) virtual world with his/her mobile terminal.

A virtual world consists of virtual architectural objects and virtual creatures. Virtual architectural objects are static objects like buildings, houses, and bridges. Virtual creatures are dynamic objects that can move or interact with other objects, or with users visiting the virtual world. In other words, a virtual creature is an active agent that can react to stimuli from the environment and dynamically execute methods like uttering words to the user. They can also exchange messages with other agents. Sometimes we call virtual creatures just as agents.

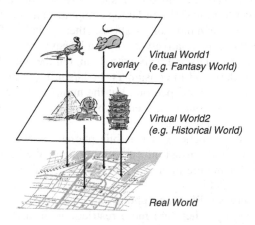

Fig. 1. Overlaid Virtual Model

From a user with a mobile phone, a virtual world can be seen with a perspective view. A far object is drawn as a small image, whereas a closer object is shown as a large image. If a face of a virtual creature can be seen from the north side of the virtual animal, its back can be seen from its south side. Location of a user can be detected by the GPS embedded on the mobile phone. Hence a user can walk in the virtual world when he/she walks in the real world. The correspondence between the two worlds is based on location.

We have two versions of the virtual world system: a *browser-based* version and a *Brew-based* version.

The browser-based version does not need any special software on a mobile phone. Only a built-in browser is used. All the necessary processing for the virtual world system is performed at the server side. However, it is a "pull" information system, so a user should manually download a new image of the virtual world, whenever he/she has moved to a new location.

On the other hand, the Brew-based version needs special software based on Brew, at the terminal side. Brew (http://brew.qualcomm.com/brew/) is a software platform for mobile terminals designed by Quallcomm, Inc. With the Brew-based version, the graphics is dynamically redrawn [9-10]. It gives more satisfying user interfaces than the browser-based version. However, since we had not completed the development of a reliable version with Brew before this study, we used the browser-based version.

Fig. 2 shows the configuration of our virtual city system prototype. It is basically a client-server system. Clients are mobile phones on the Japanese market with a GPS function (Qualcomm's gpsOne) and internet accessibility. Terminals we used for this study were A5502K, W21S, and W21SA provided by KDDI with "au" brand (http://www.au.kddi.com/), but other types of terminals can be used if they support GPS.

In Fig. 2, the server is drawn as one block, but it consists of two computers. Because the graphics processing needs computer power, one machine is used only for drawing.

The server's main function is to generate a static image of virtual city for each user. When a user accesses to the server, location parameters are attached to the request message by the gpsOne location server. The virtual city server can then detect the location of user by latitude and longitude values ("Convert (Lat, Lon) to Internal Parameters" module). These location parameters are converted to the internal coordinates, and distance and direction of virtual objects are computed ("Compute Distance and Direction" module). They are shown on the user's display like "a house, 200m west" for reference.

The "Compute Distance and Direction" module gives a default direction to the "Image Generation" module. A default direction is defined as the direction in which the closest object exists. The user can look into another direction by selecting from a direction list (its flow is shown as broken arrows). In this case, a user is asked by the server about the direction he/she wants to see. The user should select one of the eight directions: N, NW, W, SW, S, SE, E, or NE.

Data of virtual objects are stored as LightWave 3D data files on the server. A LightWave file is loaded to an image generation module written by Java using Java3D package, and is converted to a 2D image (120 x 120 pixels). An image generation process is invoked by the servlet mechanism triggered from the user's request. By

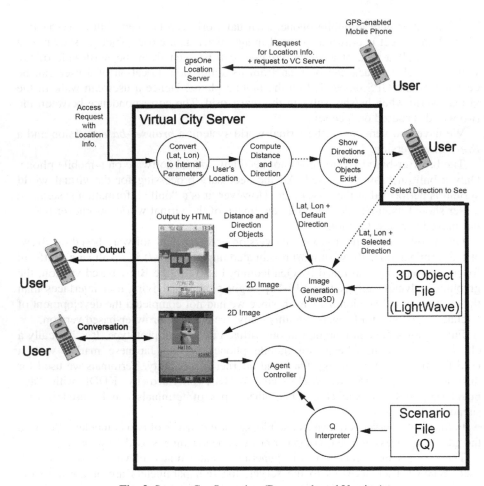

Fig. 2. System Configuration (Browser-based Version)

adopting a popular tool like LightWave, many people will have chances to take part in the activities of authoring virtual city objects. However, we cannot take full advantage of LightWave, because complex objects that have many polygons or fine textures could not be handled by Java3D and phone terminals.

In Fig. 2, two images are shown. The upper image is an example of the viewing mode. In this case, the generated page in HTML format containing an image of scenery is just sent to the user's terminal. Distance and direction parameters as texts are also attached as mentioned above.

The lower image in Fig. 2 is an example of the conversation mode. A user can enter this mode by selecting "conversation" button that is shown along with a virtual creature. Conversation of an agent is controlled by the "Agent Controller" module. This module uses the Q interpreter to control the conversation. Q is a language developed by the Q consortium [15], which is a scenario-description language based on the Scheme language. With Q, we can easily define the behavior of agents. A more detailed description of the agent control mechanism is given in [11].

3 Entertainment Applications of the Virtual World System

The virtual world system can be used for various applications [13]. For example, providing local public information or advertisement is expected as applications. However, while GPS-phones have been shipped more than ten million in Japan, we still cannot say almost all people have them. These applications are effective when most of the people can access the information services. We consider that the market for these kinds of application is immature.

Entertainment applications, on the other hands, have a considerable market even if only some people have GPS-phones. RPG (Role Playing Game) is a typical example of such application we can consider. With our system, we can control agents based on a scenario. Agents are located and move around in a virtual world that is overlaid onto the real world. Game players walk about in the real world, encounter such agents, talk with them, and play the scenario seeking the goal.

Comparing with conventional RPG on game computers or personal computers, RPG on our virtual world system has some barriers to play. Players have to walk, rather than simply inputting a "move" command or manipulating a joy stick. When it is raining, hot, or cold, players would be reluctant to go out. On the other hand, there are merits of this style of game. Players have chances to meet other players in the real world. They also have chances to discover some real objects (e.g., historic objects, curious plants, etc.) while playing a game. Walking is better for health than playing in the room. We are expecting potentials of such kind of RPG.

Sightseeing is one of the practical applications that can be mixed with games. While playing a game, players will find interesting points in a sightseeing area. They might spend money in the area to take a rest or to buy memorial items or souvenirs. In other words, such RPG has some economical effects and is anticipated by the local government, shops, and the tourist industry.

Of course, the system can be used for just showing explanations of sightseeing spots to visitors. This kind of usage is also expected. However, from the viewpoint of entertainment, we have developed and evaluated an RPG-like sightseeing support application.

4 Evaluation Sessions

In this section, we introduce an application of the virtual world system with a scenario of RPG based on a famous Japanese tale, designed for sightseeing support. We also show results of evaluation of the application.

4.1 Background: Momotaro and Megijima

The tale of Momotaro is a very well known story in Japan. All Japanese people know it. The outline of the tale is as follows. Momotaro was a boy living in a village in ancient Japan. His village was very much damaged by Oni (ogres). Momotaro went to Onigashima, which means "the ogres' island" in Japanese, with a dog, a monkey, and a pheasant, and exterminated Oni.

Fig. 3. Momotaro, Animals, and Oni designed with LightWave 3D

Today, it is believed that Megijima, which is an island located four kilometers north from Takamatsu port, is the Onigashima. In Megijima, there is an artificial cave where people believe Oni (ogres) lived. Oni are considered as pirates in ancient Japan. With this background, Megijima is one of the recommended sightseeing destinations in Takamatsu city. However, since Megijima itself is not as famous as the tale of Momotaro and people must take a boat to go to Megijima, the number of visitors is not so many. Promotion of Megijima is hence required.

4.2 Evaluation Settings

At the beginning of this project, we were planning to build a virtual world on Megijima. However, it is more important to encourage tourists to go to Megijima than to give virtual experiences in Megijima, since visitors would have nothing to do except for sightseeing in Megijima. Hence we have changed the plan to build a virtual world on Takamatsu port, where the boat departs and people can see Megijima well.

We designed Momotaro, a dog, a monkey, a pheasant, and Oni with LightWave 3D (Fig. 3). They were placed onto the area of Takamatsu Port as shown in Fig. 4. Megijima is at the left of the map. It can be well viewed from the seawall, where the Oni was placed virtually. We placed other virtual animals like a bear, a penguin, a rabbit, a giraffe, etc. within the experiment area. They could make conversation to players and give some information useful to play the game. Eight virtual buildings were also placed in the area.

A virtual Moai statue was also placed. There really is a Moai statue in Megijima, which is not well known. We placed the virtual one to give such information to players.

We recruited 21 subjects and asked them to play the game. The sessions were conducted from January 15th to 29th, 2005. Since a server trouble occurred for one subject, totally 20 sessions were completed. Six of them were male, and fourteen were female. They were university students from various faculties.

Prior to each session, we gave each subject a GPS-phone and explained how to operate it. Also we explained each subject that he/she should play as Momotaro, find a dog, a monkey, and a pheasant, and defeat Oni in cooperation with the animals. We also gave a map to him/her. The map was different from Fig. 4; it does not show virtual objects except for a house, where the game started. We also gave each subject a compass to find a correct direction.

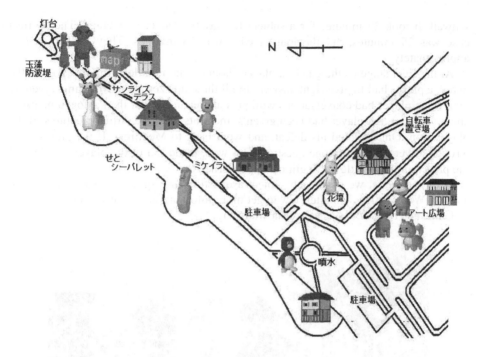

Fig. 4. Map of the Experiments Area (colored objects are virtual)

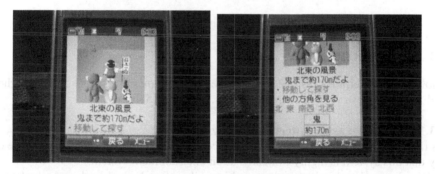

Fig. 5. Sample Displays (left: top of the screen, right: scroll-downed)

Fig. 5 shows examples of the screen. The player, Momotaro, was shown at the center, from his back. We had adopted this third person view rather than Momotaro's own view, since our previous evaluations had shown it better. A dog, a monkey, and a pheasant were displayed behind Momotaro, if they had been already found by the player. When the player scrolled down the screen, he/she could find names of virtual buildings and virtual creatures, look into arbitrary directions, or talk to virtual creatures.

During the game, we helped a subject only when he/she got lost in the virtual world and continued to proceed to an opposite direction from the final destination, the seawall. It took 35 minutes for a subject to play the game, in average. The shortest case was 25 minutes, but the longest case was 58 minutes. They walked 1.5km, approximately.

At the final stage of the game, a player should fight a battle with Oni. To win the battle, a player had to give right answers to all three quizzes about Megijima given by Oni. If the player had conversations with virtual creatures other than a dog, a monkey, and a pheasant, the player had been given some hints by those virtual creatures. If the player won, Oni declared his defeat, and went back to Megijima. If the player gave wrong answers at least to one question, Oni won, made fun of the player, challenged the player another battle in Megijima, and returned there.

After the game, we gave each subject a questionnaire sheet and asked him/her to answer. We conducted an interview to get more information from each subject.

Game and interview scenes are shown in Fig. 6.

Fig. 6. Game (left, center) and Interview (right) Scenes

4.3 Results and Discussion

Table 1 lists excerpt results of questionnaire. For each question, score 5 is the highest, and 1 is the lowest. A subject could select 1, 2, 3, 4, or 5, for each.

4.3.1 Evaluation as an Entertainment System
As the result of first question shows and according to interviews with subjects, we can say that this system is highly evaluated as an entertainment system.

We observed and videotaped one subject who often looked back and watched his friend who was also playing the game. At the interview, he said that he enjoyed competing with his friend, although we did not say this was a race. This is a typical fact of evidence that subjects are entertained.

We also observed and videotaped that another subject naturally uttered "Kandou..." (in Japanese), which meant that she was much impressed, when she found that real Megijima was in front of her at the end of the game.

In the interview, we asked all subjects what aspect of the experience was enjoyable. Answers from all subjects included "gaming by walking." We can say that it gave subjects a kind of new experience different from conventional role playing games. With all these facts, we can say that this system is successful as an entertainment system.

Table 1. Result of Questionnaire (N=20)

Question	Average Score (1:bad ... 5: good)
Did you enjoy the game?	4.60
Have you become interested in Megijima after this game?	4.10
Do you want to visit sightseeing spots introduced in the game?	4.15
Do you think that sightseeing guides using virtual and real worlds like this are effective?	4.40
Were you interested in the quiz battle with Oni?	3.90
Did you feel that you were walking in a virtual world?	3.95
Did you find some bad effects of GPS errors?	3.40

4.3.2 Evaluation as a Sightseeing Support System

Results of the second and third questions in Table 1 show that the subjects were well interested in Megijima after the game. From the fourth question we can find that subjects generally agreed that this system can be used as sightseeing guides.

However, we still need further long-time evaluations before concluding that this application has some good effects on the tourism industry. Being interested in an island and really visiting it are different things.

Besides the evaluation sessions, we also asked four tourism-promotion staffs of the local government to play the game and evaluate it. They very much agreed that this was an exciting experience and the application really entertained them. However, they expected us to provide more links to real objects from the game scenario. They were also afraid that players would be interested in the game itself, not in the sightseeing.

Providing links to real objects is not so easy because of GPS errors mentioned in the next subsection. We should find a well-balanced solution for it.

4.3.3 Technical Quality

(a) Reality of Experience

The result of the fifth question in Table 1 shows that subjects felt in a sense that they were walking in a virtual world. The score was not high enough, but it is better than our previous experiments [10]. We consider that introduction of the third person view (Fig. 5) and other minor refinements contributed to the improvement. Also, an exciting scenario of Momotaro may have also contributed to this subjective evaluation, comparing with previous evaluation sessions without scenarios.

(b) GPS Errors

According to the result of the last question in Table 1, where 5 means that they did not feel bad effects and 1 means they felt it most, subjects felt GPS errors to some extent. This score is not good, but also better than previous experiments. One reason of improvement would be that there are no tall buildings, which make GPS precision worse, at Takamatsu Port. However, GPS error is still the most serious problem for our system. Techniques to avoid the bad effect of GPS error will be described in another paper in very near future.

(c) User Interface

Since all of our subjects were young people, they quickly became accustomed to the operation of the game. However, tourists include elder people. Mobile phones are not always appropriate for them. It is a difficult problem because adopting other kinds of terminal needs additional costs and our goal of the project is to adopt popular terminals with GPS.

The browser-based system architecture was not well evaluated. Subjects needed to reload new data from the server, whenever he/she had moved to another location, or looked into another direction. Adopting the Brew-based version with a mobile-phone with electronic compass will be able to solve this problem.

(d) System Response

We received no complaints about the system response from the subjects. It took about ten seconds to detect the position using gpsOne. About five additional seconds are needed before finishing receiving contents from the server.

5   Conclusions and Future Work

In this paper, we have introduced a virtual world system for mobile phones with GPS, an RPG-based sightseeing application, and its evaluation.

According to the formal evaluation by young subjects and informal evaluation by local government staffs, we can say that this virtual world system for mobile phones with an RPG-like scenario can provide good quality of entertainment. As we designed it to minimize the additional costs paid by consumers, this system is much more realistic solution than other virtual systems using wearable computers, laptop PCs, or PDAs.

Subjects said that they became interested in Megijima, which is the theme of the game and a sightseeing spot to promote. We can expect that it can promote tourism to some extent, but more refinement of the system is needed. For example, taking real objects into the scenario is expected. This problem should be considered taking GPS errors into account.

The evaluation sessions were conducted with a browser-based version of the system. A Brew-based version will be more user-friendly, because users do not need to reload data by themselves, and they can find right directions of objects without a reference to a compass. To finish the development of a Brew-based version is our future work, but good evaluation for the browser-based version suggests that a Brew-based version be more successful.

We are planning to another future work, evaluation sessions involving many users who have mobile phones compatible to our system. As we have stated, some current mobile phones can be used to enjoy our system without any additional devices. We will announce our evaluation project to the public so that many users participate in the evaluation without our attendance.

One of the interesting characteristics of our system is the virtual creature. There are some games using GPS phones (for example, http://www.mogimogi.com/), but shared autonomous virtual creatures are not supported. We are also developing an authoring tool for virtual world, including a script editor to define behaviors of virtual creatures.

Acknowledgments

Part of the research was supported by Kagawa Industry Support Foundation (Grant for Industry-Academia-Government Liaison for Research and Development) and the Okawa Foundation. We very much appreciate the kind support by Professor Tohru Ishida's laboratory for Q language.

References

1. Cheok, A. D., et al: Game-City: A Ubiquitous Large Area Multi-Interface Mixed Reality Game Space for Wearable Computers, Proceedings of the 6th International Symposium on Wearable Computers (ISWC'02), IEEE (2002)
2. Flintham, M., et al.: Where On-Line Meets On-The-Streets: Experiences With Mobile Mixed Reality Games, Proceedings of CHI 2003, ACM (2003) 569-576
3. Tenmoku, R. Kanbara, M., and Yokoya, M.: A Wearable Augmented Reality System Using Positioning Infrastructures and a Pedometer, Proceedings of the Seventh IEEE International Symposium on Wearable Computers (ISWC'03), IEEE (2003)
4. Vlahakis, V., et al.: Personalized Augmented Reality Touring of Archaeological Sites with Wearable and Mobile Computers, Proceedings of the 6th International Symposium on Wearable Computers (ISWC'02), IEEE (2002)
5. Schnadelbach, H., et al.: The Augurscope: A Mixed Reality Interface for Outdoors, Proceedings of CHI 2002, ACM (2002) 9-16
6. Izadi, S. et al.: Citywide: Supporting Interactive Digital Experiences across Physical Space, Personal and Ubiquitous Computing, Springer-Verlag, Vol. 6 (2002) 290-298
7. Björk, S., Falk, J., Hansson, R., and Ljungstrand, P.: Pirates! – Using the Physical World as a Game Board, Proceedings of Interact 2001, IFIP TC. 13 Conference on Human-Computer Interaction (2001) 423-430
8. Cheverst, K., Davies, N., Mitchell, K., Friday, A., and Efstratiou, C.: Developing a Context-aware Electronic Tourist Guide: Some Issues and Experiences, Proceedings of CHI 2000, ACM (2000) 17-24
9. Tarumi, H., Matsubara, K., and Yano, M.: Implementations and Evaluations of Location-based Virtual City System for Mobile Phones, Proc. of 2004 IEEE Global Telecommunications Conference Workshops (Workshop on Network Issues in Multimedia Entertainment), IEEE (2004) 544-547
10. Tarumi, H., Tokuda, S., Yasui, T., Matsubara, K., Kusunoki, F.: Design and Evaluation of a Location-Based Virtual City System for Mobile Phones, Proc. of 2005 Symposium on Applications and the Internet (SAINT 2005), IEEE (2005) 222-228
11. Matsubara, K., Mizukubo, Y., Morita, T., Tarumi, H., and Kusunoki, F.: An Agent Control Mechanism in Virtual Worlds for Mobile Users, Proceedings of the 2005 International Conference on Active Media Technology, IEEE (2005) 475-480
12. Tarumi, H., Morishita, K., Nakao, M., and Kambayashi, Y.: SpaceTag: An Overlaid Virtual System and its Application, Proceedings of International Conference on Multimedia Computing and Systems (ICMCS'99), IEEE, Vol.1 (1999) 207-212

13. Tarumi, H., Morishita, K., and Kambayashi, Y.: Public Applications of SpaceTag and their Impacts, Digital Cities: Technologies, Experiences and Future Perspectives, Ishida, T. and Isbister, K. (Eds.), Lecture Notes in Computer Science (State-of-the Art Survey), Vol. 1765 (2000) 350-363
14. Tarumi, H., Morishita, K., Ito, Y., and Kambayashi, Y.: Communication through Virtual Active Objects Overlaid onto the Real World, Proc. of The Third International Conference on Collaborative Virtual Environments (CVE 2000), ACM (2000) 155-164
15. Ishida, T.: Q: A Scenario Description Language for Interactive Agents. IEEE Computer, Vol.35, No. 11 (2002) 42-47

A Tutoring System for Commercial Games

Pieter Spronck and Jaap van den Herik

Universiteit Maastricht,
Institute for Knowledge and Agent Technology
{p.spronck, herik}@cs.unimaas.nl

Abstract. In computer games, tutoring systems are used for two purposes: (1) to introduce a human player to the mechanics of a game, and (2) to ensure that the computer plays the game at a level of playing strength that is appropriate for the skills of a novice human player. Regarding the second purpose, the issue is not to produce occasionally a weak move (i.e., a give-away move) so that the human player can win, but rather to produce not-so-strong moves under the proviso that, on a balance of probabilities, they should go unnoticed. This paper focuses on using adaptive game AI to implement a tutoring system for commercial games.[1] We depart from the novel learning technique 'dynamic scripting' and add three straightforward enhancements to achieve an 'even game', viz. high-fitness penalising, weight clipping, and top culling. Experimental results indicate that top culling is particularly successful in creating an even game. Hence, our conclusion is that dynamic scripting with top culling can implement a successful tutoring system for commercial games.

1 Introduction

In computer games, tutoring systems are used for two purposes: (1) to introduce a human player to the mechanics of a game, and (2) to ensure that the computer plays the game at a level of playing strength that is appropriate for the skills of a novice human player. In our view, an 'appropriate' playing strength entails that the computer manages to play an 'even game' against the human player, i.e., a game where both players have an equal chance to win. Of course, winning a game is not a matter of chance, but a matter of applying strategies, and strategies are to be chosen at will by the players involved. To ensure that the game remains interesting, the issue is not for the computer to produce occasionally a weak move (i.e., a give-away move) so that the human player can win, but rather to produce not-so-strong moves under the proviso that, on a balance of probabilities, they should go unnoticed [1]. We refer to the automatic adaptation of the computer's playing strength to the skills of the human player as 'difficulty scaling'. Our present research investigates the second purpose of tutoring systems, i.e., the

---

[1] All software discussed in this paper can be downloaded from the first author's website: http://www.cs.unimaas.nl/p.spronck

F. Kishino et al. (Eds.): ICEC 2005, LNCS 3711, pp. 389–400, 2005.
© IFIP International Federation for Information Processing 2005

scaling of a game's difficulty level so that the computer plays an even game against even a novice human player. Our focus is on commercial games.

Especially for complex commercial games, such as Computer RolePlaying Games (CRPGs) and strategy games, where for every move the human player can choose between hundreds of different actions, tutoring systems are a necessity. When available, a tutoring system usually consists of two parts: (1) one or more 'introductory levels', to make the human player familiar with the game's mechanics, and (2) a 'difficulty setting', a discrete value that allows the human player to determine at what level of difficulty the game will be played. While the state of the art for introductory levels is of high quality, the difficulty setting commonly has some seriously challenging issues.

We indicate three different issues with the difficulty setting in games. First, the setting is *coarse*, with the player having a choice between only a limited number of difficulty levels (usually three or four). Second, the setting is *player-selected*, with the player unable to assess which difficulty level is appropriate for his skills. Third, the setting has a *limited scope*, (in general) only affecting the computer-controlled opponents' strength, and not their strategies. Consequently, even on a 'high' difficulty setting, the opponents exhibit similar behaviour as on a 'low' difficulty setting, despite their greater strength.

We propose to alleviate the three issues mentioned above by replacing the 'difficulty setting' with a tutoring system consisting of adaptive game AI and an adequate difficulty-scaling mechanism. Adaptive game AI changes the computer's strategies to the way a game is played. As such, (1) it makes changes in small steps (i.e., it is not coarse), (2) it makes changes automatically (i.e., it is not player-selected), and (3) it affects the computer's strategies (i.e., it does not have a limited scope). With difficulty scaling, the changes made by the adaptive game AI can be tuned to the human player's skills, effectively enticing an even game at all times. We demonstrate the viability of our proposal by enhancing the online adaptive game AI technique 'dynamic scripting' with difficulty-scaling enhancements, and empirically validating the effectiveness of the resulting tutoring system in a simulated CRPG.

The outline of the remainder of the paper is as follows. Section 2 provides background information on tutoring systems and adaptive game AI. Section 3 describes dynamic scripting. Section 4 deals with three difficulty-scaling enhancements to dynamic scripting. Section 5 presents the experimental results obtained from applying dynamic scripting with difficulty scaling in a simulated CRPG. Section 6 discusses the results. In Section 7, the paper concludes and points at future work.

2   Tutoring Systems and Adaptive Game AI

In analytical computer games, an interesting domain of research is online adapting strategies, i.e., strategies that adapt and learn automatically (unsupervised) while the game is being played. The application areas are (1) learning from the computer (i.e., tutoring systems), (2) teaching the computer, and (3) providing human players with sufficient entertainment that they enjoy the game. For commercial games, 'online adapting strategies' are generally referred to as 'adaptive game AI'. We believe that adaptive game AI is a prerequisite for successful commercial games [2].

In the domain of analytical two-player games such as SHOGI, CHESS, and CHECKERS we have seen many learning systems, but not so many online learning systems (apart from opening books). There is an interesting branch of opponent-model search [3] that might suit our research aim; however, in general opponent-modelling techniques are applied offline. Early ideas on tutoring strategies in game-tree search can be ascribed to Iida, Handa, and Uiterwijk [1], with their introduction of loss-oriented search (LO search), that is used to produce an even game. Iida *et al.* [1] acknowledged that their model is possibly too detailed to be realistic, and rather naively replaced the stochastic quality by a numerical value. Yet, the first ideas are there, even though they are based on an idealised opponent.

For analytical games, tutoring systems are based on adding adaptive game AI in minimax search and opponent-model search. So far, most commercial games do not rely on such advanced AI techniques [4]. Consequently, there is only a small basis in the game AI of commercial games to apply our ideas of difficulty scaling to.

The implementation of online adaptive game AI is widely disregarded by commercial game developers [4,5], even though it has been shown to be feasible for simple games [6]. Recently, Spronck, Sprinkhuizen-Kuyper, and Postma [2] introduced a set of four computational requirements for online adaptive game AI to be successful in commercial games. The four requirements are (1) speed, (2) effectiveness, (3) robustness, and (4) efficiency. Moreover, Spronck *et al.* [2] developed an online learning technique that meets the four requirements, called 'dynamic scripting'. Dynamic scripting is a straightforward technique, but nevertheless the first of its kind. It supports online adaptive game AI in an intuitive way. Dynamic scripting is the basis for our enhancements to incorporate difficulty scaling in commercial games.

3   Dynamic Scripting

In this section we present dynamic scripting as a technique that is designed for the implementation of online adaptive game AI in commercial games (henceforth called 'games'). Those interested in a more detailed exposition of dynamic scripting are referred to [2].

Dynamic scripting is an unsupervised online learning technique for games. It maintains several rulebases, one for each opponent type in the game. The rules in the rulebases are manually designed using domain-specific knowledge. Every time a new opponent of a particular type is generated, the rules that comprise the script controlling the opponent are extracted from the corresponding rulebase. The probability that a rule is selected for a script is proportional to the weight value that is associated with the rule. The rulebase adapts by changing the weight values to reflect the success or failure rate of the associated rules in

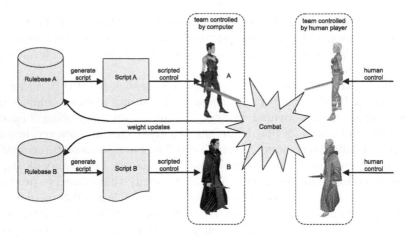

Fig. 1. Dynamic scripting

scripts. A priority mechanism can be used to let certain rules take precedence over other rules. The dynamic scripting process is illustrated in Figure 1 in the context of a game.

The learning mechanism of dynamic scripting is inspired by reinforcement-learning techniques [7,8]. 'Regular' reinforcement learning techniques, such as TD-learning, in general need large amounts of trials, and thus do not meet the requirement of efficiency [9,10]. Reinforcement learning may be suitable for online learning of game AI when the trials occur in a short time-span. Such may be the case on an operational level of intelligence, as in, for instance, the work by Graepel, Herbrich, and Gold [11], where fight movements in a fighting game are learned. However, for the learning on a tactical or strategic level of intelligence, a trial consists of observing the performance of a tactic over a fairly long period of time. Therefore, for the online learning of tactics in a game, reinforcement learning will take too long to be particularly suitable. In contrast, dynamic scripting has been designed to learn from a few trails only.

For the rules, weight values are bounded by a range $[W_{min}, W_{max}]$. The size of the weight changes depends on how well, or how badly, a team member behaved during the encounter. It is determined by a fitness function that rates a team member's performance as a number in the range $[0, 1]$. The fitness function is composed of four indicators of playing strength, namely (1) whether the member's team won or lost, (2) whether the member died or survived, (3) the member's remaining health, and (4) the amount of damage done to the member's enemies. The new weight value is calculated as $W + \Delta W$, where W is the original weight value, and the weight adjustment ΔW is expressed by the following equation:

$$\Delta W = \begin{cases} -\lfloor P_{max} \dfrac{b-F}{b} \rfloor & \{F < b\} \\ \lfloor R_{max} \dfrac{F-b}{1-b} \rfloor & \{F \geq b\} \end{cases} \tag{1}$$

In Equation 1, $R_{max} \in \mathbb{N}$ and $P_{max} \in \mathbb{N}$ are the maximum reward and maximum penalty respectively, F is the agent fitness, and $b \in \langle 0, 1 \rangle$ is the break-even value. At the break-even point the weights remain unchanged.

4 Difficulty Scaling

This section describes how dynamic scripting can be used to create new opponent strategies while scaling the difficulty level of the game AI to the experience level of the human player. Specifically, it describes three different enhancements to the dynamic scripting technique that let opponents learn how to play an even game, namely (1) high-fitness penalising in Subsection 4.1, (2) weight clipping in Subsection 4.2, and (3) top culling in Subsection 4.3. These enhancements have been discussed before by Spronck, Sprinkhuizen-Kuyper, and Postma [12].

4.1 High-Fitness Penalising

The weight adjustment expressed in Equation 1 gives rewards proportional to the fitness value: the higher the fitness, the higher the reward. To elicit mediocre instead of superior behaviour, the weight adjustment can be changed to give highest rewards to mediocre fitness values, and lower rewards or even penalties to high fitness values. With high-fitness penalising weight adjustment is expressed by Equation 1, where F is replaced by F' defined as follows.

$$F' = \begin{cases} \dfrac{F}{p} & \{F \le p\} \\ \dfrac{1 - F}{p} & \{F > p\} \end{cases} \qquad (2)$$

In Equation 2, F is the calculated fitness value, and $p \in [0.5, 1]$, $p > b$, is the reward-peak value, i.e., the fitness value that should get the highest reward. The higher the value of p, the more effective opponent behaviour will be. Figure 2 illustrates the weight adjustment as a function of the original fitness (left) and the high-fitness-penalising fitness (right), with the mapping of F to F' in between. Angles α and β are equal.

Since the optimal value for p depends on the strategy that the human player uses, we decided to let the value of p adapt to the perceived difficulty level of a game, as follows. Initially p starts at a value p_{init}. After every fight that is lost by the computer, p is increased by a small amount p_{inc}, up to a predefined maximum p_{max}. After every fight that is won by the computer, p is decreased by a small amount p_{dec}, down to a predefined minimum p_{min}.

4.2 Weight Clipping

During the weight updates, the maximum weight value W_{max} determines the maximum level of optimisation that a learned strategy can achieve. A high value for W_{max} allows the weights to grow to large values, so that after a while the

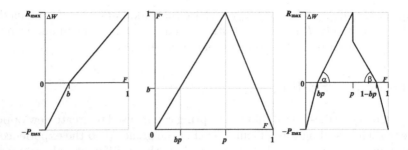

Fig. 2. Comparison of the original weight-adjustment formula (left) and the high-fitness-penalising weight-adjustment formula (right), by plotting the weight adjustments as a function of the fitness value F. The middle graph displays the relation between F and F'.

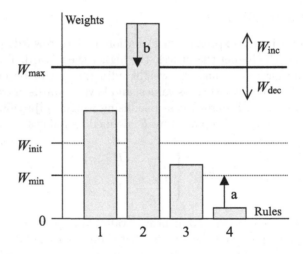

Fig. 3. Weight clipping and top culling process and parameters

most effective rules will almost always be selected. This will result in scripts that are close to a presumed optimum. A low value for W_{max} restricts weights in their growth. This enforces a high diversity in generated scripts, most of which will not be that good.

Weight clipping automatically changes the value of W_{max}, with the intent to enforce an even game. It aims at having a low value for W_{max} when the computer wins often, and a high value for W_{max} when the computer loses often. The implementation is as follows. After the computer won a fight, W_{max} is decreased by W_{dec} per cent (with a lower limit equal to the initial weight value W_{init}). After the computer lost a fight, W_{max} is increased by W_{inc} per cent.

Figure 3 illustrates the weight-clipping process and the associated parameters. The shaded bars denote weight values for arbitrary rules on the horizontal axis. Before the weight adjustment, W_{max} changes by W_{inc} or W_{dec} per cent, depending on the outcome of the fight. After the weight adjustment, in Figure 3 the weight value for rule 4 is too low, and will be increased to W_{min} (arrow 'a'), while the weight value for rule 2 is too high, and will be decreased to W_{max} (arrow 'b').

4.3 Top Culling

Top culling is quite similar to weight clipping. It employs the same adaptation mechanism for the value of W_{max}. The difference is that top culling allows weights to grow beyond the value of W_{max}. However, rules with a weight greater than W_{max} will not be selected for a generated script. Consequently, when the computer-controlled opponents win often, the most effective rules will have weights that exceed W_{max}, and cannot be selected, and thus the opponents will use relatively weak strategies. Alternatively, when the computer-controlled opponents lose often, rules with high weights will be selectable, and the opponents will use relatively strong strategies.

In Figure 3, contrary to weight clipping, top culling will leave the value of rule 2 unchanged (the action represented by arrow 'b' will not be performed). However, rule 2 will be unavailable for selection, because its value exceeds W_{max}.

5 Experimental Results

To evaluate the effect of the three difficulty-scaling enhancements to dynamic scripting, we employed a simulation of an encounter of two teams in a complex Computer RolePlaying Game (CRPG), closely resembling the popular BALDUR'S GATE games. We used this environment in earlier research to demonstrate the efficiency of dynamic scripting [2]. Our evaluation experiments aimed at assessing the performance of a team controlled by the dynamic scripting technique using a difficulty-scaling enhancement, against a team controlled by static scripts. If the difficulty-scaling enhancements work as intended, dynamic scripting will balance the game so that the number of wins of the dynamic team is roughly equal to the number of losses. In the simulation, we pitted the dynamic team against a static team that uses one of five, manually designed, basic strategies (named 'offensive', 'disabling', 'cursing', 'defensive', and 'novice'), or one of three composite strategies (named 'random team', 'random agent' and 'consecutive').

Of the eight static team's strategies the most interesting in the present context is the 'novice' strategy. This strategy resembles the playing style of a novice BALDUR'S GATE player (for whom a tutoring system is most needed). While the 'novice' strategy normally will not be defeated by arbitrarily picking rules from the rulebase, many different strategies exist that can be employed to defeat it, which the dynamic team will quickly discover. Without difficulty-scaling, the dynamic team's number of wins will greatly exceed its losses.

In our experiments we initialised $W_{max} = 2000$. We set $W_{init} = 100$, $W_{min} = 0$, $W_{inc} = W_{dec} = 10\%$, $p_{init} = 0.7$, $p_{min} = 0.65$, $p_{max} = 0.75$, $p_{inc} = p_{dec} = 0.01$,

$R_{max} = P_{max} = 100$, and $b = 0.3$. We employed the same fitness function as in previous research [2], and dynamic scripting with fitness-propagation fallback [13].

For each of the static strategies, we ran 100 tests in which dynamic scripting was enhanced with each of the three difficulty-scaling enhancements, and, for comparison, also without difficulty-scaling enhancements ('plain'). Each test consisted of a sequence of 150 encounters between the dynamic team and the static team. Because in each of the tests the dynamic scripting process starts with a rulebase with all weights equal, the first 50 encounters were used for finding a balance of well-performing weights (in an actual game, weights would be biased to prefer the best rules from the start, so this 'training period' would not be needed). We recorded the number of wins of the dynamic team for the last 100 encounters. The results of these tests are displayed in Table 1. Histograms for the tests with the 'novice' strategy are displayed in Figure 4. The length of each bar in the histograms indicates the number of tests that resulted in the number of wins (out of 100) that is displayed on the horizontal axis.

To be recognised as an even game, we decided that the average number of wins over all tests must be close to 50. To take into account random fluctuations, in this context "close to 50" means "within the range [45,55]". In Table 1, all cell values indicating an even game are marked in bold font. From Table 1 the following four results can be derived.

First, dynamic scripting used without a difficulty-scaling enhancement results in wins significantly exceeding losses for all strategies except for the 'consecutive'

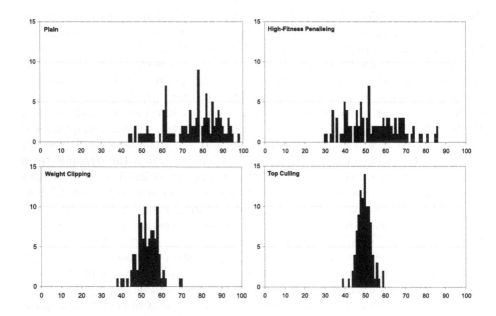

Fig. 4. Histograms of 100 tests of the achieved number of wins in 100 fights, against the 'novice' strategy

Table 1. Experimental results of testing the difficulty-scaling enhancements to dynamic scripting on eight different strategies, averaged over 100 tests. The results achieved against the 'novice' strategy (marked with an asterisk) are detailed in the histograms in Figure 4.

Strategy	Plain		High-Fitness Penalising		Weight Clipping		Top Culling	
	Average	St.Dev.	Average	St.Dev.	Average	St.Dev.	Average	St.Dev.
Offensive	61.2	16.4	**46.0**	15.1	**50.6**	9.4	**46.3**	7.5
Disabling	86.3	10.4	56.6	8.8	67.8	4.5	**52.2**	3.9
Cursing	56.2	11.7	42.8	9.9	**48.4**	6.9	**46.4**	5.6
Defensive	66.1	11.9	39.7	8.2	**52.7**	4.2	**49.2**	3.6
Novice*	75.1	13.3	**54.2**	13.3	**53.0**	5.4	**49.8**	3.4
Random team	55.8	11.3	37.7	6.5	**50.0**	6.9	**47.4**	5.1
Random agent	58.8	9.7	44.0	8.6	**51.8**	5.9	**48.8**	4.1
Consecutive	**51.1**	11.8	34.4	8.8	**48.7**	7.7	**45.0**	7.3

strategy (with a reliability > 99.9% [14]). The 'consecutive' strategy is the most difficult strategy to defeat [2]. Note that the fact that, on average, dynamic scripting plays an even game against the 'consecutive' strategy even without difficulty scaling, is not because it is unable to consistently defeat this strategy, but because dynamic scripting continues learning after it has reached a local optimum. Therefore, it can "forget" what it previously learned, especially against an superior strategy like the 'consecutive' strategy.

Second, high-fitness penalising performs considerably worse than the other two enhancements. It cannot achieve an even game against six of the eight strategies.

Third, weight clipping is successful in enforcing an even game against seven out of eight strategies. It does not succeed against the 'disabling' strategy. This is caused by the fact that the 'disabling' strategy is so easy to defeat, that even a rulebase with all weights equal will, on average, generate a script that defeats this strategy. Weight clipping can never generate a rulebase worse than "all weights equal".

Fourth, top culling is successful in enforcing an even game against all eight strategies.

From the histograms in Figure 4 we derive the following result. While all three difficulty-scaling enhancements manage to, on average, enforce an even game against the 'novice' strategy, the number of wins in each of the tests is much more "spread out" for the high-fitness-penalising enhancement than for the other two enhancements. This indicates that the high-fitness penalising results in a higher variance of the distribution of won games than the other two enhancements. The top-culling enhancement seems to yield the lowest variance. This is confirmed by an approximate randomisation test [14], which shows that against the 'novice' strategy, the variance achieved with top culling is significantly lower than with the other two enhancements (reliability > 99.9%). We observed similar distributions of won games against the other strategies, except that against some of the stronger strategies a few exceptional outliers occurred with a significantly lower number of won games. The rare outliers were caused by dynamic scripting occasionally needing more than the first 50 encounters to find well-performing weights against a strong static strategy.

6   Discussion

Of the three different difficulty-scaling enhancements we conclude the top-culling enhancement to be the best choice. It has the following three advantages: (1) it yields results with a very low variance, (2) it is easily implemented, and (3) of the three enhancements, it is the only one that manages to force an even game against inferior strategies, which is of crucial importance for tutoring systems.

We further validated the results achieved with top culling, by implementing dynamic scripting with the top-culling enhancement in a state-of-the-art computer game, NEVERWINTER NIGHTS (version 1.61). We tested it against the game AI implemented by the game developers, with the same experimental procedure as used in the simulation environment. Ten tests without difficulty scaling resulted in an average number of wins of 79.4 out of 100, with a standard deviation of 12.7. Ten tests with the top-culling enhancement resulted in an average number of wins of 49.8 out of 100, with a standard deviation of 3.4. Therefore, our simulation results are supported by the NEVERWINTER NIGHTS tests.

Obviously, the worst difficulty-scaling enhancement we tested is high-fitness penalising. In an attempt to improve high-fitness penalising, we performed some tests with different ranges and adaptation values for the reward-peak value p, but these worsened the results. However, we cannot rule out the possibility that with a different fitness function high-fitness penalising will give better results.

An additional possibility with weight clipping and top culling is that they can be used to set a desired win-loss ratio, simply by changing the rates with which the value of W_{max} fluctuates. For instance, by using top culling with W_{dec}=30% instead of 10%, leaving all other parameters the same, after 100 tests against the 'novice' strategy, we derived an average number of wins of 35.0 with a standard deviation of 5.6.

In previous research we concluded that dynamic scripting is suitable to be applied in real commercial games to improve strategies automatically [13]. With a difficulty-scaling enhancement, dynamic scripting becomes a tutoring system for novice players, improving its usefulness significantly.

7   Conclusions and Future Work

In this paper we proposed to implement a tutoring system for commercial games by enhancing online adaptive game AI with difficulty scaling. We demonstrated the viability of our proposal by testing three different enhancements to the online adaptive game AI technique 'dynamic scripting' that allow scaling of the difficulty level of game AI. These three enhancements are (1) high-fitness penalising, (2) weight clipping, and (3) top culling. Of the three difficulty-scaling enhancements tested, top culling gave the best results. We also discovered that both weight clipping and top culling, besides forcing an even game, can be used to set a different win-loss ratio, by tuning a single parameter. We conclude that dynamic scripting, using top culling, can be used as a tutoring system for commercial games.

In future work, we intend to apply dynamic scripting, including difficulty scaling, in other game types than CRPGs. We will also investigate whether offline machine learning techniques can be used to "invent" completely new rules for the dynamic scripting rulebase. First results for this research are reported by Ponsen and Spronck [15]. Finally, we will aim to investigate the effectiveness of the proposed tutoring system in games played against actual human players. While such a study requires many subjects and a careful experimental design, the game-play experiences of human players are important to convince game developers to adopt the proposed tutoring system in their games.

References

1. Iida, H., Handa, K., Uiterwijk, J.: Tutoring strategies in game-tree search. ICCA Journal **18** (1995) 191–204
2. Spronck, P., Sprinkhuizen-Kuyper, I., Postma, E.: Online adaptation of game opponent AI with dynamic scripting. International Journal of Intelligent Games and Simulation **3** (2004) 45–53
3. Donkers, H.: Nosce Hostem: Searching with Opponent Models. Ph.D. thesis. Universitaire Pers Maastricht, Maastricht, The Netherlands (2003)
4. Rabin, S.: Promising game AI techniques. In Rabin, S., ed.: AI Game Programming Wisdom 2, Hingham, MA, Charles River Media, Inc. (2004) 15–27
5. Woodcock, S.: The future of game AI: A personal view. Game Developer Magazine **7** (2000)
6. Demasi, P., Cruz, A.: Online coevolution for action games. International Journal of Intelligent Games and Simulation **2** (2002) 80–88
7. Sutton, R., Barto, A.: Reinforcement Learning: An Introduction. MIT Press, Cambridge, MA (1998)
8. Russell, S., Norvig, P.: Artificial Intelligence: A Modern Approach. Second edition edn. Prentice Hall, Pearson Education, Upper Saddle River, NJ (2003)
9. Manslow, J.: Learning and adaptation. In Rabin, S., ed.: AI Game Programming Wisdom, Hingham, MA, Charles River Media, Inc. (2002) 557–566
10. Madeira, C., Corruble, V., Ramalho, G., Ratitch, B.: Bootstrapping the learning process for the semi-automated design of challenging game AI. In Fu, D., Henke, S., Orkin, J., eds.: Proceedings of the AAAI-04 Workshop on Challenges in Game Artificial Intelligence, Menlo Park, CA, AAAI Press (2004) 72–76
11. Graepel, T., Herbrich, R., Gold, J.: Learning to fight. In Mehdi, Q., Gough, N., Natkin, S., Al-Dabass, D., eds.: Computer Games: Artificial Intelligence, Design and Education (CGAIDE 2004), Wolverhampton, UK, University of Wolverhampton (2004) 193–200
12. Spronck, P., Sprinkhuizen-Kuyper, I., Postma, E.: Difficulty scaling of game AI. In El Rhalibi, A., van Welden, D., eds.: GAME-ON 2004 5th International Conference on Intelligent Games and Simulation. (2004)

13. Spronck, P., Sprinkhuizen-Kuyper, I., Postma, E.: Enhancing the performance of dynamic scripting in computer games. In Rauterberg, M., ed.: Entertainment Computing – ICEC 2004. Lecture Notes in Computer Science 3166, Berlin, Germany, Springer-Verlag (2004) 296–307
14. Cohen, P.: Empirical Methods for Artificial Intelligence. MIT Press, Cambridge, MA (1995)
15. Ponsen, M., Spronck, P.: Improving adaptive game AI with evolutionary learning. In Mehdi, Q., Gough, N., Natkin, S., Al-Dabass, D., eds.: Computer Games: Artificial Intelligence, Design and Education (CGAIDE 2004), Wolverhampton, UK, University of Wolverhampton (2004) 389–396

Non-verbal Mapping Between Sound and Color – Mapping Derived from Colored Hearing Synesthetes and Its Applications

Noriko Nagata[1], Daisuke Iwai[2], Sanae H. Wake[3], and Seiji Inokuchi[4]

[1] School of Science and Technology, Kwansei Gakuin University, 2-1, Gakuen, Sanda, Hyogo 669-1323, Japan
nagata@ksc.kwansei.ac.jp
[2] Graduate School of Engineering Science, Osaka University, 1-3, Machikaneyama, Toyonaka, Osaka 560-8531, Japan
iwai@sens.sys.es.osaka-u.ac.jp
[3] Faculty of Human and Social Environment, Doshisha Women's College of Liberal Arts, Kodo, Kyoutanabe, Kyoto 610-0395, Japan
swake@dwc.doshisha.ac.jp
[4] Faculty of Media Contents, Takarazuka University of Art and Design, 7-27, Hanayashiki-tsutsujigaoka, Takarazuka 665-0803, Japan
inokuchi@ieee.org

Abstract. This paper presents an attempt at 'non-verbal mapping' between music and images. We use physical parameters of key, height and timbre as sound, and hue, brightness and chroma as color, to clarify their direct correspondence. First we derive a mapping rule between sound and color from those with such special abilities as 'colored hearing'. Next we apply the mapping to everyday people using a paired comparison test and key identification training, and we find similar phenomena to colored hearing among everyday people. The experimental result shows a possibility that they also have potential of ability of sound and color mapping.

1 Introduction

Musical pieces and pictures, upon their production, are often used to supplement each other to enhance the impression they give. For instance music is attached to pictures that matches its image or vice versa [1]. If it were possible to find which elements of the parameters contained in music and pictures produce such effects, it would serve as a clue in making 'hearing pictures and seeing music' possible. This in turn would enable the possibility of use in the creation of support systems for multimedia applications such as web pages.

So far in the field of affective computing, the affective correlation between the same or different sorts of media such as image and music has been mostly intervened by adjective words. This study approaches 'non-verbal mapping' as shown Fig. 1, that is to say, to clarify what kind of direct and affective correlation or mapping can be found between the mutual physical parameters of pictures and music.

As seen in such musical pieces titled 'Pastoral' or 'Planet', in many cases composers compose their work based on visual images. Also some performers use colors to

F. Kishino et al. (Eds.): ICEC 2005, LNCS 3711, pp. 401–412, 2005.
© IFIP International Federation for Information Processing 2005

express the image of the music in their performances. Particularly, when performing in an ensemble with many kinds of musical instrument, such as orchestras, many people attending the performance feel color sensations within the harmony of the instruments.

Further, in the field of musical psychology and cognitive science, there is a phenomenon referred to as synesthesia, which is the remarkable experience of cross-sensory perception where the stimulation of one sensory modality consistently causes sensations in one or more other senses. One type of synesthesia is 'colored hearing'. People with colored hearing can call to their minds a specific color when hearing an instrument's timbre or musical scale [2]. It has been reported that performers with a sense of absolute pitch have the common feature of this colored hearing [3]. The color sensation seen in colored hearing is not a phenomenon common to all those with absolute pitch. Some people see it as attributable to the recollection of experience or individual sensitivity [4].

Based on these studies, first of all, we will define 'color' in images and 'key, timbre and height' in music as physical parameters, in an attempt to clarify the correspondence when these are changed. This study will not focus particularly on the correspondences that apply to only those with such special abilities as colored hearing (the colored hearing group) but on clarifying the correspondence that apply to everyday people (the general group) with no special abilities such as absolute pitch or colored hearing. When conducting this study, we performed an experiment based on the following idea. The colored hearing group were not regarded as a group with completely different abilities as compared with the general group but as a group with sharply developed abilities of part of the senses that the general group have. In other words the colored hearing group can present a correspondence between sound and color actively while the general group, despite possessing the same kind of sense, may not be able to present it actively but can judge the superiority or inferiority in the correspondence of sound and color, given that they receive some kind of assistance.

First of all, we conducted a parameter mapping derivation experiment between a given color and given sound on the general group. In this experiment, no correspondence could be derived. Then the same experiment was conducted on the colored hearing group in an effort to derive a mapping. Next, we verified whether this mapping was acceptable or not to the general group using a method based on a paired comparison test and key identification training.

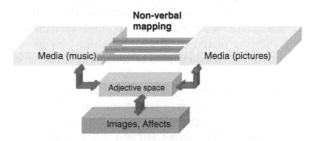

Fig. 1. Non-verbal mapping between music and pictures

2 Mapping Derivation Experiment

The object was to derive what kind of non-verbal mapping exists in the sound and color parameters from the colored hearing group and the general group.

2.1 Selection of Color and Sound Parameters

Color parameters: For color parameters, lightness, saturation, hue and tone in addition to the complex concept of lightness and saturation in the PCCS (Practical Color Co-ordinate System) system designed by the Japan Color Research Institute were used.

Sound parameters: Key, timbre and height were used as sound parameters in the experiment.

Key: The rising scales that start from each white piano key were used. The scales consist of fourteen types of C major to B major and C minor to B minor.

Timbre: There are various possible factors that affect the impression of timbre such as the power envelope. In this study, to make things simple, we focused our attention on the difference in the higher harmonic wave structure.

The timbres provided are as follows:

- Sine wave (SW): Pure sound that does not contain a higher harmonic wave.
- Harmonic series 1, harmonic series 2 (H1, H2): H1 means a higher harmonic wave component which is an integral multiple of a fundamental frequency added to a five-fold sound, and IM2, to a ten-fold sound.
- Odd harmonic series 1, odd harmonic series 2 (OH1, OH2): OH1 means a higher harmonic wave component which is an uneven number of multiples of a fundamental frequency added to a five-fold sound, and OH2, to an eleven-fold sound.
- Even harmonic series 1, even harmonic series 2 (EH1, EH2): EH1 means a higher harmonic wave component which is an even number of multiples of a fundamental frequency added to a five-fold sound, and EH2, to an eleven-fold sound.

Height: A rising scale of D major starting from height D0, D2 and D4 in the same timbre was used.

2.2 Experiment Procedure

From the parameters selected as in 2.1, the sound parameters the subjects listen to were changed in various ways to see how which sound corresponds to what color.

The following 3 types of experiment were conducted on subjects.

Mapping of key and color: Piano timbre sound samples of major and minor scales were given to the subjects randomly. Then they selected a color closest to the sample image. The color selection method is described afterwards.

Mapping of timbre and color: Eight types of timbre samples outlined in 2.1 were given randomly. The subjects selected a color close to the sample images. Sounds were given in non-scale sound order to prevent subjects from feeling key images.

Mapping of height and color: A D major scale starting with D0, D2 and D4 were given in both pure sound and piano sounds randomly to the subjects to select a color.

The experiments were conducted using the following procedure;

1.   A pccs color chart was provided so that it could be glanced through.
2.   This chart was shown to the subjects and they memorized where the colors were located.
3.   A sound sample was given with the color chart invisible.
4.   The subject imagined the color in their mind that was close to the sound sample just heard. A time limit of 10 seconds was set to allow intuitive imaging.
5.   The color chart was then shown to the subject to select the color close to the image in mind. From the same reason the time limit was 10 seconds.

2.3   Experimental Result (Colored Hearing Group)

Four females aged 23 to 25 with colored hearing were selected as subjects. The experiment using the procedure as in 2.2 was conducted on the colored hearing group.

Mapping of key and color. Table 1 shows the mapping result of key and color. The codes in the diagram indicate the number of the color and the tone symbol defined in the pccs colorimetric system.

Let's take subject A as an example. We can see that she selected white as C major, light blue as D major, green as E major, yellowish green as F major, blue as G major, orange as A major and dark blue as B major. In this way the colored hearing group shows a correspondence between each key and hue. However, there is no similarity in the correlation since all four people selected different hues for the same key. Also, in order to confirm individual repeatability, we performed the same test 3 months later, and 3 out of 4 people gave the same answers. Thus it was confirmed that although there is no common feature in this mapping, there is individual repeatability.

Mapping of timbre and color. The mapping result of timbre and sound showed no similarity of hue, with subject A giving off-neutral, B and D grey and C navy blue for the sine wave. Fig. 2 shows the change in the lightness and saturation of selected colors according to each timbre for scale sounds.

Table 1. Mapping Results of Key/Timbre and Color

	subject A		subject B		subject C		subject D	
C major	w	[W]	lt18	[B]	p18	[B]	b8	[Y]
D major	lt18	[B]	sf22	[P]	lt8	[Y]	dp12	[G]
E major	v12	[G]	g8	[Y]	sf4	[O]	p20	[V]
F major	v10	[YG]	g10	[YG]	sf10	[YG]	lt18	[B]
G major	b18	[B]	dp8	[Y]	d2	[R]	b6	[O]
A major	v4	[O]	ltg6	[O]	offN-2	[W]	b16	[B]
B major	dp18	[B]	ltg6	[O]	offN-6	[W]	ltg14	[BG]
C minor	dp24	[RP]	p18	[B]	d22	[P]	sf24	[RP]
D minor	Gy7	[gray]	g4	[O]	dk8	[Y]	d8	[Y]
E minor	dp14	[BG]	sf6	[O]	b4	[O]	sf12	[G]
F minor	d6	[O]	d16	[B]	dk12	[G]	ltg22	[P]
G minor	lt20	[V]	p22	[P]	offN-14	[O]	ltg18	[B]
A minor	v2	[R]	dk8	[Y]	sf22	[P]	d8	[Y]
B minor	v22	[P]	ltg10	[YG]	offN-6	[W]	ltg14	[BG]

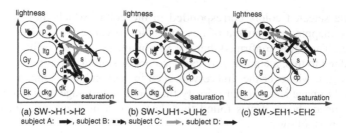

(a) SW->H1->H2   (b) SW->UH1->UH2   (c) SW->EH1->EH2
subject A: ➡, subject B: ■■➡ subject C: ➡, subject D: ➡

Fig. 2. The change in tone of colors according to each timbre for scale sounds

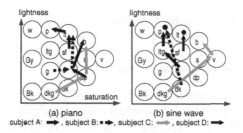

(a) piano   (b) sine wave
subject A: ➡, subject B: ■■➡, subject C: ➡, subject D: ➡

Fig. 3. The change in tone of colors when the height was changed

With Fig. 2a as an example, we will describe how to observe the graph. Fig. 2a shows the timbre of the integral multiple and the change in the lightness and saturation of the selected color. Two arrows for each subject show the change in the selected lightness and saturation when the timbre was changed SW -> H1 -> H2. In the diagram, the lightness increases in the upward direction and the saturation increases in the rightward direction. On the whole, it is seen that about 83% of arrows are directed downward and about 71% to the right. From this it can be said that, irrespective of the timbre type, the more higher harmonic wave components are contained, the higher the tendency of selecting colors of lower lightness and higher saturation.

Moreover, in spite of there being no similarity in the hues chosen by the 4 subjects, a tendency to select colors of similar hue for sound samples of the same key whatever the timbre was seen in each subject. Taking C major for example, subject C selected p18 (as piano, H1, H2, OH1, OH2 and EH1), b18 (SW) and lt18 (EH2). All these belong to blue, and correspond to the color which they selected in the mapping experiment of key and color. Therefore it is considered that the key image comes before the timbre image in colored hearing.

Mapping of height and color. As for the relation between hue and height, subject A gave blue green, B purple and C and D yellow, showing no similarity. The change in the lightness and saturation of the selected colors when the height was changed from D0 -> D2 -> D4 is shown in Fig. 3. Taking subject A as an example, in the case of the piano, when it is changed from D0 -> D2 -> D4, colors that increase in lightness are selected such as sf -> lt -> p. In the case of a sine wave, colors that increase in lightness are also selected such as d -> ltg -> p when changed as D0 -> D2 -> D4. It was found that in this way with an increase in height, the color lightness also increases.

Also, all the selected colors corresponded to the colors which they selected for D major in the mapping experiment of key and color, because the samples used were D major scales. Thus, it is confirmed that the key image has a great influence on colored hearing. Added to this, a tendency to select colors of similar hue for sound samples of the same height, whatever the timbre was seen in each subject. Thus it is considered that the height image has a higher priority than the timbre image in colored hearing.

As mentioned above, it was found that there was a mapping rule for the colored hearing group as follows:

1. Key: no common features, but individual repeatability on hue
2. Timbre: more higher harmonic wave components, lower lightness and higher saturation
3. Height: higher height, higher lightness
4. Priority: key > height > timbre

2.4 Experimental Result (General Group)

The same experiment was conducted on the general group to attempt at derivation of a mapping. The five subjects could not select colors clearly in all experiments. In the interview conducted after the experiment, the following comments were heard. "Is there anyone who can actually do this kind of thing?" "Even if I did select one color, I would choose a different color if the same experiment were conducted again."

3   Effectiveness of Mapping 1 (Paired Comparison Test)

This experiment tried to verify whether the mapping rule seen in the colored hearing group was acceptable to the general group or not when support was given. The purpose was to confirm whether the same mapping rule as the colored hearing group exists in the general group also.

3.1 Experimental Method

Forty-six subjects of men and women in their early 20s (with no such special abilities as absolute pitch) are selected to perform the following experiment.

Mapping of key and color. In the colored hearing group, a tendency of correspondence between key and hue was seen. Then, we gave a sound sample containing key information and at the same time presented two of colors that were complementary.

How the hue of the color sample should be set was a problem. In the mapping experiment of key and color conducted on the colored hearing group, no similarity was seen in the selected colors, but 3 out of 4 selected colors of the same hue for 5 types of sound sample, F and A majors and C, G and A minors. In this experiment, using these 5 types of samples, we decided to present those hues and hues that are psychologically complementary. A projector was used to project color samples. Using this task as one set, a total of 3 sets of tasks were preformed. By comparing the colors selected for each set, we verified the repeatability of mapping among the subjects.

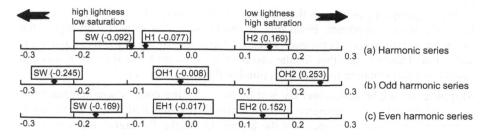

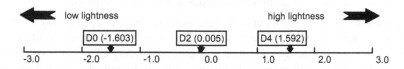

Fig. 4. The interval scales of timbres

Fig. 5. The interval scales of height

Mapping of timbre and color. In the colored hearing group, a tendency to select lower lightness and higher saturation colors was seen for sounds with higher harmonic wave component for timbre. Thus, two types of sound sample of different timbres were given continuously and at the same time color samples of high lightness and low saturation and low lightness and high saturation were presented. Then we asked for a response on which image was close to which image of the sounds heard.

Mapping of timbre and color. In the colored hearing group, a tendency was seen to select colors of higher lightness for a higher height. Two types of sound samples of different height were given continuously with high lightness color and low lightness color samples, and a response was requested on which image was close to which image of the sounds heard. We made it an obligation to create two groups for color and sound as in the experiment in the previous section. For the sound sample, a major scale starting with D0, D2 and D4 in the sine wave was used.

3.2 Result and Discussion

Mapping of key and color. Of the 5 types of scales given to the subjects, the value obtained by dividing the number of samples, in which the subjects selected the same color three times, by a full scale number of 5 was set as the repeatability rate. For instance, if the same color was selected three times for 4 types of 5, the repeatability rate was $(4/5) \times 100 = 80(\%)$. Theoretically, the repeatability rate must be more than 80% for it is estimated at the significant level of 95%, whereas, in the experiment result, no one showed results higher than 80%. From this fact, we confirmed that there is no repeatability in the answers of subjects.

Mapping of timbre and color. For each group of (SW, H1, H2), (SW, OH1, OH2) and (SW, EH1, EH2), we calculated the values on the three timbre impression interval scale, by scaling based on the comparison judgment rule. The scale values of those are shown in Fig. 4.

In any group, it can be seen that the scale value is larger for timbres with a higher harmonic wave component. From this, it can be seen that sounds with higher harmonic wave components contained correspond to colors of lower lightness and higher saturation. That is to say that for the mapping between timbre and color, it was confirmed that this mapping rule can be applied to the general group.

Mapping of height and color. By scaling based on the comparison judgment rule, values on three height impression interval scales were calculated. The scale values are shown in Fig. 5. It can be seen that the higher the height, the higher the scale value. This shows that high pitched sounds correspond to high lightness colors. In other words, it has been confirmed that also for mapping of height and color, the mapping rule of the colored hearing group can be applied to the general group.

Consideration. In the experiment, we could not confirm the repeatability of the mapping between key and color in the general group. However, a rule or similarity in the relationship between tonality and color was observed rarely even in the colored hearing group. It must be still more difficult in experiments with the general group. We next tried to apply this mapping to the general group from a different viewpoint.

4   Effectiveness of Mapping 2 (Key Identification Training)

The next experiments concerned training in key identification utilizing the mapping between key and color. The purpose of this experiment was to verify positively whether mapping as in the colored hearing group is also inherent in the general group, being brought out by effective training. The subjects who didn't have absolute pitch were trained to memorize the name of the key by hearing a sound sample of the key. At that time they were also shown a color based on the mapping and they memorized the key of the sound with the color as a cue. It was an experiment based on the hypothesis that if the general group had immanent mapping like the colored hearing group, the utilization of the color as a cue would be effective in memorizing the key.

4.1   Subjects of Experiment

Eight men and seven women around the 20 years old were selected to perform the following experiment. They didn't have absolute pitch, but were highly motivated to gain that ability. (Here, absolute pitch means the ability for long-term memory to identify or label a musical tone without reference to an external standard. For reference, perfect pitch means the ability to have some sort of super resolution in their pitch perception and to tell whether a sound is perfectly in tune or not.5, 6) The men were members of a university glee club, and the women had experience in playing musical instruments.

4.2   Training Method

The subjects were trained to listen to the sound samples while being shown the name of the key on repeated occasions for 8 minutes per day, for a period of 5 days. Then the subjects were divided into 2 groups. Group A (the 'seeing color' group) were given sound samples with a color sample based on the mapping, and Group B (the 'no seeing color' group) were given only the sound samples.

The sound samples were a piano timbre sequence of 'tonic chord (for 3 seconds), rising scale (for 6 seconds), tonic chord (for 4 seconds)' of the 7 major keys. The color samples were shown by projecting images of each color onto a screen. Here as prototypical mapping, the colors were determined based on the results of Ogushi's experiment, which included the most subjects.

The subject were training in a dark room, wearing a pair of headphones, close to a screen in order to be absorbed in the training. The name of the key of the sound was also displayed before and after giving the sound sample (for example, "next is C major"), and the subject was prompted to imagine the sound corresponding to the key in advance. For Group A, the characters of the key name were displayed with the color, and the subject was strongly requested to imagine the sound from the color as a cue. After that, in Group A, the color sample was given at the same time as the sound sample was given. In Group B, there was no color on the screen.

The training included three sets per a day (a set consisted of the sound samples of the seven keys given randomly).

4.3 Test Method

The subject was examined by being given the seven sound samples from the training randomly and requested to give the name of the key. The time limit was 10 seconds. The results of the test were evaluated by the number of correct answers. The tests were carried out three times in total. The first one was done just before the first training, the second was before the last training on the 5th day, and the third test was after the last training on the same day. Also, at the same time of the third test, the subject filled out a questionnaire about what kind of cue was used to identify the key.

4.4 Results

The results of the tests are shown in Tables 2. From the results of the first test, it was confirmed that none of the subjects had the ability of key identification because the number of the correct answers was four or under. According to the increase in correct answers in the second test, most subjects seemed to be gaining ability in key identification. In the last test, the number of correct answers was down in some subjects. This was considered to be because they were confused by the strong effect of the training.

For the above reasons, the subjects were evaluated based on the results of the second test. The subjects who had seven correct answers in the second test were called the 'short-term absolute pitch (sAP)' gainers, and those who had five or more correct answers in both the second and third tests were called the 'short-term partial absolute pitch (sPAP)' gainers. Two sAP gainers and one sPAP gainer appeared in Group A, and no sAP gainers and two sPAP gainers appeared from Group B. Therefore, it was suggested that training was more effective in Group A than in Group B.

4.5 Consideration

Next as shown in Table 3, the images and cues used in the recognition of the key obtained by the questionnaires are listed. They are divided into four categories, 'color', 'lightness', 'height' and 'other images' with their frequency as shown in Table 4.

Table 2. Results of Tests

| Subject | Correct answers | | | Effectiveness of training |
| | 1st day | 5th day | | Gaining sAP or sPAP |
	1st test	2nd test	3rd test	
A1	4	7	7	sAP gainer
A2	0	7	5	sAP gainer
A3	3	5	5	sPAP gainer
A4	0	5	4	
A5	1	2	4	
A6	1	2	2	
A7	4	2	1	
Av. A	1.86	4.29	4.00	
B1	4	5	7	sPAP gainer
B2	2	5	6	sPAP gainer
B3	0	5	3	
B4	2	4	5	
B5	0	3	2	
B6	2	3	2	
B7	1	3	0	
B8	0	2	4	
Av. B	1.38	3.75	3.50	

Independence on pitch height. It can be seen from the table that the subjects in Group B greatly depended on the pitch height. To the contrary in Group A, they seemed to identify the keys by using cues other than height, such as color and images. As for the pitch height, we must consider the fact that the key and the height of the sound samples used in these experiments were not proper because they were in a one-to-one ratio. After the experiments, such comments from subjects as "I remembered that the lowest sound was A major and the highest sound was G major" was heard. We intend to devise better sound samples in the future. However the dependence on pitch height was rarely seen in Group A in spite of the samples being the same. Therefore, it is supposed that while Group B judged the keys by the relative pitch height, Group A identified the keys by using the other images as absolute cues, which helped them gain sAP easily.

Reference to color. All the sAP and sPAP gainers referred to color as a cue in the identification of the key of the scale. Subject A3 said "Color appears when a chord sounds", in other words, the given colors themselves could be cues. Also subject A1 mentioned the given colors and images related to those. More noteworthy was that the two sPAP gainers in Group B associated color with sound by themselves in spite of seeing no colors. Subject B1 mentioned colors for every key though they gave descriptions concerning the pitch height as a cue. Subject B2 talked about color association such as "They were the same colors which I imagined" after the experiment. It follows from this that color is an important cue for key identification to the two from Group B.

Same colors in the mapping. Associations of color or images related to color were observed in most subjects in Group B, and not a few of the colors, 10/16, were the same as the mapping. Examples of these are G major as blue (subjects B3, B6 and B7), A major as red (B1 and B2) and F major as green (B1). Though subject B1 stated "I was shocked that the colors were different from those I had imagined", actually their association of C major as blue was same as 3 out of 4 of the colored hearing group selected as shown in 4.2.

Table 3. Results of Questionnaire on Cues or Images used for Key Identification

Subject	C Major	D Major	E Major	F Major	G Major	A Major	B Major	Overall impressions	To A only: Is color useful for identification?
A1 [sAP]	basic color; brand-new white	a little higher than C; uneasy	light sound; yellow	clear sound; bright green	highest sound; sky color; busy tone of cell phone	lowest sound; heavy red	dignified image; dark blue		somewhat
A2 [sAP]	obedient feel			clear feel; image of sky					somewhat
A3 [sPAP]		Takemoto piano						color appears when a chord sounds	somewhat
A4	No particular image	light, but not as light as F	a little dark image	extremely light sound	no particular image	lowness of depth	begins with higher sound than A but has a darker impression than A	impressions depending on keys are related to light/darkness of colors	somewhat
A5				light	high-pitched	Clear; heavy feel	Dim		somewhat
A6								Light or dark feeling appears more clearly than before	somewhat
A7								confused in my own mind as just after training	little

Subject	C Major	D Major	E Major	F Major	G Major	A Major	B Major	Overall impressions	To B only: To see colors of samples after experiment
B1 [sPAP]	standard sound (blue)	like F	high sound and like G (white)	begins with Fa (green)	begins with So (pink)	low sound and like B (brownish - yellow)	low sound and like A		shocked that the colors were different from those I had imagined
B2 [sPAP]						wine		the lowest sound was A and the highest sound was G	the same colors which I imagined
B3	spatial sound		gypsophila (kasumi-sou)	unexpected high sound	little blue flower	rose	tulip	images of flowers came, but didn't stay with me for long	surprised that the colors of G and A were exactly the same as I imagined
B4		time to feel sound neither C nor E	lower image than accompaniment	like accompaniment of concert	higher image than F	roughest feel	darker image than C	let F a standard	
B5	Standard-like, rather light sound	Takemoto piano	suspicious D	Maki Goto	higher than F ?	rather dark feel	time to feel sound neither A nor C	the lowest sound was A and the highest sound was G	
B6	white image		orange image		resounding highly; blue image	vibration comes up low			
B7	flattest sound; slope (uphill)	beginning of radio exercises	river; lake	like raindrops fall in petal of hydrangea	pure blue sky	muffled dark sound	nothing distinctive		
B8	solemn feel	a little solemn feel	undecided	undecided	something like white curtains	dark feel	dark feel	the lowest sound was A and the highest sound was G	

Table 4. Categories and their Frequency of Cues

Subject	Height	Lightness	Color	Other images	Main factor
A1 [sAP]	2	1	6	6	color; image
A2 [sAP]	0	0	1	2	image
A3 [sPAP]	0	0	7	1	color
A4	2	4	2	0	lightness
A5	1	1	0	2	image
A6	0	3	0	0	lightness
A7	0	0	0	0	-
AV. A	0.71	1.29	2.29	1.57	
B1 [sPAP]	4	0	5	0	color
B2 [sPAP]	2	0	2	2	color; height
B3	1	0	4	5	image
B4	3	1	0	1	height
B5	3	2	0	2	height
B6	2	0	3	0	color
B7	0	1	1	4	image
B8	2	2	1	2	height
AV. B	2.13	0.75	2.00	2.00	
AV. s(P)APs	1.60	0.20	4.20	2.20	
AV. Non s(P)AP	1.40	1.40	1.10	1.60	

Concrete images. There were more concrete images such as 'rose', 'Maki Goto' and 'white curtain' in Group B than in Group A. This can be considered to be because Group B enlarged their scope for imagination more than Group A because they had no information other than sounds, so that their concrete images increased. However it does not necessarily make mapping between key and color.

It follows from these considerations that the subjects who attempted to identify the keys with color as a cue could gain sAP more efficiently than those who applied the

412   N. Nagata et al.

pitch height or other images as cues. Especially in Group B, the 'no seeing color' group, a lot of color associations came to their minds by themselves and not a few of those corresponded to the mapping the colored hearing group had. We may therefore conclude that mapping between sound and color like colored hearing synesthetes have is inherent in the general group also.

5 Conclusion

We have presented non-verbal mapping between sound and color. Even everyday people with no special abilities such as absolute pitch or colored hearing, get a vague non-verbal sense that a picture they see and music they hear do not match or match well when they are exposed to a stimulation that contains visual and audio information. Based on this fact, we attempted deriving a mapping between selected parameters on the general group but could not find a desirable result. It is considered that the general group could passively obtain a sense from the visual and audio stimulation, but could not correspond the two parameters actively.

On the other hand, colored hearing synesthetes could correspond the two parameters actively, as they originally had the ability to clearly visualize images from auditory stimulation. Also, when the mapping rule obtained from the colored hearing group was presented to the general group, we found that this mapping was acceptable by the general group. Thus it is thought that the colored hearing group does not have a completely different ability from the general group but has more sharply developed senses than the general group.

References

1. Iwamiya, S.: Interaction between auditory and visual processing in car audio, Applied Human Science, 16, 115-119, 1997.
2. Kawamura, M. and Ohgushi, K.: Tonality of music and sense of color, Annual report for musical psychology, 160.
3. Umemoto, T. et al.: Studies in the Psychology of Music, Chapter 7, Nakanishiya Syuppann CO., LTD, 1996.
4. Saisho, H.: Absolute Pitch, Shogakukan, Inc., 1998.
5. Levitin, D.J., Absolute pitch: Self-reference and human memory, Proc. CASYS'98, 1998.
6. Fujisaki, W. and Kashino, M.: The characteristics of pitch perception in absolute pitch possessors, J. ASJ, 57, 12, 759-767, 2001.

Design and Implementation of a Pivotal Unit in a Games Technology Degree

Shri Rai[1], Chun Che Fung[2], and Arnold Depickere[3]

[1] School of Information Technology
[2] Centre for Enterprise Collaboration in Innovative Systems
[3] Division of Arts
Murdoch University, Murdoch, Western Australia, 6150, Australia
{s.rai, 1.fung, a.depickere}@murdoch.edu.au

Abstract. This paper reports the development and running of the first Games Development and Programming unit at Murdoch University, Western Australia. Unlike other Games courses which have been repackaged or re-modeled from existing multimedia courses, the proposed course and units are focused on meeting the needs of the industry and high level of academic standard. As such, great demands have been placed on the students. The unit objectives, structure and examples of assignments from the first batch of students are described in this paper. Experience has shown that the students were able to perform well with positive encouragement. Ability to work in a team also proved to be an important factor. This has shown to be related to the standard of the students' work and it is also an essential attribute expected by the industry.

1 Introduction

It has been recognized that digital and computer games is the fastest growing industry in Information Technology. According to the Game Developers Association of Australia (GDAA), an estimated amount of \$A40.9 billion dollars of interactive video games were sold in 2002 [1]. Globally, the current figure is expected to exceed \$50 billion. According to the same source, in 2002, Australians have spent \$825 million on games hardware, software and the figures are increasing quickly every year since then.

Apart from the gowing markets, computer games are also evolving and advancing rapidly in terms of complexity, realism and the overall design. Hence, there is a need for a new generation of professionals in the industry. The games industry requires not only computer programmers but also people skilled in other areas. The Australian Government's Culture and Recreation Portal [1] indicates that the games industry has a need for specialists in various areas which includes: animation skills; technical design; script or play writers; 3D graphics; game project management; film making and character design. Although not mentioned at the portal, artists are also needed along with people skilled in mathematics and physics. The government portal also indicates that just like any other industry, basic or generic skills required are: teamwork; communication skills; problem solving; adaptivity and creative thinking. In order to survive in the games industry, people working in this industry have to be prepared to face relentless challenges to their creativity and their technical skills. This

F. Kishino et al. (Eds.): ICEC 2005, LNCS 3711, pp. 413–421, 2005.

sets the games industry apart from the rest of the Information and Communication Technology industry.

In Western Australia (WA), market surveys had showed that there was a demand for a degree program in the development of computer games. However, it was discovered that there were no tertiary institutions at that time offering such a program. Since there are a number of software companies producing games in WA, it had become apparent that a gap existed between the demand of the industry and supply from the tertiary institutions.

Through extensive consultation with industry and background research it was acknowledged that a games technology degree cannot be offered as a re-packaged version of our existing Multimedia Degree although such an approach was appealing from the point of view of the costs involved. The idea of modifying several aspects of the multimedia degree to fit into a games technology degree was also rejected even though it was understood that a number of other institutions had adopted such an approach. It was decided that these two approaches would not do justice to the games technology degree we wanted to offer.

Design of the Games Technology Program has been based on the guiding document by the International Game Developers Association's IGDA Curriculum Framework [2]. Both the Games Technology degree program and the new units in the degree went through a number of formal academic planning processes required by the university and the university's academic council. Within the university, the planning processes usually happen at least one year in advance of the degree and units being offered. This gives sufficient time for the consultation and planning of the new programs and units.

After extensive consultation within the university and with the industry advisory committee, it was decided that the new degree program will have a common first year structure keeping it in line with the other current degree programs. Under such a structure, the students are prepared with common or foundation units and then they pursue specific majors or minors in the second part of the program (course). The first year included a number of introductory units such as Fundamentals of Computer Systems and Java Programming, and a Computational Mathematics (also known as Discreet Mathematics or digital Mathematics) unit. In this mathematics unit, students learn the basics of linear algebra. Due to nature of the programs, not all students will be enrolled in all the programming or the mathematics units. The units the students enrol in is largely determined by the specialisation they wish to pursue when they enter the second year of their degree program/major.

Students who wanted to specialise in games technology would need to complete a first semester, second year unit called Games Design and Programming (GDP). Failure in this unit means that students could not continue with the games technology specialisation. Students enrolling in GDP would have done at least two units with computer programming content. GDP also requires knowledge of Computer Graphics and Computational Mathematics. Hence, GDP is the pivotal unit within the Games degree course.

This paper aims to report on the detailed objectives, organisation and works submitted by the students after one year of running GDP. It is expected that through sharing of the experience and feedbacks on the program will enable further improvement of the unit and the program.

2 Games Design and Programming

As pointed out in the previous section, the Games Design and Programming unit is a pivotal unit in the Games Technology course. Subsequent core units in the games technology program/major are based on the GDP unit as a pre-requisite. Also, in order to provide flexibility and wider choices to the students, those who would like to study GDP would need to cover the elements of computer graphics and mathematics. GDP would also need to cover basic Newtonian physics, Artificial Intelligence and elements of Media Studies. All these are indicated in the IGDA's Curriculum Framework. Along with GDP, students also need separate units called Intelligent Systems and Computer Graphics Principles and Programming for the subsequent advanced units in the Games Technology degree program. It was felt that from the very first games related unit in the degree program, students would have to develop games as part of their final project. This requirement determined the content of the Games Design and Programming unit. The final description of the unit in the handbook is stated below:

> "This unit covers introduction to games design and programming from a theoretical and practical points of view. The unit includes game theory, data structures, and play-testing, as well as the physics of games programming. Further work covers non-linearity, level-design and intelligent agents. Practical rules for writing games programs are developed and applied."

The declared aims of GDP are:

1. to introduce students to the field of Games Design and Programming and to appreciate the multidisciplinary nature of this field.
2. to introduce students to the essential concepts and techniques through practice work based on developing programs that create interactive visual imagery.
3. to get students to acquire independent self-learning skills.

The listed learning objectives of the unit are:

1. to find out about current applications of computer graphics in games;
2. to learn about the techniques and algorithms used for developing games applications involving both 2D and 3D objects;
3. to learn the essential theory behind games design;
4. to be able to design and implement simple computer games in C/C++ including the use of library functions from various APIs (Application Programmer's Interface).
5. to acquire some ability to extend current skills unaided.

It was felt that students had been exposed to Java but not to C/C++. It was decided that the computer graphics unit would use C as the implementation language whereas, GDP would use C++. This was to give students exposure to these languages as well as to improve their programming skills using a variety of programming languages. Both of these units contain a heavy programming content.

As the computer graphics unit was not a pre-requisite to GDP, selected sections of the graphics unit was taught in an intensive approach in GDP. The only language used in GDP was C++. In addition, in line with other units being taught in the university, GDP was taught in a thirteen week semester. The following table lists the topics covered and their duration in weeks.

Table 1. Course structure and topics taught in GDP unit

Starting Week	No. of Weeks	Topic No.	Topic Title
1	1	1	Games in Context
2	1	2	History of Games
3, 4	2	3	Game Graphics
5, 6, 7	3	4	Game Design
8	1	5	Virtual Worlds
9	1	6	Game Physics/Mathematics
10, 11	2	7	Game AI
12	1	8	Game Engines
13	1	9	Network Games

Staff with various backgrounds was called on to teach the unit. Staff specialising in literary and media art forms taught "Games in Context", "History of Games" and part of Game Design where narrative and narrative structures are examined. A person from the games industry (game developer) was employed to teach the rest of "Games Design" as well as "Virtual Worlds, "Game Engines" and "Network Games". Staff with a Computer Science background taught "Game Graphics", "Game AI", "Game Physics/Mathematics". The finer points of object orientation using C++ were covered on demand – when students needed to know so that they could do the implementation. We would like to note that our experience in teaching Computer Science indicated that teaching object orientation in a formal and structured fashion (as taught in traditional Computer Science schools) is not as effective as teaching "on demand". As it can be seen, the topics are interdisciplinary and therefore the staff teaching the unit came from different disciplines.

The practical work that student did was a mix of individual work as well as group work. The individual assessments were needed to ensure that each student would have the necessary skills. Group work was encouraged as students needed to learn how to work co-operatively and therefore acquire group-work skills. This group-work was needed because games are not designed and built by individuals but teams of people. Although group-work was strongly encouraged when students were working on the projects and assignment, group-work was not made mandatory.

During the semester, staff handling the practical aspects of the unit kept praising the students' ability to understand the more difficult aspects of the unit. This was done to encourage them not to give up. There were some topics which some students found too difficult to follow. The first assignment was the construction of a virtual tour of part of the university's campus. This was due half way into the semester. There was approximately 50-50 split in the assignment quality. Students had to demonstrate the tour in class. To encourage the less able students, staff did not criticise the assignments. It was felt that there was no need to criticise as it was patently obvious to everyone – including the students concerned - that the work was no good when viewed alongside the better assignments. Instead staff chose to highlight something (in the poorer as well as the better assignments) that the students had spent some time on and commenting on how well that was done. The real motive for all this was that the drop out rate would not be high in the unit.

Assessment in the unit was such that to pass the unit, students needed to have an understanding of what was taught in the unit. However, to get distinction grades, students needed to go beyond what was covered in the unit. They had to find out additional tools and techniques to use to build their games. The students were also told from the very beginning that their work would be exhibited publicly and their names would be associated with the work they produced.

3   Results from the First Class of Students

All students who attempted GDP and sat the exam passed the unit. There was an unusually high number of distinction or higher grades awarded in the unit. The following are the descriptions and screenshots of some assignments produced by the students.

Fig. 1. Screen shot of "The Books are Missing"

The object of this game is to find a number of lost books. There is only a limited amount of time to get the books. Carrying the books too long would tire the player out and the player would have to drop some books to continue. The game has a 3D environment and use of graphics to illustrate a virtual world. The player has to strike a balance between time and resources.

The object of the game in Figure 2 is to capture the "nerve centre" guarded by robots. Similar to "Lost Books" this game utilised 3D graphics to create a virtual environment where the robots roam and destroy the enemies. There is a fair amount of point and shoot actions with sound. The program demands fast reaction and regeneration of the graphics.

The object of the game in Figure 3 is to destroy the robots guarding a city and capture the city. The AI in the robot guards enables the robots to chase the player if the player comes too close. In addition to the 3D environment and graphics, the students have put in a fair amount of effort in designing the robots. They even included an "Evolution" of the robots which illustrated the development of the game concept.

The objective of the game in Figure 4 is to kill the red fire ants and move on to the next level of the game. This project won the industry prize. If a wrong ant is killed, the red ant will multiply. The twist to the game is that the movement of the cursor is purposely designed to be sluggish and the player cannot just chase the ants. Strategic placement is needed. This creates a high level of addictiveness and challenge. It is the most complete game as compared to the rest. Although the graphics are not as sophisticate as the others, the students have demonstrated high level of professionalism in the organisation and concept for the games. The documentation also included marketing materials with sense of humour and fun. This captured the main objective of the game development unit.

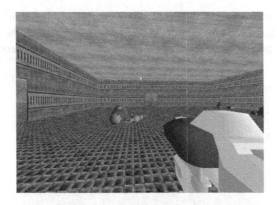

Fig. 2. Screen shot of the "Grunge"

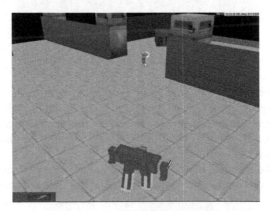

Fig. 3. Screen shot of "Robowar"

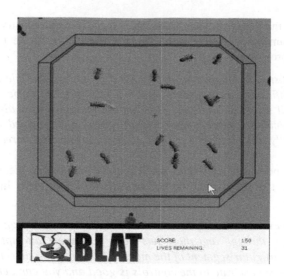

Fig. 4. Screen shot of "BLAT"

4 Discussion

Feedbacks and surveys from running of the unit for the first time have provided many lessons to be learnt – for both the students and staff. It appears that there was high level of competition amongst the various teams. It also emerged that not everyone would like to work in groups. A few students were not invited to join groups because they were known by the other students as not being capable (not technically inclined). A smaller number of students chose to work on their own because they felt that the others were not as good as they were and would therefore contributed negatively towards the quality of the project. This is a significant phenomenon as the students are unlikely to work on their own in times to come. It proved to be a challenge to encourage the students to overcome the differences and in managing the group dynamics. This inequity in group formation needs to be resolved by formal intervention. Formal intervention, however, was not used as it was felt that students would naturally form groups to reduce the workload as the both the assignment and project in the unit were made substantial to "encourage" students to work on these tasks in groups. Those students who deliberately chose to work on their own managed a credit or better. Those students who were not invited to join groups did marginally with a couple of them failing the project. Those who worked in groups usually got a distinction or a high distinction.

It was also noted that projects which had good graphics had a less sophisticated gameplay compared to those projects which had simpler graphics. This was a time problem as there was only a limited amount of time available to complete the project. Some students chose to spend more time on graphics at the expense of game play and vice versa.

A number of the better projects were short listed for an industry selected award. Eventually, a team based project won. The following is from an industry reviewer concerning this project:

> "It had a distinctive logo, reasonably good graphics; multiple levels of increasing difficulty, randomisation and it could turn out to be quite addictive. As well it had a "designed" instruction manual which also reflects a sense of humour. The accompanying documentation seemed like the authors actually still enjoy it, even after all their hard work to create it."

The only one-person project short listed had an honourable mention but industry criticised the fact that the student did not want to work in a team. In the words of an industry reviewer:

> "This is an excellent attempt by a one-person team. The design process has been thought through and there has been a genuine attempt to aim the game at a particular segment of the market. The collision detection actually works, the response rate to the controls is good and you can actually go inside the buildings – it's a pity that there is not very much in there to explore and do."

and also,

> "I would suggest that the creator learns to work in a team as future employers may see him as a potential management problem."

Obviously, working alone, the student could not put in the details inside his buildings. It appears that there were two very important motivation factors behind the students' performance. One was the knowledge that their work would be exhibited publicly and that their names would also be associated with the work they did. It is possible that Maslow's [3] "Esteem needs" may be at work here. It was obvious that for a number of students, the need to stand out was important.

The second factor appears to be the encouragement they obtained. The original intention of this encouragement was to reduce student drop-outs. This encouragement had an unforseen side-effect. It turns out that students' motivation to produce good work increased. It is possible that Attribution theory [4-6] may explain this. Students were being constantly told that there were good at the work they were doing. Staff were inadvertently encouraging students' belief that they were "actually" capable. This was not an issue with students who were actually capable but it became critical with students whose initial work was not very good. These students decided to apply themselves to show that they were good. Unfortunately, this did not work with all students as some students received a negative message from their peers who would not let weaker students join their teams.

There are some lessons to be learnt. Team building requires further attention. This is crucial as the industry representative's comments indicate. It was realised that there is a need to fine tune the way the students were treated and encouraged. The work and standard expected from the students have been very demanding and will continue to be so. A number of students whom appeared to be not able to cope have proved to be able to complete the tasks and even did well. They did this through sheer hard work at the expanse of their performance in other units. We belief that these students sacrificed their performance in their other units because they felt that they were good in GDP and were determined to prove it.

5   Conclusion

The Games Technology course is the first of its kind on offer by tertiary institutions in Western Australia. The course generated high level of interests and the number of initial applications has proved the course to be a very popular choice. The development and running of the pivotal Games Development and Programming unit have been a rewarding experience for both students and staff. While the course was initially designed to meet the needs of the industry, the concept and content of the unit have fulfilled and far exceeded the expectations from the technical, academic, education and training viewpoints. Students from the pilot second year unit have demonstrated high levels of professionalism in their ability for game development. The ability of the students was also demonstrated when one of the project submissions was awarded a prize in an industry competition. We can also report that the Games Technology students now command respect amongst their peers in other ICT majors. As one Computer Science major remarked during a staff and student discussion: "We are no match for them [Game Technology students]… they are like gods among men". One of the reasons for the success can be attributed to the positive encouragement and support given to the students. It also became clear that there were attitude and management issues which the students and staff have to deal with. In particular, the need for the students to be able to work in a team has shown to correlate with the quality and level of the work being produced. Also, the students' perceptions of their own ability determine how much work they will put in to achieve some objective even if this means sacrificing other goals. There is, unfortunately, a serious issue which is highlighted by the Computer Science major's remark: there are no female students who have survived the demands of the pivotal unit even though a number of female students were enrolled at the beginning. This is a very difficult and vexing problem that we are now grappling with. Obviously, all these issues will have important lessons for the students as well as staff and attention will be paid to subsequent offerings of the unit.

References

1. Australian Government Cultural and Recreation Portal, "Digital games industry in Australia", URL: http://www.cultureandrecreation.gov.au/articles/digitalgames/, Accessed: 25th March, 2005
2. IGDA (2003). IGDA Curriculum Framework: The Study of Games and Game Development. San Francisco, International Game Developers Association.
3. Maslow, A. H. (1971). "The farther reaches of human nature." New York, Viking Press.
4. Bem, D. (1972). "Self-perception theory." Advances in experimental social psychology,. L. Berkowitz. New York, Academic Press. **6**
5. Miller, R., Brickman, P., Bolen, D. (1975). "Attribution versus persuasion as a means of modifying behavior." In Journal of Personality and Social Psychology **31**: 430-441.
6. Heider, F. (1958). The psychology of interpersonal relations. New York, Wiley.

Interactive Educational Games for Autistic Children with Agent-Based System

Karim Sehaba[1], Pascal Estraillier[1], and Didier Lambert[2]

[1] Laboratory of Informatics Image Interaction - University of La Rochelle,
Pôle Sciences et Technologie, 17042 La Rochelle Cedex 1, France
{karim.sehaba, pascal.estraillier}@univ-lr.fr
[2] Department of Child Psychiatry - Hospital of La Rochelle,
U.P.E.A. Centre Hospitalier Marius Lacroix,
208, rue Marius Lacroix, 17000 La Rochelle, France

Abstract. This article addresses design issues that are relevant in the Autism project which aims at developing a computer games, for diagnosis and training of the children with autism and accompanying mental disorders. This approach is put in the broader context of interactive environments, which computer games are a special case. The characteristic of our approach is that it has the capability of user adaptation. The user adaptation is based on the model they maintain the observation of user interactions, the knowledge of therapists and the case-based reasoning paradigm.

1 Introduction

The characteristics of infantile autism are the severe disorder of the communication functions, the cohabitation of cognitive deficiencies and performances focalized on specific domains, and the avoidance of change, all of which often block educational attempts in a repetitive behavioural sameness.

The computer tool enables to focus the child's attention on a specific task, which also allows parameters and possible to reproduce to infinity, but which may also evolve following a model adjusted to the age, competencies and type of pathology of each child.

Computer games applied to autistic children must be sufficiently flexible to adapt to the specifices of each child and integrate the personal data of his/her own world and the beliefs attached. On the screen we therefore privilege the stimulus, which represents an object that has previously drawn the attention of the child and which carries a satisfying emotional significance. This object will then undergo physical transformations (for example in the speed of movement) which will allow the setting-up of basic categories (rough-weak, fast-slow, big-small) which the child may even mime or reproduce as well within other educational or re-educational situations.

Our research is to promote the set-up of computer games in order to :

- Complete the more traditional psychological and educational assessment procedures by offering software capable of appreciating attention spans and of

F. Kishino et al. (Eds.): ICEC 2005, LNCS 3711, pp. 422–432, 2005.

understanding the adaptive strategies of the child to the stimuli presented.(to observe whether the action produced is linked to an understanding between cause and effect).

- Allow to modify the child's beliefs by offering virtual images which inter-react with the child, but at the same time taking into account his autistic specificities, such as by slowing down their movement, so that the child can extract a general pattern, usable in the re-education of emotional, language, perceptual and cognitive problems.
- Favor the need for reassuring sameness of autistic children, while setting-up procedures for introducing the "un-sameness", so avoiding the isolation of perpetual repetition.
- Develop the encoding of time through the subordination of the software to a narrative role which specifically identifies the child within a chronology interacting with his/her environment.

We present the implementation of a prototype architecture we used in a recent field trial. The architecture draws on the educational games dedicated to children with autism. This paper is organized as follows. The next section presents and discusses a variety of systems dedicated to autistic persons. Section 3 gives a brief *Autism Project* description. Section 4 describes the principle of our architecture. The decision process is detailed in section 5. Section 6 presents the implementation. Finally, section 7 presents the conclusion and perspectives.

2   Related Works

Several interactive environments as learning and teaching tools for the reha-bilitation of children with autism have been developed (see for example [7] [8] [16] [18]). In this context a variety of different robotic and software systems can successfully interact with humans.

Among interesting interactive robotic systems are the KISMET platform [4] and the ROBOTA dolls [2] [3]. KISMET is a humanoid face that can gener-ate expressive social interactions with human 'caretakers'. Such 'meaningful' interactions can be regarded as a tool for development of social relationships between a robot and a human. The ROBOTA dolls are humanoid robots de-veloped as interactive toys for children and are used as research platforms in order to study how a human can teach a robot, using imitation, speech and gestures. Increasingly, robotic platforms are developed as interactive playmates for children [5] [16]. Besides commercial purposes (see Sony's Aibo robot), such interactive robotic systems can potentially be utilised as learning environments and in rehabilitation applications, as studied in the AURORA project [1].

Other systems [8] [17] use virtual environment for understanding the emo-tional expressions of children with autism. The emotional expressions are used in order to allow systems to enhance or subdue signals, and indeed introduce new signals to support interaction with the children. [11] is interested in the design of human-computer interfaces for children with autism.

However, to our knowledge, there is no model that proposes an adaptive approach that takes into account the experts directives in an educational context. The modeling of this approach requires modeling of the knowledge of experts, the users profile and the dynamics of their interactions.

This paper proposes an intercative model between users (children with autism) and system taking account into the expert's directives. It offers a model that analyzes children behavior from their actions. The model is based on multi-agent systems which, as will be shown in this paper, allows the simultaneous study of:

- Selection and adaptation a individualized activities plan defined by the expert. The activities plan is a sequence of educational games (called *Protocol*) dedicated to children with autism.
- Observation of the user's actions in order to ensure a real-time interactivity between user and activities of protocol.

3   Brief Project Description

Given the centrality of the interaction in a multi-agent systems, our investigations thus far have concentrated on the ability of agents to interact with children with autism in order to rehabilitate them. This is important since interaction is central on multi-agent technology, and since the understanding of their emotional expressions is important to assure a concordance of presented games and child's behavior. To facilitate such an investigation, we have defined:

- **Game** is characterized by: *statical decor*, *objets* (pictogram, music, picture...) and *functioning rules*. It has configuration parameters and the objectives to be reached.
- **Activity** is an instance of a game (with a particular configuration and, qualified and quantified objectives).
- **Protocol** is an activities sequence, given in order to make it possible to the user to reach complex objectives.
- **Directive** characterizes a system state (in particular its evolution related to the user behavior) and associates treatments which adapt during the activity execution.

The project that we carry out, called **Autism Project**, is in partnership with the psychiatric service for children with autism of *Department of Child Psychiatry of La Rochelle hospital*. Our objective is to implement a software and hardware system that could help the children with autism during the rehabilitation process. It consists in establishing a multimode and multimedia dialogue between the assisted child and the system. The role of such a system is to provide to the children the personalized activities in the form of educational games. During a session, the system collects by various devices (camera, touch screen, mouse, keyboard) the child reactions, in order to understand her/his behavior and response to it, in real time, by adequate actions considering *the expert's directives*.

The directives concern rupture, avoidance, stereotyped patterns of behavior... for instance, the system may attract child's attention by posting of a familiar image, or by launching a characteristic jingle.

4   The Multi-agent Architecture

Each child is characterized by particular competences and preferences, so he requires an adapted treatment. It is impossible to generalize activities without precaution, but we have to favour adaptability of system to take into account specific deficits observed for each child. It is important to locate and interpret carefully these intrinsic behaviors, in order to help him/her to rehabilitate.

Our approach aims to bring flexibility and modularity in the individualized rehabilitation of children with autism. Accordingly, we propose a multi-agent system architecture which allows children and experts to interact with different agents, according to the activities they will carry on and the educational approach.

In order to be able to design needs, the expert makes the following actions :

– characterizes the activities i.e defines instances of games with particular configurations.
– defines some educational objectives and associates them with appropriate protocols.
– specifies the directives.
– characterizes the children's profiles.

During the session, each child is supported by three artificial agents:

User Observation Agent (UOA): It is an agent associated with the child's interface with a wide range of goals. Mainly it observes the child's actions, notifying other agents when needed and giving access to system resources. Figure 1 gives the principle of UOA mainly inspired on *the theory of affordances* [9] [10] and *the theory of Procedural Semantics* [14] [22] [23]. From its observation, UOA associates to child's actions some states words that characterize behaviors. The

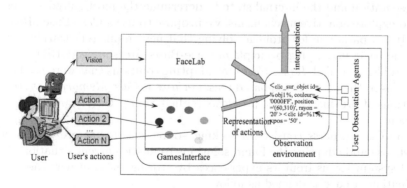

Fig. 1. User's observation mechanism

observation is based on two approaches, *Software action* and *Vision*. The first one, recovering the child's actions carried out on: mouse, touch screen, keyboard. The second one, ensured by the software/hardware system **FaceLab**, it consists in measuring the characteristics concerning the 3D representation of the face and the orientation of the gaze.

Tutor Agent (TA): A tutor agent tries to choose its strategy according to the needs and the child's profile. It can interact with UOAs and other tutor agents, access the child's profile to retrieve and adapt the protocol activities to child, retain the new experiences, and update the child's history. Tutor agents are didactic agents whose decision process is described in more detail in the next section.

Exceptions Management Agent (EMA): In order to assure an interactivity between protocols generated by TA and the child, the protocols can be modified during the training session if they are incoherent with the child's behavior. This is ensured by the Exceptions Management Agent inspired by [20]. Its role consists in identifying, indicating and treating a special cases like rupture or avoidance detected by UOA.

5   Decision Process

The selection of the most suited strategy is the result of the decision process. Several mechanisms can be used to represent this decision making process. Among these mechanisms are: Rule-Based Systems, Case-Based Reasoning Systems and Learning Classifier Systems. These mechanisms are either reactive or adaptive (see [13]).

Reactive mechanisms are based on a fixed set of rules provided by the expert before run time. The rule-based paradigm shows some drawbacks [21]: the development and maintenance of rule-based system is costly, moreover it is hard to adapt rule-based instructional planners to new domains and also to situations not foreseen in advance, e.g. children with special behaviors.

Adaptive mechanisms deal with the dynamic variations of the child behavior. Each agent builds a symbolic internal representation of child. It then uses this representation and the internal state to determine the most suited strategy.

To explore adaptive mechanisms, we propose to use a Case-Based Reasoning [15]. It is a paradigm for problem solving that has an inherent learning capability. The basic underlying principle of Case-Based Reasoning (CBR) is to solve new problems (called *Target Case*) by adapting solutions that were used to solve problems in the past. A case-based reasoner uses a *Case Memory* that stores descriptions of previously solved problems (called *Source Cases*) and their applied solutions.

The CBR process consists of seeking source cases that are similar to the target case and adapting the found solutions to fit the current situation. A case-based system learns from its experiences by storing these in new cases. In our application, a **case** is defined as follows:

```
Application Context
   [descriptors sequence]
Protocol
   [activities sequence]
```

The Application Context describes the situation in which the Protocol was applied and is implemented as a list of pairs [attribute, value]. In general, it contains information related to the children profile and the goals of case. The descriptors related to child profile define its preferences and knowledge e.g. [level-of-acquisition, high], [color, green]. Various goals can be expressed as Perception, Attention, Gaze... The descriptors of Application Context are used to calculate the similarity between cases and also to structure the case memory.

Once the basic structure has been presented, in this section we will show a deeper view of the Case memory organization, the Child's profile and the Reasoning process of Decision Agent.

5.1 Case Memory Organization

The organisation of the case memory has been based on the more general Schank's Dynamic Memory Model [19]. The fundamental idea is to organize various cases having similarities in the form of a more general structure called *Generalised Episode* or GE.

GEs generalise the common features of a set of cases. Each GE is composed of:

− *A Norm* is attached to each GE and contains the descriptors of the application context shared by a group formed by cases and GEs; it is represented by means of a list of pairs [attribute, value].

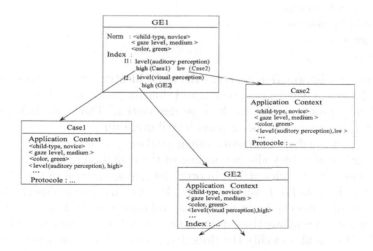

Fig. 2. Case memory organization

428   K. Sehaba, P. Estraillier, and D. Lambert

Trajectory of objects moving

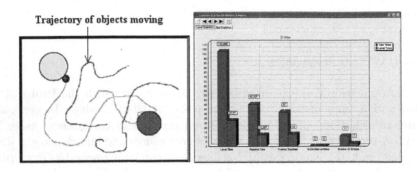

Fig. 3. Execution trace

- *The Indices* link the network elements of the memory in such a way that each GE contains a set of indices that link it with and discriminate among its descendants. Each index is related to one concrete attribute of the application context and contains a list of pairs [value, node[1]].
- *The Cases* represent a individual experiences

Thus is formed a hierarchical graph (see the example of figure 2) whose nodes are either EGs or cases. The arcs represent the links between the indices and the nodes.

5.2   Child's Profile

The child's profile has multiple functionality, used at various moments by the TA, particularly in the reasoning process (see section 5.3). It also involves in the interpretation of the child's actions by UOA. Several types of information concerning the child are present:

- General information
- Domain knowledge
- Preferences
- History

The general information concerns the child identity such as name, identifier of the child group; child's preferences and domain knowledge give a description of the child's profile similar to the case description. Thus, this information is represented by means of a list of pairs [attribute, value].

The history is a diary of activities suggested by system and the results carried out by child. The history allows tracking of the evolution of the child; it is also at the origin of many rules of TA. In order to give an interest of the history, the expert can visualize *the Execution Trace*. It concerns the child-activities interaction. Visualization can be in two forms: animation or statistics (see figure 3). The execution trace allows the expert to draw conclusions and adapt the defined protocols. He can also modify the directives, resources or functioning rules.

---

[1] Node of case or GE (see figure 2).

5.3 Reasoning Process

Tutor Agent uses the Case-Based Reasoning [15] to generate protocols by retrieving similar cases and adapting them to the current situation. We have listed three phases for reasoning process: Retrieving, Reuse and Learning.

During the *Retrieve* phase the agent obtains a set of protocols with a high level of similarity to the current situation of target case. The similarity is measured in terms of the relevant attributes that specify the application context. This task can be considered as the search of the most appropriate case through the case memory. We have used the matching method based on *the nearest neighbour matching* of REMIND [6] that calculates the similarity among cases by using a numeric function.

The similarity function ϕ is defined as the sum of the similarity measures values of each attribute in the application context of each case, multiplied by the importance of the attribute; this value is divided by the sum of the weights in order to normalise the value. The weights estimate the degree of importance of the attributes.

$$\phi(C_1, C_2) = \frac{\sum_{i=1}^{n} w_i * \varphi(v_i^1, v_i^2)}{\sum_{i=1}^{n} w_i} \tag{1}$$

Formula 1 shows the similarity function where:

- C_1, C_2 are cases defined by a set of descriptors d_i ($i \in [1..n]$) of Application Context.
- w_i is the importance of the attribute of the descriptor d_i.
- $\varphi(v_i^1, v_i^2)$ is similarity function for two primitive values v_i^1 and v_i^2 are the values for the attribute of d_i in the compared cases.

The similarity function is also defined between the application context and a GE in the Retrieve phase, in this situation the function is restricted to the attributes included in the GE norm. Therefore, the selection criterion is based on a comparison between the result of the similarity matching formula and a heuristically established threshold.

During the *Reuse* phase the decision agent combines and adapts the retrieved cases to form a protocol suitable for the current situation of target case. The adaptation of the retrieved cases to the description of target case is a knowledge-intensive task and therefore, needs a different treatment for each experience. In order to have a generic technique, two types of adaptation are identified:

- *The global adaptation* consists in replacing sub-protocols of candidates cases, selected in the Retrieve phase, by other protocols more adapted.
- *The local adaptation* consists in regulating of the activities configuration of protocol of candidat case to the target case description.

During the *Learning* phase the agent evaluates each protocol by observing the outcome of the session. The evaluation is carried out along two dimensions: *educational* and *computational*.

The relevant data of educational dimension concern just the Child Profile. Basically, the Agent revises the changes in the attributes that represent the preferences and knowledge of the child. In addition, we think that the agent's beliefs about the child should be supplemented with some feedback from the expert. Therefore, the agent interacts with the expert after each session to gather directly the beliefs of the expert about the whole session as well as her/his own knowledge of the different activities played during the session.

The objective of the evaluation along the computational dimension is to assess the goodness of each case as the basis to create the new source case.

6   Implementation

The proposed model was implemented with the platform DIMA [12]. DIMA provides a library of JAVA classes (Agent Classes and Agent Component classes) that have been used to build the various agents. In the first step, we have developed agents that ensure the user observation, reasoning process and exceptions treatment.

In the second step, we have developed an interface that allows the expert to define the activities, the cases, the directives and the distances between the various values of the attributes of each descriptor. This information as well as the child's profile are stored in a data server.

Figure 4 illustrates our example. Firstly, the user connects to the server, his profile will be loaded. The user is requested to specify the goals which wants to reach. Once this information has been entered, a target case is created. The target case is transmitted by a message to the server. The message is received by the decision agent. The role of this agent is to generate a adapted protocol to the current situation of the target case by using CBR.

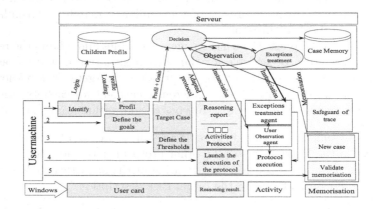

Fig. 4. Implementation

During the session the UOA and EMA assist the user. For each exception detected on the level of child's behavior by UOA, the EMA adapt the protocol by taking into account of the expert's directive.

7 Conclusion

This paper presents an architecture of interactive educational games. Our approach is applied to rehabilitation of children with autism. The application reflects significant characteristics of user-adapted interactions according to the perceived behavior. Moreover, an model was introduced. The model represents the child's profile, the expert's directives and the dynamics of their interactions.

The paper illustrated first the different robotic and software systems that exist for rehabilitation of children with autism. We propose to use agent-based systems in an educational way. The agents provide the capacity to interact with humans. It showed the observation and analyze of child's behavior in order to adapt the activities execution.

Experiments with our model have been presented. The obtained results by simulation are interesting and promising. However, more experiments are needed to validate the proposed models and architecture. Moreover, a validation of the system by experts are in current experimentation in the service of psychiatric of *La Rochelle* hospital. Future works include the dynamic generation of child's profile and the design of an agent that can request the proof verification in order to ensure the protocols coherence.

References

1. AURORA project, URL: http://www.aurora-project.com/ (last accessed 02/06/2005)
2. Billard, A., Play: Dreams and Imitation in Robota, Proc. AAAI Fall Symposium Socially Intelligent Agents - The Human in the Loop, AAAI Technical Report, AAAI Press, (2000).
3. Billard, A., Dautenhahn, K., Hayes, G.: Experiments on human-robot communication with Robota, an imitative learning and communicating doll robot, Proc. Socially Situated Intelligence Workshop, Zurich (1998).
4. Breazeal, C., Scassellati, B.: How to build robots that make friends and influence people, Proc. IROS99, Kyonjiu: Korea (1999).
5. Cañamero, L., Gaussier, P.: Emotion Understanding: Robots As Tools and Models. In J. Nadel and D. Muir (Eds.), Emotional Development: Recent research advances, Oxford University Press (2005).
6. Cognitive Systems. ReMind Developer's Reference Manual. Boston (1992).
7. Dautenhahn, K.: Design issues on interactive environments for children with autism, Proc 3rd Intl Conf. Disability, Virtual Reality & Assoc. Tech., Alghero, Italy (2000) 153-159.
8. Fabri, M., Moore, D.J.: The use of emotionally expressive avatars in Collaborative Virtual Environments, Proc of Symposium on Empathic Interaction with Synthetic Characters, held at Artificial Intelligence and Social Behaviour Convention 2005 (AISB 2005), University of Hertfordshire (2005).

9. Gibson, J.J.: The theory of affordances. R. Shaw and J. Bransford (eds.), Perceiving, Acting and Knowing. Hillsdale, NJ: Erlbaum. (1977).

10. Gibson, J.J.: The ecological approach to visual perception. Chapter 14: The theory of information pickup and its consequences, Boston: Houghton Miflin Co (1979) 238-263.

11. Grynszpan, O., Martin, J.C., Oudin, N.: Towards A Methodology For The Design Of Human-computer Interfaces For Persons With Autism. International Congress Autism-Europe. Lisboa (2003).

12. Guessoum, Z., Briot, J.P.: From active objects to autonomous agents. IEEE Concurrency, (1999)7(3), 68-76.

13. Guessoum, Z., Rejeb, L., Durand, R.: Using adaptive Multi-Agent Systems to Simulate Economic Models, AAMAS'04, ACM, New York City (2004) 68-76.

14. Johnson-laird, P.: Procedural semantics. Cognition, (1977) 189-214.

15. Kolodner, J.: Case-based reasoning. Morgan Kaufmann Pub. (1993).

16. Montemayor, J., Physical programming: tools for kindergarten children to author physical interactive environments. Doctoral dissertation, department of computer science, University of Maryland, USA (2003).

17. Parsons, S.: Social Conventions In Virtual Environments: Investigating Understanding Of Personal Space Amongst People With Autistic Spectrum Disorders. Robotic & Virtual Interactive Systems in Autism Therapy, Hatfield, U.K (2001).

18. Robins, B., Dautenhahn, K., te Boekhorst, R., Billard, A.: Effects of repeated exposure of a humanoid robot on children with autism. In S. Keates, J. Clarkson, P. Langdon and P. Robinson (eds), Designing a More Inclusive World. London: Springer-Verlag (2004) 225-236.

19. Schank., R.C.: Dynamic Memory: a Theory of Reminding and Learning in Computers and People. Cambridge University Press (1982).

20. Souchon, F., Urtado, C., Vauttier, S., Dony, C.: Exception handling in component-based systems: a first study, In ECOOP'03 international conference (2003).

21. Watson, I., Marir, F.: Case-Based Reasoning: A Review. The Knowledge Engineering Review, (1994) 327-354.

22. Wittgenstein, L.: The philosophical investigations. New York: Macmillan, (1953).

23. Woods, W.: Procedural semantics as a theory of meaning. E. of discourse understanding, (1981).

User Experiences with a Virtual Swimming Interface Exhibit

Sidney Fels[1,2], Steve Yohanan[1], Sachiyo Takahashi[2], Yuichiro Kinoshita[1],
Kenji Funahashi[1], Yasufumi Takama[1], and Grace Tzu-Pei Chen[1]

[1] Human Communication Technologies Laboratory, Department of Electrical
and Computer Engineering, University of British Columbia, Vancouver, BC, Canada
[2] Media and Graphics Interdisciplinary Centre (MAGIC),
University of British Columbia, Vancouver, BC, Canada
ssfels@ece.ubc.ca, stevey@cs.ubc.ca, taksaci@telus.net,
kino@spice.cs.ritsumei.ac.jp, kenji@center.nitech.ac.jp,
yasufumi@yamato.eeyo.jp, tzupei@ece.ubc.ca

Abstract. We created an exhibit based on a new locomotion interface for
swimming in a virtual reality ocean environment as part of our *Swimming
Across the Pacific* art project. In our exhibit we suspend the swimmer using a
hand gliding and leg harness with pulleys and ropes in an 8ft-cubic swimming
apparatus. The virtual reality ocean world has sky, sea waves, splashes, ocean
floor and an avatar representing the swimmer who wears a tracked head-
mounted display so he can watch himself swim. The audience sees the
swimmer hanging in the apparatus overlaid on a video projection of his ocean
swimming avatar. The avatar mimics the real swimmer's movements sensed by
eight magnetic position trackers attached to the swimmer. Over 500 people
tried swimming and thousands watched during two exhibitions. We report our
observations of swimmers and audiences engaged in and enjoying the
experience leading us to identify design strategies for interactive exhibitions.

1 Introduction

Our artwork, *Swimming Across the
Pacific*, takes inspiration from the
performance art piece "Swimming
Across the Atlantic" [15]. It was
performed by the artist, Alzek Misheff,
who accomplished the artistic endeavour
by swimming in the pool of the ocean
liner, Queen Elizabeth II, traveling from
South Hampton to New York as a
comment on contemporary art at the
time. In *Swimming Across the Pacific*,
we plan to swim across the Pacific
Ocean, from Los Angeles to Tokyo, in
an airplane to transform it into a
"bubble" containing a media arts festival

Fig. 1. Swimmer in swimming apparatus

F. Kishino et al. (Eds.): ICEC 2005, LNCS 3711, pp. 433–444, 2005.

for the same purpose. To do this we developed our virtual swimming locomotion interface as shown in Figure 1 so we can swim virtually rather than in real water as part of the transformation symbolism. While this swimming device is originally designed for placing in an airplane, anyone can try it to swim and enjoy the virtual water. Thus, as one step in the artwork, we designed and built an interactive installation around the virtual swimming apparatus.

We exhibited our work at the exhibitions of the 2004 International Conference on Special Interest Group on Graphics and Interaction (Siggraph'04, Los Angeles, USA) and Imagina'05 (Monte Carlo, Monaco). These provided us valuable opportunities to observe and evaluate how well our design decisions worked. During the exhibits, hundreds of people enjoyed the experience of swimming. Thousands of audience members also enjoyed watching swimmers in the exhibit. Of particular significance is that, on one hand, the virtual swimming device may be seen technically as a novel computer input device for users to interact through swimming motions with a virtual environment. On the other hand, through careful design of the user experience, we transformed the computer interface into a successful *swimming experience* exhibit.

In designing the actual device, we considered the swimmer as the user. However, in designing the exhibit, we considered three additional user types to make a successful and enjoyable experience for a wider audience. The additional three users types are the swimmer within a group of swimmers, the attendant and the audience. Our main observations during the exhibition validated our design decision to balance the fidelity of all the components. We found that amateur swimmers were more critical than novices or expert swimmers. As well, we realized that the attendants helping people at the exhibit played multiple roles. This required us to build the device and exhibit to allow attendants' full attention to be on the audience and participants rather than the system.

We begin our discussion with related work and the technical design of the novel swimming apparatus that is at the core of the exhibit. Next we describe the exhibit design itself and the workflow of the attendants. Finally, we describe the observations we made during the exhibitions.

2 Related Work on Locomotion Interfaces

"Locomotion interfaces" such as virtual walking, virtual hang-gliding, our swimming apparatus and others, are closely tied to virtual reality (VR). In an artificial reality, where the users have a presence in a 3D space and use their bodies as natural input devices, development of locomotion interfaces is vital for immersive experiences. Christensen et al. say, "Locomotion interfaces are energy-extractive interfaces to virtual environments and fill needs that are not met by conventional position-tracking approaches or whole-body motion platforms." [6] Some VR researchers particularly advocate the development of locomotion interfaces because with their improvement come many more unforeseen applications [7]. Locomotion interfaces have been created for walking and biking. Walking interfaces include the Sarcos Treadport [6, 10], CirculaFloor [11]. TorusTreadmill [12] and GaitMaster [13]. Examples of virtual reality bicycling systems are the Peloton Bicycling Simulator [5] and Trike [1].

While not requiring direct human locomotion behaviours, high-end flight simulators have been used in military and pilot training schools for a long time. Commercial systems using variations of flight simulators include Dreamality's DreamGlider, JetPack, and SkyExplorer, and HumphreyII [3] that includes force-feedback. Much like our swimming apparatus, HumphreyII places the user in a prone position; however, we argue that a flying interface is not a locomotion interface, as people do not normally fly by their own energy.

Virtual swimming offers some unique advantages over other forms of VR and locomotion interfaces. In comparison to flying interfaces such as HumphreyII, most people have experience swimming in water, whereas flying in air is not a common experience. Thus, we expect people to understand and more easily explore our type of interface when moving in a virtual world. Bicycle and treadmill interfaces share this property as well. However, with swimming there are many styles and personal techniques that provide means for people to develop complex behaviours and expertise with the apparatus. This leads to an increase in intimacy with the device [9], providing more satisfaction and enjoyment than may be possible with typical flying, bicycling and walking interfaces.

Examples of other early attempts at aquatic interfaces include Fraunhofer's Aquacave, which allows virtual interaction with cartoon fish characters, and Virtual Diver [4], which is used for artificial reef study. Aquacave used a paragliding harness and pulley system to suspend the diver in a CAVE, wherein a virtual underwater environment is displayed. Virtual Diver explores methods of mapping photographs of artificial reefs onto a 3D reef model, which is then explored using a 3D joystick. Other undersea VR marine navigation and positioning technologies can be found in [14]. In these examples the focus is on the underwater environment itself, rather than on a locomotion interface based on surface swimming that we explore.

One unique aspect of our swimming system is that it occurs at the surface of the water. In addition to our mechanical system, we have implemented dynamic waves and splash action so that the participant experiences a water surface environment while swimming. Though our scenery is intentionally simplistic as shown in Figure 2, it is a relatively straightforward effort to improve realism using caustics, fog effects and textures to achieve a different representation of sea, sky, sun and the swimmer's avatar.

While not a locomotion interface, the Aladdin system [17] is another VR-based exhibit using a magic carpet metaphor for flying around a virtual environment. Observations made during our exhibit shared some of the same ones as in Aladdin such as: the experience is more important than the technology, people like exploring and the importance of quick throughput. However, some of the observations they

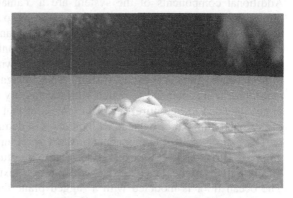

Fig. 2. Avatar in virtual Pacific Ocean

had contradict ours. Specifically, participants did not need a goal and were content with just swimming, the background story was not so important for participants and users did turn their heads constantly in yaw and pitch. We suspect the directness and affordances of the locomotion interface for swimming and the attendants interaction with the participants plays a key role in explaining the differences as discussed below.

3   Building the Virtual Swimming Device

Our current design for the swimmer consists of a combination of mechanical hardware, computer hardware and software [8]. The swimming apparatus (Figure 1) is an 8ft x 8ft x 8ft wooden structure with horizontal beams on top and bottom. The user is supported in a prone position at the shoulders and hips by running static cords through pulleys mounted on the beams and attaching the cords to the harness with carabineers. One major design goal is to give the user a sense of swimming, but not necessarily a sense of being in water. The mechanics allow the user generous freedom of motion coupled with a feeling of resistance and buoyancy. The rope-pulley system for the legs is designed to conform to several frontal swimming styles including: crawl, breaststroke, butterfly and dog paddle. Currently, there are no mechanisms designed for counterbalancing or providing feedback to the arms.

The computer hardware components of the installation were: a 1.5 GHz dual-processor Xeon Dell computer system, an NVidia Quadro4 TwinView graphics card, a video projector, two 21" LCD video monitors, a Kaiser Proview XL50 head-mounted display (HMD), two Polhemus Fastraks with 4 sensors each, and an interactive audio system. The control Tcl/tk based GUI runs on either the base computer or a remote laptop. One monitor displays a side view of the avatar for the attendants, and the other shows the swimmer's HMD view that alternates between first- and third-person perspectives. We also use rear video projection onto a screen attached to the wooden structure to show the side view to the audience as shown in Figure 1. Polhemus Fastrak sensors tracked the movement of the swimmer's head, arms, torso and legs and are attached firmly with adjustable Velcro™ straps. All the ropes and sensors cables are routed above and behind the swimmer to minimize interference.   An Apple G4 PowerBook controls the interactive audio system. Additional components of the system are a Yamaha EX5R tone generator, a CD player, and a mixing console. The result is output to a pair of powered speakers.

The virtual ocean environment includes visual and audio elements. The computer graphics are implemented in C using OpenGL running on a Debian Linux machine. Typical imagery from the graphic system is shown in Figure 2. The audio system utilizes Pure Data [19] and MIDI. The design considerations for the ocean environment are intended to match with the fidelity of the mechanical system, which is not intended to be entirely realistic. We feel that having any major component of the system being out of balance with others will detract from the user experience.

The main graphical components of the virtual environment are a sky hemisphere, an ocean surface plane, an ocean floor plane, a virtual avatar and various lighting for different times of the day. The sky hemisphere is texture-mapped with moving clouds. The ocean floor is modeled with a rugged plane that is texture-mapped with rocks. Both planes are animated to move past the virtual avatar when the user swims forward; the faster the participant swims the faster the avatar moves. As well, we simulate interactive waves and splashes on the ocean surface. The virtual avatar is a model of a gender-neutral human figure. We also created the sense of time passage through providing sunrise, daytime, sunset and nighttime by moving the sky and effects of lighting. For both aesthetic and conceptual reasons, we wanted different times of the day in order to alter the sense of reality and timing in the virtual world. Views of the virtual ocean environment are displayed to the swimmer through the HMD and alternate between first- and third-person perspectives. We provide interactive splashing sounds corresponding to the swimmer's movements for each arm and leg. We also have a continuous seaside ambient sound track that is mixed in from a CD.

The control console GUI, written in tcl/tk, is used for control and automation of the installation. Some parameters that may be manipulated are calibration of sensor data for individual swimmers, control and automation of lighting, and perspectives of the virtual environment as seen by the swimmer and audience.

4   Creating the Swimming Exhibition

Significant effort was required to shift our design from a stand-alone swimming apparatus to one that we displayed at the ACM Siggraph'04 Emerging Technologies exhibition and Imagina'05. Our major change was to focus not only on the experience of the individual within the apparatus, but also examine the other users that would be in an exhibit setting: the swimmer within a group of swimmers, the attendant and the audience. We will first address our overall constraints for the exhibit, and then we will discuss the more detailed design decision related to the stage, the cumulative experience of all participants, and attendant workflow. Of particular concern was maintaining a balance among all the components of the virtual environment, as well as focus on facilitating the attendants' workflow within the exhibit.

Overall Constraints
We based our design decisions on four main constraints: artistic, computational, robustness, and adaptability.

Artistically, we made a conscious decision not to have the virtual world look too real to match the fidelity of the rest of the system. We also put effort into making the swimmer feel like they were floating and swimming in water-like conditions. To match the other components, sound and lighting were not 100% realistic. The critical elements were to maintain balance between all the modalities, whether virtual or real. Our artistic constraints motivated implementing dynamic lighting and multiple viewing perspectives for both the swimmer and audience.

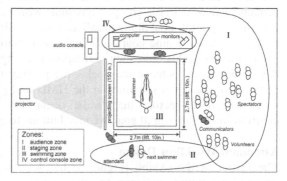

Fig. 3. Exhibit layout

We focus on aspects we consider most important to the overall experience as we have limited computational resources. We currently are not concerned with providing game-like elements or other extraneous graphics elements such as fish or ships. On the other hand, we wish the swimmer to have an engaging experience at the surface of the water. For this reason, we concentrate on synchronizing the movement of the real swimmer with the virtual avatar and having splashes and waves. We do not support diving under the water.

The Stage Design
The overall visual aspects and staging design of the swimming cage are for the audience. The layout of the swimming space is shown in Figure 3. In an attempt to attract members of the public, we made the design of the environment around the exhibit as pleasing as possible. For example, to enhance the visual aspects of the exhibit the cage is painted blue and white, there are blue spotlights and the uniforms of the attendants are coordinated. To create the feel of an open ocean space, we play a continuous ambient seaside soundtrack. We anticipated that the novel look of our apparatus coupled with the carefully designed spatial character of the exhibit and the visual and audio effect are critical to attracting the audience as noted in [2].

Both the front and sides of the installation are designed to give the audience (Zone I) an unobstructed view of the swimmer in the apparatus (Zone III). The swimmer is positioned such that their physical body is suspended in front of a rear-projected view of the avatar seen from the side pointing in the same direction as the swimmer (Figure 1). In addition, one LCD monitor (Zone IV, right-hand monitor) was placed so that audience members could see the same view as the swimmer's HMD. This allowed the participant and audience to share the swimming experience; also noted by Borchers to be a good design strategy. Posters and brochures are positioned such that they do not occlude the swimmer, but are in areas where audience members are standing.

We decided not to provide a clearly marked area for audience members waiting to try the apparatus in order to avoid making the installation appear like a theme park ride as well as avoid separating these two user groups. Instead, we wanted to create an inviting environment for both these user groups and at the same time not make a strong delineation between the two.

Cumulative Experience Design
We constructed the storyline of the experience so that individual swimmers were actually part of a larger group. Consistent with the theme of *Swimming Across the Pacific,* the overall goal of the installation was to simulate swimming across the ocean over the course of nine hours. Though each swimmer was only in the apparatus a small fraction of this time, their participation, along with all the other swimmers each day, added up to achieve the goal. We portray this by displaying a "flight map" before and after each swimmer in the HMD and projection to show progress of the swimmers flying across the Pacific ocean. In addition, to commemorate their contribution to the overall goal, we give buttons to each swimmer to wear.

Attendant Workflow Design
The layout of the exhibit (Figure 3) has four zones that the attendants navigate: staging, swimming, audience and the control console. The staging area is where

attendants move volunteers in and out of the exhibit (Zone II). Participants swim in the wooden structure in the swimming zone. We located the computers and control GUI in the control console zone (Zone IV). These zones intentionally overlapped to allow attendants to work in multiple areas. The attendants in the staging area or those working at the control console could also easily provide assistance with the swimming apparatus. This helped reduce the number of attendants and allowed them to concentrate on the area that needed the most attention at the time.

We developed a workflow to facilitate the transition from an audience member to swimmer as shown in Figure 4. The workflow begins by an audience member volunteering to try the apparatus (a). She is then led to the staging area where she is fitted into the harness while the current swimmer is still in the apparatus (b). When the current swimmer completes his swim and returns to the staging area, she would be clipped into the swimming structure (c). With the help of the attendants, she leans over until the ropes hold her in a prone position. An attendant fits the HMD on her.

Attendants attach the eight magnetic sensors and strap her feet into the leg pulley system (Figure 3). When she is ready, one attendant changes the flight map in the swimmer view with a GUI button and another provides her some basic instructions. She swims until she is done (d). Once done, one attendant switches the display back to a flight map scene and others help her get out of the swimming apparatus (e). She moves to the staging zone and is helped out of her harness and receives a button (f).

Fig. 4. Workflow to get in and out of apparatus

There were several design considerations for getting the swimmer into the cage. The HMD had to be adjustable, to fit the varied head sizes of the participants. In addition, we had to add a chinstrap to hold the HMD in place because the swimmers head would be facing downward. Since the participant was to be suspended horizontally, safety was a major concern. We ensured that the floor around the apparatus was free from obstructions such as cabling and equipment. We also provided a stepstool to aid the swimmer when being clipped into and out of the apparatus. Finally, we had two harnesses to improve throughput.

5   Users' Perspectives and Observations

Over a five-day period we exhibited the swimming apparatus at ACM SIGGRAPH'04 in the Emerging Technologies exhibit and for four days during Imagina'05. We had four to six attendants helping and observing the experiences of the participants involved while they interacted with the swimmers getting them into and out of the apparatus. We did minimal video recording and did not give participants/audience members written questionnaires to reflect on the experience during Siggraph. At Imagina'05, we distributed questionnaires and made video recordings.

At Siggraph, approximately 400 people (including about 10 children) tried the swimming device, and there were thousands of people who watched. The people who tried swimming appeared equally distributed across gender with a slight male bias. We did not notice any race bias given the demographics of the event. More often than not, audience members volunteered to swim; however, the attendants would occasionally go into the audience to solicit swimmers. Interestingly, attendants did not have success in predicting who would and who would not try swimming based on appearances.

We had 104 participants fill out questionnaires at Imagina'05 who were predominantly male (86 vs. 20) between 20 and 29 (21 under 20 years, 55 between 20 and 29 years, 23 between 30 and 39 years, 4 between 40 and 49 years and one person over 60 year old). Most were intermediate level swimmers (9 never had been swimming, 21 novices, 68 intermediate and 6 experts). Most had never tried a VR experience (78 vs. 26).

Overall, swimmers had a wonderful, engaging and enjoyable time swimming, and members of the audience had fun watching. The main comment we received is, "It was GREAT!" The main criticism we received is that people would like to have fish in the scene and better graphics. Some people commented that they preferred the third person view and/or would like to have control over the camera angle as seen in the HMD. We also had comments from people who wanted more feedback for the arms.

We consider there to be four different distinct user categories that had unique experiences with the exhibit: individual swimmer, swimmer within a group of swimmers, attendant and audience. Our design had significant impact on the way each type of user interacted and experienced the exhibit.

Individual Swimmer as User
Based on the variety of participants, we are able to group them along two dimensions that appeared to influence their experience: skill level and body size. Two additional factors in the experience were related to the HMD and user control.

We categorize each participant's swimming skill level into three types: novice, amateur, and expert. We assumed that expert swimmers would not enjoy the experience as much as participants in lower skill levels due to the low fidelity of the system. However, based on comments from the participants at Siggraph'04, what we observed was that novice swimmers and expert swimmers appeared to derive a higher amount of pleasure from the experience than amateur swimmers. Quantitatively, from our Imagina'05 questionnaires, almost everyone enjoyed the experience (4.3 score (std. dev 0.8) where 1 = strongly disagree and 5 = strongly agree, to "I enjoyed the experience" and 4.4 score (std. dev 0.8) to "I would recommend other people try it") with no obvious trends based on sex, age, skill or VR experience.

We hypothesize that novice swimmers seemed to enjoy the experience as it gave them the sensation of swimming but they were not hampered by an inability or fear of swimming. They were able to swim using simple strokes, or simply float and enjoy the environment. Expert swimmers were originally expected to be overly critical of the environment since it does not present a realistic physical or visual swimming environment. What we observed, however, was that these swimmers quickly moved past the fidelity issues and concentrated heavily on their body. It appeared that the expert swimmers were using the device to explore the way their body moves through space. In some cases, trying movements typical of swimming, while other times they appeared to be trying different motions, ones that might not be possible in water, to feel and see the results. Most expert swimmers, however, did comment that the lack of resistance on the arms is one factor that they thought detracted from the experience. The lack of feeling liquid on skin was not reported as detracting from the experience from any of the swimmers. We suspect that amateur swimmers concentrated on the visual environment and indicated verbally as well as on the questionnaires. Though many enjoyed the experience, this category of swimmers seemed to be most critical of the fact that the installation did not provide a realistic environment.

One aspect that was common to all swimmers dealt with the coupling between the movements of the swimmer and the avatar. We had two main observations: first, that the movements must look the same, and second, the approximately 100msec of latency between movements was not a significant issue. Swimmers rarely mentioned the lag in the system. We believe that the fluid nature of the environment and the fact that the swimmer only had relative position cues to gauge where they were, mitigated the effect of lag.

People with smaller bodies appeared to have a different experience than those with larger bodies, probably due to using a one-size-fits-all harness.

Head-Mounted Display Issues
Many swimmers commented that they enjoyed the third-person view in the HMD. Since the swimming apparatus affords full-body motion, it is thought that full-body perspectives helped the user maintain a stronger connection between their physical movements and those of the avatar within the virtual environment; seeing the avatar's arms, legs, head and torso moving synchronously with theirs. This connection enhances intimacy with the device [9]. One difficulty, though, was that the HMD sometimes slipped during swimming. Some users suggested substituting a wrap-around display or simply a monitor placed in front of the swimmer rather than the HMD. Pierce et al. discuss other strategies to deal with HMD problems [18].

Swimmer Control
Perspective changes in the HMD were automated by means of the control GUI. Thus, the attendant did not have to concentrate on changing it; however, the view changes seemed to confuse some swimmers. The participant was unclear who was controlling the views. Some swimmers originally thought they were able to change it even though it was just coincidence that the view changed. This suggests a user difficulty in both execution and evaluation of the interface [16]. Similarly, the swimmer did not directly control when the experience started or stopped. Rather, it required an attendant (out of the swimmer's view) to switch between the view of the flight map and the virtual ocean environment. It was observed that participants were also confused by this ambiguity.

Swimmer in a Group of Swimmers as User
The swimmer was also part of a second user group, that of a group of swimmers collectively swimming across the Pacific Ocean. Our hope was to provide swimmers

with a broader experience in the exhibit than just using a virtual reality device. However, we observed that participants were confused by the concept of collectively swimming across the Pacific Ocean. Our use of a "flight map over the ocean", to convey the idea was confusing. In addition, many users were disappointed to find that they were not swimming across the Pacific Ocean themselves, in compressed time. Quantitatively, during Imagina'05, participants judged with a score of 3.5 (std. dev = 1.0) suggestion they are between neutral and agree with being part of the team enhanced the experience. Thus, our solution to have the attendant provide the swimmer with additional instructions during the exhibit was not so effective.

Attendant as User
The primary job of the attendants is to help volunteers get into and out of the swimming apparatus according to the workflow as described in the *Attendant Workflow* section. Essentially, they were a main part of the interface between the system and the participants and audience. As such, they played three main roles during the exhibit: *system user*, *performer* and *mediator*. The attendants scored 4.8 out of 5 (std. dev. 0.66) by Imagina'05 participants when asked if they thought the attendants were helpful.

For the attendant as *system user*, we provided a robust and flexible design of our system for attendants to use. The control GUI enabled the attendants to adjust the system's parameters as needed. Initial parameters were set with only occasional adjustments afterwards, such as when an audience member or swimmer requested it. The simplicity of this interaction allowed the attendants to spend minimal time attending to the system and maximum time attending to the people.

By being a *performer* for the audience the attendants provide a theatrical and entertaining context to the audience to entice them to try it. Once an audience member agrees to become a participant, the theatrical context provides the mechanism to establish the attendant as a *mediator* that can be trusted. Trust is important since the *mediator* and participant need to have intimate interactions, so that the participant can fully enjoy the experience and feel safe. Some design elements support the role of *performer* such as a special bright T-shirt with a logo that all attendants wear. The T-shirts functioned as a uniform and costume to maintain the attendant's role as *performer*.

We observed the attendants, as *mediators*, bridged the gaps in understanding between the complex layers of the system such as the swimming gear, the VR environment, the different perspectives, and the artistic context. The mediation allows smooth human-computer interaction for the participants. *Mediators* give life to the installation beyond the technical aspects and make it accessible to the participants. As *mediators*, the attendants contextualized system deficiencies in cases where we encountered minor problems during the exhibit. Our design decision to use two harnesses influenced how the participant and the attendant related to each other. While waiting for the current swimmer, the attendant helped the participant get their gear on and continued to talk while waiting. The act of working together initiated contact that facilitated a bond that continued to grow while they waited together.

Mediators interact with participants at two levels: verbal and tactile. *Mediators* talk to the participants to help them putting on gear, explaining what he is seeing or offering support to make him feel safe when he had to place his trust in the equipment to hold him up. They also communicate and entertain participants to make them feel comfortable in swimming experience. We anticipated this aspect in our design.

We observed another important aspect of the *mediator's* interaction: **touch**. Attendants had to touch participants regularly in the staging zone and the swimming zone (Figure 3). Touching made participants feel safe and complemented the verbal instructions. We found participants responded very positively to the direct physical experience of being touched by the attendants, allowing them to enjoy the experience of being in the swimming apparatus. We believe that the theatrical context of the exhibit allowed attendants to touch people in potentially sensitive areas that could have had quite negative consequences in other contexts. However, since the response was positive, our observations suggest that touch is effective in mediating the experience in interactive installations that have complex layers of interaction. We may only hypothesize in other mediated activities such as bungee jumping and skydiving that touch plays a similar role.

Audience as User

We observed several different roles audience members played: volunteers, communicators, and spectators. *Volunteers* are audience members who wish to participant in the exhibit and try the swimming apparatus. They often interact with the current swimmer verbally as well as ask the attendant detailed questions while waiting. *Communicators*, though not interested in swimming, are the audience members who are interested in understanding the contents of the installation. They ask questions and interact with the attendants and even the swimmer. We observed that *communicators* are particularly interested in what the swimmer is seeing in the HMD. They like to follow the swimmer's experience and they often interact with swimmer verbally; encouraging them, cheering them and joking with them. *Communicators* navigate the swimmer zone and audience zone spontaneously. *Spectators*, typically stand around the swimming apparatus watching and taking photos of the swimmer but generally do not talk to the attendants. For them, the poster and brochure are useful sources of information. Our design accommodates all the types of audience members, providing information, amusement and enjoyment for everyone.

6 Summary

We were very pleased that so many people enjoyed the *Swimming Across the Pacific* exhibit at ACM SIGGRAPH'04 and Imagina'05. This result validates that our main design directions for this novel virtual swimming exhibit were correct. We made three contributions: first, we created a successful swimming experience exhibit based on a VR swimming apparatus that was enjoyed by participants and audience members; second, we identified multiple roles of the attendant to engage and enhance the participant and audience experience; and third, we developed an exhibit-oriented artistic context for the swimming apparatus. Thus, we believe that the approaches we use led to an enjoyable experience for all users informing the design of similar exhibitions that have complex interaction with technology.

Acknowledgements. We received funding from: ATR MI&C, NSERC, Polhemus Inc., Kaiser Electro-Optics Inc., MAGIC, and the Dept. of ECE at UBC. We thank: A. Gadd, A. Misheff, F. Vogt, D. Dawson, D. Chu Chong, L. Jones, the HCT lab and anonymous reviewers for their contributions.

References

1. Allison, R. S., Harris, L. R., Jenkin, M., Pintilie, G., Redlick, F., and Zikovitz, D. C., "First steps with a rideable computer", *In Proc 2nd IEEE Conf. on VR*, 2000, 119-175.
2. Borchers, J., A Pattern Approach to Interaction Design, Wiley & Sons, 2001.
3. Bruner, M., Buttner, M., Degen, S., Feldler, S., Freudling, P., Jalsovec, A., Lindinger, C., Ptzelberger, W., Weingrtner, M., and Zepetzauer, M., 2003. HumphreyII in Ars Electronica Futurelab. http://www.aec.at/en/center/project.asp?iProjectID=12280. (Feb 1, 2004).
4. Buffa, M., Diard, F., Persson, M., and Sander, P. 1995. "The Virtual Diver, an architectural `swim-around' system incorporating real imagery", In Workshop Proc Computer Graphics Technology for the Exploration of the Sea, CES'95, 1995.
5. Carraro, G. U., Cortes, M., Edmark, J. T., and Ensor, J., "The Peloton bicycling simulator", In Proc 3rd Symp on VRML, ACM Press (1998), New York, SIGGRAPH, 63–70.
6. Christensen, R., Hollerbach, J. M., Xu, Y., and Meek, S., "Inertial force feedback for the Treadport locomotion interface", In Presence: Teleoperators and Virtual Environments, 2000, vol. 9, 1–4. .
7. Durlach, N. I., and Mavor, A. S., (Eds.) Virtual Reality: Scientific and Technological Challenges, National Academy Press, Washington, D. C., 1994.
8. Fels, S., Yohanan, S., Takahashi, S., Kinoshita, Y., Funahashi, K., Takama, Y., and Chen, G., Swimming Across the Pacific: A VR Swimming Interface, Computer Graphics and Applications, Vol. 25, No. 1, pp. 24-31, 2005.
9. Fels, S., Designing for Intimacy: Creating New Interfaces for Musical Expression, Proceedings of the IEEE, Vol. 92, No. 4, 2004, pp. 672-685.
10. Hollerbach, J. M., Xu, Y., Christensen, R., and Jacobsen, S. C., "Design specifications for the second generation SarcosTreadport locomotion interface", In Proc of ASME Dynamic Systems and Control Division, vol. 69, 2000, 1293–1298.
11. Iwata, H., Yano, H., Fukushima, H., Noma, H., "CirculaFloor", IEEE Computer Graphics and Applications, vol. 25, No. 1, pp. 64 – 67, 2005.
12. Iwata, H., "Walking About Virtual Environments on an Infinite Floor", Proceedings of IEEE Virtual Reality, 286-298, 1999.
13. Iwata, H., Yano, H., and Nakaizumi, F., "Gait Master: A Versatile Locomotion Interface for Uneven Virtual Terrain," Virtual Reality (VR'01), p. 131, 2001
14. Jones, D. Case studies in navigation and positioning. Underwater Magazine, 1999.
15. Misheff, A., Swimming Across the Atlantic, Ciesse Piumini, Milano, 1982.
16. Norman, D., The Psychology of Everyday Things, Basic Books Inc. New York, 1988.
17. Paush, R., Snoddy, J., Taylor, R., Watson, S., Haseltine, Disney's Aladdin: first steps toward storytelling in virtual reality, Proc. of ACM SIGGRAPH'96, pp. 193-203, 1996.
18. Pierce, J., Paush, R., Sturgill, C., Christiansen, K., Designing a Successful HMD-Based Experience, Presence: Teleoperators and VE, 8(4), pp. 469-473, 1999.
19. Puckette, M., "Pure Data: another integrated computer music environment", Proc. 2nd Intercollege Comp. Music Concerts, Tachikawa,1996, pp. 37-41.

Toward Web Information Integration
on 3D Virtual Space

Yasuhiko Kitamura[1], Noriko Nagata[1], Masataka Ueno[1],
and Makoto Nagamune[2]

[1] Department of Informatics, Kwansei Gakuin University, Japan
{ykitamura, nagata, mueno}@ksc.kwansei.ac.jp
[2] Graduate School of Informatics, Kyoto University, Japan
nagamune@db.soc.i.kyoto-u.ac.jp

Abstract. We report an implementation of GeneSys, which is a Web information integration system on 3D virtual space. We have built Kwansei Gakuin Kobe
Sanda Campus as a virtual space called VKSC in which character agents navigate
a user. VKSC reflects the Web information concerning weather, school calendar,
and laboratories in the campus and the behaviour of agents changes depending on
the information. Conventional Web systems mainly aim at providing information
and knowledge to users, but GeneSys can additionally provide virtual experiences
to users.

1 Introduction

Character agents [6], which are also called life-like characters [8], believable agents [1],
or embodied conversational agents (ECA) [2], provide a natural and interactive interface
between computers and human users by incorporating conversational communication
technique in the interface. They become more attractive and entertaining by adding
emotional aspects to them.

A number of commercial products have been developed by Microsoft [1], Extempo [2],
Haptek [3], Artificial Life [4], and so on. These agents still need to be improved because
of their limited communication skills, but have a potential to be an ultimate interface
between computers and human users. For example, when we get in trouble to use a
computer or a software, the easiest way to fix the problem is just to ask our colleague
who knows the system well or to make a phone call to a support center of the system
developer. Unfortunately, such colleague or center is often unavailable or busy, so we
have to take an alternative way to consult Web sites that contain FAQs about the system,
but actually we often have another problem to find a right answer in the Web sites. If a
character agent is available on the Web sites and can answer our questions appropriately
through dialogue on behalf a staff of the support center, it must be very helpful and
appreciated.

---

[1] http://www.microsoft.com/msagent/
[2] http://www.extempo.com/
[3] http://www.haptek.com/
[4] http://www.artificial-life.com/

F. Kishino et al. (Eds.): ICEC 2005, LNCS 3711, pp. 445–455, 2005.
© IFIP International Federation for Information Processing 2005

We have been working on character agents as a Web interface [6,5,4]. Venus and Mars [4] is a cooking recipe search engine which employs multiple character agents. Each agent is an expert on a specific domain such as cooking recipes, health, and local specialities, respectively. These agents collaborate to answer a question such as "let me know a good recipe for recovering from cold. " This question can not be answered by a single agent because that requires both knowledge of cocking recipes and health. Recommendation Battlers [5] is a restaurant recommendation system employing two character agents. Each agent collects restaurant information from an individual Web site, and recommends restaurants to a user competing with another agent. These agents can be called presentation agents and related works have been done in DFKI [9].

In the previous applications, character agents are just attached to a Web browser, so they can move up, down, right, and left only and their actions are limited in the two dimensional space. In this paper, we extend the world where agents live from two dimensional to three dimensional space and propose a Web information integration scheme on the 3D virtual space.

2   Web Information Integration on 3D Virtual Space

In this paper, we provide a three dimensional virtual space which is tightly connected to the Web information concerning the virtual space. Character agents in the virtual space can have not only interactions through conversations with a user but also a more advanced form of interactions through taking actions in the space.

We can utilize a virtual space as a platform to integrate Web information which is distributed physically and logically. For example, in a university campus, there are many departments, and there are a number of laboratories in each department. Many of laboratories have their own Web pages, but the pages reside in an individual Web site and are maintained individually. Through a browser, it may be difficult to experience a fact that two laboratories are in the same campus. If we can integrate the Web pages related to the campus onto a 3D virtual space, it is easy for us to understand the geographical relation among the Web pages.

The 3D virtual space can be evolved by utilizing the information on the Web site. For example, by referring to the opening hours of a library that is available on the Web page, we can open and close the gate of the library on the 3D virtual space according to the time. This makes the virtual space more realistic.

Character agents take an important role as guides who navigate a user in the virtual space recommending the related Web information. For example, when the user wants to know the way from the main entrance of the campus to a laboratory which he/she wants to visit, an agent navigates the user in the virtual space. In addition, the agent recommends the related Web information, in which the user may show interest, encountered on the way to the destination.

Of course, the user can walk around the virtual space freely without character agents. He/she can get access to various information linked to the Web and can encounter various guide agents. This framework provides virtual experiences to users based on the Web information.

3   GeneSys

We are developing a system called GeneSys (world Generating System) which is a prototype to embody Web information integration on a 3D virtual space. As shown in Figure 1, we classify elements in the virtual space into a background, objects, and agents. The background and objects are static elements which do not act autonomously by themselves. On the other hand, agents are active elements which act autonomously in the virtual space. Agents can influence objects but not the background. In other words, they can change the state of the objects but not that of the background.

As shown in Figure 2, Genesys integrates real world information such as Web information and the time onto a 3D virtual space. Web information is generally specified in HTML and a wrapper is to extract information from a Web page. Genesys takes Web information and the time information as its input and produces descriptions of the background, objects, and agents as its output. These descriptions are displayed on Free-Walk3 [7] which is a tool to browse a 3D virtual space and character agents. Figure 3

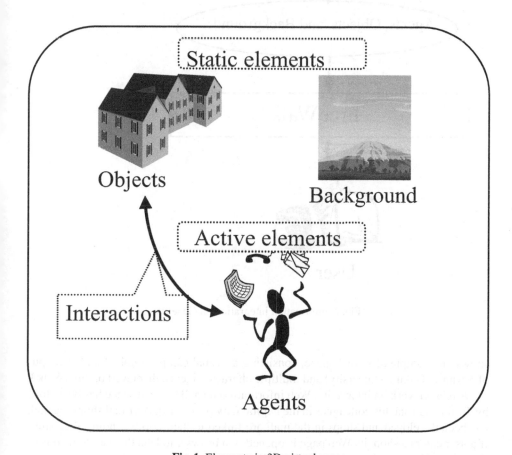

Fig. 1. Elements in 3D virtual space

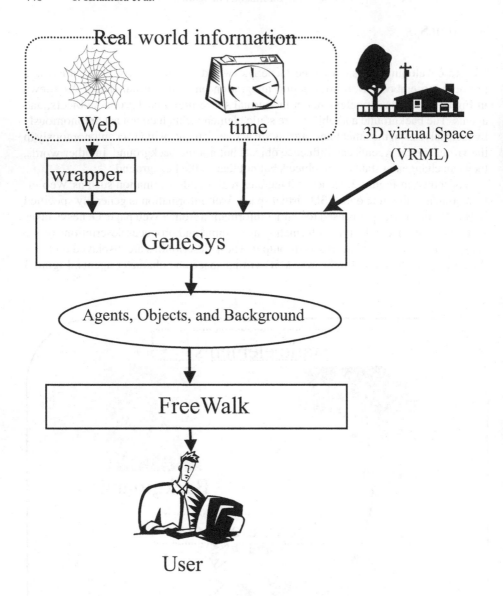

Fig. 2. Information integration on Genesys

shows an example of virtual space, consisting a virtual campus (Kobe Sanda Campus of Kwansei Gakuin University) and multiple character agents, displayed on FreeWalk3.

A related work on integrating Web information on a 3D virtual space has been done by Toru Ishida and his colleagues in the Digital City project [3]. A virtual shopping mall has been developed and shops in the mall are linked to their corresponding Web sites. If a user enters a shop, its Web page is opened in a browser to lead the user to its online shopping. The virtual space in the Digital City project is static and does not change.

On the other hand, our virtual space generated by GeneSys is dynamic and changes depending on the Web information.

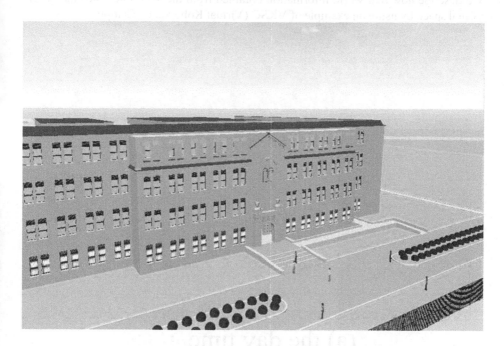

Fig. 3. Virtual campus and character agents on FreeWalk3

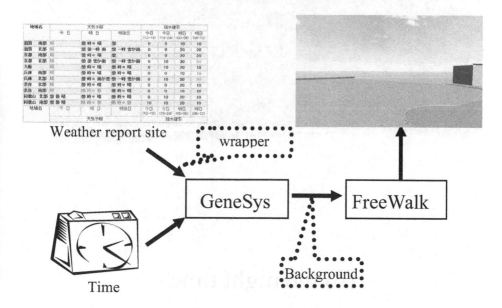

Fig. 4. Linking the Web and the background

4   Web Information Integration on GeneSys

We describe how real world information obtained from the Web integrates onto a 3D virtual space by using an example of VKSC (Virtual Kobe Sanda Campus).

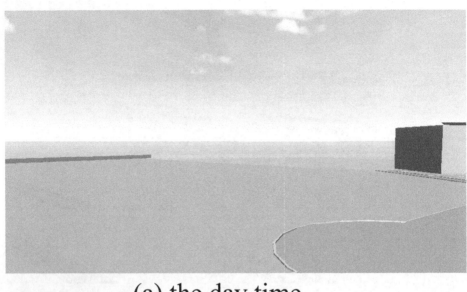

(a) the day time

(b) the night time

Fig. 5. Backgrounds in day time and night time

(a) gate closed   (b) gate open

Fig. 6. Linking the Web and objects

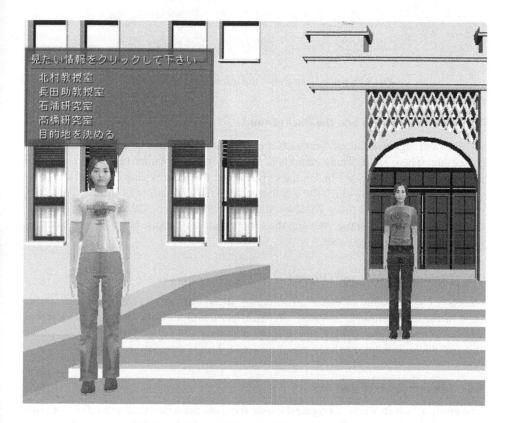

Fig. 7. A guide agent shows the list of laboratories

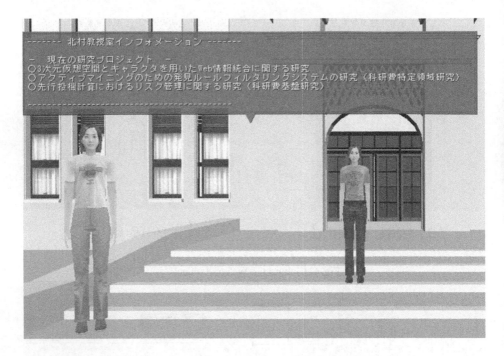

Fig. 8. A guide agent shows the information of laboratory

4.1 Linking the Web and the Background

As shown in Figure 4, Genesys collects the weather information of the southern Hyogo prefecture, where Kobe Sanda campus is located, from a weather report site[5] through a wrapper program. It also obtains the current time from the system clock. It then produces the background in which the weather reflects the Web information and the brightness reflects the current time. We show the difference between day and night of a fine day in Figure 4. Linking the Web and the time information to the background enhances the reality of the virtual space.

4.2 Linking the Web and Objects

GeneSys can make the calendar information in the university's Web site[6] reflect the state of the main entrance in VKSC. When it is on holidays, the entrance is closed as shown in Figure 6(a) and when not, it is open as shown in Figure 6 (b). Changes of the state of objects influence behaviours of character agents as mentioned later.

4.3 Linking the Web and Agents

The guide agents in VKSC navigate the user from the main entrance to a laboratory that the user wants to visit. At first, a guide in pink shows the list of laboratories (Figure 7).

---

[5] http://www.imoc.co.jp/yohou/yohou_4.htm

[6] http://www.kwansei.ac.jp/student/years_calender.html

Fig. 9. A guide agent navigates the user in VKSC

It then shows the information of the laboratory chosen by the user. (Figure 8). Finally, another guide agent in orange navigates the user from the main entrance to the laboratory chosen (Figure 9).

We can send instructions to agents through the laboratory's Web pages. For example, we insert the following description into the Web page.

```
<GeneSys:
owner = "Yasuhiko Kitamura"
affiliation = " Department of informatics"
goal = "Room 31"
information = "Our current research project includes Web
information integration on 3D virtual space."
:GeneSys>
```

In this description, owner specifies the owner of the Web page, affiliation specifies the affiliation of the owner, goal specifies the destination to which a guide agent navigate a user, and information specifies the laboratory information that the guide agents answer when asked by a user. The guide agents collect this description through a wrapper and utilize it for their navigation.

When a laboratory is chosen by the user, the guide agents show the attribute `information` and navigate the user to the place specified by the `goal` attribute.

We can easily update the description in the Web page and the agents change their behaviour depending on the change.

4.4   Interaction Between Objects and Agents

The guide agents take actions according to the state of objects. For example, when the main entrance is closed on holidays, the agents bypass the main entrance and enter through a sub entrance which is open even on holidays. To embody this function, a simple planner based on the shortest path algorithm is embedded in the guide agents.

5   Summary and Future Work

This paper proposes a framework where Web information distributed on the Internet is integrated on a 3D virtual space and introduces a prototype called GeneSys. Genesys collects Web information related to the virtual space and produces the background, objects, and agents depending on the Web information. By using this scheme, we cab enhance the virtual space to be more realistic and dynamic according to the Web information.

The main goal of conventional Web systems is to provide information or knowledge to users. By integrating the Web information onto a 3D virtual space, it also provides a field where a user virtually experiences the information. Character agents take an important role in the virtual space to provide the information and to guide in the virtual space through natural and various ways of interactions with the user.

At present, a prototype has been just developed. From a viewpoint of character agents, our future work is to enhance the functionality of the agents. By using GeneSys, the 3D virtual space is updated according to the Web information, so the agents need to be adaptive to the updates. At present, they have just a simple form of planning scheme to find a shortest path to a destination, but they need to plan more elaborate aspects of agents such as conversation, gesture, actions, and emotion, to guide users more efficiently and naturally.

References

1. Joseph Bates. The Role of Emotion in Believable Agents, Communication of the ACM, 37(7):122-126, 1994.
2. Justine Cassell, Joseph Sullivann, Scott Prevost, and Elizabeth Churchill (Eds.), Embodied Conversational Agents, MIT Press, 2000.
3. Toru Ishida. Digital City Kyoto: Social Information Infrastructure for Everyday Life, Communications of the ACM, 45(7):76-81, 2002.
4. Yasuhiko Kitamura, Teruhiro Yamada, Takashi Kokubo, Yasuhiro Mawarimichi, Taizo Yamamoto, Toru Ishida. Interactive Integration of Information Agents on the Web, Matthias Klusch, Franco Zambonelli (Eds.), Cooperative Information Agents V, Lecture Notes in Artificial Intelligence 2182, Berlin et al.: Springer-Verlag, 1-13, 2001.

5. Yasuhiko Kitamura, Toshiki Sakamoto, and Shoji Tatsumi. A Competitive Information Recommendation System and Its Behavior, Matthias Klusch, Sascha Ossowski, and Onn Shehory (Eds.), Cooperative Information Agents VI, Lecture Notes in Artificial Intelligence 2446, Berlin et al.: Springer-Verlag, 138-151, 2002.
6. Yasuhiko Kitamura. Web Information Integration Using Multiple Character Agents, Helmut Prendinger and Mitsuru Ishizuka (Eds.), Life-Like Characters: Tools, Affective Functions, and Applications, Springer-Verlag, 295-316, 2004.
7. Hideyuki Nakanishi. FreeWalk: A Social Interaction Platform for Group Behavior in a Virtual Space, International Journal of Human Computer Studies, 60(4):421-454, 2004.
8. Helmut Prendinger and Mitsuru Ishizuka (Eds.) Life-Like Characters: Tools, Affective Functions, and Applications, Springer-Verlag, 2004.
9. Thomas Rist, Elisabeth Andre, Stephan Baldes, Patrick Gebhard, Martin Klessen, Michael Kipp, Peter Rist, and Markus Scmitt. A Review of the Development of Embodied Presentation Agents and Their Application Fields, Helmut Prendinger and Mitsuru Ishizuka (Eds.), Life-Like Characters: Tools, Affective Functions, and Applications, Springer-Verlag, 295-316, 2004.

Ikebana Support System Reflecting *Kansei* with Interactive Evolutionary Computation

Junichi Saruwatari and Masafumi Hagiwara

Department of Information and Computer Science, Keio University,
3-14-1 Hiyoshi, Kohoku-ku, Yokohama, 223-8522, Japan
junnichi@soft.ics.keio.ac.jp

Abstract. In this paper, we propose an *ikebana* support system which can reflect *kansei* employing interactive evolutionary computation. In the conventional flower layout support system, users cannot adjust the presented layouts. In the proposed system, users can adjust and evaluate the presented layouts. Moreover, new functions are implemented so that the system can learn users' preferences from their adjustments and evaluations. In addition, we deal with basic styles of *ikebana* which differ in many schools of Japanese *ikebana*. From evaluation experiments, it is indicated that the proposed system can present layouts which satisfy both *ikebana* beginners and advanced *ikebana* learners.

Keywords: Evolutionary computation, *ikebana*, image scale.

1 Introduction

Since designs have become very important, there are great demand for design support which reflects individual *kansei* [1]-[5].

People enjoy *ikebana* as hobby and culture not only in Japan but also in foreign countries. There are many people who are interested in *ikebana* and want to learn. The design support system is a very useful tool in such a case.

Generally, we know that evolutionary computation is useful as a way to solve problems which involve complex various factors [6]-[8]. Interactive evolutionary computation is a method which takes in the evaluations decided by users. It is considered that interactive evolutionary computation is useful especially for the intellectual works, such as designs reflected inclinations and *kansei* of users. For example, it is applied to the field of interior design [5].

We have proposed a flower layout support system with interactive evolutionary computation [10]. The system used the image scale to deal with atmosphere of *ikebana* on the whole [14]-[17]. In general, There is a problem of the interactive evolutionary computation: exhaustion of users by long time working in the case that many design factors are needed [9]. The system reduces the exhaustion of the work by using the interface with virtual reality [11].

However, there is another problem that users cannot make improvements at all to the layouts. What users do is only evaluating the layouts after inputting

F. Kishino et al. (Eds.): ICEC 2005, LNCS 3711, pp. 456–467, 2005.
© IFIP International Federation for Information Processing 2005

their image to the system at first. So, it is not practical for advanced *ikebana* learners. They can make the *ikebana* more beautiful by changing the vase, flowers, and the angles of the flowers. Then they need to be able to make improvements to the layouts. Also, *ikebana* beginners learn the basic styles of each school at first. They arrange flowers on the basis of the styles [19]. Therefore, the system needs to show the basic styles for them.

In this paper, we improved the conventional system from these points mentioned so far. The proposed system can learn the inclinations of users from not only the evaluations of users but also the adjustments of users. The system is more practical: Users can make *ikebana*, cooperating with the system more interactive.

2   Proposed *ikebana* Support System

2.1   Outline of Proposed System

Fig.1 shows the outline of this system. Users input the season and the image which they prefer for *ikebana*. The image is input as *kansei* word on the image scale which is proposed by Kobayashi[17]. It is shown in Fig.2. Image scale works as if it is the database of image. The feature of the image is derived from the position of the word. Based on the image and the season, each individual of the first generation is made as each layout. Then, three individuals with the highest fitness level are shown to users. Users can evaluate them and adjust them in respect of the following:

  – vase and flowers
  – size and position of each flower
  – largeness of each flower

The proposed system has the interface where the layout is presented and users adjust and evaluate it. Users can see it on the screen from various angles. Based

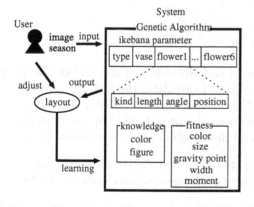

Fig. 1. Outline

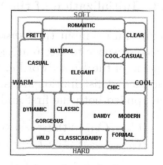

Fig. 2. Image scale

on the evaluations and the adjustments of users, the knowledge base in the system is updated. Then individuals are remade in the next generation by the framework of interactive genetic algorithm. Therefore the proposed system can learn the preferences of users.

2.2 Basic Knowledge on *ikebana*

Here we explain the basic knowledge on *ikebana*. We applied this knowledge to the proposed system. The fundamental of *ikebana* is to make the triangle with three flowers. They are the main flowers called " *Yaku-eda*". *Yaku-eda* consists of " *Shin*", " *Soe*" and " *Tai*" [20]. *Shin* is the longest, *Tai* is the shortest and *Soe* is middle in them [20]. The other flowers are called " *Ashirai*". The length of each *Ashirai* is shorter than *Yaku-eda*.

The length of each *Yaku-eda* is decided based on the size of the vase: The length of the vase is determined by its height and the diameter. The length of *Shin* is about 1.5 times of that of the vase. The length of *Soe* is about 0.75 times of that of *Shin*. The length of *Tai* is about 0.75 times of that of *Soe*.

$$l = h + d \tag{1}$$
$$a = \lambda_1 l \tag{2}$$
$$b = \lambda_2 a \tag{3}$$
$$c = \lambda_2 b . \tag{4}$$

where l is the length of the vase, h is the height of the vase, d is the diameter of the vase, a is the length of *Shin*, b is the length of *Soe*, c is the length of *Tai* and λ_1, λ_2 are the random numbers.

In the proposed system, we deal with the Upright Style and the Slanting Style[19]. We prepare the basic styles on the basis of the introductory books of *ikebana* [18]-[20]. The angle of each *Yaku-eda* is shown in these styles. At the initializing stage, the proposed system selects the style and decides the angle of each *Yaku-eda* from the style.

2.3 Initialization of the System

At first, users input the *kansei* word e and the season. Then, the system divides HS color space to 10x10 areas equally and calculates the histogram of the color scheme of the *kansei* word e. Fig.3 and Fig.4 show HS color space and the first and second distribution areas. This color scheme is decided by the *kansei* word e. We applied both the first and second distribution areas to evaluate the layouts.

(C_{e1x}, C_{e1y}) : the $x - y$ coordinate of the first distribution area for e
(C_{e2x}, C_{e2y}) : the $x - y$ coordinate of the second distribution area for e

Next, probability for selecting vase is calculated according to the position of the *kansei* word e on the image scale.

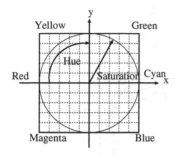
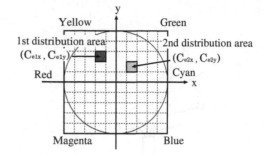

Fig. 3. HS color space   **Fig. 4.** First and second distribution area

2.4   Feature Quantities of *ikebana*

We selected the feature quantities about the color scheme and the figure.
  Four feature quantities about the figure are based on [10].

- Size V
  This is the size of the space made by the layout.
- Gravity point G
  This is the mean vector that heads from the root to the edges of the flowers.
  The slant is calculated by the ratio of x-coordinate or z-coordinate to y-coordinate of G.
- Width W
  This is the width of the layout from an anterior view.
- Complexity M
  This means the momentum.

These feature quantities are expressed as follows:

$$V = S \mid G \mid \tag{5}$$

$$G = \frac{1}{N} \sum_i^N P_i \tag{6}$$

$$W = \frac{1}{N} \sum_i^N \mid P_{ix} \mid \tag{7}$$

$$M = \frac{1}{V} \sum_i^N \mid G - P_i \mid . \tag{8}$$

where N is the number of the flowers, S is the area of the triangle made by *Shin,Soe* and *Tai*. P_i is the vector that heads from the root to the edges of the flowers, and P_{ix} is the x-coordinate of P_i. These are shown in Fig.5 and Fig.6.
  HS color space is better than RGB color space to deal with the feature quantities about the color [12][13]. HS color space consists of hue and saturation. The system divides HS color space to 10x10 areas equally and calculates the

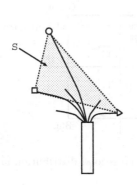

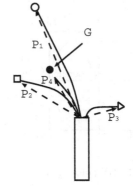

Fig. 5. Area of the triangle

Fig. 6. Vectors

histogram of the color scheme of the layout as shown in Fig.3. These feature quantities are shown as follows:

(C_{i1x}, C_{i1y}):the $x - y$ coordinate of the first distribution area for the layout

(C_{i2x}, C_{i2y}):the $x - y$ coordinate of the second distribution are for the layout.

2.5   Interactive Evolutionary Computation

We use genetic algorithm (GA) as evolutionary computation.

Each individual fitness is determined by the color and the shape.

$$E_i = E_{ic} + E_{if} . \tag{9}$$

where E_i is the fitness of individual i, E_{ic} is the color evaluation of individual i, and E_{if} is the figure evaluation of individual i.

The figure evaluation is shown as,

$$E_{if} = j(G_{ix}, G_{iy}, G_{iz})(f_v(E_{iv}) + f_g(E_{ig}) + f_w(E_{iw}) + f_m(E_{im})) \tag{10}$$

$$E_{iv} = V_i - V_{ave} \tag{11}$$

$$E_{ig} = \frac{G_{ix}}{G_{iy}} - \frac{G_{avex}}{G_{avey}} \tag{12}$$

$$E_{iw} = W_i - W_{ave} \tag{13}$$

$$E_{im} = M_i - M_{ave} . \tag{14}$$

where the subscript ave means the average of the same generation, G_x and G_y are the x and y coordinate of G, respectively, and $j(x, y, z)$ is the element(x, y, z) of the matrix J. J is the figure-learning map. All elements of J are initialized to 1.

The evaluations of each feature are calculated by the evaluation functions. The evaluation functions are decided by the position of e on the image scale. These evaluation functions are shown in Table 1.

Table 1. Functions for evaluating the figure

function	area	output	
		input $x \geq 0$	input $x < 0$
$f_v(x)$	Warm-Soft	0.5	0.5
	Warm-Hard	1.0	0.0
	Cool-Soft	0.0	1.0
	Cool-Hard	0.5	0.5
$f_g(x)$	Warm-Soft	0.0	1.0
	Warm-Hard	0.5	0.5
	Cool-Soft	0.5	0.5
	Cool-Hard	1.0	0.0
$f_w(x)$	Warm-Soft	1.0	0.0
	Warm-Hard	0.5	0.5
	Cool-Soft	0.5	0.5
	Cool-Hard	0.0	1.0
$f_m(x)$	Warm-Soft	0.5	0.5
	Warm-Hard	1.0	0.0
	Cool-Soft	0.0	1.0
	Cool-Hard	0.5	0.5

Also, the evaluated value is 0 when the ratio of G_x or G_z to G_y is larger than the golden section ratio 1.618. This means that the layout is too slant.

The evaluation value of the color is shown as,

$$E_{ic} = \frac{t(C_{i1x}, C_{i1y})}{(C_{e1x} - C_{i1x})^2 + (C_{e1y} - C_{i1y})^2} + \frac{t(C_{i2x}, C_{i2y})}{(C_{e2x} - C_{i2x})^2 + (C_{e2y} - C_{i2y})^2}. \tag{15}$$

where $t(x, y)$ is the element (x, y) of the matrix $\boldsymbol{T}$. $\boldsymbol{T}$ is the color-learning map. The map is the correspondent map where HS color space is divided 10x10 equally. All elements of $\boldsymbol{T}$ are initialized to 1.

The coding sequence of the gene is shown in Fig.7.

In the proposed system, the crossover and the mutation are carried out as the genetic operation.

- crossover
  The crossover is carried out with each *Yaku-eda* in each gene. For example, the flower used as *Shin* in an individual is crossed over the flower used as *Shin* in another individual. The same kind flower of *Yaku-eda* is used to *Ashirai* which aids *Yaku-eda*.
- mutation
  A new individual is made by mutation.

2.6   Learning

Learning is carried out to update the knowledge in the proposed system based on the adjustments and evaluations by users. When the evaluation is good, this

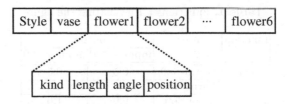

Fig. 7. Coding sequence of a gene

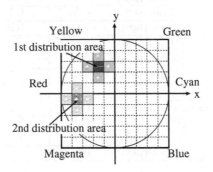

Fig. 8. Color-learning map

system learns the color, the style and the figure of the layout. Now we explain the learning.

The color-learning map is used for learning the color. Fig.8 shows the color-learning map. When the evaluation to the layout is good, the histogram of the color scheme is calculated in HS color space. Then T is updated and the elements of the first distribution area, the second distribution area and their four proximities are updated. The update procedure is the follows.

$$t_{new}(C_{i1x}, C_{i1y}) = t(C_{i1x}, C_{i1y}) + R_C \tag{16}$$

$$t_{new}(C_{i1x} + 1, C_{i1y}) = t(C_{i1x} + 1, C_{i1y}) + 1 \tag{17}$$

$$t_{new}(C_{i1x} - 1, C_{i1y}) = t(C_{i1x} - 1, C_{i1y}) + 1 \tag{18}$$

$$t_{new}(C_{i1x}, C_{i1y} + 1) = t(C_{i1x}, C_{i1y} + 1) + 1 \tag{19}$$

$$t_{new}(C_{i1x}, C_{i1y} - 1) = t(C_{i1x}, C_{i1y} - 1) + 1 \tag{20}$$

$$t_{new}(C_{i2x}, C_{i2y}) = t(C_{i2x}, C_{i2y}) + R_C \tag{21}$$

$$t_{new}(C_{i2x} + 1, C_{i2y}) = t(C_{i2x} + 1, C_{i2y}) + 1 \tag{22}$$

$$t_{new}(C_{i2x} - 1, C_{i2y}) = t(C_{i2x} - 1, C_{i2y}) + 1 \tag{23}$$

$$t_{new}(C_{i2x}, C_{i2y} + 1) = t(C_{i2x}, C_{i2y} + 1) + 1 \tag{24}$$

$$t_{new}(C_{i2x}, C_{i2y} - 1) = t(C_{i2x}, C_{i2y} - 1) + 1 . \tag{25}$$

where R_C is 4 when the evaluation by a user is very good or 3 when the evaluation is good.

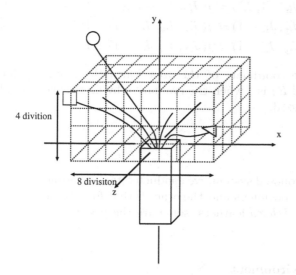

Fig. 9. Figure-learning map

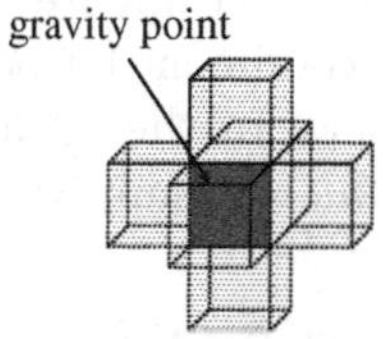

Fig. 10. Update of figure-learning map

The style learning is learning the style. When the evaluation is good, the proposed system learns the angles of the flowers in the style. The angle around z-axis is changed by this learning. By learning the style, the difference of the schools gets less. If advanced *ikebana* learners use this system, the style learning is useful for learning the style which they like.

$$\alpha_{new} = \alpha - \eta(\alpha - \alpha_u) \tag{26}$$
$$\beta_{new} = \beta - \eta(\beta - \beta_u) \tag{27}$$
$$\gamma_{new} = \gamma - \eta(\gamma - \gamma_u) . \tag{28}$$

where α, β and γ are the angle of *Shin*, *Soe* and *Tai* of a style around z-axis, respectively, α_u, β_u and γ_u are the angles adjusted by users, and η is the learning rate.

The figure-learning map is used for learning the figure. Fig.9 shows the figure-learning map. When the evaluation is good, the figure-learning map is updated. Fig.10 shows the update of the figure-learning map. The figure-learning map is the area where the layout is set. The area is divided 8x4x8 equally. This map is the matrix which corresponds to the area. Each element of this map corresponds in position to the divided area. This map learns the position of G. G can represent the largeness and stability of the layout.

$$j_{new}(J_{ix}, J_{iy}, J_{iz}) = j(J_{ix}, J_{iy}, J_{iz}) + R_J \tag{29}$$
$$j_{new}(J_{ix} + 1, J_{iy}, J_{iz}) = j(J_{ix} + 1, J_{iy}, J_{iz}) + 1 \tag{30}$$
$$j_{new}(J_{ix} - 1, J_{iy}, J_{iz}) = j(J_{ix} - 1, J_{iy}, J_{iz}) + 1 \tag{31}$$
$$j_{new}(J_{ix}, J_{iy} + 1, J_{iz}) = j(J_{ix}, J_{iy} + 1, J_{iz}) + 1 \tag{32}$$

$$j_{new}(J_{ix}, J_{iy} - 1, J_{iz}) = j(J_{ix}, J_{iy} - 1, J_{iz}) + 1 \tag{33}$$

$$j_{new}(J_{ix}, J_{iy}, J_{iz} + 1) = j(J_{ix}, J_{iy}, J_{iz} + 1) + 1 \tag{34}$$

$$j_{new}(J_{ix}, J_{iy}, J_{iz} - 1) = j(J_{ix}, J_{iy}, J_{iz} - 1) + 1 . \tag{35}$$

where (J_{ix}, J_{iy}, J_{iz}) is the coordinate of the area which the gravity point of individual i belongs to and R_J is 4 when the evaluation by users is very good or 3 when the evaluation is good.

3   Experiments

In order to evaluate the proposed system, we conducted two experiments. One is the experiment for *ikebana* beginners and the other is that for advanced *ikebana* learners. In the advanced *ikebana* learners, some are the people who practiced *ikebana* for many years.

3.1   Experimental Environment

We conducted the experiments to 8 beginners and 8 advanced learners. The experimental procedure is the following.

1. input the image and the season.
2. evaluate and adjust the layouts presented by the system.
3. order the system to remake the layouts.
4. repeat 2 and 3.

We asked them to evaluate the layouts by 5 levels. The items that they evaluated are the color, the figure and the global image. In addition, we asked the advanced learners to answer whether this system is useful for the idea generation support. The parameters used in these experiments are shown in Table 2.

3.2   Experimental Result

Fig.11 and Fig.12 show the result of advanced *ikebana* learners and that of *ikebana* beginners, respectively. From these figures we can see that the proposed

Table 2. Parameters used in the system

item	value
individual number	100
the ratio of crossover	0.5
the ratio of mutation	0.1
λ_1	1.5 - 2.0
λ_2	0.66 - 0.75
η	0.5 - 0.8

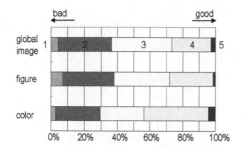

Fig. 11. Result of advanced *ikebana* learners

Fig. 12. Result of *ikebana* beginners

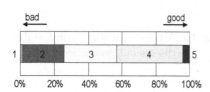

Fig. 13. Idea generation support

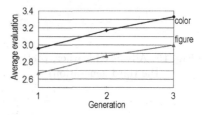

Fig. 14. Transition of the average evaluation value

system is more useful for beginners. Fig.13 shows whether this system could support them to generate new ideas. From this figure, it is considered that this system is useful for the idea generation support.

It was observed that advanced learners tend to adjust the layouts frequently. Therefore we examined the transition of the average evaluation value of each generation. The result is shown in Fig.14. It shows that the average value goes up as generation proceeds. We got some suggestions from advanced learners. We show some of them.

- I felt as if I arranged *ikebana* actually.
- When we cut a real branch too short, it cannot be restored. So, it is useful that we can simulate the length of flowers.
- It is better that the kinds of flowers and the colors increase.
- It is better that the kinds of the bend of the branches and the leaves increase.
- It is better that we can change the color of the vases.
- I enjoyed it.

The followings are suggestions from beginners.

- We can make *ikebana* which we want easily.
- I enjoyed it purely.

3.3   Examples of Layouts

Figs.15-18 show the examples of layouts. Various kinds of layouts are obtained by the proposed system.

Fig. 15. Advanced learner, pretty
(the third generation)

Fig. 16. Advanced learner, comfortable
(the second generation)

Fig. 17. Beginner, charming
(the first generation)

Fig. 18. Beginner, luxurious
(the second generation)

4   Conclusion

In this paper, we have proposed *ikebana* support system which can reflect *kansei* employing interactive evolutionary computation. From the experiments, it is considered that this system can present the layouts which satisfy both *ikebana* beginners and advanced *ikebana* learners. Also, it is shown that this system can learn the preference of users.

References

1. Mitsuo Nagamachi: "study of merchandise with Kansei," Kaibundo shuppan, 1993 (in Japanese).
2. Yositeru Nakamori: "Kansei data analysis," Morikita suppan, 2000 (in Japanese).
3. Takayuki Miyazaki, Masafumi Hagiwara: "A poster creating support system to reflect Kansei," IPSJ Trans., Vol.38, No.10, pp.1928-1936, 1997.
4. Takanobu Obata,Masafumi Hagiwara: "A color poster support system to reflect Kansei," IPSJ Trans., Vol.41, No.3, pp.701-710, 2000.
5. Motoki Korenaga, Masafumi Hagiwara:"Interior layout support system with interactive evolutionary computation," IPSJ Journal, Vol.41, No.11, pp3152-3160, 2000.
6. Haym Hirsh, Wolfgang Banzhof, John R. Koza, Conor Rya, Lee Spector, Christian Jacob: Genetic programming, IEEE Intelligent Systems and Their Applications, 15, 3, 74-84, 2000.
7. Masafumi Hagiwara:"Neuro,Fuzzy,Genetic Algorithm," Sangyou tosho, 1994(in Japanese).
8. David E. GoldBerg:"Genetic Algorithms", Addison-Wesley, 1989.
9. Hideyuki Takagi, Tatsuo Unemi, Takao Terano: "Perspective on Interactive Evolutionary Computing," JSAI Journal, Vol.13, No.5, pp.692-703, 1998.
10. Motoki Korenaga, Masafumi Hagiwara:"Flower Layout Support System with Interactive Evolutionary Computation," JSKE Journal, vol.4, no.2, pp81-88, 2004.
11. Howard Rheingold: "Virtual reality," Summit Books, 1991.
12. Saitou Takeshi, Toyohisa Kaneko: "Automatic Recognition of Wild Flowers," IEICE Journal, Vol.J84-DII, No.7, pp.1419-1429, 2001.
13. Hideaki Titiiwa: "science of color," Fukumura shuppan, 1983 (in Japanese).
14. Shigenobu Kobayashi:"Color System ," Koudansha, 1999 (in Japanese).
15. Shigenobu Kobayashi:"Colorist" Koudansha, 1997 (in Japanese).
16. Shigenobu Kobayashi: "Color Design," Koudansha, 2000 (in Japanese).
17. Shigenobu Kobayashi:"Color Image Scale" Koudansha, 1990 (in Japanese).
18. Minobu Ohi:"Flower arrangement : the Ikebana way," Shufunotomo, 1962.
19. Kou Sugita:"Easy Intorduction to Ikebana," Kin-en sha, 2004 (in Japanese).
20. Senei Ikenobou:"First Introduction to Ikenoubou Ikebana," NihonKadou sha, 1999 (in Japanese).

Effects of Team-Based Computer Interaction: The Media Equation and Game Design Considerations

Daniel Johnson[1] and John Gardner[2]

[1] Communication Design, Queensland University of Technology, Kelvin Grove,
Queensland, 4059, Australia
dm.johnson@qut.edu.au
[2] School of Business, University of Queensland, Australia

Abstract. The current paper applies media equation research to video game design. The paper presents a review of the existing media equation research, describes a specific study conducted by the authors, discusses how the findings of the study can be used to inform future game design, and explores how other media equation findings might be incorporated into game design. The specific study, discussed in detail in the paper, explores the notion of team formation between humans and computer team-mates. The results show that while highly experienced users will accept a computer as a team-mate, they tend to react more negatively towards the computer than to human teammates (a 'Black Sheep' Effect).

Keywords: Media Equation, Team Formation, Groups, Game Design.

1 Introduction

The media equation is based on the idea that people respond socially to computers. In its simplest form the media equation can be stated as 'media equals real life': more broadly it is the concept that people's interactions with televisions, computers and new media are fundamentally social and natural [1]. In media equation studies, the social dynamics surrounding human-human interactions are shown to exist in human-computer interactions. The studies conducted supporting the media equation all follow a similar research process. The process is as follows: (a) pick a social science finding (usually within social psychology or sociology) which concerns behaviour or attitudes towards humans, (b) substitute 'computer' for 'human' in the statement of the theory e.g., 'people like people that flatter them' becomes 'people like computers that flatter them' [2], (c) replicate the methodology of the social science study but replace one or more humans with computers, (d) determine if the social rule still applies [3].

A myriad of different media equation effects are described in the literature. The vast majority of this research can be considered to fall into four categories, reflecting the kinds of psychological or sociological effects that are being explored. Human research in the areas of traits, social rules and norms, identity, and communication has been shown to be applicable to human-computer interactions. Media equation research focusing on human traits includes studies on gain-loss theory [4], social facili-

F. Kishino et al. (Eds.): ICEC 2005, LNCS 3711, pp. 468–479, 2005.

tation [5], social presence [6] and principles of attraction [6-8]. For example, research has shown that people tend to prefer computers that are similar to themselves [8, 9] which parallels the tendency to prefer other people who are similar to oneself (the similarity attraction hypothesis) [10-12]. The media equation research concentrating on social rules and norms has explored reciprocity [13-16], flattery [2, 17], politeness [18], assignment of roles [19] and praise and criticism [20]. For example, there is evidence that people perceive a computer who criticises others to be smarter than a computer that praises others, which is the same process that tends to occur between people [20]. Media equation research focusing on identity incorporates studies on group formation and affiliation [21, 22], self-serving bias [23], and stereotyping [24]. For example, research has shown that people (both male and female) will apply gender-based stereotypes to a computer as a function of whether the computer communicates using a male or female voice [24]. The media equation research directed towards issues of communication has included studies exploring party host behaviour [25], balance theory [26] and emotion theory and active listening [27]. The latter researchers, for example, found that for people experiencing negative affect (e.g., frustration), interacting with a computer that provided sincere non-judgmental feedback led to a moderation of the negative feelings experienced (as often happens when people talk to other people who offer sincere non-judgmental feedback).

1.1 General Applications of the Media Equation

Recently, the media equation has been applied to the design and implementation of software programs, interfaces and electronic devices. Both the general theory, that people tend to treat computers as though they are real people and places, and specific media equation findings have proven useful to designers. Cooper [28] applied the media equation theory (particularly findings regarding politeness; see [18]) when creating a series of principles for programmers to use when designing software. Diederiks [29] analyzed 'L-icons' (virtual personal friends that make viewing recommendations for a television system) and 'Bello' (a virtual pet dog that facilitates voice control for a television set) and found evidence that animated characters deploying social behaviour and social rules make it easier to interact with consumer electronic products. Friedman, Kahn and Hagman [30] found that as a result of the social cues they provide, AIBO robots (small robotic dogs produced by SONY) provide their owners with social companionship and emotional satisfaction. Based on the media equation literature, Johnson [31] designed and implemented guidebots (or virtual tutors) based on the behaviour of actual human teachers. The results of this work are being used to create a social intelligence model to be incorporated into a guidebot-enhanced interface, which will be able to assess when pedagogical interventions are appropriate. These examples represent a sample taken from the population of published applications of the media equation, and as such do not represent the full scope of applications drawing on media equation research that are currently in existence.

1.2 Experience as a Moderator of the Media Equation

Recent research conducted by Johnson, Gardner and Wiles [17] found evidence suggesting a link between degree of experience with computers and propensity to show a media equation response to computers. An informal survey of computer users of varying levels of experience revealed that most people expect that users with high levels of experience with computers are *less* likely to exhibit the tendency to treat computers as though they were real people. This belief is based on the argument that more experienced users, having spent more time using computers, are more likely to view the computer as a tool. They are more likely to be aware of the computer's true status -- that of a machine. However, the research conducted does not support this argument, Johnson et al. found that more experienced participants were *more* likely to exhibit a media equation response.

Specifically, participants of high experience, but not low experience, displayed a media equation pattern of results, reacting to flattery from a computer in a manner congruent with peoples' reactions to flattery from other humans. High experience participants tended to believe that the computer spoke the truth, experienced more positive affect as a result of flattery, and judged the computer's performance more favorably (for a detailed discussion of these findings, their relation to the media equation and it's theorized relationship to mindlessness the reader is directed to the original paper [17]).

1.3 Group Identity and the Media Equation

One of the strongest findings in intergroup behaviour research is the minimal group effect [32]. The minimal group paradigm is an experimental methodology developed by Tajfel and colleagues in order to explore the minimal conditions required for intergroup behaviour (including team formation) [33]. In Tajfel and colleague's original study, participants were invited to take part in a study on decision making and assigned to one of two groups on the basis of their reported preference for paintings by either the artist Klandinski or Klee. Participants were then given the opportunity to allocate money to pairs of fellow participants identified only by group membership. The results indicated that participants tended to strongly favor their own group [33]. The striking feature of this and subsequent minimal group paradigm (MGP) studies is that team affiliation effects resulted even though the categorisation was on the basis of a largely arbitrary criterion, the groups created had no history or future, and self-interest was not a motivating factor for participants [32].

More recently, MGP studies have shown categorisation and associated affiliation effects on the basis of coin toss allocations to groups K or W [34], painting preferences [35, 36], line length estimation (overestimators and underestimators) [37], random categorisation to groups X and Y [38], figural versus grounded perceptual style [39], shape dependency and independency [40], and concave and convex attention styles [41].

1.4 The Current Study

The current study was designed to test whether minimal categorisation could be used to create a sense of team affiliation between human participants and computers. It was hypothesized that participants would show group affiliation effects as a result of being placed on a team with a computer (H1). Moreover, it was hypothesized (based on previous research) that this effect would be stronger for participants with a greater degree of experience with computers (H2).

2 Method

2.1 Procedure

Sixty University of Queensland students participated in the study (40 females and 20 males). Participants ranged in age 17 to 35, with an average age of 19.8 years.

Participants were initially told that the study dealt with decision making with computers. Participants were informed that the computers they were working on had been trained to use neural networks to complete two different tasks: a text rating task (TRT), and a desert survival task (DST).

For the TRT, participants read a body of text and rated the extent to which six words (descriptive, emotive, intriguing, factual, stimulating, entertaining) accurately described the text. Then the computer presented its own ratings. Ostensibly, the computer ratings were based on the neural network it employed; in fact, the computer ratings were systematically different to the participants' ratings. After viewing the computer's ratings, participants were allowed to alter their original ratings.

For the DST, participants were asked to imagine they were stranded in the desert and to rank 12 items according to their importance for survival. When participants had completed their ranking, the computer gave a suggested ranking and listed a rationale for its suggestions. Ostensibly, the computer used a neural network to rank the items; in fact, the computer's ranking was systematically different from the participant's. After viewing the computers' suggested ranking and rationale, participants were allowed to alter their own rankings.

The experiment had three conditions: control (N = 25), human team (N = 19), and human-computer team (N = 17). In the control condition, participants were told they would be working on their own during the experiment, and the experimental materials and procedures were designed to promote the notion of individual work. In the human team condition, participants told they would be working as part of one of two teams, and materials and procedures were set up to promote the distinction between the people in the teams. In the human-computer team condition, participants were also told they would be working as part of one of two teams, but materials and procedures were set up to include the computers as part of each team.

2.2 Measures

After all interaction with the computer was complete, participants completed the written questionnaire. Participants' degree of experience with computers was assessed, and they were classified as having low or high experience. To assess mood, the questionnaire included the Positive and Negative Affect Scale; 20 mood descriptors designed to assess mood states [42]. Participants' attitudes towards the TRT and the DST were assessed; participants also rated the quality of the information provided by the computer. To assess their openness to influence from the computer, participants rated seven items drawn from prior research [21, 22]. For each task, participants were asked to assess the extent to which their ratings/rankings had changed: a *subjective* measure of the degree to which respondents were influenced by the computer. *Objective* measures of the extent to which participants were influenced by the computer were also recorded by summing numerical changes in participants' ratings and rankings. Demographic data were also collected.

Exploratory factor analyses were conducted to identify variables to be combined into scales. Analysis of the PANAS items showed a two-factor solution, with the 10 positive mood descriptors loading on one factor (Positive mood; Cronbach's $\alpha = .78$) and the 10 negative mood descriptors loading on another factor (Negative mood; $\alpha = .74$). The three items assessing ratings of the TRT loaded on a single factor (TRT rating; $\alpha = .91$). Similarly, the three items assessing ratings of the DST loaded on a single factor (DST rating; $\alpha = .87$). The three items rating the quality of the computer information loaded on a single factor (Information quality; $\alpha = .85$), as did the seven items assessing respondent's openness to influence (Openness to influence; $\alpha = .91$).

3 Results

A series of one-way ANOVAs were conducted on the dependent measures, with the experimental manipulation (control, human team and human-computer team) as the independent variable. Results from these initial analyses were non-significant. Prior findings suggest that media equation effects are more apparent amongst people with more extensive experience with computers [17], so the sample was split into respondents with low and high experience with computers. Subsequent one-way ANOVAs were conducted separately for these two groups. The ANOVAs conducted on the low-experience respondents (N = 32) showed no significant effect of experimental manipulation for any of the dependent measures.

The ANOVAs conducted on the high-experience respondents (N = 28) showed significant effects across the experimental manipulation for several measures. There were significant differences across conditions for the ratings of both the TRT ($F(2,25) = 3.87$, $p < .05$) and the DST ($F(2,25) = 3.90$, $p < .05$). Examination of the mean scores indicated that high experience participants in the human team and human-computer team conditions rated both tasks more positively than their counterparts in the control condition (see Table 1). No such pattern existed for low experience participants. This finding suggests that for high experience (but not low experience) respondents, simply being placed in a team was sufficient to promote more positive attitudes to the tasks than working alone (in the control condition).

For high experience respondents' subjective measures of how much they were influenced by the computer, there were significant differences across conditions for the text rating task ($F(2,25) = 4.10$, $p < .05$), but not the desert survival task. Mean scores for the TRT suggested that respondents reported less alteration of their responses in the human-computer team condition than in the control and human team conditions (see Table 1). High experience respondents, who were working in a team with other people and a computer, subjectively rated themselves as being less influenced by the computer in the TRT than high experience participants in either the control condition or the human team condition.

High experience respondents showed significant differences across conditions for both their ratings of the quality of information provided by the computer ($F(2,25) =$

5.01, p < .05), and their openness to influence from the computer (F(2,25) = 3.77, p < .05). Mean scores for these measures indicated that high-experience respondents in the human-computer team condition rated the quality of information from the

Table 1. Mean Scores for Dependent Measures Across Conditions

Measure	Low Experience			High Experience		
	Control	Human	Human-Comp	Control	Human	Human-Comp
TRT Rating	4.0	3.3	3.2	2.5	4.5	4.4
DST Rating	5.7	4.6	5.1	4.4	5.7	6.1
TRT Subjective Infl.	2.1	1.0	1.6	1.0	1.7	0.6
Information Quality	5.5	5.6	6.0	6.1	5.8	4.6
Openness to Infl.	5.8	5.2	5.2	6.1	6.0	4.5
TRT Objective Infl.	118.6	122.1	115.3	121.1	107.2	143.6
DST Objective Infl.	27.0	28.2	25.7	20.8	13.7	32.7

computer lower, and reported lower openness to influence from the computer than those in the control and human team conditions (see Table 1). When high experience participants were placed in a team with a computer as well as other humans, they were less positive about the quality of information provided by the computer, and reported being less open to being influenced by the computer.

Amongst high experience respondents, there were significant differences across conditions for the objective measures of the computer's influence for both the text rating task (F(2,25) = 6.07, p < .01) and the desert survival task (F(2,25) = 4.00, p < .05). Mean scores for these measures indicated that high-experience respondents in the human-computer team condition had ratings/rankings that were *further* from the computer's suggestions in both the TRT and the DST than their counterparts in the control and human team conditions (see Table 1). In both tasks, high experience participants in a team with a computer were *less* influenced by the computer, than were high experienced participants in the human team and control conditions.

4   Discussion

Consistent with previous media equation research [17], a media equation pattern of behaviour was exhibited by participants who had high experience with computers but not by participants with low experience with computers (supporting H2). An unexpected but consistent pattern of results arose for high experience participants across the human team and human-computer team conditions. Broadly, high experience participants in the human-computer team condition rated the quality of information from the computer lower, felt they were less open to influence from the computer, perceived their own responses to the text rating task to be less influenced by the computer's ratings, and were actually less influenced by the computer's response in both the text rating and desert survival tasks than were high experience participants in the human team condition (contrary to H1). This finding is in contrast to the findings of

Nass and colleagues [21, 22] in which participants (on a team with a computer teammate) perceived the computer as having more influence, rated the quality of information from the computer more highly, and conformed more to the computers recommendations when the computer was made a part of the team.

The contrary pattern of results obtained in the current study is intriguing, as it is not possible to conclude that the identity manipulation did not work. Firstly, team affiliation effects are present for high experience participants in terms of rating of the tasks. Secondly, those in the human-computer team condition did not show the same attitudes and behaviour as those in the human team condition. Those who had a computer teammate as well as human teammates generally reacted negatively towards the computer in comparison to those who were part of a team without the computer as a teammate. This finding suggests that there is something unique about being on a team that includes a computer, which evokes a negative reaction towards that computer.

This result raises the question of why these high experience people would be inclined to disregard or undervalue the computer's recommendations. Our initial consideration of the social identity literature led us to hypothesise the opposite pattern of results. We expected high experience participants to be more likely to treat the computer as a team member and thus, expected them to be more likely to be influenced by the computer's ratings and rankings in the two tasks, when the computer was made part of the team. The pattern of results obtained contradicted these expectations; high experience participants working with the computer as a team member were less influenced by the computer than either low experience participants or participants in which the computer was not a team member.

However, further exploration of the social identity literature leads to explanations of these results that are in line with the media equation explanation of people's reactions to computers. Research has been conducted identifying a phenomenon known as the 'Black Sheep Effect', whereby group members may reject another group member based on that group member's deviation from the group prototype [43-50]. These studies highlight unfavourable evaluations and derogation of ingroup members as a form of ingroup bias that marginalises members who threaten positive ingroup identity. If the current findings are considered in light of the 'black sheep effect', then they can be interpreted as a clear example of media equation behaviour. Specifically, high experience participants placed on a team with the computer (but not low experience participants) treat the computer like a person to the extent that they perceive the computer as a member of the ingroup, albeit a member of the group that does not contribute positively to their group identification. As a result, high experience participants derogate this less positively perceived group member (the computer) by placing less value on its recommended ratings and rankings and generally perceiving its contribution to be of less value. This derogation of the computer and the information it provides does not occur among high experience participants unless the computer is implied to be a member of the team. Low experience participants, on the other hand, do not exhibit a media equation pattern of results; even when it is implied that the computer is a team member, the computer is not perceived as a member of the group, and thus no negative reaction towards the computer as a group member occurs. This explanation is strengthened by the fact that the results extend beyond subjective ratings and into objective behaviour. The pattern of results was consistent for subjective ratings of the quality of information provided by the computer, subjective ratings of the degree to which participants felt they were open to influence from the computer, subjective ratings of the degree to which participants thought they were influenced by the computer in one of the tasks, and objective measures of the degree to which participants actually were influenced by the computer in both tasks.

It would seem that while high experience computer users tend to treat computers like real people to the extent that they will accept the categorisation of the computer as a fellow group member, the effect is not strong enough for them to perceive the computer as a positive addition to the group. Rather, high experience users seem to be prepared to accept the computer as a teammate, but presumably because of deviations from the assumed group prototype, the computer is reacted to negatively and its input is marginalized or disregarded. According to the black sheep theory of group formation, this derogation of the marginal ingroup member (in this case the computer) serves to strengthen and protect the existing team identity.

An alternative explanation for this pattern of results would be that participants found the concept of having the computer as a teammate ridiculous. In response to being forced into an absurd situation, participants became belligerent and deliberately changed their responses to be contrary to the recommendations made by the computer. However, this explanation cannot account for the fact that only high experience participants rated the information provided by the computer as less useful, perceived themselves as less influenced by the computer, perceived themselves as less similar to the computer, and changed their responses away from the recommendations made by the computer. Nor can it account for the fact that high experience participants reported enjoying the task more when they worked as part of a team regardless of whether the computer was part of the team.

4.1 Application of Current Findings to Games

Within the arena of video games, the most obvious applicable finding is that people tend to enjoy a task more when placed within a team environment (whether or not a computer is a member of the team). This suggests that enjoyment of tasks in single-player games can be improved by helping the player feel like they are part of a team. This technique (increasing enjoyment of tasks by creating a sense of being on a team) is already utilised in many games (for example, Jak 3 or Half Life 2, in which the player is led to believe they are acting in concert with, or for the benefit of, other non-player characters (NPCs)).

The aforementioned application relates specifically to the player's attitude towards the *tasks* being undertaken within a game. The current findings are also relevant to the player's attitude towards the other *characters* within the game. Specifically, consideration should be given to games in which the player controls a character in a team setting and the computer controls NPCs on the team (role playing games, real-time strategy games and first-person shooters). The current research suggests that players (at least those of high experience) will accept computer players as part of the team, but may react negatively towards them or value them less than other human members of the team (as they deviate from the group prototype in the same way as the computer team-members in the current study – they are not human). At first glance, it might appear that this is something to be avoided by game developers on the basis that a negative reaction on the part of the player towards an NPC is a bad thing. However, the research on the black sheep effect shows that derogation of a marginal in-group member (in this case a NPC) serves to strengthen and protect the existing team identity. Thus, it is quite possible that NPCs on teams in videogames can and do play a "scapegoat" role, becoming a target towards which the human members of the team can release their frustration, direct blame and generally release negative emotions. Ultimately, NPCs placed in such a role would strengthen the sense of identity amongst the human members of the team.

4.2 Application of General Media Equation Findings to Games

From the myriad of media equation findings there are a wide variety that can be applied to the development of video games. What follows is by no means an exhaustive list, rather the aim is to provide a few examples of how media equation research can be applied to video games and thereby highlight the fact that the media equation is a ready source of design principles and techniques that can be applied in video game development.

One of the strongest and most consistent findings in psychological research is that perceptions of similarity increase attraction between people [51]. Nass and colleagues [4, 8, 9, 52] were able to show that computers exhibiting similar levels of extroversion, introversion, submissiveness or dominance (displayed via the style of text based communication or tone of voice) as their human users were perceived far more positively than computers which were not doing so. To this end, it seems safe to assume that videogames that contain NPCs with personalities similar to those of the player will be more positively perceived. For example, in an action adventure game, a short questionnaire or observation of the player's choices in the early stages of the game could allow for the facilitation of the player interacting with NPCs who exhibit similar personality traits to the player; this would facilitate greater positivity on the part of the player towards the NPCs.

Research has also shown that the gain/loss theory of interpersonal attractiveness (which suggests that individuals will be more attracted to others who initially dislike them and then come to like them, than to others who consistently like them) is applicable to interactions between people and computers [4]. This could be a useful technique for games in which players continually interact with one particular NPC across the course of a game (for example a game in which a particular NPC is a 'sidekick' or a tutor/helper). Such characters, if they initially treated the player negatively and became more positive or friendly over time, should become far more well-liked by the player than an NPC that is consistently positive.

In the context of the social norm that 'we should treat others the way they treat us', there is a great deal of research showing that if people receive a favour from others they feel obligated to reciprocate [32]. A series of media equation studies [14-16] demonstrated that people will feel indebted to a computer that provides a benefit, and subsequently reciprocate to that computer. The notion of the player receiving 'favours' or 'benefits' from a game or NPCs within a game is quite common ('power-ups', weapon upgrades, bonus levels etc.). It may be that these benefits can be leveraged by developers to encourage players to meet other objectives, such as the completion of specific tasks requested by NPCs. This technique may also be useful outside the game environment, for example; providing players with a bonus level or weapon in return for the completion of an online survey focussed on future game development.

One of the areas of media equation research most obviously applicable to video games is the research conducted on flattery. Just as people tend to react positively to flattery from others, researchers [2, 17] have shown that when flattered by computers, people tend to believe that the computer spoke the truth, experience more positive affect as a result of the flattery, and judge the computer's performance more favourably. This is one design technique identified in media equation research that is being applied in existing video games. Many first-person shooters (such as Quake, Unreal Tournament and Halo 2) use a voice-over or on-screen text to flatter players when they are performing well. This technique may well prove effective in other video games where little or no feedback is provided to the player while playing the game.

It is hoped that the suggested applications of the current study in combination with the aforementioned general examples of design principles derived from media equation research will inspire academics and game developers to further explore the potential synergies between the media equation and video game design.

References

1. Reeves, B. and C. Nass, The Media Equation: How People Treat Computers, Television and New Media Like Real People and Places. 1996, Cambridge: Cambridge University Press.
2. Fogg, B.J. and C. Nass, Silicon sycophants: the effects of computers that flatter. International Journal of Human Computer Studies, 1997. **46**: p. 551-561.
3. Nass, C., J. Steuer, and E. Tauber. Computers are social actors. in CHI 97. 1994. Boston.
4. Moon, Y. and C. Nass, How "real" are computer personalities?: Psychological responses to personality types in human-computer interaction. Communication Research, 1996. **23**(6): p. 651-674.
5. Rickenberg, R. and B. Reeves. The effects of animated characters on anxiety, task performance, and evaluations of user interfaces. in CHI 2000. 2000. Amsterdam.
6. Lee, K. and C. Nass, Designing social presence of social actors in human computer interaction, in CHI Letters. 2003, ACM: Ft. Lauderdale. p. 289-296.
7. Gong, L. and J. Lai, Shall we mix synthetic speech and human speech? Impact on users' performance, perception and attitude. CHI Letters 2001, 2001. **3**(1): p. 158-165.
8. Nass, C. and K.M. Lee, Does computer-synthesized speech manifest personality? Experimental tests of recognition, similarity-attraction, and consistency-attraction. Journal of Experimental Psychology: Applied, 2001. **7**(3): p. 171-181.
9. Nass, C. and K.M. Lee. Does computer-generated speech manifest personality? An experimental test of similarity-attraction. in CHI 2000. 2000. Amsterdam: ACM.
10. Duck, S.W., Personality similarity and friendship choice: Similarity of what, when? Journal of Personality, 1973. **41**(4): p. 543-558.
11. Byrne, D., G.L. Clore, and G. Smeaton, The attraction hypothesis: Do similar attitudes effect anything? Journal of Personality and Social Psychology, 1986. **51**: p. 1167-1170.
12. Neimeyer, R.A. and K.A. Mitchell, Similarity and attraction: A longitudinal study. Journal of Social and Personal Relationships, 1988. **5**(2): p. 131-148.
13. Fogg, B.J. and C. Nass. How users reciprocate to computers: An experiment that demonstrates behaviour change. in CHI 97. 1997. Atlanta.
14. Takeuchi, Y., et al. Social response and cultural dependency in human-computer interaction. in PRICAI 98. 1998.

15. Nass, C. and Y. Moon, Machines and mindlessness: Social responses to computers. Journal of Social Issues, 2000. **56**(1): p. 81-103.
16. Takeuchi, Y., et al. A cultural perspective in social interface. in CHI 2000. 2000. Amsterdam.
17. Johnson, D., J. Gardner, and J. WIles, Experience as a moderator of the media equation: the impact of flattery and praise. International Journal of Human Computer Studies, 2004. **61**: p. 237-258.
18. Nass, C., Y. Moon, and P. Carney, Are people polite to computers? Responses to computer-based interviewing systems. Journal of Applied Social Psychology, 1999. **29**(5): p. 1093-1110.
19. Nass, C., B. Reeves, and G. Leshner, Technology and roles: A tale of two TVs. Journal of Communication, 1996. **46**(2): p. 121-128.
20. Nass, C., et al., Machines, social attributions, and ethopoeia: performance assessments of computers subsequent to "self-" or "other-" evaluations. International Journal of Human-Computer Studies, 1994. **40**: p. 543-559.
21. Nass, C., B.J. Fogg, and Y. Moon, How powerful is social identity? Affiliation effects in human-computer interaction. 1995.
22. Nass, C., B.J. Fogg, and Y. Moon, Can computers be teammaters? International Journal of Human-Computer Studies, 1996. **45**: p. 669-678.
23. Moon, Y. and C. Nass, Are computers scapegoats? Attributions of responsibility in human-computer interaction. International Journal of Human Computer Studies, 1998. **49**: p. 79-94.
24. Nass, C., Y. Moon, and N. Green, Are Computers Gender Neutral? Gender Stereotypic Responses to Computers. Journal of Applied Social Psychology, 1997.
25. Isbister, K., et al. Helper agent: designing an assistant for human-human interaction in a virtual meeting space. in CHI 2000. 2000. Amsterdam.
26. Nakanishi, H., et al. Can software agents influence human relations? Balance theory in agent-mediated communities. in International Conference on Autonomous Agents and Multiagent Systems. 2003. Melbourne, Australia: ACM.
27. Klein, J., Y. Moon, and R. Picard, W., This computer responds to user frustration: Theory, design, results and implications. submitted to Interacting with computers, 1999.
28. Cooper, A., 14 Principles of Polite Apps. Visual Basic Programmers Journal, 1999(June): p. 62-66.
29. Diederiks, E. Buddies in a box. Animated characters in consumer electronics. in International Conference on Intelligent User Interfaces. 2003. Miami, Florida: ACM.
30. Friedman, B., P. Kahn, and J. Hagman, Hardware companions? - What online AIBO discussion forums reveal about the human-robotic relationship. CHI Letters 2003, 2003. **5**(1): p. 273-280.
31. Johnson, W. Interaction tactics for socially intelligent pedagogical agents. in International Conference on Intelligent User Interfaces. 2003. Miami, Florida: ACM.
32. Vaughan, G.M. and M.A. Hogg, Introduction to social psychology. 1995, Upper Saddle River, NJ: Prentice-Hall Inc. xv, 438.
33. Tajfel, H., et al., Social categorization in intergroup behavior. European Journal of Social Psychology, 1971. **1**: p. 149-177.
34. Gagnon, A. and R. Bourhis, Discrimination in the minimal group paradigm: Social identity or self interest? Personality and Social Psychology Bulletin, 1996. **22**(12): p. 1289-1301.
35. Gaertner, L. and C. Insko, Intergroup discrimination in the minimal group paradigm: categorisation, reciprocation or fear? Journal of Personality and Social Psychology, 2000. **79**: p. 79-94.
36. Gaertner, L. and C. Insko, On the measurement of social orientations in the minimal group paradigm: Norms as moderators of the expression of intergroup bias. European Journal of Social Psychology, 2001. **31**: p. 143-154.

37. Dobbs, M. and W. Crano, Outgroup accountability in the minimal group paradigm: Implications for Aversive Discrimination and Social Identity Theory. Personality and Social Psychology Bulletin, 2001. **27**(3): p. 355-364.
38. Grieve, P. and M. Hogg, Subjective uncertainty and intergroup discrimination in the minimal group situation. Personality and Social Psychology Bulletin, 1999. **25**(8): p. 926-940.
39. Otten, S. and G. Moskowitz, Evidence for implicit ingroup bias: Affect biased spontaneous trait inference in a minimal group paradigm. Journal of Experimental Social Psychology, 2000. **36**: p. 77-89.
40. Hertel, G. and N. Kerr, Priming ingroup favouritism: The impact of normative scripts in the minimal group paradigm. Journal of Experimental Social Psychology, 2001. **37**: p. 316-324.
41. Otten, S. and D. Wentura, Self-anchoring and ingroup favoritism: An individual-profiles analysis. Journal of Experimental Social Psychology, 2001. **37**: p. 525-532.
42. Watson, D., L.A. Clark, and A. Tellengen, Development and validation of brief measures of positive and negative affect: The PANAS scales. Journal of Personality and Social Psychology, 1988. **54**: p. 1063-1070.
43. Biernat, M., T. Vescio, and L. Billings, Black sheep and expectancy violation: Integrating two models of social judgment. European Journal of Social Psychology, 1999. **29**: p. 523-542.
44. Branscombe, N.R., et al., Ingroup or outgroup extremity: Importance of the threatened social identity. Personality and Social Psychology Bulletin, 1993. **19**: p. 381-388.
45. Hogg, M., E.A. Hardie, and K.J. Reynolds, Prototypical similarity, self-categorization, and deperonalized attraction: A perspective on group cohesiveness. European Journal of Social Psychology, 1995. **25**: p. 159-175.
46. Jetten, J., R. Spears, and A.S.R. Manstead, Distinctiveness threat and prototypicality: Combined effects on intergroup discrimination and collective self-esteem. European Journal of Social Psychology, 1997. **27**: p. 635-657.
47. Marques, J.M., et al., The role of categorization and ingroup norms in judgments of groups and their members. Journal of Personality and Social Psychology, 1998. **75**: p. 976-988.
48. Marques, J.M., D. Paez, and D. Abrams, Social identity and intragroup differentiation as subjective social control, in Social identity: International perspectives, S. Worchel, et al., Editors. 1998, Sage: London, England. p. 124-141.
49. Marques, J.M. and V.Y. Yzerbyt, The black sheep effect: Judgmental extremity towards ingroup members in inter- and intra-group situations. European Journal of Social Psychology, 1988. **18**: p. 287-292.
50. Matheson, K., B. Cole, and K. Majka, Dissidence from within: Examining the effects of intergroup context on group members' reactions to attitudinal opposition. Journal of Experimental Social Psychology, 2003. **39**: p. 161-169.
51. Smith, R., E., Psychology. 1993, Minesotta: West Publishing.
52. Moon, Y. and C. Nass. Adaptive agents and personality change: complementarity versus similarity as forms of adaptation. in CHI 96. 1996. Vancouver Canada: ACM.

The Ethics of Entertainment Computing

Andy Sloane

School of Computing and Information Technology, University of Wolverhampton,
Wulfruna Street, Wolverhampton, WV1 1SB
A.Sloane@wlv.ac.uk

Abstract. This paper investigates a number of issues that relate to the development of entertainment computing (EC) and the home environment. The consumption of EC is closely related to the efforts of companies to market it. At the same time there are many different factors that affect the quality of life of the individual consumers that participate in the entertainment. There are a number of unresolved conflicts that are currently not answered by the providers of EC software and the manufacturers of hardware. These conflicts are explored and the ethics of an example scenario is discussed.

Keywords: Ethics, home, leisure, quality of life.

1 Introduction

The use of Entertainment Computing (EC) is rooted in the home environment where much of the product is consumed. The home has an influence on the type of EC consumed and on the way it is consumed. The home is a concept that is dependent on the many traditions and cultures of the world [1]. Different concepts of home are relevant in different cultures; and within these there are many different instances of "home". This has made generic study of "home-life" very difficult over the years for the many researchers that are interested in the subject. [2] This variability in the manifestation of the home concept has led to many generalisations in the design and production of EC and these do not necessarily give the optimum service for individuals as the development of EC tends to encapsulate the culture within which it is developed.

The rooting of the home in its culture is fundamental - it is not a standalone concept devoid of influence from the embedding social fabric, but an integral part of society, neighbourhood and culture. In many modern societies there is a move towards multiple co-existing cultures with a wide variety of home styles and configurations in evidence. This leads to even more disparity between the perceived usefulness of EC design and its use. To encompass this diversity is one of the challenges of EC for the future, but to do so requires a more ethical approach to the development EC that will enable users to be better informed and assisted in their "leisure", when they are being entertained.

There is also a wider need to incorporate the cultural diversity in different countries, and the diversity in multi-cultural environments. The development of EC should aid and assist the user where necessary without causing more problems than it

F. Kishino et al. (Eds.): ICEC 2005, LNCS 3711, pp. 480–487, 2005.

solves. Central to the development of ethical EC is the recognition of the conflicts of everyday life that are exacerbated by the wider provision and use of EC and the inherent conflicts inside the various EC components that can be manifest in everyday home situations.

2 Scope of Entertainment Computing

There is a wide range of what constitutes entertainment computing product and service. The traditional concept of the computer game is one that appeals to one part of the consumer market. The use of computer-mediated entertainment is much more widespread and the blurred boundaries between leisure, education, work and home life all goes to make the definition of EC all the more difficult.

As an example, a household may use computers, and particularly the Internet, for gaming, messaging, discussion forums, teleconferencing, web browsing, information gathering and many more activities. These can be termed EC or may be a hybrid between EC, work and educational uses.

Entertainment computing can be seen to be many different types of system and service provided for users in their homes or elsewhere that gives them some form of leisure activity or a means of social support.

3 Conflicts

Within the wider domain of EC the different activities provide many opportunities for conflict. These can arise in a number of different ways and in different arenas: design, development, deployment, use, upgrade and obsolescence. In the following sections there are two areas of conflict that are of interest: that between users of systems, and that between the design goals of systems.

3.1 Conflicts Between Users

The use of many different types of EC in the home can often lead to conflicts for the participants where there are different pulls on time and resources. With the widespread use of computers and networked resources there is now little need to restrict the home to one computing device. Indeed, it now makes sense to have a number of different devices networked together so that they and share data and provide users with a suitable standardised platform [3] for the exchange of information between the various devices and between users (both in the home and elsewhere). This allows users to customise their environment to their own particular needs and avoid conflicts with other users in the same home. This may, however, reduce the communication between the users and actually degrade the quality of their real-time experience. An ethical perspective on provision or design of EC would assist in reducing this problem.

3.2 Design Goal Conflict

There are also conflicts in the provision of computer-mediated leisure, particularly in the home environment. For example, it is possible to build "smart" homes [4] with labour-saving features that allow users to have automatic control of various facilities such as lighting, audio-visual entertainment and climate control. At the same time there is a need for the human body to get regular exercise and there are tools ad devices to monitor activity levels. There seems little point in building a home that has a number of labour-saving devices if the occupants then need to take more exercise because of them!

The provision of EC in any environment that is not strictly controlled, which includes most of the application areas of EC, could modify its design goals to account for the wider perspective of users. It is unlikely to do so where commercial pressure is the main driving force for development.

The design of EC that can take account of this conflict and incorporate it into the design cycle could be more useful to end-users. The capability of EC to incorporate such ideas would benefit the quality of life and user experience of the users and purchasers of the EC system - and be more ethical.

4 Quality of Life

The quality of life aspects of systems development are only recently coming into the equation for entertainment computing and other general systems that are used in the home. A number of studies have shown that some Internet uses can enhance quality of life whilst others have shown a detrimental correlation [5]. This may also be true of other EC technologies such as computer games, although with the increased range of interactions possible in modern gaming there is scope for the quality of life to be enhanced.

Examples of this enhancement to the quality of life are the increasing use of Internet forums for information and discussion. Many members of these forums use them as a means of gaining useful and timely information from a pool of "experts" – these are mainly those that have experience of the activity that is the focus of the discussion. Other forum members use the opportunity to gain social support and form networks of contacts that may or may not interface with their real-life or non-Internet activities.

As the above study found [5] there are some who tend to rely too heavily on this virtual support mechanism and they are less happy with this than those who use more proximate support. This finding echoes earlier work and is a common feature of many Internet support networks where the participants are relatively distant from each other.

To summarise the findings it would appear to be appropriate to point out that there is no substitute for the human touch, even the computer-mediated version is not able to fulfil the role. However, these Internet opportunities form a useful alternative place for people to gain support if traditional resources are not available.

5 Market-Driven Development

The main source of devices, systems and services for EC users is the industry that sells these to consumers. The marketing push in the industry is to engage a wide range of users in the process of purchasing new equipment and systems for entertainment. Some technologies have been more successful than others and there are a number of historical studies that show that wider take-up is not necessarily because of superior technology (see Liebowitz and Margolis, [6]) and the outcome is often closer related to marketing, advertising and other non-technical factors rather than any technological, or even usability, superiority.

The market background document from the TEAHA project (Homega Research, [7]) gives some insight into the status of various technologies and their take-up around the world. This allows some perspective on the market for connected home products and as such gives some idea of the EC systems that are related to these technological advances. As is pointed out in this report the prediction of markets is fraught with danger and simple extrapolation is not a reliable indicator of future trends in such diverse markets as home electronics and leisure equipment.

The market-led nature of this technology is also a factor that does not lead to the most ethical style of development for the systems in question. The primary goal of manufacturers is to sell goods, to make profits and to continue to operate. They do not necessarily have any "emotional capital" in the goods that they sell and promote. In fact there are a number of conflicting goals for manufacturers that do not assist the user. Amongst these are the problems of compatibility and standards.

5.1 Compatibility Issues

There are some complex economic issues involved in the production of goods for the EC market, as for many other markets for electronic goods and services. Many of these issues are related to the compatibility of different software and systems. The issue for companies and the goods they produce (i.e. do they produce them to be compatible with others or not?) rests on many factors and is too complex to discuss in this paper. However, the more significant side of this argument, from the EC perspective, is summarized by the following [8]:

"Society reaps significant benefits from compatibility and standardization"

It is this factor and the incompatibility of much market-driven production that are the opposing forces in the EC arena and that can determine the outcome of technological developments.

The compatibility of devices, systems, services and software is not a pre-requisite for successful EC development but it has a considerable influence on the take-up and spread of the technology. It is also clear that the ethical development of home systems, devices and services requires them to be developed using an ethical perspective which must account for the societal need for standardization in addition to the commercial requirement for profit.

5.2 Standardisation

The issue of standardization is quite complex. The opposing views are that: on the one hand, standards are necessary to ensure compatibility of equipment and, on the other, that standards are a restriction to the successful development of new devices and systems. Both of these viewpoints are, to some extent true. The use of standardization has helped many systems to gain a bigger share of the market and many manufacturers are able to compete in a market that is led by standardization activities. Examples of this are: the CD audio and DVD video standards. These have led to many different devices being available to users to play the standard software.

Standardisation of media, such as DVD, helps both equipment manufacturers and content producers provide users with compatible devices and useable content. Indeed, without the standardization effort the market may not reach critical mass before the device or system becomes obsolete. There have been many different proprietary media standards that have faltered without the back-up of a wide variety of content to enhance sales.

The opposite problem of standards: that of restricting innovation is only problematic when the devices that are standardized become widespread and the standard becomes technically limited compared to other competing standards. This situation is the case with video recording equipment. There is a large-scale legacy investment in VCRs around the world and they are now much more limited than the digital replacements: DVD recorders. However, there is still a need to support the VCR user with software content, consumables and maintenance for some time into the future. There are some moves to end support for VCRs by ending sales but the legacy of many old devices will continue for a number of years and there are still manufacturers supplying new devices for users.

The move from video-cassette to DVD as the medium of choice for consumers is likely to be driven by a number of factors: wider DVD content provision, compatibility with other devices such as PC drives, multi-function capabilities (e.g. on-screen viewing of photos), digital input, output quality factors, price (although VCRs are currently much cheaper than DVD recorders of an equivalent functionality), and media cost (DVD+RW and Video-cassette prices are roughly comparable). However, one of the most useful and attractive characteristics of using discs is the indexing and random-access capabilities of the device. All these factors and the market-push of the manufacturers are likely to see the replacement of VCRs by DVD devices in a fairly short time.

The next problem that will be faced by DVD/VHS users is then likely to be the recording of family archives of legacy content onto new media. This has been an issue in the past, albeit on a smaller scale, when the introduction of home video recorders made home use of cine film unattractive. Some content was moved onto videocassette by specialist companies. Upgrading to digital formats will see more legacy content being moved to new media systems.

In other spheres of EC there are similar problems. Many computer games are marketed alongside the platforms that support them, as the platforms develop, the games are replaced by new ones. The original games may be enough for some users and the upgrade inappropriate. However, the obsolescence that is inherent in the process militates against using software for longer than the original hardware support is available.

6 Social Activity

The social support mechanisms of the Internet have been discussed above. These form a small part of the wide range of social activities that take place on the Internet and between the connected systems of different users. The use of Internet forums, bulletin boards and other, more direct, Internet communication tools has revolutionised the contact between people separated by space and time. It is now commonplace to use email as a primary means of communication, although the more personal SMS text messaging seems to be common amongst certain groups, especially the young, where individual control of the "message terminal" may be an issue.

Email provides a useful means of communicating information and allows most of what can be sent with more personal means, but there is still a problem with the "sense" and "meaning" that is implied with tone of voice that is missed when email is used. This makes email useful as a social tool but not as a sole means of communication. It is often a more useful instrument when the communicators have prior knowledge of each other and they are familiar with "idiosyncrasies" and "style".

Having said that, it is possible to conduct successful online conversations with total strangers via email and in forums when each participant has a good knowledge of the other from the "clues and cues" that are part of everyday net use. One of the activities that seems to bind online groups together is a real-life meeting. The two-way exchange of information can be used to facilitate a successful outcome.

7 Ethical Development

There have been a number of studies that have used co-operative design methods (for example, [9]) these are perhaps the most appropriate for the design of entertainment computing systems as they involve the end-user in the design process, although there are problems with the application of any methods to the design of systems that are primarily used for leisure purposes.

However, there remains the problem of how the design of EC systems can be made more ethical. The initial problem of how to design EC system needs to be replaced by an extra stage of analysis that asks the fundamental question "Should this device or system be designed and made?" and if it is, "How should it be made so that it can be used ethically?" and finally "Is it possible to make an ethical version by excluding or enhancing certain functionality?"

With the use of a comprehensive ethical analysis of the situation of the user and the device, put into the context of the leisure environment, devices can be designed to include a more ethical dimension for the type of device that is in use by people for a significant amount of their free time. The idea of an ethical dimension to EC system design will be explored in the following section where a typical design scenario of an EC device will be outlined and discussed.

7.1 Design Scenario – Internet Forum Software

It is worth considering the three questions from the previous section: "Should this device or system be designed and made?" "How should it be made so that it can be used ethically?" and "Is it possible to make an ethical version by excluding or enhancing certain functionality?"

Should this device or system be designed and made? Internet forum software can be designed that allows many types of transaction and allows users to provide and use information in different ways. A software system for multiple users can be designed that allows any user to post any information into the system. This can clearly be abused and there are usually functions available to allow moderation of posts on a forum.

How should it be made so that it can be used ethically? If the moderation option is not provided there is clearly an ethical lapse by the software developers. Allowing users to abuse systems is not in the interest of those that run the forums, and some form of "control" would seem to be the most ethical approach to a harmonious use of such a system.

Is it possible to make an ethical version by excluding or enhancing certain functionality? The levels of control by different groups of user is generally the way that Internet forums are run. The various levels of control of post information are designed to allow a hierarchy of control with minimal input from those with highest level of access. This has been seen to wok well when the members of the forum conduct their "business" in a way that is a parallel of real-life.

To exclude the facility of all users to have wide control would appear to be an option that works. To enhance the control options at the various levels also gives an approach that is workable.

8   Conclusions

Entertainment computing covers a wide area of human life and there are many ways in which the development of services and systems can take a "less then ethical" road. What is clear is that there is an ethical route through the design, development, deployment and use of systems that can lead to a much wider acceptance by the users of the systems and services, and enhance their quality of life in the process. This will need further study to determine how an ethical approach can be embedded within the full lifecycle of products and services in this domain. The main area of study has been the use of Internet forums and the approaches used by product developers and users.

The use of computer-mediated communication technology is not new, but the rapid growth on recent years has been aided by the increase in Internet speed and wider access to it by people in every walk of life. This use of the Internet as a leisure activity is one of the aspect of "Entertainment Computing" that provides both an element of leisure and an element of social activity in much the same way as more formal face-to-face gatherings have done in the past.

References

1. Sloane A (2003) "The Internet in the home: Changing the domestic landscape" in Harris D, Duffy V, Smith M and Stephanides C (Eds.) Human-Centred Computing, Volume 3 of the proceedings of HCII2003, Crete, June 22-27. ISBN0-8058-4932-7. pp1126-1130.
2. Sloane A (2002) "Methodologies for studying the home user" - World Computer Congress - Tutorial, Montreal, August 2002.
3. Sloane A, Harris A, and Huang W (2000) "Home Information Systems: The storage problem" in van Rijn F. and Sloane A. (eds.) Home-oriented informatics and telematics: Information, Technology and Society, Proceedings of HOIT 2000, Wolverhampton, U.K., June 2000, Kluwer. ISBN 0-7923-7867-9.
4. Sandström G, Gustavsson S, Lundberg S, Keijer U, Junestrand S. (2005) " Long-term viability of smart-home systems", Home-oriented informatics and telematics, in Sloane A (ed.) Home-Oriented Inforamtics and Telematics", Proceedings of HOIT2005, York April 2005, Springer, pp71-86.
5. Leung L and Lee P S N (2005) "Multiple determinants of life quality: the roles of Internet activities, use of new media, social support and leisure activities" Telematics and Informatics 22, pp161-180.
6. Liebowitz S J and Margolis S.E (1995), "Path Dependence, Lock-In and History "Journal of Law, Economics and Organization
7. Homega Research (2004) "The worldwide markets for the Connected home: status and trends", TEAHA background document, Available from http://www.teaha.org/ project_outputs.php (Downloaded 9th November 2004)
8. Economides N (1999) "Competition and Vertical Integration in the Computing Industry", in Eisenach J. A. and. Lenard T M (eds.), *Competition, Innovation, and the Role of Antitrust in the Digital Marketplace,* Kluwer Academic Publishers 1999
9. Kristensen J F, Eriksen M A, Iversen O S, Kanstrup A M, Nielsen C and Petersen M G (2003) "Young People in Old Cars - Challenges for Cooperative Design", Electronic Proceedings of the 26th Information Systems Research Seminar in Scandinavia/IRIS26, Haikko Manor, Finland, August 9-12, 2003.

Notes on the Methodology of Pervasive Gaming

Bo Kampmann Walther

Centre for Media Studies, University of Southern Denmark,
Campusvej 55, 5230 Odense M, Denmark
+45 65 50 36 16
walther@litcul.sdu.dk

Abstract. The paper introduces four axes of pervasive gaming (PG): mobility, distribution, persistence, and transmediality. Further, it describes and analyses three key units of PG (rules, entities, and mechanics) as well as discusses the role of space in PG by differentiating between tangible space, information embedded space, and accessibility space.

Categories and Subject Descriptors: H.5.1 [Multimedia Information Systems]: Artificial, augmented, and virtual realities.

General Terms: Performance, Human Factors, Theory.

Keywords: Pervasive gaming, game rules, gameplay, game theory, ludology, game space.

1 Introduction

New technology and new methods for networking digital systems are essential for the development, implementation, and conceptual understanding of complex adaptation in computer mediated games and play. At the same time, we must identify and rethink the social interactions as well as the formalisms and theories that are deployed in pervasive gaming. Since 'real life' is part of the game and the gaming arena itself, including rules and game parameters, concepts such as *probability*, *uncertainty*, and *contingency* gain importance in the design and understanding of PG.

First, I will depict the four axes of pervasive games: the mobility axis, the distribution axis, the persistence axis, and the transmediality axis. In the second part of the paper we shall look deeper into game rules, game entities, and game mechanics. Third, we shall concern ourselves with the renewed focus on space or spatiality in relation to PG.

2 PG Formalisms

I define 'pervasive game' as an over-arching concept or activity subsuming the following post-screen gaming sub-genres [9]:

F. Kishino et al. (Eds.): ICEC 2005, LNCS 3711, pp. 488–495, 2005.
© IFIP International Federation for Information Processing 2005

- A *mobile game* is a game that takes changing relative or absolute position/location into account in the game rules. This excludes games for which mobile devices merely provide a delivery channel where key features of mobility are not relevant to the game mechanics. Hence, one could distinguish between *mobile interfaced games* and *mobile embedded games*.
- A *location-based game* is a game that includes relative or absolute but static position/location in the game rules.
- A *ubiquitous game* uses the computational and communications infrastructure embedded within our everyday lives.
- *Virtual realities games* are games generated by computer systems. The goal is to construct is to construct wholly autonomous and completely surrounding game worlds.
- *Augmented reality games* and *mixed reality games* are an interesting approach to the creation of game spaces that seek to integrate virtual and physical elements within a comprehensibly experienced perceptual game world.
- *Adaptronic games* are games consisting of applications and information systems that simulate life processes observed in nature. These games are embedded, flexible, and usually made up of 'tangible bits' that oscillate between virtual and real space.

Two essential qualities of pervasive computing stand out; 1) the explicitness of *computational tasks*, and 2) the all-importance of *physical space*. The former implies that actions are carried out in ways that transcend the traditional screen-facilitated environment; embedded computing shifts our attention from metaphorical data manipulation to simulated and natural interactions with things and physical objects. This interweaves with the second aspect of pervasive computing as objects obeying the laws of natural physics are open to (digital) manipulation and thus take on a double meaning: they are objects within the outside non-game world; yet they can also be objects within a game world.

Following this I will propose a general or 'classic' definition of PG:

Pervasive gaming implies the construction and enacting of augmented and/or embedded game worlds that reside on the threshold between tangible and immaterial space, which may further include adaptronics, embedded software, and information systems in order to facilitate a 'natural' environment for gameplay that ensures the explicitness of computational procedures in a post-screen setting.

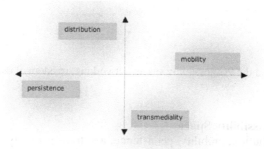

Fig. 1. Four axes of PG

2.1 The Four Axes of PG

We will zero in on four axes that together mark the possible domains of PG. The four axes can be illustrated like this:

- *Distribution.* Pervasive computing devices are frequently mobile or embedded in the environment and linked to an increasingly ubiquitous network infrastructure composed of a wired core and wireless edges. This combination of embedded computing, dynamic networking, and discrete information sharing clearly affects and strengthens the distribution paradigm of IT. One example of a distribution system designed to work in huge networks is the so-called Twine resource discovery system. It uses a set of resolvers Twine nodes that organize themselves into an overlay network to route resource descriptions to each other for storage, and to collaboratively resolve client queries [1].
- *Mobility.* New challenges of pervasive computing further include mobility, i.e. computing mobility, network mobility, and user mobility, context aware (smartness), and cross-platform service. Particular interesting to the field of PG is the growth in mobile 3G technologies, Bluetooth, and LAN-LAN Bridging.
- *Persistence.* The idea of creating an online world in a mobile phone is the driving force behind the Danish company Watagame's *Era of Eidolon.* The persistence factor here touches upon the notion of temporality. Persistence means total availability all the time.
- *Transmediality* relates to modes of media consumption that have been profoundly altered by a succession of new media technologies, which enable average citizens to participate in the archiving, annotation, appropriation, transformation, and re-circulation of media content [7]. No medium in the present day can be defined as a self-sufficient application based on partial groupings. The junction of multiple media spread out over huge networks and accessible through a range of devices is rather a nice instance of how media commune in circular, not linear, forms.

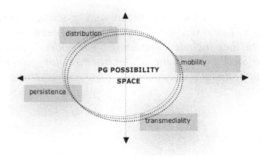

Fig. 2. Four axes and the PG possibility space: networking, freedom of device, non-closure, and circular storytelling

2.1.1 The PG Possibility Space
Combining distribution, mobility, persistence, and transmediality we embark upon the 'PG possibility space'. It is a space that deals in *networking* given the focus on non-locality, non-metric systems, and constant accessibility. It is a space that celebrates

the *freedom of device* – games can be played on anything; and game devices may trigger anything, anywhere, anytime. It is further a space that favors *non-closure*; although pervasive games still cling to the law of goal-orientation (closure) they open up new ways of collaborative world building as well as invite continuous structural expansion. Finally, the PG possibility space embraces *circular* storytelling as *the* norm of mediated entertainment.

2.2   The Three Key Units of PG

Games can be divided into three key units that are strongly interlaced: 1) Game *rules*, 2) game *entities*, and 3) game *mechanics*.

2.2.1   Game Rules

In Jesper Juul's generalized model there are six invariant parameters of game rules:

1) Rules: Games are rule-based. **2) Variable, quantifiable outcome:** Games have variable, quantifiable outcomes. **3) Value assigned to possible outcomes:** That the different potential outcomes of the game are assigned different values, some being positive, some being negative. **4) Player effort**: That the player invests effort in order to influence the outcome. (I.e. games are challenging.) **5) Player attached to outcome**: That the players are attached to the outcomes of the game in the sense that a player will be the winner and "happy" if a positive outcome happens, and loser and "unhappy" if a negative outcome happens. **6) Negotiable consequences**: The same game [set of rules] can be played with or without real-life consequences [8].

It is evident that some of these rule parameters are altered with respect to PG. Let me narrow this alteration down to two issues:

1) Take the vital concept of variable, quantifiable outcome. To Juul, this mean that the outcome of a game is designed to be beyond discussion, and that this trait is an instinctive token of game rules. This fits perfectly well with practically all computer games. However, when moving the logic structure of the digital computer into the tangible world the quantifiability of a rule system seems to shift into a more fuzzy type of interaction between constitutive and regulative rules. In *The Construction of Social Reality* Searle explains that social rules may be regulative or constitutive [12]. *Regulative* rules legalize an activity whereas *constitutive* rules may create the possibility of an activity. It is the constitutive rules that provide a structure for institutional facts. In the context of explaining the (extended) rule system of PG, computation can be regarded as a conceptual framework that constitutes the possibility space for regulative behavior. Constitutive rules belong to the set of quantifiable norms while the regulative rules govern the ad hoc player interference with the game world. Another way of distinguishing the computational rule logic from the real-time interaction pattern of gameplay would be to differentiate between *global regulations* (provided by the computer's state machine) and *local operatives* (controlled by the player's behavior with the physical as well as information embedded game world).

2) Next, we should consider the term 'negotiable consequences'. In pervasive gaming 'real-life consequences' is exactly that which drives the play experience forward. The entire teleology of gameplay in fact rests on these outcomes that transpire and are enacted on the physical arena. A game of chess might have ferocious consequences if played out in real life. However, since the movement of pieces across the board

merely *represents* physical structures it follows that the rules of chess apply to the discrete topology of the game and not the phenomenological experiences that this topology may cause. In the domain of pervasive gaming it is precisely the 'negotiability' signifying the toggling back and forth between real-life consequences and discrete representations that pushes gameplay forward. Thus, the 'tangibility consequence' of PG brings forth a level of uncertainty to the gaming phenomenology; and this uncertainty becomes part of the rule structure, as it must be inscribed in the computational representation.

2.2.2 Game Entities

In line with the Object Oriented Programming paradigm I define a game entity as an *abstract class of an object that can be moved and drawn over a game map.* There can be an enormous amount of entities in a game; inventory objects in an adventure game; Non Playing Characters (NPC's) in a FPS (First Person Shooter); or a text message in a strategy game. Since a game has more entities, the ways that they can react together increases geometrically.

A PG entity can take the shape of a) *game object*, i.e. any object that can be encountered, seen, or interacted with during gameplay; b) a *human agent*, since an essential part of a pervasive game is to collaborate and engage in conflict with 'flesh polygons'; and c) a *physical object*.

It is the negotiability or uncertainty principle that do the trick. Pervasive gameplay implies *contingency handling*.

2.2.3 Game Mechanics

Lundgren & Björk define game mechanics, as simply *any part of the rule system of a game that covers one, and only one, possible kind of interaction that takes place during the game, be it general or specific.* A game may consist of several mechanics, and a mechanic may be a part of many games [10].

Thus, one can generally define game mechanics as an *input-output engine.* The task of this engine is to ensure a dynamic relation between game state and player interference, and it is responsible for simulating a direct connection between the I/O system of computational, discrete logic and the continuous flow from initial to final state in a physical setting. Game mechanics postulates a deep transport from the laws of computation to the natural laws of physics.

The following issues of mechanics are specifically noteworthy:

- *Physically embedded game mechanics.* Frontrunner in pervasive gaming, German-based Fraunhofer FIT, has designed *Net Attack* (www.fit.fraunhofer.de). The game is presented as a new type of indoor/outdoor Augmented Reality game that makes the actual physical environment an inherent part of the game itself. The mechanics apply to the outdoor environment where players equipped with a backpack full of technology rush around a predefined game field trying to collect items as well as to the indoor setting where a player sits in front of a desktop computer and supports the outdoor player with valuable information. In order to control the information flow linking physical and virtual space the various components communicate via events and a TCP/IP-based high-level protocol. A central component guarantees consistency and allows the configuration of the game. Before starting to play the game, the outdoor game area must be modeled and the game levels configured. In other words: modeling the game means embedding the necessary mechanics into physical space. The configuration is done with XML.

- *Input-output engine with dual purpose.* Since interaction with tangible objects in PG implies, as noted above, a level of contingency handling the input-output engine must be constructed in such a fashion so that it provides a probability algorithm for the actual interaction as part of the rules and dictates a global, discrete and binary rule (state) to the interaction. That is why PG mechanics may serve a dual purpose; on the one hand maintaining and stimulating the contingency of interaction with real-life objects, and on the other hand structuring the controlled set of actions embedded in the state rules.

3 PG Space

Space differs when we look at it from a human and a strictly mathematical angle [11; 14]. The space of every day life is *heterotrophic* because it confronts its user with a surplus of potential, spatial strategies. The space of mathematics is *isotropic* in which all matter and every coordinates are evenly spread in all directions. When a human subject navigates through space it becomes *contingent* and *intentional*. Suddenly, space *matters.*

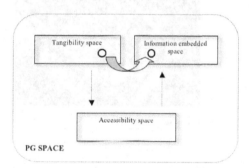

Fig. 3.

The point here is that the space of pervasive gaming mixes the isotropic and heterotrophic space. The teleological goal structure of a game necessitates *accessibility* by which the user can obtain information about space and proceed from e.g. one level to the next [13]. A PG space must amalgamate the physical *metric* space and the informational and networked *non-metric* space and, finally, merge these into the accessibility space [4]. A metric space consists of a non-empty universe of points together with a family of distance relations satisfying the axioms of distance [3]. A non-metric space may be defined as a topological or nodal connected space. 'Real life' as such would not alone be interesting in a gaming sense. We need to organize and structure the non-teleological and open meaning of the mundane space in order to make it playable. Therefore, accessibility is the portal to the information embedded spatial game world.

3.1 Tangibility Space

The whole idea of 'playability' in PG is the player's interaction with the physical reality. The tangibility space, however, is not just the sum total of this available, real-time world and the vast amount of objects it possesses. Rather, it must be understood as the *heterotrophic organization of potential spatial patterns of behavior*. This organization or vectorization of space facilitates a 'playground' and is often aided by multiple information units located in material objects as 'tangible bits' [6].

3.2 Distributed Information Space

PG involves the blending of physical and virtual space. In spatial terms this means that the tangibility space is facilitated by and projected onto information embedded space. This kind of space is the digital representation of the tangibility space. Yet, besides serving as a map of the gameworld, it may also function as a phenomenological space in its own right.

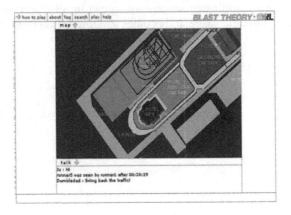

Fig. 4. Information embedded space [2]

3.3 Accessibility Space

Finally, we have the accessibility space that is the key to the oscillation between embedded and tangible information. One way of explaining the delicate relation between the triadic space structures is to say that accessibility space *maps* the information embedded space system that is in turn *mapped* onto the tangible reality.

4 Conclusion

A great many challenges await us in the field of post-screen gaming. On the analytical side it may be rewarding to think PG in terms of axes, key units, and space modalities, as I have suggested in this context. Regarding the continuous innovation of production schemes and technology enhancement it might prove equally gratifying to integrate the rising world of adaptronics in tomorrow's pervasive games.

References

[1] Balazinska, Magdalena & Balakrishnan, Hari (2001). Twine: A Scalable Peer-to-Peer Architecture for Intentional Resource Discovery (http://sow.csail.mit.edu/2001/).

[2] Benford, Steve et al. (2003). Coping With Uncertainty in a Location-Based Game, *EEE CS and IEEE ComSoc*, 1536-1268.

[3] Bricker, P. (1993). The Fabric of Space, in *Midwest Studies in Philosophy XVIII*, Notre Dame: Norte Dame University Press.

[4] Bøgh Andersen, Peter (2002). Pervasive Computing and Space. In L. Kecheng, Clarke, R. J., Andersen, P. B. Stamper, R. & El-Sayed Abou-Zeid (Eds.): *Organizational Semiotics: evolving a science of information systems. IFIP TC8/WG8. 1 working conference of organizational semiotics, July 23-25, 2001, Montreal, Quebec, Canada.* Kluwer: Boston/Dordrecht/London, pp. 133-152.

[5] Ishii, Hiroshi and Ullmer, Brygg (1997). Tangible Bits: Towards Seamless Interfaces between People, Bits and Atoms, in *The Proceedings of CHI '97*, March 22-27.

[6] Jenkins, Henry (2003). Transmedia Storytelling, *Technology Review*, Jan.

[7] Juul, Jesper (2003). The Game, the Player, the World: Looking for a Heart of Gameness, in Marinka Copier & Joost Raessens (Eds.): *Level Up: Digital Games Research Conference Proceedings.* Utrecht: Universiteit Utrecht, 2003, pp. 30-45.

[8] Lindley, Craig (2004). Trans-Reality Gaming. In *Proceedings of the Second Annual International Workshop in Computer Game Design and Technology*, 15-16 November, Liverpool John Moores University, UK.

[9] Lundgren, Sus & Björk, Staffan (2004). Game Mechanics: Describing Computer-Augmented Games in Terms of Interaction (retrieved from http://www.playresearch.com).

[10] Nielsen, Arno Victor (1996). A Space Odyssey, in *K & K*, no. 82.

[11] Searle, John (1995). *The Construction of Social Reality.* New York: The Free Press.

[12] Walther, Bo Kampmann (2003a). Gaming and Playing, in *Game Studies*, vol. 3, issue 1.

[13] Walther, Bo Kampmann (2003b). La représentation de l'espace dans les jeux vidéo : généalogie, classification et réflexions, in Melanie Roustan (Ed.): *La pratique du jeu vidéo. Réalité ou virtualité*, Paris

From Hunt the Wumpus to EverQuest: Introduction to Quest Theory

Espen Aarseth

Center for Computer Games Research,
IT-University of Copenhagen, Rued Langgaardsvej 7,
2300 Copenhagen, Denmark
aarseth@itu.dk
+45 3253 4567

Abstract. The paper will explore how the landscape types and the quest types are used in various games, how they structure the gameplay, how they act as bones for the game-content (graphics, dialogue, sound) and how they sometimes form the base on which a story is imposed and related to the player. The question then becomes, how does the quest structure influence the story structure? How do the limitations of the quest combinations limit the kinds of story that are possible? How rich can the imposed story be, without breaking the gameplay? Are landscape and quest-structure the dominant factors in quest game design, to which the story-ambitions must defer? The main thesis of the paper is that if we understand the powerful but simple structure - the grammar - of quests (how they work, how they are used) we can understand both the limits and the potential of these kinds of games.

1 Introduction

This paper will lay out the foundations of a theory of quests in computer games. Quests are a basic, dominant ingredient in a number of types of games in virtual environments, from the early adventure games to today's massive multiplayers, and by understanding their functions and importance for game design and game aesthetics we can contribute to many of the current debates in game studies, such as the question of genres and typologies, the question of narrativity in games and cross media productions, and the crucial issue of playability and replayability.

This work builds on efforts by Tronstad [8], Tosca [7] and Aarseth [1]. Previous attempts at describing quests and their importance for computer games have fallen short of defining the concept, except for Tosca:

> A quest, as we said earlier, brings some or all the storytelling elements (characters, plot, causality, world) together with the interaction, so that we can define it as the array of soft rules that describe what the player has to do in a particular storytelling situation. ([7], section 4.2)

However, Tosca's definition relies on too many unnecessary elements (characters, plot, storytelling, "soft rules") to be generally applicable. E.g., in a labyrinth game

F. Kishino et al. (Eds.): ICEC 2005, LNCS 3711, pp. 496–506, 2005.
© IFIP International Federation for Information Processing 2005

such as Gregory Yob's *Hunt the Wumpus* (1972), what are the "soft rules" and the storytelling situation? In this paper, I propose two definitions of quest games. A quest game can be defined as

a game with a concrete and attainable goal, which supercedes performance or the accumulation of points. Such goals can be nested (hierarchic), concurrent, or serial, or a combination of the above.

Or, minimally, as

a game which depends on mere movement from position A to position B.

The minimal definition should not be seen as descriptively exhaustive; most games framed by it would also have a number of additional elements and features, such as characters, dialogue, setting, music, a semiotic universe, etc. But they would involve the necessity of moving from A to B, in a way that games like chess, *Tetris*, football, multiplayer *Starcraft*, and *Quake Arena*, or quest games such as *Morrowind* and *EverQuest*, do not. (While some other non-quest game types, e.g. racing games, also do depend on movement from A to B, in these cases mere movement is not sufficient to win.) Hence, not all games containing quests are framed by the minimal definition (only by the first definition above); such is its weakness. But the specificity of the minimal definition overlaps nicely with the set of games that are usually seen as "narrative," i.e. games that contain a storyline, e.g. a fixed sequence of predetermined events that cannot be circumlocuted through gameplay. There seems to be few, if any "narrative" games that do not also conform to the "A to B" formula, so until proven wrong by example, I will assume that "narrative" games and "A to B" games are the same, at least for the purposes of this paper.

2 The Basic Quest Types and Combinations

Since, content-wise, quests can appear in innumerable variations (e.g. go to X, ask for object Y, take it to place Z), it is on the grammatical level that we must look for structure and design principles. Evidently, quest games come in many forms and shapes - just compare *Doom3* to *Pikmin2* - but underneath their colorful and varied appearance there is a very simple variation of skeletal patterns, consisting of a few elemental figures.

Fig. 1. Time, place, and objective, the three basic quest types

There are three basic quest types: 1) Place-oriented, 2) time-oriented and 3) objective-oriented. These can then be combined in various ways, to form complex and elaborate games where quests are weaved, mixed, parallelized and sequentialized.

Place-oriented quests are the simplest type, where the player typically has to move the avatar from a starting position in the game world to a target position (cf. definition two above). Games of this type include *Doom* and *MYST* (both 1993) and *Adventure* (1976). Such games may also typically include puzzles that require the player to manipulate objects found along the way, but in its most basic form the place-oriented quest is a labyrinth, where the players simply have to find their way.

Time-oriented quests may seem rare in pure form, but they do exist, usually as part of a larger game. A typical example is found more than once in games like *Call of Duty* (2003), where sometimes the only quest-task is to stay alive for a fixed number of minutes. I distinctly remember a railway station level in *Call of Duty: United Offensive* (2004), where I (or rather my avatar) spent the last minute and a half of the time-quest lying still, hidden between the train and the platform, with enemies all around, who were unable to find me and kill me before my reinforcements, finally, arrived.

The third basic type is the objective-oriented quest, where the task is to achieve a concrete result, such as an object that must be taken by force from a non-player character (NPC). This object may not be in the same place, but could be moving freely in the game world. Typical examples can be found in *Hunt the Wumpus,* or in the *Heroes of Might and Magic* series, where an enemy hero might possess a magical item (a powerup) which, when acquired, defines the winning condition of the level.

In a recent empirical study of 80 "significant games of 2003" Jeffery Brand and Scott Knight [2] found that 73% of the games were place-oriented, 43% were time-oriented, and 83% were objective-oriented. They also found a strong correlation between place-oriented (topological) rules and "embedded narrative," which tells us that "narrative" games can usually and more sensibly be identified as place-/A-to-B-oriented quest games.

The three basic quest types can be combined, and in four fundamental ways. The combinations are

Fig. 2. a) Time&Place ("get there before…");   b) Time&Objective ("Get it before…")

Fig. 3. a) Place & Objective ("Get there and…");   b) Time&Place&Objective ("Get there before … and …")

In addition, games can combine, nest and serialize these seven types, resulting in rich and highly complex quest worlds, where the player feels free to decide what to do next, and can solve the quests in many orders. Typical games of this kind are *Fable* (2004), *Knights of the Old Republic* (2003), *EverQuest* (1999-) and *World of Warcraft* (2004-).

If we compare quest structures in a number of games, it can clearly be shown how they form the backbone of the gameplay:

- *Half-Life*: Serial quest; place and (occasionally) objective-oriented
- *Halo*: Serial quest; place and (occasionally) time-oriented
- *Knights of the Old Republic*: Nested and concurrent quests; place and objective-oriented
- *Morrowind*: Concurrent quests; place and objective-oriented
- *GTA3*: Serial and nested quests; place, time and objective-oriented
- *EverQuest*: Concurrent quests; place, time and objective-oriented

3 The Quest Game Landscape

The complementary, equally important structure is of course the game landscape. Quest and space are intrinsically linked: Level design in quest games is structured by the types of quests the game uses, and vice versa. There are three basic quest game landscapes:

Fig. 4. The linear corridor (e.g. *Half-Life*)

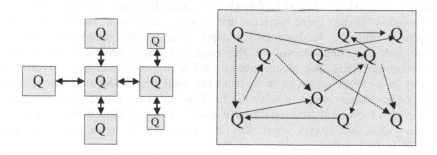

Fig. 5. The semi-open, often star-shaped hub (e.g. *Knights of the Old Republic)* and the open landscape (e.g. *Morrowind*)

Moreover, games that might appear open-landscaped, such as the 2D strategy series *Heroes of Might and Magic* or the *Warcraft* series, will often feature maps/landscapes that consist of a uni- or multi-cursal labyrinth or hub, where mountain ranges, oceans or impenetrable forests form natural boundaries of the game labyrinth.

Fig. 6. Heroes of Might and Magic: Armageddon's blade. A multicursal labyrinth, where the hero can move through open glades only.

4 Storylines vs. Gameworlds

Ever since the first literary article on adventure games [6], and the first dissertation [3], questions have been raised about the relationship between narratives and games. Though these questions have been formulated in many ways and from many needs and perspectives (e.g. technical, utopian, critical, and pragmatic), little progress has been made in these two decades. This lack can be explained by 1) little or no awareness of previous work and of work in parallel disciplines; 2) little progress in the evolution of the game systems themselves, and 3) a lack of theoretical engagement with the fundamental concepts (story, game, interactive, narrative, fiction) and their implications for the empirical basis, especially in the more utopian/technical/pragmatic contributions. While a more thorough investigation resulting in a clearer notion of these concepts, their limitations and their relevance might not have been enough to solve the fundamental issue, it might have resulted in a better set of concepts, that could have modeled and explained the relationships between games and stories where the first generation of terms (e.g. "interactive fiction") clearly failed.

For instance, if we go back to the first academic use of "interactive fiction", the authors (Niesz and Holland [6]) do not attempt to explain in what way the adventure games they discuss actually are fiction, how the concept of fiction is expanded by their use of it, or how they would re-define it, in light of the new material. Rather than to take this wonderful opportunity to explore the generality and scope of the concepts, the new empirical evidence was forced to fit the pre-conceived semantics of the old concepts. This unfortunate tendency is still evident in recent studies: For instance, in the article "Games and Stories" [9] the authors, strangely, criticize the profoundly successful dungeon game *Diablo* (1996) for failing to comply with the principles of narrative communication. This is just one example among innumerable; they can be easily spotted by either their lack of a clear, empirically grounded definition of the key concepts (story, narrative, fiction, etc), or when new attempts at definitions of narrative are provided, these definitions are usually so broad as to be useless. A good test is to see whether the definitions also will include obviously non-narrative phenomena and activities such as, say, elevators, meals, or shopping. One such term is "emergent narratives" negatively defined by Henry Jenkins [5] as "not pre-structured or pre-programmed, taking shape through the game play, yet they are not as unstructured, chaotic, and frustrating as life itself". Jenkins does not offer a definition that allows us to positively discriminate between emergent narratives and "life itself" – or between "life itself" and any part of "life itself" that may appear structured, un-chaotic and un-frustrating.

The current state of affairs (i.e. the "ludology-narratology" war) has been lamented many times (see Frasca [4]) and this is not the place to rehash that meta-debate. Instead, it is time to examine and perhaps explain the apparent dichotomy or (as also claimed) synergy between games and stories. To do so, we must first return to the roots of computer games and "interactive fiction". The first modern computer game was no doubt *SpaceWar!* (Russell et al. 1961-2). It was a space combat simulation, a fight between two player-controlled spaceships where the laws of gravity and the players' ingenuity determined the outcome. *SpaceWar!* is a simulation, a set of automatic rules represented on a graphics screen. While the game was inspired by science fiction, it was pure action, and could produce an infinite variety of slightly different game events. *SpaceWar!* was the start of the action/arcade genre, that today contains a rich diversity of games which let the player move through simulated space.

An equally important root was *Dungeons and Dragons* (D&D) by Gary Gygax and Dave Arneson (1974), the pen-and paper game which simulated fantasy combat through a system later known as the D20 rules, named after the 20-sided dice used to produce random results in the game. *D&D* was a set of rules, inspired by tactical war games, which would let a game master lead a team of adventurers through a medieval-fantasy landscape. Games could last for months, and players nurtured their characters and co-produced the unfolding of an improvised fantasy narrative through their interaction with the game master's prepared landscape and schemes.

The D&D system has been immensely influential across many game genres, from singleplayer games such as Richard Garriott's *Ultima* Series, *Rogue/Nethack,* strategy games such as *Heroes of Might and Magic,* the original *Multi-User Dungeon* (Bartle and Trubshaw 1979), and newer games like *Baldur's Gate, Morrowind* and *Knights of the Old Republic,* not to mention MUD-style "massively" multiplayer games like *Ultima Online* and *EverQuest.* The elegant, easily implementable simulation of monsters, heroes, skills, spells and weapons has proved a powerful base for computer game development for more than two decades.

But while "interactive storytelling" as a collaborative effort between game master and players is an important aspect of many D&D sessions, the computer games based on the D20 rules are less creative than human authors, as they lack the human intelligence needed to create or co-create a story in real time. Instead, they rely on other tricks to present successive events in a story-like order.

Another origin game was Crowther and Woods' *Adventure* (1976), which started as a cave simulation, based on William Crowther's exploration of Colossal Cave in Kentucky. Donald Woods turned the cave simulation into a puzzle-solving and treasure hunting game, which in turn inspired the very popular genre of textual adventure games, later known as "interactive fiction." Unlike the creators of *MUD*, *Rogue*, *Ultima* etc; Woods was not familiar with the *D&D* system, and, perhaps for that reason, produced a game which was much simpler in terms of simulation and rules, and whose main gameplay elements were the labyrinth and the verb-object puzzle. While the textual adventure game died commercially in the late 80s, the basic linear labyrinth structure survives in the graphical puzzle and action adventure games such as *MYST*, *Half-Life*, *Max Payne*, *Halo* and numerous others.

The two root structures (unicursal labyrinth and D20) are still present in modern games, and typically, they do not overlap. D20 games tend to be more open-landscaped and open-ended, while linear games (*Half-Life 2, Halo*) do not make use of D20 rules.

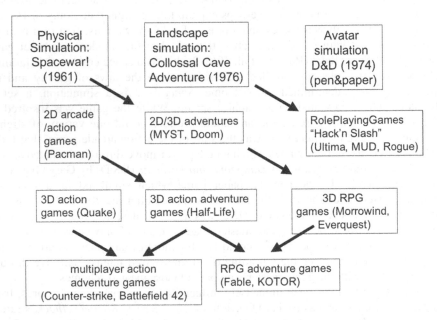

Fig. 7. The three origins of modern computer games, with cross-strain influences

Are unicursal adventure games a form of narrative, while D20 games are too open for that term to make sense? Is it possible to draw a narratological demarcation line between these two genres? In almost all "new media" theory, we find a basic pair of opposites: text/hypertext; linear/nonlinear; fiction/hyperfiction; static/interactive; progression/emergence; representation/simulation; narrative/database. If this sounds familiar, it may be because the rhetoric is not at all far from the literary structuralists' distinction between *closed* and *open* (Eco), or *lisible* and *scriptible* (Barthes).

But as examples such as *Final Fantasy*, *The Legend of Zelda*, and *Grand Theft Auto* (incidentally, all series) or even *Ludo* show us, the dichotomy is far from absolute. There can be no robust demarcation between simulation games and "narrative" (quest) games. While *Half-Life* and *Halo* do not use D20, there is no reason why they couldn't. And it is easy to imagine a *Grand Theft Auto*, which, *Matrix Reloaded*-style, solely takes place on a unicursal motorway. So perhaps the solution is to use the term "story-game hybrid"?

The problem with *terms* like story, fiction, and game is that they, unlike the phenomena they give name to, do not exist in the real world. Our use of them will always remain pragmatic, no matter how carefully we define them. A better approach than to fight over the meaning of words like "narrative" might therefore be to temporarily remove the problem-word from our analysis, and instead try to come up with a finer set of terms and models that can describe the differences between so-called stories, games, and game-story hybrids.

What is called for, in other words, is a work-specific analysis, a close look at the individual specimen to identify similarities and differences from other specimens.

What is common for all computer games with virtual environments is that they are based on a simulation, a dynamic model/rule set. Also, like board games, they take place in a virtual space, where the player moves the pieces/avatars and manipulates the objects in the game environment according to the rules. In addition, there may be times when the player can do nothing, because the game system refuses or even terminates player control. Without these conditions, there can be no game; however, a closed sequence of events (a story) could easily be presented by the same system. In other words, there is no real dichotomy between a story and a computer game system; the production of story is merely a constraint of the system's user. A game engine can be used to present animated sequences, but, on the other hand, a story cannot be used to play games (although it can tell us how it is done). The relationship between games and stories is a hierarchical one: game engines are also potential story-producing devices, but not vice versa. So the game system is the more basic, fundamental, encompassing structure; the story is merely one of its possible uses. This becomes clear in the opening sequences of *Half-Life* and *Half-Life 2*, where the user-avatar is free to move inside a train car, listening to a voice-over, but nothing the user does has any effect on the avatar's situation. Later, towards the end of *Half-Life 2*, the avatar is enclosed in a transportation device inside the enemy complex, and the player can only watch as the avatar is transported through the building. There is space, but no room to move, only to be moved around in.

Constrained space and forced movement, however, is not in itself a narrative device. A unicursal labyrinth, a structure known from antiquity, is not a story, but a trial, a place of testing, a game. However, given its sequential structure, it can easily be ornamented with story-like elements: other characters, causes and effects, descriptive passages in meaningful, orderly sequences. By far the best story-like device is the quest, which provide the purpose that the naked space and mere exploration may lack. The quest gives direction, action, and resolution, a sense of ourselves as participants in the game world. As Tronstad (2001) pointed out, successfully accomplished quests are the stuff stories are made from, but they should not be confused with the stories that can be told about them. Quests force players to experience the game world, to go where they have not gone before, and barely can. The quest is the game designer's main control of the players' agenda, forcing them to perform certain actions that might otherwise not have been chosen, thus reducing the possibility space offered by the game rules and the landscape.

Such enforced spaces and quests may be used to convey information that may pass as stories, but these "stories" are not co-told by the players, only uncovered and observed by them.Not gamer-as-author, but (at best) gamer-as-archaeologist. In most linear corridor games, like *Max Payne*, the player can ignore the information, with no strategic penalty. Unlike *D&D*, there is no *narrative* improvisation on the player side (though there may be gameplay improvisation), and no collaboration or even information exchange bwtween gameplayer and game designer. The only creative possibility for the player is to subvert the system, to play against the designers, to try to sabotage the intentions by exploiting a flaw in the programming of the system. What is created by such actions, however, is not a new "interactive" story, but an exposure of the non-caring simulation system beneath the fragile, easily broken and unconvincing storyline.

Successful productions of this type, whether we call them stories, games or story-game hybrids, must find a balance between the landscape and the path forward. The landscape must disguise its unicursal nature, and the true path must appear as though it was one choice among many. The creative ingenuity of the quest game designers hinges not on their ability to create story-building elements (believable characters and events) but on their spatial design: how well the path is disguised by the landscape, and discoverable by a balanced amount of player effort. Games like *Half-Life* is an exercise in spatial exploration and discovery, and what makes *Half-Life 2* better than its predecessor is its tighter, better staged levels.

Fig. 8. Half-Life 2 (2004): A single path through the landscape; the mysterious man with suitcase (blowup, right) is merely narrative ornament

Other games open up the game landscape and create more freedom and choice for their players. One alternative model to the unicursal corridor is the *hub-structure* (or multicursal labyrinth) we find in games like *Knights of the Old Republic* (2004), a game set in the Star Wars universe, where the avatar must progress, D20-like, from apprentice to Jedi, while choosing between the light and dark side of the Force. The game allows the user to move between several planets (level clusters) while solving progressively harder tasks, given by many minor game characters. The player can move at will, revisiting the same places with new objectives. As the avatar becomes stronger, the range and freedom of safe movement grows. Here, too, the object of the game is to discover new areas, which may reveal "story" elements in a carefully orchestrated way.

Finally, we have games with completely open landscapes; where the challenge of navigation is mainly a matter of moving safely, and not of maze-solving. A recent example is *Morrowind (2002)*, where the game consists of one huge, continuous world/level (and some underground "dungeons") and where the avatar may move in any direction, as long as the monsters in our path can be conquered. In *Morrowind*, we may eventually discover story-elements in the form of a "central quest" that one is free to pursue, but given the open landscape, one can play for a very long time doing anything one pleases.

5 Conclusion

Comparing these games shows us that what may resemble narrative structures is actually spatial (A to B) structures, and that the games that may seem most story-like are the most spatially constrained and place-quest oriented. The challenge for game designers who want to create rich, open game worlds and tell interesting stories at the same time, is to move beyond the constraints of unicursal corridors or multicursal hub structures while keeping the player's attention on a storyline. And that is no easy task. But perhaps presenting an interesting landscape with challenging quests is enough? The most original quest games of 2004, such as *Far Cry* and *Fable,* presented shallow characters and utterly traditional gameplay, but their worlds and landscapes were rich and varied.

References

1. Aarseth, Espen. "Quest Games as Post-Narrative Discourse" in Marie-Laure Ryan (ed.): *Narrative Across Media.* University of Nebraska Press, (2004) 361-76.
2. Brand, Jeffrey and Scott Knight. "The Narrative and Ludic Nexus in Computer Games: Diverse Worlds II," paper presented at the DIGRA conference in Vancouver, (2005).
3. Buckles, Mary Ann. *Interactive Fiction: The Storygame "Adventure."* Ph.D.-dissertation, UCSD. (1985)
4. Frasca, Gonzalo. "Ludologists love stories, too: notes from a debate that never took place," Proceedings, Level Up 2003 Conference. (2003)
5. Jenkins, Henry. "Game Design as Narrative Architecture," in Pat Harrigan and Noah Wardrip-Fruin (eds.) *First Person.* MIT Press, (2004) 118-130.
6. Niesz, Anthony J. and Norman N. Holland. "Interactive Fiction" in *Critical Inquiry* Volume 11, Number 1, (1984) 110-129.

7. Tosca, Susana. "The Quest Problem in Computer Games" presented at the Technologies for Interactive Digital Storytelling and Entertainment (TIDSE) conference, in Darmstadt (2003)
    http://www.itu.dk/people/tosca/quest.htm
8. Tronstad, Ragnhild: "Semiotic and Non-Semiotic MUD Performance", paper presented at the COSIGN conference, Amsterdam, (2001)
    http://www.kinonet.com/conferences/cosign2001/pdfs/Tronstad.pdf
9. Wibroe, M., K.K. Nygaard and P. Bøgh Andersen. "Games and Stories," In Lars Qvotrup (ed.) Virtual Interaction, Springer (2001) 166-81.

A Computerized Interactive Toy: TSU.MI.KI

Yuichi Itoh, Tokuo Yamaguchi, Yoshifumi Kitamura, and Fumio Kishino

Graduate School of Information Science and Technology, Osaka University,
Japan Yamada-oka 2-1, Suita, Osaka, Japan 565-0871
{itoh, yamaguchi.tokuo, kitamura, kishino}@ist.osaka-u.ac.jp
http://www-human.ist.osaka-u.ac.jp/ActiveCube/

Abstract. Young children often build various structures with wooden blocks; structures that are often used for pretend play, subtly improving children's creativity and imagination. Based on a traditional Japanese wooden block toy, Tsumiki, we propose a novel interactive toy for children, named "TSU.MI.KI", maintaining the physical assets of wooden blocks and enhancing them with automation. "TSU.MI.KI" consists of a set of computerized blocks equipped with several input/output devices. Children can tangibly interact with a virtual scenario by manipulating and constructing structures from the physical blocks, and by using input and output devices that are integrated into the blocks.

1 Introduction

Young children often construct various structures with blocks and also play with the constructed structure in pretend play. As an example of such blocks, we have Tsumiki-toy which is a Japanese traditional toy made of wooden blocks. Despite Tsumiki's simple form, children assemble and play with it, while at the same time unconsciously learn and enhance their creativity and imagination. However, since the toy consists of wooden blocks, the interaction has been limited to be only one-way – from children to Tsumiki blocks. If this interaction could be bidirectional and supported by rich multimedia contents on a computer, it could stimulate children's creativity and imagination even further.

On the other hand, in order to realize intuitive interaction with computers, approaches of direct manipulation have been focused on. These approaches can make user interfaces easy to learn, to use, and to retain over time [1]. Based on this idea, researches have recently commenced on user interfaces that use physically substantial objects to improve the intuitiveness of interactions with the computer [2]–[4]. Such interfaces do not require computer expertise, nor do they depend on users' cultural background and age. In addition, if the shapes of these interfaces in the physical environment matched their representation and function in cyberspace, users could interact with cyberspace via these physical objects more intuitively and easily.

Our main research goal is to bridge the gap that separates cyberspace and the physical environment by using physical objects as user interfaces. In this paper we present such interface, "TSU.MI.KI", a novel interactive story-telling system

F. Kishino et al. (Eds.): ICEC 2005, LNCS 3711, pp. 507–510, 2005.

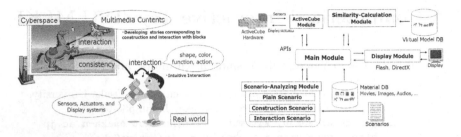

Fig. 1. Overview   **Fig. 2.** System architecture

for stimulating children's creativity and imagination by supporting multimedia contents intuitively and easily (see in Fig. 1).

2   TSU.MI.KI.

We describe TSU.MI.KI's general flow of events. First, by using a set of computerized blocks, children construct a shape with which they want to play in cyberspace. The computer automatically recognizes the constructed structure in real time, and then retrieves some candidate 3D virtual models closely matching the constructed structure. After that, children select one of the candidates, and the computer starts to play the virtual model's multimedia contents. Children can play in cyberspace while holding the constructed object in their hands. This interaction is supported by input and output devices fitted to each block, and by the computerized cube structure being self-aware of its geometry. In order to realize this system, we have designed the system architecture shown in Fig. 2.

The TSU.MI.KI system supports this flow of events in all its applications by three different scenarios that follow each other sequentially: plain, construction and interaction scenarios. The plain scenario displays non-interactive contents, such as a movie, an image or a music clip, explaining to the children what happens in cyberspace. In the construction scenario, children construct a shape with which they want to play in cyberspace. The computer then displays candidate virtual models that closely match the constructed structure. After children choose one of the candidates in the construction scenario, the interaction scenario starts playing. In this scenario, children play in cyberspace with the structure they constructed earlier through input and output devices fitted to each block.

To allow children to input the shape with which they want to play and input their intention into the interaction scenario, and to show the result of children's interaction to them, we use the ActiveCube system [5] as the physical object. All scenarios for the application are defined and recorded as files on the computer in advance. In the construction scenario, children construct their desired shape tangibly, and the ActiveCube module recognizes its structure in real time. After that, the main module gives data of the structure to the similarity-calculation module, which calculates similarities between all of the virtual models and the constructed structure by using a method [6]. The main module acquires the results of this calculation and presents some virtual model candidates corresponding to the results. The display module presents TSU.MI.KI's multimedia and virtual contents. To realize an immersive environment for children, the display module is designed to be capable of presenting realistic and interactive multimedia contents.

3 Application

We expect that the TSU.MI.KI system can be applied to various applications for children and can stimulate children's creativity and imagination. As one typical example of this system and to provide confirmation of our assumptions and claims, we implemented an application that consists of one quest with several scenarios. The application follows this story outline:

A girl, Alice, has lost her way home and has been wandering in a magical world. Then, she encountered an elderly lady, who was a good witch. The witch gave her magical blocks to help her overcome difficulties on her way home. When she constructs an object with these magical blocks to form a desired shape, it transforms itself into an object that forms the same shape as the constructed blocks. Next, Alice faces a wide river and somehow has to cross it. How can she get across this wide river, and can she reach her home safely?

In order to implement this story-telling application, we prepared seven scenarios: three plain, one construction, and three interaction scenarios. Fig. 3 shows a scene which a girl is constructing and selecting her desired object.

At first, a plain scenario explains the situation that the children are facing by presenting some images; the scenario explains the approximate story as described above and displays to the children the wide river and indicates the need to cross it.

Then, in the construction scenario, they construct a shape which they consider the most appropriate to get Alice across the river, using trial and error

Fig. 3. Shape selection from several candidates

Fig. 4. Interaction with ship

(repetitions of connection and disconnection of blocks). The constructed shape is transformed into several virtual objects as candidates in real time.

After completing construction, the children have to select one of the appropriate objects from the presented candidates. The current selected object is changed by rotating the circle of candidates and executed by tilting the physical object to the right or to the left. When they decide on their desired object, they push down on the physical object. The scenario branches off corresponding to the chosen object into three interaction scenarios.

The interaction scenario shown in Fig. 4 is the most specific and novel part of the TSU.MI.KI system. With the traditional Tsumiki wooden block toy, children only play in their imagination with static blocks; there is no response from blocks and no spread of the story. In contrast, the TSU.MI.KI system enables children to play in cyberspace, where there are no limitations to representation and imagination.

4   Conclusion

In this paper, we proposed a novel user interface named TSU.MI.KI that bridges the gap between cyberspace and the physical environment, and provide a unique and innovative "edutainment" (educational-entertainment) experience for children. We briefly described the design approach and implementation method of our system and of the prototype quest game that used it as infrastructure.

References

1. Shneiderman, B.: Designing the user interface - strategies for effective human-computer interaction - third edition, Addison-Wesley (1998)
2. Ishii, H., Ullmer, B.: Tangible Bits: towards seamless interfaces between people, bits and atoms. in Proc. of Conference on Human Factors in Computing Systems (CHI '97) (1997) 234–241
3. Anderson, D., Frankel, J., Marks, J., Agarwala, A., Beardsley, P., Hodgins, J., Leigh, D., Ryall, K., Sullivan, E., Yedidia, J.: Tangible interaction + graphical interpretation: a new approach to 3D modeling. in Proc. of SIGGRAPH2000 (2000) 393–402
4. Gorbet, M. G., Orth, M., Ishii, H.: Triangles: tangible interface for manipulation and exploration of digital information topography. in Proc. of Conference on Human Factors in Computing Systems (CHI '98) (1998) 49–56
5. Kitamura, Y., Itoh, Y., Kishino, F.: Real-time 3D interaction with ActiveCube. CHI 2001 Extended Abstracts (2001) 355–356
6. Ichida, H., Itoh, Y., Kitamura, Y., Kishino, F.: Interactive retrieval of 3D shape models using physical objects. in proc. of ACM Multimedia 2004 (2004) 692–699

Multimodal Wayfinding in a Driving Simulator for the ^S_cha$_i$r^e Internet Chair, a Networked Rotary Motion Platform

Kazuya Adachi, Ken'ichiro Iwai, Eiji Yamada, and Michael Cohen

Spatial Media Group, University of Aizu,
Aizu-Wakamatsu, Fukushima-ken, 965-8580; Japan

1 Multimodal Display/Control

We are exploring IDSS (intelligent driver support systems), especially including way-finding presented via spatial audio. ("Way-finding" refers to giving a driver directions, as via car navigation ["*Car-Nabi*"] GPS/GIS systems.) We have developed a networked driving simulator as a virtual-reality based interface (control/display system) featuring integration with the ^S_cha$_i$r^e rotary motion platform for azimuth-display, stereographic display for 3D graphics, and spatial audio (sound spatialization) way-finding cues.

As a haptic output modality, chairs with servomotors (shown below in Fig. 1) can render force-display, turning themselves under networked control, to respond to driving control. Our chairs are deployed with augmented reality visual scenes (via QTVR-enabled browsers, Swing-conformant dynamic maps, and Java3D) and sounds, using laptops integrated via wireless communication (using Wi-Fi, 820.11). As a visual output modality, a mixed perspective or stereoscopic rendering of a scene, fusible via special eyewear, allows spatial graphics. As an audio output modality, transaural speakers (without crosstalk), "nearphones" embedded in the seat headrest, can present unencumbered binaural sound with soundscape stabilization for multichannel sound image localization. These sensory modalities are reviewed in the following subsections.

1.1 Haptic Modality: Driving Control and Azimuth-Display

We developed a second-generation prototype of our Internet Chair [1] deployed as an output device, a rotary motion-platform information appliance [2,3]. Dubbed "^S_cha$_i$r^e" (and pronounced /schaire/, for 'share-chair'), our prototypes can twist under networked control, synchronized with visual displays and spatial audio for propriocentric consistency. We extended our ^S_cha$_i$r^e to support networked driving simulation, including a steering wheel controller and foot pedals (accelerator and brake).[1] The ^S_cha$_i$r^e Internet Chair motion platforms don't translate, but their rotation is synchronized with the turning of the respective virtual vehicle.

F. Kishino et al. (Eds.): ICEC 2005, LNCS 3711, pp. 511–514, 2005.
© IFIP International Federation for Information Processing 2005

512   K. Adachi et al.

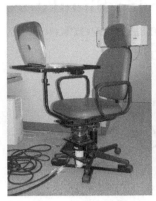

(a) Second Generation Prototype. (Developed with Dept. of Mechanical Engineering Systems, Yamagata University and Mechtec.)

(b) Java3D Virtual Internet Chair (Developed by Daisuke Kaneko, and extended by Shiyota Nakayama with Alam Bolhassan.)

(c) Stereographic viewer on the ^S_cha$_i$r^e desk, used to fuse dynamic stereograms on the laptop.

Fig. 1. For its haptic output modality, servomotors render kinesthetic force display, rotating each ^S_cha$_i$r^e under networked control. Note the nearphones straddling the headrest for binaural display without cross-talk.

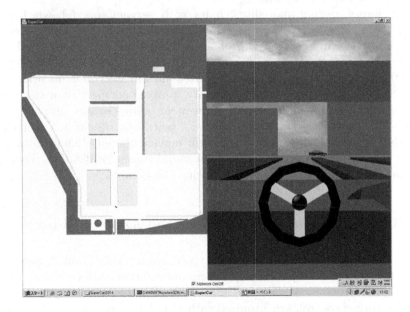

Fig. 2. Double-paned driving simulator window showing exocentric (left, bird's eye) and egocentric (right, driver's perspective) views. (Originally developed by Hideto Shimizu.)

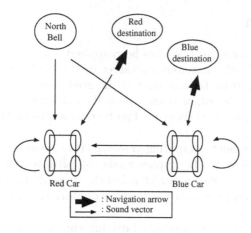

Fig. 3. Sound vector modeling

1.2 Visual Modality: Mixed Perspective or Stereoscopic Display

Using Java3D[2] [4,5,6], we developed an interface for a driving simulator, shown in Fig. 2, featuring a model of our campus and controls for time-of-day (day- or night-time) and visibility (clear or foggy). Graphical way-finding is augmented by arrows that fly from each car's current position towards the goal. We have deployed a stereoscopic display, programming parallel windows presenting visual perspectives whose standpoints may be coupled, separated by an interocular displacement, fusible with a viewer like the "Screen Scope,"[3] shown in Fig. 1(c).

1.3 Auditory Modality: Spatial Audio Wayfinding via Nearphones

Anticipating a convergence of GPS/GIS and spatial audio [7], we are experimenting with audio cues for wayfinding. Besides each driver's own "driving music," various tones and sounds are emitted from other salient objects. As illustrated by Fig. 3, each driver may **attend** or **mute** four sound sources: one's own car's music, another's car's music, "North bell" (an audio compass), and navigation (way-finding) beacon.

A 'simplex' mode couples the local control and display, while an alternative 'duplex' mode disables such immediacy, relying instead upon returned network events to update the visual and displays. This scheme accommodates network delays and client latency, synchronizing the multimodal display. For particular instance, the ^S_chair^e Internet Chair has significant sluggishness, a consequence of mechanical inertia (seatee payload) and user comfort.

---

[1] www.logitech.com, www.logicool.co.jp
[2] www.java.com/products/java-media/3D/
[3] www.berezin.com/3d/screenscope.htm

2   Conclusion

Our driving simulator application has been applied to a race game. A game manager program randomly determines a target in the field, and locates the audio beacon at that position. Drivers race to the goal— using a steering controller with foot pedals, keyboard, or both— with the encouragement of arrows flying towards and sound emitted from it. The first to arrive at the goal position is declared the winner.

In this entertainment computing research, three senses— touch, sight, and hearing— are employed. The duplex mode establishes that when the motion platform controller receives a target azimuth, it sends updates on a separate channel while twisting towards the target, coupling the proprioceptive, visual, and auditory displays.

Using spatial audio, our networked driving simulator is enhanced regarding both realism and augmented reality capability. In conditions of good visibility, the dynamic stereographic arrows are effective way-finding cues, but especially in conditions of reduced visibility— night-time and/or fog— spatial audio cues complement the arrows for way-finding and situation awareness.

References

1. Cohen, M.: The Internet Chair. IJHCI: Int. J. of Human-Computer Interaction **15** (2003) 297–311 www.u-aizu.ac.jp/~mcohen/welcome/publications/ic4.ps. Special Issue: Mediated Reality. ISSN 1044-7318.
2. Duminduwardena, U.C., Cohen, M.: Controlling the $_c^S$ha$_i$r^e Internet Chair with a Mobile Device. In: Proc. CIT: Fourth Int. Conf. on Computer Information Technology, Wuhan, China (2004) 215–220
3. Adachi, K., Cohen, M., Duminduwardena, U., Kanno, K.: "*Kuru-kuru* Pitcher": A Game for the $_c^S$ha$_i$r^e Internet Chair. In: Proc. ICEC: Third Int. Conf. on Entertainment Computing, Eindhoven, Netherlands (2004) 35–45 ISBN 3-540-22947-7.
4. Matsubara, S., Monobe, K., Miura, S., Miyawaki, Y., Hattori, H., Kobayashi, R., Yamada, K., Tanaka, S.: Java3D Graphics Nyumonn. Tokyo: Morikita Syuppann Sha (2002) ISBN 4-627-84391-7.
5. Walsh, A.E., Gehringer, D.: Java 3D API jump-start. Prentice-Hall (2002) ISBN 0-13-034076-6.
6. Sowizral, H., Rushforth, K., Deering, M.: The Java 3D API Specification. Addison-Wesley (1997) ISBN 0-201-32576-4.
7. Holland, S., Morse, D.R., Gedenryd, H.: AudioGPS: Spatial Audio Navigation with a Minimal Attention Interface. Personal and Ubiquitous Computing (2002) 253–259

Making Collaborative Interactive Art "Ohka Rambu"

Ryota Oiwa, Haruhiro Katayose, and Ryohei Nakatsu

School of Science and Technology, Kwansei Gakuin University,
Sanda 669-1337, Hyogo, Japan
{for_you, katayose, nakatsu}@ksc.kwansei.ac.jp

Abstract. This paper describes an environment for editing and performing interactive media art/entertainment. The design background is to provide artistic/entertainment pieces, in which multiple people can participate without special sensory equipment. This paper introduces a gesture input function using color tags in the image and some matching functions to be used for writing a piece. This paper shows an example of interactive media art/entertainment, called "Ohka Rambu," and describes the usage and possibilities of the environment.

1 Introduction

Modern computer technologies on real-time gesture sensing and fast audio and visual rendering techniques have brought about a brand-new art genre called interactive art, and video games appealing to body sensation [1]. Nowadays, interactive art has become popular, and the number of galleries or artistic events featuring interactive art is increasing. Also body action games are very popular, especially for the young generation. The main stream of the game centers (arcade) has been changing to the gesture games. Interactive technology is one of the crucial keywords, when we think of new entertainment.

In this paper, we are going to describe one of the endeavors to realize interactive art/entertainment, in which plural participants can enjoy collaborative media performance. In Section 2, we introduce some related works and our design concept. Section 3 describes technical overview of the developed environment on which we edit and perform contents. In section 4, we present a concrete work called "Ohka Rambu," implemented on the proposed environment. Finally we discuss the possibilities of the presented system.

2 Related Works and Design Concept

There have been many technological activities explored with the goal of assisting to edit (compose) interactive performances efficiently. These endeavors are mainly classified into one of the following three types; 1) authoring environment for multi-media, 2) media-rendering techniques, and 3) gesture information processing. In the research field of music, authoring environments for designing sound and music

F. Kishino et al. (Eds.): ICEC 2005, LNCS 3711, pp. 515–518, 2005.
© IFIP International Federation for Information Processing 2005

have been developed since the 80's. We can find its developed form as a visual iconic authoring environment for multimedia, like a commercial product Max/msp [2]. Max/msp provides an interface to use external objects that third parties have developed. Currently, objects for computer graphics, video effects, and image sensors are available. There also are some activities to employ multiple sensors with some pat-tern matching functions for writing performing art for Max/msp [3, 4].

Rendering techniques and gesture acquisition are related to virtual reality technology. Recently, higher-level APIs for virtual reality have been open to the public. Among these open APIs, a free toolkit called ARToolkit [5] that supports image processing for object tracking is widely used for the implementation of virtual reality applications. Recently various high quality software video effect APIs are also available [6].

As mentioned above, we can choose and combine free tools as they may be fit for the intended design of the artistic/entertainment work. Although the freedom of editing interactive art/entertainment work is expanding, it is not useful enough, when we once set the concrete system configuration resulting from the artistic goal. Here, we focus on making interactive art/entertainment pieces, in which one or multiple audience members can participate without special sensors. In addition, we intended to edit a competitive mass game on the same environment. For this goal, we decided to design an environment for editing and performing interactive art/entertainment, which detects and reports movement of some color regions in video image, as shown in the following chapter.

3   System

The system consists of a PC and video cameras. The main functions provided in the environment are movement detection of the given color regions and some feature

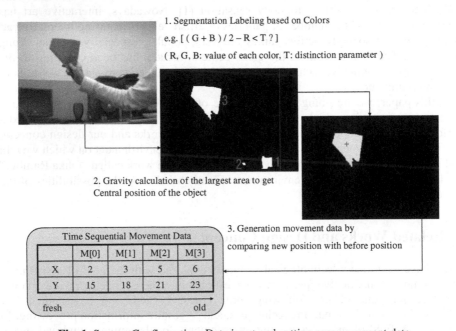

Fig. 1. System Configuration. Data input and getting raw movement data

extraction functions for the obtained movement. Processing flow from video image to movement calculation is shown in fig 1. We utilize color codes for identifying multiple gesture input.

The system captures the gravity of the registered color at the frame rate. Users of the environment may use similarity values between registered movements (template), as well as the time sequential gravity data. One of the points that we set in designing the system is to measure and utilize information regarding synchronicity of the participants to the works. Therefore we prepared for an API which reports the movement similarities of the selected two color regions. Combining these APIs, the content programmer can write cooperative and competitive contents efficiently.

4   Implementing "Ohka Rambu"

We edited a Japanese-taste piece called "Ohka Rambu" (Dancing with Cherry blossoms) using the environment described in chapter 2. The artistic concept of "Ohka Rambu" is derived from typical Japanese spring scenery where plenty of pedals of cherry blossoms are dancing fanned by a wind. In this piece, one or two persons play by producing winds using blue and red paper fans. Some of the rules are implemented in a production system manner are:

Utilization of Reported Data

0. Raw data
1. Function1. Similarity to registered movement patterns
2. Function2. Synchronicity detector of plural color data

1. Visual Effect for keeping moving (0,1)

2. Visual Effect for Stop and Move (0,1)

3. Visual Effect When Synchronizing Movement (1,2) is detected.

Fig. 2. Some pictures of "Ohka-Rambu

1. For each fan, if a movement over a certain threshold has been detected, pedals falls down around the center of the fan, with ambient sound.
2. If fans stay at the same place for a while, a big cherry blossom emerges at the position of the fan. After the cherry blossom has fully grown and movement of the fan has been detected, plenty of pedals are blown up with a flash sound and imaging effect.
3. If the movement of two fans is synchronized, a motion blur effect emerges.

The image sample corresponding to the rules are shown in fig 2.

5   Concluding Remark

This paper has presented a framework that is intended to write interactive art/entertainment efficiently, and introduced a piece "Ohka Rambu" (Dancing with Cherry blossoms) edited on the framework. "Ohka Rambu" is supposed to demonstrate at any event including ICEC2005.

The system uses color markers for identifying gestures. Although participants of the have to wear or have colored markers, it is not a strong constraint com-pared with wearing the electric sensors. Moreover, this configuration allows many people to enjoy mass games. For instance, we implemented a preliminary mass game, in which the audience is divided into a blue team and a red team, having a blue penlight and a red penlight respectively. If each of the team members moves the penlight in the same way, we can detect this regularity from the gravity data. To the contrary, if the team members move the penlight at random, the gravity data does not produce meaningful data. We used this constraint in implementing the mass game.

We would like to demonstrate the system together with the media piece "Ohka Rambu," at some events, including the ICEC2005. We would like to gather comments from participants who experienced "Ohka Rambu", for evaluating the system and piece as future work.

References

1. Katayose, H.: Using Multimedia for Performance, Y. Anzai (Ed.), Multimedia Informatics "Self Expression", Iwanami-Shoten (in Japanese) (2000) 67-113
2. http://www.cycling74.com/products/maxmsp.html
3. Mulder, A.: The I-Cube system: Moving towards sensor technology for artists. Proc, the 6th International Symposium on Electronic Art (1995).
4. Katayose, H. Kanamori, T. and Inokuchi, S.: An Environment for Interactive Art, Proc. International Computer Music Conference (1996) 173-176
5. http://artoolkit.sourceforge.net/
6. Kentaro Fukuchi: "EffecTV: a real-time software video effect processor for entertainment, Sam Mertens, Ed Tannenbaum: Entertainment Computing - ICEC 2004 (LNCS 3166) (2004) 602-605

Agents from Reality

Kazuhiro Asai, Atsushi Hattori, Katsuya Yamashita, Takashi Nishimoto,
Yoshifumi Kitamura, and Fumio Kishino

Graduate School of Infomation Science and Technology, Osaka University,
2-1 Yamadaoka, Suita, 565-0871 Osaka, Japan
{asai, a-hattori, katsuya, nishimoto.takashi, kitamura,
kishino}@ist.osaka-u.ac.jp
http://www-human.ist.osaka-u.ac.jp/

Abstract. A fish tank is established in a cyberspace based on a real world in which autonomous fish agents, generated from images captured in an actual world, swim. The behavior of each fish is determined by an emotional model that reflects personality according to encountered events and user interactions.

1 Introduction

Environment of the earth is one of the most vital themes in these days. Therefore, computer simulations of natural ecological systems have an increasingly important role in various fields. Moreover, sophisticated interactive simulation systems are expected to be established for the purpose of assessment of the environment, enlightenment or education of the theme, and expandion of the range of the research field, and so on.

We are exploring a novel approach to interactive ecosystem simulation, carefully addressing the fragile balance and tradeoff between the autonomy of the simulated ecosystem and the freedom of user interaction. In this paper, a fishtank in a cyberspace is described. Goldfish swimming in a tank is used as an example and an interactive simulation system of an ecosystem is established.

2 System

Our project establishes a fish tank in a cyberspace based on video images taken from the real world.

2.1 Outline

Each fish in a fish tank in cyberspace is an autonomous agent generated from images of real fish from the real world. All fish motions, shapes, and textures are extracted from live video of real fish from a tank by using an image processing technique, which is then applied to the fish agents. The behavior of each autonomous fish agent is determined by an emotional model with fuzzy logic. Here, the emotions of each

F. Kishino et al. (Eds.): ICEC 2005, LNCS 3711, pp. 519–522, 2005.

agent are generated and based on individual personality and physiological parameters of the agent, which vary according to encountered events and user interactions. After an agent's behavior is determined, a sequence of video images that most matches the determined behavior is retrieved from a database in which a variety of video clips of real fish behavior are stored. Then the retrieved images are applied to the fish agent.

By using a mouse or other adequate interaction device, users can interact with fish agents to perform such interactions as feeding, copying, deleting, dragging, and so on. Users can also customize the fish tank by changing its brightness, temperature, water quality, time transition, and so on (Fig. 1).

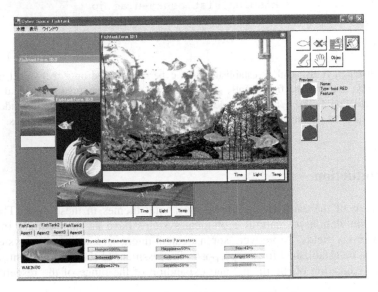

Fig. 1. The interface of Cyberspace fish tank

2.2 Configuration

The basic flow is as follows: a camera is used to extract living individual objects present in the real world by image processing techniques, and these extracted objects are presented in real time in a computer-generated virtual space. Each living individual has virtual sensors such as temperature, olfactory, and visual sensors. For example, the visual sensor is used to discover the status of the other living individuals, and the visual and olfactory sensors are used to discover the availability of food. Each living individual agent is provided with six types of behavior patterns (searching, eating, sleeping, approaching, avoiding, and escaping).

When the behavior of each agent is determined, suitable behavior is called up from a wide variety of scene video examples of this living individual in a pre-prepared database, and this is displayed in the virtual space after performing any video editing that may be required.

Figure 2 shows the configuration of a system configured as an application example. As an example, consider an application where the video objects are goldfish inside a fish tank, and each goldfish is an individual living agents. A database is pre-loaded with scenes consisting of several tens of frames depicting a goldfish swimming in various different directions at different speeds and with different postures, inclinations, and so on. This database is indexed using information such as the direction and speed of the goldfish, its posture, inclination and so on is added on a per-scene or per-frame basis. When the behavior of a fish has been determined, a search is applied to the index information of this video database to call up a suitable scene for the behavior of the goldfish, and this is displayed in the virtual space after applying any video editing that may be necessary.

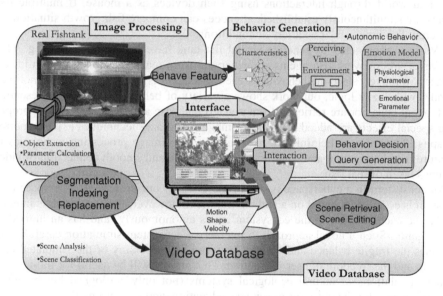

Fig. 2. System overview

3 Method

Core technical innovations of the system are the following:

1. Image Processing: accurate extraction and tracing of target fish from roughly installed cameras (Fig. 3).
2. Behavior Generation: behavior of each autonomous agent is determined by an emotional model with fuzzy logic.

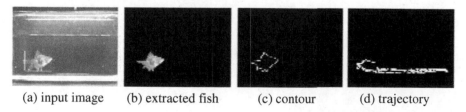

(a) input image   (b) extracted fish   (c) contour   (d) trajectory

Fig. 3. A sequence of video image processing to extract goldfish

3. Video Database: automatic generation/maintenance of a video database and automatic editing of retrieved video clips based on context.
4. User Interface: presentation of a cyberspace fish tank and an interactive environment with autonomous fish agents.

4 Conclusion

The users will enjoy a cyberspace fish tank generated from video images taken from the real world through interactions using such devices as a mouse. If multiple fish tanks are simultaneously established, attendees can compare fish growth situations in different fish tanks under a variety of conditions.

Various approaches to generate virtual fist tank have been presented (e. g., [1]), however, in our work fish agents are generated from real video images taken in real space. Moreover, since the behavior of each fish agent is determined by an emotional model with fuzzy logic, our work shows a variety of behaviors. Images representing fish agent behavior are retrieved from a video database and displayed after appropriate special effects are added. The video image processing techniques [2] and motion graphs [3] were very helpful. We use similar video image processing techniques in feature based extraction and classification of real fish and smooth connection of video frames taken of real fish.

An ecosystem in a cyberspace is one of the goals of our project. A cyberspace ecosystem is established based on a real environment; however, the ecosystem is interactive, and each creature in the ecosystem exists autonomously and has an individual personality. Such a novel approach to interactive ecosystem simulation carefully addresses the fragile balance and tradeoff between the autonomy of the simulated ecosystem and the freedom of user interaction. This project will be useful for future computer simulations of natural ecological systems (not only zoological but botanical environments) for the purposes of science, education, and relaxation.

References

1. Tinsley Galyean et al. Virtual fishtank, Conference Abstracts and Applications, p. 116, SIGGRAPH Enhanced Realities, 1998.
2. Arno Schodl, Richard Szeliski, David H. Salesin, and Irfan Essa. Video Textures, Computer Graphics Proceedings, Annual Conference Series (Proc. of SIGGRAPH), pp. 489-498, 2000.
3. Lucas Kovar, Michael Gleicher, and Frederic Pighin. Motion Graphs, ACM Transactions on Graphics, Vol. 21, No. 3 (Proc. of SIGGRAPH), pp. 473-482, 2002.

AR Pueblo Board Game

Jong Weon Lee and Byung Chul Kim

Game Interface Research Center,
Sejong University, 98 Kunja-dong, Kwangjin-ku,
Seoul 143-747, Korea
jwlee@sejong.ac.kr, psycokim2@hotmail.com

Abstract. This paper considers a new tangible interface for vision-based Augmented Reality (AR) systems. Tangible AR interfaces provide users seamless interaction with virtual objects in AR systems but with the restriction of user's motions. A new tangible AR interface is designed to overcome this limitation. Two hexahedral objects are attached together to create the new tangible AR interface. The shape of the new tangible AR interface removes the restriction of user's motions in existing tangible AR interfaces. Users can move and rotate the new interface freely to manipulate virtual objects in AR environment. This improvement is useful for applications that require unrestricted rotation motions of virtual objects. The Pueblo board game is developed to demonstrate the usability of the new tangible AR interface.

1 Introduction

Augmented Reality (AR) merges real and virtual worlds to provide users useful information that cannot be achieved by users own senses. From the end of the last decade, AR gains much interest from researchers in various fields (i.e., computer science, architecture, industry design, and psychology), and they develop applications in diverse areas (i.e., industry, medical, mobile, and entertainment). Although many researchers have explored AR, the interface design has not been actively studied. General AR applications mainly provide users limited viewing or browsing of augmented information.

This paper considers an interface technique that provides users natural interaction with vision-based AR systems through a tangible 3D object. Recently, researchers apply the tangible user interface [1] to AR systems and develop tangible AR interfaces. Generally, these interfaces are composed with a real object and markers. One or

Fig. 1. Tangible AR interface and occlusion problems (a) Board interface (b) Cube interface (c) Occlusion problems

F. Kishino et al. (Eds.): ICEC 2005, LNCS 3711, pp. 523 – 526, 2005.

more markers are attached on the real object as shown in Figure 1, and the pose of the interface is computed based on these markers and used to manipulate virtual objects.

Many researchers use a flat board with a marker (a Board interface) as a tangible interface for their AR systems, Figure 1(a). The Board interface is used to manipulate corresponding virtual objects [3], [4], [5]. Frequently, the Board interface is attached on a real object such as a paddle [3], and a cup [5]. A cube can be used instead of a flat board. More than one marker are attached on sides of the cube, and users can manipulate this Cube interface to interact with AR systems [2], [6], Figure 1(b). The main advantage of using these tangible AR interfaces is that users interact with virtual objects as they do with real objects. The tangible AR interfaces provide users more realistic interaction than using special-purpose input devices, which cause interaction discontinuity [4]. However, the current tangible AR interface has limitations.

The current tangible AR interface cannot be rotated freely to interact with virtual objects because a marker on the tangible AR interfaces is not always viewable to the camera in AR systems. Users can rotate the Board interface along the up axis, but users cannot rotate it along other axes. The marker on the Board interface is not viewable to the camera for these rotation motions. For the Cube interface, users can rotate it along any axes, but users have to place their hand(s) in special locations of the interface (i.e., corners of the Cube). If users were not careful, user's hand(s) would occlude markers partially or entirely as shown in Figure 1(c) and result the failure of pose estimation. This requirement causes uncomfortable interaction with virtual objects.

This restricted motion is critical for applications that require varied rotation motions. To overcome this limitation, a new design of the tangible AR interface is presented in this paper. Two hexahedral objects are attached together to create the new tangible AR interface as shown in Figure 2(a). We call this interface as the Pueblo interface because the shape is similar to the building blocks of the Pueblo board game.

In the next section, the key aspects of the Pueblo interface are introduced, and the pilot application, AR Pueblo board game, is presented in section 3. The conclusion will follow the description of the pilot application.

2 Pueblo Interface

This section discusses key aspects of the new 3D tangible interface, i.e., basic design, tracking, and interaction. We designed the Pueblo interface considering one aspect of interface principles, seamless interaction with an AR system.

(a)   (b)   (c)

Fig. 2. Pueblo interface (a) Shape of the interface (b) Visible markers at varying positions (c) Two-hand interaction

The Pueblo interface is an object that is created by aligning two hexahedral objects as shown in Figure 2(a) with markers. Eighteen distinguishable markers are attached to the Pueblo interface, so it can be viewable from the camera of AR systems at any orientation as long as the interface is located inside the viewing area of the camera.

The pose of the Pueblo interface is estimated using the vision-based AR library, ARToolKit [7]. The camera views the Pueblo interface, and the AR system detects markers on the Pueblo interface and estimates pose of the Pueblo interface using the detected markers.

The Pueblo interface provides natural interaction to users. Users hold the Pueblo interface and move or rotate it freely to manipulate the corresponding virtual object. At least one marker of the Pueblo interface is always visible to the camera as long as the interface is viewed by the camera, Figure 2 (b). Users can also hold the Pueblo interface with one or two hands not occluding all markers on the Pueblo interface, Figure 2(c).

3 Pilot Application: AR Pueblo Board Game

The main application of the Pueblo interface is 3D AR board games. One of the popular board games is the Pueblo shown in Figure 3, and we implemented it to demonstrate the capability of the Pueblo interface. The game requires complex 3D manipulations of building blocks to play it. Players have to rotate and move their building blocks to build a large pueblo on a game board.

The AR Pueblo board game consists of four components, a main board, building blocks, a camera, and a display. The main board is used to place and to manipulate a virtual Pueblo board, and it is the main coordinate of the system, Figure 4(a). Every virtual object on the system will be located relative to the origin of the main board.

Fig. 3. Pueblo board game

The building blocks are manipulated by the Pueblo interface. Users interact with the Pueblo interface to locate their building blocks on the virtual board to build a virtual pueblo. While users are manipulating the Pueblo interface, the camera is used to track the pose of the Pueblo interface, and the system locates the corresponding virtual building blocks in the AR environment.

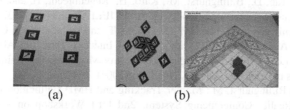

(a)   (b)

Fig. 4. AR Pueblo board game (a) Main board (b) Rotate the main board to view at varying locations

HMD and a desktop monitor can be used as a display of the game. When HMD is used, the camera is attached on the front side of the HMD. Players can move their heads to view the game in various locations. When a desktop monitor is used, the camera is attached on the top of the monitor. Players can rotate the main board to view the other side of the game, Figure 4(b). Each display has its own advantages. Players wearing HMD could view the game freely and realistically. When a desktop monitor is used as the display, players are free from wearing a cumbersome HMD, so they can play the game longer than players wearing a HMD.

Using these elements, up to 3 players can play the AR Pueblo game. After selecting the appropriate building block, the player manipulates the Pueblo interface to interact with the selected building block. The player can rotate the Pueblo interface freely as he/she does with a real building block used in the real Pueblo board game.

4 Conclusion

This paper introduces the new tangible AR interface called the Pueblo interface. The Pueblo interface is built by attaching two hexahedral objects, so users can move and rotate the Pueblo interface freely to manipulate 3D virtual objects. This freedom is the main advantage of the new interface over existing tangible AR interface, the Board and the Cube interfaces. By improving the freedom of the interface motions, the Pueblo interface provides natural interaction with AR applications that require unrestricted motions of virtual objects.

Currently, the Pueblo interface is only tested empirically to demonstrate that the interface can provide users natural 3D interactions. The Pueblo interface has not been proven as the optimal interface that provides unrestricted 3D motions to users. The way to design the optimal Pueblo interface is left for the future work.

References

1. Ishii, H. and Ullmer, B.: Tangible bits: towards seamless interfaces between people, bits and atoms. Proc. Conference Human Factors Computing Systems (CHI'97), 234–241
2. Hong, D. and Woo, W.: I^2-NEXT: Digital Heritage Expo. Proc. 14th International Conference Artificial Reality and Telexistence (ICAT 2004), 120-125
3. Kato, H., Billinghurst, M., Poupyrev, I., Imamoto, K. and Tachibana, K.: Virtual Object Manipulation on a Table-Top AR Environment. Proc. ISAR 2000, 111-119
4. Poupyrev, I., Tan, D., Billinghurst, M., Kato, H., Regenbrecht, H. and Tetsutani, N.: Developing a Generic Augmented-Reality Interface. IEEE Computer, 35, 3, 44-50 (2002)
5. Kato, H., Tachibana, K., Tanabe, M., Nakajima, T. and Fukuda, Y.: A City-Planning System based on Augmented Reality with a Tangible Interface. Proc. ISMAR'03 (2003)
6. Park, J. and Lee, J.: Tangible Augmented Reality Modeling. Entertainment Computing, Lecture Notes in Computer Science, No. 3166 (2004), 254-259
7. Kato, H. and Billinghurst, M.: Marker Tracking and HMD Calibration for a Video-based Augmented Reality Conferencing System. 2nd Int'l Workshop on Augmented Reality (1999), 85-94

Aesthetic Entertainment of Social Network Interaction: Free Network Visible Network

Adrian David Cheok[1], Ke Xu[1], Wei Liu[1], Diego Diaz Garcia[2], and Clara Boj Tovar[2]

[1] Mixed Reality Lab, National University of Singapore
[2] Laboratorio de Luz, Polytechnic University of Valencia

Abstract. Free Network Visible Network is an active media system that uses the possibilities of the new technologies to create new landscapes in the public space by means of the visualization of the data that ow between digital networks. It changes our perception of the world with the "invisible meanings" that are around us. Mixed Reality Technology and Internet Traffic Listening system are adopted in this project in order to visualize, floating in the space, the interchanged information between users of a network. The people are able to experience in a new exciting way about how colorful virtual objects, representing the digital data, are flying around. These virtual objects will change their shape, size and color in relation with the different characteristics of the information that is circulating in the network. By the use of the objects exciting movement through space, users will feel fun and aesthetic entertainment at observing the social digital communications in their physical space and city streets.

1   Introduction

In the last 20 years the digital information has flooded the world in which we live. No matter where we are, even if we are not able to see it, we can imagine ourselves surrounded by data. The space of digital networks is also the space of *invisible meanings* that represents relations between people and a very dynamic knowledge interchange. By the metaphorical representation of these *invisible meanings*, our project here wants to establish a hybrid space where the visualization of the invisible data can help persons to understand the information society in an exciting way.

By Free Network we mean any computer network that allows free information flowing through the network [1]. Figure 1 shows how our system will represent those *invisible meanings* between the networks in a real public space.

2   Related Work

Our project uses visual metaphors to represent network traffic creating an analogy between natural systems and online information sets, highlighting, as Christian

F. Kishino et al. (Eds.): ICEC 2005, LNCS 3711, pp. 527–530, 2005.

528   A.D. Cheok et al.

Fig. 1. Screenshot of our system running besides one busy street in Kyoto

Paul says, *relationships between data elements that might not be immediately obvious and that exists beneath the surface of what we usually perceive* [2]. Our project is also related conceptually and formally with other initiatives as the "warchalking" [3], a term developed by Matt Jones that refers to the act in which people walk through the cities in search of WiFi nodes, and leaves a simple chalk drawing for others to find it without difficulty. In which is referred to the representation of invisible meanings in the real space, our project has also some relations with Remain in Light, a piece of the Japanese artist Haruki Nishijima [4].

Nevertheless our project is the first art project based on the real coexistence of physical and virtual objects by means of the Mixed Reality technologies. It uses art to built communities, and uses technologies to play in the street.

3   System Design

The first step of our project is to indicate the presence of a wireless networking node. We place visual marks wherever there is a working Free Network (Figure 2), and each node in this network becomes an urban symbol that can be easily identified.

In this project, we establish direct relations between visual physical messages placed in the street and the virtual digital information that is floating in the air. Real messages and virtual information are connected by the a software named Visible Network Client that converts the data captured from a network into virtual objects, and superimposes them in real time to the real space. This software is mainly based on the Mixed Reality technology using MXRToolKit [5] and CarnivorePE, a software that listens to all Internet traffic (email, web surfing, etc.) on a specific network. The union between these two technologies has made possible a new innovative system to visualize in Mixed Reality the metaphorical representation of the data that are continuously around us. MXR-ToolKit is used to develop the tracking part of the system, and the Internet

Fig. 2. Markers indicating Free Network access around the city

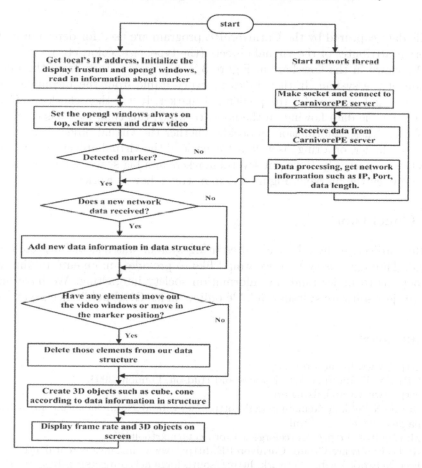

Fig. 3. Markers indicating Free Network access around the city

Fig. 4. Relation between markers and data visualization

traffic data captured by the CarnivorePE program are used for determining the different attributes of the virtual objects (the type, size, color, etc.)

As shown in the flowchart in Figure 3, the program starts from the initialization of the system. It then takes in every frame from the incoming video sequence, and searches for the predefined marker. It will then check the CarnivorePE for the data flowing on the network which this computer has connected to. We use these information to decide whether the virtual object is a cube, a cone, a cylinder, or a ring, as well as the scale of the virtual object in x, y, and z direction respectively. If we put several markers in a big space, virtual data may flow between the markers. Figure 4 demonstrates how it works.

4   Conclusion

In this project, a digital data representing system was successfully built and tested. Through this system, we would like to provide a more entertaining way for persons to understand the information society interacting. We have made this project software system available online under GNU public license at [7].

References

[1] http://www.freenetworks.org
[2] GREEN, R. Internet Art. Thames and Hudson, London, 2004.
[3] http://www.warchalking.org
[4] Haruki Nishihima, Remain in Light http://www.fundacion.telefonica.com/at/vida/paginas/v4/eharuki.html
[5] MxrToolKit, http://sourceforge.net/projects/mxrtoolkit/
[6] Radical Software Group, CarnivorePE. http://www.rhizome.org/carnivore/
[7] Free Network Visible Network, http://sourceforge.net/projects/visiblenetwork/

Motion Illusion in Video Images of Human Movement

Kiyoshi Fujimoto and Akihiro Yagi

Department of Psychology, School of Humanities, Kwansei Gakuin University,
1-1-155 Uegahara, Nishinomiya, Hyogo, 662-8501, Japan
{kys.fujimoto, yagi}@kwansei.ac.jp
http://www.h6.dion.ne.jp/~fff/backscroll/
http://www.dips-kwansei.gr.jp/Yagi's%20HP/top.htm

Abstract. We found a novel motion illusion; when a video clip presents a moving person, the background image appears to move incorrectly. We investigated this illusion with psychophysical experiments using a movie display that consisted of a human figure and a vertical grating pattern. The grating periodically reversed its light-dark phase so that it was ambiguous in terms of motion directions. However, when the human figure presented a walking gait in front of the grating, the grating appears to move in the opposite direction of her/his locomotion. This illusion suggests that human movements modulate perception of video images, and that creators of entertainment images need to pay attention to background images in videos used in animation and computer graphics.

1 Introduction

Viewing human movement has an important role in societal survival, and in enjoying entertainment such as sports, dance, cinemas, TV shows and video games. The latter field has been enlarged by computer graphics that easily create animation of moving people in virtual environments such as walkers on the moon, swimmers in the sky, runners in an imaginary street, and so on. However, we have found that seeing human movements accompanies visual motion illusions. When a person presents a walking or running gait, specifically, a background pattern appears to move in the opposite direction of his/her locomotion. We have called this illusion the 'backscroll illusion' because it is apparently created by backward display scrolling. Here we present some demonstrations, an overview of psychophysical experiments, and the implications of this illusion for entertainment computing.

2 Methods

To demonstrate motion illusions, researchers have used patterns of ambiguous movements. The backscroll illusion appears optimally in dynamic grating backgrounds, as illustrated in Fig.1. These gratings reverse dark-light phases periodically so that they have two motion components in opposite directions at an equal speed. An individual grating is made by the linear summation of two gratings that move in opposite direc-

F. Kishino et al. (Eds.): ICEC 2005, LNCS 3711, pp. 531–534, 2005.

tions at equal speeds. Gratings are also suitable for visual stimuli in psychophysical experiments because their physical properties such as luminance contrast, spatial frequency, temporal frequency and velocity can be independently controlled. In addition, and known as motion cancellation methods, the strength of the illusion is physically represented by controlling the ratio of luminance contrasts between the two component gratings [8].

Fig. 1. Snapshots of video clips used in our experiments. The video images presented either a walker or a runner; they remained stationary as if stepping on a treadmill, and were seen against a counterphase grating background. The grating appeared to drift in the direction opposite to the gait despite there being no prominence of any physical components corresponding to such a perception. Demonstration movies are on the website at http://www.h6.dion.ne.jp/ ~fff/back-scroll/.

The human figures are presented in walking or running gaits, as if they stepped on a treadmill. There is no body-translation. Each body part moves along a pendulum-like trajectory with anti-phase to its counterpart (e.g. left vs. right elbows, wrists, knees, ankles, etc.). Thus, in physical terms the human figures also have no directional bias. In our experiments and demonstrations, the human figures were designed with Curious Poser 4/5 software, and superimposed on the gratings using a chroma key technique.

In our experiments, the size of the movie stimuli was about 8 cm width and height from 256 pixels on a 17 inch CRT monitor. Observers viewed the display from a distance of 90 cm, which resulted in a retinal size of 5 deg of visual angle. Other details about the experimental methods have been described in our papers [3] [4].

3   Results

Psychophysical experiments showed that the backscroll illusion was optimally perceived under the following conditions: velocity match between the grating and the human gait, temporal frequency of grating at 10-20 Hz, and presentation time between 0.5 and 4 s [4]. Strength was as much as that of the well-known motion after effect (induced by prolonged observation of unidirectional motion [8]). Another experiment indicated that the effect corresponded to micro-stimulation of the motion-specific brain area of macaque monkeys [2] [9].

Further, we recently found involvements of a social factor. The backscroll illusion was enhanced when video clips were presented in peripheral visual fields and the walker appeared to go away from the fovea on the retina. In this case, a walker gradually disappeared due to decreasing acuity in peripheral vision unless observers tracked the walker with increasing attention.

We have reported another experiment using a point-light biological motion display in which only small light sources attached on the main joints of actors are visible [1]. Such fragmented human figures also affected observers' perceptual judgments, although they poorly produced illusory impression. The most important result was that the illusion disappeared when the point-lights were spatially scrambled without any change of moving trajectory of each joint. This emphasizes that there is no involvement of a physical motion bias in the backscroll illusion.

4 Discussion

Our psychophysical results have consistently suggested that the backscroll illusion involves high-level perception mechanisms. Physiological studies showed that recognition of human movements is mediated by the highest brain area of the visual system [6]. On the other hand, grating movements are analyzed in lower areas [7]. Thus, the backscroll illusion will find feedback streams in the neural network in the visual system.

We do not believe that it is only video images that produce the backscroll illusion. It should exist in natural scenes and influence our behavior. For example, seeing others' gaits upsets our vision enough to cause collisions in a crowded street. When driving at night, the sudden appearance of pedestrians attracts a driver's attention to produce illusory spatial perception, which can lead to a crash. We think that the backscroll illusion is likely to appear when background images are ambiguous.

We have reported elsewhere that background motion affects the perception of human gaits [5], which is a counter effect to the backscroll illusion. Our findings suggest that creators of images need to take care with background images in animation or computer graphics. If not, audiences will receive wrong information and experience feelings of unpleasantness. Rather, we hope that new entertainment vehicles will apply the visual illusions of human movements.

Acknowledgments

This study was supported by grants from the Hoso-Bunka Foundation, the 2004 Satow's Research Fund for Behavioral Science, and the Grant-in-Aid for Scientific Research in Academic Frontier Promotion Project provided by the Japanese Ministry of Education, Culture, Sports, and Technology.

References

1. Fujimoto, K.: Motion induction from biological motion. Perception. 32 (2003) 1273-1277
2. Fujimoto, K., Sato, T.: Motion induction by biological motion. Journal of Vision. 2 (2002) 337
3. Fujimoto, K., Sato, T.: Backdrop motion illusion from images of a walking human figure. Japanese Journal of Psychonomic Science. 22 (2003) 27-28
4. Fujimoto, K., Sato, T.: Backscroll Illusion: Apparent motion in the Background of Locomotive Objects. Vision Research. (submitted)
5. Fujimoto, K., Yagi, A.: Translational motion alters the visual perception of articulatory movements of human gait. Perception, 29 (supplement) (2000) 76
6. Giese, M. A., Poggio, T.: Neural mechanisms for the recognition of biological movements. Nature Reviews Neuroscience. 4 (2003) 179-192
7. Heeger, D. J., Boynton, G. M., Demb, J. B., Seidemann, E., & Newsome, W. T.: Motion opponency in visual cortex. Journal of Neuroscience. 19 (1999) 7162-7174
8. Nishida, S., Ashida, H.: A hierarchical structure of motion system revealed by interocular transfer of flicker motion aftereffects. Vision Research. 37 (2000) 265-278
9. Salzman, C. D., Britten, K. H., Newsome, W. T.: Cortical microstimulation influences perceptual judgments of motion direction. Nature. 346 (1990) 174-177

A Chat System Based on Emotion Estimation from Text and Embodied Conversational Messengers

Chunling Ma[1], Helmut Prendinger[2], and Mitsuru Ishizuka[1]

[1] Graduate School of Information Science and Technology, University of Tokyo,
7-3-1 Hongo, Bunkyo-ku, Tokyo 113-8656, Japan
{macl, ishizuka}@miv.t.u-tokyo.ac.jp
[2] National Institute of Informatics, 2-1-2 Hitotsubashi, Chiyoda-ku, Tokyo 101-8430, Japan
helmut@nii.ac.jp

Abstract. This short paper contains a preliminary description of a novel type of chat system that aims at realizing natural and social communication between distant communication partners. The system is based on an Emotion Estimation module that assesses the affective content of textual chat messages and avatars associated with chat partners that act out the assessed emotions of messages through multiple modalities, including synthetic speech and associated affective gestures.

1 Introduction

An important issue in meeting the needs of the spatially distributed knowledge society is to provide natural and intuitive communication tools. In order to improve textual methods such as e-mail and online chat systems, some recent systems are based on like-like embodied agents as a new multi-modal communication means [9]. Most prominently, the BodyChat system [2] employs embodied conversational avatars to mimic human-human face-to-face communication. The TelMeA system [11] uses embodied agents to deliver messages in an asynchronous online community system. Other work employs agents as personal representatives to express the user's point of view of (personal) documents [1].

Although avatars may improve the expressivity of online communication, it remains within the responsibility of the user to carefully prepare the affective content of the textual message. Picard [8] provides a suggestive example: " 'How many of you have lost more than a day's work trying to straighten out some confusion over an email note that was received with the wrong tone?' A majority of hands usually go up when I ask an audience this question. Email is an affect-limited form of communication." [8, p. 87]

In order to increase the 'affective bandwidth' of computer-mediated exchange, the internet community typically uses special ASCII symbol combinations, so-called 'emoticons', to express the emotional tone of the message (e.g. ":-)" for "happy"). As a complementary technique, work on 'textual affect sensing' proposes to analyze the textual message itself for affective qualities. In the e-mail composer EmpathyBuddy [5], emotional content of text is processed by an approach based on large-scale real-world knowledge. The assessed emotion is then attached to the textual message in the form of a caricature face that displays the relevant emotion.

F. Kishino et al. (Eds.): ICEC 2005, LNCS 3711, pp. 535–538, 2005.

The concept presented in this paper can be conceived as an alternative to the EmpathyBuddy system [5]. Our approach is based on the following methods: (i) the affective content of the textual message is recognized by an advanced keyword spotting technique, (ii) syntactical sentence-level processing is applied for detection of affective meaning, and (iii) animated 2D full-body agents perform the emotional coloring of the message using synthetic affective speech and appropriate gestures.

2   Calculating Emotion Estimation from Text

The approach for providing emotional estimations for natural-language texts is based on a keyword spotting technique, i.e. the system divides a text into words and performs an emotional estimation for each of these words (see [7] for an extensive discussion of this approach), as well as a sentence-level processing technique, i.e. the relationship among subject, verb and object is extracted to improve emotion estimation.

The initial step of analyzing an emotional scenario is to define the emotions relevant to the application scenario. In the chat system, we use the six (basic) emotions from Ekman's research [3]: *happiness*, *sadness*, *anger*, *fear*, *surprise* and *disgust*. We employ WordNet-Affect Database [12] of ITS-irst (The Center for Scientific and Technological Research of Autonomous Province of Trento, Italy) with WordNet 1.6 [4] to first find synonyms sets of these six emotion categories and to assess their emotional weight, and then compute the weight of a sentence by combining the weights of its parts. However, the word spotting method is too simple to deal with sentences such as "I think that he is happy" since here, the speaker is not necessarily happy.

We hence perform the following two types of *sentence-level processing*. First, we eliminate 'non-emotional' sentences: (i) sentences without emotional words, (ii) questions, (iii) sentences without first person pronouns (as the example sentence above). Second, we detect 'negation' in sentences. Since negatively prefixed words such as "unhappy" are already included in the emotion database, they do not have to be considered. On the other hand, negative verb forms such as "have not", "was not", "did not" are detected and flip the polarity of the emotion word.

3   Embodied Conversational Messengers

Based on the engine for textual emotion estimation from text, we built a chat system that extracts the emotion from the user's input sentence. In the following, we briefly describe our chat system where animated life-like agents with synthetic speech and gestures serve as user avatars and conversational messengers.

Fig. 1 shows an example of a chat client, where three persons are involved in a chatting activity. Among them, "norogo" refers to the user as one chat client, the other two (named "holala" and "koko") are displayed by their own avatar characters. When the chat partner called "holala" types the message "I am very happy for her", her avatar character expresses the "gladness" emotion. The relevant emotion word in the sentence is the word "happy", which is defined as "gladness" in the emotion database. The words "very" add to the intensity of the emotion conveyed by "happy". The emotional content of the message "I am very happy for her." is expressed through the avatar by synthetic speech and a (exaggerated) non-verbal expression of gladness.

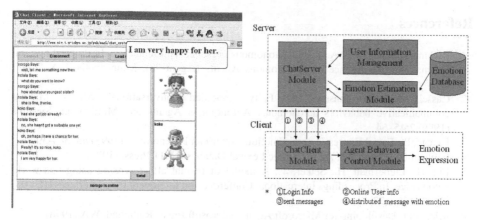

Fig. 1. Chat Client   **Fig. 2.** Architecture of the chat system

The architecture of the chat system is depicted in Fig. 2. On the server side, the ChatServer module is used to listen to the clients' connection and incoming messages. The Emotion Estimation module analyzes the emotion tendency of the incoming messages and returns the result back to the ChatServer Module. In our current system, emotion detection is context independent, i.e. we currently do not consider the current mood or emotion of a chat partner. Once the emotion of a message is estimated, the avatar will perform the message with affective expression. The analysis of emotion is based on an emotion database and the algorithm mentioned in Sect. 2. The chat system has been implemented using the Java platform, JavaScript, the Microsoft Agent package [6], and Stanford javaNLP API [10]. The behavior sequence and messages to be spoken out are sent to JavaScript functions as parameters. Currently we use a light client design in the system; that is, the client side essentially sends connection requests to the server module, and sends or receives messages. When the connection is established, the client will request the server to send its information, e.g. to a particular agent character. The server will update its online list of the clients for each client. Then the user can choose the chat user to talk with in the animated style. After a chat user is chosen, the Agent Behavior Control module is called to generate a behavior expression corresponding to the emotion estimation value. On the server side, we also maintain a user information database.

4   Future Work

In our future work, we plan to improve the Emotion Estimation module, specifically by combining past emotional states as a parameter for deciding the affective meaning of the user's current message. In addition, the speaker's mood will be associated with the topic of the conversation. In this way, we hope to obtain a better identification of the relation between speaker and topic terms in the sentence.

References

1. Bickmore, T.W., (ed.): Animated autonomous personal representatives. In Proceedings 2nd International Conference on Autonomous Agents (Agent-98), Minneapolis, MN (1998) 8-15
2. Cassell, J., Vilhj´almsson, H.: Fully embodied conversational avatars: Making communicative behaviors autonomous. Autonomous Agents and Multi-Agent Systems (1999) 2:45–64
3. Ekman, P.: Facial Expression and Emotion. American Psychologist (1993) 48, 384-392
4. Fellbaum C.: WordNet: An Electronic Lexical Database. MIT Press. (1982)
5. Liu, H., Lieberman, H., Selker, T.: A model of textual affect sensing using real-world Knowledge. In Proceedings International Conference on Intelligent User Interfaces (IUI-03) (2003) 125–132
6. Microsoft. Developing for Microsoft Agent. Microsoft Press. Redmond, WA (1998)
7. Osherenko., A.: Modeling Emotions Using a Shallow Natural Language Processing Technique. Humboldt University Berlin, Institute of Informatics (2004) Master's thesis.
8. Picard., R. W.: Affective Computing. The MIT Press, Cambridge, MA (1997)
9. Prendinger, H., Ishizuka, M.: editors. Life-Like Characters.Tools, Affective Functions, and Applications. Cognitive Technologies. Springer Verlag, Berlin Heidelberg (2004)
10. Stanford NLP Group (2005) URL: http://nlp.stanford.edu
11. Takahashi, T. (ed.): TelMeA—Expressive avatars in asynchronous communications. International Journal of Human-Computer Studies (2005) 62:193–209
12. Valitutti, A., Strapparava, C., Stock, O.: Developing Affective Lexical Resources. PsychNology Journal. (2004) Volume 2, Number 1, 61-83

Author Index

Lecture Notes in Computer Science

For information about Vols. 1–3606

please contact your bookseller or Springer